Dudley's first Charter of Incorporation, 1865. (By permission of Birmingham Reference Library)

TOWN RECORDS

TOWN RECORDS

John West

Phillimore

1983

Published by
PHILLIMORE & CO. LTD.
Shopwyke Hall, Chichester, Sussex

ISBN 0 85033 472 1

Typeset in the United Kingdom by:
Fidelity Processes - Selsey - Sussex

Printed and bound in Great Britain by
BILLING & SONS LTD.
Worcester, England

This book is dedicated to
Margaret, my wife

CONTENTS

LIST OF PLATES

(between pages 338 and 339)

Dudley

1. The 'Chairing' of Thomas Hawkes in 1834
2. Tower Street, 1900
3. Tower Street, 1983
4. Dudley Old Town Hall
5. The Dudley Fountain
6. View of Dudley *c.*1775
7. Dudley High Street, 1812
8. George Mason's shop *c.*1900
9. Stane Street 1983

Birmingham

10. The 'Theatre Royal', 1834
11. Holder's Concert Hall *c.*1851-7
12. Lench's Trust Almshouses
13. Moor Street, 1886
14. New Street, 1886
15. No. 6 Court, Bagot Street, 1903
16. Toll Gate, Perry Barr, *c.*1870
17. High Street, Harborne *c.*1905

Worcester

18. Elgar Brothers' Music Shop, *c.*1906
19. Friar Street, 1829
20. Fish Street, now Deansway
21. The Cross, *c.*1910
22. The Volunteer Training Corps, 1915
23. Foregate Street, 1893

LIST OF TEXT ILLUSTRATIONS

ACKNOWLEDGEMENTS

I should like to thank the following institutions for permission to reproduce material in their possession as text illustrations: The British Library, nos. 1, 29 and 30; Birmingham Public Libraries Service, nos. 6b, 13, 14, 16, 20, 23, 24 and 33; Dudley Public Libraries Service, nos. 6a, 6c, 8b, 15, 17, 18, 19, 34; the Superintendent Registrar of the Guildhall in Worcester, nos. 8a and 11; The Public Record Office, no. 33; The Ordnance Survey, nos. 35 and 36. Frank Power of Dudley took the photographs used in nos. 6a, 6b, 8b, 17, 18, 22, 34, 35 and 36 and Tom Bader of Worcester took the photographs used in no. 11.

INTRODUCTION

IN 1972 PARLIAMENT changed the course of a thousand years of urban history; as a result of the Local Government Act of that year the English borough was abolished. Municipal and county boroughs ceased to exist and their status was, in many cases, subtly altered to that of 'districts' in their counties. Ancient cities which claimed their burgage rights from kings of Wessex and Viking pirates reverted to the rank of parish; places which were powerful 'ports' in Domesday were amalgamated anonymously into metropolitan districts. Boroughs whose charters were wrested from Norman barons, bought from Plantagenet kings or pledged in support to the Victorian Liberal Party were at one stroke combined with less ancient urban districts. Cities which grew prosperous on Tudor or Victorian favours are now reduced to a new dependence upon the 'principal council'. Just as the earliest burgage rights were claimed from the crown in terms of independence from the shire, its courts and officers, so the end of borough government was marked by the reversion of scores of townships into county districts. The history of every place is as real as it ever was. Government may have robbed those towns of their identity; their history cannot be as conveniently erased.

We shall see in the early chapters of this book that 'township' was always a difficult and imprecise quality to define. Many anomalies of size, of antiquarian decline and upstart wealth or fashion were once resolved only in the common factor of autonomous town government. Moreover, that autonomy was deliberately devised to emphasise the *separate* nature of the town and its government from the county around it. Some towns were important and separate enough to be counties in their own right. This essential feature of autonomy was removed, or at best drastically altered, by the Local Government Act of 1972. Growth in size and population may continue until the English countryside becomes one sprawling conurbation; then every town's identity will finally be lost as 'regional' government inexorably imposes the 'single tier' overall. All that will remain will be each town's history, preserved in the countless records of ancient boroughs like Halesowen, Ripon, Monmouth, Beccles, Bideford, Chippenham and two hundred more which have lost their borough status.

There is indeed a wealth of town records. Such is the new power of centralization that these could disappear into county store-rooms unless determined townsmen value their retention in their proper places. It may be that in the past busy town clerks and under-staffed borough librarians have sometimes been unable to make adequate provision for more than the mere custody of their borough's records; the same will now apply to overworked county archivists. In many towns, however, provision was always made, not only for storage, but also for cataloguing, preserving and displaying the local records of civic history. Any student who has been fortunate enough to work with the local history collections of Liverpool, Dudley, or any similar borough collection will know that not all the resources were confined to the county record offices. There were many towns before 1974 which made admirable provision for the access of students and searchers to the essential documents and reference books. The advantages of accessibility, of the records' identity with the town in which they were housed, usually made long journeys to search them out unnecessary. It is therefore more important than ever before that we remember where our town records were kept, are aware if they have been removed and are prepared to make full use of the information which they will provide. This book will endeavour to help the searcher, however unskilled, to find and use the essential records of his own town. *Town Records* does not pretend to be a 'history' of individual towns, nor yet a complete narrative of urban change; it is rather a gazetteer or index to other local sources of information, with examples and illustrations of what the student may expect to find in searching out the past history of his own home town.

The base-line of this survey (see Gazetteer on p. 12) is a handlist of 375 county and municipal boroughs which existed in 1971, just before the implementation of the Local Government Act of the following year. Some of those towns were old incorporated boroughs like York (1160), Bristol (1188) and Norwich (1194), whose civic history and archives pre-date the Municipal Corporations Act of 1835 by several centuries. Others on the base-list are the newer creations of 19th-century parliamentary and municipal reform; these are the great Victorian cities like Birmingham (1838), Huddersfield (1868) and Manchester (1838). The records which one will find for each group are very different. The records of old incorporated towns will include such early records as poll books, apprenticeship registers, assembly books and hall papers, freemen's lists, mayors' accounts and the like, none of which exist for the typical unincorporated towns before 1835; yet those older boroughs, often smaller and nowadays more rural than the conurbations, are precisely those which have been most vulnerable to change and loss of status.

It might have been considered advisable to separate the two types of town completely, dealing with them as separate subjects in different volumes. Instead, we shall endeavour to use an example of each type of borough as a model, each of its own state of development at different times, each with its similar or different archives. As an ancient town we shall portray the city of Worcester, first incorporated in 1189; a nearby neighbour, the metropolitan district of Dudley, itself possessing a medieval castle, market place and burgage tenements but not incorporated until 1865, will illustrate the expansion of the small latecomer to civic dignity; finally, the metropolitan city of Birmingham (1838) will be used to exemplify the fortunes of the greatest but less continually documented towns. This is in fact a book about the 'town-ness' of towns.

'Town' is a difficult concept to define precisely; the essential difference between the large market 'village' and the small urban district may sometimes be difficult to perceive. Certainly many thriving Anglo-Saxon communities, ancient in their history, prosperous in their pursuits, may be offended not to find themselves on our basic list — such towns as Chipping Campden, Stourport-on-Severn or Prescot may, with many a score more, spring immediately to mind. Is our criterion of township to be sheer size? If so, the metropolitan districts merit their automatic borough status. Or should we be more concerned with administrative and cultural influence in the locality, than with antiquity and civic pride? For antiquity all the choices of the present cities were inevitable.

'Continuity' may also be an elusive concept to define and identify with certainty. Continuity of existence may easily be demonstrated in Birmingham or Dudley as in

Worcester, but continuity of development is another matter. Again, the classic historical problem of interpreting the extent of 'continuity' of Roman township in cities where 2nd-century walls are fossilized into streets, castle and market place are only a starting point to the same problem in later ages. Dudley was reasonably continuous in its growth from the foundation of William FitzAnsculf's castle to the achievement of municipal status. Others, such as Clun, preserve civic monuments and relics, as important in their time as Dudley's, which are no longer seen to be as important to modern local government. Some cities, such as Birmingham, started small and remained small for many centuries, bursting lately into industrial wealth and international status. Others, such as Winchelsea or Ironbridge, were once important but for one economic reason or another progressively, or suddenly, declined. A few, like York, Bristol and Worcester, were great and independent from ancient days until 1974.

The urban criteria chosen for the 375 towns used as reference points throughout this book are therefore a mixture of all those features which remained significant in 1971, a combination firstly of antiquity, secondly of corporate identity, thirdly of municipal privilege, whenever this was gained, fourthly a measure of self-government and finally of relative size. What all our towns have in common is their *borough status* in 1971. This was the characteristic which quite deliberately set them apart from the rural areas, the villages and markets around them. Today the student of urban economics and sociology inevitably draws attention to the inter-dependence of town and countryside, to the network of relationships which welds suburbs into conurbations, villages into suburbs and boroughs into metropolitan districts. There was a time, historically, when identity was more clearly perceived; this book intends to remind ourselves of that time and that identity.

This is also a book about the *accessibility* of urban archives, whether or not these are peculiar to urban growth and status. As in our companion volume, *Village Records*, certain documentary landmarks are taken as reference points from chapter to chapter. Each document is explained by reference to the three models, Dudley, Birmingham and Worcester, with illustrations of the archives available, notes as to their whereabouts and bibliographies of further reading and reference. Similar information is then more briefly given by reference to the gazetteer of boroughs in the base-list. From Celtic, Roman and Anglo-Saxon origins, through the common record of Domesday Survey and the borough charters of the Middle Ages we follow a series of 'peaks' of urban development, from Tudor local government, through Whig revolution to the Municipal Corporations Acts of Victoria's reign and the final reorganization of 1974. In all these records, from age to age, the essential elements of township will have been preserved.

It is now more than ever before essential that any towns-man or -woman with a stubbornly surviving civic pride should be able to verify the history of his own town. Students and young people should be encouraged to remember that their own town is more than the dominant stereotype of a plastic shopping precinct surrounded by high-rise living units. The beauty of each English town has always been its *difference*; even where the bulldozers have erased the physical features of the old town, the archives will have preserved reminders and evidence of its unique character; its history.

ACKNOWLEDGEMENTS

The author wishes to acknowledge the considerable amount of helpful advice and encouragement offered by the good friends listed alphabetically below: Paul Anness, representing Geographia Ltd., for their generous permission for reproduction of their invaluable street maps of Birmingham, Dudley and Worcester taken from the *Geographia Street Atlas and Index to Birmingham and the West Midlands* as base-maps in several of the illustrations; the staff of the many Departments of Birmingham Reference Library, particularly in Local Studies and Archives, History and Geography and Social Sciences, for their frequent help in searching out difficult references; John M. Buck, Managing Director of the Francis Frith Collection for his helpful correspondence about the Collection and about the Gazetteer to Chapter Twelve; Frances Condick of Phillimore's, for her unfailing care and patience in editing the text so sensitively; and Ann Hewitt, who drew the maps and, indeed, dealt with all the artwork; the staff of Dudley Reference Library; particularly the Archivist and librarians in the Local History Department for their unfailing helpfulness over many years; and to the Chief Librarian; C. R. Elrington, General Editor of the *Victoria County Histories*, for helpful information about the various Domesday Chapters and Tables of Population (1801–1901), and for his permission to reproduce the facsimile page from the Worcester Volume on page 93; Robin and Joan Evans (Mayor and Mayoress of Newport, Dyfed, in 1982–3) and all the friendly townspeople who preserve the traditions of a small and ancient borough; Dr. John Fines, for his cheerful encouragement throughout the task and especially for his constructive advice on unavoidable cuts in the text and Gazetteers; Jeremy W. S. Gibson and the Federation of Family History Societies, for advice on many of the most useful bibliographical references; John Hardeman, Director and Editor-in-Chief of Berrow's Newspapers, for his advice on the origins of the *Worcester Postman* and *Berrow's Worcester Journal*; Margaret Henderson, formerly Deputy Archivist at St Helen's Record Office, Worcester, for her professional interest and support, which endured from *Village Records* (1963) to *Town Records* (1983); A. S. (Stan) Hill, Warden of Dudley Teachers' Centre, for his continuing help and for his insight into the municipal history of the Black Country; Arnold Ivell and William J. West, mathematicians both, for their help with diagrams and statistics; John F. Mulvehill, Chief Executive of Dudley Metropolitan Borough, for his authority to photograph the borough charter. Anthony Phillips, Superintendent Registrar at the Guildhall, Worcester, for obtaining permission for the use of original documents of the City and its gilds; Frank Power of Dudley, for his photographs of the town and its records, and for much invaluable advice on illustrations; Sheila Screen, Computer Research Assistant at Dudley Teachers' Centre, for making the Dudley Census workable for the local historians; William Wall, archaeologist, for his knowledge of the Burghal Hidage and the origins of Saxon towns; John Westmancott, Chief Librarian of the Newspaper Library at Colindale, for a great deal of helpful advice on the composition of the Gazetteer to Chapter Ten.

An especial debt of gratitude is owed to numerous borough librarians and county archivists, who gave so much essential information and advice on the interpretation of the archives in their care. This indebtedness is so long-standing as to require an explanation of the many now out-of-date designations.

In December 1973 the author sent out a well-intentioned but singularly ill-timed questionnaire as a preliminary to beginning this book. The immediate result was two-fold; firstly a predictably dusty answer from the Society of Archivists, and secondly a wealth of information from many hard-pressed county and borough archivists. This book is therefore, to some extent, a belated apology to the first group and a heart-felt expression of thanks to the second. Many offered encouragement and sound advice and the librarians and archivists of the following then-existing boroughs completed both the first and a second, overlong questionnaire, often accompanying it with valuable typescripts and printed guides. All these have been thoroughly used in the course of writing *Town Records*: Aldeburgh, Arundel, Ashton-under-Lyne, Aylesbury, Bacup, Barrow-in-Furness, Batley, Birmingham, Blackburn, Blandford Forum, Bodmin, Bolton, Bootle, Bridport, Burnley, Bury St Edmunds, Buxton, Cambridge, Castleford, Chatham, Chichester, Chipping Norton, Colchester, Colne, Conwy, Coventry, Croydon, Darlington, Dartford, Dorchester, Dudley, Dukinfield, Dunstable, Ealing, Epsom and Ewell, Ely, Fleetwood, Gateshead, Gillingham, Godalming, Grantham, Greenwich, Grimsby, Hackney, Halifax, Harwich, Hedon, Hemel Hempstead, Hillingdon, Honiton, Hounslow, Hyde, Hythe, Ilkeston, Keighley, Launceston, Leamington Spa, Lichfield, Liverpool, Llandovery, Luton, Maidenhead, Mansfield, Middleton, Morecambe and Heysham, Newcastle-under-Lyme, Newham, Nuneaton, Pembroke, Port Talbot, Radcliffe, Rochdale, Romsey, Rotherham, St Ives (Cornwall), Sale, Salford, Scarborough, Solihull, Southampton, Southwold, Stalybridge, Stratford-upon-Avon, Stretford, Sunderland, Sutton, Swinton and Pendlebury, Tenby, Tenterden, Torbay, Wallasey, Walsall, Wandsworth, Warley, Wells, Weston-super-Mare, Weymouth, Worksop, Wrexham, Yeovil and York. Apologies are offered to any contributors whose questionnaires were mislaid in the intervening decade; the others are well-kept and highly valued as a mine of further information on particular towns.

Further thanks are due to the following individuals who, in returning the questionnaires — or in some cases unable to do so — offered further advice, even in some cases where this had to be negative. Many added particular words of encouragement without which *Town Records* would never have been completed. Designations are in most cases as they were in 1973, as are also the employing authorities. Qualifications and titles are given on the letterheads; in some cases letters were written by assistant members of staff, these are acknowledged here. Other more recent or up-to-date designations may duplicate the title of some posts; many of those who helped in 1973 are now, like the author, retired. Each of the following wrote one or more helpful letters about the book: E. J. Adsett, F.L.A., Borough Librarian, London Borough of Merton; P. Anderton, Reference Librarian, Divisional Library Morecambe and Heysham; A. T. Arber-Cooke, Hon. Sec., Friends of Llandovery; Patrick Baird, Librarian of the Local Studies Department, Reference Library, Birmingham; W. F. Bergess, County Reference Librarian, Kent County Council; A. Betteridge, Archivist to the County Borough of Halifax; Norman E. Binns, Borough Librarian of Ealing; A. F. Bottomley, Borough of Southwold; K. F. Bowden, A.L.A., Borough Librarian, Bacup; W. G. B. Brown, F.L.A., Borough Librarian and Curator, Royal Borough of Kingston-upon-Thames; George A. Carter, F.L.A., Chief Librarian, County Borough of Warrington; Miss M. E. Cash, B.A., County Archivist and Diocesan Record Officer to Hampshire; Ivor P. Collis, Somerset

Record Office; C. R. Davey, Deputy County Archivist, Hampshire Record Office; Harrison Dean, M.A., F.L.A., County Librarian, Kent County Council; S. C. Dean F.L.A., A.M.B.I.M., Borough Librarian and Curator, County Borough of Darlington; G. A. Dickman, A.L.A., County Librarian, Pembrokeshire; D. G. T. Eddershaw, B.A., Dip.Ed., Museum Education Officer, Oxford City Museum; M. W. Farr, M.A., F.S.A., F.R.Hist.Soc., County Archivist, Warwickshire County Council; J. M. Farrar, M.A., County Archivist, Cambridgeshire and Isle of Ely County Council; Miss F. Foster, Park Lane Cottage, Southwold; Dr. Levi Fox, O.B.E., D.L., Shakespeare Birthplace Trust, Stratford-upon-Avon; Robert Frost, Principal Archivist, West Yorkshire Archives Service; R. M. Gard, M.A., County Archivist, Northumberland County Council; Miss M. Gooding, Borough Librarian of Ealing; K. Hall, B.A., Dip.Archive Admin., County Archivist, Lancashire County Council; H. A. Hanley, County Archivist, Buckinghamshire County Council; D. E. Hayward, F.L.A., Borough Librarian and Curator, Grantham Library and Museum; M. J. Hayward, Hon. Muniments Officer, Dunstable; M. Higson, M.A., County Record Office, East Riding of Yorkshire; Jennifer Hofman, Assistant Archivist, Dorset County Council Record Office; C. W. T. Huddy, F.L.A., Borough Library of Evesham; A. D. Johnson, Town Clerk and Borough Accountant, Honiton; Derek Jones, M.A., F.L.A., Borough Librarian, London Borough of Richmond-upon-Thames; Ernest W. Kirtley, A.L.A., Acting Director, County Borough of Sunderland Public Libraries, Museum and Art Gallery; D. Larkin, Rye Branch Librarian, County Library, East Sussex; J. W. Lendon, F.L.A., Borough Librarian of Solihull; Miss S. J. MacPherson, B.A., Archivist-in-Charge, The Record Office, Kendal; R. J. Marsh, F.L.A., City Librarian, Rochester; Mrs. Patricia Moore, B.A., F.S.A., Archifydd Morgannwg; C. C. Morris, Assistant Librarian, Surrey County Library; Miss U. B. Murphy, B.A., A.L.A., Morecambe Divisional Library; Miss M. Patch, B.A., D.A.A., County Archivist, Pembrokeshire; T. Prideaux, The Guildhall, St Ives, Cornwall; Maurice R. Rathbone, A.L.A., County and Diocesan Archivist, Wiltshire County Council; Ernest W. Redmond, Deputy Borough Librarian, Grantham Library and Museum; Brian C. Redwood, M.A., County Archivist, Cheshire County Council; H. J. Ridler, Saffron Walden Area Librarian; Miss Anne Roper, M.B.E., F.S.A., Hon. Archivist, Borough of Hythe; Ian M. Seddon, A.L.A., Malmesbury Regional Librarian, Wiltshire County Council; R. Sharpe France, M.A., County Archivist, Lancashire Record Office; R. A. Shaw, Local History Librarian, London Borough of Wandsworth; Janet Smith, Liverpool Record Office and Local History Department; H. C. Stacey, Saffron Walden; F. Sunderland, A.L.A., Borough Librarian, Radcliffe Public Library; Miss J. F. K. Swinyard, A.L.A., Wells Areas Librarian, Somerset County Council; Marjorie Teathen, Branch Librarian, Woodstock; Isabella B. Thomson, A.L.A., Borough Librarian and Curator, Goole Public Library, Museum, and Art Gallery; A. B. Venning, Hon. Borough Archivist, Lancaster; The Committee of Wallingford Archaeological and Historical Society; Peter Walne, as Secretary to the Society of Archivists in 1974; Julian Watson, Local History Librarian and Archivist, London Borough of Greenwich; I. Webster, A.L.A., Senior Librarian, Public Library, St. Ives, Cornwall; Christine M. Whitehead, A.L.A., Branch Librarian, North Riding County Library; K. J. Westmancoat, Information Officer, Newspaper Library (Colindale), The British Library; A. P. Whittaker, M.A., City Archivist of Winchester; G. Haulfryn Williams, M.A., D.A.A., Is-Archifydd y Sir ac Archifydd Rhanbarth, Caernarfon; Michael Winton, B.A., Dip.Ed., A.L.A., Local History Librarian, Borough of King's Lynn; Mrs. Woodward, Hon. Sec., Woodstock History Society; and W. Nigel Yates, Archivist Designate of North Tyneside Metropolitan District.

Finally, any remaining errors are, of course, my own.

CHAPTER ONE

THE PRESENT STATE OF THE TOWNS 1971–1981

IN 1971 NATIONAL census returns classified 14% of the land of England and Wales as 'urban areas' and 78% of the population as inhabitants of towns. Almost exactly one-third of the population lived in the six great conurbations of Greater London, West Midlands, West Yorkshire, South-East Lancashire, Merseyside and Tyneside, a score of cities ranging in size from 100,000 to 1,000,000; each metropolis spreading across several hundred square miles. In 36 other towns outside the conurbations, each numbering more than 100,000 people – towns like Blackburn, Norwich, St Helens, Reading and York – lived another eight million residents; together with the conurbations they numbered half the population of England and Wales. Although some of the largest cities such as Liverpool, Newcastle and Manchester have steadily declined since 1901 and more particularly in the late 1960s, most towns of the middle and upper rank continue to grow, often, as in the case of the Midland boroughs, by extension of their boundaries with local government reorganization. Our Gazetteer of 375 incorporated towns was in 1971 the composite home town of about 30,000,000 people. Their individual towns ranged in size from fewer than 1,000 inhabitants in Montgomery to more than 1,000,000 in Birmingham. Their townsfolk were 60% of our total population.

In 1971 there were 83 county boroughs, 259 municipal boroughs, the City of London with 32 boroughs of Greater London and the exceptional City of Ely which was an urban district but is included in our list. These are the towns, ancient and modern, large and small, which we shall endeavour to follow through a thousand years of documentary history, from the place-names which indicate their various starting-points as Roman *ceasters* or Saxon *ports* standing at fords and bridges, through the vicissitudes of historical growth and decline.

What were the main differences from one to another of those towns? First in order of historical growth stood the chartered municipal boroughs whose privileges and rights originated in the early Middle Ages. Originally the designation of a fortified town or *burh*, the term 'borough' came to mean a town which returned burgesses to Parliament. By virtue of their charters those towns obtained the right to own property and exercise their corporate identity in the name of Mayor and Council, and by the first Municipal Corporations Act of 1835, 178 of those ancient chartered boroughs were given a uniform system of elected councils, thus becoming 'municipal' boroughs. As such they took over the organization of public services previously in private hands. Trevelyan notes that: 'From this beginning there grew up a concentration of new functions; throughout the coming century powers were perpetually being added to the Municipal Corporations. Finally they dealt with almost all aspects of local government except public house licensing and judicial power, which were regarded as

1

unfit functions for an elective body. In 1835 very few foresaw that the new Municipalities would end in educating the children of the people and in supplying the public with trams, light, water and even houses, or that they would become traders and employers of labour on a large scale.'[1] It is significant that the creation of the municipal boroughs preceded the existence of county councils by more than fifty years. By 1971 these more than twelve-score towns were members of the counties alongside the urban districts which shared similar functions and frequently petitioned for their own charters of incorporation. Fifteen of the boroughs were also cities; this dignity was usually bestowed by virtue of a bishop and cathedral church in the town. One of the 'municipal' cities, Lichfield, was a county of itself, as was Poole, another non-county borough. The term 'city' was merely an honorific title without legal significance.

County boroughs — there were 83 of these in 1971 — were a further creation of 19th-century local government reform, in their case the outcome of the Local Government Act of 1888. This Act, having created 62 new administrative counties almost identical with the geographic shires, made further provision for 61 county boroughs of more than 50,000 population (plus Burton, Canterbury, Chester and Worcester). These were to be independent of the administrative counties, with equivalent powers and functions to those of the counties themselves. Thus the Act enunciated the firmly held principle of English local government, that the administration of the towns was separate from the rural countryside around them. Municipal boroughs which failed to gain this status were, for the first time, subordinated to the administration of the county council. A dual system of urban and county government was thus established which survived until 1974. Most of the new county boroughs were relatively late arrivals, first incorporated between 1835 and 1888, but about a dozen towns like Ipswich, Portsmouth, Preston, Walsall, Reading and Wigan were boroughs of the early Middle Ages. Thirty of the county boroughs were also cities, all medieval in origin except Leeds, which was incorporated in 1626; half the cities were also counties in their own right — Bristol had first achieved that status in 1373. The real significance of the county boroughs lay in their peculiarity as the only 'all-purpose' authorities in local government, for, unlike the counties, they did not share their functions with subordinate districts. Instead they were fully responsible for the administration of highways, housing, health, education, libraries, children's services, planning, fire-fighting and police in their towns.

The four maps reveal the chronological and geographical distribution of charters of incorporation from a time before the Norman Conquest down to the 1972 Act. In the first map we see the importance of communications to the growth of the first chartered towns, for almost all the earliest boroughs, well distributed over England and Wales, are evidently closely adjoined to the coastal harbours, the Roman road system and above all, to the navigable rivers and estuaries which made trade possible. With the reigns of Tudors and Stuarts we see a change in distribution. Then, although many of the earlier gaps were filled from north to north-west, the main areas of new grants of incorporation were concentrated in the south-eastern and midland region of the cloth-producing Cotswolds and East Anglia. The last two maps record the massive outcome of the Acts of 1835 and 1888; equally they map the intensity of the 19th-century industrial boom and the consequent growth of urban population, most particularly in Lancashire and Yorkshire. Here we see the municipal origins

CREATION OF BOROUGHS

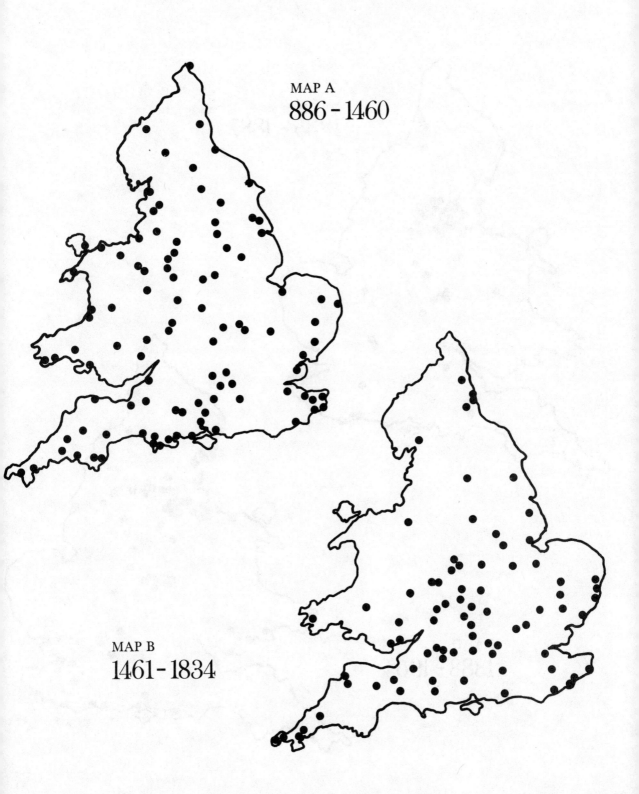

MAP A
886 - 1460

MAP B
1461 - 1834

CREATION OF BOROUGHS

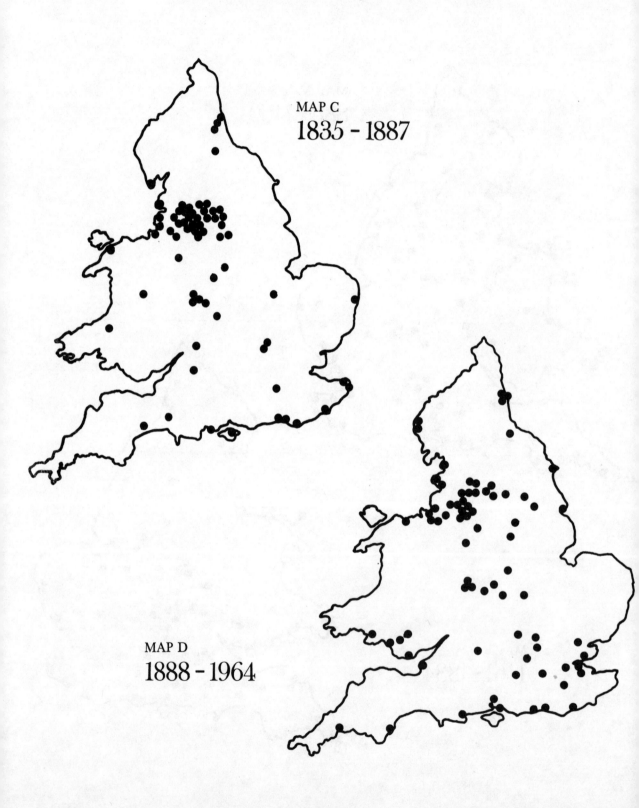

MAP C
1835 - 1887

MAP D
1888 - 1964

of the modern conurbations and the metropolitan counties. Here are the signs of commercial and industrial life in Manchester, Birmingham, Wakefield, Halifax, Jarrow, Rochdale, West Bromwich and dozens more Victorian county boroughs in England; though not, at first, in Wales.

NUMBER OF BOROUGHS FOUNDED

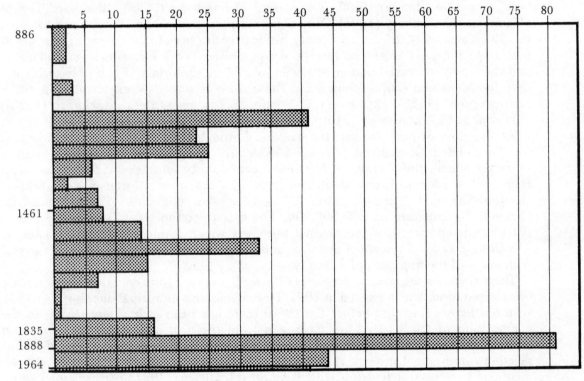

DATES OF FOUNDATION OR INCORPORATION

Graph of Distribution of Borough Creation 886 - 1964 (See previous maps A - D)

The above graph clearly reveals three peaks of municipal development, in the 13th 16th and 19th centuries; it shows two inactive periods when no new boroughs were created and existing municipal privileges were left undisturbed, even by extension. These are the troughs of 15th-century recession and political anarchy and of complacent Whig oligarchy in the 18th century. The graph also shows that the process of borough creation was continuing up to and after the Second World War, for as late as 1954–55 incorporation was granted to Solihull, Whitley Bay, Castleford, Ellesmere Port and Rhondda. Later still, on the very eve of complete reorganization, the Local Government Commission's *Reports on Special Review Areas* resulted in last-minute creation of new county boroughs and extension of the boundaries of many more. Then we see the creation, often abortive, of new towns like Teesside, Warley and Torbay, whilst others like Dudley and Wolverhampton gained at the expense of their neighbouring county.

In 1971 the chief distinctions in urban government were between large and small towns, between old towns and new. Frequently the correlation of those differences was the distinction between county and municipal boroughs. Broadly speaking, with the exception of the great ancient cities, the county boroughs were larger and newer, whilst the municipal boroughs were smaller and older. Thus it is no surprise to find that of the 16 non-county boroughs with populations fewer than 4,000 only three were incorporated after 1600. These were Malmesbury (1885), Blandford Forum (1605), and Shaftesbury (1604). Only Cambridge was larger than 100,000 and founded in 1207. Conversely, of the 26 county boroughs with populations more than 100,000 (excluding the great cities like Liverpool, Manchester, York etc., which were all older, and the newly created London boroughs which are uniformly large), only eight pre-date the Municipal Corporations Act. These were Newport (Mon.) created in 1623, Northampton (1189), Reading (1253), South Shields (1550), Stockport (1220), Sunderland (1634), Swansea (1169), and Walsall (1159).

At the time of our base-list, the London boroughs had already been reorganized by the London Government Act of 1963. This amalgamated the former London County Council, the County of Middlesex and County boroughs of East Ham, West Ham and Croydon with several adjacent boroughs and urban districts of Kent, Surrey, Hertfordshire and Essex to form 32 new London boroughs of the supposedly 'optimum' population of 200–300,000. The Gazetteer (pp. 10–27) gives the earlier dates of incorporation of the original boroughs which formed these amalgamations. The City of London remained inviolate and unique, governed by its Common Council with many of the functions of a county.

These then, are the several categories of 'town', all sharing the common characteristic of incorporation, which existed in 1971. If we compare a municipal directory for 1930 with our list we find that before the 1960s there had been little if any change in the composition of the list. As we have seen from the map and graph, 34 towns had aspired to borough status of one kind or another between 1930 and 1968, but deletions from the list were rare. The amalgamation into Greater London already mentioned removed a few towns like Acton (Middlesex), Ilford (Essex) and Leyton (Essex) from the 1930 directory while Torbay experienced the latest amalgamation of all, in 1968. Otherwise the main losses were those in rural areas like Lostwithiel in Cornwall and above all in Shropshire. There a few ancient towns like Bishop's Castle, Bridgnorth, Ludlow and Wenlock are missing by 1971, usually to form the newly created rural boroughs.

The Local Government Act of 1972 abolished, as from 1 April 1974, the 58 county councils which had previously existed in England and Wales. They were replaced by six metropolitan and 47 non-metropolitan counties. Eighteen newly named counties were created in England and Wales and 26 shires, or their Ridings, were abolished, amalgamated and re-named. In all, 36 new metropolitan districts and 333 county districts were created; these replaced all the previous boroughs, urban districts and rural districts, which were abolished. The metropolitan counties are virtually the six great conurbation regions of the north, north-west and midlands; they resemble in their structure the Greater London Council. In each case the new metropolitan districts have as their administrative centre, and usually as their name, the largest county borough or city which they included. Except in three cases (Trafford and Tameside in Greater Manchester and Knowsley in Merseyside), a municipal borough or an urban district houses the district offices. In most large districts which contain several previous small authorities there are usually 'area offices' in one or more of the original boroughs or urban districts; occasionally one or more of the local government departments such as finance, engineers, recreation and libraries, will be housed in outlying offices. The Gazetteer indicates in the 1981 column of districts which original boroughs contain the *central* district office.

The principal functions of the new counties are strategic planning, highways, reserve powers on housing, police, fire-services, libraries, museums and art galleries education, social services and refuse disposal. The metropolitan counties' functions are more limited in that responsibility for education, social services and public libraries are functions of the metropolitan districts. The non-metropolitan districts are subsidiary authorities with no responsibility for major functions unless as 'agencies' of their county. They are 'autonomous', taking their own rates, but in a smaller way of business than the metropolitan districts. Only the metropolitan counties preserve the real division of major functions between county and borough. There are no authorities other than the non-metropolitan counties which are all-purpose authorities in the same way that only the county boroughs were before 1974. It is an over-simplification to refer to our Gazetteer and note the consequences of the 1972 Act in terms of 'gain' and 'loss' by borough or county. The Act appears at first sight to have stricken both with impartiality; the 'losses' of Somerset, Gloucestershire, Lancashire, Berkshire, Cheshire and the West Riding are exceeded only by the total elimination of Middlesex in 1963 and of Anglesey, Rutland, Westmorland and Huntingdon in 1972. Similarly, in 1966 it was counties like Staffordshire which suffered from the 'gains' of county boroughs like Dudley and Wolverhampton. Ever since the earliest Norman boroughs' insistence upon the exclusion of the sheriff from their affairs, the gains and losses of towns and counties have swung from one to the other at different times. The Local Government Act of 1972 must be seen as a further step from those taken in 1835, 1888 and 1963.

It might be argued that many county boroughs have also 'gained' from the provisions of the 1972 Act. The majority, after all, have retained their names, the central administrative offices of their new districts and so-called 'borough' status. Some, like Plymouth, Southampton and Brighton, now comprise as districts the exact area of their earlier boroughs which ceased to exist in 1974. Many more have received additional areas from the adjacent county, so that the borough may seem to have grown or 'gained' in area and population by becoming a district. In some metropolitan districts like Dudley, neighbouring municipal boroughs have been added from a county to form a district named after the original county borough. In other cases, such as Halifax and Huddersfield, it may appear to be only an emotive issue that, in gaining the administration of Calderdale (including the previous boroughs of Brighouse and Todmorden as well as several neighbouring urban districts) or Kirklees (including the former county borough of Dewsbury, the municipal boroughs of Batley and Spenborough and several more urban districts) both great Yorkshire towns could be deemed the 'loser' of nothing but their names. Each district has regained the town's former borough status. This is to misunderstand the real nature of the change, as well as to underestimate the 'losses' of Brighouse, Todmorden, Dewsbury, Batley and Spenborough. None of these, including Halifax and Huddersfield, is any longer a town, none of them is any longer an all-purpose authority; they are all now districts of a county. Some towns have lost their administrative offices, some have lost their names; 130 towns have lost both identity and influence of any kind; none is in any sense, other than in the survival of the honorific title and office of Mayor, any longer a borough in the original sense of its charter of incorporation or the provision of the Municipal Corporations Act.

Nowhere is the difference between town-as-borough before 1974 and district-as-borough in 1981 more clearly seen than in the different identity of the new non-metropolitan districts and the wholesale grants of borough status to hills and valleys, fields and rivers. As we have seen, the majority of the 333 new county districts, are the results of the amalgamation of urban and rural districts, in some cases around one or more municipal boroughs or, in some cases, without a recognizable town centre. A large number of urban districts were about to be granted borough status by charter immediately before the reorganization of 1974; a list in Hansard gives their names. (*23.3.74: Cols. 185-6*) The new Act made provision (*Sections 245-6*) for districts to apply for borough status after reorganization. In 1981, 167 district councils had made successful applications, with King's Lynn about to be added to the list. Of these, 91 are included in our base-list as original county or municipal boroughs which have regained their former status, as districts. This leaves a majority, 282 in all, which have been deprived of their status.

Of the remaining 76 'new' boroughs, Middlesbrough had previously been a county borough, first chartered in 1165, and Stockton-on-Tees was once a municipal Borough, incorporated in 1283; both towns lost their identity in the premature reorganization of 1968. Other new boroughs had been urban districts like Ashford and Stevenage, some were civil parishes like Halton in Cheshire. Yet they were at least named for earlier townships; the majority are notionally named after natural or geographical features, even in cases where an ancient borough is contained. Many district-boroughs take the names of rivers — Tameside, Afan, Swale, Taff, Ely, Medina and Calderdale; others are named after forests such as Wyre and Rossendale. Some districts are merely named after their locality — North Bedfordshire, South Wight or North Tyneside; all are now 'boroughs'. A few have been given up-to-date names which, in the same way that new counties such as 'Avon' and 'Cleveland' smack more of Independent Television companies than of ancient shires, remind us of suburban houses — Gravesham (Kent) and Hertsmere (Hertfordshire), for example. A few of these can take us by surprise with their antiquity; the councillors of Cleveland will no doubt remind us that 'Clivelanda' was 'the hilly region' as early as 1110, and Trafford (Greater Manchester) is surely named after the park of the 1206 Pipe Rolls rather than any more modern recreation ground? But the appeal to antiquity is belated: to be a hilly region was never before a qualification for borough status and Runnymede, however famous a meadow, is still a field rather than a town. The full extent and nature of the changes brought about the towns by the 1972 Act can best be summarised by means of the following Table:

CHANGES OF IDENTITY AND STATUS OF BOROUGHS 1971–1981
LB = London Borough: CB = County Borough: MB = Municipal Borough: Met = Metropolitan Borough

Nature of Change:		LB	CB	MB	Total
Towns which are now districts in their previous name, with borough or city status:		33	70	59	162
	Met:	—	26	—	
	Non-Met:	—	44	—	
Towns with full district identity (name and district offices) *without* borough status:		—	—	14	14
Towns with district offices under new names:		—	6	63	69
	Met:	—	6	2	
	Non-Met:	—	—	61	
Towns which have lost both status and identity:		—	7	123	130
TOTALS:		33	83	259	375

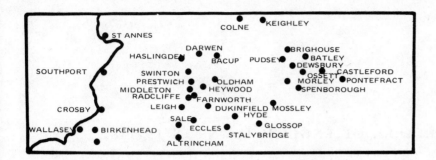

The Lost Boroughs
1974

GAZETTEER OF ENGLISH TOWNS IN 1971–81

Let us now turn to the base-list which names those towns which we shall document in the following Chapters. The first column gives the name of each town which was incorporated in 1971. In **BOLD CAPITALS** (e.g. **BARNSLEY**) are those which have retained their identity and status as new districts, some as boroughs; these are the survivors. Towns named in CAPITALS (e.g. ABERYSTWYTH) are those which house the offices of a district with another name; some of those districts also have borough status. These are the anonymous towns. Those listed in *ITALIC CAPITALS* (e.g. *STOUR-BRIDGE*) are the towns which retain neither status nor identity, their only existence is now that of a parish, where once they were boroughs; these are the losers. There are some cosmetic devices by which a few of these towns — or even cities such as Ripon — have retained their civic pride and endeavoured to conserve their original borough identity. These devices include the establishment of charter trustees (CT) by 31 towns such as Aylesbury, Kidderminster and Yeovil; the trustees may annually elect a mayor and have 'any powers to appoint local officers of dignity exercisable immediately before 1st April 1974 by the corporation of the city or borough'. A few towns or cities, such as Bangor, Chichester, Ely, Truro, Ripon and Wells are 'parish councils which have adopted town status' (TC) and Rochester is now a city by Special Letters Patent. Of the largest cities 21 still have Lord Mayors; all these dignities are noted in the base-list.

The Gazetteer is divided into two parts. Firstly, for 1971, its columns give the original county in which each town was situated and its status as MB, CB or LB; Cities (C) and Cities as Counties(Co) is also noted, then the date of each borough's incorporation. The population as recorded by the 1971 Census follows, with reference finally to any recognized county record office, city record office or borough archives recognized by the handlist of *Record Repositories in Great Britain* (4th edition, 1971). The 1981 section of the list parallels the earlier information, beginning with the present county of each borough, its district whether in its own name (in **BOLD CAPITALS**) or another and its present status, if any. Population in 1981 is given only for the districts which are identifiably the original towns in the first column of all. Finally the continuing existence of the local record repositories is noted by reference to the 6th edition (1979) of *Record Repositories in Great Britain*.

This books is mainly about the *identity* of boroughs: it is, therefore, also concerned with the accessibility of the archives which preserve that identity. The present position, as far as one can find any definite information, is unclear, except that in theory the counties are intended to be responsible for the archives of their districts; as we have seen, the non-metropolitan counties are responsible for their library provision, the metropolitan counties are not. There has certainly been some local apprehension, shared particularly by borough librarians before 1974, that there might be a county 'take-over' of borough archives, but there is little purpose at this stage in making this an emotive issue. One should fear rather the dangers of economies, staff shortages and 'rationalization' of resources, than any sinister plot by hard-worked county archivists. There has been, inevitably, some closure or amalgamation of uneconomic outlying archive repositories; shortage of staff will continue to bedevil the situation at county and district levels. Yet we must recognize that occasionally the current urge to centralization is strong; the present 'Measure' by the Church of England, which requires 'adequate' custody of all parish records in the diocesan (usually the county) record office, will remove countless archives from their parishes. This is not a reassuring precedent and will probably create far more work than can be done by record office staff in the near future.

Our base-list is not an encouraging record of enhanced provision. There have been, it is true a few new appointments of district archivists by new boroughs which evidently place priority on the custody of archives. Dudley was for many years an example of the best provision a student could hope for at borough archives level; the provision continues, but with an immense additional responsibility for the archives of Stourbridge and Halesowen. Most of the new London boroughs have appointed archivists since their reorganization and outside London several new appointments are recorded; in some towns there are evidently new record offices for the new district. Yet, regrettably, the total of all archivists in post is less promising than these good examples would seem to indicate.

The *Municipal Year Book* of 1981 lists 53 fewer archivists than there were in the 1971 edition and *Record Repositories in Great Britain* in its 5th edition (1973) states plainly that since their previous issue of 1971 '. . . the number of repositories included has fallen by nearly a third.'

The county record offices appear to survive intact, even where amalgamations with other counties have made dual arrangements for more than one major repository in the new county (such as Hereford and Worcester) inevitable. As yet however (1982), there is no mention of archivists' appointments in Avon, Clwyd, West Midlands, Cumbria and others where, presumably the earlier provisions of Bristol, Hawarden, Carlisle and Kendal will suffice. In view of the present economies the discrepancies, for example in the provision mentioned for Cumbria in 1979 (*R.R.G.B.*) and 1981 (*Municipal Year Book*), are ominous. The total of county archivists appears to have been reduced from 49 to 24 and the 26 district appointments previously noted are less than half the 53 borough archivists' posts which were recorded ten years ago. Even the encouraging example of the London Boroughs is, overall, one appointment fewer than the previous boroughs' total number of posts. It is noticeable from our list that the public libraries previously recorded as being also record repositories are in some cases missing from the current list. It may be that some of these are merely omissions or the failure of a new authority to acknowledge the provision of a subordinate repository which is still, nevertheless, thriving.

In compiling the base-list and verifying the data given in this chapter, reference has been made to the *Annual Abstracts of Statistics* published by the Central Statistical Office (H.M.S.O.), to the *Municipal Year Books* of 1971 and 1981 and to *Whitaker's Almanacks (Municipal Directory)* for the same years. Other reference books such as current *A.A. Members' Handbooks* and the A.A.'s *Book of British Towns* (1979) are also useful, as is Lewis Braithwaite's *Historic Towns of Britain* (1981). The index to a good Atlas of Great Britain is essential and the *Readers' Digest 'Complete Atlas of the British Isles'* in its 1965 edition has the additional value of being itself an historic document of British towns and counties as they were before reorganization. Bartholomew's *Gazetteer of Great Britain* (1st edition, 1977) is an essential guide to the new districts and their populations and the topography of local government is most clearly delineated in the Ordnance Survey maps of *Local Government Boundaries, England and Wales* (two sheets, North and South). A comprehensive outline of the organization, past and present, of all the ancient parishes and boroughs of southern England (below a line Severn to Wash) is published by the Royal Historical Society as the first volume of two which will cover all England. This is the *Guide to Local Administrative Units of England* by Frederic A. Youngs, Jnr. (Royal Historical Society, 1979). This reference book is indispensable in tracing the sequences of all the different units of local government down to the reorganization of 1974. From all this data we produce the following Gazetteer which will act as a base-list for each documentary chapter which follows. Population figures are taken from the Registrar-General's *Estimates* for 1979 (for 1981); and from the Census of 1971 for that year. The London boroughs as listed here were created by the London Government Act 1963 which reorganized three county boroughs, 28 metropolitan boroughs, and 15 urban districts. In each case the earlier boroughs will be noted in the Secondary notes at the end of the Gazetteer, for example (i).

ABBREVIATIONS USED IN THE GAZETTEER

(1) in the columns headed 'Status'

B	=	Borough
C	=	City
CB	=	County Borough
Co	=	County
CT	=	Charter Trustees
D	=	District
LB	=	London Borough
LM	=	Lord Mayor
MB	=	Municipal Borough
MD	=	Metropolitan District
Met	=	Metropolitan borough of the County of London, pre-1965
TC	=	'Parish Council having adopted Town status' (*Municipal Year Book*)
UD	=	Urban District

(2) in the columns headed 'Archives'

Arch	=	entry in *Municipal Year Book* of an archivist appointment other than CRO
BRO	=	Borough Record Office
CRO	=	County/City Record Office
GLRO	=	Greater London Record Office
Mus	=	Museum
NLW	=	National Library of Wales
PL	=	Public Library
*	=	entry in *Record Repositories of Great Britain* (4th edn., 1971)
**	=	appointed by the Lord Chancellor as a repository for specified classes of records.
nc	=	no charter
RB	=	Royal Borough

Note: the names of many counties have also been abbreviated, but are not listed here. The last column of the Gazetteer includes certain items of detailed information which cannot be shown in tabular form.

Name of Town	1971: County	Status	Inc.	Pop.	Archives
ABERGAVENNY	Mon	MB	1542	9,401	
ABERYSTWYTH	Card	MB	1277	10,688	NLW**
ABINGDON	Berks	MB	1556	18,610	Arch
ACCRINGTON	Lancs	MB	1878	36,894	
ALDEBURGH	E.Suffolk	MB	1529	3,180	
ALDERSHOT	Hants	MB	1922	33,390	Arch
ALTRINCHAM	Cheshire	MB	1937	40,787	
ANDOVER	Hants	MB	1175	25,881	
APPLEBY	Westmld	MB	1179	1,890	
ARUNDEL	W.Sussex	MB	1586	2,990	
ASHTON-UNDER-LYNE	Lancs	MB	1847	48,952	
AYLESBURY	Bucks	MB	1916	40,569	CRO**
BACUP	Lancs	MB	1882	15,118	
BANBURY	Oxon	MB	1554	29,387	
BANGOR	Caern	C:MB	1883	14,558	UCNW**
BARKING	London	LB	1965	153,870	
BARNET	London	LB	1965	305,700	PL*
BARNSLEY	W.R.Yorks	CB	1869	75,395	Arch
BARNSTAPLE	Devon	MB	930	17,317	
BARROW-IN-FURNESS	Lancs	CB	1867	64,034	PL*
BARRY	Glam	MB	1939	41,681	
BASINGSTOKE	Hants	MB	1392	52,587	
BATH	Som	C:CB	1590	84,670	GH:PL*
BATLEY	W.R.Yorks	MB	1868	42,006	
BEAUMARIS	Anglesey	MB	1294	2,102	
BEBINGTON	Cheshire	MB	1937	61,582	
BECCLES	E.Suffolk	MB	1584	8,015	Arch
BEDFORD	Beds	MB	1166	73,229	CRO**Arch
BERWICK-UPON-TWEED	Northld	MB	1302	11,647	
BEVERLEY	E.R.Yorks	MB	1573	17,132	CRO**
BEWDLEY	Worcs	MB	1462	7,237	PL*
BEXHILL	E.Sussex	MB	1902	32,898	PL*
BEXLEY	London	LB	1965	216,400	
BIDEFORD	Devon	MB	1573	11,802	
BIRKENHEAD	Cheshire	CB	1877	137,852	
BIRMINGHAM	Warks	C:CB:LM	1838	1,014,670	
BLACKBURN	Lancs	CB	1851	101,806	
BLACKPOOL	Lancs	CB	1876	151,860	
BLANDFORD FORUM	Dorset	MB	1605	3,647	
BLYTH	Northld	MB	1922	34,653	

981: ounty	District	Status	Pop.	Archives
	*indicates that the *main* District office is here			
went	Monmouth (1)			
yfed	Ceredigion* (see Cardigan and Lampeter)			NLW** CRO**
xon	Vale of White Horse*			
ancs	Hyndburn D & B*			
uffolk	Suffolk Coastal			
ants	Rushmoor D & B			
tr Manchester	Trafford MD & B			
ants	Test Valley D & B* (see Romsey)			
umbria	Eden			(CRO Kendall)
. Sussex	Arun			
tr Manchester	Tameside MD & B*			
ucks	Aylesbury Vale* (see Buckingham)	D & B		CRO**
ancs	Rossendale D & B			
xon	Cherwell*	CT		
wynedd	Arfon D & B* (see Caernarvon)	C:CT		UCNW*
ondon	**BARKING AND DAGENHAM**	LB(i)	149,300	Arch
ondon	**BARNET**	LB(ii)	290,400	PL:Arch*
.Yorks	**BARNSLEY**	MD:B	221,800	
evon	N.Devon*			
umbria	**BARROW-IN-FURNESS**	D:B	71,100	CRO**
.Glam	Vale of Glamorgan D & B* (see Cowbridge)			
ants	**BASINGSTOKE AND DEANE***	D:B	127,200	
von	**BATH***	C:D	83,900	CRO**Arch(D)
.Yorks	Kirklees MD & B			
wynedd	Ynys Môn (Anglesey) D & B*			CRO Llangefni
erseyside	Wirral MD & B			
uffolk	Waveney			
eds	N.Beds D & B*			CRO**Arch
orthld	**BERWICK-UPON-TWEED***	D:B	25,500	
umberside	**BEVERLEY***	D:B	106,600	CRO**
& W	Wyre Forest			
. Sussex	Rother*	CT (see Rye)		
ondon	**BEXLEY**	LB (iii)	213,000	Arch
evon	Torridge* (see (Great) Torrington)			
erseyside	Wirral MD & B			DRO Arch
.Midlands	**BIRMINGHAM(2)***	C:MD:LM	1,033,900	PL:Arch**
ancs	**BLACKBURN(3)***	D:B	142,500	
ancs	**BLACKPOOL***	D:B	145,400	
orset	N.Dorset* (see Shaftesbury)			
thmb	Blyth Valley D & B			

Name of Town	1971: County	Status	Inc.	Pop.	Archives
BODMIN	Cornwall	MB	1798	9,207	
BOLTON	Lancs	CB	1838	154,199	
BOOTLE	Lancs	CB	1868	74,294	
BOSTON	Lincs	MB	1545	26,025	
BOURNEMOUTH	Hants	CB	1890	153,869	
BRACKLEY	Northants	MB	1260	4,480	
BRADFORD	W.R.Yorks	C:CB:LM	1847	294,177	PL*Arch
BRECON	Brecon	MB	1412	6,304	
BRENT	London	LB	1965	280,257	
BRIDGWATER	Som	MB	1200	26,642	
BRIDLINGTON	E.R.Yorks	MB	1899	26,776	
BRIDPORT	Dorset	MB	1253	6,369	
BRIGHOUSE	W.R.Yorks	MB	1893	34,141	
BRIGHTON	E.Sussex	CB	1854	161,351	
BRISTOL	Glos	Co:C:CB:LM	1188	426,657	CRO**Arch
BROMLEY	London	LB	1965	306,680	PL*
BUCKINGHAM	Bucks	MB	1554	5,076	
BURNLEY	Lancs	CB	1861	76,513	
BURTON-ON-TRENT	Staffs	CB	1878	50,201	PL*
BURY	Lancs	CB	1876	67,849	
BURY ST. EDMUNDS	W.Suffolk	MB	1606	25,661	CRO**Arch
BUXTON	Derbs(7)	MB	1917	20,324	
CAERNARFON	Caern	MB (RB)	1284	9,260	CRO**
CALNE	Wilts(8)	MB	1565	9,688	
CAMBRIDGE	Cambs	C:MB	1207	98,840	CRO**
CAMDEN	London	LB	1965	203,640	PL
CANTERBURY	Kent	Co:C:CB	1448	33,176	CRO:Arch
CARDIFF	Glam	C:CB:LM	1680	279,111	NMW:CRO:PL**
CARDIGAN	Card	MB	1230	3,810	
CARLISLE	Cumb	C:CB	1158	71,582	CRO**Arch
CARMARTHEN	Carm	MB	1313	13,081	CRO**
CASTLEFORD	W.R.Yorks	MB	1955	38,234	
CHARD	Som	MB	1570	7,908	
CHATHAM	Kent	MB	1891	57,153	
CHELMSFORD	Essex	MB	1888	58,194	CRO**
CHELTENHAM	Glos	MB	1876	74,356	
CHESTER	Cheshire	Co:C:CB	1506	62,911	CROs**Arch
CHESTERFIELD	Derbs	MB	1598	70,169	PL*:Arch
CHICHESTER	W.Sussex	C:MB	c.1150	20,649	CRO**
CHIPPENHAM	Wilts	MB	1554	18,696	
CHIPPING NORTON	Oxon	MB	1606	4,763	
CHORLEY	Lancs	MB	1881	31,659	
CHRISTCHURCH	Hants	MB	1886	31,463	
CLEETHORPES	Lincs	MB	1936	35,837	
CLITHEROE	Lancs	MB	1147	13,194	
COLCHESTER	Essex	MB	1189	76,531	PL*
COLNE	Lancs	MB	1895	18,940	
COLWYN BAY	Denb	MB	1934	25,564	Arch
CONGLETON	Cheshire	MB	1272	20,341	
CONWAY	Caern	MB	1284	12,206	
COVENTRY	Warks	C:CB	1345	335,410	CRO**Arch
COWBRIDGE	Glam	MB	nc	1,350	
CREWE	Cheshire	MB	1877	51,421	
CROSBY	Lancs	MB	1937	57,497	

981: ounty	District	Status	Pop.	Archives
ornwall	N.Cornwall* (see Launceston)			
tr Manchester	BOLTON(4)*	MD:B	260,100	BRO*
erseyside	Sefton MD & B* (see Crosby and Southport)			
ncs	BOSTON*	D:B	51,500	
orset	BOURNEMOUTH*	D:B	144,200	Arch
orthants	S.Northants			
.Yorks	BRADFORD(5)*	C:MD:LM	461,600	CRO:PL,Arch** (Northallerton)
owys	BRECKNOCK*	D:B	39,000	
ondon	BRENT	LB(iv)	251,900	
om	Sedgemoor*	CT		
umberside	N.Wolds D & B*			
orset	W.Dorset			
. Yorks	Calderdale MD & B			
Sussex	BRIGHTON*	D:B	152,700	
von	BRISTOL*	C:D:LM	408,000	CRO**Arch(D)
ondon	BROMLEY	LB(v)	290,700	PL*Arch
ucks	Aylesbury Vale			
ancs	BURNLEY*	D:B	92,300	
affs	E.Staffs*	CT		Arch (from CRO)
tr Manchester	BURY*	MD:B	178,600	
uffolk	St. Edmundsbury D & B*			CRO**
erbs	High Peak D & B			
wynedd	Arfon D & B			CRO**
ilts	N.Wilts			
ambs	CAMBRIDGE*	C:D:	101,600	CRO**
ondon	CAMDEN(v)	LB(vi)	190,900	PL*
ent	CANTERBURY*	C:D	118,600	CRO**Arch(D)
Glam	CARDIFF*	C:D:LM	282,000	NMW:CROs**(9)
yfed	CEREDIGION(10)	D	60,400	
umbria	CARLISLE*	C:D	98,300	CRO**
yfed	CARMARTHEN*	D	49,900	CRO**
.Yorks	Wakefield MD & C			
om	Yeovil			
ent	Rochester-upon-Medway			
ssex	CHELMSFORD*	D:B:CT	134,600	CRO**
los	CHELTENHAM*	D:B:	85,000	
heshire	CHESTER*	C:D	116,300	CROs**Arch(D)
erbs	CHESTERFIELD*	D:B	96,300	
.Sussex	CHICHESTER*	C:D:TC(11)	96,500	CRO**
ilts	N.Wilts* (see Calne and Malmesbury)	CT		
xon	W.Oxon			
ancs	CHORLEY*	D:B	88,500	
orset	CHRISTCHURCH*	D:B:	38,600	
umberside	CLEETHORPES*	D:B	68,400	
ancs	Ribble Valley D & B*			
ssex	COLCHESTER*	D:B	137,500	Arch
ancs	Pendle D & B			
wyd	COLWYN D & B			
heshire	CONGLETON*	D:B	78,900	
wynedd	Aberconwy D & B			
. Midlands	COVENTRY*	C:MD:LM	339,300	CRO**
Glam	Vale of Glamorgan D & B			
heshire	CREWE AND NANTWICH*	D:B	97,500	
erseyside	Sefton MD & B			

Name of Town	1971: County	Status	Inc.	Pop.	Archives
CROYDON	London	LB	1965	333,840	PL**
DARLINGTON	Co.Durham	CB	1867	85,938	
DARTFORD	Kent	MB	1933	46,510	
DARTMOUTH	Devon	MB	1341	5,707	
DARWEN	Lancs	MB	1878	28,926	
DAVENTRY	Northants	MB	1595	11,815	
DEAL	Kent	MB	1699	25,432	
DENBIGH	Denb	MB	1290	8,101	Arch
DERBY	Derbs	CB	1154	219,582	PL**
DEVIZES	Wilts	MB	1605	10,179	
DEWSBURY	W.R.Yorks	CB	1862	51,326	PL*
DONCASTER	W.R.Yorks	CB	1194	82,668	BRO*
DORCHESTER	Dorset	MB	1324	13,736	CRO**
DOVER	Kent	MB	1278	34,359	
DROITWICH	Worcs	MB	1215	12,748	
DUDLEY	Staffs	CB	1865	185,581	PL*Arch
DUKINFIELD	Cheshire	MB	1899	17,315	
DUNSTABLE	Beds	MB	1864	31,828	
DURHAM	Co.Durham	C:MB	1602	24,776	CRO**
EALING	London	LB	1965	300,580	
EASTBOURNE	Sussex	CB	1883	70,921	
EASTLEIGH	Hants	MB	1936	45,361	
EAST RETFORD	Notts	MB	1246	18,413	
ECCLES	Lancs	MB	1892	38,502	
ELLESMERE PORT	Cheshire	MB	1955	61,637	
(ELY) (12)	Cambs	C:UD	nc	9,020	
ENFIELD	London	MB	1965	266,230	
EPSOM AND EWELL	Surrey	MB	1937	72,301	
EVESHAM	Worcs	MB	1604	13,855	
EXETER	Devon	Co:C:CB	1156	95,729	CRO**
EYE	E.Suffolk	MB	1206	1,603	
FALMOUTH	Cornwall	MB	1661	18,041	
FARNWORTH	Lancs	MB	1939	26,862	
FAVERSHAM	Kent	MB	1252	14,818	
FLEETWOOD	Lancs	MB	1933	28,599	
FLINT	Flints(15)	MB	1284	14,662	
FOLKESTONE	Kent	MB	1313	43,801	
GATESHEAD	Co.Durham	CB	1835	94,469	PL**Arch
GILLINGHAM	Kent	MB	1903	86,862	
GLASTONBURY	Som	MB	1705	6,558	
GLOSSOP	Derbs	MB	1866	24,272	
GLOUCESTER	Glos	Co:C:CB	1483	90,232	
GODALMING	Surrey	MB	1575	18,669	
GOOLE	W.R.Yorks	MB	1933	18,072	
GOSPORT	Hants	MB	1922	76,116	
GRANTHAM	Lincs	MB	1463	27,943	
GRAVESEND	Kent	MB	1562	54,106	
GREAT YARMOUTH	Norfolk	CB	1208	50,236	BRO Arch
GREENWICH	London	LB	1965	217,790	
GRIMSBY	Lincs	CB	1201	95,540	BRO**Arch
GUILDFORD	Surrey	LB	1257	57,214	Mus**(15) Arch
HACKNEY	London	LB	1965	219,240	PL*
HALESOWEN	Worcs	MB	1936	53,980	

ounty	District	Status	Pop.	Archives
ondon	**CROYDON**	LB(vii)	320,500	
urham	**DARLINGTON***	D:B	95,000	
ent	**DARTFORD***	D:B	81,300	
evon	S.Hams			
ancs	Blackburn D & B			
orthants	**DAVENTRY***	D:CT	56,400	
ent	Dover	CT		
lwyd	Glyndŵr			
erbs	**DERBY***	C:D	215,900	
ilts	Kennet*			
	(see Marlborough)			
.Yorks	Kirklees MD & B			
.Yorks	**DONCASTER***	MD:B	286,500	BRO
orset	W.Dorset*			CRO**
	(see Bridport and Lyme Regis)			
ent	**DOVER*(13)**	D:CT	98,700	
& W	Wychavon			
.Midlands	**DUDLEY*(14)**	MD:B	296,000	PL**Arch
tr Manchester	Tameside MD & B			
eds	S.Beds*			
urham	**DURHAM***	C:D	87,200	CRO**
ondon	**EALING**(vi)	LB(viii)	289,400	
.Sussex	**EASTBOURNE***	D:B	73,100	
ants	**EASTLEIGH***	D:B	88,000	
otts	Bassetlaw			
tr Manchester	Salford MD & B			
heshire	**ELLESMERE PORT AND NESTON***	D:B	85,100	
ambs	E.Cambs*	C:TC		
ondon	**ENFIELD**	LB(ix)	258,800	Arch
urrey	**EPSOM AND EWELL***	D:B	90,500	Arch
& W	Wychavon			
evon	**EXETER***	C:D	95,600	CRO**
uffolk	Mid-Suffolk*			
ornwall	Carrick			
tr Manchester	Bolton MD & B			
ent	Swale D & B			
ancs	Wyre D & B			
lwyd	Delyn D & B			
ent	Shepway*			CRO:PL**
	(see Hythe, Lydd and New Romney)			
yne and Wear	**GATESHEAD***	MD:B	212,200	PL**
ent	**GILLINGHAM***	D:B	92,800	
om	Mendip			
erbs	High Peak D & B			
los	**GLOUCESTER***	C:D	91,300	CRO**
urrey	Waverley*			
umberside	Boothferry D & B*			
ants	**GOSPORT***	D:B	79,400	
incs	S.Kesteven*			
	(see Stamford)			
ent	Gravesham D & B*			
orfolk	**GREAT YARMOUTH***	D:B	79,700	
ondon	**GREENWICH**	LB(x)	204,400	PL*
umberside	**GREAT GRIMSBY***	D:B	91,900	'Area'RO**
urrey	**GUILDFORD***	D:B	117,400	CRO**
ondon	**HACKNEY**	LB(xi)	190,700	PL*Arch
.Midlands	Dudley MD & B			

Name of Town	1971: County	Status	Inc.	Pop.	Archives
HALIFAX	W.R.Yorks	CB	1848	91,272	PL*Arch
HAMMERSMITH	London	LB	1965	184,750	PL*
HARINGEY	London	LB	1965	238,200	PL*
HARROGATE	W.R.Yorks	MB	1884	62,427	PL*
HARROW	London	MB	1965	205,000	
HARTLEPOOL	Co.Durham	CB	1201	97,094	
HARWICH	Essex	MB	1603	14,926	
HASLINGDEN	Lancs	MB	1891	14,924	
HASTINGS	E.Sussex	CB	1588	72,410	Mus
HAVERFORDWEST	Pemb	MB	1479	9,140	CRO**
HAVERING	London	LB	1965	246,700	
HEDON	E.R.Yorks	MB	1154	2,530	
HELSTON	Cornwall	MB	1201	9,978	
HEMEL HEMPSTEAD	Herts	MB	1898	76,000	
HENLEY-ON-THAMES	Oxon	MB	1526	11,431	
HEREFORD	Herefs	C:MB	1189	46,503	CRO:PL**
HERTFORD	Herts	MB	1555	20,362	CRO**
HEYWOOD	Lancs	MB	1881	30,400	
HIGHAM FERRERS	Northants	MB	1251	4,390	
HIGH WYCOMBE	Bucks	MB	1237	59,530	
HILLINGDON	London	LB	1965	230,020	
HONITON	Devon	MB	1846	5,072	
HOUNSLOW	London	LB	1965	206,650	PL*
HOVE	Sussex	MB	1898	73,086	PL*
HUDDERSFIELD	W.R.Yorks	CB	1868	131,190	PL*
HUNTINGDON AND GODMANCHESTER	Hunts	MB	1202 1212	16,557	CRO**Arch
HYDE	Cheshire	MB	1881	37,095	
HYTHE	Kent	MB	1575	11,959	Mus* Arch
ILKESTON	Derbs	MB	1887	34,134	
IPSWICH	Suffolk	CB	1200	123,312	CRO**Arch
ISLINGTON	London	LB	1965	200,730	PL*
JARROW	Co.Durham	MB	1875	28,907	
KEIGHLEY	W.R.Yorks	MB	1882	55,345	
KENDAL	Westmld	MB	1575	21,596	CRO**
KENSINGTON AND CHELSEA	London	LB	1965	186,570	PL*
KETTERING	Northants	MB	1938	42,668	
KIDDERMINSTER	Worcs	MB	1636	47,326	PL**
KIDWELLY	Carm	MB	temp.Hen I	2,290	
KING'S LYNN	Norfolk	MB	1204	30,107	
KINGSTON-UPON-HULL	E.R.Yorks	Co:C:CB:LM	1440	285,970	CRO* Arch
KINGSTON-UPON-THAMES	London	LB	1965	140,550	CRO**BRO**
LAMBETH	London	LB	1965	304,410	PL*
LAMPETER	Card	MB	1884	2,189	
LANCASTER	Lancs	C:MB	1193	49,584	PL*
LAUNCESTON	Cornwall	MB	1199	4,670	Arch
LEEDS	W.R.Yorks	C:CB:LM	1626	496,009	PL** Arch
LEICESTER	Leics	C:CB	1589	284,208	CROs**Mus*Arch
LEIGH	Lancs	MB	1899	46,181	
LEOMINSTER	Herefs	MB	1554	7,079	
LEWES	Sussex	MB	1881	14,159	CRO**
LEWISHAM	London	LB	1965	266,700	PL*
LICHFIELD	Staffs	Co:C:MB	1594	22,600	CRO** Arch
LINCOLN	Lincs	Co:C:CB	1154	74,269	CRO**PL*Arch
LISKEARD	Cornwall	MB	1240	1,289	
LIVERPOOL	Lancs	C:CB:LM	1207	610,113	CRO** Arch
LLANDOVERY	Carm	MB	1485	2,002	

981: ounty	District	Status	Pop.	Archives
.Yorks	Calderdale MD & B*(17)			Arch(D)
ondon	HAMMERSMITH AND FULHAM	LB(xii)	161,800	PL*
ondon	HARINGEY	LB(xiii)	223,900	PL* Arch
.Yorks	HARROGATE*(18)	D:B	134,500	
ondon	HARROW	LB(xiv)	196,600	
leveland	HARTLEPOOL*	D:B	95,100	(CRO:Middlesbro)*
ssex	Tendring			
ancs	Rossendale D & B			
.Sussex	HASTINGS*	D:B	74,200	Mus*
yfed	Preseli*			CRO**
ondon	HAVERING	LB(xv)	239,900	
umberside	Derwentside			
ornwall	Kerrier			
erts	Dacorum*	CT		
xon	S.Oxon			
& W	HEREFORD*	C:D	46,800	CRO**
erts	E.Herts			CRO**
tr Manchester	Rochdale MD & B			
orthants	E.Northants			
ucks	Wycombe*			
ondon	HILLINGDON*	LB(xvi)	228,700	
evon	E.Devon			
ondon	HOUNSLOW	LB(xvii)	201,300	Arch
.Sussex	HOVE*	D & B	87,800	
.Yorks	Kirklees* MD & B(19)			PL** Arch
ambs	HUNTINGDON*(20)	D	125,500	CRO**
tr Manchester	Tameside MD & B			
ent	Shepway			
erbs	Erewash D & B*			
uffolk	IPSWICH*	D & B	118,900	CRO**
ondon	ISLINGTON	LB(xviii)	167,400	
yne & Wear	S.Tyneside MD & B			
.Yorks	Bradford MD & C			
umbria	S.Lakeland			
ondon (ROYAL)	KENSINGTON AND CHELSEA	RLB(xix)	149,900	PL* Arch
orthants	KETTERING*	D:B	70,500	
& W	Wyre Forest			
yfed	Llanelli D & B			
orfolk	W.Norfolk*			
umberside	KINGSTON-UPON-HULL*	C:D:LM	274,500	CRO** Arch
ondon (ROYAL)	KINGSTON-UPON-THAMES	RLB(xx)	135,700	CRO**BRO*Arch
ondon	LAMBETH(xviii)	LB(xxi)	266,400	PL* Arch
yfed	Ceredigion			
ancs	LANCASTER*(21)	C:D	123,400	
ornwall	N.Cornwall			
.Yorks	LEEDS*(22)	C:MD:LM	724,300	PL** Arch
eics	LEICESTER*	C:D:LM	276,600	CRO**
tr Manchester	Wigan MD & B			
& W	LEOMINSTER	D	37,400	
.Sussex	LEWES*	D	76,600	CRO**
ondon	LEWISHAM(xix)	LB(xxii)	238,100	PL*
taffs	LICHFIELD*	C:CT	86,700	CRO**
incs	LINCOLN*	C:D	71,900	CRO**
ornwall	Caradon* (see Saltash)			
erseyside	LIVERPOOL*	C:MD:LM	520,200	CROs**
yfed	Dinefwr D & B			

Name of Town	1971: County	Status	Inc.	Pop.	Archives
LLANELLI	Carm	MB	1913	26,383	
LLANFYLLIN	Mont	MB	c.1290–95	1,120	
LLANIDLOES	Mont	MB	1280	2,350	
LONDON	London	Co:C	1067	4,245	GLRO**CRO
LOUGHBOROUGH	Leics	MB	1888	45,875	
LOUTH	Lincs	MB	1551	11,170	
LOWESTOFT	E.Suffolk	MB	1885	52,267	
LUTON	Beds	CB	1876	161,405	
LYDD	Kent	MB	1885	4,800	
LYME REGIS	Dorset	MB	1284	3,290	
LYMINGTON	Hants	MB	1150	35,733	
LYTHAM ST. ANNES	Lancs	MB	1922	40,299	
MACCLESFIELD	Cheshire	MB	1261	44,401	
MAIDENHEAD	Berks	MB	1582	45,288	
MAIDSTONE	Kent	MB	1549	70,987	CRO** Arch
MALDON	Essex	MB	1171	13,891	
MALMESBURY	Wilts	MB	1885	2,680	
MANCHESTER	Lancs	C:CB:LM	1838	543,650	PL**
MANSFIELD	Notts	MB	1891	57,644	
MARGATE	Kent	MB	1857	50,347	Arch
MARLBOROUGH	Wilts	MB	1575	6,108	
MERTHYR TYDFIL	Glam	CB	1905	55,317	
MERTON	London	LB	1965	177,150	
MIDDLETON	Lancs	MB	1886	53,512	
MONMOUTH	Mon	MB	1447	6,570	
MONTGOMERY	Mont	MB	1885	990	
MORECAMBE AND HEYSHAM	Lancs	MB	1902	41,908	
MORLEY	W.R.Yorks	MB	1885	44,345	
MORPETH	Northld	MB	1662	14,054	
MOSSLEY	Lancs	MB	1885	10,086	
NEATH	Glam	MB	1685	28,619	Arch
NELSON	Lancs	MB	1890	31,249	
NEWARK	Notts	MB	1549	26,646	
NEWBURY	Berks	MB	1506	23,634	Arch
NEWCASTLE-UNDER-LYME	Staffs	MB	1173	77,126	
NEWCASTLE-UPON-TYNE	Northld	Co:C:CBLM	1175	222,209	CROs**PL*Arch
NEWHAM	London	LB	1965	236,490	PL**
NEWPORT	I of W	MB	Hen II	22,309	
NEWPORT	Mon	CB	1623	112,286	
NEW ROMNEY	Kent	MB	1563	3,650	
NORTHAMPTON	Northants	CB	1189	151,000	CRO**PL*Arch
NORWICH	Norfolk	Co:C:CB:LM	1194	122,083	CROs** Arch
NOTTINGHAM	Notts	Co:C:CB:LM	1155	300,630	CROs**PL*Arch
NUNEATON	Warks	MB	1907	67,027	
OKEHAMPTON	Devon	MB	1272	3,830	
OLDHAM	Lancs	CB	1849	105,913	
OSSETT	W.R.Yorks	MB	1890	17,183	
OXFORD	Oxon	C:CB	Hen II	108,805	CRO**
PEMBROKE	Pemb	MB	1100	14,197	
PENRYN	Cornwall	MB	1275	5,135	
PENZANCE	Cornwall	MB	1614	19,415	
PETERBOROUGH	Hunts	C:MB	1874	87,568	

1981:

County	District	Status		Pop.	Archives
Dyfed	**LLANELLI***(23)	D:B		75,500	
Powys	Montgomery				
Powys	Montgomery				
London	**LONDON**(xxiii)	Co:C	(night)	6,800	GRLRO**Gh**
			(day)	340,000	CRO**
Leics	Charnwood D & B*				
Lincs	E.Lindsey*				
Suffolk	Waveney*				
	(see Beccles and Southwold)				
Beds	**LUTON***	D:B		160,300	
Kent	Shepway				
Dorset	W.Dorset				
Hants	New Forest				
Lancs	Fylde D & B				
Cheshire	**MACCLESFIELD***	D:B		149,800	
Berks	(ROYAL)**WINDSOR AND MAIDENHEAD***	D:RB(24)		131,500	
Kent	**MAIDSTONE***	D:B		128,700	CRO**
Essex	**MALDON***	D		45,500	
Wilts	N.Wilts				
Gtr Manchester	**MANCHESTER***(25)	C:MD		479,100	CRO**PL**Arch
Notts	**MANSFIELD***	D		97,900	
Kent	Thanet				
Wilts	Kennet				
Mid.Glam	**MERTHYR TYDFIL***	D:B		60,700	
London	**MERTON**(xxi)	LB(xxiv)		162,100	
Gtr Manchester	Rochdale MD & B				
Gwent	**MONMOUTH***(26)	D		70,300	
Powys	**MONTGOMERY***(27)	D		47,200	
Lancs	Lancaster				
W.Yorks	Leeds MD & B				
Northld	Castle Morpeth D & B*				
Gtr Manchester	Tameside MD & B				
W.Glam	**NEATH***	D:B		65,000	
Lancs	Pendle D & B*				
	(see Colne)				
Notts	**NEWARK***	D		100,800	
Berks	**NEWBURY***	D		123,400	
Staffs	**NEWCASTLE-UNDER-LYME***	D:B		116,700	Arch
Tyne & Wear	**NEWCASTLE-UPON-TYNE***	C:MD		287,300	CROs**
London	**NEWHAM**(xxii)	LB(xxv)		224,300	
I of W	Medina D & B*				CRO**
	(see Ryde)				
Gwent	**NEWPORT***	D:B		132,800	
Kent	Shepway				
Northants	**NORTHAMPTON***	D:B		154,900	CRO**PL*
Norfolk	**NORWICH***	C:D		119,300	CRO**
Notts	**NOTTINGHAM***	C:D		278,600	CRO**
Warks	**NUNEATON***	D:B		110,300	
Devon	W.Devon				
Gtr Manchester	**OLDHAM***	MD:B		223,500	
W.Yorks	Wakefield MD & C				
Oxon	**OXFORD***	C:D		122,400	CRO**
Dyfed	S.Pemb*				
	(see Tenby)				
Cornwall	Carrick				
Cornwall	Penwith*				
	(see St. Ives, Cornwall)				
Cambs	**PETERBOROUGH***	C:D		129,300	Mus*Arch

Name of Town	1971: County	Status	Inc.	Pop.	Archives
PLYMOUTH	Devon	C:CB:LM	1493	239,452	PL** Arch
PONTEFRACT	W.R.Yorks	MB	1194	31,364	
POOLE	Dorset	Co:MB	1248	107,161	Arch
PORTSMOUTH	Hants	C:CB:LM	1194	197,431	CRO** Arch
PORT TALBOT	Glam	MB	1921	50,729	
PRESTON	Lancs	CB	1179	98,088	CRO**
PRESTWICH	Lancs	MB	1939	32,911	
PUDSEY	W.R.Yorks	MB	1899	38,143	
PWLLHELI	Caern	MB	1355	4,180	
QUEENBOROUGH-IN-SHEPPEY	Kent	MB	1968	28,630	
RADCLIFFE	Lancs	MB	1935	29,278	
RAMSGATE	Kent	MB	1884	39,561	
RAWTENSTALL	Lancs	MB	1891	21,432	
READING	Berks	CB	1253	132,939	CRO**BRO*Arch
REDBRIDGE	London	LB	1965	239,880	
REIGATE	Surrey	MB	1863	56,223	
RHONDDA	Glam	MB	1169	88,994	
RICHMOND	N.R.Yorks	MB	1093	7,245	
RICHMOND-UPON-THAMES	London	LB	1965	174,310	
RIPON	W.R.Yorks	C:MB	886	10,989	
ROCHDALE	Lancs	CB	1856	91,454	
ROCHESTER	Kent	C:MB	1189	55,519	
ROMSEY	Hants	MB	1607	10,043	
ROTHERHAM	W.R.Yorks	CB	1871	84,801	Arch
ROYAL LEAMINGTON SPA	Warks	MB	1875	45,064	PL*
ROYAL TUNBRIDGE WELLS	Kent	MB	1889	44,612	Arch
RUGBY	Warks	MB	1932	59,396	
RUTHIN	Denb	MB	1282	3,920	
RYDE	I of W	MB	1868	23,204	
RYE	Sussex	MB	1289	4,434	
SAFFRON WALDEN	Essex	MB	1513	9,971	
ST. ALBANS	Herts	C:MB	1553	52,174	
ST. AUSTELL WITH FOWEY	Cornwall	MB	1968	32,265	
ST. HELENS	Lancs	CB	1868	104,341	PL*
ST. IVES	Cornwall	MB	1639	9,839	
ST. IVES	Hunts	MB	1874	5,501	
SALE	Cheshire	MB	1935	55,769	
SALFORD	Lancs	C:CB	1835	130,976	
SALISBURY	Wilts	C:MB	1227	35,302	PL*
SALTASH	Cornwall	MB	1199	9,926	
SANDWICH	Kent	MB	1226	4,467	
SCARBOROUGH	N.R.Yorks	MB	1181	44,440	
SCUNTHORPE	Lincs	MB	1936	70,907	
SHAFTESBURY	Dorset	MB	1604	3,976	
SHEFFIELD	W.R.Yorks	C:CB	1843	520,327	PL** Arch
SHREWSBURY	Shrops	MB	1189	56,188	CRO**BRO**PL*
SLOUGH	Bucks	MB	1938	87,075	
SOLIHULL	Warks	CB	1954	107,095	
SOUTHAMPTON	Hants	Co:C:CB	1447	215,118	CRO** Arch
SOUTHEND-ON-SEA	Essex	CB	1892	162,770	PL*
SOUTHPORT	Lancs	CB	1867	84,674	
SOUTH SHIELDS	Co.Durham	CB	1550	100,659	
SOUTHWARK	London	LB	1965	260,780	PL*
SOUTHWOLD	E.Suffolk	MB	1489	1,992	

1981:

County	District	Status	Pop.	Archives
Devon	**PLYMOUTH***	C:D	255,500	CRO**
W.Yorks	Wakefield MD & C			
Dorset	**POOLE***	D:B	115,500	Arch
Hants	**PORTSMOUTH***	C:D	191,000	CRO**
W.Glam	Afan D & B*			
Lancs	**PRESTON***	D:B	126,200	CRO**
Gtr Manchester	Bury MD & B			
W.Yorks	Leeds MD & B			
Gwynedd	Dwyfor*			
Kent	Swale			
Gtr Manchester	Bury MD & B			
Kent	Thanet			
Lancs	Rossendale*			
	(see Bacup and Haslingden)			
Berks	**READING**	D:B	138,400	CRO**
London	**REDBRIDGE**(xxvi)	LB	239,880	
Surrey	**REIGATE AND BANSTEAD***	D:B	114,000	
Mid-Glam	**RHONDDA***	D:B	81,800	
N.Yorks	Richmondshire*			
London	**RICHMOND-UPON-THAMES**	LB(xxvii)	161,700	
N.Yorks	Harrogate D & B	C:TC		
Gtr Manchester	**ROCHDALE***(28)	MD:B	209,000	
Kent	**ROCHESTER-UPON-MEDWAY***	C:SLP:B	147,700	
	(see Chatham)			
Hants	Test Valley D & B			
S.Yorks	**ROTHERHAM***	MD:B	248,800	PL*
Warks	Warwick*			
Kent	**(ROYAL) TUNBRIDGE WELLS***	D:RB	95,700	
Warks	**RUGBY***	D:B	83,800	
Clwyd	Glyndŵr*			CRO*
	(see Denbigh)			
I of W	Medina D & B			
E.Sussex	Rother			
Essex	Uttlesford*			
Herts	**ST. ALBANS***	C:D	124,300	
Cornwall	Restormel D & B*			
Merseyside	**ST. HELENS***	D:B	188,700	Arch
Cornwall	Penwith			
Cambs	Huntingdon			
Gtr Manchester	Trafford MD & B			
Gtr Manchester	**SALFORD***(29)	C:MD	252,600	CRO* Arch
Wilts	**SALISBURY***(30)	C:CT	103,100	
Cornwall	Caradon			
Kent	Dover			
N.Yorks	**SCARBOROUGH***	D:B	99,900	
Humberside	**SCUNTHORPE***	D:B	67,200	
Dorset	N.Dorset			
S.Yorks	**SHEFFIELD***	C:MD	544,200	CRO** Arch
Salop	**SHREWSBURY AND ATCHAM***	D:B	85,700	CRO:BRO**
Berks	**SLOUGH***	D:B	98,400	
W.Midlands	**SOLIHULL***	MD:B	198,300	
Hants	**SOUTHAMPTON***	C:D	207,800	CRO**
Essex	**SOUTHEND-ON-SEA***	D:B	154,700	CRO*
Merseyside	Sefton MD & B			
Tyne & Wear	South Tyneside MD & B			
	(see Jarrow)			
London	**SOUTHWARK**(xxviii)	LB	219,200	Arch
Suffolk	Waveney			

Name of Town	1971: County	Status	Inc.	Pop.	Archives
SPENBOROUGH	W.R.Yorks	MB	1955	40,690	
STAFFORD	Staffs	MB	1206	55,001	CRO**
STALYBRIDGE	Cheshire	MB	1857	22,806	
STAMFORD	Lincs	MB	1461	14,662	
STOCKPORT	Cheshire	CB	1220	139,644	
STOKE-ON-TRENT	Staffs	C:CB:LM	1910	265,258	
STOURBRIDGE	Worcs	MB	1914	54,344	
STRATFORD-ON-AVON	Warks	MB	1553	19,452	
STRETFORD	Lancs	MB	1933	54,297	
SUDBURY	Suffolk	MB	1554	8,166	Arch
SUNDERLAND	Co.Durham	CB	1634	217,079	
SUTTON	London	LB	1965	168,090	
SUTTON COLDFIELD	Warks	MB	1528	83,291	
SWANSEA	Glam	CB	1169	173,413	UCL*
SWINDON	Wilts	MB	1900	91,033	
SWINTON AND PENDLEBURY	Lancs	MB	1934	40,167	
TAMWORTH	Staffs	MB	1560	40,285	
TAUNTON	Som	MB	1627	37,444	CRO**
TEESSIDE	N.R.Yorks	CB	1968	396,230	PL*
TENBY	Pemb	MB	1402	4,994	
TENTERDEN	Kent	MB	1449	5,930	
TEWKESBURY	Glos	MB	1547	8,749	
THETFORD	Norfolk	MB	1573	13,727	
TIVERTON	Devon	MB	1615	15,566	
TODMORDEN	W.R.Yorks	MB	1896	15,163	
TORBAY	Devon	CB	1968	109,257	
TORRINGTON (GREAT)	Devon	MB	1554	3,536	
TOTNES	Devon	MB	1206	5,772	
TOWER HAMLETS	London	LB	1965	164,650	PL*
TRURO	Cornwall	C:MB	1589	14,849	CRO**
TYNEMOUTH	Northld	CB	1849	69,338	
WAKEFIELD	W.R.Yorks	C:CB	1848	59,590	
WALLASEY	Cheshire	CB	1910	97,215	
WALLINGFORD	Berks	MB	1155	6,182	
WALLSEND	Northld	MB	1901	45,797	
WALSALL	Staffs	CB	1159	184,734	
WALTHAM FOREST	London	LB	1965	233,960	PL*
WANDSWORTH	London	LB	1965	300,530	PL*
WAREHAM	Dorset	MB	1211	4,379	
WARLEY	Worcs	CB	1966	163,567	PL*
WARRINGTON	Lancs	CB	1847	133,400	PL*
WARWICK	Warks	MB	1545	18,296	CRO**
WATFORD	Herts	MB	1922	78,465	
WELLS	Som	C:MB	1201	8,604	
WELSHPOOL	Mont	MB	1263	7,030	
WEST BROMWICH	Staffs	CB	1882	166,593	
WESTMINSTER	London	C	1256	218,500	PL* Arch
WESTON-SUPER-MARE	Som	MB	1937	50,894	
WEYMOUTH AND MELCOMBE REGIS	Dorset	MB	1280	42,349	
WHITEHAVEN	Cumb	MB	1894	26,724	

1981: County	District	Status	Pop.	Archives
W.Yorks	Kirklees MD & B			
Staffs	**STAFFORD***	D:B	113,700	CRO**
Gtr Manchester	Tameside MD & B			
Lincs	S.Kesteven			
Gtr Manchester	**STOCKPORT***	MD:B	219,700	PL*Arch
Staffs	**STOKE-ON-TRENT***	C:D	257,200	
W.Midlands	Dudley MD & B			
Warks	**STRATFORD-ON-AVON***	D	99,200	
Gtr Manchester	Trafford MD & B*			
Suffolk	Babergh			
Tyne & Wear	**SUNDERLAND***	MD:B	300,800	
London	**SUTTON**(xxix)	LB	166,600	
W.Midlands	Birmingham MD & B			
W.Glam	**SWANSEA***	C:D	186,900	CRO**Arch
Wilts	Thamesdown D & B*			
Gtr Manchester	Salford C & MD*			
Staffs	**TAMWORTH***	D:B	60,300	
Som	**TAUNTON DEANE***	D:B	83,100	CRO**
Cleveland	Stockton-on-Tees: Middlesbrough: Langbaurgh Ds & Bs			
Dyfed	S.Pemb			
Kent	Ashford D & B			
Glos	**TEWKESBURY**	D:B	80,200	
Norfolk	Breckland			
Devon	Mid-Devon*(36)	D		
W.Yorks	Calderdale MD & B			
Devon	**TORBAY***	D:B	108,700	
Devon	Torridge			
Devon	S.Hams* (see Dartmouth)			
London	**TOWER HAMLETS**(xxx)	LB	149,200	
Cornwall	Carrick* (see Falmouth and Penryn)	C:TC		CRO*
Tyne & Wear	N.Tyneside MD & B (see Wallsend and Whitley Bay)			
W.Yorks	**WAKEFIELD***(31)	C:MD	309,700	CRO**DRO*Arch
Merseyside	Wirral MD & B * (see Bebington and Birkenhead)			
Oxon	S.Oxon* (see Henley-on-Thames)			
Tyne & Wear	N. Tyneside D & B			
W.Midlands	**WALSALL**	MD:B	263,400	PL**Arch
London	**WALTHAM FOREST**	LB(xxxi)	218,400	Arch
London	**WANDSWORTH**	LB(xxxii)	272,800	
Dorset	Purbeck*			
W.Midlands	Sandwell MD & B*(32)	MD:B		PL**
Cheshire	**WARRINGTON***	D:B	168,200	
Warks	**WARWICK**	D	116,000	CRO**
Herts	**WATFORD***	D:B	76,500	
Som	Mendip* (see Glastonbury)	C:TC		
Powys	Montgomery			
W.Midlands	Sandwell*			
London	**WESTMINSTER**	C(xxxiii)	211,900	PL:Arch**
Avon	Woodspring*			
Dorset	**WEYMOUTH AND PORTLAND***	D:B	57,700	
Cumbria	Copeland D & B			

Name of Town	1971: County	Status	Inc.	Pop.	Archives
WHITLEY BAY	Northld	MB	1954	37,817	
WIDNES	Lancs	MB	1892	56,949	
WIGAN	Lancs	CB	1246	81,147	BRO**
WILTON	Wilts	MB	1100	3,815	
WINCHESTER	Hants	C:MB	1155	31,107	CROs**
(NEW) WINDSOR AND MAIDENHEAD	Berks	MB	1277	30,114	
WISBECH	Cambs	MB	1549	17,016	
WOKINGHAM	Berks	MB	1583	21,069	
WOLVERHAMPTON	Staffs	CB	1848	269,112	
WOODSTOCK	Oxon	MB	1543	1,940	
WORCESTER	Worcs	Co:C:CB	1189	73,452	CRO**
WORKINGTON	Cumb	MB	1888	28,431	
WORKSOP	Notts	MB	1931	36,098	
WORTHING	Sussex	MB	1890	88,407	PL*
WREXHAM	Denb	MB	1157	39,052	
YEOVIL	Som	MB	1854	25,503	
YORK	W.R.Yorks	Co:C:CB:LM	1160	104,782	CRO**

NOTES TO PRECEDING TABLE:
    1. The following notes show which boroughs have been absorbed and lost their names; 2. Birmingham incl. Sutton Coldfield MB (1528); 3. Blackburn incl. Darwen MB (1878); 4. BOLTON incl.Farnworth MB(1939); 5. Bradford incl. Keighley MB (1882); 6. BURY incl. Prestwich MB (1939) Radcliffe MB (1935); 7. Derbyshire CRO at Matlock; 8. Wiltshire CRO at Trowbridge; 9. (Cardiff entry Glamorgan Archive Service administers archives of former Cardiff PL (*RRGB*); 10. CEREDIGION D &] incl Aberystwyth MB (1277), Lampeter MB (1884); 11. TC = 'Parish Council adopting Town status'; 12 ELY, a City and Urban District, is not a Borough; 13.DOVER incl Deal MB (1699); 14. DUDLEY incl Stourbridge MB (1914), Halesowen MB (1936); 15. Flintshire CRO at Hawarden; 16. Guildford Museum an Muniment Room; 17. CALDERDALE incl. Brighouse MB (1893), Todmorden MB (1896); 18. HARRO GATE incl. Ripon C & MB (886); 19. HUNTINGDON incl. St. Ives MB (1874); 20. KIRKLEES incl Batley MB (1868), Dewsbury CB (1862), Spenborough MB (1955); 21. LANCASTER incl. Morecamb and Heysham MB (1902); 22. LEEDS incl. Pudsey MB (1899), Morley MB (1885); 23. LLANELLI incl Kidwelly MB (temp. Hen I); 24. WINDSOR AND MAIDENHEAD, Royal Borough; 25. MANCHESTER (Co) incl. Altrincham MB (1937); Ashton-u-Lyne MB (1843); Hyde MB (1881): Sale MB (1935); Oldham CB (1849); Mossley MB (1885); Stockport CB (1220); Stalybridge MB (1857); Stretford MB (1933) Dukinfield MB (1899); & Bolton CB (1838) which also incl. Farnworth MB (1939); Bury CB (1876) Rochdale CB which incl. Middleton MB (1886) & Heywood MB (1881); Salford C:CB (1835) which incl Eccles MB (1892); Swinton & Pendlebury MB (1934); Wigan CB (1246); which incl. Leigh MB (1895) 26. MONMOUTH incl. Abergavenny MB (1542); 27. MONTGOMERY incl. Llanidloes MB (1286) & Welshpool MB (1263) & Llanfyllin MR; 28. ROCHDALE incl. Middleton MB (1896), Heywood MB (1881) 29. SALFORD incl. Eccles MB (1892), Swinton and Pendlebury MB (1934), Wigan CB (1246) which incl Leigh MB (1895); 30. SALISBURY incl. Wilton MB (1100); 31. WAKEFIELD incl. Castleford MB (1955) Ossett MB (1890), Pontefract MB (1194); 32. SANDWELL incl. Warley CB (1966), & West Bromwich C1 (1882); 33. WIGAN incl. Leigh MB (1895); 34. WINDSOR AND MAIDENHEAD is Royal B; 35. YEOVII incl. Chard MB (1570); 36. TIVERTON was a District in its own name until 1978 when it was re-name 'Mid-Devon'. ROCHESTER on the other hand regained its name, 'upon-Medway', in 1979.

1981: County	District	Status	Pop.	Archives
Tyne & Wear	N.Tyneside D & B* (part Blyth Valley)			
Cheshire	Halton D & B*			
Gtr Manchester	WIGAN*(33)	MD:B	311,200	BRO** Arch
Wilts	Salisbury			
Hants	WINCHESTER*	C:D	88,900	CRO**
Berks	WINDSOR AND MAIDENHEAD	D:RB(34)	131,500	BRO*
Cambs	Fenland			
Berks	WOKINGHAM*	D	111,000	
W.Midlands	WOLVERHAMPTON*	MD:B	258,200	Arch
Oxon	W.Oxon			
H & W	WORCESTER*	C:D	75,000	CRO**
Cumbria	Alerdale			
Notts	Bassetlaw* (see East Retford)			
W.Sussex	WORTHING*	D:B	90,600	
Clwyd	Wrexham Maelor D & B*			
Som	YEOVIL(35) *	D	129,300	
N.Yorks	YORK*	C:D	100,900	CRO** Arch

SECONDARY NOTES TO PRECEDING TABLE

(i) Barking incl. Dagenham MB (1938), Essex; (ii) Barnet incl. Finchley MB (1933) Mx., and Hendon MB (1932) Mx.; (iii) Bexley incl. Erith MB (1938) Kent; (iv) Brent incl. Wembley MB (1937) Mx., Willesden MB (1933) Mx.; (v) Bromley incl. Beckenham MB (1935) Kent; (vi) Camden incl. Hampstead (Met), Holborn (Met), St. Pancras (Met); (vii) Croydon, MB inc. 1883, became CB 1889; (viii) Ealing incl. Acton MB (1921) Mx., Southall MB (1936) Mx.; (ix) Enfield incl. Edmonton MB (1937) Mx., Southgate MB (1937) Mx.; (x) Greenwich incl. Woolwich (Met); (xi) Hackney incl. Shoreditch (Met), Stoke Newington (Met); (xii) Hammersmith incl. Fulham (Met); (xiii) Haringey incl. Hornsey MB (1903) Mx., Wood Green MB (1933) Mx., Tottenham MB (1934) Mx.; (xiv) Harrow formerly MB (1954) Mx.; (xv) Havering incl. Romford MB (1937) Essex; (xvi) Hillingdon incl. Uxbridge MB (1955) Mx; (xvii) Hounslow incl. Brentford-and-Chiswick MB (1932) Mx.; (xviii) Islington incl. Finsbury (Met); (xix) Kensington and Chelsea were amalg. 1963: now Royal B.; (xx) Kingston-upon-Thames, Royal B., incl Malden (MB) and Surbiton (MB) in 1963; (xxi) Lambeth incl. some former wards of Wandsworth (Met.); (xxii) Lewisham incl. Deptford (Met); (xxiii) London's constitution is unique. It is governed by the Court of Common Council and its Corporation has many of the functions of a County; (xxiv) Merton incl. Mitcham MB (1934) Surrey; (xxv) Newham incl. East Ham CB (1904) Essex, West Ham CB (1886) Essex and parts of Barking MB (1931) Essex & Woolwich (Met); (xxvi) Redbridge incl. Ilford (MB), Essex, Wanstead and Woodford (MB), Essex & part of Dagenham MB, Essex; (xxvii) Richmond-upon-Thames incl. Twickenham MB (1926) Mx., Barnes MB (1932), Surrey; (xxviii) Southwark incl. Bermondsey (Met), Camberwell (Met); (xxix) Sutton incl. Sutton-and-Cheam MB (1934), Surrey, Beddington-and-Wallington MB (1937), Surrey; (xxx) Tower Hamlets incl. Bethnal Green (Met), Poplar (Met), Stepney (Met); (xxxi) Waltham Forest incl. Chingford MB (1938), Essex, Leyton MB (1926) Essex, Walthamstow (MB), Essex; (xxxii) Wandsworth incl. Battersea (Met); (xxxiii) Westminster incl. Paddington (Met), St. Marylebone (Met).

CHAPTER TWO

THE ORIGINS OF THE TOWNS c. A.D. 60-1066

CONTINUITY OF SETTLEMENT in or nearby most areas of present-day habitation is more prevalent than we sometimes suspect. This is all the more true wherever a settlement has proved to be especially well-founded, potentially prosperous, or capable of sustained and continuing growth. The impression is sometimes given by history textbooks that there was a complete separation of Anglo-Saxon settlement — in which most modern English places are certainly most widely, if not most deeply rooted — from all that went before. We might conclude that the separation was also a long inactive period, a Dark Age of total loss or complete cessation of growth. That is not invariably the case. In county after county we find prehistoric and post-Saxon sites in relatively close proximity. Near the city of Chichester, for example, are found the Neolithic barrow on Stoughton Down, the causewayed camp of Barkhale, Bronze Age barrows on Bow Hill and the Iron Age hill-forts of Trundle and Chichester Dykes. Celtic hillforts match the modern towns of Newbury, Chester, Lewes, Warwick, Colne, Portsmouth, Andover, Bristol, Hereford, Sheffield, Stourbridge, Colchester and Tunbridge Wells; these sites were often tribal centres. At Dunstable and Luton, Neolithic and Bronze Age origins are found at Maiden Bower and Walud's Bank. Brighton's racecourse preserves the Neolithic camp of Whitehawk and is overlooked by Hollingbury hillfort. Eastbourne, Chipping Norton, Cheltenham, Dorchester, Winchester, Warminster, Chippenham, Basingstoke and countless other modern towns had prehistoric neighbours. At Monmouth there is even a paleolithic cave.

The importance of site and situation are vital in the almost inevitable survival and continuity of some settlements throughout the ages. Such essentials as water supply, drainage, inter-communication and above all, safely defensible positions, often dictated a limited choice of desirable position and comfortable settlement. Reference to a modern atlas will usually reveal the dominant factors in the positioning of a modern town. These may combine, for example, the bend in a river and a fertile terrace; an accessible river-crossing point; the junction of two or more intersecting roadways; a pass or saddle between surrounding high ground and, above all, space for growth if a town is to prosper. These factors are common to widely differing tribal economies. Given a five-mile radius, an aerial survey, or an archaeological investigation, many of the modern boroughs on our base-list will reveal their pre-Roman or non-Saxon antecedents. Given only a one-kilometre Ordnance Survey map, some of those formative features could be predicted.

Towns as we recognize them today were first established in Britain by the Romans in successive phases of building between the 1st and 4th centuries, more particularly from about A.D. 80-130, although some of those places, like Colchester, Cirencester,

St Albans and Canterbury were already important Celtic tribal capitals, capable of maintaining their own coinage and of sending out diplomatic emissaries. Historians distinguish between three main types of Romano–British town: these are the *civitas*, *colonia* and *vicus*. *Civitas* capitals, promoted from tribal centres, were established at Caerwent, Caistor-St-Edmund near Norwich, Canterbury, Carmarthen, Chichester, Dorchester, Exeter, Leicester, Silchester, Winchester, Wroxeter, Cirencester and Aldborough. These were capital towns of self-governing British areas, with Roman citizenship as a special privilege for their inhabitants. There were also four special *coloniæ* for time-expired legionaries and other Roman citizens, governed by charters based upon the constitution of Rome itself; such were the settlements at York, Gloucester, Colchester and Lincoln. These typically Roman towns, both *coloniæ* and *civitates*, were defended by stone walls and gatehouses, dignified by well-planned civic centres, amphitheatres, public bath-houses and colonnades, along well-paved streets with main drainage, regularly laid out to a standard grid pattern of craftsmen's shops and centrally-heated town-houses. Their distinctive feature as 'towns' is that they were all *planned* and carried out specific administrative functions in the regions in which they were central.

The most convenient and explicit source of information on the whereabouts of these and other Roman towns is the Ordnance Survey *Map of Roman Britain* in the Fourth Edition (1978) published by HMSO. The map itself is in two sheets, North and South, to a scale of about ten miles to the inch, and is accompanied by a handbook and index of all known Roman settlements. These list 55 other major towns which are sometimes referred to as *vici*. These were often connected with Roman forts and posting stations and though of a lower legal status than the tribal cities, they represent a widespread Roman urban influence which runs from Carlisle to Chelmsford and from Chester to Brough in Northumberland. Many of these are found on our later list of municipal boroughs, as at Ewell, Worcester, Cambridge, Rochester, Caerleon and Droitwich, with the exceptional spas at Bath and Buxton. Other major settlements developed in places which are no more than market towns or villages today: these include such places as Alcester (Warw), Bourton-on-the-Water (Glos), Camerton (Avon), and Leintwardine (H & W).

The Ordnance Survey map also identifies a further 104 places which are classified as 'minor settlements', other than the multitude of villas which represent a different type of estate-management. These smallest towns are defined as those which lacked substantial buildings with stone foundations. Strung out along the Roman roads of Britain, occasionally marked out by ramparts and ditches and still today yielding up fragments of mosaic pavement, artefacts, pottery, coins and other relics, and sometimes identified with a Latin place-name, these small 'towns' or large market-villages are the early foundation of many modern parishes and some boroughs. They survive at different levels of present-day 'township' such as Ambleside (Cumbria), Ilkley (W.Yorks), Caernarvon (Gwynedd), Cricklade (Wilts) and Great Dunmow (Essex). A few achieved lasting status as major English or Welsh boroughs; our base-list includes Caernarvon, Manchester, South Shields, Doncaster, Cardiff, Wareham and Kettering.

Romano–British industrial centres are rarely continuous with modern manufacturing towns, though many potteries, tile kilns, mines, quarries and salt-working sites are identified. The few exceptions include Derby, Lincoln and Luton, where pottery kilns were found, tile-works at Epsom, iron mines at Monmouth, saltpans at Droitwich and the spas at Bath and Buxton; these are the modern towns which have been 'busy' more or less continuously since Roman times. Of these Droitwich is possibly the most consistently important manufacturing town. The Roman *burgi* which in the 4th century were selected and developed as strongpoints for the protection of imperial supplies and communications were rarely of long-lasting significance. Those six *burgi* which defended the line of Watling Street from *Bannaventa* in Northamptonshire to *Vxacona* in Shropshire are now insignificantly situated, at such places as Caves Inn, Mancetter and Water Eaton. Ports and harbours such as Dover and Pevensey continued, almost inevitably, to maintain their strategic position, though others such as Rich-borough, Reculver, Lympne, Bradwell, Walton Castle and Burgh Castle yielded their places to later coastal ports. In terms of defence and sea-trading the later Saxon organi-zation of hided *burhs* made new towns at Southwark, Hastings, Southampton, Lewes, Stamford, Wallingford and Winchester; of these *burhs* only Portchester, Chichester and Bath continue the existence of important Roman sites.

Continuity of 'settlement' and of 'township' are not the same thing; one place remains a hamlet for centuries and a neighbouring new town mushrooms in the artificial environment provided by electricity, rail transporters and container lorries. The mere fact that a place was 'there' in prehistoric times and is now a town does not prove continuity. We shall find many places which retain little more than their names for centuries; we shall need to re-define out criteria for 'township'.

Those elements which tended to set Roman municipal life apart from what came immediately before and immediately after were: citizenship, standardised planning, and a high material standard of life. If we are prepared to accept Celtic tribal capitals such as Colchester and Saxon *burhs* such as Winchester as full-scale towns, on the strength of their administrative importance and the element of planning in their foun-dations (as well as an obvious continuity of site) then the differences are relative. The obvious discrepancies between *civitas* and *borough*, between *forum, via principalis* and baths on the one hand and gildhall, street-grid and cathedral on the other, between the stone-built streets of *Corinium Dobunnorum*, and the half-timbered jetties of Cirencester, are differences of degree not of kind. Those cases where the difference is total, where *Viroconium* falls back to fields and farmyards at Wroxeter, were not the inevitable rule. Several Celtic capitals, most of the Roman *civitates* and all the *coloniæ* are still recognizably major towns. A tradition of 'township' does appear in more of the places on our municipal base-list than might have been expected.

The first verbal record of any place is its name. Archaeology and earthworks apart, a place-name may be the earliest record of all and possibly the only one. Fortunately, England is well served by a full complement of reliable place-name dictionaries. A full county handlist is given in Chapter II of *Village Records*. In the Gazetteer to this present Chapter, Ekwall's *Concise Oxford Dictionary of English Place-names*[1] has been the sole source of information except for Roman origins where *Place-Names of Roman Britain* by A. L. F. Rivet and Colin Smith[2] has been used. Place-name dictionaries are doubly useful to the student of local history in that not only do they give the linguistic derivation, but also the sources of documentary information for each phase of a name's development. Thus a complete entry refers to many of the earliest documents which trace the history of any town or village. For the purposes of our own Gazetteer (pages 45–52) Ekwall's first reference only has been used, as we are here concerned with origins. Further reference to his Dictionary will lead to other, later sources and this enables us to distinguish certain common features in the origins of many English towns.

The earliest names are Celtic in origin or contain originally British elements in Anglo-Saxon form, as Celtic place-names were adopted by the Germanic settlers. Most Celtic derivations describe natural features such as rivers, streams, hills and forests, but the existence of some British cantonments and hillforts is also confirmed, as at London, Dover and York. Many Saxon towns preserve the record of an earlier Roman settlement in the English name of their *ceastre* and many of those Roman origins acknowledge a Celtic source. Romano–British settlement and fortification is evident in the names of 10 per cent of the modern towns on our base-list. When we add to these the 31 purely Celtic derivations which refer only to natural elements rather than to actual settlement, a significant 20 per cent of the names of later municipal boroughs are found to be of pre-Saxon derivation. It is relatively rare for the original Latin name itself to be preserved, as in Manchester (from *Mamucium*). In some cases, as at York and Gloucester, the Romano–British origin undergoes a Germanic change of sense in translation, but in many other names the Celtic, Latin and German are intermingled and continuous in meaning. Often the name of the Roman site was added to a British river-name, which had previously provided a Roman translation. Thus both *Isca Dumnoniorum* and *Escan-ceastre* name Exeter from the British river-name of Exe; the same name was used by Celts, Romans and Saxons in turn. Usually the Roman site is described entirely in Saxon, as at Castleford (Ceaster-ford: the ford by the Roman fort – of *Lagentium*).

Certainly most settlement names in south, south-western and midland England are predominantly Anglo–Saxon with a wealth of Scandinavian derivations in the Danelaw of East Midlands and Northumbria. The most basic names of all refer to the original tribal areas, for instance the kingdoms of the East Saxons in Essex, the Cantiani in Kent and the South Saxons in Sussex. In the same way the earliest colonization by Germanic immigrants is commemorated in those place-names which contained *-saetan* as in Somerset and Dorset, or *-waru* as in Canterbury (*Cant-wara-burg*: the town of the people of Kent). Of our three West Midland 'models' the name of Worcester falls into this earliest category, being 'the Roman fort of the people called Wigoran'; this name is also preserved in the more recent 'district-name' of Wyre, 'the forest of the Wigoran tribe'. Many of the Saxon settlement names were possessive, commemorating the personal names of a tribal chieftain. Of these, the *-ingas* names are most ancient, as at Hastings, 'the home of Haesta's people' the Haestingas; and at Reading, 'the land of the people of Raeda' which means the Red. Many more habitation names are denoted by the suffix *-ham*, the 'home' or homestead of a tribe. Thus in our second Midland example we have Birmingham as '*Beormund-inga-ham*' or 'Beorma's people's homestead'. Some of the earliest homesteads were clearings or glades, in the ancient forest; previous clearing of the wild wood and its undergrowth are now thought to be more extensive around British settlements in the valleys than was once supposed. Such 'forest-names' usually end in *-leah-* or *-ley*, and their extensiveness is an indication of the widespread woodland of the Dark Ages. Thus our third Midland borough commemorates the *leah* of Dudda at Dudley, which can be compared with countless similar examples such as Barnsley, Batley, Burnley and Chorley.

The most significant Anglo-Saxon place-names to illustrate the study of towns should, naturally, be those which describe a place as a 'town' at an early date. For

The Burhs of the Burghal Hidage
C. 914 - 918 A.D.

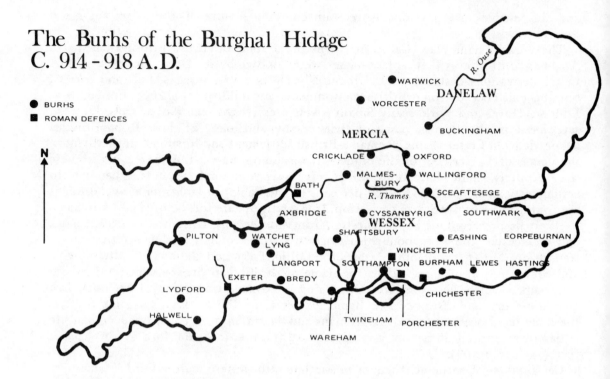

● BURHS
■ ROMAN DEFENCES

N

WARWICK
WORCESTER
DANELAW
BUCKINGHAM
MERCIA
CRICKLADE   OXFORD
MALMES-   WALLINGFORD
BURY
BATH   SCEAFTESEGE
R. Thames
CYSSANBYRIG   SOUTHWARK
AXBRIDGE   WESSEX
SHAFTSBURY
PILTON   WATCHET   EASHING   EORPEBURNAN
          LYNG   WINCHESTER
LANGPORT SOUTHAMPTON BURPHAM LEWES HASTINGS
EXETER   BREDY
LYDFORD   CHICHESTER
HALWELL
                TWINEHAM PORCHESTER
        WAREHAM

this purpose the common Saxon suffix *-ton* as in Luton, Workington, Okehampton, Nuneaton and many more is no indication of early urban life. The old English *-tun* was an enclosure, a fenced settlement or homestead, a village rather than a town; *-tun* is a later equivalent to *-ham* and, as in these earlier examples, is often combined possessively with a personal name, as in Bebington (*Bebbe-ing-tun*: 'the village of Bebbe's people'). More significant is the OE suffix *-burg* or *-bury* from the Saxon *-burge* or *-byrh*. This means a fortified manor and may in many cases refer to a Roman fort or a Saxon defensive ditch. It may also imply the existence of a town or 'borough'. Thirty of our base-list towns such as Bury, Dewsbury, Malmesbury and Shaftsbury originated as 'burhs'; this is almost three times as many as will be found in a random sample of 30 consecutive places in the *Place-Names Dictionary*. Thus a great deal of the place-name evidence for early town development occurs in terms of their defences. Once again care is essential as the similar suffix *-beorg*, a hill, will give a misleading place-name, as a Marlborough in Wiltshire and Shuckburgh in Warwickshire. Stantonbury in Berkshire is more exceptional; this is no 'borough' but the record of a French family name at Stanton Barri. From this point on we are entering an area of long-standing academic dispute. One school of historians, led by Carl Stephenson[3] have maintained the view that the military character of the 'burh' is the most prevalent *raison d'être* for British towns; more generally accepted is the contention of James Tait[4] that their more significant element is mercantile.

In the north-east large numbers of Scandinavian place-names remind us of widespread and long-lasting Norse immigration during three centuries before the Conquest and a time only a generation before, when England was part of an Anglo–Norse kingdom. Beginning in piracy the Viking invasion resulted in long-lasting colonization of the northern and east Midland counties. From the Scandinavians we received many *-by* towns, as in Derby, Crosby, Grimsby and Appleby. These are the only Old Norse names on our base-list; Rugby was originally derived from the English *Hroca's Burg*; only later was the Scandinavian *-by* substituted. In Danelaw too were the Five Boroughs of Derby, Leicester, Lincoln, Nottingham and Stamford which began as headquarters of the Danish host and became under their jarls the first county boroughs after which the shires themselves were named, different from those which had originated in the tribal *saetan* of Somerset and Dorset, the kingdoms of Essex, Sussex and Middlesex, or the 'folk' names of Norfolk and Suffolk.

Place-name references to trade, as in the added Chipping, (from *ceping* the Old English word for 'market' from which 'cheap' goods and Cheapside also originate) are later medieval additions, as at Chipping Norton from 1280. This applies also to most of the *-ports*, more particularly the New-ports of the 13th century which record instances of new town planning. If we total all the elements found, some in combination, in English place-names of the towns on our list, we find that by far the most widespread single element is that of natural features, particularly of streams and rivers but also sites of pasture, groves, glades and valleys; these account for one-third of all our towns' names. References to church sites, monasteries, and minsters together account for 16 origins of later municipal boroughs (4 per cent). Most (about 25 per cent) towns begin with personal and tribal ownership, often recording the sites of Romano–British camps. If any one factor emerges, apart from the burghal defences, as being especially significant to the further growth of potential boroughs, it is found in the prevalence of references to communications by road and river. We find that about one in every ten borough names originates at Roman 'street', at ford, bridge, landing-place or harbour. Such names are numerous, as in Oxford, Bridgestowe (Bristol), Stratford, Bridport (an earlier 'port' than most), Chelmsford, Gosport, Hereford, Stamford and 30 more. A few town-names are very new indeed. This applies particularly to Victorian seaside resorts, though some of these, too, like Brighton, may be found in Domesday Book; Southport and Southend, however, are both new. Nelson in Lancashire is named after an inn and a hero; Morecambe is an 18th-century invention and Sir Peter Fleetwood gave his name to the Lancashire town in 1836. Otherwise all our modern boroughs were named by the end of the 13th century.

Roman inscriptions and some early British coins apart, the earliest written place-names are found in Anglo-Saxon charters of the 7th to the 11th centuries. There are two types of documents which are loosely described as 'charters'; both share the common feature of a grant by a king, prelate or lord to his dependents. In the earliest Anglo-Saxon documents these are usually gifts or bequests of land, standing as deeds which often define the boundaries of the grant. These charters are often called 'landbooks'; they are written in Latin and Old English and include many blatant forgeries. Saxon charters of this type are described and illustrated in *Village Records*, with a list of county examples. Many charters are grants by a king or ealdorman to his favoured monastery, witnesssed by his household officers and the thanes and bishops of his council.

A later development of this document is the early medieval charter of privileges, of which Magna Carta is the supreme example. More usually these delegate local rights and authority. Medieval borough charters will be described in Chapter Four; in this Chapter we are concerned only with the earlier 'land-books'. The information given in a typical charter is mainly topographical, if not entirely formal, mentioning only the place-names amongst a profusion of prayer of good intentions. The actual gifts are made in agrarian terms with rustic boundaries; occasionally, however, a few places are already referred to as 'towns'. More usually grants are recorded in such terms as swine pasture at Bexley and Cheam, meadows at Basingstoke and a marsh at Rochester. Only at London do we find references, as early as 733 and 743, to grants of tolls on ships and the grant of privileges at a wharf in 1012. Similarly any charter references which appear to mention recognizably urban tenements are also late, relatively close to the Conquest and the Domesday Survey, which makes such burgage tenures more familiar. 'Messuages and a croft' are mentioned at Worcester as early as 904 and 972, but these are not exclusively 'urban' terms. More significant for the future growth and planning of towns, perhaps, are the references to a *mansus* at Thetford in 1040 and the later very familiar *hagæ* or town building sites (see e.g. p. 51 'Warwick') mentioned in land-grants at Hereford in 958, Warwick in 1016 and at Canterbury in 1045. Borough courts are mentioned in a collection of Devonian charters at Barnstaple, Exeter, Lydford and Totnes, all important towns on our borough-list. Otherwise specific evidence of early 'town-ship' is scanty and it will take a minute scrutiny of all available leases, wills and writs with boundary clauses to discover any more meaningful evidence of town-houses and markets. The Saxon charters are primarily concerned with the wealth and welfare of the monasteries which they favour and enrich. Abingdon, Worcester, Evesham and Peterborough figure prominently in the cartularies, mainly as recipients of lands in villages elsewhere. We learn little of their development as monastic towns, though other evidence will show that especially at Peterborough and Bury St Edmunds, the abbeys' enrichment of their own boroughs could be considerable. In this context we are particularly fortunate in the survival of such an important early 'burghal' charter as the model for 9th-century Worcester (between pp. 41–4) with its references to defences and a market.

Early charter evidence is not yet well arranged or indexed for specifically urban studies. However, Beresford and Finberg's *Handlist* has collected most of the known examples, as for instance that of Taunton where a grant by the Bishop of Winchester conceded market tolls and burgage rents in 943–51. The best evidence of the quality of Saxon town-life is gleaned from a combination of archaeological evidence — hall and house-sites, pottery and coins — with the little available documentary material. This is well done in *The Archaeology of Anglo-Saxon England* edited by D. M. Wilson (1981) more particularly in M. Biddle's chapter on 'Towns'. His description of 9th-century Canterbury is the most graphic to be found: 'A royal residence there must have been, though its location is unknown; the cathedral inside the walls and four extra-mural churches date from the early seventh century if not before, and at least three other churches were in existence by the early ninth century; by this date the land inside the walls was divided up into a number of large enclosed holdings. There was a market place and the community could be described as a *port* or trading-place, its citizens as *portware* or *burgware*, dwellers in the *port* or *burh*, the defended place. Canterbury was also a mint and it is altogether clear that by the ninth century it was a fully urban community'.[5] The student is fortunate in that the earliest charters have been very thoroughly calendared and indexed, though without much specific reference to early urban development. Massive collections from the earliest cartularies are available in the larger reference libraries, though usually in the original Latin and Old English with only partial translation. These and the reference books which lead us to the charters are listed in the bibliography to this chapter.

Additional information on the early existence and some of the history of many Saxon towns can be gleaned from the *Anglo-Saxon Chronicles*. This primary source of the history of Britain during and after the Dark Ages of Saxon and Viking invasion has been published.[6] The chronicles were at first little more than annotated calendars of the monastic year. Only gradually did these monastic annals assume the character of 'a book of events and laws'. There are in all seven surviving manuscripts designated alphabetically by scholars as Chronicles A, B, C etc., some being transcripts of one of the other versions. The four outstanding versions were those kept at the abbeys of Winchester, Worcester, Abingdon and Peterborough, all sharing the name 'Anglo-Saxon Chronicle'. These are an essential source for the formative period of the kingdoms of Wessex and Mercia, the settlement of the Danelaw, the dynastic politics of pre-Conquest England and overall, year after year and generation by generation, the roaming and ravaging of 'the host'. Thus they become the contemporary history of the establishment of a single kingdom of Anglo-Saxon, Norse and Celtic Britain, continuing into the 12th century. In the earliest Anglo-Saxon Chronicles we find a considerable amount of reference to many of the towns on our base-list.

As to how towns are described, we are at the mercy first of the chronicler, next of the translator; proof of a town's significance may become merely a matter of words. As early as 577 Gloucester, Cirencester and Bath are described as 'cities' but *tunas* might be anything from a village to a town and *civitas* may be no more reliable. Thus Rochester is a 'city' as early as 885, London certainly by 895; Christchurch and Wimborne on the other hand, although evidently important places with gates and defences, are described as 'manors' in 901. It is relatively rare for a place to be described as *tunas*, as in the cases of Aylesbury (571), Huntingdon (656) and Andover (994); usually the only description is by name. Some towns were evidently important as royal centres, capital towns or seats of great councils and synods. Such was Chester, rebuilt in 907, where in 972 six kings made submission to King Edgar of Wessex. Regularly Winchester, Oxford, Gloucester, Wilton and other royal boroughs were the centre of royal government. In the morbidly negative sense of so much of the Saxon evidence — where a town was only important enough to be burnt down — some boroughs were mostly dignified as royal deathbeds or burial-places. Naturally this often reflects the importance of the monastery rather than the town. Sadly, the best indication of a Saxon town's wealth was its capacity of providing booty for the Danish host. So many ancient boroughs were still worth sacking — Colchester in 920, Wilton in 1003, Cambridge in 1010, Norwich and Thetford in 1004, Oxford in 1009 and Wallingford in 1006. Just as monasteries were the richest prey in the 8th century, so by the 10th and 11th centuries the attacks were directed against towns. The large numbers of prisoners and hostages and the quantity of silver and gold taken from so many ransacked towns are significant evidence of their early wealth.

We learn more from the Chronicles, as from the charters, about the estates and influence of the monasteries than of any towns, yet the distinction during the 300 years before the Conquest is sometimes a narrow one. Winchester withstood Danish attacks in 860 and 879 as both Old Minster and capital city; in the early 10th century it would be rated for 2,400 hides. In fact abbey and borough had much in common, above all the wealth which would draw down Danes and destruction upon them both. Both defended themselves with walls, both were especially protected by kings and ealdormen, both tended to raise dependent communities of laymen and priests. At Canterbury in 1010 when the Danes 'seized all those in holy orders who were within the borough it was impossible for any man to say how great a part of the inhabitants that was ...'. At York, Ripon, Gloucester, Evesham, Lincoln, Westminster, Malmesbury, Worcester and many more of our later boroughs, monastic sites laid the town's foundations.

Many southern boroughs were notable as having provided convenient winter quarters for the Danish host. Cirencester, Chippenham, Fulham, Huntingdon, Thetford, Cambridge and in 872 London itself enjoyed this doubtful distinction. Indeed, the Danes appear to have introduced the very idea of the 'county town' with the surrounding region said to owe allegiance to the borough; this was the case at Cambridge, and indeed at all the Five Boroughs where jarls ruled. Other towns grew, or suffered, because of their accessibility. Harbours, landing-places, *hythes* and *staithes* and all the many *-fords* were at once potentially important and vulnerable. Such are Portsmouth as early as 501, Southampton in 840, Folkestone in 993 and Greenwich in 1013, all ports of call or beach-heads for the Danish host. As far as the evidence shows, Southwark was as important as London and Sandwich was the most thriving seaport on the southeast coast. We may be in danger of overlooking the importance of many places for want of written evidence; yet the names which occur most frequently in the Chronicles are those which are important towns today. It is true that we also learn something of places such as Pucklechurch, Shifnal, Dyrham and Tettenhall which barely outlived the chronicles themselves and some, like Torksey, Cricklade, Cirencester and Selsey which would still be found to rate highly in the Domesday Survey; these are, however, outnumbered by the municipal and county boroughs of our base-list.

We have seen the importance of communications, royal favour and religious foundations to the early development of towns, but none of these factors is as evidently important as that of fortification. As with the place-name evidence, it is apparent from the Chronicles that the 'borough' was primarily a stronghold. This is the more true after the extensive fortifications made by King Edward and Lady Aethelflaed from 913 to 922. Tamworth, Stafford, Bedford, Buckingham, Nottingham, Warwick, Stamford, Hertford, Maldon and Manchester were all fortified during their period of command. It is at this time, the early 10th century, that we find the last and in some ways the most precise of our Saxon documents to verify the early importance of our county towns. This is the list of towns known as the *Burghal Hidage*. The document is dated 944 and is found amongst the wills and charters collected by Birch (*BCS 1335*). It lists 32 West Saxon towns and two in Mercia which were to stand as defensive points against the Danish host, supported and maintained by an extensive *hidage* of surrounding land. The *hide* was a unit by which the scale of maintenance and garrison for each town's walls would be calculated 'for the maintenance and defence of an acre's breadth of wall'. Every hide supported one defender and every 5½ yards of wall was manned by four men. Thus 'for the maintenance of a circuit of 12 furlongs (1½ miles) of wall, 1,920 hides are required'. The calculations in each town's case deliberately omit any length of the perimeter which was guarded by a river. As the map shows (page 32) the rated boroughs lined the south and south-west coastline from Sussex, round Hampshire to Somerset, including that county's northern coast and estuary. They also cover inland Wessex, across Dorset, Hampshire, Oxfordshire and Wiltshire and even begin to move into Mercia at Worcester and Warwick, towns which, like the Danish Five Boroughs, would give the counties their names. The *Burghal Hidage* includes at one end of the scale the cities of Exeter, Bath, Southampton, Winchester, Lewes, Chichester, Oxford and Buckingham and at the other places which are now no more than market towns or villages. The measurement of the *hide*, usually equated with an extent of 120 acres (though more usually a rateable value rather than a precise area) became the basis of the feudal five-hide unit which produced a knight and the tax-assessment of countless Domesday towns and manors. It is significant that the hidage recorded in 944 at Worcester (1200 in all) is almost exactly the rating of the Domesday county.

Tait, in *The Medieval English Borough*, gave as the four essential criteria which distinguish the early boroughs from other towns: a market, a court, heterogeneous burgage tenure and a mint. Anglo-Saxon coins are remarkable documents in their own right, recording, with other significant details, the name of the borough in which it was struck and the moneyer responsible. There were, at any given generation of Saxon rule, at least 60 mints in operation throughout the land: tens of thousands of their coins have survived. They record the existence of mints not only in the already great capital centres such as London, York, Lincoln, Chester and Winchester but also in unexpectedly small towns such as Quatford, now a hamlet on the outskirts of Bridgnorth in Shropshire, or Bedwyn, now a village in Wiltshire. Decentralized sites were safer and more convenient and, as H. R. Loyn puts it: 'Towns needed mints; mints helped to confirm towns as boroughs'.[7] Most of the present-day small towns, like Watchet, Pershore, Milborne Port, Cricklade, Torksey and Lydford, for example, are recognizably important Anglo-Saxon places from other contemporary references. Some we find also included in the *Burghal Hidage*, some we shall find with important markets, such as Launceston, in Domesday England. The full list indexed in the recent study, *Anglo-Saxon Coins*, is of almost exactly 100 places. Of these, more than half — 60 in all — are towns on our base-list which were to become permanently important boroughs; similarly almost one in five of that base-list's towns had Saxon mints. Evidently 'when all is taken into account, possession of a mint remained a spectacular test of immediate borough status and a hint at the hope of permanence'.[8] Of our three West Midland 'models' only Worcester had a mint.

The city of Worcester's Mercian origins are fairly well documented and provide us with a useful resumé of several of the sources reviewed in this Chapter. Its status as a Roman *ceastre* is mainly vouched for by some coins of the 1st to 4th centuries and a few other fragments. The problematic *Ravenna Cosmography* of the early 8th century leads to the possible identification of a town named *Vertis*, but the place-name bears no relation to the later *Wigoran*.[9] The church of St Peter was built in the later 7th century and became the diocesan seat of the bishops of the Hwiccas. For some time the identity of the town and bishopric was inseparable; a charter of Earl Aethelred of Mercia to Bishop Oftfor in the last decade of the 7th century grants land to the church which stood *in Uuegorna civitate*. This charter, listed in this Chapter's Gazetteer, is printed in *BCS 75* and confirmed by Finberg as having an 'authentic basis' as a later document or interpolation (Sawyer 77). There was at this time an extensive area of land around, and dependent upon, the city. *The Victoria County History of Worcestershire* reviews the evidence for the growing tactical importance of the city: 'With the Danish wars of the 9th century begins the second phase in the history of Worcester. At an unknown date between 872 and 899 the city was fortified by Aethelred, Earl of the Mercians and Aethelflaed his wife with the assent of King Alfred and of the Mercian Witan. The work was undertaken at the request of Bishop Werfrith "for the protection of all the people" and the bishop's friendship with the earl and his wife obtained for the church of Worcester a grant of privileges within the borough recorded in a document which has happily been preserved'.[10] That document is illustrated between pp. 41–4. It is printed in *BCS 579*; it has been verified by Finberg, and is listed by Sawyer (*223*). In return for psalms and masses, Aethelred and Aethelflaed granted to the bishop half the fines levied as regards the market place and streets 'both within the fortification and outside it' and in respect of land rent, with fines for fighting, stealing, dishonest trading or damage to the borough wall.

This document is of the highest value, as well for general as for local history. It is one of the earliest records to imply the existence of a borough court, and it enumerates the more important matters which were likely to fall within its province. It reveals the early market of Worcester, and suggests with some force that the duty of maintaining the borough wall was laid at this date upon the townsmen rather than on the men of the shire. It tells of an early bishop's quarter within the borough distinct from the market-place and the streets where jurisdiction was the king's.[11]

At about this time the city is included, with two other boroughs outside Wessex, Warwick and Buckingham, in the *Burghal Hidage*, where it is rated at 1,200 hides. As we have seen, this would mean a calculation of 1,650 yards of wall, excluding the river-side. Significantly, this hidage is almost exactly that of the Domesday county's assessment, when the city is rated at only 15 hides. There is here a valuable indication of the pre-Conquest dependence of the entire region on the county town which gave the shire its name. Birch also prints (*BCS 608*) one of those relatively rare town charters which offer some insight into the building of the borough. This is a charter of 904 in which Bishop Waerforth grants to Aethelred and Aethelflaed the lease of a *haga* or messuage within the walls of Worcester. The boundaries of this early example of a burgage plot are given as 'From the water by the north wall, eastwards 28 rods long and then southwards 24 rods broad, and again then westwards to the Severn 19 rods long'.[12] The lease also included meadows across the river and two separate parcels of 60 acres each, possibly indicating their situation in an open two-field system, an unusual reference to the relationship of town tenement with outlying borough fields.

As we have already seen, Worcester became a mint at some time between the reign of Alfred and 1066. 'A solitary moneyer by name Alfwold first appears in the reign of Aethelred II, two moneyers only struck the extant Worcester coins of Cnut: Under Edward the Confessor the number was suddenly increased to seven'. The *VCH* refers to the *British Museum Catalogue of English Coins, Anglo-Saxon Series (ii)* and identifies two Scandinavian moneyers at work in the city, Arncetel and Wicing by name: 'we might have expected a stronger alien element to appear in a city which for a time was the centre of a Danish earldom'.[13] This is a large number of coiners for any town, comparable with Hereford at the time of Domesday and certainly one of the best tests of the relative prosperity of a pre-Conquest borough. The town is not very fully represented in the chronicles, except by repeated notices of the deaths and succession of its bishops. The most sensational instance is a dramatic illustration of an early assertion of burghal independence. In the year 1041 the *Chronicle* of Worcester's abbey reads: 'In this year Harthcnut had all Worcestershire harried on account of his two housecarles who were collecting the heavy tax: the inhabitants slew them within the town, inside the minster.' The story is extended in the *Chronicle* of Florence of Worcester: 'after six months' preparation a royal array, led by Godwin, Siward and other earls, reached the county. But the citizens in the long interval had formed a camp of refuge in the island of Bevere and now stoutly resisted. The avenging force sacked and burnt the city: but after this a settlement was effected and the *men of Worcester* returned to build again their ruined homes'.[14]

We see, in all, that the Saxon foundations of many of our modern boroughs were firmly laid during the reigns of the Saxon and Mercian kings, and indeed, that many of them continued in a position of eminence which had its origins in Roman township. Trade and industry were not as yet so important in their growth as were defence and religion, though a commanding site and accessible position were essential to growth. The extent of markets and trade is an unknown quantity which reflects the lack of adequate documentary evidence. What is certain is that from the earliest dates, county boroughs stand between kingdom and county; the later institution of the administrative shire is usually pre-dated by the emergence of a strong and influential borough and depends upon the town for defence and centralized administration.

FURTHER READING

See the comprehensive bibliography in Sawyer, P. H., *Anglo-Saxon Charters; An Annotated List and Bibliography* (Royal Historical Society 1968), also

Biddle, M., Chapter 3 on 'Towns' in *The Archaeology of Anglo-Saxon England* (1976); 'Winchester, the development of an early capital' in *Vor- und Frühformen du europaischen Stadt in Mittelalter* (1973).

Brooke, N., 'Anglo-Saxon Charters, the work of the last 20 years' in *Anglo-Saxon England,* 3 (1974)

Gelling, M., 'Recent work on Anglo-Saxon Charters', *Local Historian*, Vol. 13, No. 4, (1978).

Hill, D., *An Atlas of Anglo-Saxon England* (1981).

Lobel, M. D., *Historic Towns* (Vol. I: Banbury, Caernarvon, Glasgow, Gloucester, Hereford, Nottingham, Reading and Salisbury; Vol. II: Bristol, Cambridge, Coventry, Edinburgh, Winchester and Windsor) (*British Committee of the International Commission for the Study of Town History*, from 1969.)

EARLY CHARTERS : NOTE ON THE FACSIMILE DOCUMENTS

The amateur student, beginner or self-taught, cannot expect to become a capable paleographer with Saxon or medieval scripts, nor can *Town Records* pretend to be a paleographer's handbook. The problems are twofold; firstly, the illegibility of the script and secondly, the translation of a foreign, archaic language, either Anglo-Saxon or medieval Latin. With much practice and an elementary knowledge of the language, even an unqualified searcher can begin to recognize words, names and simpler constructions, but to transcribe an abbreviated shorthand *in extenso* is too complex, requiring special training. In fact, many professional scholars who use documents rarely attempt a complete transcription.

Even so, the author still maintains that the amateur student, however modest, should not be discouraged from searching out and recognizing original documents, even when these are illegible; otherwise he becomes dependent upon the scholars' observations on a third-hand translation. Problems of paleography can be avoided by several available aids. Simplest of all is avoidance of impossible hands; it will be noticed that in this book only the earliest documents fall into that category, the rest are in English. Those of us who are content to browse through ancient newspapers or analyse 19th-century census returns will experience no insoluble problems. 15th- to 17th-century records in English can be mastered with patience and practice, as our later examples will show. For the earliest records which demand at the very least an 'O-level' in Latin or a course on Anglo-Saxon, the student is dependent upon various aids and 'cribs' which lead him more closely towards the original which he cannot transcribe. The route is fully illustrated by the following extensive study of our first illustration, which reproduces the original Anglo-Saxon charter made about or between 889-899 by Aethelred and Aethelflaed in favour of the monks of Worcester. The original, a manuscript held by the British Library, is largely illegible, in some parts almost vanished or destroyed, and for that reason only part of the charter is illustrated opposite.

The student's route towards a better understanding of this document lies firstly through Professor Sawyer's indispensable *List*, which under No. 223 offers all the available transcriptions and translations as follows:

> A.D. 884 x 901. Æthelred, *ealdorman*, and Æthelflæd, to the church
> of St Peter, Worcester; grant of rights at Worcester. *English*.
>
> *MS.:* B.M., Cotton Tib. A xiii, fos 1^v–2 (s.xi[1]).
>
> *Printed:* B 579; Harmer 1914, pp. 22-23 (no. 13) with translation,
>   pp. 54-55; Hearne, *Heming*, pp. 3-5; K 1075; Thorpe, pp. 136-39,
>   with translation.
>
> *Translated:* Whitelock 1955, p. 498 (no. 99).
>
> *Comments:* Harmer 1914, pp. 106-7; Stenton, *V.C.H. Worcs.*, iv. 377,
>   genuine; Tait 1936, pp. 19-23; Stenton 1947, p. 521; Harmer
>   1950, p. 339 n. 4, pp. 343-44; Whitelock 1955, p. 498; Finberg
>   1961, no. 268, authentic.

The reference B579 is to W. de Gray Birch's *Cartularium Saxonicum*, a massive work in 3 volumes, published 1885-1899. This prints hundreds of Anglo-Saxon Charters and deciphers the British Library manuscript for us on pages 221-2. Note that the reproduction shows only the *second half* of the charter, and therefore the printed version shown below applies to that reproduction from the part marked *.

From the British Library Dept. of Western MSS (Cotton Tib. A xiii fo. 2). Actual size 6 in. x 9 in.

579. *Grant by Æðeldred, alderman, and Æðelflæd, of privileges to*
Worcester Monastery.   A.D. 873 × 899.

Ðæm ælmihtigan Gode þære soðan annesse ⁊ ðære halgan ðry-
nesse on heofonum sie lóf ⁊ puldor ⁊ dæda þoncung ealra þæra goda
þe he us forgifen hafað . for ðæs lufan æt ærestan ÆÐELDRED
ealdorman ⁊ ÆÐELFLÆD ⁊ for sancte Petres ⁊ ðære cyricean æt
Peogerna ceastre ⁊ eac for Pærferðes bisceopes bene heora freondas
hehtan bepyrcean þa burh æt PEOGERNA CEASTRE eallum þæm folc[1]
to gebeorge ⁊ eac þær on Godes lóf to arærenne ⁊ heo nu cyðað on
Godes gepitnesse on þisse béc þ heo pillað on ælcum þæra gerihta
þe to heora hlaford dome gebyrað oððe on ceapstowe oððe on
stræte ge binnan byrg ge butan geunnan healfes Gode ⁊ S̆. Petre ⁊
þære cyrcean hlaforde þ þy arlicor on þære stope beon mæge ⁊ eac
þy eaðr[2] be summum[3] dæle þæs heoredes helpon ⁊ þ heora gemynde[4]
on ecnesse ðy fæstlicor on ðære stope seo ða hpile ðe Godes hear-
sumnes on ðam mynstre beo .*

On[d][5] PÆRFERÐ bisceop ⁊ se heored habbað/gesetted þæs god-
cundnesse beforan ðære þe him mon dæghpamlice/deð ge be heora
life ge æfter heora life þ ðonne æt eolcum/uhtsonge ⁊ æt ælcum
æfensonge ⁊ æc eolcum undern song "de/profundis" ðone sealme[6]
ða hpile þe heo lifgeon ⁊ æfter heora life "laudate/dominum" ⁊ ælce
sæternes dæge on S. Petres cyrcean ðrittig sealma/⁊ heora mæssan
ægðer ge for heo lifgende ge eac forð geleorde ./ Ond þone cyðeð
Æþelred ⁊ Æþelflæd þ he pillað mid estfullan/mode ðisses unnan
Gode ⁊ sancte Petre on Ælfredes cyninges gepiþnesse ⁊ ealra ðæra
pitena ðe on Myrcna land[7] syndon . buton/þ se þægn scilling ⁊ se
seam pending gonge to dæs cyninges handa/. spa he ealning dyde
æt Salt píc .   Ah elles ge land feoh ge fihte/pite ge stale ge poh
ceapung ge burh pealles sceatinge ge ælc/þæra ponessa ðe to ænigre
bote gebyrie þ hit age healf ðære cyrcean hlaford Godes þances ⁊
sancte Petres spa spa hit mon to ceapstope gesette ⁊ on strætum .
Ond piðutan ða ceapstope seo se bisceop his landes ⁊ ealra his
gerihta pyrðe spa hit ær ure foregengan/gesetton ⁊ gefreodan . ⁊
Æðelræd ⁊ Æðelflæd ðis dydon on Ælfredes/cyninges gepitnesse ⁊
on Myrcna pitena ðæra naman her be/æftan apritene standað ⁊ on
Godes ealmihtiges naman halsiað/ealle heora æfter fylgendan þ
nænig mon ðæs ælmæssan ne panige þe/heo for Godes lufan
⁊ sancte Petres to ðære cyricean geseald habbað /

[A.] MS. Cotton, Vespasian A. v, f. 148b.   [T.] Thorpe, *Dipl.*, p. 136.
[K.] Kemble, *Cod. Dipl.*, No. MLXXV ; from [A.]

[1] Folce, **T.**   [2] Eað, **T.**   [3] Sumum, **T.**   [4] Gemynd, **T.**
[5] On, MS.   [6] Sealm, **T.**   [7] Lande, **T.**

Transcription of the Worcester charter reproduced from *Cartularium Saxonicum*, by W. de Gray
Birch (1885–1899), No. 579.
Facing page: Translation of same, reproduced by permission from *English Historical Documents*,
vol. I (c.500–1042), edited D. Whitelock (1975), pp. 540–1.

99. Arrangements about the building of fortifications at Worcester (about 889-899)

This is an Old English document of great importance in relation to Alfred's "burghal system", and to the organisation of a town. It survives in B.L. Cott Tiber. A. xiii, fol Ib (see p. 289). A paper manuscript of the sixteenth century, B.L. Cott. Vespas. A. v, is useful for filling the lacunae where the Tiberius text is now illegible. The best edition is by Harmer, No. 13, with translation. It is No. 1075 in Kemble, No. 579 in Birch, and is edited with translation in Thorpe, *Diplomatarium*, pp. 136-9.

To Almighty God, the True Unity and the Holy Trinity in heaven, be praise and honour and thanksgiving for all the benefits which he has granted us. For whose love in the first place, and for that of St Peter and of the church at Worcester, and also at the request of Bishop Wærferth their friend, Ealdorman Ethelred and Æthelflæd ordered the borough of Worcester to be built for the protection of all the people, and also to exalt the praise of God therein. And they now make known, with the witness of God, in this charter, that they will grant to God and St Peter and to the lord of that church half of all the rights which belong to their lordship, whether in the market or in the street, both within the fortification and outside; that things may be more honourably maintained in that foundation and also that they may more easily help the community to some extent; and that their memory may be the more firmly observed in that place for ever, as long as *obedience to God shall continue in that minster.

And Bishop Wærferth and the community have appointed these divine offices before that which is done daily, both during their life and after their death; i.e. at every matins and at every vespers and at every tierce, the psalm *De profundis* as long as they live, and after their death *Laudate Dominum*; and every Saturday in St Peter's church thirty psalms and a mass for them, both for them living and also departed.

And moreover Ethelred and Æthelflæd made known that they will grant this to God and St Peter with willing heart in the witness of King Alfred and of all the councillors who are in the land of the Mercians; except that the wagon-shilling and the load-penny[1] go to the king as they have always done at Droitwich. But otherwise, land-rent, the fine for fighting, or theft, or dishonest trading, and damages[2] to the borough-wall, and all the [fines for] offences which admit of compensation, are to belong half to the lord of the church, for the sake of God and St Peter, exactly as it has been laid down as regards the market-place and the streets. And outside the market-place, the bishop is to be entitled to his land and all his rights, just as our predecessors established and privileged it.

And Ethelred and Æthelflæd did this in the witness of King Alfred and of all the councillors of the Mercians whose names are written hereafter.[3] And they implore all their successors in the name of Almighty God that no one may diminish this charitable gift which they have given to that church for the love of God and St Peter.

1 The payments on a cart-load or pack-load of salt.
2 Accepting Bosworth-Toller's emendation of *sceatinge* to *sceapinge*.
3 These were omitted in the cartulary.

Professor Sawyer's printed references are to F. E. Harmer's *Select English Historical Documents of the Ninth and Tenth Centuries* published in 1914 (Cambridge), which offers a translation; and to T. Hearne's *Hemingi Chartularium Ecclesiae Wigorniensis*, an eighteenth-century cartulary of Worcester Abbey (Oxford 1723). K 1075 is another massive transcription series the *Codex Diplomaticus Aevi Saxonici* in 6 volumes, between 1839 and 1848; like Birch's volumes these will be available only in the larger reference libraries. This is also the case with reference to Thorpe, or *Diplomatiarium Anglicum Aevi Saxonici* edited by B. Thorpe in 1865; this also offers a translation.

We are offered three English translations of the Worcester charter. Of these the most readily accessible is 'Whitelock 1955'; this refers to the series of *English Historical Documents*, edited by Professor D. C. Douglas. In this case the translation appears in Volume I of the series (*c*.500-1042) edited by D. Whitelock, now in a new edition of 1975 which prints the full English translation of the charter as No. 99 on pages 540-541, with notes on the great importance of the document 'in relation to Alfred's 'burghal system' and to the organization of a town'. Note that the editor also gives a reference to a later, 16th-century, manuscript in the British Library which has filled the gaps in the original manuscript. Like Sawyer's *List*, the set of *English Historical Documents* will be found in any town library. On page 43 is the clear translation of an otherwise insoluble paleographical problem, taken from Whitelock; once again the point corresponding to the portion of the charter illustrated above is marked with an *.

GAZETTEER OF ANGLO-SAXON REFERENCES TO ENGLISH TOWNS

Saxon charters listed here are taken from Birch (BCS) and confirmed by Sawyer (S). However, references marked 'S*' are said by Sawyer to be 'spurious'. References to the Anglo-Saxon chronicles are to page numbers in Garmonsway's edition (ASC). Places listed in the *Burghal Hidage* are marked BH, with the number of hides allocated. Mints are noted from the lists in R. H. M. Dolley, *Anglo-Saxon Coins* (1961). Smaller towns not on the municipal base-list, but listed in the *Burghal Hidage* or possessing a mint, are listed in lower-case **bold print**, e.g.: **Burpham**. Any of the base-list boroughs which according to any of these sources was evidently a substantial Saxon town is listed in **BOLD CAPITALS**, e.g.: **BATH**. All other towns with place-names including the suffixes '-bury', '-caster', '-chester' or '-cester' are also shown in **BOLD** print. Boroughs on the base-list which are mentioned only as rural sites in these sources are given in normal capitals, e.g.: BARNSLEY. Modern boroughs for which no significant Anglo-Saxon references have been found have their earliest place-name citation listed with its date. These are taken from E. Ekwall, *The Concise Oxford Dictionary of English Place-Names*. The derivation of the place-name usually indicates the town's rural origins. Those towns cited in Domesday Book (1086) have the notation 'DB'. L (Latin); E (English); B (Bounds).

ABINGDON: BCS 155 (c. 730): BCS 850 (811); S 241/BCS 101 (699; L); S 567/BCS 906 (955; L/E) S 605/BCS 924 (956; L/E). S. Also refs. to Abbey: founded 675, destroyed by Danes c. 790, refounded c. 964. ASC: 122; 124-5; 153; 155; 164-6; 170; 208; 247.

ACCRINGTON: PND: Akarinton — Aecern-*tun*; Tun where acorns grow (1194).

ALDEBURGH: PND: Aldeburc — Alde-*burga*; Old fort (DB).

ALDERSHOT: PND: Alreshete — Alder-*sceat*; Alder copse (1248).

ALTRINCHAM: PND: Aldringeham — Aldhere-*ing-ham*; home of Aldhere's people (1290).

ANDOVER: BCS 912 (955; L/OE and ME) S 1515; ASC: 128-9.

APPLEBY: PND: Aplebi — Aeppel-*by*; Apple-homestead (N.B. Sc element) (1130).

ARUNDEL: PND: Harundel — Harhun-*dell*; Hoarhound valley (DB).

ASHTON-UNDER-LYNE: PND: Eston — Aesc-*tun* village where the ash grows (1212).

Axbridge: (Som): BH: 400; Mint.

AYLESBURY: BCS 1174 (968x971: E) S 1485; ASC: 18-19, 101. Mint.

BACUP: PND: Fulebachope — Baec-*hop*; valley by a ridge (c. 1200).

BARKING: S 1246/BCS 87 (695): S 1171/BCS 81 (685x694; L/B) Nunnery founded c. 666, destroyed by Danes, refounded c. 975.

BARNET: BCS 1263 (966; L); S 1293 and 1295*.

BARNSLEY: PND: Berneslai — Beorn's-*leah*: Beorn's glade (DB).

BARNSTAPLE: BH (as Pilton) 360; **Mint**.

BARROW-IN-FURNESS: PND: Barrai — Barr-ey island (ON element).

BASINGSTOKE: S 874: (990; L/EB).

BATH: (The Roman Baths of *Aquæ Sulis*) BCS 277 (796: *in celebri vico*); BCS 43 (676 *civitati quæ vocatur Hat Bathu*); BCS

(Bath — continued)

814 (Weston 946; L/EB); BCS 1009 (Weston 961 L/EB); S 51, 508, 661; ASC: 18-19, 94-5, 118-9, 144, 223, 240 (577 refers to three 'cities', Bath, Gloucester, Cirencester: BH: 100; **Mint**.

BATLEY: PND: Bateleia — Bata's-*leah*; Bata's glade (DB).

BEBINGTON: PND: Bebinton — Bebbe's-*ing-tun*; place of Bebbe's people (c. 1100).

BECCLES: PND: Becles — Bec-*laes*; pasture on the stream (DB).

BEDFORD: ASC: 100-101 (fortifications along river, jarls who rule the Danish boroughs, region owing allegiance to Bedford); **Mint**.

Bedwyn: **Mint**.

BERWICK-UPON-TWEED: PND: Berewich — Berewic; Corn farm or grange (1167).

Berkeley: (Glos): Mint.

BEVERLEY: S 1067 (1060x1065; L/E); ASC: 39, 43.

BEWDLEY: PND: Beuleu — Beau-lieu; beautiful place (1275).

BEXHILL: BCS 208 (772 . . . 'viii *cassatos*, L/EB); S 108.

BEXLEY: BCS 260 (765x785 L/EB); BCS 346 (814 L/EB); S 37 and 175.

BIDEFORD: PND: Bedeford — Bieda's *ford* (DB)

BIRKENHEAD: PND: Birkened — Bircen-*heved*; headland overgrown with birches (c. 1150).

BIRMINGHAM: PND: Bermingeham — Beornmund-*inga-ham*; Homestead of Beornmund's people (DB).

BLACKBURN: PND: Blacheburne — Blaec-*burna*; dark stream (DB).

BLACKPOOL: PND: Blacke Pull (1661).

BLANDFORD FORUM: PND: Blaneford — Blaegna-*ford*; ford with gudgeons (DB); '*Cheping*' Blandford (1288), '*Forum*' (1291) refer to market.

BLYTH: PND: Blida — River-name; gentle or
  merry (1130).
BODMIN: PND: Bodmine — Cornish *bot-meneich*;
  house of monks (DB). Priory founded c. 944,
  destroyed by Danes, restored c. 1124.
BOLTON: PND: Bodeltun — Botl-*tun*; Home-
  stead-place (DB).
BOOTLE: PND: Bodele — Botl; dwelling
  (DB).
BOSTON: PND: Botuluestan — Botulf's-*stan*;
  Botulf's stone house or church (1130).
BOURNEMOUTH: PND: La Bournemowthe —
  mouth of stream (1407).
BRACKLEY: PND: Brachelai - Braccas-*leah*;
  Braccas glade (DB).
BRADFORD: PND: Bradeford — Broad *ford*
  (DB).
BRENT: S 1436/BCS 384 (825 L); also
  WILLESDEN: S* 453/BCS 737 (L).
Bredy: (Dorset): BH: 760.
BRIDGWATER: PND: Brugie — Brycg; bridge
  (DB).
BRIDLINGTON: PND: Bretlinton — Beorhtel-
  ingas-tun; village of Beorhtel's people (DB).
Bridgnorth: (Salop): Mint.
BRIDPORT: PND: Brideport — Bredy's port
  (DB); Mint.
BRIGHTON: PND: Bristelmestune — Beorh-
  thelm's-*tun* (DB).
BRIGHOUSE: PND: Brighuses — houses by
  bridge (1240).
BRISTOL: ASC: 175, 191, 203, 223, 256, 266
  (see 1052 'borough'—; Mint.
BUCKINGHAM: ASC: 100 (918: fortifications
  along river); BH: 1, 600; Mint.
BROMLEY: S 331/BCS 506 (862 L/EB); S 671/
  BCS 1295 (955 x 973 L/EB); S 1457/BCS
  1296 (late 10th c. E); S 1511/BCS 1132
  (973 x 987 L/EB) S 864 (987 L/EB); S 893
  (998 L/EB); also Beckenham, BCS 506,
  1295.
Bruton: Mint.
BURNLEY: PND: Brunlaia — Brun-*leah*; glade
  on river Brun (1124).
Burpham: Mint.
BURTON-UPON-TRENT: S 906 (1004);
  929 (1012); 1536 (1002-4 E). Abbey
  founded 1002.
BURY: PND: Biri — Byrig; burgh, fort (1194).
BURY-ST-EDMUNDS: S 1494/BCS 1288 (962-
  991 E); ASC: 166, 234, 241, 245, 252 refers
  to Abbey only; Mint.
BUXTON: PND: Buchestanes — buc-*stane*;
  ancient monument (c. 1100).
Cadbury: Mint.
Caistor: Mint.
CALNE: S 1515/BCS: 912, 913 and 914 (951 x
  955 OE, ME and L); ASC; 123.
CAMBRIDGE: ASC: 74-5, 103, 140; see 1010
  destroyed by fire; Mint.
CAMDEN: BCS 1309 (978 L/EB); BCS:
  1351 (866 L/EB); S 805, 894, 1040, 1043,
  1450 (as HAMPSTEAD).

CANTERBURY: S 2/BCS 4 (605 L/B: S*);
  S 3/BCS 5 (605 L/B: S*); S 323/BCS 407
  (833 x 858 L); S 1204/BCS 519 (868 L);
  S 1209/BCS 733 (939 L/B); S 160/BCS 317
  (804 L/B); S 168/BCS 335 (811 L); S 187/
  BCS 373 and 374 (823 L/B); S 287/BCS 426
  (839 L/E); S 905 (1002 L/E); S 1414/BCS
  402 (833 L); S 1471 (c. 1045: a 'haga' in
  Canterbury OE and ME); ASC: 20, 23, 46--7,
  131, 139, 141, 156-7 (see 1009 ref. to
  'borough'); Mint. Priory founded 598,
  refounded 997, sacked by Danes 1011,
  destroyed 1067, refounded 1071. Abbey
  founded 598-605.
CARLISLE: Rom.: Luguvallium from British
  name Luguvalos. Then Caer-*deol*, Welsh
  'Caer', a city. ASC: 227 (William I restored
  town, built castle 1093).
CASTLEFORD: PND: Caesterford — ford by
  Rom. fort (Ermine Street crosses R. Aire
  here, Rom. station *Lagentium* or
  Legeolium here), ASC: 112 (see 948).
CHARD: S 1042 (1065 L).
CHATHAM: PND: Cethaema-mearc — from
  Celtic *Kaito* — a forest, British *ceto*. Thus:
  homestead by forest (995).
CHELMSFORD: PND: Celmeresfort —
  Ceolmaer's-*ford* (DB).
CHELTENHAM: S 1431/BSC 309 (803 L),
  Minster at.
CHESTER; Rom. Deva; later OE Ceaster —
  fort. ASC: 22-3, 88, 94, 119, 133, 147, 186,
  229, 249, 251, 266 (893; ref. to 'deserted site
  called Chester; 907; 'Chester rebuilt'. Mint.
CHESTERFIELD: S 569/BCS 911 (955 L).
CHICHESTER: Romano-British Noviomagnus
  Regnorum capital of Civitas Regnorum
  S 47/BCS 212 (n.d. 13th c. Ms. L) S*;
  ASC: 88, 222, 245, 260, 895; BH: 1,500;
  Mint.
CHIPPENHAM: S 1507/BCS 553 (873 x 888
  OE, ME, L); ASC 74-77.
CHIPPING NORTON: PND: Norton Mercatoria,
  Chepyngnorton Ceping (OE 'market town'),
  by 1246-80.
Chisbury: (Wilts): BH: 700.
CHORLEY: PND: Cherleg — Ceorla - leah;
  glade of ceorls/peasants (1246).
Cissbury: (Sussex): Mint.
CHRISTCHURCH: Orig. Twinham 'tween-eam';
  place between streams (1177); ASC: 92-3;
  S 391/BCS 738 (934 L and E; poss. S*)
  S 1741 (954); BH: 470 (ASC: 901 refers
  to 'manor').
CLEETHORPES: PND: Cleia — Claeg-thorp;
  Hamlet on clay (DB).
CLITHEROE: PND: Cliderhou — Klithra-haugr
  (ON); Song-thrush hill (1102).
COLCHESTER; Iron Age Camulodunon, later
  Rom. Colonia Camulodunum. PND: Cair
  Colun or Colneceaster — Rom. station on R.
  Colne (c. 800). ASC: 102-3 (see 920: ref.
  fortress destroyed, rebuilt). Mint.

COLNE: PND: Calna – Colne, British river-name, see CALNE (Wilts) 1124.

CONGLETON: PND: Cogeltone – ON *kang* – a bend (in R. Dane DB).

COVENTRY: S 1226: (1043, S*); ASC: 184, 188, 198, 260.

CREWE: PND: Creu – Welsh *Cryw* – ford or stepping stones (DB).

Crewkerne: Mint.

Cricklade: (Wilts) BH: 1500; Mint.

CROSBY: PND: Crosebi – Sc. Krossa-*byr*; homestead by cross (DB).

CROYDON: S 1202/BCS 529 (c. 871 OE and ME).

DARLINGTON: PND: Dearthingtun – Deornoth-*ingas-tun*: town of Deornoth's people (c. 1050).

DARTFORD: PND: Tarentefort – *ford* over R. Darent (DB).

DARTMOUTH: ASC: 168–9.

DARWEN: PND: Derewent – British r. name (1208).

DAVENTRY: PND: Daventrei–poss. r.-name Dane, personal name Dafa (DB).

DEAL: PND: Addelam – *dael*, a valley (DB).

DERBY: ASC: 101, 110–11. 167 (see 917 ref. to 'borough' and region it controlled); Mint.

DEWSBURY: PND: Deusberia – Dewi's-*burg*, or *Deaw*, a stream-name (DB).

DONCASTER: S 906 (1004 L/E); 1536 (1002 x 1004 E).

DORCHESTER: Rom. Durnovaria, later Dornuuarana Ceaster (c. 894); Mint.

DOVER: Rom. Novus Portus or Dubris, later Dofras (696); S 22/BCS 91 (696 x 716); S 1439/BCS 445 (844 L): ASC: 172–3, 179, 230; Mint.

DROITWICH: Romano–British Salinæ; S 83/BCS 134 (716 L); S 97/BCS 138 (716 x 717): 'part of building' L); S 1301/BCS 1087 (962 L/EB: 'saltpans'); S 786/BCS 1282 (972 L/EB; poss. S*); S 788/BCS 1284 (972 L: S*); S 1384 (1017 L/EB: 'ovens'); S 1824 (716 x 757 L; part of building and two salt-furnaces *in vico emptorio salis*); ASC: 167.

DUDLEY: PND: Dudelei – Dudda's *leah*; Dudda's glade (DB).

DUKINFIELD: PND: Dokenfeld – Ducena-*feld*; ducks' field (12th c.).

DUNSTABLE: Romano–British Durocobrivis.

DURHAM: S 1659, 1661/BCS 1256 (10–11th c. E).

EALING: S 1783 (693 x 704 L).

Eashing: (Surrey) BH: 600.

EASTBOURNE: PND: Burne – stream name (DB).

EASTLEIGH: PND: Estleie – *leage*, clearing or glade (DB).

EAST RETFORD: PND: Redforde – red *ford* (DB).

ECCLES: PND: Eccles – British Ecles; Welsh Eglwys, church (c. 1200).

ELY: S 646/BCS 999 (957 L); S 1051 (1042 x 1066 L), ASC: 34–5, 115, 157, 160, 205, 207–8, 241.

ENFIELD: PND: Enefelde – Eana's *feld* or open lands (1190).

EPSOM and EWELL: S* 1181/BCS 39 (727 L); S* 420/BCS 697 (933 L); S 752/BCS 1195 (967 L S*); S 1035 (1062 L: S*).

EVESHAM: S 80/BCS 125 (709 L/EB); S 1250/BCS 130 (16 c. L); S 1591a (12th c. Ms L): ASC: 160, 165, 184–5, 213 (mainly Abbey).

EXETER: Rom. Isca Dumnuniorum, later Ad-Escancastre (Rom. station on R. Exe) ASC: 74–5, 86–7, 134–5, 201, 263 (877 ref. to 'fortress', 1003, destruction of 'borough'); Mint; BH: 734.

EYE: ASC: 116 monastery founded 963, no jurisdiction of K. or Bp.

FALMOUTH: PND: Falemuth – obscure Cornish r.-name (1235).

FARNWORTH: PND: Farnewurd – enclosure round homestead with ferns (1185).

FAVERSHAM: PND: Fefresham – Latin, Faber's-*ham*; smith's homestead (811).

FOLKESTONE: S 1439/BCS 445 (monastery founded 1095); S 398/BCS 660 (927 L); S 981 (11 c. E/L); 1047 (1042 x 1066 E/L); 1643 (1038 L); ASC: 126, 179.

Frome: Mint.

GATESHEAD: PND: Ad Caprae Caput and Gateshaphed – wild goats' *headland* (c. 730).

GILLINGHAM: PND: Gyllingeham – Getlingas – place of the people of Gylla (10th c.).

GLASTONBURY: S 246/BCS 109 (704 L: S*); S 257/BCS 169 (745 L, poss. S*); S 1666 (678); ASC; 40, 110, 152–3, 159, 184–5, 200, 214–5, 252, 260.

GLOSSOP: PND: Glosop – Glott's-*hop* or valley (DB).

GLOUCESTER: S 70/BCS 60 (674 x 679 L); S 74/682 E, S*; S 1424 etc. (all ref. to Abbey; ASC: 18–19, 98–9, 105, 111, 163, 173, 175, 182, 186, 189, 191, 216, 219, 227–8, 235, 238, 244, 250–1, 253, 256, 266–7 (577 ref. to, as 'city'). Romano–British: Colonia Nerviana Glevensium, British: Glevum.

GODALMING: S 1507/BCS 553, 554 and 555 (873 x 888).

GOOLE: PND: Gowle – small ditch (1553).

GOSPORT: PND: Goseport – goose-market (1250).

GRANTHAM: PND: Grantham – Granta's-*ham* (DB).

GRAVESEND: PND: Gravesham – Grafes-*end*; end of grove (1157).

GREENWICH: S 728 (964 L); S 1002 (1044 L); ASC; 144–5, 148–9.

GRIMSBY: PND: Grimesbi – Grim's-*by* (Sc. for 'village' c. 1115).

GREAT YARMOUTH: PND: Gernemwa – mouth of Yare, or Ear-mouth, gravelly harbour (DB).

GUILDFORD: S 1507/BCS 553–555 888 OE, ME and L); Mint.

HACKNEY: PND: Hakney — Haca's Island or
   hook in r. (1231).
HALESOWEN: S 906 and 1536 (1002 x 1004
   L/E).
HALIFAX: PND: Feslei, later Haliflex — holy
   flax-field (1086 and 1175).
Halwell: (Devon): BH: 300.
HAMMERSMITH: PND: Hameresmythe —
   hammersmith's smithy (1312); as FULHAM:
   ASC: 76-7.
HARINGEY (formerly Harringay): PND: Harin-
   geie (1201) (changes to Harnesey, Hornsey, c.
   1543). *Haering-gehaeg*; greywood enclosure.
HARROGATE: PND: Harlo-gate (Sc. 'gate')
   grey-hill road (1512).
HARROW: S 106/BCS 201 (767 L); S 1414/BCS
   402 (833 L); S 1436/BCS 384 (825 L).
HARTLEPOOL: PND: Herterpol — Heoroteg-
   pol; pool by Hart (Bay?) c. 1180.
HARWICH: PND: Herwyz — Herewic; soldiers'
   camp (1238).
HASLINGDEN: PND: Heselingedon — Haselen-
   dun; valley of hazel trees (1241).
HASTINGS: S 133/BCS 259 (790 L); S 686/BCS
   1057 (960 L); S 1186 (795 L); ASC: 141,
   170, 178-9, 198-200, 220; BH: 500; Mint.
HAVERING: PND: Haueringas — Haeferingas;
   Haefer's peoples' place (DB).
HEDON: PND: Heldone — Heath-*dun*; heather-
   grown hill (1115).
HELSTON: PND: Henlistone — Cornish Henlis-
   tun; Old Court *tun* (DB).
HEMEL HEMPSTEAD: S 1784 (704x709 L).
HENLEY-ON-THAMES: PND: Heanlea — Hean-
   leage; high wood, clearing (1186).
HEREFORD: S 677/BCS 1040 (958 L/EB:
   '*haga* in Hereford'; cites Finberg's *Charters of
   the West Midlands* (1961) for discussion of
   bounds.) ASC: 98-9, 185-7, 189, 200, 223;
   Mint.
HERTFORD: ASC: 34-5, 96-7, 134 (see 913:
   ref. to fortresses); Mint.
HEYWOOD: PND: Hewude — high wood (1246).
HIGHAM FERRERS: PND: Hehham — *heah-
   ham*; high hamlet (1066-75); Count of
   Ferrers held in 1166.
HIGH WYCOMBE: S 106/BCS 201 (764-767
   L/EB): S 1485/BCS 1174 (968x971 E); S
   1497/BCS 812 (10th c. Ms. E/L).
HILLINGDON: PND: Hildedun — Hilla's-*dun*
   (1078-85).
HONITON: PND: Honetone — Huna's-*tun* (DB).
Horncastle: (Lincs): Mint.
Horndon: Mint.
Horsforth: Mint.
HOUNSLOW: PND: Honealaw — Hund's barrow
   (DB); ASC: 150-1.
HOVE: PND: Houue — *Hufe*, a hood or shelter
   (1296).
HUDDERSFIELD: PND: Oderesfelt — Huder's-
   feld (DB).
HUNTINGDON: S 792/BCS 1297 (973 L);
   ASC: 31, 101, 103, 116 (656 ref. to as

(Huntingdon — continued)
   'town', fortress at Tempsford, 920 fortress,
   963 'market' there.)
HYDE: PND: Hyde — *Hide* of land (1285).
HYTHE: S 1047 (1042 x 1066 E/L); S 1221
   (1026 L); ASC: 179; Mint.
Ilchester: (Som); Mint.
ILKESTON: PND: Tilchestune — Ealac's-*tun*
   (DB).
IPSWICH: S 1526/BCS 1008 (942 x 951 E);
   ASC: 126-7, 140; Mint.
ISLINGTON: PND: Gislandun — Gislas's-*dun*
   (c. 1000).
JARROW: ASC: 57 (794, monastery looted).
KEIGHLEY: PND: Chichelai — Cyhha's-*leah*
   (DB).
KENDAL (originally Kirkby Kendal): PND:
   Cherchebi — valley of the R. Kent (DB).
KENSINGTON: PND: Chenesitun — Cynesige's-
   tun.
KETTERING: S 68/BCS 22 (664 L/B, S*); S
   592/BCS 943 (956 L/EB): S 787/BCS 1258
   (972 L) poss. S*; S 1448/BCS 1128 (963 E);
   ASC: 116-7.
KIDDERMINSTER: PND: Chideminstre —
   Cydda's *minster* (DB).
KING'S LYNN: PND: Lynware — Lynn
   people (DB).
KINGSTON-UPON-HULL: PND: Wyk (c. 1160);
   Portus de Hull (1276).
KINGSTON-UPON-THAMES: S 1438/BCS 421
   (838 L).
LAMBETH: S 1036 (1062 L/EB); ASC: 163.
LANCASTER: PND: Loncastre — Rom. fort
   on R. Lune (DB).
Langport: (Som): BH: 600; Mint.
LAUNCESTON: perhaps Rom. fort named
   Tamara, see Rivet and Smith, p. 464. PND:
   Lanscavetone — old Cornish name with -*tun*
   (DB); Mint.
LEEDS: perhaps Rom. fort named Cambodunum
   PND: Hledes — Hlyde, loud brook (DB).
LEICESTER: Rom. Ratæ Coritanorum, capital
   of Civitas Coritanorum; PND: Legorensis
   civitas — dwellers on R. *Legra-ceastre*; ASC:
   98, 101, 105, 110-11 (921 ref. 'borough',
   943 'city' and Five Boroughs (Leicester,
   Lincoln, Derby, Stamford and Nottingham).
   Mint.
LEIGH: PND: Leeche — *leage*, glade,
   clearing (1276).
LEOMINSTER: ASC: 164, 176 (1052 'French-
   men at the castle of').
LEWES' BH: 1,300; Mint.
LEWISHAM: S 728 (964 L); S 1002
   (1044 L).
LICHFIELD: Rom. Letocetum, 2½ m S, later
   Lyccidfelth ASC: 42-3, 45, 160, 182.
LINCOLN: Rom. Lindum Colonia; ASC: 25,
   110-11, 202, 251, 253, 266, 268 (mostly
   post-1066, 942, one of Five Boroughs conq.
   by K. Edmund, 1069; K. William builds
   castle). Mint.

LISKEARD: PND: Lyscerruyt — from Cornish *lis*, 'a hall' with *caer*, 'a town' and *ruid*, 'free' (11th c.).

LIVERPOOL: PND: Liuerpul — lifrig-*pul*; pool thick water (1194).

LONDON: Rom. Londinium, later Lundonia, personal/tribal name. S 88/BCS 152 (734 L: toll on one ship); S 86/BCS 149 (733 L: takes tolls); S 98/BCS 171 (743x745 L: takes toll); S 133/BCS 259 (790 L: S*); S 208/BCS 492 (857 L: land in) S 346/BCS 561 (889 L: poss. S*, land in); S 940 (1006x1012 L: wharf in): S 1002 (1044 L); S 1096 (1058x 1066 E); S 1234 (1052x1070 E); S 1246/ BCS 87 (677 L); S 1488 (1003x1004 E/L); S 1489 (1035x1040 E: messuage in); S 1497/BCS 812 (10th c. E/L); S 1526/BCS 1008 (942x951 E); ASC: 13, 24, 64-5, 72-3, 80-1, 114, 124, 126-7, 150-3, 213, 218, 266 etc. (Refs. to fires, 961, 982, 1071); St Paul's rebuilt, 961: Mint.

LOUGHBOROUGH: PND: Lucteburne — Luhhede's-*burg* (DB).

LOUTH: S 68/BCS 22 (644 L/B: S*); ASC: 54 (re monastery); Mint (?).

LOWESTOFT: PND: Lothu Wistoft — Hlothver's *toft* from ON personal name (1212).

LUTON: S 133/BCS 264 (795-792 L); ASC: 98-9.

LYDD: S 111/BCS 214 (774 L/B).

Lydford: (Devon): BH: 140; Mint.

LYME REGIS: S 263/BCS 224 (774 L); S 442/BCS 728 (938 L/EB); S 895 (998 L); S 644/BCS 995 (957 L/EB).

Lympne: (Kent): Mint.

LYMINGTON: PND: Lentune — Limen-*tun*, stream-name.

Lyng: (Som): BH: 100.

LYTHAM ST ANNES: PND: Lidun — *hlith* (ON), slope (DB).

MACCLESFIELD: PND: Maclesfeld — Macca's forest *field* (DB).

MAIDENHEAD: PND: Maydehuth — *mayden-hyth*, maiden's landing-place (1248).

MAIDSTONE: PND: Mæidesstana — poss. maiden's *stone* (10th c.).

MALDON: ASC: 96-7, 100, 102, 126-7; Mint.

MALMESBURY; S 1245/BCS 37 (657 L). Sometimes called Ealdemsburg after founder. S 243/BCS 103 (701 L); S 322/BCS 447 (884 L); ASC: 146; Mint; BH: 1,200.

MANCHESTER: Romano–British Mamucio-ceast, Mameceaster ASC: 104 (repaired, garrisoned by K. Edward, 922).

MANSFIELD: PND: Mamesfeld — Mam's hill-*feld* (DB).

MARLBOROUGH: PND: Merleberge — Maerle-*beorg*, Maerla's hill (DB).

MERTON: S 551/BCS 878 (949 L); S 747/BCS 1196 (967 L/EB); ASC: 46; also: MITCHAM: S1181/BCS 39 (727 L; S*); S 420/BCS 697 (933 L; S*); S 1035 (1062 L: S);

(Merton — continued) also WIMBLEDON: S 1526/BCS 1008 (942 x 951 E). (Wunnemannedune ?)

Milborne Port: (Som): Mint.

MIDDLETON: PND: Middeltun — Middel-*tun*, middle place (1194).

MONMOUTH: Rom. settlement, Blestium.

MORLEY: PND: Moreleia — *leah* by fen, moor (DB).

MORPETH: PND: Morthpath — *morth-paeth*, murder-path. (c. 1200).

NEATH: Rom. fort, Nidum.

NEWARK: S 1233 (1054x1057 L: S*); Mint.

NEWBURY: PND: Neuberie — new *burgh* or castle (c. 1080).

NEWCASTLE-UNDER-LYME: PND: Novum Oppidum sub Lima (post-Conquest castle 1168).

NEWCASTLE-UPON-TYNE: Rom. fort, Pons Aelius. PND: Novum Castellum (post-Conquest castle, 1130).

NEWHAM: S 676/BCS 1037 (958 L/EB: poss. S*); S 774/BCS 1228 (969 L); S 1040 (1065 L; poss. S*); S 1043 (1066 L: S*).

NEWPORT (I.o.W.): PND: Novus Burgus — New town (temp. Henry III).

NEW ROMNEY: ASC: 178; Mint.

NORTHAMPTON: ASC: 98-101, 103, 141, 190, 192-3, 223, 240, 245, 250, 267-9; Mint.

NORWICH: S 1489 (1035x1040 E, messuage in) ASC: 134-5, 210-12, 223, 250, 260, 265 (see 1004: sack of 'the borough'); Mint.

NOTTINGHAM: ASC: 68-9, 104, 110-11, 202 (see 922-4 K. Edward repairs & garrisons, 'borough'); Mint.

OKEHAMPTON: S 303/BCS 472 (854 L: poss. S*); S 1696 (839x855).

OLDHAM: PND: Aldholm — Old Holm from Sc. *holmr* a small island in fens (1226).

OSSETT: PND: Osleset — Osla's *geset* or fold (1275).

OXFORD: S 964 (1032 L/EB); ASC: 95-7, 105, 139, 143, 145, 159, 161, 192, 263, 267-8 (see 1009 Danes burn 'the borough'); BH: 1,400; Mint.

PENRYN: PND: Penrin — Cornish *penryn* a promontory (1259).

PENZANCE: PND: Pensans — Cornish *pen* is 'cape' and *sans* is 'holy' (1332).

Pershore: Mint.

PETERBOROUGH: PND: Medeshamstedi (c. 730): Burh (972): Burgus Sancti Petri (1225). Monastery, destroyed by Danes, was Mede's *homestead*: new borough Peterborough, after church. S 68/BCS 22 (664 L/B): S 1448/BCS 1128 (963 E): ASC: 117, 171, 183, 187-9, 198-9; As Medeshamstede 29, 33, 35-7, 52-3, 65, 71, 115-7; as Burh 117. (Ms. E of ASC once here). Mint.

PLYMOUTH: PND: Sutton (DB) becomes Plimmue (1231), Plummuth (1235).

Petherton: (Som): Mint.
PONTEFRACT: PND: Fracti-pontis — broken bridge (1069).
POOLE: PND: Pole — the *pool* (1194).
Porchester: (Hants) BH: 500.
PORTSMOUTH: PND: mouth of Port harbour (501); ASC: 14–15, 237, 246, 253.
PRESTON: PND: Prestune — preosta-*tun*; town of priests (DB).
PRESTWICH: PND: Prestwich — priests' *wic*, parsonage (1194).
PUDSEY: PND: Podechesaie — Pudoc's island (DB).
Quatford: (Salop); Mint.
READING: S 1494/BCS 1288 (962 x 991 E); as ASC: 70–3, 137, 263 (1004; ref. to food depot there; Mint.
REDBRIDGE: As WANSTEAD: S 1040 (1065 L: S*); S 1043 (1066 L: S*); also WOODFORD: S 1036 (1062 L/EB: S*); also DAGENHAM: S 1171/BCS 81 (690 x 694 L/B); S 1246/BCS 87 (677 L: poss. S*).
RICHMOND-ON-THAMES: Sheen until 1485; S 1526/BCS 1008 (942 x 951 E); see Unwin, R. C. B., *Saxon Twickenham: the Evidence of the Charter 704–948 A.D.* (Twickenham Loc. Hist. Soc., 1981).
RIPON: S 456/BCS 646 (13th c. Ms. L: S*); ACS 41, 53, 112 (see 948 monastery destroyed).
ROCHESTER: S 1/BCS 3 (604 L/EB: poss S*); S 32/BCS 193 (762 L/B); S 34/BCS 196 (765 L); S 131/BCS 255 (789 L/B); S 165/BCS 339 (811 L/B); S 266/BCS 242 (781 L/EB: poss. S*); S 291/BCS 439 (842 L); S 299/BCS 460 (850 L: poss. S*); S 315/ BCS 486(i); (855 L); S 327/BCS 502 (790 for 860 L/EB: S*); S 339/BCS 518 (868 L/EB); S 349/BCS 571 (895 L/EB: S*); S 1514/BCS 486(ii) (c. 855 E); ASC: 20, 23–4, 26–7, 29–30, 32, 37, 43–5, 58–9, 64–5, 78–9, 86–90, 125, 131, 156, 188–9, 223–4, 245, 252, 254, 261, 267; (see 885: ref. to siege of 'city' & 'citizens' defending it.) Mint.
ROMSEY: S 812/BCS 1187 (c. 970 L/EB: poss. S*); ASC: 118, 217.
ROYAL LEAMINGTON SPA: PND: Lamintonetun, on River Leam (DB).
RUGBY: PND: Rocheberie — Hroca's *burg* (OE *burgh* replaced by Sc. *-by*: DB).
RYDE: PND: La Ride — *rith*, a small stream.
RYE: PND: Ria — *aet thaere-iege*, at the island (1130).
SAFFRON WALDEN: PND: Waledana — Walhdene; valley of the Britons.
ST ALBANS: S 138/BCS 264 (792 L: S*); S 645/BCS 994 (957 L/EB); S 888 (996 L); S 912 (1005 L: S*).
ST AUSTELL and FOWEY: PND: Austol — Saint's name of church (1138); Fawe — beeches, beech-river (c. 1200).
SALE: PND: Sale — *salh*, sallow (1260).

SALFORD: PND: Salford — *salh*-ford, sallow *ford* (DB).
SALISBURY: At Old Sarum, Rom. Sorviodunum; removed to New Sarum by Bp. Poore in 1220. ASC: 16–17, 134--5; Mint.
SANDWICH: S 808/BCS 1185 (963 x 971 L: poss. S*); S 959 (1023 L and E: poss. S*, 'port of'); S 1047 (1042 x 1066 L and E); S 1467 (1037 x 1040 E); S 1636 (979 L and E); ASC: 64–5, 126, 136, 138–9, 143, 145–6, 157–8, 161, 164, 166–70, 177–9, 194–6; refs. to naval base, port, harbour dues); Mint.
SCARBOROUGH: PND; Escardeburg — Skarthi (harelip's)-*burg* (c. 1160).
SCUNTHORPE: PND: Escumethorp — Skuma'storp (DB).
SHAFTESBURY: S 655/BCS 1026 (958 L/EB): ASC: 124–5, 158–9; BH: 700; Mint.
SHEFFIELD: PND: Scafeld — open land on R. Sheaf (DB).
SHREWSBURY: ASC: 147; Mint.
SLOUGH: PND: Slo — *sloh*, a mire or slough (1196).
SOLIHULL: PND: Sulihull — *sulig-hyll*, pigsty-hill (1242).
SOUTHAMPTON: S 701/BCS 1094 (962 L); ASC: 62–3. 124–5, 129, 229; BH: 150; Mint.
SOUTH SHIELDS: Rom. fort, Arbeia.
SOUTHWARK: PND: Suthgeweork — southern fortification; Suthriganaweorc — fort of the Suthrige, Surrey People (10th c. and 1023); ASC; 156, 175, 180–2; BH: 1,800; Mint.
SOUTHWOLD: PND: Sudwolda; Southern-*wald*, wood (DB).
STAFFORD: ASC: 96–7 (see 913: Aethelflaed of Mercia-built fortress): Mint.
STAMFORD: S 787/BCS 1258 and 1280 (972 L: poss. S*); ASC: 31, 103, 110–11, 116, 148–9, 205, 258, 267 (see 921: K. Edward had fortress); Mint.
Steyning: (W. Sussex): Mint.
STOCKPORT: PND: Stokeport — poss. originally Stockford — stock port or town (1190).
STOKE-ON-TRENT: PND: Stoche — *stoc*, an outlying cattle-farm (DB).
STRATFORD-ON-AVON: PND: Aet Stretfordae, *straet*-ford, ford on Rom. road (691–2); S 198/BCS 450 (845 L: poss. S*); S 1251/ BCS 131 (714 L: poss. S*); S 1252/BCS 76 (699 x 717 L); S 1257/BCS 241 (781 L).
STRETFORD: PND: Stretford — *straet*-ford, ford on Rom. road (1212).
SUDBURY: S 1486/BCS 1289 (1002 E); S 1501 (961 x 995 E); ASC: 56; Mint.
SUNDERLAND: PND: Sunderland — *sundorland*; separate (c. 1168).
SUTTON: S 1181/BCS 39 (727 L: S*); S 420/ BCS 697 (933 L: S*); S 752/BCS 1195 (967 L: S*); S 1035 (1062 L:S*); S 1047 (1042 x 1066 E and L; poss. S*); S 1504 (946 x 947 E) (including CHEAM).

SUTTON COLDFIELD: PND: Sutone — suth-*tun;*
southern *tun* (DB); Colfeld — open land where
charcoal burned.

SWINDON: PND: Svindune — pig-hill (DB).

SWINTON and PENDLEBURY: PND: Suinton —
pig-farm (1258); Penelbiri — *tun* by Pendle
Hill (1202).

TAMWORTH: S 906 and 1536 (1004 E); ASC:
96–7, 103, 105, 111 (see 913 Aethelflaed of
Mercia built fortress); Mint.

TAUNTON: S 254/BCS 158 (737 L/EB: poss.
S*); S 311/BCS 476 (854 L/EB: S*); S
1491/BCS 652, 653, 654 (955 x 958 OE, ME
and L); S 443/BCS 727 (938 L/EB: S*); S
521/BCS 813 (947 L: S*); S 825/BCS 1149
(963 x 975 L); S 818/BCS 1159 (963 x 975 L);
S 806/BCS 1219 and 1220 (978 L and E,
poss. S*); ASC: 43 (see 722, Aethelburgh
destroyed); Mint.

TENTERDEN: PND: Tentwardene — *Tenet-
waru-denn,* swine pasture of people of Thanet.

TEWKESBURY: PND: Teodechesberie —
Teodec's-*burg* (DB).

THETFORD: S 996 (1040 x 1042 L: *mansus* or
mansio in); ASC: 70–1, 112, 135, 140, 229
(see 952 and 1004 ref. to 'borough'); Mint.

TIVERTON: S 1507/BCS 553, 554, 555 (873 x
888 OE, ME and L).

TODMORDEN: PND: Tottemerden — Totta's
gemaer-denu, Totta's boundary-valley (1246).

Torksey: (Lincs); Mint.

TORRINGTON: PND: Toritona — *tun* on R.
Torridge (DB).

TOTNES: PND: Totanaes — Totta's-*naess,* headland (979); Mint.

TOWER HAMLETS: see STEPNEY: PND:
Stybbanhyth — Stybba's *hyth,* landing-place
(c. 1000); POPLAR and BETHNAL are later
names).

TRURO: PND: Triuereu — Cornish *tri-* three
(1285).

TYNEMOUTH: ASC: 55, 231.

WAKEFIELD: PND: Wachefeld — field where
wake-feast held (DB).

WALLASEY: PND: Walea — *Wala-eg;* island of
Welsh (DB).

WALLINGFORD: S 517/BCS 810 (945
L/EB: poss. S*); S 1488 (1003–4
E and L): ASC: 137, 144, 256, 267 see
1006 town burnt down BH: 2,400;
Mint.

WALLSEND: PND: Wallesende — end of (Rom.)
wall (c. 1085).

WALSALL: PND: Aet Walesho — Wealh's *halh*
or valley (1002).

WALTHAM FOREST: S 1056 (1042 x 1066
L: S*); also LEYTON: S 1040 (1065 L: S*);
S 1043 (1066 L:S*).

WANDSWORTH: S 1246/BCS 82 (693 L: S*);
see BATTERSEA: S 1248/BCS 82 (693
L/EB: poss. S*).

WAREHAM: ASC: 52–3, 74–5, 123–5, 244;
BH: 1,600; Mint.

WARRINGTON: PND: Walintune — *tun* of
Waer's people, or at weir (DB).

Warminster; Mint.

WARWICK: S 1388 (1016 L/EB, *haga* in);
ASC: 98–9 (see 914: fortress); BH: 1,200;
Mint.

Watchet: (Som): BH: 513; Mint.

WATFORD: S 1497/BCS 812 (10th c. E and L);
S 1517 (1053 L).

WELLS: S 1042 (1065 L: S*).

WEST BROMWICH: PND: Bromwic — *wic*
where broom grows (DB).

WESTMINSTER: S lists 47 charters or Abbey;
many are forgeries or 'embellished', or ref.
to lands in various counties, only one or two
to London. 'Authentic' ones include: S 670/
BCS 1048 (951 L/EB: estate N of river);
S 903 (1002 L/EB; *Berewican,* near Tyburn);
S 1119 (1042 x 1044 E: wharf, portreeve);
S 1142 (1053 x 1066 E: *Staeningahaga).*

WEYMOUTH: S 391/BCS 738 and 739 (934 L
and E: poss. S*).

WIDNES: PND: Wydnes — wide promontory
(c. 1200).

WIGAN: PND: Wigan — Wigan's homestead
(1199).

WILTON: S 767/BCS 1216 (968 L/EB); S 870
(988 L/EB: 'messuage'); S 1774 (984:
mansa); ASC: 72–3, 114, 134–5; BH: 1,400;
Mint.

WINCHESTER: Romano–British Venta Bel-
garum, later Uintanceastir (c. 730). Some
charters unreliable, or deal with land at a
distance. The following ref. to Winchester: S
488/BCS 786 (943 L/EB: *haga*): S 689/BCS
1080 and 1144 (961 L/EB: 13 *predia);* S
807/BCS 1302 (984 for 963 x 970 L); S 845
(983 OE, ME and L); S 889 (996 L/EB); S
925 (1012); S 1153 (1052–3 E); S 1560/
BCS 630 (9th c.); ASC: 26–7, 46–9, 67–9,
105–7, 112–7 etc. BH: 2,400; Mint.

WINDSOR: S 1040 (1065 L); 1043 (1066 L);
1141 (1042 x 1066 E) all S*.

WISBECH: ASC; 30 (see 656).

WOKINGHAM: Wokingeham — Wocca's peoples'
place (1227).

WOLVERHAMPTON: S 860 (985 L/EB); S 1155
(n.d. E); 1380 (996 for 994): L/EB: grants
land at Bilston, Willenhall, Wednesfield etc.):
S*.

WORCESTER; poss. Rom. town Vertis otherwise Uuegorna civitas — Rom. fort of Wigoran
people (692); 98/BCS 171 (743–5 E: toll
grants); S 223/BCS 579 (884 x 901: grants
to Bp.); S 1280/BCS 608 (904 L and E;
incl. messuage); S 1367 (972 x 992 L and E:
incl. messuage and croft); S 1369 (983 x 985
E and L/EB: messuage by gate); S 1408
(1052–6 L: messuage); S 1158 (1062 E;
third pt of *seamtoll* and *ceaptoll);* ASC: 127,
159, 162, 165, 167, 244 (mainly re Bps.
except 1041. Two collectors of taxes, slain by
inhabitants); BH: 1,200; Mint.

WORKINGTON: PND: Wurcingtun — *tun* of
  Weorc's people (946).
WORKSOP: PND: Werchessope — Weorc's *hop*,
  valley (DB).
WORTHING: PDN: Ordinges — Wurth's people
  (DB).
YEOVIL: S 1057/BCS 553, 554, 555 (873 x 888
  OE, ME and L).

YORK: Romano-British Eburacum,
  legionary fortress and *colonia*. Later,
  Eferwic from British personal name *Eburos*
  changed to Eofor — (a boar). Scandinavians
  changed name to Iorvik, thus Iork.
  ASC: 8, 10, 25, 39, 46, 68–9, 105,
  149–9, 184, 190, 196–8, 202–4, 210, 212;
  Mint.

CHAPTER THREE

BOROUGHS IN THE DOMESDAY SURVEY, 1086

DOMESDAY BOOK is our oldest national record. In 1086 William the Conqueror ordered that a survey of the whole of England be undertaken to provide a detailed account of the manorial population and productive resources of the country, and a record of the value and the ownership of all the land. Although it did not, for various reasons, cover the entire country, its scope and detail was unmatched in Europe for many centuries. The text of the Survey has only once been set and printed — in 1783 — and then in an edition of only 1,250 copies. Translations have been published over the years for most counties, but they have been of varying quality. Fortunately, it is now possible to obtain an up-to-date translation and copy of the text in the new Phillimore edition of Domesday. This will be available for the whole of England by 1986, the ninth centenary of the original Survey.

Domesday Book is essentially a manorial survey. As we have seen in *Village Records* it is a primary source of information on feudal tenures in the counties and on the agricultural economy of villages. Manor by manor, listing first the *demesne* lands of the King, then those of each tenant-in-chief, barons and churchmen, the Survey is mainly concerned with the *hidage* or taxable value of each village. Each entry separates the ploughlands held in *demesne* in each manor from the number of ploughs worked by the villagers. The population of each place is set out in separate classes, giving the numbers of *villeins, bordars, cottars* and *serfs*, with occasional details of the priest and his church. Land use is next described in terms of arable land, pastures, meadows and woodland with additional information on fisheries and other more unusual manorial assets such as hawks' eyries, vineyards, lead-mines, beehives and salt-pans. One or two counties, such as Devon, Cornwall, and Somerset give exceptional detail of the numbers of sheep, cattle, horses and oxen in each manor; pigs are more commonly recorded elsewhere as a measurement of the feeding-capacity — and thus the tax — of each wood. A glossary of technical terms and Latin words used in Domesday will be found at the end of this chapter.

Domesday says little about the economic organization of the manors, apart from the measure of the ploughlands in *carucates* or individual *virgates* and the significant ratio of estate-managed *demesne* and land let out to *villein* tenants. Agrarian services are rarely mentioned and place-names within a village are not given unless as manors in their own right. The Survey is concerned only with manorial tenure and customary dues in money and in kind, primarily concerned with the king's assets and income from all sorts of rents, taxes, tributes and tolls. If a place, a person or a possession could be profitable it was usually recorded. In one county a tenure is held in return for embroidery lessons for the sheriff's daughter, in another for the training of the royal hunting dogs. Thus, although it is frustrating to search vainly for institutions which the Domesday commissioners never intended to describe for us, the king's profit-motive often ensures that items not exactly feudal were nevertheless recorded.

Each manorial entry concludes with the total valuation of the holding — in each case a comparison is made between its value before the Conquest, (T.R.E. or Tempore Regis Edwardi), and its value at the time of the Survey (T.R.W. or Tempore Regis Willelmi). In the case of the towns the second phase is often divided to compare value at the time of the Norman tenant's acquisition of the property and 'now', that is in 1086. Most county surveys begin with a numbered 'contents-list' of the tenants-in-chief, beginning with the king, but in some cases the chief town of the county is first described. The county-town survey often runs on into a resumé of the special laws or 'customs of the county', usually a criminal code of penalties for especially dire offences against 'the king's peace': sometimes also, as at Chester, it includes a set of special commercial bye-laws. Rarely is more than one county town sufficiently important to be described 'above the line'; Norfolk includes as 'lands of the burgesses' not only Norwich but also Yarmouth and Thetford, but this is in the main body of the Domesday text. Colchester is surveyed at length but is recorded at the end of the Essex Domesday, which has no other town 'above the line'; Chelmsford is entered as a manor of the Bishop of Ely. Dorset, exceptionally, precedes the list of tenants-in-chief with four towns, Dorchester, Bridport, Wareham and Shaftesbury, though only Shaftesbury is described as a 'borough'; in all four there had been a great loss of houses. (Slightly expanded descriptions of the same towns are also given in the *Exon Domesday*.) Many counties record no separate boroughs; Somerset, Rutland, Essex, Surrey, Sussex, Middlesex, Derbyshire and Cornwall record all their towns as manors within the lordship of king, barons or churchmen. In those cases where a pre-entry is made it appears to be assumed that the town is royal *demesne*, a 'royal borough' or that the king is chief landlord there; in some cases however there is an impression that a few towns were already literally separate from the county and from the 'feudal system' of the normal Domesday record.

Some of the pre-Survey town records are brief and not particularly urban in character; Bedford, Buckingham and Gloucester are typical examples of predominantly rustic boroughs. Other towns appear amongst the manors of the tenants-in-chief. In these cases the ploughland and economy of the manor is usually dealt with first and the tenure of the burgesses is recorded separately. Thus we find such typical entries, after the details of ploughlands and pasture, as: 'In the same Maldon the King has 180 houses held by burgesses . . . . or 'In this manor (Rye) is a new borough; 64 burgesses pay £8 less 2s. . . . '. Often a group of burgesses appears among the bordars and the pigmen with no further explanation, as in Pocklington and Bridlington in Yorkshire. If this type of entry is combined with that of a market or a castle we may assume that the place was in some small sense a 'borough', but this is a dangerous assumption, because of Domesday's widespread method of recording extra-mural burgesses of boroughs elsewhere in the county. Many towns had residents who belonged to rural manors at a distance; the existence of such 'contributory manors' in fact is one of the criteria of a real Domesday borough. A typical manorial entry is, for example: '18 burgesses of Stafford belong to this manor . . . ' at Marston, a hamlet three miles north of Stafford. Such tenancies could be substantial. At Saltwood in Kent we find that ' . . . to this manor belong 225 burgesses in the borough of Hythe . . . '; Saltwood is now a suburb of Hythe. So when a manor at Stanstead, four miles from Hertford, includes '. . . 7 burgesses who pay 23s.' with no reference to any neighbouring town, it is difficult to know whether this may not have been omitted. As well as burgesses, town houses and burgage tenements are recorded as manorial property. This was presumably a town-house and country-house arrangement for the burgesses.

Towns to the Domesday Commissioners were an innovation, relatively unfamiliar; they did not fit easily into the format and terminology of the rest of the Survey, which was arranged on the basis of county and manor. The existence of the larger towns literally did not fit the general arrangement of shire and hundred. Yet many towns did exist in Norman England and the Survey recognizes their existence in several different ways. Moreover, it acknowledges that borough tenures and rights were recognizable before the Conquest. Domesday's problem is to find suitable language to describe these tenures and make them fit, as far as possible, the 'customary dues' and feudal relationships of the surrounding counties. The Gazetteer at the end of this Chapter will show that about 70 of our modern towns were already 'boroughs' in 1086 or were demonstrating strong signs of urban life. Of our base-list of later municipal boroughs about 40% are not recorded in any form at all, as unfortunately the Survey is incomplete. Whole counties such as Durham, Northumberland and most of Cumberland and Westmorland were either not surveyed or appeared in the Survey of Yorkshire. Lancashire did not exist and manors in the northern part of the county, including such later Lancastrian strongholds as Preston and Lancaster are recorded as 'lands of the king in Yorkshire'. South Lancashire, 'between Ribble and Mersey', including Liverpool and much of modern Merseyside, is found with the Cheshire Domesday, as are parts of North Wales. Most of Wales was not surveyed and two of the most important towns in England, London and Winchester, were surveyed but not recorded in the transcription.

Another 40% of the modern boroughs are recorded in Domesday Book but their descriptions are simply manorial and agrarian with no sign of town life whatever. The remaining 20% show some signs of urban growth and about half of these are quite substantial towns which continue to flourish throughout the Middle Ages and afterwards. Most of the county towns such as Bedford, Nottingham, Shrewsbury, Lewes, Dorchester, Huntingdon and others are all clearly identified, are usually surveyed 'above the line' and are usually described as 'boroughs'. All the ancient cathedral cities are clearly identified and described. Chester, Chichester, Worcester, Hereford, Norwich and York are prominent, each with hundreds of houses and populations of 1,000 or 2,000 families. Most modern industrial cities, however, were rural vills in the time of King William and were long to remain so. Birmingham was open fields for six ploughs, worth in all 20s. Bradford, Huddersfield, Lancaster, Luton and Manchester were similarly manorial. There were other small towns which are recorded in Domesday as having castles, markets, burgesses and even mints of their own. Though some of these were described in 1086 as 'boroughs', today they are no more than villages or small market towns. Some of these 'non-survivors' are included with our base-list in the Gazetteer, for comparison; they include such places as Ashwell in Hertfordshire, Pershore in Hereford–Worcester, Bradford-on-Avon in Wiltshire, Lydford in Devon and Milborne Port in Somerset. Cricklade in Wiltshire had dozens of dependent burgesses in many Wiltshire manors; other small towns like Wigmore in Herefordshire were reclaimed from waste and returned to obscurity.

Domesday's usual words to describe a town are *burgus* or *civitas*; the word *villa* is used less specifically and often means only 'manor', though *manerium* is the more exact description of the rural *demesnes*. It is inadvisable to assume too much precision in any of these terms, particularly in the case of the *civitates* or 'cities'. There were 13 so named: York, Lincoln, Chester, Shrewsbury, Hereford, Worcester, Gloucester, Leicester, Exeter, Oxford, Chichester, Canterbury and Rochester. Chester, Worcester and Leicester are described variously as both borough and city. Exceptionally, Lydford in Devon, having been described as a 'borough with 69 burgesses and 40 ruined houses' is said to have land for the burgesses's two ploughs 'outside the city . . .'. The Hertfordshire Survey complicates the terms by referring to 'the borough of the town' at Berkhamsted and the 'borough-town' or *suburbium* of Hertford. It is tempting to think of the *burgus* as the walled enclosure of the towns; walls there certainly were. At Oxford there were 20 'wall-dwellings', so-called because 'if there is need and the king commands their owners repair the wall'. At Chester, 'for the repair of the wall and the bridge the reeve used to call out one man to come from each hide in the county'. It is commonplace for town surveys to record burgesses living both within and without the walls as at Hereford; at Canterbury, Nottingham and York dwellings are actually recorded as being 'in the town ditch'. In smaller places castle and borough seem almost synonymous; at Tutbury in Staffordshire, now a village, there was 'a borough round the castle where 42 men live only by their trading who, with a market, pay £4 10s. . . .'. Other small fortified places like Clifford and Wigmore, both in Herefordshire, and now villages were Domesday 'boroughs'; Wigmore paid the comparatively large sum of £7 in *ferm* and Clifford housed 16 burgesses. The impression gained in the smallest castles is of the 'borough' as the bailley of the castle, where the burgesses, as at Monmouth, might alternatively be knights with ploughs.

The actual town survey, when it is separately recorded, consists of an account of the king's property and rights in the borough, usually in terms of a number of burgesses. 'In Northampton there were 60 burgesses in the king's lordship before 1066 who had as many residences . . .'. The king's holding may be given in terms of property: 'In the city of Exeter the king has 300 houses all but 15 of which pay the customary due . . .'. Unfortunately, the numbering of the burgage tenements in any town is usually done in at least three ways: firstly, the king's houses, then a list of lords both great and small with more houses; other houses may, as we have seen, be separately concealed in the main text of the manorial surveys. This makes a total population difficult to calculate. Some larger cities were divided into wards or districts. In York there were seven 'shires', one belonging entirely to the archbishop who also held the third part of another. In the borough of Huntingdon there were four quarters or *ferlingi* and Stamford was divided into six wards or '*custodiæ*', five in Lincolnshire, the sixth in Northamptonshire, 'across the bridge but paying all customary dues with the others except tribute and tolls'. Nine of the ten wards of Canterbury are precisely described, with roughly equal numbers of 30–50 burgesses in each ward. In several cases there are references to a 'new borough' and at Nottingham it appears as if Hugh the Sheriff had built 13 additional houses 'in the new borough' within the existing town. Chester's survey, too, distinguishes between 'the bishop's borough' and the other parts. Winchester is surveyed separately in the later *Winton Domesday* where individual streets are identified; this is unusual but may be compared with Colchester's survey, exhaustively house by house, repeating the names of the same tenants at intervals, which suggests that actual streets are being listed. In the survey of Dorset, Wareham has 'the part belonging to St Wandrille' and 'the parts belonging to the other barons'; and at Shaftesbury 104 houses were 'in the king's demesne' and 153 more were 'in the part belonging to the Abbess of Shaftesbury'.

Property within the borough or city is described in several ways, either as *hagæ* or sites, *masuræ* and *mansiones* or tenements, and *domus* or houses. 'Sites' appear to be subdivided into smaller holdings or messuages but the *domus* is usually an individual burgage tenement. At Wallingford there were 276 *hagæ* on eight virgates of land, which suggests an acre site. At Guildford there are two burgesses to each *haga*, which further indicates a half-acre burgage. At Shrewsbury and Northampton the survey specifically states that there are as many burgesses as there are *mansiones*. Colchester's houses are coupled with acreages of land; 393 houses are associated with a total acreage of 1,318 acres, which suggests a larger average burgage tenement of 3½ acres. It is usually difficult to arrive at a complete total of population for any town. The largest single entries are those for York, with 1,418 burgesses and Norwich with 1,320. Other towns range from Barnstaple with at least 47 burgesses; Bath with 64 and Hereford with 103; to Cambridge with 332; Canterbury with 267; and Oxford with 279. The smaller numbers, however, may record only the king's tenants and omit baronial owners; Northampton starts with a figure of 87 houses, then lists an additional 227 in private hands. Small boroughs not included in our modern base-list include Ashwell (Herts) with 14 burgesses; Bedwyn (Wilts) with 25; Bradford-on-Avon with 33; Fordwich in Kent with 96; Langport in Somerset with 34; and Milborne Port, also in Somerset, with 56. Some of these 'non-survivors' rival the smaller county towns in Domesday population; Ilchester in Somerset had 107 burgesses, Pevensey 110 and Steyning 123. The most peculiar obstruction to precision in arriving at possible totals of Domesday town-dwellers is explained quite graphically in the survey of the city of Lincoln which reveals the 'English mode of computation' by the 'long hundred' where 100 = 120. Thus 'of the beforementioned mansions which T.R.E. were inhabited, there are now 200 decayed, that is to say 240 according to the English way of counting'.

The payments due from burgesses and presumably the sizes of their tenements are fairly consistent from borough to borough, allowing for vagaries of medieval mathematics. We have already seen a suggestion of half-acre and one-acre burgages; at York we learn that seven small dwellings measured 50 feet in breadth. As to value, there is a built-in hazard in calculating individual rents from a document which invariably omits the word 'each'. Thus '2 houses at 16d.', a very common entry, might mean either 8d. or 1s. 4d. per house. As far as averages can be meaningful in towns where individual burgages pay anything from 1d. to 6s. or more, burgesses and burgages seem to pay a fairly regular 7½d. or 10½d. each, whereas 'sites' tend to average about twice as much, possibly another indication of a two-house burgage plot. In the new borough of Rye and at Reading where sites pay 30d. to 35d. the exceptionally high rate may also indicate development plots capable of subdivision by an enterprising landlord. Southampton's returns make it clear that there was more likely to be a sliding scale of rents rather than an overall average; here the burgage list of 76 [*sic*] is subdivided into 27 who pay 8d., 2 who pay 12d. and 50 who pay 6d. Hereford's average return on 'each whole burgage' was 7½d. but those without the walls paid only 3½d. and there were 'other men who had not whole burgages . . .'. Some of the smaller 'unofficial' boroughs were evidently cheaper concerns. At Fordwich the burgesses paid only 1½d. each, at Ilchester 2d. and at Langport 5d. Others, though small, paid the usual standard rate; Steyning had paid 8d. each but this had recently increased to 10½d.; Cricklade and Pevensey both average 8½d. per burgess.

In some towns there is evidence of a hierarchy of residents. In Huntingdon there were 166 burgesses and 'under them 100 smallholders who aid them in discharging the tax . . .'. Similarly, at Norwich there were 665 burgesses who paid full customary dues, and 480 bordars who 'on account of their poverty pay no dues . . .'. In the borough of Nottingham there were 173 burgesses and 19 villeins; in Derby a distinction was made between 100 burgesses and 40 'lesser burgesses' (*minores*). At Hereford the more substantial citizens could provide a horse for escort duty, the lesser sort 'did duty in the Hall'. As we have seen, there was also a hierarchy of housing, with different rates paid for 'the better houses' and frequent distinction between houses within the walls and without.

The king and other overlords exacted several types of payment from their burgesses. Above all was the king's geld from which, according to the survey of Guildford, 'no man escapes'. In fact a few royal manors, like Basingstoke, had before the Conquest never paid geld 'nor was it assessed in hides'. Utter poverty might cancel the obligation; at Bridport there were 20 houses 'so impoverished (*destitute*) that those who dwell in them are not prosperous enough to pay geld . . .'. Some towns, like Exeter, never paid geld 'except when London, York, and Winchester paid it'. Usually, however, even when other payments are relinquished geld will be the one exception. Next there was 'borough-right', as at Taunton, variously referred to as 'tribute, land-tax or gable' due to the burgess's immediate landlord. To this might be added various payments in kind, such as salt from Droitwich, herrings from Sandwich, wheat and corn from Arundel, honey and iron rods from Gloucester and horse-shoes from Hereford. There were also tolls on trade to be paid, '*theloneum*, team and port-dues, ship-customs and market rents'. Where there was a mint – there were seven moneyers in Hereford, three in Huntingdon and three in Shrewsbury; even small towns like Rhuddlan and Malmesbury had their mints – each moneyer paid 20s. for new dies whenever the coinage was renewed. Finally the king took all fines levied in the local court; the town was often a hundred court. If these were commuted the king usually retained the three major offences of housebreaking, highway robbery and breach of the king's peace. Of all 'customary dues' the king usually took two-thirds, giving the 'third penny' to the earl of the county. Originating before the Conquest the 'third penny' may be taken as one of the signs of 'borough-right'.

Occasionally, and this is important enough to be interpreted with caution, the townsmen already appear to have secured some sort of down payment or rent in place of customary dues, services and payments in monies or in kind. Not until the reign of Henry I at the earliest, more generally not until that of King John, were specific grants of *fee-farm* made by charter to any towns; this was to be the first criterion of borough independence after recognition of burgage tenure. Any premature instances of commutation are therefore significant indications of royal recognition of a borough's identity. Several boroughs' Domesday returns give the impression that T.R.E. the burgesses had owed service, but that 'now' King William took silver. For instance, at Leicester: 'King William has £42 10s. by weight for all payments of the city and county' and Colchester's returns clearly state that 'now the burgesses do not render dues, save on their polls . . .'.

Similarly, any evidence in Domesday Book of property owned in common by burgesses is important early recognition of corporate identity which was not to become prevalent until the reigns of the Conqueror's descendants. As yet the burgesses' common assets are usually agricultural; we have seen instances of land outside the town walls let out to a proportion of the townsmen and their ploughs. In Oxford the burgesses owned a common pasture paying 6s. 8d. and at Colchester the town commons were 80 acres and 8 perches, 'about the wall', from which 'all the burgesses have 60s. a year for the king's service if there be need of it and if not, they divide it in common'. At Cambridge the burgesses complain that their common pasture has been 'removed' by Picot the Sheriff, who had built three profitable mills there. At Canterbury 'the burgesses have 45 burgages outside the city for which they themselves receive rent and customary dues . . . the same burgesses have from the king 33 acres of land for their gildhall'. Fifteen of Norwich's churches belonged to the burgesses with 181 acres of land in alms and at Dover there was 'a gildhall of the burgesses'. Merchant gilds were already an essential feature of early borough growth (see Chapter Five on this subject). The rustic quality and basically agrarian economy of medieval towns, both great and small, is a textbook commonplace; nowhere is it more evident than in Domesday, even in boroughs which were destined to become the chief county town. Okehampton is typical of the very small 'borough' which probably had little pretension to urban privileges or status. Indeed Okehampton is called a manor, in spite of its castle, four burgesses and a market paying 4s. a year. At the extreme end of the scale is the 'small borough' of Seasalter in Kent which belonged to the Archbishop's private kitchen with one plough, no market, no castle and a valuation of 100s. in all.

Burgesses were occasionally expected to perform — or be responsible for — agricultural labouring services for their tenure. At Cambridge the burgesses had lent their plough-teams to the sheriff thrice yearly; now they were demanded nine times a year, in addition to carrying and cartage services never required before. To the borough of Derby belonged 12 carucates of taxable land 'which 8 ploughs can plough'. The land was divided between 41 burgesses (there were 242 in all in the town) who also had 12 ploughs. At Huntingdon there was a similar allocation of ploughland to the burgage tenants: 'In the lands of this borough lie 2 carucates and 40 acres of land and 10 acres of meadow . . . the burgesses cultivate this land and let it through the officers of the king and the earl . . .'. The more important services rendered by the town-dwellers were military and naval. The men of Dover supplied the king with 20 ships for 15 days in each year; in each ship were to be 21 men. At Colchester each householder paid 6d. a year to support the king's soldiers for war service by land and sea. Whenever the king 'wished to send his men in his absence to guard the sea' the townsmen of Lewes collected 20s. for those who had charge of the arms in the ships. The military aspect of feudal society was often evident, as for example at Westminster where 25 houses provided billets for the Abbot of Westminster's men-at-arms. Such military commitment was inevitably intensified by the presence of the lord's castle on the town site.

Many Domesday boroughs were overlooked by Norman castles and it is clear that of the two, the town was usually older than the castle. In several cases burgage tenements had been recently destroyed to clear a castle-site. At York a whole 'shire' of the city containing possibly as many as 300 houses had been razed on the land where Clifford's Tower now stands. At Wallingford only eight burgages were lost, at Norwich 17; in Canterbury the Abbot of St Augustine's had received 14 other houses in compensation for the castle site; in Huntingdon there had been 20 *mansiones* paying 16s. 8d. a year *in loco castri*. At Shrewsbury the burgesses complained bitterly that they were expected to pay the same amount of geld as before 1066 even though the earl's castle had removed 51 burgage tenements. The building of a castle, however small, had recently resulted in the creation of many a 'new borough' of the smaller sort, as we have seen at Clifford and Wigmore in Hereford. Small, ruined castle sites abound, in villages like Quatford which never sustained their Domesday position, at Penwortham in Cheshire, Bramber in Sussex, Ewias Harold and Richards Castle in Herefordshire, Montacute in Somerset and Castle Holgate in Shropshire.

There is ample evidence of both contraction and expansion of towns in many different parts of the Survey. Generally the king's income from individual towns had increased, as most towns were valued at a higher rate T.R.W. than they were T.R.E. This however might not reflect equally increasing prosperity. In the older cities there was dramatic evidence of dilapidation and destruction, beyond that already caused by castle-building. At Oxford 'within and without the walls are 243 houses which pay tax. Apart from these there are 478 houses so derelict and destroyed that they cannot pay any tax ...'. Dover had been destroyed by a fire in recent times 'so that a right evaluation could not be made of what it was worth when the Bishop of Bayeux received it ...'. The Conquerer's harrying of the north and west of England had taken its toll of town prosperity. York recorded 391 houses in the king's hands; 400 not regularly inhabited, which rendered 1d. or less; and 540 dwellings so empty 'that they render nothing at all'. At Thetford in Norfolk there had been 943 burgesses before the Conquest; in 1086 there were 720 burgesses and 224 empty messuages. It is not unusual to find fewer occupants still assessed for an earlier total tribute; at Fordwich, in the lands of the Church of St Augustine of Canterbury, there had formerly been 96 burgesses paying 13s.; 'there are now 73 burgesses paying the same amount'. The Surrey Commissioners report that: 'In Guildford King William has 75 sites in which dwell 175 men. Before 1066 they paid £18 0s. 3d.; now they are assessed at £30; however they pay £32.' Rochester, valued at £20, paid twice that sum; everywhere supplementary rate demands appear to have been the order of the day.

One cannot escape the impression that some post-Conquest decline in urban tenancies might have been due to over-stringent demands for service and tribute; the burgesses of Shrewsbury made their grievances very clear. 'The English-born burgesses of Shrewsbury maintain that it is very hard on them that they now pay the same geld as they used to pay T.R.E. although the earl's castle has occupied 51 burgages and 50 others are waste and 43 French-born burgesses occupy burgages geldable T.R.E. and the earl has granted the abbey which he is forming there 39 burgesses formerly geldable in like manner with the others. In all there are 200 burgesses all but 7 who do not pay geld.' The townsmen of Norwich also itemise the various causes of oppression: 'those fleeing and those remaining have been entirely ruined, partly by reason of the forfeitures of the earl, partly by reason of a fire, partly by reason of the king's geld . . .'. Predatory barons were a hazard, but the king's tenants were equally at risk. In Bath 64 'royal burgesses' paid a high average rent of 15d. each, whereas 90 'burgesses of other men' paid the more usual rent of 8d. At Derby, Cambridge, Huntingdon and Maldon there are similar records of burgage tenements lying waste and unoccupied — yet often taxed at higher valuations than pre-Conquest.

In other places there were, however, signs of renewed growth. Several towns had evidently received plantations of French immigrants; these we find in Shrewsbury, Southampton, Wallingford and York. At Norwich the French have a separate new borough to themselves and, as an incentive to the colonists, the customary dues were only 1d. each. At Northampton deliberate attempts were being made to revitalize the town. There had been 60 burgesses there in the Confessor's day; now 14 tenements were derelict but 'besides those there are now 40 burgesses in the new borough in King William's lordship'. Similarly, at Nottingham Hugh son of Baldric the Sheriff had found 136 men living there. Before 1066 there had been 173, now there were only 120. 'However, Hugh erected 13 houses himself which were not there before in the New Borough, and placed them amongst the dues of the old borough . . .'. Once again, the main emphasis is on the product of tax.

Reference to markets are frequent in Domesday and many of the manors which were eventually to achieve full county borough status already held their weekly market. Basingstoke, Lewisham, Bodmin, Liskeard, Worksop, Luton, Newark and many more besides paid regular market tolls. Many other small manors, which included a handful of burgesses, were also market towns. Such are Bradford-on-Avon (Wilts), Eaton Bishop (Herefordshire), Kings Sutton and Oundle (Northants), Melton Mowbray (Leics), Tutbury (Staffs). We are left with the impression that local markets were usually rustic affairs, reminiscent more of the small modern 'market town' than of the municipality. Yet there is no doubt that local trading rights could be profitable and their monopoly attractive. In Cornwall at St Germans a Sunday market had been 'reduced to nothing by the Count of Mortain's market, which is nearby, in a castle of his own and held on the same day'. The rival was probably Trematon, where we find that 'the count has a castle and a market which pays 3s.' The same count had 'taken away' another market from St Stephens by Launceston which had been worth 20s. before 1066 and 'put it in his castle' of Launceston.

Trade certainly existed in these early towns, and would be well protected by the nearby castle and its lord; but Domesday is not concerned to describe that trade for us, except to record the amount of market dues in each case. In Tutbury Henry of Ferrers had the castle and 'in the borough around this castle are 42 men who live only by their trading; with the market they pay £4 10s.' At Nottingham, William Peverel had 48 merchants' houses clearly distinguished from the 'horsemen's houses' and the bordars' cottages. There were 10 merchants at Cheshunt in Hertfordshire, nowadays a centre for market gardening; but there is comparatively little if any detail of trading conditions or customs. Exceptions exist, as at Chester, where the customs of the port and its merchants are explicitly stated at length. Ships arriving at the city port, or leaving it, must have clearance from the king's officials or pay 40s. a man. 'If a ship arrived against the king's peace and despite his prohibition, the king and the earl had both the ship itself and its crew, together with everything in it.' The Normans were close enough to the days of the Viking host to see trade and piracy as very closely allied; control of both was essential. Chester gives a good example of official

pre-emption of imported goods. Those who shipped marten skins, presumably from
Ireland and the northern coast of England, were not to sell to anyone before the
king's reeve had been given first sight and made his purchases. The Bishop of Chester
also had his purview of trade. If a merchant opened a bale of goods between Saturday
noon and Monday or on any other holy day without permission from the bishop's
officer the bishop had 4s. fine therefrom. By contrast, at Dover we learn that a fully
paid-up resident of the borough was exempt from tolls all over England.

There is rarely any reference in Domesday Book to an industrial activity or craft as a
basis for the towns' economy. Droitwich is probably the only example of a commercial town almost totally specialized to the production and distribution of a staple
industrial commodity, salt; comparable growth is seen in Cheshire at Nantwich,
Middlewich and Northwich. The two lords of the new borough of Rhuddlan share
the proceeds of the iron mines there, and there were evidently other ironworks around
Gloucester which paid 36 *dickers* of iron and 100 iron rods 'drawn out for making
nails for the king's ships'. Yet in Derbyshire the towns reflect no commercial
development of the lead mines which are recorded at Matlock, Wirksworth, Bakewell
and Ashford, all of which are otherwise totally manorial, as was Hope which had
(T.R.E.) paid its dues with five wagon-loads of 50 lead sheets but 'now' paid £10 6s.
in lieu. Indeed, any of these 'industrial' centres is as likely to pay as much in honey
or in eels as in heavy metal. Smiths are occasionally mentioned — there were six in
Hereford, but only very few of the burgesses' surnames, such as Otto the Goldsmith
in Colchester, Turstin the Engineer at Southampton, and William the Artificer at
Northampton reflect their crafts or trades. Most burgesses are described only by
their Christian names. Any occupational names are more likely to be those of minor
officials, the Dapifers, Cooks, Ushers, Interpreters, Chamberlains, Reeves and Sheriffs.
Stephen the Carpenter is as likely to hold a village manor in Earlscourt, Wiltshire,
though he also has a garden in the town of Cricklade; and another Goldsmith, Grim-
bald, holds the villages of Manningford and Stanton Fitzwarren, with no mention of
a burgage tenement or town house. Other townsmen are more likely to be Thanes and
Archers, Crossbowmen, Housecarles, Gunners, Steersmen, Priests and Canons rather
than tradesmen by name.

Incidentally, the Survey of some towns includes occasional items of a particular
interest and unusual detail. For example, at Hereford we learn how a man might sell
his house with the consent of the reeve and how he might lose it if he became too poor
to perform his due service. In Lewes 'whoever sells a horse in the borough gives a
penny to the reeve; the buyer gives another; for an ox ½d. *and for a man 4d.*, where-
ever he buys within the Rape'. Details of fire insurance are given for Shrewsbury:
'Should the house of any burgess be burned by accident or misfortune or by negligence he pays 40s. to the king by way of forfeit and 2s. to each of his two nearest
neighbours'. Strict observation of holidays was the responsibility of the bishop of
Chester, where murder was more heavily punished if committed on a Sunday but was
at no time more seriously considered than the crimes of housebreaking or rape. Upkeep
of roads and river-ways was seen to be especially important in several towns. Special
punishments were reserved at Dover, Canterbury and Nottingham for those who
interfered with the public way: 'In Nottingham the river Trent and the road to York
are so protected that if anyone hinders the passage of ships or if anyone ploughs or
makes a ditch within 2 perches of the king's road, he has to pay a fine of £8.'

The full descriptive account of the town of Bury St Edmunds, which had grown up 'towards the provision of the monks' of St Edmund's shrine is quite exceptional. Having described the town as it was in the reign of King Edward, one and a half leagues square with a hierarchy of freemen who could give or sell their lands with 52 dependent *bordars*, 54 freemen 'poor enough' and 43 almsmen each with a subordinate *bordar*, the scribe explains that all this has changed since the Conquest. 'But this refers to the town as it was, as if it was still so . . .'. Now, we are told, the town is contained in a greater circle of land which was once ploughed and sown but is so no longer. Here there are 342 new houses on the demesne with 58 religious, nuns, priests and deacons to pray for the king and all Christian people. Thirteen reeves 'over the land' have their houses in the town, with five of their own *bordars*. There was also a garrison of 34 knights, both French and English. Most exceptional of all is the register of 75 tradesmen who wait upon the monks at the abbey. These include: 'bakers, ale brewers, tailors, washerwomen, shoemakers, robe-makers, cooks, porters, and agents.' This is the most complete description of any Domesday borough, though here there is no mention of burgesses as such; all are seen to be either manorial tenants or servants of the abbey.

By far the largest number of towns which were destined to develop and grow into modern boroughs were those which began as royal manors; two-thirds of the towns with borough or city status recorded in Domesday belonged to the king; some, like Stamford, were named as 'King's Boroughs'. This applies as well, as our Gazetteer will show, to those modern towns which were still rural and manorial at the time of the Conqueror; a high proportion of later municipal boroughs began their development as royal manors. For the rest there appear to have been certain barons and churchmen who were more aware than others of the possibilities of town growth and the profitability of burgage revenues. Some magnates, like the Count of Mortain and the Bishop of Coutances, were prominent in more widespread towns than their local political importance would ensure. William FitzAnsculf is particularly notable in that he was overlord of two of the three Midland towns which are our documentary examples. FitzAnsculf was lord of the manor of Birmingham, but it was in the nearby town of Dudley that his castle stood, on a hill above the High Street, with its castle church of St Edmund at the gate.

Our three regional examples are illustrations of each of the three main types of origins which we find for modern towns in Domesday Book. Worcester was in 1086 by far the most ancient and well-established of the three, as we have seen from earlier evidence; it was still, however, a city of chiefly ecclesiastical importance. Birmingham was as yet recorded only as a rustic manor with land for six ploughs and nine villeins. Dudley (at a later period to be the smallest of the three until local government reorganization gave it precedence over Worcester) was in feudal terms the most important of the three. As a manor, Dudley was of moderate size, rated for 11 ploughs and one hide for geld. It was not yet recognized as a borough in the way that Worcester was recognized as a city, borough and county-town. But William FitzAnsculf held Dudley 'and his castle is there'. That castle was in fact the 'caput' or centre of a vast 'honour' or 'barony of Dudley' which comprised estates in 11 counties, mainly in Buckinghamshire, but also in Stafford, Warwick, Worcester, Surrey, Berkshire, Northampton, Rutland, Oxford, Middlesex and Huntingdon. Dudley's feudal position can be equated with the ecclesiastical or county status of Worcester city.

As a borough, nascent as yet, Dudley was one of those small Norman–English towns of the middle rank which, though as yet still essentially manorial with only one smith recorded as a forecast of its later industries, was chiefly outstanding in the locality for the lord's castle which dominated its market street and protected its householders. There was, as yet, no mention in Domesday of burgesses in Dudley, certainly not of walls or gates; even the market, which is still set out in the typical pattern of early medieval tofts and crofts, is not recorded as markets were in so many more insubstantial places. Yet of the three Midland towns it would be the village of Birmingham which would grow most vast and the City of Worcester which would most decline. Dudley would, as ever, hold the middle ground and prosper.

To sum up the Domesday evidence of town development we can review the main criteria of township. If we are expecting to see our own home town as an early borough we should expect to find the following essential characteristics in 1086. Only if several of these are found together can we claim any real importance for the place. The signs of 'town-ship' in Domesday are: a pre-county entry 'above the line' of the main survey; the descriptive title of 'borough' or 'city'; the residence there of numerous burgesses in burgage tenements; the payment by those tenements of unusual, non-manorial dues and services; the physical boundaries of walls and ditch and possibly the site of a castle; the presence of official mints and moneyers; a market from which substantial tolls are paid; the residence in neighbouring manors of 'contributory' burgesses, who live and work in the village, but own town houses; and finally the presence of more than one lord, other than the king or the lord of the manor, with tenants of their own either within the town or in the 'contributory manors'. A town which fulfilled all these qualifications was almost certain within the next century to receive the grant of a charter from the king, or from its secular or religious overlord. Our next Chapter examines the nature of those charters more closely, and will show how many of our base-list towns became chartered boroughs.

FURTHER READING

Ballard, A., *The Domesday Inquest* (1906).

Clifford, H. C., *Domesday Gazetteer* (1975).

Douglas, D. C., 'The Genesis of Domesday', in *Domesday Monachorum of Christ Church, Canterbury* (1944).

—— 'Historical Revision – The Domesday Survey', in *History*, vols. 21, 33 (1936).

Ellis, Sir H., *A General Index to Domesday Book* (1st edition 1833, reprinted 1971).

Fines, J., *Domesday Book in the Classroom; A Guide for Teachers* (1980).

Franklin, T. Bedford., 'Domesday' (a series of three articles), in *Amateur Historian*, vol. 1, (1953–54).

Galbraith, V. H., *The Making of Domesday Book* (1961).

—— *Domesday Book: its place in administrative history* (1974).

Maitland, F. W., *Domesday Book and Beyond* (1897; reprinted 1960).

Round, J. H., 'The Domesday Manor', *Eng. Hist. Rev.*, vol. XV (1910).

—— 'Introduction to Domesday' (*VCH Essex*, vol. 1, 1903).

Harvey, S. P., 'Domesday Book and Anglo-Norman Governance', *Trans. Royal Hist. Soc.*, vol. 25, 1970).

Welldon Finn, R., *Domesday Book: A Guide* (1973).

'Satellite' surveys similar to, or derived from, Domesday will be found in:

Inquisitio Comitatus Cantabrigiensis (or *Inquisitio Eliensis*). An edition edited by N. E. S. A. Hamilton published 1874; a translation is given in *VCH Cambridgeshire*, vol. I.

The *Exon Domesday* (or *Liber Exoniensis*). An edition edited by Sir H. Ellis published by the Record Commission, 1816.

The *Feudal Book of the Abbot Baldwin of Bury St Edmunds*. An edition edited by D. C. Douglas appears in his book *Feudal Documents from the Abbey of Bury St Edmunds* (1932).

The *Christ Church, Canterbury Survey* is included in D. C. Douglas, *Domesday Monachorum* (1944).

St Augustine, Canterbury Inquest. See A. Ballard, *An Eleventh Century Inquisition of St Augustine's, Canterbury* (1920).

The *Worcester Survey* (temp. Hen. I); see T. Hearne's edition of Heming's *Chartularium Ecclesiae Wignorniensis* (1723).

Liber Winton (concerning Winchester): an edition edited by Sir H. Ellis for the Record Commission, 1816.

The *Lindsey Survey* (concerning Lincoln), 1115-1118. An edition produced by J. Greenstreet (1884).

The *Leicestershire Survey* (c. 1130): edited by C. F. Slade, *University College of Leicester Occasional Papers*, no. 7 (1956).

The *Herefordshire Domesday* (c. 1160-70). A facsimile edition was produced for the *Pipe Roll Society*, New Series, vol. XXV (1950), edited by V. H. Galbraith and J. Tait.

The Boldon Buke (concerning Durham), 1183, was edited by the *Surtees Society* by W. Greenwell (1852); it may also be found in *VCH Durham*, vol. I, with a translation by G. T. Lapsley, and in 1983 Phillimore published an edition, edited by David Austin which may be found as vol. 35 in their Domesday Book series.

Notes to the illustrations:

The full Domesday entries for each of the three towns of Worcester, Dudley and Birmingham are shown here, with translations. These latter are taken from the Phillimore edition of the county's Domesday. The Phillimore Domesday is the first *complete* translation of Domesday ever undertaken; it incorporates the most up-to-date and thorough linguistic and historical information. It replaces the only previous translation available — and then not for all counties — which was that published in the appropriate volumes of the *Victoria County History* series. The Phillimore Domesday offers a parallel Latin text and translation, with a wealth of maps, notes on the text, indexes, and glossaries. It is available for each county in a hardback or paperback edition. The facsimiles of the original text for each example are taken from a photo-zincography copy which was made of the entire Survey by the Ordnance Survey Department in 1861-62; bound copies of county facsimiles are usually available in county record offices and reference libraries.

These entries are from the Ordnance Survey facsimile volumes for Worcestershire (1862) and Warwickshire (1862) at Birmingham and Dudley Reference Libraries. Each entry is approximately 10 cm wide. The illustrations are not uniformly enlarged.

In Civitate Wirecestre habebat Rex Edw hanc c̄suetudinē. Quando moneta uertebat: qsq; moneta rius dabat. xx. solid ad lundoniā p cuneis moneta accipiend. Quando comitat geldabat: p. xv. hid se ciuitas adqetab. De ead ciuitate habeb ipse rex. x. lib. 7 comes Eduin. viii. lib. Nullā aliā c̄suetudinē ibi rex capiebat: pter censū domoꝛ sicut uniciuiq; ptinebat.

172 a

In Civitate Wirecestre Habebat Rex Edw̄

hanc c̄suetudinē. Quando moneta ue̊rtebat: qsq; moneta
rius dabat. xx.solid ad lundoniā p cuneis monetæ accipiend.
Quando comitat geldabat: p. xv. hid se ciuitas adqetab.
De ead ciuitate habeb ipse rex. x. lib. 7 comes Eduin. viii. lib.
Nullā aliā c̄suetudinē ibi rex capiebat: pter censū domoꝛ
sicut unicuiq; ptinebat.

[C] [WORCESTERSHIRE CUSTOMS] 172 a

1 In the City of WORCESTER King Edward had this customary due:
whenever the coinage was changed each moneyer gave 20s at
London for receiving the dies for the coinage. Whenever the
County paid tax the city settled for 15 hides. Also from this city
the King used to have £10 himself and Earl Edwin £8. The
King received no other customary due from it except for the
dues on the houses as each was liable.

De. W. ten Ricoard. iiii. hid in Beramwicha tra e. vi. car. In dnio. e una. 7 v. uilli 7 iiii. bord cū. ii. car. Silua dim leuu lg. 7 ii. quaretn lat. Valuit 7 ual. xx. sol. Vluuin libe tenuit T.R.E. In Cudulvestan hd.

Ꝼ De.W.ten̄ Ricoarđ.ıııı.hiđ in *BERMINGEHA*.Ꞇ̄ra
ē.vı.car̄.In dn̄io.ē.una.7 v.uiłłi 7 ıııı.borđ cū.ıı.car̄.
Silua dim̄ leuū l̄g.7 ıı.q̄rent lat̄.Valuit 7 uał.xx.ſoł.
Vłuuin̄⁹ liꝺe tenuit.T.R.E. *IN CVDVLVESTAN HĐ.*

[Held of W(illiam) fitz Ansculf]

5　Richard holds 4 hides in BIRMINGHAM.　Land for 6 ploughs.
In lordship 1;
　　5 villagers and 4 smallholders with 2 ploughs.
　　Woodland ½ league long and 2 furlongs wide.
The value was and is 20s.
　　Wulfwin held it freely before 1066.

in CUTTLESTONE Hundred (in Staffordshire)

Iſđ.W.ten̄ *DVDELEI*.7 ibi eſt caſtellū eius.Hoc m̄
tenuit Eduinus.Ibi.ı.hida.　In dn̄io.ē.ı.car̄.7 ııı.uiłł
7 x.borđ 7 un̄ faber.cū.x.car̄.Ibi.ıı.ſerui.7 ıı.leuueđ
filuæ.T.R.E.uałꝺ.ıııı.liꝺ.Modo.ııı.liꝺ.

[The same W(illiam fitz Ansculf) holds]

10　DUDLEY. His castle is there. Earl Edwin held this manor. 1 hide. . . .
In lordship 1 plough;
　　3 villagers, 10 smallholders and 1 smith with 10 ploughs.
　　2 slaves.
Woodland, 2 leagues.
Value before 1066 £4; now £3.

GLOSSARY OF TECHNICAL TERMS USED IN DOMESDAY:

Note: The Phillimore edition definitions have been added where they seem to shed further light on the meaning of the term.

Beadle: Bailiff or local officer.

Berewick: A grange or outlying part of a manor.

Bordar: Smallholder with a little land; found in towns as subordinate tenants of burgesses.

Burgage: The town unit of tenancy, including a plot for house and garden often still identifiable on town High Streets.

Burgess: A townsman holding a burgage tenement under special conditions of rent or service; he may also be a manorial tenant elsewhere.

Burgus: Township or borough; more specific than *tun* which means 'village'.

Carucate: A ploughland both a measure of land and a rateable value.

Civitas: City.

Comes: Count or earl.

Cottar: Smallholder similar to a bordar. [Phillimore edition: 'Inhabitant of a cottage, often without land'].

Customs, customary dues: Rates of tax, revenue and rents or services due to an overlord. 'Customs' of the county are local bye-laws.

Demesne: The lord's own part of his manor, cultivated for himself. Domesday's main division of each manor is between demesne and villeinage, measured in ploughlands.

Descriptio: The Survey.

Domus: A house, particularly a town-house.

Farm: Written as *firma, feorm* or *ferm*; a fixed revenue paid in place of miscellaneous dues; thus *firma burgi*, the commutation of townsmen's dues for a fixed rate.

Fee: A feudal holding or *fief*; the tenants lands and rights. See also 'honour'.

Freemen: Men who could sell their land or bequeath it without obligation to an overlord and not bound by manorial services. A man with his own *sac and soc* (q.v.).

Gable: *Gabol* or *gafol*; tribute, tax or rent. [Phillimore edition: 'tribute or tax paid to the king or a lord'].

Geld: The main national tax in Saxon and Norman days; derived from the original Danegeld paid to Viking raiders; raised at irregular intervals in emergency.

Haga: Building plot in a town; a multiple burgage tenement.

Hide: Rateable value usually reckoned at about 120 acres. The basic Domesday rating of county and manor, as in the *Burghal Hidage*, c. 944. [Phillimore edition: 'A unit of land measurement or assessment'].

Housecarles: The Saxon royal guard or household troops.

Hundred: Administrative subdivision of the county; also the court or jury of that division. [Phillimore edition; 'A district within a shire, whose assembly of notables and village representatives usually met about once a month'].

Honour: Similar to 'fee'; the entire holding of a major tenant.

League: Measure of land in length, usually the bounds of woodland, about 1½ miles.

Manor: The basic unit of feudal tenancy and farming economy. Usually one village but not necessarily identical; some villages may contain more than one manor each appearing under the same village-name for several tenants. Modern hamlets within a villages were often separate manors. Domesday is essentially a manorial record; free relationships outside manorial jurisdiction tend to be omitted from manorial records, thus losing sight of non-manorial population as, e.g., wage-labourers or forest dwellers.

Mansio, masura: A messuage or tenement in a town; a burgage plot.

Port: Market or town.

Prepositus: See Reeve.

Quit: Exempt from a customary due.

Reeve: Local official in manor or county; from which 'shire-reeve' or 'sheriff'. There is early evidence of 'port-reeves'.

Riding-men or *Radknights*: Freemen who provided escort service on horseback.

Sac and Soc: Jurisdiction over minor offences or the obligation, and right, to respond personally, not through a lord; thus a man 'had his own sac and soc' which could be granted him as a privilege.

Seisin: Possession (nine-tenths of the law); actual tenancy or right to a property; proof of possession.

Sheriff: The king's chief officer in the county.

Shire: The administrative county and its court.

Sokeman: Freemen with their own *sac and soc*.

Tenant-in-chief: The major barons, churchmen and officials holding directly of the king, with their own sub-tenants under them. Domesday Survey is arranged by tenancies-in-chief within each county.

T.R.E.: 'Tempore Regis Edwardi'. In the time of King Edward (the Confessor) 1042–66. The Survey often takes as its reference point 'the day when King Edward was alive and dead'.

Serf: A slave.

T.R.W. 'Tempore Regis Willelmi'. In the time of King William (the Conqueror) 1066–1086; more precisely, for the Survey, two points in time, 'then' in 1066 at the Conquest and 'now' at the time of the Survey, 1086.

Vicecomes: The sheriff.

Villa: The Saxon *tun* or village, sometimes synonymous with 'manor'. [Phillimore edition: 'The later distinction between a small "village" and a large "town" was not yet in use in 1086'.]

Villein: A villager bound by services and payments in money and kind to the lord and his demesne (q.v.). The villein was the main manorial tenant, holding a virgate (q.v.) or multiple parts of virgates. Owing various 'suits' to the lord's court and certain 'fines' or fees for various aspects of his domestic life he was not a free man.

Virgate: A ploughland or yardland; literally the amount of land ploughed by one 8-oxen team annually. Usually reckoned as 30 acres. [Phillimore edition: 'A quarter of a hide'.]

Wapentake: Division of a county equivalent to the Hundred; found in the Danish regions of East Midlands and northern England.

GAZETTEER OF MODERN BOROUGHS AS
RECORDED IN THE DOMESDAY SURVEY

As many of the boroughs on the base-list as possible have been traced in Domesday Book. Where no entry has been found the borough is omitted from this list but will return as it occurs in other records. The names of those towns which are named as 'boroughs', 'towns' or 'cities' during the reigns of Edward the Confessor and William the Conqueror, or which have one or more significant elements of township, are printed in **BOLD CAPITALS** (e.g.: **WORCESTER**) and a fairly full extract of the most important 'town' elements of their entry is given. As the complete entries of the larger cities run to several pages of transcription, a great deal of detail is omitted from the extracts; in small towns, this results in the significant omission of what is usually their major part, i.e. the manorial, agricultural aspects. Towns listed in *ITALIC CAPITALS* (e.g.: *ALDEBURGH*) will be found in their county Survey as stated, but their entries will be found to be entirely manorial, with no sign of other than a rural economy. Also added to our list are some towns which, although not included in our base-list of those which retained borough status in 1971–72, reveal early elements of burghal life and property as great or greater than some later towns. These are named in **bold lower case print** (e.g.: **Steyning**, in Sussex). The chief criteria used to identify Domesday towns are: those named as 'burgus' or 'civitas' ('villa' may mean 'town' or 'village'); evidence of *burgage plots* (*hagæ*, *masuræ*, *mansiones* etc.) and *burgesses*. The Gazetteer endeavours to avoid ascribing borough status to manors which housed burgesses of a neighbouring town or had town-houses belonging to them elsewhere. The site of a castle is usually noted, especially if it includes a borough, and the payment of tolls, land-gable or the 'third penny' is taken to be significant. The existence of a market, though usually noted, is not taken alone to indicate conclusive town status, as many of these were evidently village markets at that time; the existence of a mint is more significant. Folio references are taken from Phillimore editions where these have been published, otherwise from the *Victoria County Histories*; fo. = folio number of original Domesday volume for that county. The basic reference is shown within parentheses, and is followed in most instances by a quotation illustrative of the status of the place in question in 1086.

ABINGDON: Abbendone (Berkshire: Land of Abingdon Church fo. 58c) at Barton: '10 merchants dwelling in front of the church pay 40d.'

ALDEBURGH: Aldeburc (Suffolk, Land of Robert Malet's mother fo. 316.)

ANDOVER: Andovere (Hampshire, King's lands fo. 39.)

ARUNDEL: Castrum Harundel (Sussex: Land of Earl Roger fo. 23a) . . . 'the borough and the harbour (*portus aquæ*) and the ship-customs (*consuetudines navium*) between them pay £12'. Refs. to *hagæ*, tolls, custom-dues, sites with named tenants.

Ashwell: Asceuuelle (Hertfordshire, Westminster Abbey fo. 135b-c) '14 burgesses from tolls and other customary dues of the borough 49s. 4d.'

AYLESBURY: Eilesberia (Buckinghamshire, King's lands fo. 143b) 'from tolls (*de theloneo*) £10'.

Axbridge: Alseburge (Somerset, King's lands fo. 86b) '32 burgesses pay 20s.'

BANBURY: Banesberie (Oxfordshire, Bp. of Lincoln fo. 155b).

(BARNET): See: HENDON; (Handone, Middlesex. Abbot of Westminster fo. 128d.)

BARNSLEY: Berneslai (Yorkshire, Ilbert de Laci fo. 316.)

BARNSTAPLE: Barnestaple (Devon: King's lands fo. 87b). 'The king has 40 burgesses

(Barnstaple – continued)
within the borough and 9 without and they pay 40s. by weight to the king and 20s. by tale to the bishop of Coutances . . . 3 houses . . . have been laid to ruins since K. William had England . . . (in Baldwin the Sheriff's lands there are) . . . 7 burgesses in Barnstaple and 6 houses lying in ruins [which] pay 7s. 6d. a year.

BASINGSTOKE: (Basingestoches, Hampshire, King's lands fo. 39) 'a market worth 30s. . . . and in Winchester 4 inhabitants of the suburbs (*suburbani*) pay 12s. 11d.'

BATH: Bade, Somerset (King's lands fo. 87b) 'king has 64 burgesses who pay £4; 90 burgesses of other men pay 60s. there. The king has 4 derelict houses. This borough with the said Batheaston pays £60 at face value and one gold mark . . . the mint pays 100s.' Burgesses and town houses of, recorded in Keynsham, Chewton Mendip, Batheaston, Bishopsworth, High Littleton, Hinton Charterhouse and Weston. See Whale, T. W.: 'The principles of the Somerset Domesday', *Bath Nat. Hist. & Antiq. Field Club*, vol. 10 (1902).

BATLEY: Bateleia and Bathelie (Yorkshire: Ilbert de Laci fo. 317).

BECCLES: Becles (Suffolk: fo. 283b) . . . 'market, customs'.

BEDFORD: Bedeford (Bedfordshire: fo. 209a) 'Bedford answered for half a hundred before before 1066 and does so now in military expeditions by land and in ships'. Land of the burgesses of Bedford by names of burgesses in Biddenham, Hinwick, Sharnbrook, Beeston, Henlow, Arlesey. See Fowler, G. H., 'Domesday Notes', *Beds. Hist. Rec. Soc.*, vol. I (1913), vol. 5 (1918).

Bedwyn; Bedvinde (Wiltshire: King's lands fo. 64d.) . . . 'to this manor belong 25 burgesses'

Berkhamsted: Berchehamstede (Hertfordshire: Count of Mortain fo. 136c.) . . . 'In the borough of this town (*in burgio hujus villæ*) 52 burgesses who pay £4 from tolls'. . .

BEVERLEY: Bevreli (Yorkshire: Archbishop of York fo. 304).

BEXHILL: Bexelei (Sussex: Count of Eu fo. 18b).

BEXLEY: Bix (Kent: Archbishop of Canterbury fo. 3).

BIRMINGHAM: Bermingeham (Warwickshire: William fitzAnsculf fo. 243a).

BLACKBURN: Blacheburne (Cheshire: Roger of Poitou fo. 270a).

BLANDFORD FORUM: Bleneford (Dorset; Count of Mortain, fo. 194).

BODMIN: Bodmine (Cornwall: Land of St Michael fo. 120d) . . . '64 houses and market'

BOOTLE: Boltelai (Cheshire: Roger of Poitou fo. 269c).

BRACKLEY: Brachelai (Northamptonshire: Earl Aubrey fo. 224b).

BRADFORD: Bradeford (Yorkshire: Ilbert de Laci fo. 317b) . . . 'Waste'

Bradford-on-Avon: Bradeford (Wiltshire; Church of Shaftesbury fo. 67c) . . . '33 burgesses who pay 35s. 9d. . . . a market which pays 45s.'

BRIDGWATER: Brugie (Somerset: Walter of Douai fo. 95b).

BRIDPORT: Brideport (Dorset: pre-entry fo. 75) 'T.R.E. there were 120 houses and . . . one moneyer rendering to the king 1 silver mark and 20s. when the coinage was changed. Now there are 100 houses and 20 are so impoverished that those living in them are not prosperous enough to pay geld'

BRIGHTON: Bristelmestune (Sussex; William of Warenne fo. 26c).

BURY ST EDMUNDS (Suffolk: St Edmund's lands fo. 372). The town is now contained in a greater circle including land which used to be ploughed and sown . . . (there are) . . . 75 bakers, ale-brewers, tailors, washerwomen, shoemakers, robe-makers, cooks, porters and agents . . . 13 reeves who have their houses in the said town . . . 34 knights, French and English . . . Now altogether there are 342 houses on the demesne land of St Edmund which was under the plough T.R.E.'

BRISTOL: Bristou (Gloucestershire: pre-entry fo. 163); burgesses; . . . 'houses in Bristol recorded under Westbury-on-Trym and Bishopsworth'.

BROMLEY: Bronlei; also Bacheham (Beckenham) (Kent: Bp. of Bayeux fo. 5b).

BUCKINGHAM: Bochingeham (Buckingham: pre-entry fo. 143a) . . . 26 burgesses; . . . 'Bp. Remigius holds the church of this borough'; list of 12 tenants with 27 burgesses; incl. Bp. of Coutances, Robert d'Oilly.

BURTON-UPON-TRENT: Bertone (Staffordshire: Land of St Mary's Burton fo. 247c) probably entered in error as 'Stafford'.

CALNE: Cauna (Wiltshire: King's lands fo. 64d) . . . 'borough of Calne'; 45 burgesses; houses and burgesses also recorded under Bps Cannings and Calstone (Wellington).

CAMBRIDGE: Grentebrige (Cambridgeshire: pre-entry). 'Assessed as one hundred T.R.E. In this borough were and are 10 wards. In the first ward there were 54 burgages (*masurae*) but two of these are waste. In the first ward Count Alan has 3 burgages etc. . . . This ward was reckoned as two T.R.E. but 27 houses were destroyed for the castle . . . In the second ward there were 48 burgages T.R.E., 2 of them are waste. Of these, 13 pay nothing, the remaining 32 pay all customary dues . . . 9 dwell in the land of the English. In the third ward there were 41 burgages T.R.E. Of these 11 are waste . . . In the fourth ward . . 45 burgages T.R.E. Of these 24 are waste . . . in the fifth ward . . . 50 burgages T.R.E.; one of these is waste . . . (sixth ward omitted) . . . seventh ward: there were 37 burgages T.R.E. Three Frenchmen have 3 of these but pay nothing . . . eighth ward . . . 37 burgages T.R.E. . . . ninth ward: 32 burgages . . . three waste . . . tenth ward: . . . 29 burgages. Of these 6 are waste yet they are assessed . . . T.R.E. the burgesses lent the sheriff their plough teams thrice yearly; now they are demanded nine times'.

CAMDEN: As Rug More; district re-named Camden Town in 1795; Rugemere (Middlesex; Bp. of London fo. 127d); also Hampstead; Hamstede (Middlesex: St Peter Westminster fo. 128b); Holborn: Holeburne (Middlesex; King's lands fo. 127a); St Pancras-Ad Sanctum Pancratium (Middlesex: Bp. of London fo. 128a).

CANTERBURY: Cantuaria (Kent: King's lands fo. 2). In the City of Canterbury K. Edward had 51 burgesses paying rents (*gablum*) and 212 others over whom he had sac and soc and 3 mills worth 40s. The burgesses now paying rents are 19; the houses of the 32 others are desolated, 11 are in the defences (*fossato*) of the city; of the others the Archbishop has 7 and the Abbot of St Augustine 14 in exchange for the site of the castle. And

(Canterbury – continued)–
there are still 212 burgesses over whom the
king has sac and soc and 3 mills paying 108s.
and toll amounting to 68s. . . . the burgesses
have 45 burgages outside the city for which
they themselves received rent and customary
dues . . . the same burgesses also had from the
king 33 acres of land for their gild [long
extent of named burgage tenants] . There is
an agreement as to the direct roads which
have entry to and exit from the city. . . . A
certain reeve, Bruman by name, took customary dues from foreign merchants on the
land of Holy Trinity and St Augustine . . .
Burgesses and sites (*hagæ*) recorded under
manors of Faversham, Westgate, Aldington,
St Martin, Northgate, Otterdean, Wickham-
breux, Westleave, Wichling, Nackington,
Chilham, Throwley, Ospring, Arnoldton,
Perry, Luddenham, Denton, Langport and
Newington.

CASTLEFORD: Manorial entries under Holtune
(Glasshoughton), Queldale (Wheldale), Friston
(Fryston) and Whitwode (Whitwood).

CHARD: Cedre (Somerset: Bishop of Wells
fo. 89b).

CHATHAM: Ceteham (Kent: Bp. of Bayeux
fo. 8b).

CHELMSFORD: Celmeresfort (Essex: Bp. of
London fo. 10b).

CHELTENHAM: Chinteneham (Gloucestershire:
King's lands 162d).

Cheshunt: Cestrehunt (Hertfordshire: Count
Alan fo. 137a) '10 merchants pay 10s. in
customary dues'.

CHESTER: Civitas de Cestre (Cheshire: pre-
entry fo. 262c) paid tax on 50 hides; Ref. to
431 houses, 7 moneyers, repair of the city
wall, ships at the city port, and merchants'
regulation. Includes the Laws of Chester
and the Bp. of Chester's Customary Dues.
Burgesses and houses of Chester are recorded
under the manors of Weaverham, Dunham
Massey, Hawarden and Claverton. See Tate,
J. (ed.)., 'Domesday Survey of Cheshire',
Chetham Soc., vol. 75 (1916).

CHESTERFIELD: Cestrefeld (Derbyshire: King's
lands fo. 272b).

CHICHESTER: In Cicestre Civitate (Sussex:
Land of Earl Roger fo. 23a.). 'In the city of
Chichester before 1066 there were 100 sites
(*hagæ*) less 2½ and 3 crofts. In the same
dwelling-sites (*masuræ*) there are 60 more
houses (*domi*) than there were before'. More
than 90 sites in Chichester are recorded
under the manors of Bosham, Pagham,
Tangmere, E. Lavington, Donnington, Fel-
pham, Racton, Bepton, Petworth, Fishbourne,
Selham, Westbourne, Marden, Donnington,
Singleton, Lavant, Harting, Linch, Tillington,
Duncton, Stopham, Compton, Westhamp-
nett, Selsey and Strettington; see Round,
J. H., 'Note on the Sussex Domesday',

(Chichester – continued)
Sussex Arch. Soc., vol. 44 (1901).

CHIPPENHAM: Chepeham (Wiltshire: King's
lands fo. 64d.)

CHIPPING NORTON: Nortone (Oxfordshire:
Arnulf de Hesdin fo. 160a).

Clifford: Cliford (Herefordshire: Ralf de Todeni
fo. 183) 'Ralf holds the castle of Clifford:
Earl William erected in on waste land . . .
Gilbert the Sheriff holds it at farm with the
borough and the plough; named tenants;
16 burgesses.

Clare: Clara (Suffolk: Richard son of Count
Gilbert fo. 389b); market and 43 burgesses.

COLCHESTER: Survey of Colecestra (Essex:
separate entry fo. 104). Refers to burgesses'
common about the wall and to moneyers.
List of named burgesses totals 285 entries,
393 houses and 1,318 acres. The burgesses
now pay 'only on their polls'.

CONGLETON: Cogeltone (Cheshire: Bigot of
Loges fo. 266 d).

COVENTRY: Coventreu (Warwickshire:
Countess Godiva fo. 239c).

CREWE: Crev (Cheshire: Richard of Vernon
fo. 265a) found waste.

Cricklade: Crichelade (Wiltshire: Church of St
Peter, Westminster etc. fo. 67b). 'It has
there many burgesses and the third penny
of the same town', See Wiltshire Customs
fo. 64c 'from the third penny of Cricklade,
£5'. Burgesses of Cricklade are recorded
under manors of Aldbourne, Ramsbury,
Badbury, Purton, Chisledon, Liddington,
Liddington, Lydiard Tregoze, Clyffe Pipard,
Calcutt and Earlscourt.

CROSBY: Crosebi (Cheshire: Roger of Poitou
fo. 269c).

CROYDON: Croindene (Surrey: Archbishop of
Canterbury fo. 30d).

DARTFORD: Tarentefort (Kent: King's lands
fo. 2b).

DAVENTRY: Daventrei (Northamptonshire:
Countess Judith fo. 228c).

DEAL: Addelam (Kent: Canons of St Martin,
Dover fo. 1)

DERBY: In Burgo Derby (Derbyshire: pre-
entry 280b). 'To this borough were attached
12 carucates of land taxable, which 8 ploughs
can plough. The land was divided between 41
burgesses who also had 12 ploughs. From dues
and tolls and fines and all customary dues,
two parts were the king's, the third part the
Earl's . . . Now there are 100 burgesses and
40 lesser burgesses (*minores*); 103 *mansæ*
which used to pay dues are unoccupied'.

DEWSBURY: Deusberia (Yorkshire: King's lands
fo. 299d). 'This land belongs to Wakefield,
nevertheless K. Edward had a manor in it'.

DONCASTER: Donecastre (Yorkshire: Count
of Mortain fo. 307b).

DORCHESTER: Dorecestre (Dorset: pre-entry
fo. 75) 'In Dorchester T.R.E. there were

(Dorchester — continued) –

172 houses ... there were 2 moneyers ... now there are 88 houses and 100 were completely destroyed from the time of Sheriff Hugh until now'.

DOVER: Dovere (Kent: pre-entry fo. 1). 'The burgesses supplied the king once a year with 20 ships for 15 days and in each ship were 21 men ... Whenever the king's messengers came there they paid 3d. for the passage of a horse in winter and 2d. in summer, the burgesses finding a steersman and one other helper ... A permanent settler in the town paid customary dues to the king and was exempt from tolls throughout England ... just after (K. William) came to England, the town was burned down and therefore a right valuation could not be made of what it was worth when the Bp. of Bayeux received it ... In Dover there are 29 burgages from which the king has lost his customary dues ... amongst which was the gildhall (*gilhalla*) of the burgesses ... The king's laws for Dover follow'.

DROITWICH: Wich (Worcestershire: King's lands and St Peter, Westminster fos. 172 and 174b). The king had 11 houses and in 5 brine-pits K. Edward had his share ... 4 furnaces ... 54 saltpans ... and 31 burgesses who render 15s. 8d.' Saltpans in Droitwich are recorded under manors of Tardebigge (7), Holt (1), Northwick (1), Oddingley (1), Hallow (1), Hampton Lovett (7), Crowle (3), Ombersley (2), Salwarpe (6), Horton (1), Pershore (1), Astley (1), Hadsor (7), Belbroughton (1), Witton (4½), Doverdale (1), Chaddesley Corbett (5), Feckenham (4), Hampton Lovett (1), Princes Risborough (Bucks) etc. Also burgesses and houses in the town belonging to the manors of Kidderminster, Northwick, Hallow, Elmley Lovett, Hartlebury, Wychbold, Crowle, Sakwarpe and Mitton.

DUDLEY: Dudelei (Worcestershire; William Fitz Ansculf fo. 177). 'The same William holds Dudley and his castle is there'.

Dunwich: Duneuuic (Suffolk: land of Robert Malet's mother fo. 312) 'T.R.E. ... 2 carucates of land, now 1; the sea carried away the other and then 120 burgesses now 236 and 180 poor men, less 2' [Land of St Ethelreda at Alnet'ne fo. 385b], '... to this manor belong 80 burgesses in Dunwich and they dwell on 14 acres'.

EASTBOURNE: Burne and Borne (Sussex: Count of Eu fo. 19c).

EAST RETFORD: Redforde (Nottinghamshire: Archbishop of York fo. 283b).

ELY: Ely (Cambridgeshire: Abbot of Ely fo. 192).

ENFIELD: Enefelde and EDMONTON as Adelmetone (Middlesex: Geoffrey de Mandeville fo. 129d).

EPSOM AND EWELL: Etwelle (Surrey: King's lands fo. 30c) and Evesham (Surrey: church of Chertsey fo. 32c).

EVESHAM: Evesham (Worcestershire: church of Evesham fo. 175b). 'The town where is situate the Abbey'.

EXETER: Essecestra (Devonshire: King's lands fo. 88) 'the City of Exeter the king has 300 houses all but 15 which pay the customary dues ... This city did not pay geld T.R.E. except when London, York and Winchester paid it and that was half a mark of silver for the hired troops (*ad solidarios*)'. List of tenants includes the Bp. of Coutances, Baldwin the Sheriff, Alvered the Breton; almost uniform rent of 8d. a house.

EYE: Eia (Suffolk: land of Robert Malet's mother fo. 320). 'One market and a park. And in the market 25 burgesses have their dwellings'. (See Hoxne, below).

FAVERSHAM: Favreshant (Kent: King's lands fo. 2b).

FLINT: See: Tait, J., 'Flintshire in Domesday Book', *Flint Hist. Soc. Pubs.*, vol. 11 (1926).

FOLKESTONE: Fulchestan (Kent: Bp. of Bayeux fo. 9) 5 churches, £100 value.

Fordwich: Forewick (Kent: land of St Augustine fo. 12). 'The Abbot himself holds a small borough which is called Fordwich ... there were 100 burgages all but 4, paying 13s. There are now 73 paying the same amount'.

GILLINGHAM: Gelingeham (Kent: Archbishop of Canterbury fo. 3b Bp. of Bayeux fo. 8).

GLASTONBURY: Glaestingeberia (Somerset; St Mary, Glastonbury fo. 90a).

GLOSSOP: Glosop (Derbyshire: King's lands fo. 273a).

GLOUCESTER: Glowecestre (Gloucestershire: pre-entry fo. 162d). 'T.R.E. the city of Gloucester paid £36 by tale and 12 sestiers of honey according to the measure of the borough and 36 dickers of iron and 100 rods of iron drawn out for making nails for the king's shops and certain other small customs in the hall and chamber of the king. The City now pays the king £60 at 20d. in the *ora* and the king has £20 for the liberty of coining'. List of named tenants of *mansiones* including Bp. Osbern, Geoffrey de Mandeville, Roger de Laci.

GODALMING: Godelminge (Surrey: King's lands fo. 30d).

GRANTHAM: Grandham (Lincolnshire: King's lands). 'There are here 111 burgesses and 92 small messuages belonging to the sokemen and thanes'.

GRAVESEND: Gravesham (Kent: Bp. of Bayeux fo. 7b).

GREENWICH: Grenviz (Kent: Bp. of Bayeux fo. 6b).

GREAT YARMOUTH: Gernemwa (Norfolk: land of the Burgesses fo. 118) was held by

(Great Yarmouth – continued) –
K. Edward. 'Then as now 70 burgesses'.
GRIMSBY: Grimesbi (Lincolnshire: Bp. of
Bayeux fo. 343b) references to ferry and a
'new toll'.
GUILDFORD: Gildeford (Surrey: King's lands
fo. 30a) K. William has 75 sites (*hagas*) on
which dwell 175 men.
HALESOWEN: Hala (Worcestershire: Earl Roger
fo. 176).
HALIFAX: Feslei (Yorkshire: King's land fo.
299b). 'A bailiwick of Wakefield'.
HAMMERSMITH: see Fuleham (Middlesex: Bp.
of London fo. 127c). 'Between the French-
men and some London burgesses, 23 hides of
villagers' Lands'.
HARINGEY: see Toteham (Middlesex:
Countess Judith fo. 130d).
HARROW: Herges (Middlesex: Archbishop of
Canterbury fo. 127a).
HASTINGS: see RYE.
HAVERING: Haveringas (Essex: King's lands
fo. 1b) tenants at Leyton and Chafford.
HELSTON: Henlistone (Cornwall: King's lands ᶥ
120a); burgus de . . .
HEMEL HEMPSTEAD: Hamelamstede (Hertfordshire: Count of Mortain fo. 136d).
HEREFORD: Hereford Civitate (Herefordshire:
pre-entry fo. 179a). 'In the City of Hereford
T.R.E. there were 103 men dwelling together
within and without the wall and they had the
following customs . . . There were six smiths
in the city, each of them rendered 1d. from
his forge and each made 120 shoes of the
king's iron . . . there were seven moneyers
there; one was the Bishop's moneyer . . . Earl
Harold had 27 burgesses who had the same
customs as the other burgesses . . . the king
now has this City of Hereford in demesne and
the English burgesses dwelling there have their
former customs, but the French burgesses are
quit for 12d. from all their forfeitures except
[breach of the peace etc.] '. See: Bannister,
A. T., 'The Herefordshire Domesday', *Woolhope Nat. Field Club Trans.* (1902–4).
HERTFORD: Burgus Hertforde (Hertfordshire:
pre-entry 132a). 'The Borough of Hertford
answered for 10 hides before 1066 but does
not now. There were 146 burgesses in K.
Edward's jurisdiction. This borough-town
(*suburbium*) pays £20 assayed and weighed
3 mills pay £10'; list of named tenants.
Hoxne: Hoxana (Suffolk: land of William, Bp. of
Thetford fo. 379). 'A market T.R.E. and it
went on after K. William came hither . . . on
Saturdays. And William Malet made his castle
at Eye and on the same day as the Bp's
market used to be held, he made another
market at his castle and the Bp's market
has been so far spoiled that it is of little
worth and is now set up on Fridays'.
HIGHAM FERRERS: Hecham (Northamptonshire: William Peverel fo. 225d).

HIGH WYCOMBE: Wicumbe (Buckinghamshire:
Robert d'Oilly fo. 149b).
HONITON: Honetone (Devon: Count of Mortain
fo. 84 and 215b) paid 30d. a year to
Axminster, ceased T.R.W.
HUDDERSFIELD: Oderesfelt (Yorkshire: Ilbert
de Laci fo. 317b).
HUNTINGDON: In Burgo Huntedone
(Huntingdonshire: pre-entry 203a). 'In the
borough . . . there are four quarters (*ferlingi*).
In two quarters there were 116 burgesses
before 1066 and still are . . . under them are
100 smallholders who assist them in paying
the tax . . . On the castle site there were
residences liable for all customary dues
which paid 16s. 8d. to the king's revenue;
they are not there now'. Ref. to 60
unoccupied sites, 140 burgesses with 139½
houses and customary dues on 80 sites, also
to market rights, mint-tax, £10 land-gable
and third penny, 20 residences 'where the
castle is' and 3 moneyers, 'not there now'.
See also Godmuncestre (Huntingdonshire:
King's land fo. 203c). See: Ladds, S. I.,
'The Borough of Huntingdon and Domesday Book', *Cambs. and Hunts. Arch. Soc.*,
vol. 5 (1937).
HYTHE: Hede (Kent: Archbishop of Canterbury's lands fo. 8b) at Saltwood: 'To this
manor belong 225 burgesses in the borough
of Hythe. Borough and manor together it
was worth £16 T.R.E. When received it was
worth £8, now £29 6s. 4d.'
ILKESTON: Tilchestune (Derbyshire: Gilbert
of Ghent fo. 277a).
IPSWICH: Gepeswiz (Suffolk: of this Roger
Bigod has charge in the king's hands fo. 290).
'In the borough there were T.R.E. 538
burgesses rendering custom to the king and
they had 40 acres of land. But now there are
110 who render customs and 100 poor burgesses who cannot render to the king's geld
but one penny a head. . . . and 328 burgages
(*mansiones*) within the borough lie waste
which T.R.E. paid scot towards the king's
geld . . . and the moneyers used to render
annually £4 for the mint, now they ought to
render £20'.
ISLINGTON: Isendone (Middlesex: Bp. of
London fo. 128a).
KEIGHLEY: Chichelai (Yorkshire: King's lands
301b).
KENDAL: Cherchebi (Cheshire: King's lands in
Yorkshire fo. 302a).
KENSINGTON AND CHELSEA: Chenesitun
(Middlesex: Aubrey de Vere fo. 30d) and
Chelched (Middlesex: Edward of Salisbury
fo. 130d).
KETTERING: Cateringe (Northamptonshire:
Peterborough Abbey fo. 221c).
KIDDERMINSTER: Chideminstre (Worcester-
shire: King's lands fo. 172b) . . . all waste.
KING'S LYNN: Lena (Norfolk: Encroachments

(King's Lynn — continued) —
fos. 273 and 275) possibly a 'simple borough' see *VCH Norfolk*, vol. II, p. 37.

KINGSTON-UPON-HULL: (?) Totfled (Yorkshire: Ralf de Mortemer fo. 325) part of the manor of Ferriby.

LAMBETH: Lanchei (Surrey: Lambeth church 34ab) '19 burgesses in London, 36s.'

LANCASTER: Loncastre (Cheshire: lands of the king in Yorkshire fo. 301d) see Farrer, W., 'The Domesday Survey of N. Lancs . . .', *Lancs. & Ches. Antiq. Soc.*, vol. 18 (1901).

Langport; Lanport (Somerset: King's lands fo. 86b). 'A town (*burgus*) . . . in which 34 burgesses live who pay 15s. . . . Of the third penny of Ilchester, William de Mohun pays £6, of Milborne Port 20s., of Bruton 20s., of Langport 10s., of Axbridge 10s., of Frome 5s.' There were burgesses of Langport in North Curry.

LAUNCESTON: Dunhevet (Cornwall: Count of Mortain fo. 121d) the Count's castle is there.

LEEDS: Ledes (Yorkshire: Ilbert de Laci fo. 315).

LEICESTER: Civitas de Ledecestre (Leicestershire: pre-entry fo. 315). 'The city . . . paid to the king £30 a year T.R.E. at face value, at 20d. to the *ora* and 15 sesters of honey. When the king went on campaign by land 12 burgesses from the borough went with him, but when he went by sea they sent him four horses from the borough as far as London . . . from the moneyers, £20 a year . . . the king has 39 houses . . . the Archbishop of York 2 houses, Hugh of Grandmaisnil 110 houses and 2 churches . . . , list of houses and tenants by name, also manors with houses in town'.

LEOMINSTER: Leofminstre (Herefordshire: King's lands fo. 180).

LEWES: Burgus de Lewes (Sussex: William of Warenne fo. 26a). 'The borough of Lewes before 1066 paid £6 4s. 1½d. from tribute and toll (*de gablo et de theloneo*) K. Edward had 127 burgesses in lordship. Their custom was that if the king wished to send his men in his absence to guard the sea, they collected 20s. from all men wheresoever the land was and those who have charge of arms in those ships had the shillings'; laws of the town follow; refs. to moneyers and uninhabited houses; manors with 189 sites (*hagæ*) in Lewes include: Rodmell, Patcham, Ditchling, Harpingden, Pangdean, Keymer, Westmeston, Orleswick, Ovingdean, Brighton, Winterbourne, Pawthorne, Saddlescombe, Plumpton, Bevendean, East Chillington, Perching, Clayton, Wickham, Preston, Aldingbourne, Alciston, Southease, Stanmer and Malling.

LEWISHAM: Levesham (Kent: St Peter of Ghent fo. 12b) 'market'.

LICHFIELD: Lecefelle (Staffordshire: Bp. of Chester fo. 247ab).

LINCOLN: Lincolia (Lincolnshire; pre-entry fo. 336a). 'In the city . . . there were 970 inhabited *mansiones*; these being reckoned after the English measure of computation, that is 120 to the hundred . . . there are now 200 decayed *mansiones*, that is 240 by the English way of counting and they are uninhabited, while, according to the same way of reckoning, the remaining 760 are still inhabited . . . of the above-mentioned decayed *mansiones*, 156 have been pulled down to make room for the castle; the remaining 74 are within the bounds of the castle, still standing in their decayed condition, not because of any oppression by the sheriff or his officers, but because of mishaps, poverty and fire'; list of named tenants. (For all Lincs entries see: Foster, C. W. & Langley, T., 'Lincolnshire Domesday & Lindsay Survey', *Lincs. Rec. Soc.*, vol. 19 (1924).

LISKEARD: Liscarret (Cornwall: Count of Mortain fo. 121c) 'market'.

(LONDON): The survey of London was never transcribed. See occasional refs. in other Middlesex manors, e.g.: Fulham.

LOUGHBOROUGH: Lucteburne (Leicestershire: Hugh de Grandmaisnil fo. 237a). Has one house in Leicester (fo. 230a).

LOUTH: Ludes (Lincolnshire: Bp. of Lincoln fo. 345a). 'The Bp. has there now in demesne 3 carucates and 80 burgesses and a market worth 29s. yearly'.

LOWESTOFT: Lothu Wistoft (Suffolk: King's lands fo. 283b).

LUTON: Loitone (Bedfordshire: King's lands fo. 209b). 'Tolls and market 100s.'

Lydford: Lydford (Devon: King's lands fo. 87b). 'The king has the borough of Lydford (Note *VCH:* 'where there was a castle') which K. Edward held before 1066. There the king has 28 burgesses within the borough and 41 without and they pay £3 a year . . . there are also 40 houses which have been laid in ruins since K. William had England. The aforesaid burgesses have land for 2 ploughs outside the city (*foras civitatem*). If an expedition goes forth by land or sea, this borough renders the same service as Totnes or Bodmin'.

LYME REGIS: Lime (Dorset: Bp. of Salisbury, fo. 76d).

LYMINGTON: Lentune (Hampshire: Lands in the New Forest and round about it; Roger of Shrewsbury fo. 51).

LYTHAM ST ANNES: Lidun (Cheshire: lands of the king in Yorkshire fo. 301d).

MACCLESFIELD: Maclesfeld (Cheshire; King's lands fo. 263d).

MAIDSTONE: Meddestane (Kent: Archbishop of Canterbury fo. 36).

MALDON: Melduna (Essex: King's lands fo. 5b). 'In the same Maldon the king has 180 houses held by burgesses and 18 *mansuræ* which are uninhabited. Of which burgesses, 15 hold

(Maldon – continued) –
half a hide and 2 acres, whilst the others hold
no more than their houses in the borough'.

MALMESBURY: Burgo Malmesberie (Wiltshire:
pre-entry fo. 64c). 'The king holds 26 unoccupied dwellings (*masuras*) and 25
dwellings where there are houses which do
not pay tax any more than waste land; each
of these pays 10d. in tribute, that is 43s. 6d.
altogether . . . from its mint the borough pays
100s. . . . When the king went on expedition
by land or sea he had from this borough
either 20s. to feed his boatmen or he took
with him one man from each honour of five
hides'. List of named tenants; also Wiltshire
Customs. Burgesses of Malmesbury are
recorded under Somerford, Hullavington,
Alderton, Castle Combe, Wootton Bassett
and Foxley.

MANCHESTER: Mamecestre (Cheshire
'between Ribble and Mersey' fo. 270a).

MANSFIELD: Mamesfeld (Nottinghamshire:
King's lands 281b).

MARLBOROUGH: Merleberge (Wiltshire
Customs fo. 64c). 'From the third penny
of Marlborough the king has £4'.

MERTON: Meretone (Surrey: King's lands fo.
30b). 'In Southwark 16 dwellings at 18s. 2d.
belong to this manor'.

Milborne Port: Mileburne (Somerset: King's
lands fo. 86c). 'In this manor 56 burgesses
who pay 60s. with the market: at Ilchester
107 burgesses who pay 20s'.

MONMOUTH: In Monemude Castle (Herefordshire, lying in Worcestershire: King's lands
fo. 180b).

MONTGOMERY: Montgomeri (Shropshire: Earl
Roger fo. 253) 'castle'.

MORLEY: Moreleia (Yorkshire; Ilbert 317b).

MORECAMBE AND HEYSHAM: Hessam
(Cheshire: lands of the king in Yorkshire
fo. 301d).

Nantwich: Wich (Cheshire; King's lands 268b)
customs related to saltworks.

NEWARK: Newerche (Nottinghamshire: Bp. of
Lincoln fo. 283d). 'Bp. Remigius has . . .
56 burgesses; Countess Judith has market
rights'.

Newport Pagnell: Neuport (Buckinghamshire:
William Fitz Ansculf fo. 148d). 'The burgesses have 6½ ploughs'.

NEW ROMNEY: Romenel (Kent: Archbishop
of Canterbury, fo. 4b) at Langport; '21
burgesses who are in Romney', also 85 burgesses at Aldington and 50 more belonging
to the Hundred of Langport.

NORTHAMPTON: Northantone (Northamptonshire: pre-entry 219a). 'There were 60 burgesses in the king's lordship before 1066 who
had as many residences (*mansiones*), now 14
of them are derelict; 47 are left. Besides these
there are now 40 burgesses in the new borough
in K. William's lordship . . . Northampton

(Northampton – continued) –
pays three nights' revenue £30 by weight'.
Named tenants of town houses include Bp.
of Coutances, Count of Mortain, Countess
Judith etc.; in all 227 houses at an average
payment of 11d. a house.

NORWICH: Noruic (Norfolk: King's lands fo.
116). 'There were 1,320 burgesses T.R.E. . . .
now there are in the borough 665 English
burgesses and they pay the customary dues,
and 480 bordars . . . and on the land of which
Harold had the soke there are 15 burgesses
and 17 empty messuages which are in the
occupation of the castle. In the borough there
are in addition 50 houses from which the king
has not his custom . . . List of named tenants
and messuages . . . and the Bp's men 10
houses and in the Bp's own court 14 dwelling
houses . . . and in the borough the burgesses
hold 43 chapels . . . Those fleeing and those
remaining have been entirely ruined, partly by
reason of the forfeitures of Earl Ralf, partly
by reason of a fire, partly by reason of the
King's geld, partly by Waleran . . . in this
borough the king can have one moneyer if he
wishes . . . Land of the burgesses . . . In the
new borough are 36 burgesses and 6 English-
men and each one used to pay 1d. . . . now
there are 41 French burgesses on the demesne
of the king'. . . . See Tingey, J. C., 'Notes on
the Domesday Assessment of Norfolk', *Norf.
& Nor. Arch. Soc.*, vol. 21 (1923).

NOTTINGHAM: Burgo Snotingeham (Nottinghamshire; pre-entry 280a). 'There were
T.R.E. 173 burgesses and 19 villagers . . . 6
carucates . . . this land was divided between
38 burgesses, from the dues of the land and
the work of the burgesses it pays 75s. 7d.;
from 2 moneyers 40s. . . . Hugh son of Baldric
the Sheriff found 136 men living there, now
there are 16 less. However, Hugh erected 13
houses himself in the new Borough and placed
them amongst the dues of the old borough . . .
the burgesses have 6 carucates of land for
ploughing . . . William Peverel has 48 merchants' houses which pay 36s. and 12 horsemen's houses and 8 *bordars*. Ralf of Buron
has 13 horsemen's houses; a merchant lives in
one of them . . . In the borough ditch (*fossato*)
are 17 houses and 6 others . . . In the priest's
croft are 65 houses . . . In Nottingham the R.
Trent and the dyke and the road to York are
so protected that if anyone hinders the
passage of ships, or if anyone ploughs or
makes a dyke within 2 perches of the king's
road, he pays a fine of £8'.

NUNEATON: Etone (Warwickshire: Earl Aubrey
fo. 239c and Turchil of Warwick fo. 241d).

Okehampton; Ochenemitona (Devon: Baldwin
the Sheriff fo. 268). 'On this land stands
the castle of Okehampton. There, Baldwin
has 4 burgesses and a market paying 4s.
a year'.

OSSETT: Osleset (Yorkshire):

Otterton: Otritone: (Devon: Abbey of St Michael's Mount fo. 194). 'A market is held there on Sundays'.

OXFORD: Oxeneford (Oxfordshire: pre-entry fo. 154a). 'Before 1066, Oxford paid £20 a year to the king and 6 sesters of honey, for tolls, tribute and other customary dues, and the Earl Algar £10 in addition to the mill which he had within the city. When the king went on an expedition 20 burgesses went with him for all the others, or they gave £20 that they might all be free. Now Oxford pays £60 . . . In this town, within and without the wall, are 243 houses which pay tax; apart from these there are 500 houses less 22 so derelict and destroyed that they cannot pay tax. The king has 20 wall-dwellings (*mansiones murales*) which were Earl Algar's before 1066 and paid 14s. less 2d. then and now . . . the reason they are called "wall-dwellings" is that, if there is need and if the king commands, they repair the wall . . . If the wall is not repaired when needed by him whose job it is, either he shall pay the king 40s. or he loses his house. All the burgesses of Oxford have a pasture outside the wall in common, which pays 6s. 8d'. At manors outside the Oxford entry, a further 81 houses are listed, at Streatley, Steventon etc. List of named tenants of town houses, including the Archbishop of Canterbury, Bp's of Winchester, Bayeux and Lincoln, listing 198 houses, average rent 9d.

Pershore: Persore (Worcestershire: St Peter of Westminster fo. 174b). 'There are 28 burgesses who render 30s. . . . toll renders 12s.'.

Pevensey: Pevenesel (Sussex: Count of Mortain fo. 20c). 'Before 1066 there were 24 burgesses in the king's lordship, they paid 14s. 6d. in tribute, 20s. from the toll, 35s. from port-dues and 7s. 3d. from pasture. . . . When the Count of Mortain acquired it, only 27 burgesses; now he has 60 burgesses himself in lordship who pay 39s. in tribute, toll £4, the mint 20s'. List of 110 burgesses by name, paying on average 8½d. each *de gablo.*

PONTEFRACT: as Tateshalle (Tanshelf) (Yorkshire: Ilbert fo. 316b).

PORTSMOUTH: see Buckland (Hampshire: Hugh de Port fo. 45).

PRESTON: Prestune (Cheshire: lands of the king in Yorkshire fo. 301d).

PUDSEY: Podechesaie (Yorkshire: Ilbert fo. 317b).

Quatford: Quatford (Shropshire: Earl Roger fo. 254). 'A burgh called Quatford yielding nothing. T.R.E. it was worth 40s., now 30s.'

READING: Reddinges (Berkshire: King's lands fo. 85a). 'Borough . . . the king has 28 sites which pay £4 3s. for all customary dues; however their holders pay 100s'.

REDBRIDGE: see ILFORD; Ilefort (Essex; Gilbert the Lorimer fo. 94).

WOODFORD: Wodefort (Essex: land of Canons of Holy Cross, Waltham fo. 15b) and WAN-STEAD: Wenesteda (Essex: Bp. of London fo. 9b).

REIGATE: Cherchefelle (Surrey: King's lands fo. 30b).

Rhuddlan: Roelend (Cheshire: land of Earl Hugh and his men in Wales fo. 269ab). 'Earl Hugh holds Rhuddlan from the king; before 1066 Englefield lay there and was all waste . . . now he has the lordship of half the castle which is the head (*caput*) of this land. He has there 8 burgesses, half the church and the mint, half the iron mines . . . half the waters of Clwyd, half the toll . . . Robert has 10 burgesses, half the church, mint, iron mines etc. . . . In the manor of Rhuddlan a castle has been built, likewise called Rhuddlan. There is a new borough and 18 burgesses in it, divided as stated above . . . they accorded to these burgesses the laws and customs which are observed in Hereford and Breteuil'.

RICHMOND-ON-THAMES: see Urarh, A. C. B., 'Twickenham & Isleworth in Domesday Book', *Twick. Loc. Hist. Soc.* Paper 34 (1976).

RIPON: Ripum (Yorkshire: Archbishop of York and King's lands fo. 303b).

ROCHDALE: Recedham (Cheshire: between Ribble and Mersey fo. 270a).

ROCHESTER: Rovescestre Civitas (Kent: Canons of St Martin, Dover fo. 2). 'Was worth 100s. T.R.E. . . . now valued at £20, yet he who holds it pays £40 . . . Bp. of Rochester . . . (holds land) in exchange for the land on which the castle stands'; there are sites and burgesses recorded under the manorial entries of: Aylesford, Darenth, Frinsbury, Borstall, Eccles, Luddesdon, Offham, Burham, Allington, Hoo, Waterin-bury, Chalk and Newington. Note importance of Rochester's Bridge; see also W. de Gray Birch, *Cartularium Saxonicum* (1885-99), 1321-2.

ROMSEY: Rumeseai (Hampshire: Abbey of Romsey fo. 43b); 14 burgesses in Winchester.

ROYAL LEAMINGTON SPA: Lamintone (Warwickshire; Earl Roger fo. 239b).

RYE: Rameslie (Sussex: land of Fécamp church fo. 17b). 'In this manor is a new borough; 64 burgesses pay £8, less 2s.'

SAFFRON WALDEN: Waledana (Essex: Henry de Ferrers fo. 62).

ST ALBANS: S. Albani (Hertfordshire: St Albans church fo. 62). 'The town answers for 10 hides . . . there are 46 burgesses; from tolls and other payments of the town £11 14s. a year'.

SALFORD: Salford (Cheshire: between Ribble and Mersey fo. 270a). Long manorial entry including Manchester, Rochdale and Radcliffe as 'berewicks' of Salford.

SALISBURY: Sarisberie (Wiltshire Customs fo. 64c). '7 burgesses who belong to manor pay 65d.'

SANDWICH: Sandwice (Kent: land of the Archbishop of Canterbury fo. 2). 'Lies in its own Hundred. This borough the Archbishop holds; it is assigned to the monks and renders the same sort of service that Dover renders . . . T.R.E. there were 207 burgages occupied and there are now 76 more'.

SCUNTHORPE: Escumestorp (Lincolnshire: land of the king fo. 338b).

Seasalter: Seseltre (Kent: Archbishop of Canterbury fo. 5). 'A small borough called Seasalter which belongs to the Archbishop's private kitchen'.

SHAFTESBURY: Sceptesberie (Dorset: pre-entry fo. 75). 'In the borough T.R.E. were 104 houses in the king's demesne. There were 3 moneyers each rendering 1 silver mark . . . now there are 66 houses and 38 were destroyed from the time of Sheriff Hugh until now. In the part belonging to the Abbess of Shaftesbury there were 153 houses T.R.E. Now there are 111 houses and 42 were utterly destroyed. There the Abbess has 151 burgesses and 20 vacant plots and one garden; worth 65s.'

SHREWSBURY: Civitas de Sciropesberie (Shropshire: pre-entry fo. 252a). 'T.R.E. there were 252 houses and the same number of burgesses rendering yearly £7 16s. 8d. *de gablo*. There K. Edward had these under-mentioned privileges [over infringements of the peace] . . . when the king lay in this City 12 citizens of the better class (*de melioribus civitatis*) had to serve him as guards and when he went hunting there the better class of burgess possessing horses guarded him armed. . . . Should the house of any burgess be burned by accident or misfortune or by negligence he paid 40s. to the king by way of forfeit and 2s. to each of his two nearest neighbours . . . the moneyers the king had there paid the king 20s. each on any change of coinage. In all the city paid annually £30 . . . and was assessed T.R.E. at 100 hides. . . . The English-born burgesses of Shrewsbury maintain that it is very hard on them that they now pay the same geld as they used to pay T.R.E. although the Earl's castle has occupied 51 burgages and 50 others are waste and 43 Frenchmen occupy burgages geldable at the time of K. Edward and the Earl has granted the Abbey which he is founding there 39 burgesses formerly geldable. In all there are 200 burgesses all but 7 who do not now pay geld . . .'. [Land of the Bp. of Chester] '16 burgages and an equal number of burgesses . . . now 10 are waste . . . In Shrewsbury City Earl Roger is making an abbey . . . and has given to it as many of his burgesses and mills as yield £12 annually'; manors with burgesses in the city include Emstrey, Woodcote and Meole Brace.

SOLIHULL: see Longdon (Warwickshire: church of Worcester fo. 173d) and Ulverley

(Solihull – continued) –
(Warwickshire: Christina fo. 244b).

SOUTHAMPTON: Hantune (Hampshire: in the New Forest fo. 52). 'In the borough . . . the king has 76 men who pay £7 for land-tax (*de gablo terræ*) as they did T.R.E. 27 of these pay 8d., 2 pay 12d. and the other 50 pay 6d.' List of tenants of houses includes Bp. of Coutances, Count of Evreux; town-houses recorded under manors of Shirley in Millbrook and Chilworth.

SOUTHWARK: Svdwerche (Surrey: Bp. of Bayeux's lands fo. 32a). 'The Bp. has a monastery and a tidal waterway himself . . . the king has two parts of the income from the waterway where the ships moored, Earl Godwin the third part. The men of Southwark testify that, before 1066 no-one but the king took toll (*theloneum*) on the shore or on the waterfront (*in vico aquæ*)'. Dwellings in Southwark are recorded under manors of Merton, Walkingstead, Oxted, Chivington, Blechingley, Walton-on-the-Hill and Beddington. (Average rent 8d.). See also Bermundesye (Surrey: King's lands fo. 30b), 'a new and beautiful church . . . in London 13 burgesses at 44d'; and Cambrewelle (Surrey: Hamo the Sheriff fo. 36c).

SOUTHWOLD: Sudwolda (Suffolk: land of St Edmund fo. 371b).

STAFFORD: In Burgo de Stadford (Staffordshire: pre-entry 246a). 'The king has 18 burgesses and 8 unoccupied dwellings; besides this he has 22 dwellings of the Earl's honour, 5 unoccupied, the others inhabited'. List of other tenants of dwellings 'within the wall' includes: Bp. of Chester, Earl Roger, William fitz Ansculf; houses in Stafford recorded under manors of Marston, Cresswell, Chersey and others. See Daniel, A. T., 'Staffs. Domesday Book', *Staffs. Field Club*, vol. 37 (1903).

STAMFORD: Stanford (Lincolnshire: pre-entry fo. 336a). 'The Royal Borough of Stamford paid tax T.R.E. after the rate of 12½ Hundreds towards Danegeld or any expedition by land or sea. There were, and still are, in the borough six wards, five being in Lincolnshire and the sixth in Northamptonshire, which is over the bridge. The latter ward nevertheless pays all the same customs as the others with the exception of land-gable and toll which belong to the Abbot of Peterborough. In the five wards T.R.E. were 141 *mansiones* and half a mill . . . and there are as many *mansiones* at present with the exception of 5 which have been destroyed to build the castle . . . there were 12 lawmen who had *sac and soc* over their own houses. . . . The king has 600 acres of arable land outside the town in Lincolnshire, the lawmen and burgesses have 272 acres exempt from customary payments . . . for all customary rents it pays £28'. Details of *mansiones* and their tenants.

Steyning: Staninges (Sussex: land of Fecamp church fo. 17b). 'In the borough there are 118 dwellings; they paid £4 2s. Now there are 123 dwellings, they pay 100s. and 100d. Their owners have 1½ ploughs. Before 1066 they worked like villeins'.

STRATFORD-UPON-AVON: Stradforde (Warwickshire: Bp. of Worcester fo. 238d).

SUDBURY: Sutberia (Suffolk: land of Earl Morcar's mother fo. 286b); 'and 63 burgesses attached to the Hall . . . and 55 burgesses on the demesne . . . and 9 acres of land belonging to the burgesses. And one market and therein are moneyers'.

SUTTON: Sudtone (Surrey: Abbot of Chertsey fo. 32c). Also CHEAM: Ceiham (Surrey: Archbishop of Canterbury fo. 30d); BEDDINGTON: Beddintone (Surrey: Richard son of Count Gilbert fo. 34d–35a) and (Surrey: Miles Crispin fo. 36c) . . . 21 dwellings which Earl Roger alleges to have been taken from this manor: 13 in London, 8 in Southwark. They pay 12s. . . . : also WALLINGTON: Waletone (Surrey: King's lands fo. 30b).

SUTTON COLDFIELD: Svtone (Warwickshire: King's lands fo. 238b).

SWINDON: Svindvne (Wiltshire: Bp. of Bayeux fo. 66b: Alfred of Marlborough fo. 70b; the king's thanes fo. 74b; Odin the Chamberlain fo. 74d and King's lands fo. 64d).

TAMWORTH: Tamuuorde (Staffordshire: King's lands fo. 246) 'at Wigginton; . . . 4 burgesses in Tamworth . . . at Drayton Bassett: . . . 8 burgesses in Tamworth belong to this manor and work there like the other villagers'.

TAUNTON: Tantone (Somerset: Bp. of Winchester fo. 87c). '64 burgesses who pay 32s. . . . a market which pays 50s.; from the mint 50s. . . . when Bp. Walkelin acquired it, it paid £50, now it pays £154 0s. 1d. with all its dependencies and customary dues . . . these dues belong to Taunton; borough-right, thieves, etc.' List of places paying dues to Taunton: Tolland, Oake, Holford, Upper Cheddon, Cheddon Fitzpaine, Maidenbrooke, Ford, Hillfarrance, Hele, Nynehead, Norton Fitzwarren, Bradford on Tone, Halse, Heathfield, Shopnoller and Stoke St Mary; 'from all these lands those who have to make an oath or bear judgement come to Taunton. When the lords of these lands die they are buried in Taunton'. Hillfarrance and Hele could not be separated from Taunton before 1066.

TEWKESBURY: Teodekesberie (Gloucestershire-King's lands 163b) 13 burgesses and a market.

THETFORD: Tetfort (Norfolk: land of the burgesses fo. 118b). 'In the borough were 943 burgesses T.R.E. . . . now there are 720 and 224 empty messuages. Of these burgesses, 21 have 6 ploughlands and 6 acres . . . and 2

(Thetford – continued) –
burgesses have 1 mill . . . now it also renders to the king £40 from the mint'. List of tenants: Abbot of St Edmunds, Abbot of Ely, Roger Bigod, etc.'

Tilshead: Theodvlveside (Wiltshire: King's lands fo. 65a). '66 burgesses who pay 50s.'

TIVERTON: Tovretone (Devon: King's lands fo. 110b).

Torksey: Torchesey (Lincolnshire: pre-entry fo. 337a). 'T.R.E. there were 213 burgesses all of whom had the same customs as the citizens of Lincoln and so many more that whosoever held a mansion in the town paid no toll, neither when they entered it nor when they left it; but it was expected of them that whenever the king's commissioners came that way, the watermen of the town with their boats and all other necessary things should convey them as far as York. . . . The king now has the same in demesne and the burgesses there number 102, but 111 of the mansions are decayed'.

TORRINGTON: Torintona (Devon: Odo, son of Gamelin fo. 376b).

TOTNES: Totenais (Devon: lands of Juhel fo. 334). 'Juhel has a borough called Totnes which K. Edward held . . . There, Juhel has 100 burgesses, all but 5 within the borough and 15 without the borough who work the land . . . This township (*villa*) does not pay geld unless Exeter pays; when it used to pay geld the payment was 40d. If an expedition goes forth by land or sea, Barnstaple, Totnes and Lydford between them pay the same service as Exeter'.

(TOWER HAMLETS): See STEPNEY: Stibenhede (Middlesex: Bishop of London fo. 127; Robert son of Fafiton fo. 130b and Robert son of Rozelin fo. 130c).

Tutbury: Toteberia (Staffordshire: land of Henry Ferrers fo. 248c). 'Henry de Ferrers has Tutbury castle. In the borough around the castle are 42 men who live only by their trading; with the market, they pay £4 10s.'

WAKEFIELD: Wachefeld (Yorkshire: King's lands fo. 299b).

WALLASEY: Walea (Cheshire: Robert of Rhuddlan fo. 264d).

WALLINGFORD: In burgo de Walingeford (Berkshire: pre-entry fo. 56b). 'K. Edward had 8 virgates of land and on these were 276 sites (*hagæ*) which paid £11 in tribute . . . there are now fewer sites; 8 were destroyed for the castle, a moneyer has one exempt so long as he coins money . . . in addition there are 22 Frenchmen's dwellings which pay 6s. 5d. K. Edward had 15 acres in which his huscarles lived'. List of tenants totals 467 'sites' of which 32 are probably in Abingdon; ref. to 5 smithies; manors with *hagæ* in the town include: Basildon, Sutton Courtenay, Harwell, Sotwell, Brightwalton and Wittenham.

WALTHAM FOREST: see WALTHAMSTOW: Wilcumestou (Essex: Countess Judith fo. 92) and CHINGFORD: Cingefort (Essex: Robert of Gernon fo. 64).

WANDSWORTH: Wendelesorde (Surrey: church of Westminster fo. 32b).

WAREHAM: Warham (Dorset: pre-entry fo. 75). 'There were 143 houses in the king's demesne, 2 moneyers each rendering 1 silver mark to the king. Now there are 70 houses and 73 were completely destroyed from the time of Sheriff Hugh. In the part belonging to St Wandrille there are 45 houses standing and 17 are waste. In the part belonging to the other barons, there are 20 houses standing and 60 were destroyed'.

Warminster: Gverminstre (Wiltshire: King's lands fo. 64d). '30 burgesses'.

WARRINGTON: Walintune (Cheshire: Roger of Poitou fo. 269d).

WARWICK: Burgo de Warwic (Warwickshire: pre-entry fo. 238a). 'The king has 113 houses in his lordship and the king's barons have 112 from all of which the king has his tax . . . The custom of Warwick was that when the king went on an expedition by land 10 burgesses of Warwick went for all the others . . . but if the king went by sea, they sent him either 4 boatmen or £4 of pence'. List of tenants includes the Bp. of Worcester, Bp. of Chester, Abbot of Coventry, Bp. of Coutances, Count of Meulan. See Walker, B., 'Some Notes on Domesday Book (esp. Warwick Co.)', *Birm. Arch. Soc. Trans.*, vol 26 (1901).

WELLS: Welle (Somerset: Bp. of Wells fo. 89b).

WEST BROMWICH: Bromwic (Staffordshire: William Fitz Ansculf fo. 226b).

WESTMINSTER: Westmonasterium (Middlesex: St Peter's, Westminster fo. 128b). '25 houses of the Abbot's men-at-arms and other men who pay 8s. a year'.

WILTON: Wiltune (Wiltshire Customs: fo. 64c). 'The King has £50 from the borough of Wilton'. Burgesses of Wilton belong to Netheravon (5), Salisbury (7), Stratford Tony (1), Fifield Bayant (2), Sherrington (1), Castle Combe (1) and Odstock (1); also houses belonging to Dunford (4) and Marden (1).

Wigmore: Wigemore (Herefordshire: Ralf de Mortemer fo. 183c). 'Ralf de Mortemer holds Wigmore Castle; the borough there renders £7'.

WINCHESTER: *Note:* Winchester was separately surveyed in the two 12th century documents known as the 'Winton Domesday'; there is no account of the city in the earlier Domesday Survey, but several town-sites occur in other

(Wiltshire − continued) −
manors, including: Over Wallop, Cladford, Basingstoke, Faccombe by Netherton, West Meon, Mottisfont, Preston Candover, Corhampton, Headborne Worthy, Norton and Ashley in Milton.

Winchcombe: Wincelcumbe (Gloucestershire: King's lands fo. 126c); 'a borough with 29 burgesses'.

WINDSOR: Windesores (Berkshire: King's lands fo. 56d). 'There are 100 sites less 5 in the town; 26 of them are exempt from tribute and 30s. comes from the others.'

WISBECH: Wisbece (Cambridgeshire: Abbot of Ely fo. 192).

WOLVERHAMPTON: Hantone (Staffordshire: Canons of Wolverhampton fo. 247d).

WOODSTOCK: Wodestoche (Oxfordshire: King's lands fo. 154d).

WORCESTER: Wirescestre (Worcestershire: pre-entry fo. 172).

WORKSOP: Werchesope (Nottinghamshire: Roger de Bully fo. 285b).

WORTHING: Ordinges (Sussex: William de Braose fo. 28d).

YEOVIL: Givele (Somerset: Count of Mortain fo. 93c). 'To this manor have been added 22 plots of land (*masuræ*) which 22 men held jointly.'

YORK: Euruic (Yorkshire: pre-entry fo. 298). 'In the city . . . there were, as well as the shire of the Archbishop, 6 shires. One of these is spoiled for the castles [*VCH York, Note:* "The castles were destroyed in 1069; one is now the site of Clifford's Tower, the other a mound on Bayle Hill on the other side of the river"]. In 5 shires there were 1,418 inhabited dwellings (*mansiones hospitate*) . . . In these no-one else had custom, unless a burgess . . . Of all the above-mentioned dwellings, there are now inhabited in the hands of the king and rendering custom, 400 less 9 great and small, and 400 dwellings not regularly inhabited which render the better ones 1d. and the others less; and 540 dwellings so empty that they can render nothing at all. And foreigners (*Francigenæ*) hold 145 dwellings . . . The Count of Mortain has 14 dwellings there and 2 stalls in the Shambles (*duos bancos in macello*) . . . Nigel de Monneville has 1 dwelling, namely of a certain moneyer . . . Hamelin has 1 dwelling in the ditch of the city . . . the same William (de Percei) avows that he holds of Earl Hugh the church of St Cuthbert and 7 small dwellings containing 50 feet in breadth . . . T.R.E. the city was worth £35 to the king, now £100 by weight'. List of tenants of other houses.

CHAPTER FOUR

MEDIEVAL BOROUGH CHARTERS c. 1042-1500

THE KEYSTONE of a medieval borough's independence was its charter. Although this is by no means the only documentary evidence which reveals a borough's status, it is certainly the most explicit summary of the various privileges which a medieval township might enjoy. Many surviving charters have been extensively calendared, so that the origins of the most ancient boroughs on our base-list can be confirmed. The absence of a charter is not conclusive evidence of non-borough status; many records of petty seigneurial boroughs have undoubtedly been lost over the centuries. Some small towns may never have possessed written evidence of their claims, relying only upon oral evidence, folk-memory and the familiarity of custom. Thus, many quite important towns still claim their borough origins 'by prescription'. Confirmation of many charters can be traced in the great *Calendars* of the Chancery records, but this enrolment, too, may have been omitted by some seigneurs. A high proportion of our modern towns, nevertheless, do possess charter evidence of their medieval origins.

Once more the student is fortunate in access to many standard editions which will assist his search for a town's foundation. The massive collection and careful analysis of Ballard for the years 1042-1216 (published in 1913), of Ballard and Tait for the ensuing period from 1216-1307 (published in 1923) and Weinbaum's completion of this series for the centuries 1307-1660 (published in 1943), survey most available charter evidence which would otherwise have to be searched out from the many-volumed *Calendars* of the Public Record Office Rolls. More recently, Professors Beresford and Finberg published in 1973 an invaluable *Handlist of English Medieval Boroughs*, which not only collates the charter evidence of Ballard, Tait and Weinbaum, but also draws our attention to other indirect evidence of more than 400 boroughs for which charters are not available. This *Handlist*'s sources for the 9th to the 11th centuries, in Saxon charters, chronicles and Domesday Book, confirm a large number of references given in the Gazetteer to our previous Chapter. All these sources of information are drawn together in the Gazetteer at the end of this Chapter, giving references to those towns on our base-list which, by one means or another, can lay claim to medieval borough status.

Any effort to define at all precisely the specific features of 'burghality', particularly at an early stage, is almost as fraught with danger as it was in the pre-Conquest centuries; to seek a recognizable progression or hierarchy of such features is doubly dangerous. The most concise analysis of borough growth which has been recently published is that given by Colin Platt in *The Medieval English Town*.[1] In a chapter on 'The Borough Constitution', he traces development from the earliest concession of burgage tenure and grants of fee-farm to the ultimate recognition of corporate identity and occasional county-borough status in the 15th century.

The first concession made by king or overlord was the right of burgesses to own and dispose of their property by sale or hereditary bequest. Next came commutation of miscellaneous tolls and dues, which were replaced by a 'farm' or fixed payment by the whole borough, free from the financial demands of the sheriff. Other commercial advantages included the right to membership of a gild merchant or the recognition of a 'port-moot' with 'all liberties and free customs'. Ballard concluded that the only reliable indicators of full borough status were 'the application of burgage tenure to all tenements within its borders and the possession of a law court with jurisdiction over all the inhabitants of those tenements . . . Every borough had indeed a court and the court of the old royal boroughs was of pre-Conquest origin, parallel with the hundred court and not infrequently so called . . .'.[2] In those courts the burgesses benefited from a lower scale of *amercements* than was the case in manorial courts and courts baron. Moreton-in-the-Marsh (Gloucs) was ruled by a port-moot in 1273, with an officer entitled 'catchpole', and similar courts are found at Ormskirk (Lancs) in 1286, at Yeovil (Som) in 1305, and at Westbury (Wilts) in 1361. Sometimes the lord's concession was limited by conditions, or even subject to withdrawal. For instance, a 12th-century charter by King Stephen exempted the burgesses of Bury St Edmunds from all taxation — except when levied by the abbey: and at Newent (Gloucs) the Abbot of Cormeilles granted a borough court in 1298, but reserved a right of appeal from it to the parental manor-court. Ecclesiastical overlords often seem more reluctant than barons to relinquish liberties to their tenants. Of the two criteria used by Ballard, burgage tenure is still most generally accepted as a reliable test for the lowest common denominator of those rights which effectively separate a town from its neighbouring manor, lordship or county. Some grants of markets and fairs to smaller towns may imply the recognition of burgage tenure, even without the confirmation of a charter, but this is uncertain. Thirteenth-century tax rolls differentiate between chartered boroughs and *villæ mercatoriæ*, as well as between borough and vill; unfortunately these terms are frequently applied differently to the same place in successive years.

Another class of privileges gained by medieval burgesses was concerned with the legal identity of the borough. This was recognized by the grant of a common seal, the earliest of these belonging to Oxford in 1191. Next came the right to elect their own officials, 'capital portmen', bailiffs, coroners and reeves; Ipswich led the way from 1200, also providing an official roll which recorded the laws and free customs of the town. By 1215 only London had gained the right to elect a mayor, an office which did not become widespread before Nottingham was given that privilege in 1284. By 1368, however, even relatively small towns such as Queenborough on Sheppey might have the right to elect a mayor and two bailiffs. At an earlier stage other towns elected four coroners and two bailiffs; among the first to do so were Northampton (1189), Shrewsbury (1200), Lincoln (1194) and Gloucester (1200).

The expanding jurisdiction of the borough court was another aspect of increasing independence in the towns. The first extension of their rights was the privilege of 'return of writs' which once again excluded the sheriff, now from the legal as well as the fiscal business of the borough. The first exercise of this power was by Colchester and Canterbury, in 1252; it became widespread during the reign of Henry III. The ultimate stage of independence from shire and sheriff came with the creation of county boroughs which were elevated to the same status as counties in themselves with their own sheriff. The first of these was Bristol in 1373, made free from both Somerset and Gloucester almost exactly 600 years before 'Avon' existed. The grant by Edward III provided that Bristol 'should be a county by itself, to be called the county of Bristol in perpetuity . . .'. Other county boroughs were created in the 15th century; York in 1396, Newcastle-upon-Tyne in 1400, Norwich in 1404, Lincoln in 1409 and Scarborough in 1485. Such independence was in 1440 taken a step further by Hull with full incorporation, perpetual succession and the identity to sue and be sued as a borough, not as individual citizens: 'the town of the mayors and burgesses shall be a perpetually corporate commonalty of the town so incorporated under the name of the mayor and burgesses of that town . . .'.

The incorporated borough could maintain its existence by the right to purchase, own, and lease common property in the town's name, and could profit from business ventures on the town's behalf. At the same time the responsibilities and costs of town maintenance were also increasing: 'Stone defensive circuits, work on which was to begin at many towns from early in the 13th century, would prove a continual charge, considerably more expensive than the earlier ramparts, ditches, and palisades. The paving and proper drainage of the streets, scarcely an issue before the 14th century, would become the urgent concern of late medieval municipalities. There would be a gildhall to maintain, a weigh-house, prison and other buildings, municipal water supplies, wharves, cranes, quays, wash-houses and public lavatories'.[3]

Finally, the work of all this administration demanded the emergence of an increasing number of full-time salaried officers of town government, town clerks, recorders, chamberlains, sword-bearers, common sergeants and constables: 'There might be coroners, a recorder and town clerk with a host of lesser officials, some paid and some not, including the beadles, the ale-tasters, the sealers, searchers, weighers and keepers of the market, the ferrymen and porters, the clock-keepers and criers, the paviours, scavengers and other street-cleaners, the gate-keepers and watchmen of several ranks and kinds. A wealthy borough in the 15th century might keep two or three minstrels of its own and few would have been without a chaplain'.[4] Some of these officials would keep records and accounts of their activities. Thus many towns achieved their full medieval identity with some functions of what are recognisably the later municipal and county boroughs of our base-list. Of these 161 have surviving medieval charters; Beresford and Finberg's *Handlist* adds another 31 which, although without charters, record other documentary evidence of borough status. This comprises almost exactly half the towns on our list of surviving boroughs.

Fortunately for the student, Ballard and Tait have analysed each town's charter and tabulated all their liberties in separate categories. The eight main headings under which any one or more of a particular town's privileges may be indexed are as follows:

    i. *Formation of the Borough:* this section includes ratification of the customs of Domesday boroughs such as Barnstaple (1154–58), Cambridge (1201), Chichester (1135–54) etc. and many more: grants of other towns' customs to the chartered borough; confirmation by re-grant or *inspeximus* ('we have inspected' a previous charter); grant of *liber burgus* and further enlargement of the borough.

    ii. *Burgage tenure and other tenurial privileges:* including grant of burgages; liberty of sale; assessment of rents; and other rights.

iii. *Burgess franchise:* concerning freedom to marry; rights of widowhood; freedom of residence for a year and a day; and enfranchisement of serfs.

iv. *Jurisdictional privileges:* regarding courts and modes of trial; freedom from shire and hundred courts; the liberty to have a town prison and details of procecure, including the times and places for courts and scales of punishment. One clause in this category might give the power to make ordinances and agreements.

v. *Mercantile privileges:* particularly the grant and regulation of a market; grants of tolls with schedules; details of stalls and arrangements for restrictions on foreign merchants' goods. Separately listed here are also the details of grants of gilds, both gild merchant and later craft-gilds; special arrangements for Jews and foreigners; monopolies of inn-keeping and brewing, and a general monopoly of all trade to the burgesses and their gild.

vi. *Borough finances:* dealing with the *firma burgi*; the rights of lords and earls within the borough, and the grant of a court and its profits.

vii. *Borough officers:* listing those charter clauses which provided for election by the burgesses of sheriff, justiciar, reeves, coroners, mayor, stewards and other officials, each separately entered.

viii. *Public services:* including rare references to morals, public health and roads.

In Ballard and Tait's tables, not only these main sections, but also their sub-headings, of which only a few examples are given above, are itemised and numbered in full. In the Gazetteer at the end of this Chapter each town's charter is given, with the main sections identified for each document; further reference to the standard reference books will provide additional details of any town's grants and privileges under each heading. There will also be found full references to the original documentary or printed sources of each charter identified, so that a copy of the original can be found if required.

Worcester City, at this time still the largest of our three West Midland examples, provides typical examples of charter evidence. The 12th-century history of the city, as recorded by its own chronicler and others, is a narrative of disaster. The town was burned down four times in 80 years, so regularly that one chronicler records the city burning in 1131 'as often happened'. During the anarchy of Stephen's reign Worcester supported the King against the Empress his rival, coming into disastrous conflict with her supporters in neighbouring Gloucester who, in 1139, captured the city. 'A part of the city was burned, the whole was sacked, and many of the citizens were carried off for ransom, but no attempt was made to hold the place for the empress, and within a week it was re-occupied for the king by the Count of Meulan. In 1189 another fire destroyed the city.'[5]

Worcester's first royal charter was received in 1189 from Richard I in payment for support for his crusade, at the same time as many other towns. The city received its belated grant of the *firma burgi*, excluding the sheriff of Worcestershire, for a fixed payment of £24 a year directly to the royal Exchequer. The city's second royal charter granted by Henry III in 1227, which is illustrated on page 92, offered a wider range of liberties. This added to the farm of the borough (now increased to £30) the right to exclude the sheriff from 'any plea belonging to the city other than pleas of the Crown'. Equally important was the grant of a merchant gild so that no foreign merchant could trade within the city or its suburbs without the gild's consent. Next came the well-known 'year-and-a-day' clause which provided that any lord's villein who could maintain himself for that time as a member of the gild and 'at scot and lot' with the burgesses could claim his freedom. This was the traditional clause which caused men to say that 'town air makes a man free'. The final clauses of the 1227 charter deal with franchises and immunities from tolls, and exactions such as 'lastage, passage, pontage, stallage, levy, Danegeld and gaiwite' in all other towns of England 'saving the liberty of the city of London'. This charter was extended with a 'return of writs' clause in 1257 and confirmed in 1264.

The grant of a gild merchant is most important here as in so many other towns. Merchant gilds were a regular feature of charters between 1086 (Burford, Oxon), and 1303 (Newborough, Anglesea); during that period 71 towns listed by Ballard and Tait were granted merchant gilds. It is noticeable that most of those towns which were destined to survive, most of the county towns, Leicester, Derby, Hereford, Salisbury, Chester and others, had their gilds by an early date. There are only a few smaller towns which having once had the benefits of the gild lapsed into comparative obscurity in terms of lasting municipal status. These include Burford (Oxon: 1087–1103), Dunwich (Suffolk: 1200), Haverfordwest (Dyfed: 1219), Bridgnorth (Salop: 1227), Deganwy (Gwynedd: 1252), Builth (Powys: 1278), Criccieth (Gwynedd: 1284), Altrincham (Gtr Manchester: 1290) and Knutsford (Ches: 1292). The gild merchant was essentially a trading monopoly, as the charter to Worcester shows; membership gave favoured terms of trade and the exclusion of foreign competitors, with reduction of tolls and general preferential treatment. The gilds were powerful enough to be usually equivalent with the borough; the gild's aldermen were the same burgesses as the town's 'capital portmen' and reeves. The identity of borough and commerce are very close in this respect. Other aspects were more related to feudal protection.

About half the chartered boroughs listed by Ballard were seigneurial or *mesne* towns under the protection of a baron, prelate, or lesser feudal overlord. The element of protection of trade, religion and domestic life had been a strong feature of town growth since the 10th century, as in 1001 when Ethelred II granted the nuns of Shaftesbury a place that would be 'an impenetrable refuge from the barbarians' at Bradford-on-Avon in Wiltshire. Sometimes the seigneurial towns had once been royal boroughs, such as Chester or Salisbury, which the king himself had granted to a bishop or an earl. A lord might seek royal confirmation of his grants but this was not essential, so that some seigneurial boroughs may never have been chartered. Sometimes we learn indirectly of the license granted by a lord to make a free borough in one of his manors, or when the grant of free borough market or fair is given to the lord by the king, on behalf of the town.

As is often the case in grants by the crown, a group of boroughs in the same feudal honour might share the privileges of an earlier creation by the same lord. Maurice Paynel in 1207 granted to the burgesses of Leeds all the customs of Pontefract, where in 1194 Roger de Lacy had previously given the liberties and free customs of the king's burgesses of Grimsby. Other seigneurial grantors include William de Berkeley, who granted the customs of Breteuil to Tetbury, c. 1200 and Joan de Berkeley, who granted the customs of Tetbury to Wotton-under-Edge in 1253; this 'chain-effect' is not unusual. Beverley was granted the liberties of York by one archbishop in 1130 and Brough-on-Humber received the liberties of Beverley from another archbishop in 1239. The customs of London and Winchester, usually paired, were more often royal

grants; to Gloucester by Henry II in 1155, to Taunton by Stephen in 1135–39, to
Wilton by Henry I in 1129–35 and to Marlborough by King John in 1204. In some
cases a seigneurial grant was changed; John, Count of Mortain, gave Lancaster the
rights of Bristol in 1193 (these were based on the rights of Dublin in 1711), but King
John substituted those of Northampton in 1199. We know very little of the medieval
borough of Birmingham, our second Midland town, except that, in about 1280 a
burgage in Solihull was to be held freely 'according to the customs of Birmingham'.
Ballard and Tait indicate by a sub-category (No. 8) all those towns which, under their
main section (i), received another borough's customs at their foundation. These are
marked with an asterisk (i*) in the Gazetteer to this Chapter.

Dudley, our other West Midlands model, is a good example of a seigneurial borough
of some importance. Overlooked by the castle of the Domesday tenant, William Fitz-
Ansculf, son of Ansculf of Picquigny, the manor passed by marriage to the Pagenals.
Gervase Pagenal's castle was demolished by Henry II as a penalty for his support of
Prince Henry's rebellion in 1173–74. At that time Gervase's barony included 55
knights' fees subinfeudated to his tenants. It is an indication of the relative importance
of both Dudley and Worcester City that in the previous generation Gervase's father,
Ralf, had held his castle for the Empress Maud against Stephen's attack at the same
time that Worcester was sacked by the Empress's supporters. Gervase had given the
two parish churches of Dudley, the castle church which was an early dedication to St
Edmund, the Saxon martyr-king (d. 870) and the later 'town' church of St Thomas
to the Cluniac priory which he founded at the foot of the castle hill. There are other
examples of boroughs, such as Devizes in Wiltshire, with two churches marking the
seigneurial and burghal bounds of the medieval town.

A distinctive feature of most medieval boroughs is the characteristic shape and
uniform size of the burgage tenements which line the High Street. Similar at first to
the manorial crofts and tofts of any medieval vill the earliest tenements are unmis-
takably the ploughland strips of an agrarian settlement. They have the flattened,
elongated 'S' bend of the medieval open-field furlongs, lined along the street with
house or shop on a narrow street frontage. In many modern market towns such as
Burford or Chipping Campden in Oxfordshire, they provide long secluded gardens at
the back of every house; in busier towns the crofts have been over-built with outbuildings and back-to-back shops. The oldest croft is usually an acre or half-acre
strip; at Charmouth in Dorset the Abbot of Ford's charter of 1320 provided burgage
plots measuring 20 perches (110 yards) long, and 4 perches (22 yards) wide at an
annual rent of 6d.

Dudley's tenements are no exception, except that their size is small. Their shape is
unmistakable and the present-day alley-ways between Boots and Marks and Spencers
follow the recognizable curving gait of the medieval oxen-team (see illustration
p. 87). The burgage plots appear to have been laid out in two main blocks of about
eight acres each on each side of the market street, with St Edmund's church occupying
the top north-east quadrant. There has been some considerable subdivision of the
original plots, particularly at the backs and along intersecting streets. The length of
each block (that is, its depth from the road) is as in so many other cases still almost
exactly 110 feet (later road-widening will account for a few lost feet on every
boundary). The frontage of each of the blocks is a remarkably uniform 570 feet
which is today as equally divided into 28–30 modern frontages. (More recent crossing

Dudley in 1936

(From the O.S. Survey of 1936, actual scale.)

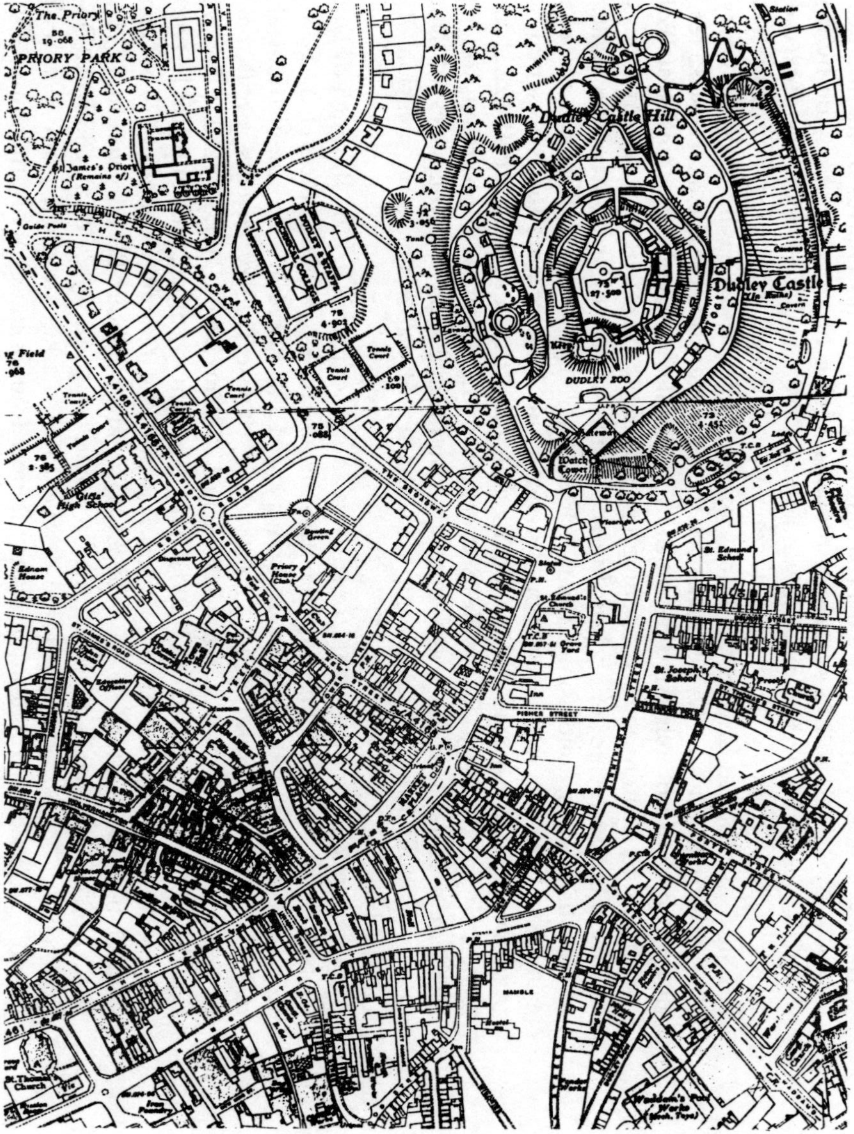

Medieval Dudley

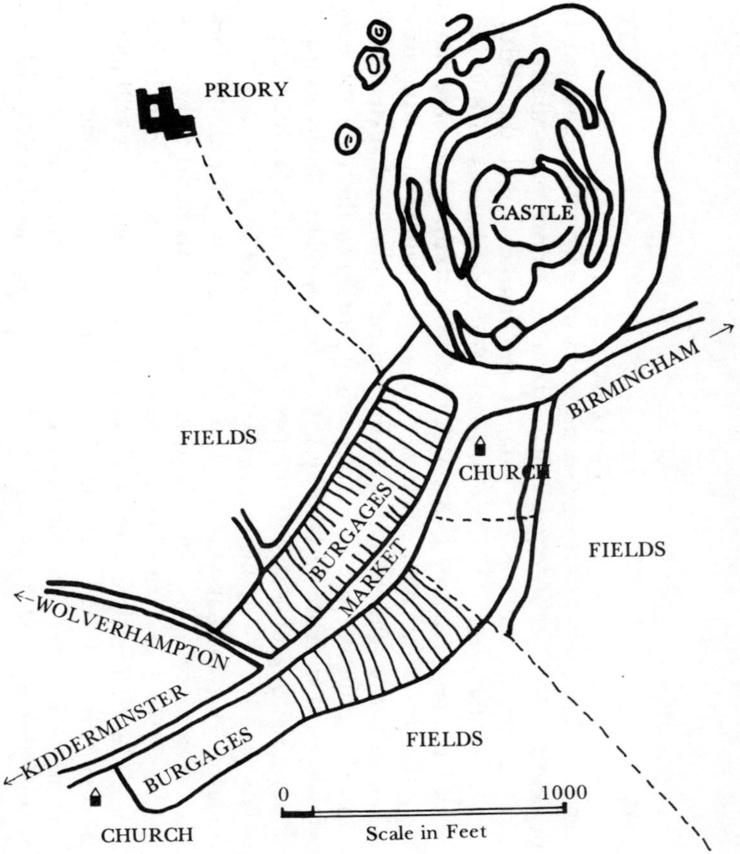

CASTLE

BIRMINGHAM

CHURCH

FIELDS

PRIORY

FIELDS

BURGAGES

MARKET

FIELDS

WOLVERHAMPTON

KIDDERMINSTER

BURGAGES

CHURCH

1000

Scale in Feet

0

(Author's reconstruction).

streets may have taken out one or more of the original tenements.) There seems to be a perceptible 21-foot integral unit of frontage, more particularly to the east of the market cross; on the western side of the market street the width of each strip is smaller, usually about 11–15 feet. In spite of the changes of 800 years of building, a medieval burgage tenement of an original one-sixth of an acre can still be detected. Only later, in those 'planted towns' where the common, waste, or even arable land, was laid out to a grid pattern was this typically manorial system likely to be squared off into more regular sub-divided building plots. For the 12th and early 13th centuries there was land to spare in Dudley for extension of building towards the 'top church' and along the outgoing streets such as Smythelane, now Wolverhampton Street, and in the Foreign. By 1314, however, the central sites were already being subdivided by speculators, for in that year we learn of a grant by John de Somery to one Richard Russell of a piece of land in the town 'on which to build a shop between the land of Matthew Russell and the land of Alan Phillips, extending in length 40 feet and in width 20 feet'. This is a very small fraction of an acre, but still preserves the 20-foot frontage. This could well be one of the shops lining a crossing street to a depth of two of the original 'strips'; the medieval foundations of many towns are very long-standing. An Enclosure Act of 1784 still referred to 'burgage houses within the Borough of Dudley'.

Dudley is also a typical seigneurial borough in that no charter of its liberties has survived, though there is a somewhat dubious 17th century copy of a grant by Roger, son of Roger de Somery, supposedly made in 1218. As J. S. Roper, has observed: 'it seems highly probable that Roger conceived the idea of laying out Dudley as a borough, granting to his tenants among other privileges, a measure of control over the number of burgesses to be permitted in the growing town'.[6] The alleged charter also gave freedom from tolls to the burgesses of Dudley in the market towns of Wolverhampton and Birmingham; it is sometimes difficult to calculate how any one town found its borough 'monopoly' profitable when so many other towns were made free of its tolls in their concessions. Charter apart, there is adequate indirect or non-charter evidence of the status of the town. Beresford and Finberg note the representation of the town as 'borough, vill and manor' by a jury of its own at the Eyre of 1221, and an agreement in 1261 by Roger de Somery that the Dean of Wolverhampton might establish a market in his town made it conditional that the burgesses of Dudley be free of tolls there. (Wolverhampton's charter of 1263 makes no mention of this concession.)

More explicit are the extents, or surveys and descriptions, of the Borough of Dudley to be found in the *Inquisitiones post mortem* of Roger de Somery I in 1273, of Roger II in 1291 and of John de Somery in 1322; there are also inquisitions at the death of important sub-tenants in the town.[7] These Dudley extents reveal that the burgesses' annual rents were £5 15s. 5d. in 1273 and £6 0s. 10d. in 1291. (This would represent at least 120 burgesses at 1s. rent per annum, more, indeed possibly twice or three times as many if the rent were less and the tenements smaller.) This can be compared with Bradford (Yorks) at £1 17s. 6d. for about 29 burgages in 1311, and Somerton, now a small market town in Somerset at £6 14s. 0d. in 1330. At Dudley between 1273 and 1294 the value of the town market dropped from 40s. to 20s., possibly because of competition from the new foundation at Wolverhampton. On the one hand, there were still villein tenants in the town at the end of the 13th century and Philip Burnell's main holding was 48 acres of arable land with certain meadow and pasture lands. At the same time 'mines of sea-coal and iron', with 'two great smithies' are also recorded, forecasting this Black Country town's industrial future. On the mercantile side a grant to John Somery in 1315 mentions 'pavage upon all wares brought for sale into the town of Dudley for a period of five years'.

Beresford and Finberg identify more than 40 boroughs for which Ballard and Tait list no charters, by means of extents and inquisitions. These occur mostly in the 14th century and, except for Penzance in 1327, relate to smaller boroughs which did not achieve the lasting borough status of our base-list. These include, for example, Fenny Stratford (Bucks) 1370, and Westbury (1361) in Wiltshire. These were mostly seigneurial boroughs.

Another means of identifying boroughs for which no charters survive is their appearance on taxation or 'subsidy' rolls with a higher rating than the 'vills'. Boroughs paid a higher proportion, one-tenth of their taxable wealth, whereas vills paid one-fifteenth. 'The greater fraction of wealth paid by the boroughs was a recognition not only of the wealthiness but of the indebtedness of the traders and craftsmen within them to the Crown for providing order and good government.'[8] What the lords gave they could also take away; ecclesiastical landlords could be particularly obstructive to their burgage tenants. At Bury St Edmunds the abbot abolished the gild merchant and there were similar disputes between abbot and burgesses at Tavistock. At Coventry the burgesses hired a wizard to rid them of an oppressive prior by spells and curses and at Cirencester the abbot enlisted the support of the Court of Chancery to suppress 'any borough, its court of customs'. In some places the lord's steward was even more difficult to exclude from a seigneurial or ecclesiastical borough than was the sheriff from a royal town.

Drawing particularly upon J. F. Willard's identification of 'taxation boroughs', we can identify in the *Subsidy Rolls* from 1294 to 1307 several more of our longer-standing boroughs, such as Old Windsor, Aylesbury, and Warwick.[9] Amongst these we find our other West Midlands example, Birmingham; we have little other evidence of the town's borough status other than their taxation rating in 1306–7. Other boroughs which did not survive, though taxed as such at the turn of the 13th century includes Leighton Buzzard, Watchet, Cricklade and Boroughbridge. Some of these, like Watchet and Cricklade can be recognized as ancient *burhs* of long standing in Saxon history, yet already their medieval importance was declining.

About a quarter of the chartered boroughs were ecclesiastical foundations, especially in Durham and Hertfordshire. It is evident that the towns of Berkshire, Dorset, Huntingdonshire and Lincolnshire on the other hand, were predominantly royal creations; those in Buckinghamshire, Devonshire and the West Riding were more usually of seigneurial origin. Beresford and Finberg tabulate the relative density of boroughs in each county, demonstrating that the highest incidence of town growth occurred in Devon, Gloucestershire, Huntingdon and Cornwall. The counties least propitious to burghal development were Cambridgeshire and Norfolk. There is however an inevitable correlation of acknowledged burghal history with the present availability of original and printed sources: 'if history is forced to rely on a small number of sources, there will be particular problems where those sources are defective'.[10]

From the 13th century onward we can trace the physical growth of successful borough developments in terms of their expansion into new areas around the town centre. Usually the original borough, as at Dudley, huddling for protection, both market and priory, at the castle gate, will extend itself into 'foreigns', outlying streets and suburbs, sometimes extending beyond earlier walls, across a bridge, on to a well-drained river terrace or newly-drained marshland. Sometimes, as at Salisbury, Launceston and Bridgnorth, the burgesses moved to an entirely new site. Elsewhere, expansion creates a pattern of streets which can be seen as successive phases of growth.

In some boroughs extensions went on piecemeal, street by street. At Burton-on-Trent the abbot created the first borough towards the end of the 12th century 'that is, the vill and the new street'. Successive abbots extended borough status street by street and in 1214 Abbot William made a 'new' borough from the Great Bridge to the New Bridge. These extensions were continuing at Burton from 1281 to 1305. At Wimborne Minster in Dorset the town consisted in 1362 of two streets named 'East Borough' and 'West Borough'. It is not unusual to find a 'New Borough' in an old town, as for instance at New Kington in Herefordshire in 1267, or with the old and new boroughs of Durham and Elvet, the latter one mile south-west of the cathedral. We may recollect that some 'New Boroughs' were already as old as Domesday; others such as Buckingham (914) were even older. Baschurch in Shropshire was *Novus Burgus* in 1227 and again *Nova Villa* in 1339. The entire picture reflects continuous growth based on the incentive of profits to be made from new ventures in trade. Overlords advertised their intentions of making a new town profitable. In 1150–59 Robert de Ferrers, Earl of Derby, expressed his intention of making Tutbury grow even further than it had under his father and in 1169 John, Bishop of Worcester, offered burgages at Stratford-on-Avon to any who would come and occupy them.

In most large medieval towns at least three main phases of extension can be traced on a large-scale map, though it may well be as many as seven stages, as at Ludlow. Often the undesirable 'noxious' trades such as tanning and the fire-hazards like forges and kilns were relegated, at first to a separate 'east-end' annexe of the main town, possibly, as at Bristol, over the bridge. As the town grew these were encompassed by new bounds or walls. Sometimes new growth was planned and drafted *en bloc* for 'new towns' where a lord or king would advertize the availability of building plots and market sites with protection of trade guaranteed and the added inducements of preferential treatment for burgesses, trading monopolies, advantageous tolls, lower rents, and less stringent fines in the local courts to those who would take up residence and business in his town. These are the origins, particularly from c. 1290, of the more than 200 'Newports', 'Newburghs', 'Newcastles' and 'Newburys' which any modern atlas will index. These planned towns are fully documented and listed with examples of their street-plans in Beresford's *New Towns of the Middle Ages*.[11]

At the height of the Middle Ages there was little that we would recognize today as 'local government'; there seemed to be little need of the many functions which are so expensive and essential today. The manor was a going concern as yet, but it was an economic unit rather than a department of local government. The functions of the parish and various constables, guardians and wardens were yet to emerge; the administrative role of the county, except as shire and hundred court with the sheriff and his agents exercising a general supervision of geld and subsidy, was part of an even more distant future. Administration, such as it was, was still basically feudal, managed by the stewards and bailiffs of the local overlords and reviewed at their courts baron and courts leet.

Standing out from this general picture is the exceptional nature of town governance; here we see a situation that is organized with responsible officers and recognizable functions. Town government was already local government as we have seen it for centuries before the Municipal Acts. It was, as we have seen, the outcome in nearly 200 of our modern townships of a process of continuous growth, if not from the Roman *civitas*, then certainly from the Saxon *burh* and the Domesday borough. Its main, essential, feature was that of independence, of overlord, steward and sheriff. The 'county borough' in particular was the first effective method of local government in England and certainly the most historically well-grounded.

FURTHER READING

For reference to the original sources and charters:

Ballard, A., *British Borough Charters 1042–1216* (1913).
—— and Tait, J., *British Borough Charters 1216–1307* (1923).
—— 'The English Borough in the Reign of John' *Eng. Hist. Rev.*, xiv (1899).
Bateson, M., 'The Laws of Breteuil', *Eng. Hist. Rev.*, xv (1900); xvi (1901).
—— 'Borough Customs', in *Selden Soc.*, xviii (1904); xxi (1906).
Beresford, M. W., *New Towns of the Middle Ages* (1967).
—— and Finberg, H. P. R., *English Medieval Boroughs, a Handlist* (1973).
Griffiths, R. A. (ed.), *Boroughs of Medieval Wales* (1978).
Martin, G. H., 'The English Borough in the thirteenth century', *Trans. Roy. Soc.*, 5th series, xiii (1963), and 'The origins of borough records', *Jnl Soc. Arch.*, ii (1960-64).
Weinbaum, M., *British Borough Charters 1307–1660* (1943).

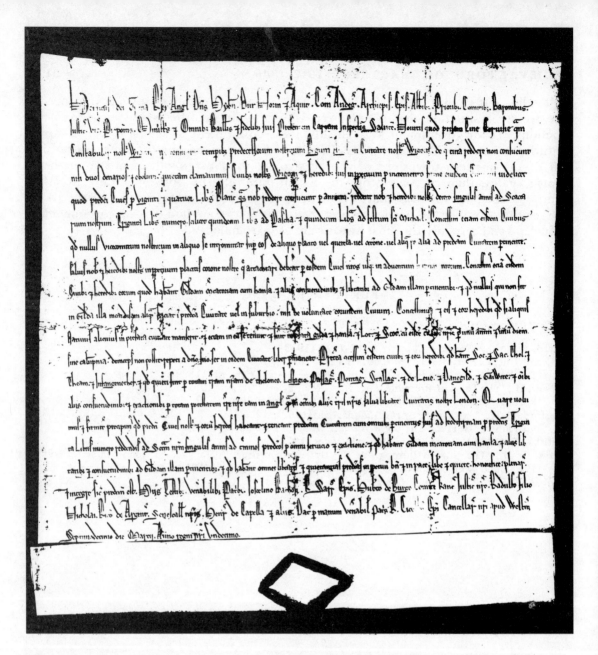

Henry III's charter to the city of Worcester, 1227, from the Superintendent Registrar's Office at the Guildhall in Worcester. Actual size: 12¼ inches square.

Extract from the *Victoria History of Worcestershire*, Vol. IV, p. 381, reproduced by permission of the General Editor. See footnote 49: VCH footnotes are an essential guide towards original sources.

It is to Henry III that Worcester owes its first detailed grant of chartered liberties.[49] In 1227, on 17 March, the king issued a charter, still preserved by the corporation, though ignored by most historians of Worcester, in which the essential privileges enjoyed by the borough in the later middle ages are explicitly conveyed. The charter opens by asserting that the royal constables, in whom we must recognize the hereditary castellans of Worcester, had been accustomed to exact from the town, apparently yearly, a tun of beer, rendering therefrom to the king only $2\frac{1}{2}d$. This demand was remitted to the town for the future, but its *firma* was simultaneously raised from £24 in assayed money to £30 by tale, to be paid at the Exchequer in two equal portions at Easter and Michaelmas respectively. For the future the fee-farm rent of Worcester was fixed at £30.[50] In the second place, it was granted that no sheriff for the future should intervene in any plea belonging to the city, saving pleas of the Crown, which ought to be attached by the citizens pending the arrival of the king's justices. The third clause of the charter is of greater interest; by it the king granted that the citizens should have a merchant gild, with a hanse and all proper liberties, and that no one outside the gild should make any merchandise within the city or its suburb without the citizens' consent.

12TH-CENTURY SEAL OF THE CITIZENS OF WORCESTER

[49] *Cal. Chart. R.* 1226-57, p. 23. Original in the archives of the corporation.

[50] The fee farm was frequently granted out by the Crown and formed part of the dower of many of the Queens of England (*Rot. Lit. Claus.* [Rec. Com.], i, 453; *Cal. Chart. R.* 1226-57, p. 218; *Cal.*

Extract from *Calendar of Charter Rolls 1226-57*, page 23, as cited in VCH footnote 49, above:

(1227)

March 17.
Westminster.
146.

Quitclaim to the citizens of Worcester, and their heirs, of the prise of the vat (*tina*) of ale, which the king's constables of Worcester were wont to take, paying thereof to the king only $2\frac{1}{2}d$. on each vat, in consideration of an increase of the farm of the city from 24*l*. blanch to 30*l*. tale, payable half at Easter and half at Michaelmas: grant also to the same that no sheriff shall hereafter meddle with them for any plea, plaint, or occasion or other matter pertaining to the said city, saving to the king the pleas of the crown, which shall be attached by the citizens until the coming of the king's justices; and the said citizens shall have their merchant gild with a hanse and other customs of the said gild, and none who are not of that gild shall do any merchandise in the said city or suburb, save at the will of the said citizens; moreover if any man's bondman shall abide in the said city and maintain himself there, and be in the said gild and hanse and lot and scot with the said citizens for a year and a day without being claimed, he shall not thereafter be reclaimed by his lord, but shall remain free in the said city; and the citizens shall have sac and soc, tol and theam, infangthef, and be quit through all the king's land, both in England and elsewhere, of toll, lastage, passage, pontage, stallage, and of lene and danegeld and gaywite and all other customs, saving the liberties of the city of London.

The above is a photograph of John de Somery's grant of the site for a shop to Richard Russell of Dudley in 1314. The original is in Dudley Public Library's archives. There is no available transcription of the Latin, the student is left to his own devices, to find that the document reads:

1. 'Sciant p(re)sentes & futurii q(uo)d ego Jo(hann)es de Som(er)y d(omi)n(u)s de Duddel' dedi (con)cessi & hac p(re)senti carta mea

2. (con)firmavi Ric(ard)o fil' Agnet(is) Ruscel de Duddeleg' pro quad' s(er)vic' pecunie quam m' dedit p(ro)manibus unam

3. placea(m)t(er)ra(e) cu(m) p(er)tinencs in Duddel' ad qua(dam) celda(m) si' edificanda(m) q qde(m) placea t(er)r(ae) scita est int(er)t(er)ra(m)

4. Mathei Ruscel & t(er)ra(m) Alani fil' Ph(illip)i. Et (con)tinet in Longitudi(n)e q(uat)tuordeci(m) pedes & in Latitudine

5. duodeci(m) pedes H(abe)nda(m) & tenenda(m) p(re)d(ict)a(m)plac' t(er)r(ae) cu(m) p(er)tinent' de me & h(er)edibus meiis p(re)d(ict)o Ric(ard)o

6. & h(er)edibus suis Lib(er)e q'ete jur' & h(er)editar' imp(er)petuu(m) cu(m) om(ni)bus Lib(er)tatibus & aysiament' ad P(re)d(ic)tam pla

7. ceam t(er)r(ae) in villa de Duddel' et ext(ra) p(er)tinentibus Reddendo inde annuati(m) m' et h(er)edibus meiis du . . . [damaged]

8. solidos argenti ad duos anni t(erm)i(n)os in villa de Duddel' (con)stientos p(ro) om(n)ibus Et ego vero p(re)dict' Johe . . . [damaged]

9. de Som(er)y & h(er)edes mei' p(re)d(ic)tam placea(m) t(er)r(ae) cum p(er)tinent's p(re)d(ic)to Ric(ard)o & h(er)edibus suis contra o(m)nes mortales

10. p(ro) p(re)d(ic)to s(er)vicio inp(er)petuu(m) Warantizabim(us) acquetabimus & defendem(us) In cui'(us) rei testi(m)oniu(m) huic presenti

11. carte sigillu(m) meu(m) apposui. Hiis testibus Will(elm)o Frebody Will(el)mo de Wytemor

Joh(ann)e de Mere Ric(ard)o
12. Lonckyn Elya P(er)kyn & aliis. Dat' apud Duddeleg' die Lune p(ro)xi(m)a post f(est)u(m) Asscenc(i)onis d(omi)ni Anno
13. Regni Reg(is) Edwardi fil' Reg(is) Edwardi septi(m)o

Note: The description of Russell's shop as a 'celda' or selda', a stall; the seventh year of Edward II's reign was 8th July 1313-7th July 1314.

TRANSLATION

The student can turn to a convenient translation of this document, given in *Dudley, the Medieval Town* by J. S. Roper, published by the County Borough of Dudley's Libraries Department, Transcript No: 8 (1962). The translation is printed as footnote 81, on page 24 and reads as follows:

'Know all persons present and future that I John de Somery Lord of Duddeley have given granted and by these present writings confirm to Richard son of Agnes Russell of Duddeley in return for certain services, all that piece of land with its appurtenances in Duddeley on which to build a shop (erect a stall) between the land of Matthew Russell and the land of Alan Phillips extending in length 40 feet and in width 20 feet; to have and to hold the aforesaid piece of land from me and my heirs to the aforesaid Richard and his heirs for ever, paying annually to me and my heirs (two) silver shillings. And I the said John de Somery and my heirs warrant the said piece of land with its appurtenances to the said Richard and his heirs against all people. In witness whereof I have placed my seal. Witnessed by William Frebody, William de Wytmor, John de Mere, Richard Lonckyn, Elias Perkyn and others. Dated at Dudley on Monday next after Ascension in the Seventh year of the reign of Edward son of King Edward (1314)'.

From the Archives and Local History Department of Dudley Public Libraries. Dudley Estate Archives Box 18; bundle 11. Actual size of original: 8½ inches x 4 inches (enlarged here).

GAZETTEER OF MEDIEVAL BOROUGHS:
CHARTERS AND OTHER EVIDENCE

The following handlist refers to 194 of our base-list of 375 English and Welsh towns which have reasonably explicit records of their status as boroughs during the Middle Ages. Towns for which a medieval charter survives are listed in **BOLD CAPITALS** (e.g.: **WORCESTER**). The date of each charter for the town is given first, then its grantor. Dates of charters given *in italics* indicate the confirmation of an earlier charter by re-grant or *inspeximus*. In each entry reference is then made to the numbers of the main categories of liberties granted to each town, as tabulated by Ballard and Tait (see pp. 83-4 above). These are given in small Roman numerals i-viii, with references to Ballard's *British Borough Charters 1042-1216* as B, to Ballard and Tait's *British Borough Charters 1216-1307* as BT and to Weinbaum's *British Borough Charters 1307-1660* as Wbm. BMW refers to Griffiths, R. A. (ed.), *Boroughs of Medieval Wales* (1978). Towns for which no charter has survived, but for which other evidence has been cited by Beresford and Finburg in *English Medieval Boroughs, A Handlist*, are listed in lower-case print (e.g.: Dudley) with the date of the evidence and the reference EMB. Identification of any town by Beresford in *New Towns of the Middle Ages* is indicated by the reference as NT. References to Ballard and Tait's Section i (formation of a borough) which are asterisked thus: i* were granted the privileges of another borough at their foundation; those similarly asterisked under Mercantile Privileges, as v* were granted the rights of a gild merchant in that charter (see Chapter Five). Names of towns in parentheses and printed in lower-case after the listed name of the borough (e.g.: **BARNSTAPLE**: (London)) indicates Gross's attribution of 'parent status' to the town in brackets in his *Gild Merchant* (Appendix E pp. 243-281). This means that the newer town was granted the privileges, or some of the customs, of the earlier town. Note how some towns benefit from a chain of 'mother-towns' (e.g.: **LEEDS**: (Pontefract–Grimsby–Northampton–London). Some towns (e.g.: **BATH** (London: Winchester)) claimed parentage from more than one town. Gross also lists (pp. 244-253) the documentary sources of each affiliation. Key to Ballard and Tait's Tabulation of Charter Privileges: (main headings, see further sub-divisions given there); i. Formation of borough; ii. Tenurial privileges; iii. Burgess franchise; iv. Jurisdictional privileges; v. Mercantile privileges; vi. Borough finances; vii. Borough officers.

ABERYSWYTH (Montgomery–Hereford); 1277: Edward I: i*, ii, iii, iv, v*. BT: NT, BMW.

ABINGDON: 1327: Abbot of Abingdon: vii (later revoked) EMB.

ANDOVER (Winchester): 1175: Henry II; v*. B:EMB; 1201: John vi. B; 1205: John: v*; vi. B:EMB; 1213; John: vi. B: 1228: Henry III: i. BT; Collier, C. and Clutterbuck, R. H.: *Archives of Andover* (2 vols., n.d.), vol. 2.

APPLEBY (York): 1179: Henry II EMB; 1181: i*, B; 1200: John: i*, v, vi: B:EMB; 1232: Henry III: i. BT; 1286: Edward I; i, vi. BT.

Arundel: (1248) EMB.

Aylesbury: (1227, 1307-32), EMB; Hollis, E.: 'The original charter of Aylesbury', *Archit. & Arch. Soc. for County of Bucks.*, vol. 11 (1926).

Banbury: (1163, 1166, 1247, 1296), EMB.

BARNSTAPLE (London): 1154: Henry II: i. B; 1200: John: i. B; 1237: Henry III: i, BT; 1272: Edward I: i. BT:EMB; Chanter, J. R.: 'Barnstaple Records', *North Devon Journal* (newspaper) (Jan.–May 1879-81); and Chanter, J. R. and Wainwright, T.: *Barnstaple Records*, 2 vols. (Barnstaple 1900).

BASINGSTOKE: 1228: Henry II: vi. BT:EMB; 1256: Henry III: ii, iv, v. BT.

BATH (London: Winchester) 1189: Richard I: i. B; 1246: Henry III: i, v. BT; 1256; Henry

(Bath — continued) —
III: i, ii, iv, vii. BT; 1275: Edward I: v. BT; 1500: inc. Wbm: EMB; King, A. J., and Watts, B. H.: *Municipal Records of Bath 1189-1604* (London 1885).

BEDFORD: 1166: Henry II: i. B:EMB; 1189: Richard I, i, ii, iv, v*. B; 1227: Henry II: i, vi. BT; *Schedule of the Records of the Corporation of Bedford* (Bedford, 1883).

Berwick: (1302) EMB.

BEVERLEY (London: York): 1115-28: Thurstan Archbishop of York: i*, ii, v*. B:EMB; 1124-35: Henry I; i*, v. B; 1154: Archbishop William: i*, ii, v*. B; 1181-5: Pope Lucius: i. B; 1182: Henry II: i*. B; 1200: John: i*. B; *1230:* Henry III: i. BT; *1237:* Henry III: i. BT; *1307:* Edward I: i. BT; Leach, A. F.: 'Beverley Town Documents', *Selden Soc.* 14 (1900).

BEWDLEY: 1472: Edward IV: i. EMB.

BIDEFORD (Bristol); 1204-17: Richard de Grenville: i*, ii, iv, v, vi, vii. B.EMB.

Birmingham: (1306 onward) EMB; c. 1280. See **SOLIHULL**; 'according to the customs of Birmingham' EMB.

BLANDFORD: (1244. 1272-1307, 1306) EMB; 1605: inc. Wbm:EMB.

BODMIN: 1225-57: Richard, Earl of Cornwall: ii, iii, iv, v*. BT:EMB.

BOLTON: 1253: William de Ferrers: i, ii, iv, v, vii. BT:EMB; Bateson, M.: 'The creation of boroughs', *Eng. Hist. Rev.* xvii (1902).
BOSTON (Winchester): (1279–85) EMB; 1545: inc. Wbm:EMB.
Bradford: (1311, 1327) EMB.
BRECON: 1270: Humphrey de Bohun: i, BT; 1277–82: Humphrey de Bohun: iii, iv, v*, vi. BT:BMW.
BRIDGWATER: 1200: John: i, iii. B:EMB; Dilks, T. B.: 'Bridgwater Borough Archives 1200–1468', *Somerset Record Soc.*. vol. 48 (1933), vol. 53 (1938), vol. 58 (1945), vol. 60 (1948).
BRIDPORT: 1253: Henry III: i, vi, vii. BT.
BRISTOL: (London): 1164: Henry II: v. B; 1171: i*, ii, B; 1185: John Count of Mortain: ii, B; *1227:* Henry III: i. BT; 1230: Henry III: vi. BT; 1252: Henry III: i, ii, iv, vi. BT; 1256: Henry III: i, ii, iv, vii. BT; 1300: Edward I: i, vii. BT; 1373: Ii: EMB; Harding, N. D.: 'Bristol Charters 1155–1373' *Bristol Record Soc. Pubns.*, i (1930); Cronne, H. A.: 'Bristol Charters 1378–1499', *Bristol Record Soc. Pubns.*, xi (1946); Seyer, S.: *Charters and Letters Patent granted by the Kings of England to the City of Bristol* (Bristol 1812). Veale, E. W. W.: 'The Great Red Book of Bristol', *Bristol Record Soc.*, vols. 2, 8, 16, 18 (1932–53); Bickley, F. B.: *Little Red Book of Bristol* (2 vols., Bristol 1900).
BURTON-ON-TRENT: 1197–1213: Abbot William: i, ii. B:EMB; 1273: Abbot John: ii. BT; 1286: Abbot Thomas: ii, iv. BT; Black, W. H.: 'Ancient Charters relating to the Abbey and Town of Burton-on-Trent', *British Arch. Assn. Jnl.*, vol. 7 (1852).
BURY ST EDMUNDS: 1102–3: Henry I: i, iv, v. B:EMB; 1135–54: Stephen: ii. B:EMB; 1121–38: Abbot Anselm: i, ii, iii, iv. B; 1182–1212: Abbot Samson: i, ii, iii, iv. B; 1256: Henry III: iv. BT; 1281: Edward I: i. BT; Lobel, M. D.: *The Borough of Bury St Edmunds* (Oxford 1935).
CAERNARVON (Hereford): 1284: Edward I: i, ii, iii, iv, v*, vii. BT; 1306: Edward, Prince of Wales: i. BT:NT. BMW.
Calne: (1194 and c. 1306 onward). EMB.
CAMBRIDGE: 1120–31: Henry I: iv, v. B:EMB; 1185: Henry II: vi. B:EMB; 1201: John: i, ii, iv, v*. B; 1207: John: vi, vii. B; 1227: Henry III: i, v. BT; 1256: Henry III: iv, vii. BT; 1280: Edward I: i. BT; Maitland, F.W. and Bateson, M.: *Charters of the Borough of Cambridge* (Cambridge 1901); Palmer, W. M.: *Cambridge Borough Documents* (Cambridge 1931); Bateson, M.: 'The origin of the Borough of Cambridge', *Camb. Ant. Soc. Communications*, xxxv (1935).
CANTERBURY (London): 1104: Henry I: iii. B; 1234: Henry III: vi, vii. BT; 1252: Henry III: iv. BT; *1256:* Henry III: i, iv, v. BT; (1294) EMB; 'Civis' (Bunce, C. R.):

(Canterbury – continued) –
Translation of the Charters etc. granted to the Citizens of Canterbury (Edward IV–Charles II) (Canterbury 1791).
CARDIFF (Hereford): 1147–83: William and Robert, Earls of Gloucester: i, ii, iii, iv, v. B:BMW.
CARDIGAN (Newborough-Rhuddlan): 1199: John: v. B; 1230: Henry III; v. BT; 1249: Henry III: v*, vi. BT; 1284: Edward I: i*, ii, iv, v, vii. BT.
CARLISLE (Bristol): (1130) EMB: 1154–89: Henry II; ii, v*. B: 1221: Henry III: vi. BT; 1231: Henry III: vi. BT: 1234: Henry II: ii, vi. BT; 1251: Henry III: i. BT; 1285: Edward I: i. BT; Ferguson, R. S. 'Royal Charters of the City of Carlisle'; *Cumb. & Westm. Ant. Arch. Soc.* (1894).
CARMARTHEN: 1154–89: Henry II; v. B; 1201; John: v, B; *1227:* Henry III: i. BT; 1254–7: Edward, son of Henry III: i, ii, iv, v. BT; *1257:* Henry III: i. BT: 1285: Edward I: ii, BT: BMW.
CHARD: 1234–5: Bp. Jocelin of Bath and Wells: i, ii, iv, v. BT:EMB; 1271–2: Bp. William II: ii, iv, v. BT; *1280:* Bp. Robert Burnell: i. BT: 1286: Edward I: i. BT.
CHELMSFORD: (1200 and 1382) EMB.
Cheltenham: (1307 and 1377) EMB.
CHESTER (London: Bristol): c. 1136: Stephen: i. EMB; 1171: Henry II: v. B:EMB; 1189–99: John, Count of Mortain and Richard I: i, ii, v. B:EMB; 1190–1212: Earl Ranulf of Chester: ii, iv, v*. B:EMB; 1202: John: i, B; 1208–26: Earl Ranulf: i, v. B; 1233–7: Earl John le Scot: i, ii, v, vi. BT; *1237:* Henry III; i. BT; *1239:* Henry III. i. BT; *1300:* Edward I: i, ii, iv, v, vi, vii. BT; Hall, J.: Royal Charters and Grants to the City of Chester, *Chester & N. Wales Arch. Soc. Jnl.* (new series) xviii (1911).
CHESTERFIELD (Nottingham-Coventry-Lincoln–London); 1204; John: i*. B:EMB; 1213: John: i, iii, v. B; 1215: John: i, iii, v. B; 1226–7: William Brewer II; i*, ii, v, vi, vii. BT; 1232: Henry III: i*. BT; 1294: John Wake: i*, ii, iii, iv, v*, vii. BT; Yeatman, J. P.: *Records of the Borough of Chesterfield* (Chesterfield 1884).
CHICHESTER: 1135–54: Stephen: i. B:EMB; 1155: Henry II: i, v*. B; Ballard, A.: 'The Early Municipal Charters of the Sussex Boroughs', *Sussex. Arch. Collections*, lv (1912). 'A Descriptive List of the Archives of the City of Chichester' (W. Sussex Record Office) (1949); Steer, F. W.: *Chichester City Charters*, Chichester Papers No. 3, 1956.
Chippenham: (1154–89, 1255, 1306 onwards); EMB.
Chipping Norton: (1296); EMB.
Chorley: (1250, 1257); EMB.
CHRISTCHURCH: 1245–62: Earl Baldwin IV of Devon; ii, iii, v, BT.

CLITHEROE (Chester-London): 1272-91: Henry, Earl of Lincoln: i*, ii, iv, v, vi. BT: EMB; Harland, John: *Ancient Charters and other Muniments of the Borough of Clitheroe* (c. 1283-1674) Manchester 1851.

COLCHESTER: 1120-30: Henry I: iii. B; 1120-35: Henry I: iv. B; 1189: Richard I: i, ii, iv, v, vi. B:EMB; 1252: Henry III: i, iv. BT; Benham, W. G.: The Town Charters and other Borough Records of Colchester, *Roy. Arch. Inst. G.B. & Ireland*, vol. 64; Harrod, H.: *Report on the Records of the Borough of Colchester* (Colchester 1865).

CONGLETON: 1272-74: Henry, Earl of Lincoln: i, ii, iv, v*, vii. BT:EMB.

CONWAY (Hereford): 1284: Edward I: i, ii, iii, iv, v*, vii. BT:NT.

COVENTRY (Lincoln-London): 1149-53: Ralph II, Earl of Chester. EMB; 1181-86: Earl Ralph of Chester: i*, ii, iv, v, vii. B; 1186: Henry II: i*, ii, iii, iv, v, vii. B; *1267:* Henry III: i, iv, v*, vii. BT; 1268: Henry III: i. BT; 1345: inc. Wbm:EMB; Harris, M.: *Ancient Records of Coventry*, Dugdale Soc. Occas. Papers No. 1, 1924; Whitley, T. W.: *Charters and Manuscripts of Coventry* (Warwick 1897-98).

Darlington: (1183) EMB:BMW.

DARTMOUTH: 1341: EMB (also 1227 and 1249).

DENBIGH (Hereford): 1283-90: Henry, Earl of Lincoln: ii, iv, v. BT; 1290: Edward I: v. BT.

DERBY (Nottingham-Coventry-Lincoln-London) 1204: John: i, ii, iii, iv, v*, vi, vii. B:EMB; *1229:* Henry III: i, v. BT; 1256: Henry III: iv, vii. BT; 1260-61: Henry III: iii. BT; 1216-72: Henry III: iv. BT.

DEVIZES (Oxford: Winchester: Marlborough): 1135-39: Empress Maud: i, ii, v. B:EMB:NT; 1200: John: v. B; *1229:* Henry III: i. BT.

DONCASTER: 1194: Richard I: vi. B:EMB; Hardy, W. J.: *Calendar to the Records of the Borough of Doncaster* (4 vols.: Doncaster, 1899-1903).

Dorchester: (1106, 1204) EMB; Mayo, C. H.: *The Municipal Records of the Borough of Dorchester* (Exeter 1908).

DOVER: 1154-89: Henry II: iv, v. B:EMB; 1201: John: i, iv, v. B:EMB; 1205: John: iv, v. B:EMB.

DROITWICH: 1215: John: iv, v, vi. B:EMB.

Dudley: (1221, 1261): EMB.

DUNSTABLE (London) 1112-17: Henry I: i*, ii, iv. B:EMB:NT.

DURHAM (Bristol): 1153-81: Bp. Hugh de Puiset: i*, v. B:EMB. (See also Old Borough, i.e. Crossgates: EMB).

ELLESMERE: 1216-37: Joan of Wales: i*. BT.

Evesham: (1055, 1221) EMB.

EXETER (London): 1154-58: Henry II: i. B; 1189 Richard I: v. B; 1189-99: John, Count of Mortain: i, B; 1200: John: i, v. B; 1237:

(Exeter − continued) −
Henry III; i. BT; *1259:* Richard, Earl of Cornwall: i, ii, vi. BT; *1286:* Edmund, Earl of Cornwall: i. BT; *1300:* Edward I: i. BT; Schopp, J. W. and Easterling, R. C.: *Anglo-Norman Custumal of Exeter*, History of Exeter Research Group Papers No. 2. (1925); Exeter City Muniments in *Notes and Gleanings of Devon and Cornwall*, vols. 2-4 (Exeter 1889-92).

Eye: (1228, 1408) EMB.

FAVERSHAM: 1252: Henry III: ii, iv, v. BT: EMB; 1261: Henry III: iv. BT; 1302: Edward I: i, ii, iv, v, vi. BT.

FLINT (Rhuddlan): 1284: Edward I: i, ii, iii, iv, v*, vii. BT:NT.

FOLKESTONE: 1135-41: Stephen: v. B.

GATESHEAD (Bristol): 1153-95: Bp. Hugh de Puiset: i*, ii, iv. B:EMB. Drinkwater, G. N.: Gateshead Charters and Companies from the 12th to the 17th centuries and later. *Arch. Aeliana* (4th series) xxxvi (1958).

Glastonbury: (1319, 1517) EMB.

GLOUCESTER: (London: Winchester): 1155-58: Henry II; i. B:EMB; 1155-66: Henry II: iii. B; 1163-74: Henry II: v. B; 1194: Richard I: i, v. B; 1200: John: i, ii, iv, v, vi, vii. B. *1227:* Henry III: i, iii, iv. BT; 1256: Henry III: i, iv. BT; 1483: inc. Wbm: EMB. City of Gloucester: notes as to ancient charters etc. Leics. Arch. Soc. ix (1900). Stevenson, W. H.: *Calendar of Records of the Corporation of Gloucester* (Gloucester 1893).

GRANTHAM: 1463: inc. Wbm:EMB.

GREAT YARMOUTH: (Oxford) 1208: John: i, ii, iv, v*, vi, vii. B; 1215: John: iv. B; 1256: Henry III: iv. BT.

GRIMSBY (Northampton-London) 1201, 1207: John: i, ii, iv, v. B:EMB; 1227: Henry III: vi. BT; 1256: Henry III: vi. BT; 1258: Henry III: i, iv, v. BT; 1298: Edward I: ii, v, vi. BT. Gillett, E.: *A History of Grimsby* (London 1970).

GUILDFORD (Winchester): (1130-31) EMB; 1129-35: Henry I: iii. B:EMB. 1154-58: Henry I: iii. B; (1235) EMB; 1257: Henry III: ii, iv. BT.

HALESOWEN: *1216-72:* Henry III: EMB.

HARLECH: (Hereford): 1283-84: Edward I: i, ii, iii, iv, v, vii. BT:NT.

HARTLEPOOL (Bristol) 1162-85: Adam de Brus: i*. B:EMB; 1201: John i, iii. B:EMB; 1230: Bp. of Poore of Durham: ii, iii, v*, vi. BT; 1234: Henry III: i. BT: (c. 1380) EMB.

HARWICH: (1227-74) EMB; 1318: EMB.

HASTINGS: 1154-8: Henry II: ii, v. B:EMB.

HAVERFORDWEST (Hereford): 1189-1219: William Marshall, Earl of Pembroke: i, ii, iii, iv, v. B; 1219: William II, Earl of Pembroke: i, BT; 1219-29: William II, Earl of Pembroke: ii, iv, v*. BT; 1219-31: William II, Earl of Pembroke: ii, iv, v. BT; 1234-41: Gilbert, Earl of Pembroke: v. BT; 1291: Edward I: i*, ii, iv, v, vii. BT.

HEDON (Lincoln–London: York): 1167–70: Henry II: ii. B:EMB; Boyle, J. R.: *The early History of the Port and Town of Hedon* (Hull 1895).

HELSTON: 1201: John: i*, iii, iv, v*. BT:EMB; *1225–40:* Richard, Earl of Cornwall: i. BT; 1260: Richard, Earl of Cornwall: iv, vi. BT.

HENLEY-ON-THAMES: (1179, 1241, 1296, 1300) EMB.

HEREFORD: (Bristol): 1154–58: Henry II: vi. B; 1189: Richard I: ii, iv, vi. B:EMB; 1215: John: iii, iv, v*, vi. B:EMB; *1227:* Henry III: i, v. BT; 1256: Henry III: i, ii, iv. BT; 1256: Henry III: i, ii, iv. BT; 1267: Edward, son of Henry III: i. BT. Johnson, R.: *The Ancient Customs of the City of Hereford, with Translations of the Charters* (London 1868).

HIGHAM FERRERS: *1251:* William Ferrers, Earl of Derby): i, ii, iii. BT:EMB; 1300: Edward I: v. BT; Bateson, M.: 'The creation of boroughs' *Eng. Hist Rev.*, xvii (1902).

HIGH WYCOMBE: 1226: Alan Bassett: i, ii, iv, v, vi. BT:EMB; *1237:* Henry III: i. BT:EMB; *1285:* Edward I: i. BT.EMB; *Charters and Grants to the Borough of Chepping Wycombe in the County of Bucks* (5 John–4 Eliz.: Wycombe 1817).

HONITON: 1193–1217: William Vernon, Earl of Devon: i. EMB (also 1224 and 1238).

HUNTINGDON: 1100–24: Henry I: iii. B:EMB; 1205: John: i, iv, vi. B; 1252: Henry III: v. BT; also: **GODMANCHESTER**: 1212: John: EMB; Griffith, E.: *Collection of Ancient Records relating to the Borough of Huntingdon* (London 1827).

HYTHE: 1156: Henry II (refers back to Edward the Confessor): iv, v. B:EMB; 1205: John: i, iv, vi. B; 1261: Henry III: v. BT.

IPSWICH: 1200: John: i, ii, iv, v*, vi, vii. B:EMB; 1256: Henry III: iv, v, vii. BT; *1291:* Edward I: i, vi. BT; Canning, R.: *Principal Charters which have been granted to the Corporation of Ipswich (1199–1688)* London 1754; Martin, G. H.: 'The records of the Borough of Ipswich to 1422', *Jnl. Soc. Arch.*, vol. 11 (4), (1956).

KENDAL: 1222–46: William of Lancaster: i. BT:EMB.

Kidderminster: (13th. c., n.d. and 1254) EMB.

KING'S LYNN (Norwich–London: Oxford): 1204: John, Bp. of Norwich, confirmed by K. John: i, v., B:EMB; *1233:* Henry III: i. BT; 1234: Henry III: vii. BT; 1255: Henry III: iv. BT; 1257–66: Simon, Bp. of Norwich: vii. BT; *1268:* Henry III: i, BT; *1280:* Edward I: i. BT; 1305: Edward I: i, iv, v, vi. BT; Harrod, H.: *Report on the Deeds and Records of the Borough of King's Lynn* (King's Lynn 1874).

KINGSTON-UPON-HULL (Scarborough–York): 1299: Edward I: i*, ii, iii, iv, v, vii. BT:EMB. Boyle, J. R.: *Charters and Letters Patent granted to Kingston-upon-Hull (1299–1897)*

(Kingston-upon-Hull — continued) –
Hull, 1905; Stanwell, L. M.: *Calendar of the Ancient Deeds, Letters and Miscellaneous Documents in the Archives of the Corporation of Hull* (Hull 1951).

KINGSTON-UPON-THAMES: (Guildford–Winchester): 1256: Henry III: ii, iv, v, vii. BT:EMB; Roots, G.: *Charters of the Town of Kingston-upon-Thames (1208–1662)*, London, 1797.

LANCASTER (Northampton–London: Bristol): 1193: John, Count of Mortain: i*, ii. B:EMB; 1199: John: i*, ii. B:EMB; *1227:* Henry III: i. BT.

LAUNCESTON: 1141–67: Reginald, Earl of Cornwall: EMB; 1274: Edmund, Earl of Cornwall: v, vi. BT; see also DUNHEVED-BY-LAUNCESTON: 1227–42: Richard, Earl of Cornwall: i, ii, iii, iv, v, vi, vii. BT:EMB.

LEEDS: (Pontefract–Grimsby–Northampton–London): 1207–8: Maurice Paynel: i*, ii, iii, iv, v, vi, vii. B:EMB; Thompson, A. H.: 'The Charters of Leeds', *Leeds. Phil. & Lit. Soc. i* (1925); Patourel, J. le: *Documents relating to the Manor and Borough of Leeds (1066–1400)*, Thoresby Soc. Pubns., xlv (1957).

LEICESTER: 1103–18: Robert, Count of Meulan: v. B; 1118–35: Henry I: v. B; 1159–62: Earl Robert Bossu: i. B; 1118–68: Henry I: ii, iv, v*. B: 1191–1204: Earl Robert Bossu: ii. B: 1199: John: ii, v. B; 1229: Henry III: v. BT: 1231–9: Simon, Lord of Leicester: ii, vi. BT; 1239; Simon, Earl of Leicester: ii, vi. BT; c. 1254: Simon, Earl of Leicester: v, vi. BT; 1255: Simon, Earl of Leicester: ii. BT; 1256: Henry III: ii. BT; Bateson, M.: *Records of the Borough of Leicester 1103–1603* (1899–1905); *Records of the Corporation of Leicester* (1956); Hartopp, Henry: *Register of the Freemen of Leicester 1196–1930: Vol. 1: 1196–1770* (1927–33); Jeaffreson, J. C.: *Index to the Ancient Manuscripts of the Borough of Leicester* (Westminster, 1878); Nichols, J. (ed.), 'Charters of the Borough of Leicester' in *Bibliotheca Topographica Brittanica*, vol. 8 (1790).

Leominster: (1221) EMB.

LEWES: 1148: Reginald de Warenne: v*. B:EMB.

LICHFIELD (Bristol): (1155–59, 1176, 1199 and 1307) EMB.

LINCOLN (London): 1154–58: Henry II: v. B:EMB; 1154–63: Henry II: iii. B; 1155–75: Henry II: v. B; 1154–79: Henry II. v. B; 1154–71: Henry II: iii. B; 1157: Henry II: iii, v*. B; 1194: Richard I: i, ii, iv, v, vi, vii. B; 1200: John: i, ii, iv, v, vi, vii. B; *1227:* Henry III: i. BT; 1255: Henry III: iv. BT; *1262:* Henry III: i. BT; 1272: Henry III: i, iv. BT; *1301:* Edward I: i, v. BT; Ross, J.: *Civitas Lincolnia* (Lincoln 1870); Hill, J. W. F.: *Medieval Lincoln* (Cambridge 1965).

LISKEARD: 1240: Richard, Earl of Cornwall: i, ii, iii. BT:EMB; 1266: Richard, Earl of

(Liskeard – continued) –
    Cornwall and king of the Romans: v. BT;
    1275: Edmund, Earl of Cornwall: ii, iv, vi,
    BT.
LIVERPOOL: 1207: John: i*. B:EMB; 1229:
    Henry III: i, iv, v*, vi. BT; *1266:* Robert
    Ferrers, Earl of Derby: i. BT; Picton, J. A.:
    City of Liverpool; Selections from the
    Municipal Archives (2 vols.) (Liverpool
    1883–86) and: 'Notes on the Charters of the
    Borough of Liverpool', *Hist. Soc. Lancs. &*
    Ches. xxxvi (1887); Platt, E. M.: *A History*
    of Municipal Government in Liverpool to
    1835 (London, 1906).
LLANFYLLIN: post-1266: Llewellyn ap
    Gruffydd ab Gwenwynwyn: i*, iii, iv, v*. BT.
LONDON: 1066–75: William I (refers back to
    Edward the Confessor): i, ii. B:EMB; 1131:
    Henry I: ii, iv, v, vi, vii. B; 1155: Henry II:
    i, ii, iv, v. B; 1194: Richard I: i, ii, iv, v. B;
    1196: Richard I: v. B; 1199: John: i, ii, iv,
    v. B; 1215: John: i, vii. B; *1227:* Henry III:
    i, ii, v. BT; 1247: Henry III: iv. BT; *1253:*
    Henry III: i, v, vi, vii. BT: 1266: Henry III:
    i. BT; 1268: i, ii, iv, v, vi. BT; 1299: Edward
    I: i. BT; Birch, W. de G.: *Historical Charters*
    and Constitutional Documents of the City of
    of London (London, 1887); Evelyn, J.:
    Charters of the City of London (London,
    1745); Luffman, J.: *Charters of London*
    (London, 1793); Noorthouck, J.: *A New*
    History of London, inc. Westminster and
    Southwark (London, 1773); McDonnell, K.:
    Medieval London Suburbs (1978).
Luton: (1202 and 1221) EMB; Austin, W.:
    History of Luton & its hamlets (1928).
LYDD (Hastings): 1155–58: Henry II: ii, v.
    B:EMB; 1290: Edward I: i, ii. BT.
LYME REGIS (London): 1284: Edward I: i*, iv,
    v*. BT:EMB; 1285: Edward I: i*, ii, iv, v, vi.
    BT:EMB.
LYMINGTON: 1184–1216: William de Redvers:
    i. EMB; 1257 to Baldwin de Redvers: v. EMB;
    1271: Isabella de Fortibus: EMB.
MACCLESFIELD: 1261: Prince Edward: i, ii, iv,
    v*, vii. BT:EMB; Clarke, W. H.: 'Charters,
    documents and insignia belonging to the
    ancient manor and borough of Macclesfield',
    Lancs. & Ches. Ant. Soc., vol. 22 (1904).
MAIDSTONE (Canterbury–London): 1549: inc.
    Wbm:EMB; (also 1474) EMB.
MALDON: 1166–75: (Henry II: ii, iv, v. B:EMB;
    1290: Edward I: i. BT.
MALMESBURY: 1205–22: Abbot Walter: iv. B;
    (1249) EMB.
MANCHESTER: 1301: Thomas Grelby: i, ii, iv,
    v, vii. BT:EMB.
MARLBOROUGH (Oxford: Winchester): 1204:
    John: i*, ii, iv, v*. B:EMB.
MONMOUTH: 1256: Henry III: ii, iv. BT;
    Bayley, D.: 'Monmouth Borough Charters',
    in *Memorials of Monmouth* (n.d.).
MONTGOMERY (Hereford): 1223: NT; 1227:

(Montgomery – continued) –
    Henry III: i*, ii, iii, iv, v. BT; 1228–29:
    Hubert, Earl of Kent: ii, v*, vii. BT; *1229:*
    Henry III: i. BT; 1267: Henry III: v. BT.
MORPETH: 1188–1249: Roger de Merlai: i.
    B:EMB:NT; *1239–66:* Roger de Merlai III:
    i, ii, v. BT; 1246–62: Roger de Merlai III: ii.
    BT; 1294: John de Greystoke: v. BT.
NEATH:(Cardiff–Hereford): 1147–73: William,
    Earl of Gloucester: i*. B; 1280: Gilbert de
    Clare: v. BT.
Newbury: (1189–1217 and 1225) EMB.
NEWCASTLE-UNDER-LYME: (1173 and 1203)
    EMB; 1235: Henry III: i, v*. BT:EMB; 1251:
    Henry III: vi. BT; 1281: Edward I: v. BT;
    1292–97: Mayor and community: vi. BT.
    Adams, D. W.: *An Octocentenary Guide to*
    sources of information (Newcastle Public
    Libraries, 1973). A13: an MS set of tran-
    scriptions/translations of N-u-L town and
    manor charters & deeds available at ref.
    library; Pape, T.: *Medieval Newcastle-under-*
    Lyme as a Trading Centre (Chamber of Trade,
    1934). 'The Borough Museum has the follow-
    ing Charters; 1281, 1344, 1372, 1378, 1590,
    1664 and 1685, also a facsimile of the 1251
    charter and a copy of the 1235 charter from
    the Rolls at the P.R.O.'
NEWCASTLE-UPON-TYNE: (Winchester):
    1100–35: Henry I, ii, iii, iv, v. B:EMB; 1154–
    89: Henry II: vi. BT; 1201: John: v, vi. B;
    1213: John: iv, vi. B; 1216: John: i, ii, iv, v*.
    B; *1234:* Henry III: i, iii. BT; 1252: Henry
    III: vii. BT; 1256: Henry III: vi. BT; 1276:
    Edward I: ii. BT; *1293:* Edward I: i. BT;
    1298: Edward I: i, ii, iii, iv, v. BT; (1296)
    EMB; 1400: inc. Wbm:EMB; Oliver, A.: Early
    Deeds relating to Newcastle-upon-Tyne,
    Surtees Soc. cxxxvii (1924).
NEWPORT (I.o.W.): 1177–84: NT; 1262–93:
    Earl Richard II de Redvers: ii, iv, v, vi, vii.
    BT: EMB.
NEW ROMNEY: 1154–89: Henry II: i, v.
    B:EMB; 1200: John: i, v. B.
NORTHAMPTON: (London): 1189: Richard I:
    i, ii, iv, v, vi, vii. B:EMB; 1200: John: i, ii, iv,
    v, vi, vii. B; 1224: Henry III: vi. BT; *1227:*
    Henry III: i, BT; 1252: Henry III: vi. BT;
    1255: Henry III: iv. BT; 1257: Henry III: i,
    iv. BT; 1268: Henry III; i, BT; 1270: Henry
    III: ii. BT; 1284: Edward I: vi. BT; 1299:
    Edward I: i. BT; 1301: Edward I: vi. BT;
    Markham, C. A. & Cox, J. C.: *Records of the*
    Borough of Northampton (2 vols.: Northamp-
    ton, 1898).
NORWICH: (London): 1154–58: Henry II: i, iii.
    B; 1191: Richard I: vi. B; 1194: Richard I: i,
    ii, iv, v, vi, vii. B; 1199: John: i, ii, iv, v, vi,
    vii. B; *1229:* Henry III: i, iii. BT; 1255: Henry
    III: iv. BT; 1256: Henry III: iii, iv, v. BT;
    1285: Edward I: i. BT; 1305; Edward I: i, iv,
    v, vi, vii. BT; Hudson, W. & Tingey J. C.:
    Revised Catalogue of the Records of the City

(Norwich – continued) –
of Norwich (2 vols.) (Norwich 1898) and:
Records of the City of Norwich (2 vols)
(Norwich 1906–10).

NOTTINGHAM: (Coventry–Lincoln–London):
1157: Henry II: i, ii, iii, iv, v, vii. B:EMB;
1189: John, Count of Mortain: i, ii, iii, iv, v,
vii. B; 1200: K. John: i, ii, iii, iv, v, vii. B;
1230: Henry III: i, iv, v, vii. BT; 1255: Henry
III: i. BT; 1265: Henry III: ii. BT; *1272:*
Henry III: i. BT; 1284: Edward I: v, vi, vii.
BT; 1449: inc. Wbm:EMB; Stevenson, W. H.:
*Records of the Borough of Nottingham
(1155–1702)* (5 vols: London 1882–1900)
and *Royal Charters Granted to the Burgesses
of Nottingham 1155–1712* (London, 1890).

NUNEATON: 1227: Sybil, Prioress and Robert,
Prior of Nuneaton: EMB.

OKEHAMPTON: 1194–1242: Robert de
Courtenay: i, ii, iii, iv, v, vi, vii. B:EMB; 1291:
Hugh de Courtenay: ii. BT.

OXFORD (London): 1156: Henry II: i, ii, iv, v*.
B :EMB; 1229: Henry III: i, v, vi. BT; *1301:*
Edward I: i. BT; Davis, R. H.: 'An Oxford
Charter of 1191 and the beginnings of
municipal freedom', *Oxoniensia* xxxiii (1968);
Ogle, O.: *Royal Letters Addressed to Oxford
and now Existing in the City Archives*
(Oxford 1892); Salter, H. E.: 'Medieval
Oxford', *Oxford Hist. Soc.*, vol. 100 (1936).

PEMBROKE: 1154–89: Henry II: i, ii, iii, iv, v*.
B; 1201: John: v. B; *1256:* Henry III: i. BT.

PENRYN: 1236: William Brewer, Bp. of
Exeter, ii, iv. BT: EMB: NT; 1275: William
Bronscombe, Bp. of Exeter: i. BT.

Penzance: (1327) EMB.

Peterborough (1125–28), EMB.

PLYMOUTH (Oxford): as Sutton Prior: (1253,
1276, 1306) EMB; inc. as PLYMOUTH in
1439: Wbm:EMB; Welch, C. E.: *Plymouth
City Charters, A Catalogue* (Corporation of
Plymouth 1962); Rowe, J. B.: 'Plympton, the
Borough and its Charters (1242–1790)' (*Devon
Assoc. for Adv. of Sci. Trans.*, 19, 1887);
Worth, R. N.: *Calendar of the Plymouth
Municipal Records* (Plymouth 1893).

PONTEFRACT (Grimsby–Northampton–
London): 1194: Roger de Lacy: i*, ii, iii, iv,
v, vi, vii. B:EMB; *1278:* Henry, Earl of
Lincoln: i, vi. BT; 1484: inc. Wbm:EMB.

POOLE (Southampton–Winchester): c. 1248:
William de Longuespee: i, ii, iv, v, vi, vii.
BT:EMB; 1371: William de Montacute: i,
vii. EMB.

PORTSMOUTH (Oxford: Winchester): 1106:
Henry I: EMB; 1194: Richard I: i*, ii, iv, v.
B:EMB:NT; 1201: John: i*, iv, v. B; *1229:*
Henry III: i, vi. BT; 1255: Henry III: i. BT;
1256: Henry III: i, ii, iv, v*. BT; Murrell, R. J.
and East, R. *Extracts from Records in the
Possession of the Borough of Portsmouth*
(Portsmouth 1884, 1891).

PRESTON: (London): 1179: Henry II: i. B:EMB;

(Preston – continued) –
1188–99: John Count of Mortain: i, ii, v. B;
1199: John: i, ii, v. B; *1227:* Henry III: i,
BT; 1252: Henry III: vi. BT. Addison, J.:
*Extracts from Ancient Documents in the
Archives of Preston* (Preston 1842); Lingard,
J.: *Charters granted to the Burgesses of
Preston* (Preston 1821).

QUEENBOROUGH: 1368: Edward III: EMB:
NT.

READING: 1253: Henry III: iv, v*. BT.

RICHMOND: 1093–1136: Count Alan III:
EMB; 1136–54: Count Alan III: i, ii, v, vi.
B:EMB; 1145–75: Count Conan: i. B; 1268:
John, son of Duke of Brittany: iv, vi. BT.

Ripon: (1316, 1341) EMB.

ROCHESTER: 1227: Henry III; ii, iv, v*, vi.
BT:EMB; *1266:* Henry III: i, ii, vi. BT; 1446:
inc. Wbm:EMB.

Romsey: (1236) EMB.

RYE (Hastings): 1140–89: Henry, Abbot of
Fécamp: iv, vi. B; 1189–1219: Robert, Abbot
of Fécamp: ii, iii, iv, vi. B :EMB.

St Albans (London): (1248) EMB.

SALFORD: c. 1230: Ranulf, Earl of Chester:
i, ii, iv, v. vii. BT:EMB.

SALISBURY (Winchester): As *Old Sarum:*
1100–35: Henry I; v*. B:EMB; (1194) EMB;
1229: Henry III: i. BT; As SALISBURY:
1219: NT; 1225: Bp. Poore: ii. BT:EMB;
1270: Henry III: v. BT; *1285:* Edward I: i.
BT; 1306: Edward I; vi. BT.

SALTASH: pre-1246: Reginald de Valletort:
i, ii, iv, v, vii. BT; (1201) EMB.

SANDWICH: 1070–86: Odo, Bp. of Bayeux and
William I; vi. B:EMB; 1155–58: Henry II; ii,
iv, v. B; 1155–72 vi, B; 1205 John ii, iv, v. B.

SCARBOROUGH: (York): 1155; Henry II: i*, ii.
B:EMB; 1200: John; i*, ii. B; 1201: John: vi.
B; 1253: Henry III: i, ii, iii, iv, v, vi. BT;
1256: Henry III: i, ii, iv, v*, vi, vii. BT; 1485:
Inc. Wbm: EMB; Forster, G. C. F.: *A Descriptive Catalogue of the Records in the
Possession of the Corporation of Scarborough*
(Borough of Scarborough 1968). Section AA:
Charters and White Vellum Book; Baker, J. B.:
A Catalogue of Charters Corporate Transactions, Letters, Records (1893); Jeayes,
I. H.: *Catalogue of Ancient Documents
belonging to the Corporation of Scarborough*
(1915): *Description of Documents contained
in the White Vellum Book* (1914) and *Copy
Translations of the Charters* (1912).

SHAFTESBURY: (1244) EMB; 1252: Henry
III: iv, vii. BT.

SHEFFIELD: 1297: Thomas de Furnival: iv, v, vi.
BT:EMB; Hall, T. W.: *Catalogue of the Ancient
Charters of Sheffield* (Sheffield 1913).

SHREWSBURY (London: Bristol): 1154–89:
Henry II. i. B; 1189: Richard I: vi. B: 1200:
John: i, vi, vii. B; *1227:* Henry III; i, ii, iii,
iv, v*. BT; 1256: Henry III: i, ii, iv, v, vi. BT;
1265: Henry III; v. BT; 1267: Henry III: v.

(Shrewsbury — continued) –
BT; 1284: Edward I: vi. BT; (no author):
*Calendar of the Muniments of the Borough
of Shrewsbury* 1896).

Solihull: (c. 1280 and 1300-1475) EMB.

SOUTHAMPTON (Winchester): 1154-66: Henry
II: i. B; 1189: Richard I: v. B:EMB; 1199:
John: v, vi. B; *1227:* Henry III: i. BT; 1249:
Henry III: vii. BT; 1252: Henry III: v. BT;
1256: Henry III: i, iv, vii. BT; 1303: Edward
I: iii. BT; Chapman, A. B. W.: *Black Book of
Southampton (c. 1388-1620)*, Southampton
Rec. Soc. Pubns., vols. 13, 14, 17 (1912-15);
Gidden, H. W.: *Charters of the Borough of
Southampton (1199-1836)* (2 vols.:
Southampton Rec. Soc. Pubns., 1909-10).

Southwark: (1253 and 1294 onward) EMB.

SOUTHWOLD: 1490: inc. Wbm:EMB.

STAFFORD: 1206: John: i, iii, iv, v, vi.
B:EMB; 1228: Henry III: i. BT; 1261:
Henry III: v. BT; Bradley, J. W.: *Royal
Charters and Letters Patent granted to the
Burgesses of Stafford 1206-1828)* Stafford
1897.

STAMFORD: (1202) EMB; 1257: Henry III: ii.
BT; Rogers, A.: *The Making of Stamford*
(Leicester 1965).

STOCKPORT: c. 1260: Robert de Stockport:
i, ii, iv, v, vii. BT:EMB.

STRATFORD-ON-AVON: (Bristol): 1196: John,
Bp. of Worcester: ii, v. B:EMB.

SUNDERLAND: As *Wearmouth:* 1180-86: Bp.
Hugh de Puiset: i, ii, iii, iv, v. B:EMB.

SWANSEA: 1153-84: William, Earl of Warwick:
i, ii, iv, v, vi, vii. B; 1215: John: v. B; *1234:*
Henry III: i. BT; Edward I: i, ii, iii, iv, v, vi,
vii. BT.

Tamworth (London); (1199 and 1307 onward)
EMB; *Tamworth Borough Records* (Tamworth 1952).

TENBY: 1265-94: William de Valence: ii, iv,
v, vi, vii. BT:BMW.

TENTERDEN: 1449: inc. Wbm:EMB.

TEWKESBURY: 1122-47: Robert, Earl of
Gloucester: EMB; 1153-83: William and
Robert, Earls of Gloucester: ii, iii, iv, v, vii.
B:EMB; 1314: Gilbert, Earl of Chester:
EMB.

Thetford: (1250) EMB.

Tiverton: (1224 and 1238) EMB.

TORRINGTON: (1135-94, 1238 and 1306
onward) EMB.

TOTNES (Exeter-London): 1199-1216: John:
i, iv, v*. B; ('spurious' EMB) 1306: BT.

TRURO: 1166: Reginald, Earl of Cornwall: i, iv,
v. B:EMB; 1174-86: Henry II: i. B; *1285:*
Edward I: i. BT.

WAKEFIELD: (1180: Hamelin, Earl of Warenne
and his wife, Isabella) EMB.

WALLINGFORD (Winchester): 1156: Henry II: i,
ii, iv, v*, vi, vii. B:EMB; 1267: Henry III: i, BT.

WALSALL: c. 1198: William Ruffus: ii, iv, vi.
B:EMB; *The Charter of the Borough of
Walsall*, Walsall. Hist. Assoc., 1926; Sims, R.:
*Calendar of the Deeds and Documents
belonging to the Corporation of Walsall*
(Walsall 1882).

Waltham: (c. 1235) EMB.

WARRINGTON: 1300: William le Botiller:
iv. BT:EMB.

Warwick: (1306 onward) EMB; Tibbits, E. G.:
Ancient Records of Warwick, Dugdale Soc.
Occ. Papers No. 5 (1938).

Watford: (1290): EMB.

WELLS: 1174-80: Bp. Reginald: i, ii, iv, v.
B:EMB; c. 1201: Bp. Savaric: i, ii, iv, v. B;
1290: Edward I: i. BT; Shilton, D. O. and
Holworthy, R.: *Wells City Charters*, Som.
Rec. Soc., xlvi (1932)|

WEYMOUTH: (Portsmouth-Southampton-
Winchester): 1252: NT; 1252: Prior and
convent of Winchester: i, ii, iii, iv, vi, vii.
BT:EMB; (1248) EMB; Moule, H. J.: *Descrip-
tive Catalogue of the Charters, Minute-Books
and other Documents of the Borough of
Weymouth and Melcombe Regis 1252-1800*
(Weymouth 1883); also MELCOMBE REGIS
(London): 1280: Edward I: i*, ii, iv, v, vi.
EMB.

WIGAN: 1246: Henry III: i, iv v*. BT:EMB;
Charters of the Borough of Wigan
(Warrington 1808).

WILTON (London: Winchester): 1129-35:
Henry I: i, v. B:EMB; *1229:* Henry III: i.
BT.

WINCHESTER (London): 1155-58: Henry II:
i, ii, v. B:EMB; 1190: Richard I: i, ii, iv,
v. B; 1203: John: iv. B: 1215: John: i, ii, iv,
v, vi. B; *1227:* Henry III: i. BT.

WINDSOR: 1277: Edward I: i*, ii, iii, iv, v*.
BT:EMB.

WOLVERHAMPTON: 1263: Dean of
Wolverhampton: i. EMB.

WORCESTER: 1189: Richard I: vi. B:EMB;
1227: Henry III: iii, iv, v*, vi. BT; 1256:
Henry III: iv. BT; 1264: Henry III: i, ii, iv,
v. BT (see pages 92--93 (i.e. deeds) above);
Bloom, J. H.: 'Original Charters Relating to
the City of Worcester in the possession of the
Dean and Chapter', *Worcs. His. Soc.* (1909).

YEOVIL: 1305-6: Robert de la More: iv, vii.
BT:EMB.

YORK: 1154-58: Henry II (refers back to Henry
I): i, v*. B; 1188-99: Richard I: iv, v. B;
1200: John: i, v. B; 1212: John: vi. B; *1252:*
Henry III: i, ii, iv, v. BT; 1267: Henry III: vii.
BT; 1396: inc. Wbm:EMB.

CHAPTER FIVE

GILD AND BOROUGH ORDINANCES c. 1066–1600

GILDS WERE a characteristic feature of medieval town life, prominent in the social and economic order, often identical with the borough administration. The present-day convention is usually to refer to 'medieval gilds' rather than 'mediaeval guilds' though the 19th-century spelling will still be found in indexes and titles. Many a local Guildhall preserves the older spelling, as do Townswomen, Needlewomen and the City and Guilds Examining Board. The persistence of these alternatives can cause problems for searchers. *British Books in Print* (London 1982) indexes *Gilds*: see *Guilds*, but the *Cumulative Book Index* (New York 1980) lists *Guilds*: see *Gilds*. Of the major reference works, both Toulmin Smith (1870) and Gross (1890) refer to *English Gilds* and *The Gild Merchant*. The original Latin word was in fact *gilda* though documents may often refer instead to the 'commune' (*comuna*) or 'brotherhood' (*fraternitas*). The searcher is well advised to check both spellings in any index. Here the term 'gild' will be used except where reference is made to an earlier title or quotation.

By whatever name, the association of merchants, tradesmen and craftsmen into self-governing corporations with their own lands, property, meeting-houses and regulations dominated the social life and hierarchy of most substantial English towns from the Norman Conquest to the 16th century and still survives in many local traditions and charities. In some towns the achievement of gild status was earlier and more effective than the development of local government or borough incorporation; in many towns the two processes went hand-in-hand. In any case the records, functions and membership of gild and borough are inextricably entwined, so that it becomes an academic exercise to attempt to differentiate between gildsman, alderman and councillor. Every aspect of gild life was so typically medieval that the story of the prosperity of many ancient towns from the 11th to the 14th centuries and their eventual decline in the 15th and 16th centuries is equally the story of the rise and fall of the gilds.

The functions of gilds in modern terms were manifold. They were by turn chambers of commerce, monopolies, insurance companies, friendly societies, family trustees, religious foundations, burial clubs, institutes of good practice and quality control and, to a very limited extent, trade unions. Although at a late date in the period of gild decline there was a vigorous emergence of 'journeymen', 'yeomen' and 'servants' gilds, which set up combinations of wage labourers against their employers, the essence of the original gilds was an association of owners, freemen-burgesses, merchants and capitalist masters, securing their vested interests against 'strangers' and 'the middle sort'.

There were, in fact, three types of gild, though their functions overlap so much that one may often be confused with another. Firstly, the Gilds Merchant emerge at the end of the 11th century; we have already seen evidence of their existence in Domesday Book, at Canterbury and Dover (page 59) and in the earliest borough charters of the Norman kings and earls (see pages 84–85). These continue in combination with the development of borough corporations into the 16th century. Meanwhile, in the 13th and 14th century, as some towns began to decline, the craft gilds were founded to regulate particular trades and industries, usually under the direct supervision of the borough or gild officials. During the 16th century many of the craft gilds amalgamated to form incorporated livery companies, many of which survive today, particularly in London. During the 14th century there was also a widespread development of religious gilds, some at a parochial level, endowing property in order to pay priests for saying prayers for the dead, and also for other charitable works. These religious foundations came to grief in the 16th century, with the Tudors' theft of chantry lands and property. Their existence is still commemorated in many a town in the foundation charters of grammar schools and charitable trusts. The religious fraternities with their endowment of lady-chapels and mass-priests closely resemble chantries, which, as in Dudley, had their own 'Lady's Lands' and altars and their own obligations to the dead; these are not 'gilds' in the strict sense. Like the gilds, however, they are an interesting early development of a sense of neighbourhood and community service, which in smaller towns may anticipate the aspirations of incorporation.

Extensive records of gilds are sadly lacking; this is the set of urban documents for which of all our choices there may be least local evidence. Although in 1389 Richard II ordered writs to be sent to every county requiring returns of 'all the ordinances, usages, properties etc.' of the English gilds, unfortunately, the returns of the 'mysteries and crafts' cannot be found at the Public Record Office. Those which do survive mainly record the ordinances of the religious fraternities, of which the records of more than 100 have been published.

The student is fortunate in that there are at least two massive standard works of reference which include extensive transcriptions of the available evidence. These are for the Gilds Merchant the essential work of Charles Gross *The Gild Merchant*; and for the religious fraternities and a few craft ordinances that of Joshua Toulmin Smith and his daughter Lucy on *The English Gilds*.[1] Locally, the original gild ordinances, minute books and accounts are less accessible than other sources; Toulmin Smith (writing in 1870) commented frequently on town archives which have no recognition of surviving gild documents. A century later Charles Phythian-Adams described the gild sources as 'a virtually unploughed field'.[2] In 1897 Gross observed that 'a general collection of the ordinances of the craft gilds is needed; abundant material for such a work is accessible in the Public Record Office and the town archives . . .'.[3] Fortunately, the close association of gilds and borough corporation has preserved the ordinances of the craftsmen amongst borough archives, so that many a town's *Red Book, Corporation Ledger* or *Ordinances* (as at Worcester), contain resumés and confirmation of various gilds' purposes and regulations. The volumes of the *Victoria County History* are sometimes a useful starting-point; information on each county's gilds will be found in the *VCH* chapter on 'Social and Economic History', or in the histories of individual boroughs. The volumes for Leicestershire, Warwickshire, Wiltshire and Gloucestershire are particularly informative. Some older county histories by contrast ignore the gilds completely, lacking even an index reference, being more concerned with manorial, religious and political affairs.

Nevertheless, some early town histories are the chief sources of information on gilds, occasionally referring to ancient records long since lost. More recent periodical publication is sparse; nevertheless, our Gazetteer can muster gild records of one sort or another for about half of the later incorporated municipal boroughs. An important article refers, in the context of pre-Conquest development, to the differences between 'organic', 'planted' and 'primary' towns.[4] The latter are those which were predestined to an urban future before and after the Conquest by virtue of ancient prehistoric settlement, early religious foundation, royal estate or regional market site. More small scale industry develops in these market towns than is usually acknowledged. 'It is a mistake to think of them either as industrial towns which never quite made the grade or as merely decaying centres of pettifogging shopkeepers'. The great majority of surviving English towns did in fact originate as medieval market centres with 'a characteristic mixed economy of trades, craft and manufacture'. In this sense, more than half the boroughs of 1974 were 'primary towns'; their medieval gild foundations are often the most convincing evidence of their primary growth.

Some areas such as Cornwall, Shropshire and Wales, preserve gild records for what are now mere villages, never having become municipal boroughs. The first rank of these include substantial small towns such as Burford (Oxon) with one of the earliest Gilds Merchant in England (1087–1107), or Thaxted in Essex with its Cutlers' Gild. Far smaller now are Caerwys in Clwyd (1290) or Kenfig in Glamorgan (1360) with its 11th century castle site. It is certain, in view of the relative paucity of surviving records, that the existence of thriving local gilds was even more widespread than the substantial Gazetteer indicates. There is certainly more work to be done in this field.

Indications of the existence of crafts which might have fostered gilds can be traced in indirect evidence other than actual gild ordinances, though this must be cautiously interpreted, especially at an early date. Borough charters, as we have seen, occasionally refer to craft and merchant gilds. Licenses to endow or found a gild appear quite frequently in the printed *Calendars of Patent Rolls* and *Close Rolls* available in most reference libraries. There was, for instance, a dramatic affray at Coventry in 1268, which was recorded in the *Patent Rolls* of 52 Hen. III, when the Prior's townsmen were prevented from operating their Gild Merchant. When the situation was investigated by the sheriff, his clerk met with armed force by townsmen who imprisoned him, trampled on the king's rolls and writs, and beat and maltreated the prior's servants. At King's Lynn in 1393 (*Cal. Pat. 16 Ric. II*) the Merchant Gild of Holy Trinity paid £120 for permission to alienate 5 messuages, one quay, rents of £11 6s. 8d. and the profits of a ferryboat across the harbour, in order to support various works of charity. Most of the licences listed in that year are for religious gilds, at Warwick, Northampton, Chesterfield, and Leicester – where ten shops were alienated – at Hedon, Ludlow, Birmingham and Coventry and many more towns year by year. Taxation records too (the great *Pipe Rolls, Subsidy Rolls* and *Poll Taxes*, similarly printed) refer to craftsmen by name and trade, and measure the relative wealth of each familiar town. Here the study of surnames can be a useful guide to industrial development with many an early Tucker, Weaver and their like.[5]

Gilds Merchant were the earliest form of gild, and the most influential upon town government and the regulation of trade. Professor Sawyer has drawn attention to the mercantile prosperity of England in the 11th century and our Domesday Chapter has shown that many towns in Sussex, for example, had increased in prosperity from

1066–1087.[6] The emergence of a Gild Merchant is a reflection of this progress. The Gild Merchant was primarily a protection society, founded by the mercantile establishment of a town to ensure their own prosperity. Its chief provision was usually that none but those who had been admitted to freedom of the borough could be gild members, and that only those members could take part in the wholesale and retail trade of the town. Although the exact provisions of any gild varied from town to town, there was a general similarity between them, and some tendency to the adoption of the customs of one town by another. All gilds were 'consistently inconsistent' in their stated intentions to protect the interests of both producer and consumer, even when these were inevitably opposed to each other. There was always a preoccupation with profit, and at the same time with the reputation of trade; an insistence on honest practice, and a blatant intention to maintain vested interests and enforce the monopoly of a few against all comers. The gild usually assumed responsibility for the enforcement of the various national 'assizes' of weights and measures, quality-control and price, with penalties for malpractice, which ranged from public punishment of offenders pilloried with offensive goods round their necks, to money-fines and dismissal from the gild.

Resistance to 'strangers' of all sorts, whether from the next county or from overseas, was in direct opposition to the proclamation by some gilds that members need not be resident in the town and that gild privileges could be claimed, if paid for, by the very 'foreigners' who were otherwise excluded. The gildsmen of one town could sometimes expect their membership to extend to privileges in other places, depending on the reputation of their own gild. Freedom from local tolls was a profitable advantage shared by gild members who themselves enforced tolls on the uninitiated. Some of their regulations amounted to downright exploitation, imported goods being reserved for the first or sole choice of gild members. The principle of the dealers' 'ring' was strictly enforced, to the extent of occasional joint-stock purchasing by the gild. On the other hand, there was a contradictory self-interest in 'fair shares for all', so that one gildsman could be compelled to share a good buy with his brethren and individual cases of 'engrossing' goods or 'forestalling' the market were regularly prosecuted.

The Gild Merchant held a regular court, sometimes indistinguishable from the borough 'port-moot'. Most important of all, the gild was incorporated for the ownership of property, its meetings being held in a gildhall which was also used as a town hall; this identity is still preserved in many ancient towns such as Birmingham and Worcester. Identity of gild and town government is a peculiar feature of medieval boroughs, but it cannot be taken for granted. The officers of the gild were usually designated 'wardens' and 'aldermen'; in some towns the term 'master' and 'mayor' became interchangeable. In other cases a distinction was preserved; as at Reading, where the abbot refused to acknowledge the warden of the gild as mayor. It was against the interests of an overlord for too much power to be consolidated in the hands of the burgesses of 'his' town. Royal licence, except when the king's own interests were at stake, was easier to obtain than the acceptance of baron, abbot or 'middle lords'. Some towns have a long history of violent disputes, even to the occasional suppression of the gild by an overlord. In other cases, as at Exeter, a newly-established gild could fall foul of a well-established town council. Yet relationships could also remain harmonious wherever profitable interests were shared by a well-organized oligarchy of lord, burgess and merchant. Freedom of gild and borough set up a different pattern of relationships from the older obligations of manorial service and feudal dues. Traditionally, 'town air made a man free' and any villein born could claim his freedom from manorial bondage if he proved himself 'in scot and lot and in the Gild Merchant as a free burgess'. Thus at Salisbury in 1248 Robert of Alderbury proved his right to be a merchant rather than a peasant; the usual qualification was residence for a year and a day.

Often lord and mayor endeavoured to exert dual control over the gildsmen, sharing the right to admit members and dividing admission fees and money-fines. At Salisbury the bishop exercised this right so effectively that the records of the town's gild were kept in the episcopal archives and eventually lost. The gild's considerable income from fees and fines was often the town's only independent source of revenue not subject to deductions by earl or overlord. Indeed, at Leicester the Gild Merchant ultimately became the 'finance department' of the borough, leaving jurisdiction over civil affairs to the borough court. In some towns there was a notable absence of any Gild Merchant, the most prominent case being that of London and those towns whose constitutions were modelled upon those of the capital. There the burgesses alone ruled, so that freedom of the borough encompassed and took precedence over commercial custom or gild membership.

In other towns the ordinances of the borough and rules of the gild were identical. At Berwick-upon-Tweed in 1283 the gild regulated everything from trade in wool and hides to the seasonal prices of ale and mutton. Conditions were imposed on the sale of fish, hay, oats, cheese, butter, hemp, leather and corn. 'Engrossing' was prevented by a ruling that 'no burgess shall have more than one buyer of wool making purchases on his behalf'. All seaborne goods bought 'at the Bray' must be carried away before sunset and butchers must not 'forestall' the market by buying up beasts beforehand. Purchases were to be shared by all members and only gildsmen were eligible to trade. In typical medieval fashion matters both great and small were treated with equal significance. At Berwick there was a strict exclusion of lepers from the town; if any forced an entry the sergeant was to strip them, burn their clothes and turn them naked from the gate: 'for we have taken care a proper place shall be kept, outside the town'. The same records prescribe compensation for customers misled by 'false top samples' (the best apples at the front of the stall). There was to be no tipping of refuse or dung-heaps on the banks of the Tweed and no-one was to make a mess 'against the walls of the gildhall whilst a meeting is being held'. The borough was governed by 24 'discreet men' with a mayor and four provosts chosen by the whole community and all separate gilds 'heretofore existing in the borough' were amalgamated in one gild. The Berwick Ordinances conclude with a plaintive statement that 'It took up five days to treat of and settle these ordinances'.

At Winchester, which had a gild merchant during the reign of Henry II, the relationship between borough and gild was also close and, apparently, harmonious. The 'Old Usages' of the city refer to mayor and council rather than warden and gild, but endorse all the familiar regulations of quality control in the manufacture of cloth; the times and places for markets with regulation of booths on High Street; and rents to be paid by butchers, fishmongers, tanners, poultry sellers and bakers (who must put their seal on each loaf). Tolls were paid on iron, steel, mill-stones, fur, lead, barrels, tanned leather, saddles, madder and woad, all by the horse-load or cart.

Of our three Midland towns, only the city of Worcester had a Gild Merchant. Birmingham's important Gild of the Holy Cross, licensed in 1383, though established by the whole community for the welfare of the town, remained technically a religious fraternity rather than a Gild Merchant. Holy Cross was particularly concerned with public works, the maintenance of the town's 'two great stone bridges and divers foul and dangerous highways'. Worcester's gild, as we saw in Chapter Four, was the main provision of the city's charter, obtained from Henry III in 1227. The city's ordinances which survive at the Guildhall (see illustrations on pages 119–121), are a compilation of the reign of Edward IV in 1467, though evidently a resumé – by royal command – of long-standing ancient customs. Like the ordinances of Berwick, they regulate the whole panorama of marketing, merchandise, public works and social welfare. There are ordinances for the butchers, brewers, woolmongers, fishmongers and keepers of hostelries; bye-laws for the maintenance of the Severn bridge, the slips and quays are included and several regulations for the upkeep of the gildhall. By this late date the union of Gild Merchant, commonalty, craftsmen and borough is almost complete, for although the emphasis of Worcester's ordinances is continually upon the burgesses, the common council, the town clerk, the bailleys and the citizens, yet the whole constitution was drawn up 'by hole assent of the citizens inhabitant in the Citye of Worcester *at their yeld merchaunt*'. This is an excellent example of the identity of gild and corporation. The ordinances show an interesting development of municipal works and building regulations. Firehooks were to be set at three stations in the city: ('And grete helpe and nede be that God defend . . .'). No chimneys 'of tree' nor thatched houses were to be allowed within the walls 'but that the owners make them of bryke or stone'.

The original Gilds Merchant included members from all types of occupation and craft, though their main preoccupation was with retail trade. At first all the master craftsmen, at least in the more prestigious trades, were members of the same gild; the emergence of self-governing craftsmen's gilds was a relatively late development.[7] Thus the sequence of the gild movement is successively amalgamation, fragmentation and regrouping, until the final supremacy of the town council and the decline of all gilds to a convivial or charitable roll in the background of town life. Ballard and Tait found craft gilds 'poorly illustrated' in borough charters, but do refer to charter evidence of the weavers of London and the weavers and cordwainers of Oxford. The street plans of many medieval boroughs suggest the existence of separate communities of craftsmen at an early date. Wells has its Walkers' Lane and Tewkesbury its Fullers' Street. Even where there is no clearly named segregation of trades, tax lists show larger numbers of a given craft in particular wards; at Salisbury most tuckers were residents of St Martins.

Most craft gilds emerge during the 14th century, the fishmongers (1339) and the weavers, dyers, fullers and tailors (1346) at Bristol; the skinners of Salisbury (1380) and the barber-surgeons of Cambridge (1348) are typical examples. Usually emergent craft gilds were kept under the control of the merchant oligarchy, their ordinances confirmed by permission of the wardens of the Gild Merchant or the mayor of the town and enrolled in the borough statutes, as at Worcester. Just as some Gilds Merchant had contested with their overlords and burgesses for their right to combine, so many newer craft gilds challenged the supremacy of their town's Gild Merchant. In some cases, as in Reading, an abbot might support the town's craftsmen as a new measure of contest with his burgesses. Sometimes, as at Cirencester, the gild was suppressed.

A note of caution is necessary about the documentation of gilds and its dating, for these are occasionally inconsistent. The licence to found a gild, or the resumé of its ordinances may be recorded late in the gild's existence. Many of the surviving documents refer, perhaps optimistically, to their origins 'beyond the memory of man'. On the other hand, the latest date of a set of ordinances is not necessarily contemporary with the foundation of the gild. Some evidence of gilds, as in the *Pipe Rolls*, is premature; some, like the later ordinances, is too late.

Craft gilds, like the earlier Gilds Merchant, were associations of capitalist owners, master craftsmen who must be freemen of the borough. The purpose of their association was, once again, to preserve their monopoly of manufacture, to exclude 'strangers' and to prevent the engrossing of production by individuals. In some towns, such as Nottingham, their monopoly of cloth-making extended for a radius of ten leagues around the town. At the same time, standards of workmanship were enforced by overseers appointed to supervise work in progress or offered for sale. Above all, the craft gilds preserved the status of the qualified master-craftsman. Membership of the gild demanded a substantial entry-fee with preferential rates for the heirs of established craftsmen. The chief control of membership was by means of a term of apprenticeship, usually for seven years, with the final submission of an expensive 'masterpiece' as a test of competence. Restrictive practices included the limitation of servants or workmen per master, the regulation of working hours to those of daylight only, with a total prohibition of work on Sundays and holy-days. Weavers' looms must stand in open view of the street, not hidden in basement cellars or upstairs rooms; working by artificial light was not allowed. The right of search by the gilds' overseers was regularly applied and the standards set are, by modern consumers' experience, high; at Buckingham, for instance, shoemakers were fined for making *inner* soles of horse-leather. An illuminating set of memoranda of the belligerent tailors of Exeter records how, when a master-tailor was accused of wasting his customer's material in making a gown by faulty workmanship or theft, the gild's model patterns on black paper were produced from the common coffer, to prove that the garment was made to the required standard. In other cases, where a master was at fault for lack of 'connyng' (skill), he repaid the cost of the cloth.

Some towns supported very few manufacturing industries except a few staple textile, leatherworking and metal crafts. Most of Hull's enrolled freemen from 1370-1499 were retail tradesmen or shipowners: craft gilds do not emerge there until late in the 15th century, when the weavers, fullers, glovers and merchants produced their ordinances. In other counties the development of natural resources such as stone, coal and timber precluded much development of manufacture by gildsmen. We must not expect to find an invariable pattern in all towns.

A primary function of every craft gild was provision for the welfare of its members and their families. In times of hardship, sickness, old age or mishap, insurance was available and the widows and orphans of the brethren were protected. The souls of departed craftsmen were also a matter of great concern, with funds being reserved for the provision of seemly funerals and masses for the dead. In all these respects the craft gilds overlap the similar functions of the contemporary religious fraternities who also called themselves 'gilds'. Some religious gilds were actually created to mask the activities of craft gilds, just as some merchant gilds had been used as a commercial 'front' for aspiring local politicians.

The gilds' attitude to women was ambivalent and varied from place to place. Sometimes wives and widows were welcome to trade in their husbands' right; elsewhere they might be expressly forbidden any access to trade. In Berwick, no married woman might buy wool; at Leicester the gild was open to all but women; and at Bristol in 1461, wives and daughters were forbidden any employment at weaving. The chauvinist cappers of Coventry rated all wives as 'of apprentice status'. Elsewhere, and particularly in the religious gilds, the 'sisteren' were offered equal treatment with the brethren; a master's widow was usually expected to continue his trade if she went unmarried.

The activities of a gild could encompass many strange and varied events: the presentation of a pageant-with-giant and sword-bearers by the tailors of Salisbury; the prohibition of shaving one's neighbour if not a barber surgeon; the founding of a Christian school for the education and conversion of Jews at Bristol; the teaching of an essential foreign language to apprentices in the Taunton cloth-trade; or the undertaking by the barbers at Oxford not to divulge the personal secrets of any client's 'abomination of stinking breath'.

The supremacy of borough over gilds was frequently enforced. In many towns, craftsmen had to be burgesses before they could practice their trade. At Coventry, the relationship was one of frequent conflicts; in other places, such as Leicester, the situation was usually harmonious. At Exeter the gild ordinances of the cordwainers and bakers were obtained by permission of the corporation, and all fines were paid half to the city and half to the gild. Any article deemed to be contrary to the city's liberties was to be redrafted, and the cordwainers surrendered their constitution annually to the corporation, receiving it back formally on payment of a 4d. fine.

In the case of the gilds' surviving records, more so than for most documents of English towns, the picture is bedevilled by the loss of evidence. In so many town histories we are told that 'there must have been . . .' or that 'perhaps there was . . .' a gild of weavers, glovers or some other well-known local craft, but that no evidence of their existence has survived. In some towns the existence of a 'portmanmoot book' may overemphasise the town's importance at the expense of the gilds; in another place the massive survival of ordinances may reveal the merchants and craftsmen in a stronger light.

Textile and leather crafts are usually well to the fore in most towns. At Oxford a dozen trades included cordwainers, weavers, fullers, bakers, butchers, barbers, tailors, skinners, mercers and woollen drapers, brewers, glovers and smiths. In some towns a particular industry is thoroughly documented, as with the tallow-chandlers of Leicester, the bakers of Bristol or the cappers of Coventry. It is noticeable that although the cloth trade, metalwork and leather goods tend to dominate some counties, most small towns could muster a full range of essential industries. At Salisbury in the 15th century, the city's *Ledger Book* lists the numbers of tradesmen as follows: 66 weavers, 44 tailors, 30 fullers and shearers, 24 smiths, 21 dubbers (leather-dressers), 18 tanners, 14 butchers, 13 barber-surgeons, 11 corn factors, eight innkeepers and three pewterers. The Salisbury gilds, as in other towns, were important contributors to national taxation, paying towards the muster of 'hobblers' and archers for the Agincourt campaign.

In the earlier stages of craft development there was intense specialization. Labour tended to be rigidly divided, so that each process of production supported its own gild.

Clothiers were divided into the various gilds of shearers, spinners, carders, weavers, fullers, dyers, tailors and drapers. Demarcation disputes were inevitable; cases occur of tailors being prohibited by the furriers from trimming gowns with fur. At a later stage in the gilds' development, during the 15th and 16th centuries, a reverse tendency towards the amalgamation of separate gilds into 'fellowships' or trading companies emerged. In Buckingham about 36 gilds were combined into four companies each of like trade, though some of the associations seem tenuous to modern eyes. These were the mercers, cordwainers, tailors and butchers. 'Mercers' now included most of the retail shopkeepers — the grocers, haberdashers, linendrapers, woollen drapers, clothiers, silkmen, goldsmiths, apothecaries, satters, chandlers, hatters and cappers. 'Cordwainers' comprised all the leather trades, such as shoemakers, tanners, glovers, parchment-makers, saddlers, collar-makers (for horses), girdle-makers, paynters and point-makers. 'Tailors' combined the dyers, fullers, weavers, smiths, glaziers, pewterers, braziers, fletchers, furbishers and painters and the 'Butchers' incorporated the bakers, brewers, cooks and millers. Buckingham's *Ledger Book* preserves these gilds' ordinances.

Nowhere are a city's companies and gilds more fully documented than in London, where the full range of records has been recorded and analysed by George Unwin.[8] Unwin's references to the documents and his bibliography are indispensable aids to the study of medieval London. Here it will suffice to refer to his transcription of a list of names 'of all the crafts exercised in London from of old and still continuing in the ninth year of King Henry V' (1421-22). This list, which Unwin reproduces in facsimile and transcribes in an appendix, was preserved in the records of the Brewers Company. No document could portray more concisely such a vivid picture of the commercial activities of a great medieval town; this array of trades will also provide a useful check-list for provincial towns. There were 111 crafts listed in all. Whitaker's current (1983) *Almanack* lists under London's present-day *City Gilds (Livery Companies)* 12 surviving companies in order of civic precedence, from mercers to clothworkers, with their present addresses and names of officials.

The pageantry of the names of the livery companies reminds us of the most familiar aspect of gild life to survive as tradition and literature, the 'mystery plays' of medieval England. For here 'mystery' means 'craft' and much of the language and liveliness of the gilds, as well as their religious faith, has been preserved in these cycles of plays, many of which are still regularly performed to modern audiences. In every town of note, the gilds were responsible for preparing an annual pageant of morality plays, based upon the scriptures, in some cases (as at York) encompassing the whole story of God and Man from Creation to the Resurrection and Doomsday. Each craft took an appropriate section of the Bible, according to its down-to-earth associations, so that the carpenters or shipmen would portray the making of Noah's Ark. With an eye to the shepherds the Shearmen of Coventry presented the Nativity; tragically the gild's manuscript of the play was burned in 1879. Plays are preserved at Chester (24 plays), York (48 plays), Coventry (42 plays); there are also the Towneley Mysteries which were probably acted in or near Wakefield.

No other gilds are as characteristic or as evocative of medieval society as are the religious fraternities. These were concerned primarily with the care of souls after death, by a prudent investment in prayers and masses for the dead, and an equal regard for the social welfare of the living. In many cases the ordinances of a religious gild place the social responsibility above the religious, requiring that the poor be fed before the cost of a priest is undertaken 'if the fund can afford him'. We gain a fairly complete picture of these medieval societies because their responses to the separate writ of Richard II (see page 104) have survived. A more deceptive reason for the predominance of religious fraternities may be that, with so much overlap of functions, a 'religious' gild's returns may be the record of the religious functions of an otherwise 'craft' gild. Certainly there were gilds which combined craft and religious functions. The gilds of furriers, barbers, tailors, carpenters and saddlers of Norwich, make no reference in their ordinances of 1350–1380 to craft byelaws but were concerned only with requiem masses, help to the poor and maimed, burial of the dead and insurance of those who fall upon hard times 'if not brought about by folly and riotous living...'. The tailors and fullers of Lincoln, on the other hand, interspersed regulation of labour amongst their more pious intentions. The medieval tendency to treat dissimilar ideas and functions as if they were of the same intent and value can be very misleading. Most of the socio-religious gilds are identifiable by their title, which is almost always ecclesiastical; fraternities of Our Lady, Corpus Christi, the Discovery of the Cross or St Helen, the Holy Trinity and many saints or martyrs are commonplace. It is, however, always worth discovering whether a saintly designation may not match the patron of a particular craft, as does St Crispin for the shoemakers.

Although each fraternity would almost certainly found and finance a lady-chapel for its own use within the parish church, the gild's saint and the patron saint of the church were not essentially the same. See for instance Unwin's *Appendix of London Parish Gilds*, where the dedications of church and gilds rarely match.[9] Sometimes one parish church might house several differently named saints' gilds; St Giles-in-Cripplegate, in the City of London housed five gilds, only one of which was named after St Giles. Where a religious gild was the only one in a town or the most important of several, it was usually called by the name of the place or parish, even if it had another special dedication to a patron saint of its own; as for example, the *comuna* of St Nicholas 'of Worcester'. Provision of chantries was similar to the formation of parish gilds and should not be confused. At Dudley we find no craft gilds, though the proclamation of Richard II's writ was read in Dudley Market Place, nor any true religious gild. There was a chantry of St Mary in St Edmund's church, but none of its foundation charters, licenses or chantry certificates survives. This was certainly an important feature of Dudley's medieval communal life, leaving its legacy of 'Lady Lands' to the town's once-distinguished grammar school.[10]

Richard II's writ demanded information on the date of foundation of each gild; a statement of its ordinances; and an account of its property (an ominous forewarning of royal depredations yet to come). A typical religious gild's responses, usually of a foundation licensed c. 1350–1379, but often claiming great antiquity, run very closely to a pattern. The ordinances usually outline a constitution of masters, aldermen or wardens with assistant stewards, fellas, skeveynes or bailiffs, and officials such as dean, beadle, summoner or clerks. If an aim is stated, as for the Gild of Galrekhithe in London, 1375, it might be 'to nourish good fellowship'; at Ludlow in 1284, 'to be a member of the Gild shall be an assurance of help in time of trouble...'.

There was in the religious gilds a more equitable treatment of 'brethren and sisteren' whose names are often listed — 13 men and 11 women at Wiggenhall in Norfolk.

Next, the ordinances will set up an annual procession, church service, and feast or 'drinking' to be held once a year on the eve and day of the patron saint. There was much emphasis on the necessity of good repute and godly living amongst the brethren. Contentious men and 'janglers' were to be excluded, and there are frequent prohibitions of swearing, quarrelling, adultery and drunkenness 'or other such by which the fraternity might be ensclaundered . . .'. As well as the annual feast there were usually three or four business meetings or 'morningspeches' during the course of the year. Entrance fees, gifts and bequests were specified and accounted for yearly. Often the gild's members must wear a livery suit or hood and occasionally were expected to provide a 'breakfast' on joining the gild. There was careful attention to the burial of the dead, and arrangements would be made for a wake and dirge or night-watch, with a specified number of large candles placed around the bier, sometimes held by paid mutes acting as torch-bearers. At Ludlow there is a strange injuction in the ordinances of the Palmers' Gild in 1284, that 'no ghosts nor spectres shall be called up at the night-watch, no mocking of the body or its good name . . .'.

The funds of the gild were allocated to the salaries of mass-priests, sometimes of schoolmasters 'of grammar', with details of daily or weekly prayers and masses for the souls of the dead, often mentioned by name. Burials of brethren were to be attended, even at a distance from the town, 'as if he were at home among them . . .'. Those who died in poverty were to be decently buried at the gild's expense. Producers of wax and ale must have made considerable profits from their local gilds as the specification of 32 lb. candles for altars, biers and processions, and fines in gallons of ale, are prodigious. The intention to preserve a seemly relationship in the community sometimes forbade brethren to go to law against each other or to take a suit to any court but the gild's. Payments of poor relief vary considerably; at Norwich the 'croked and blynd' were to receive 7d. a week. In the same city the furriers paid out twice as much (14d.) from regular subscriptions of ¼d. per member.

The religious gilds also had their gildhalls, like that of the Gild of Blessed Mary at Chesterfield in 1218. At Coventry the Gildhall is inventoried, room by room. There was an open hall, buttery, pantry and kitchen. At Exeter the Tailors' Gildhall furnished a parlour, hall, buttery, chamber next the hall and outer chamber. The history and structure of provincial gildhalls would merit many a careful survey and record by local students.

Of our three specimen West Midland towns, Dudley had no gild but a chantry; Birmingham offers the example of an important religious gild and a separate society for the hamlet of Deritend. The ancient City of Worcester affords each type of association: a Gild Merchant, craft gilds and at least two important religious fraternities. For Worcester, apart from the origin of its Gild Merchant recorded in the town's 13th-century charter (see illustration on page 92) the surviving gild records are late and fragmentary. They are preserved amongst the city's ordinances at the Guildhall and are dated 1467. These order specifically (Ordinance 22) that five pageants be held amongst the crafts, with another reference (Ordinance 78) to strangers, journeymen and payments of entry fees to the Wardens, Stewards or Master of each craft. A late 17th-century edition of the ordinances of the Worcester Gild of Carpenters and Joiners also survives. These contain the customary regulations on apprenticeship, journeymen's wages and the sharing of bulk purchases of timber. None of the city's responses to the writ of 1389 are to be found at the Public Record Office; we have only what survives at the Guildhall. As to religious gilds, the *comuna* of St Nicholas was, by 1547, primarily concerned with the upkeep of 23 cottages or almshouses adjoining Trinity Hall and the salary of a schoolmaster, John Oliver, B.A., who was paid £6 13s. 4d. The gild's seal survives and is illustrated here:

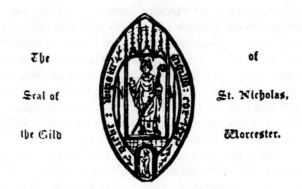

The Seal of the Gild of St. Nicholas, Worcester.

Other Worcester gilds were the Cordwainers whose 16th century Book of Ordinances was found in the care of a local shoemaker in 1857. These regulated conditions of apprenticeship and entry-fee, and provided for the continuation of a master's trade by his widow. There was also provision for a morality play to be staged by the gild on the feast of St Crispin. This Company continued to meet until the 18th century.[11] The Worcester Company of Clothiers ambitiously claimed their origins from the reign of King Wulfhere of Mercia in the 7th century.[12] There are several references to their gild in the city ordinances and other, later account books. The Company, though in debt by 1711, was still dispensing charity in the 19th century, and survives as a social group undertaking various charitable works.

Fifteen Worcester gilds re-established themselves during the years of the 16th, 17th and 18th centuries. These were the clothiers (1590), glovers (1497), cordwainers (1504), bakers (1528), mercers (1545), tailors (1504), ironmongers (1598), butchers (1604), carpenters (1661), bricklayers (1713), coopers (1726), masons, fishmongers and parish clerks (1730) and barbers (1677). Only the clothiers' gild survived into the late 19th century; some of the others, like the Merchant Taylors, invested their funds in a state lottery which failed, or became dining clubs and friendly societies.

At Birmingham the Gild of Holy Cross was licensed in 1583 for the allocation of 18 messuages, 3 tofts, six acres of land and rents worth 40s. in Edgbaston and Birmingham, to support two chaplains and undertake certain 'works of charity', which were in fact the public service of bridge and road repairs. In Tudor times the Gild also looked after 12 poor people, with rent-free housing and 'all kinds of sustenance, food and clothing'. At Deritend, across the town bridge, the Gild of St John the Baptist was founded. The Bishop of Coventry and Lichfield consented to the provision of a chapel there, because the inhabitants were two miles distant from the parish church, so that 'in the winter season the said parishioners could not go to church without great danger of perishing . . .'. By Tudor times there were 200 'houseling' people in Deritend, with two priests, one 'serving the cure of souls', the other teaching a Grammar School. The annual income of the Gild was £13 1s. 7d.; that of the Holy Cross was £31 2s. 10d.

It is ironic that the craft gilds and religious fraternities came to their flowering just as the towns began to decay. The best of English medieval urban development took place from 1066–1377. By the beginning of the 15th century a decline had set in. This was to some extent due to the disasters of the Black Death and the wastage of warfare at home and abroad. The towns' decay was even more the result of a combination of economic pressures familiar today: chiefly the costs of excessive taxation and inflation. Already in the 12th century some market towns like Oxford were feeling the strain of competition from more recently established markets, like nearby Abingdon. As the deterrent of the local castle or the economic protection of an abbey became less effective, so the towns which had grown up in their shadow began to languish. This was not the result of the isolated cataclysm of a 14th-century plague, but a more relentless economic force, which in towns like Bristol created reaction against foreign immigrants and the influx of villeins escaping from manors around the city. As a result of such pressures the gildsmen became over-protective and increasingly restrictive in their practices. In a decaying economy the merchants and craftsmen clung to their privileges, thus destroying themselves and their commerce.

In order to survive, enterprising craftsmen were forced out of the town into the neighbouring villages and countryside. This emigration was further encouraged by the opening of new pack-routes and more convenient bridges; at the same time the innovation of water-powered mills and workshops fostered a premature rural industrial revolution. Most towns had already a network of village contacts in the surrounding countryside; bricks and tiles were made for Hull in the villages of Myton and Tripett as early as 1303, and earlier still, the weavers of Worcester took in spun wool from the country. The closed shop of freemen-burgesses and gild brethren, exacting exorbitant entry fees, could work only to the destruction of gilds and towns alike. As the gilds endeavoured to enforce their control for several leagues around each town, so the enterprising newcomers went farther afield. Many ancient towns like Stamford, Northampton and Lincoln were, in the words of Edward Miller, 'permanent casualties' of the economic changes of the 13th and 14th centuries.[13]

The *Subsidy Rolls* of the 16th century reveal changes in the comparative wealth of old-fashioned towns like Oxford against those of rising towns like Abingdon, Burford, Henley and Chipping Norton as the increasing petulance of the later gild ordinances reveal a decline in trade. Sudden slumps in the admission fees in a town may indicate the imminence of collapse. At Gloucester in 1462 there were protests against weavers who 'receyven Allions' and in Bristol there were similar complaints against employment of Irish weavers who avoided the local rules of apprenticeship. By the 15th century many small villages were developing their own industrial system with its own gilds. Somerset is an outstanding example of an early rural cloth industry, with gilds of 'webbers', tuckers and fullers at Croscombe. Their gild records are preserved in the churchwardens' accounts.

Another feature of the disruption of the medieval craft structure was increasingly violent conflict between masters and their workmen. We now begin to see the only 'labour' aspects of the medieval gild system, with the emergence of militant 'journeymen gilds'. Journeymen were the wage earners of the gild system; time expired apprentices working for hire by the day (*journée*) as 'servants' to their masters. At a time of recession they saw fewer prospects of advancement or independent business for themselves and low wages, with prohibitive charges for full master craftsmanship confirmed their sense of exploitation. The masters' reaction to an uneasy labour force was the imposition of still more enforcement; wages were regulated, conditions of employment were restricted.

'Yeomen gilds' were particularly widespread in Warwickshire. In Coventry, the Journeymen Cappers were forbidden to work 'against their masters', and the 'serving men' of the Drapers' Company were refused permission to join together in their own association. In many towns the 'youths, servants and apprentices' became increasingly 'insolent' in their demands and increasingly violent in their assemblies and protests. The Coventry religious gilds were not entirely innocuous. In 1386 the 'Gild of the Nativity' was said to be a 'cover' for discontented labourers and artificers 'of the mediocre sort'. The Gild was suppressed. Increasingly the older gilds' measures became more repressive and less effectual. Soon the decay of town life became apparent in the failure of public works, the collapse of town walls, gates and castle towers, the failure to maintain roadways and bridges. By 1512 Parliamentary statutes were looking back on 200 years of decline, 'many and the most parte of all the cities, boroughs and townes corporate wythin this realme of Englonde be fallen into ruyne and decaye and not inhabited with merchauntes and men of such substaunce as they were . . .'.[14] John Leland in his *Itinerary* (c. 1535–43) laments the ruination of many a town castle. The walls of many towns were in disrepair and in Lincoln the citizens could not afford to rebuild their gildhall; indeed, in 1470 there had been 'scarce 200 citizens' still resident there. According to Leland, however, Lincoln was far from alone in its plight; he claimed that other towns like Boston, Carlisle, and Coventry were also in ruins.

To the gilds' own decline was added the confiscation of their property by Henry VIII and his son. In theory, the government of the Reformation pillaged only the religious element of the gilds and chantries. Some of the gilds' religious land and income went to school endowment: far more lined the pockets of the Tudor gentry. The unscrupulous nature of the attack was blatant, often based upon false evidence of the gilds' aims and purposes. A proportion of the profits went to found or maintain the grammar schools of Edward VI; far more was lost and stolen. At Worcester, the Gild of St Nicholas's school and 23 almshouses were at risk. Henry VIII's commissioners ruled, in a terse marginal note: 'continue clothes to the poor but shut up the schole for there is one other in the towne of the King's own foundation and this is no schole of any purpose as it is credibly said'. In fact, Henry VIII's school in Worcester accommodated 40 pupils when the school of St Nicholas taught more than 100. The school had existed 'since tyme out of mynde'.

Birmingham was more fortunate. Indeed, the town's condition was more favourable than many others for, although the roads and bridges tended to fall into disrepair 'the charge whereof the town of itself is not able to maintain', being dependent for this upon the Gild of Holy Cross, nevertheless Leland reported it to be a town of remarkable new 'bewty'. The response to Edward VI's commissioners claimed the town as 'one of the fairest and most profitable towns to the King's Highness in the shire' with 1,800 'houseling people'. 'The said town of Birmingham', the commissioners reported, 'is a very mete place'. To this author, the town is perhaps more memorable for the joyous accident of the survival of Lench's Trust, which by prudent forethought outwitted the Tudor raiders.

William Lench was a Birmingham tanner who lived in Moor Street. In 1525 apprehensive of death – which came only a year later – and mindful of his bad conscience about 'tithes forgotten', he endowed a trust as an offshoot of the gild of Holy Cross. Fortunately, mindful of his wife Agnes's welfare, Lench set up a 'deed of feoffment' which prevented the property being merged entirely with that of the Gild. His forethought saved the investment, and Lench's Trust is now the oldest – and most prosperous – of 81 surviving trusts and almshouses listed in the *Birmingham Post Yearbook and Who's Who* for 1982–83. Until recently William's original grants of land between Lancaster and Loveday Streets, intersected by streets named for Lench and his feoffee Vesey, still belonged to the Trust with his two 'closes' at Hawkes's Croft and Loveday Croft but the recent developments of Queensway, Moor Street Station, and the University of Aston have taken their toll. So the bulldozers and the planners have destroyed what even Henry VIII could not take. Even so, it is reassuring to see in a great modern city, this careful maintenance of the 'will and intent' of a Tudor tanner and gildsman.

In the changes which were overtaking 16th-century English towns, the relative decline of Worcester's cloth trade and prosperity is matched by the rising prosperity of that 'mete place' Birmingham. As many of the most ancient towns declined, so 'new towns' came to the fore with 'factory' crafts and industries. In the next Chapter we shall see the state of old and new towns graphically delineated in maps and plans. Dudley and the other 'new towns' would need to look, in that coming age, for effective substitutes for the older corporate institutions of the Middle Ages – the monastery and the gilds, now in decline or dissolution – in their provision of funds for education, hospitals, almshouses, poor relief, public works and the regulation of community affairs. Later Chapters will reveal whether or not these substitutes were adequate for the urban situation of the 18th and 19th centuries.

FURTHER READING

Abrams, P., 'Towns and economic growth; some theories and problems', in *Essays* . . . (Past & Present pubns.) (1978).

Ashley, W. J., *An Introduction to Economic History and Theory* (1888–93).

Cook, G. H., *Medieval Chantries and Chantry Chapels* (1947).

Clark, P. and Slack, P., *Crisis and Order in English Towns, 1500–1700* (1972).

Cunningham, W., 'The formation and decay of craft gilds', *Trans. Roy. Hist. Soc.*, N.S. iii (1886).

Fisher, D., 'Economic Institutions in the Towns of Medieval England', *La Ville; Receuils de la Societe Jean Bodin*, vii (1955).

Gross, C., *The Gild Merchant* (1890).

Kramer, S., *English Craft Gilds and the Government* (1905).

—— *English Craft Gilds: Studies in their progress and decline* (1927).

Maitland, F. W., *Township and Borough* (1898).

Marshall, T. H., 'Capitalism and the decline of the English Gilds', *Cam. Hist. Soc.*, vol. iii (1923).

Meyer, E. F., 'English Craft Gilds and Borough Governance in the Later Middle Ages', *Univ. Colorado Studies*, xvi (1929).

FURTHER READING: – continued

Phythian-Adams, C., 'Sources for Urban History: (3) The Crafts Gilds', *Loc. Historian*, vol. 9, No. 6, May 1971.

Smith, J. T. and L., 'English Gilds', *Early English Text Society*, vol. 40 (1870).

Thrupp, S. L., 'Medieval Gilds reconsidered', *Jnl. Econ. Hist.*, ii, (1942).

Unwin, G., 'Medieval Gilds and Education', *Studies in Economic History*, ed.: R. H. Tawney (1927).

—— *The Gilds and Companies of London* (1908: reprinted 1966).

Westlake, H. F., *The Parish Gilds of Medieval England* (1919).

No. *11*

CLOTHIERS' COMPANY.

Give to *Widow Walker* ....

FOUR POUNDS OF BREAD,

On THURSDAY, the 10th APRIL, 1879.

JOHN W. WILLIS BUND,

High Master.

To Mrs. SURMAN,
Angel Street,
Worcester.

CLOTHIERS' COMPANY.

BREAD TICKET.

No. *3* .... *Good Friday* 186*1*

Give to the Bearer, *Harriett Brewer*
                                          St Andrew

ONE LOAF OF BREAD.

c.c.

....
for Sir C A H Lechmere Bt.
H. M. C. Company.

The charitable survival of the Clothiers' Company in nineteenth-century Worcester (see page 114). Bundles of these tickets, many unused, are kept at the County Record Office at St Helen's Church in Fish Street.

Extracts from (1) the Ordinances of Worcester of 1467 referring to the regulations for bakers; (2) to the performance of pageants; (3) the Glovers' Book showing minutes and accounts for 1586. (*From the Guildhall at Worcester. The pages of the Ordinances Book are 7½ ins. wide, and those of the Glovers' Book are 5½ ins. wide.*)

Transcripts (1) and (2) from J. Toulmin Smith, *English Gilds*; (3) transcript by the author.

(1)   IX. Also, that Bakers make no fyne with the Bailly for ther offencz of bakynge, but that they haue the punysshement of every defaute accordynge to the Statute, and to the lawe. And that they bye no corne vn the market day, in somer tylle xj. of the Belle, and in Wynter tyme tylle xij. of the belle. And p^t the seid Bakers bye no corne ne mele in hur houses aforn the seid owres vppon the market day.

Regulation of bakers

(2) XXII. Also it myght be ordeined a substancialle rule, that v pagentes amonge the craftes, to be holden yerly, shuld not be to seche when the[y] shuld go to do worshippe to god and to the cite, and to better and more certenly kept then they hauc be before this tyme, vppon peyn of euery crafte founde in defaute of xl.*s.*; the oon half to be payd to the Baillies and the other half to the comyn treso^r. And that the stewards of euery crafte that ben contributory, shullen be called to the accompte to knowe the charge, so that the Stuards of euery crafte may haue levey as for ther parte, in peyne of hym that ys founde in defaute, iiij.*s.* iiij.*d.*; half to the Bailly, and half to the comyn treso^r. Also that yerly, at the lawday holdyn at hokday, that the grete enquest shalle provide and ordeyn wheþer the pageant shuld go that yere or no. And so yerly for more surete.

The five crafte pageants to be more strictly kept:

the contribution due from each craft to be settled and levied;

and the Hock-tide lawday yearly to fix whether the pageant shall go or not.

Also it myght be ordemed a substanciall rule that v pageantes amonge the craftes to be holden yerly and not be to seche when when shuld go to do worshipp to god and to the cite And to bette and more certonly kept then they hauo be bifore this tyme vppon poyn of ony crafte founde in defaute of xl d the oon half to be payd to the Baillt And the other half to the comyn treso And that the Stewardes of ony crafte that beu contributory shull be called to the acompto to knowe the charge so that the Stuard of ony crafte may hano lovoy as for ther parte in poyne of hym that ys founde in defaute iij d my A half to the Baillt And half to the comyn tresó Also that yerly at the lawday holdon at hok day that the grete enqueft shult pvide And ordem whon the pageant shuld go that yes or no And os yerly for more surete

1586

Ite(m) layd out for the Clarkes Wagis the vith
of Aprill vjd & iijd for Roger Clarke and iijd for
Cunnand Wyld/Roger Clarke accompte

Ite(m) laid oute for standing x viijd
It(em) for a paire of gloves to the alderman sargeaunt
; iiijd
It(em) to Hughe Chaddocke xviijd
It(em) payd to Hugh Chaddocke at sundry times
; ijd
It(em) paid to the clark for his wages vjd
vjs xd

GAZETTEER OF SOURCES ON
MEDIEVAL GILDS AND TRADE 1066-1600

The principal references here are: Ballard, A., *British Borough Charters 1042-1216* (1913), referred to as BBC, Ballard, A., and Tait, J., *British Borough Charters 1216-1307* (1923), referred to here as BTC; and Weinbaum, M., *British Borough Charters 1307-1660* (1943), referred to here as WBC. Where charters refer to gilds, markets and fair, F = fair, M = market, MG = Gild Merchant, and CG = craft gild(s). (On fairs and markets, which have not been dealt with in this chapter, see the *Report of the Royal Commission on Market Rights and Tolls* (1889), which lists 2,713 markets and fairs granted between 1199-1483). RCHM=the volumes published by the Royal Commission on Historical manuscripts.

An asterisk, * by a date indicates a substantial reference to, or a transcription of, documents concerning the town in question from one of the following works: Gross, C., *The Gild Merchant* (1890, repr. 1964), referred to here as GM; Toulmin-Smith, J., 'English Gilds', (*Early English Text Society*, vol. 40, 1870), referred to here as EG; the *Victoria County History* volume for the appropriate county (VCH); Douglas, D. C. (ed.), *English Historical Documents 1327-1495* (1969) (EDH iv). Names in **BOLD** print (e.g., **ABERYSTWYTH** or **Axbridge**) had Gild Merchants. Towns with names printed in lower case (e.g. **Axbridge**) were not municipal boroughs in 1974, but had had gilds etc. For further information besides the books already cited, see Gross, C., *A Bibliography of British Municipal History* (1897, repr. 1966) and Graves. E. B., *A Bibliography of English History to 1485* (1975). Gross's bibliography to *The Gild Merchant* also lists many local works. CRO = County Record Office, as before.

ABERYSTWYTH: GM, 1277; BTC, 1277 (MG, F&M).
ABINGDON: RCHM i, 98, 99.
ALDEBURGH: WBC, 1567 (M).
ALNWICK: GM, 1611*.
ALTRINCHAM: GM, 1290: BTC, c. 1290.
ANDOVER: GM, 1175-76*; BBC, 1157, 1194, 1205 (F); WBC, 1511 (F).
Axbridge: GM, temp. Ric. I*.
AYLESBURY: VCH iii.
Bala (Gwynedd): GM, 1324.
Bamborough: (Nmbd): GM, 1332; WBT, 1332 (MG, F&M).
BARNSTAPLE: GM, 1303; Chanter, J. R., 'Vestiges of an early Gild of St Nicholas at Barnstaple', *Trans. Dev. Assoc. Advancement of Science*, vol. 11 (1879).
BASINGSTOKE: WBC. 1449 (F); Millard, J. E., *The Book of Accounts of the Wardens of the Fraternity of the Holy Ghost in Basingstoke 1557-1645* (1882); Loggan, S., *The History of the Brotherhood or Guild of the Holy Ghost near Basingstoke . . .* (1742).
BATH: GM, 1189*; Shickle, C. W. 'The Guild of the Merchant Taylors', *Bath Nat. Hist. & Field Club Proc.*, vol. 9 (1901).
BEAUMARIS: GM, 1296*; BTC, 1296.
BECCLES: 'Guild of the Holy Ghost, Beccles', *East Anglian Notes and Queries*, vol. iii (1867).
BEDFORD: GM, temp. Ric. I*; BBC, 1189.
Bere (Devon): BTC, 1284.
BERWICK-UPON-TWEED: RCHM, iii 308-10; GM, temp. Ed. I*; BTC, 1302 (GM?, F&M); *Gild of Berwick-upon-Tweed* (Ord 1283-84); EG, XVIII, p. 338; Innes, C., 'Statuta Gildæ', in *Ancient Laws of the Burghs of Scotland (1249-1294)* (1868); Scott, J..

(*Berwick-upon-Tweed — continued*) —
Berwick-on-Tweed; the History of Town and Guild (1888).
BEVERLEY: GM, 1119-35*; BBC, 1130; WBC, 1554 (M&F); EG, III, 148-50; * Gild of St Elene (1378); EG, iii, p. 148; *Gild of St Mary (1355); EG, iii (b), p. 149; Great Gild of St John of Beverley in the Hanshouse (n.d.); EG, iii (c), p. 150; Leach, A. F., 'Beverley Town Documents', *Selden Soc.*, 14 (1900); Witty, J. R., 'The Plays of Beverley 1377-1467', vol. 4, *Yorks. Dialect Soc.*, EHD, iv, No. 621*.
BEWDLEY: WBC, 1507 (F).
BIRMINGHAM: *Gild of the Holy Cross (lic, 1383), EG, XIII, p. 239; 'Lenche's Trust' (1525), EG, XIII (d), p. 251; *Gild of St John the Baptist, Deritend (n.d.), EG, XIII, p. 258; Smith, J. T., *Memorials of Old Birmingham* (1863); Smith, L. T., *The Gild of Holy Cross, Birmingham* (1894).
BODMIN: GM, 1225-72; WBC, 1415 (F).
BOSTON: GM, 1260* (?); WBC, 1573 (M); Dover, P.. *The Early Medieval History of Boston 1086-1400* (1970).
Bridgnorth (Salop): GM, 1227; BTC, 1227; WBC, 1359 (F).
BRIDGWATER: GM: temp. Ed. I; RCHM, i, 99, iii, 310; BBC, 1200 (F&M).
BRISTOL: GM: 1188*; BBC, 1188; *Weavers' Ordinances 1346*, EHD, iv, No. 610*; Miscellaneous Ordinances c. 1350 (EHD, iv, No. 611*); Bickley, F. B., *The Little Red Book of Bristol* (1900); Carus Wilson, E. M., 'The Merchant Adventures of Bristol in the fifteenth century', *Trans. Roy. Hist. Soc.* 4th series, vol. 11 (1928); Fox, F. F., 'The History

(Bristol – continued) –
of the Guilds of Bristol, especially the Bakers' Guild', *Bristol & Gloucs. Arch. Soc. Trans.*, vol. 3 (1878); Fox, F. F., *Some Account of the Ancient Fraternity of Merchant Tailors with transcripts of ordinances and other documents (1392-1832)* (1880); Fox, F. F. and Taylor, J., *Some Accounts of the Guild of Weavers in Bristol* (1889); Latimer, J., *The History of the Society of Merchant Venturers in Bristol* (1903); Orme, N., 'The Guild of Kalendars, Bristol', *Bristol & Gloucs. Arch. Soc. Trans.* vol. 96 (1978); Ralph, E., *Guide to the Bristol Archives Office* (1971), see index under *City Companies*; Rogers, H., *The Calendars of All Hallowen, Bristowe* (1846); Sherborne, J. W.: *The Port of Bristol in the Middle Ages* (Bristol Branch of the Historical Association, 1966); Taylor, J., *A Book About Bristol* (1872); Taylor, L. G., 'The Merchant Venturers of Bristol', *Bristol & Gloucs. Arch. Soc. Trans.*, vol. 71 (1952); Toulmin Smith, L., 'The Maire of Bristowe is Kalendar, by Robert Ricart', *Camden Soc. N.S.*, vol. 5 (1872); also John Latimer in *Bristol & Gloucs. Arch. Trans.*, vol. 15 (1891); VCH ii, p. 152.

BUCKINGHAM: VCH iii, p. 479, refers to *Ledger Book* at CRO.

Builth (Powys): GM, 1278*; BTC, 1278.

Burford (Oxon.): GM, 1087-1107*; BBC, 1087-1107; 1147-73; 1156; WBC, 1497 (F).

BURY ST EDMUNDS: RCHM, xiv (part viii), 121-58; Weavers and clothiers, W. Suffolk C.R.O. 9/1.

CAERNARVON: GM, 1284; BTC, 1284.

Caerwys (Clwyd): GM, 1290*; BTC, 1290.

CALNE: GM, 1565*.

CAMBRIDGE: GM, 1201*; BBC, 1201; E.G., XIV, 262-272 (5 gilds); *Gild of Holy Trinity (1377), EG, XIV, p. 262; *Gild of Blessed Virgin Mary (n.d.), EG, XIV (b), p. 269; *Gild of the Annunciation (1379), EG, XIV (c), p. 270; *Gild of Blessed Virgin Mary juxta Forum (n.d.), p. 271; *Gild of St Clement (n.d.), EG, XIV (e), p. 272; Bateson, M. (ed.): 'Cambridge Gild Records 1298-1389', *Cambridge Antiq. Soc. Proc.*, vol. 39 (1903); Palmer, W., 'Village Gilds of Cambridgeshire', *Cambs. & Hunts. Arch. Soc. Trans,*, i (1904); Siraut, M., 'Accounts of St Katherine's Guild at Holy Trinity Church Cambridge 1514-1537', *Cambridge Antiq. Soc. Proc.*, vol. 67 (1977); Ordinances in *Corporation Common Daybook*, quoted in C. H. Cooper, *Annals of Cambridge*, vol. 2 (1842-53).

CANTERBURY: GM, 1093-1109*; WBC, 1453 (F); 'Civis': *Minutes collected from the ancient records and accounts in the Chamber of Canterbury . . . from 1234* (1801-2). The ordinances of several craft gilds are given in full.

CARDIFF: GM, 1341*; WBC, 1341 (MG); WBC, 1340 (F).

CARDIGAN: GM, 1249*; BTC, 1249; WBC, 1340 (M).

CARLISLE: GM, temp. Hen. II*; BBC 1154-89; Ferguson, R. S. and Nanson, W., 'Some Municipal Records of the city of Carlisle', *Cumberland & Westmorland Antiq. & Arch. Soc.* (1887). Incl. rules and orders of 8 trade guilds and extracts from Minutes of the Corporation and Gilds.

CARMARTHEN: WBC, 1340 (M).

CHARD: BTC, 1271-72 (F&M).

CHESTER: GM, 1190-1201*; BBC 1190-1212: BTC, 1233-37; RCHM, viii, 355-403; Hibbert, F. A., 'The Gild History of Chester', *Jnl. Arch. & Hist. Soc., Chester & N. Wales*, vol. 5 (1894); Rideout, E., 'The Chester Companies and the Old Quay', *Hist. Soc. Lancs. & Cheshire*, vol. 79 (1927); Deimling, H., 'The Chester Plays', *Early English Text Soc.*, vol. 62 (1892). Extract from *Noah*, 1377, EHD, iv, 620*.

CHESTERFIELD: GM, 1294*; BBC, 1213 (M); BTC, 1294; *Gild of the Blessed Mary (1218), EG, VI, p. 165; *Gild of the Smiths (n.d.), EG, VI (b), p. 168. Jacques, W., 'Chesterfield 2: Gilds and Corporate Insignia', *Derbs. Arch. & Nat. Hist. Soc.*, vol. 43 (1921).

CHICHESTER: GM, temp. Stephen*; BBC, 1155; WBC, 1500 (F); Turner, E., 'The Merchant Guild of St George at Chichester', *Sussex Arch. Soc. Collections*, vol. 15 (1863).

Chipping Sodbury (Avon): BTC 1227 (M&F).

Cirencester (Gloucs.): GM, 1403*; WBC, 1403 (MG); Fuller, E. A., 'Cirencester Manor and Town', *Bristol & Gloucs. Arch. Soc. Trans.* vol. 9 (1885); Fuller, E. A., 'The Gild Merchant in Cirencester', *Bristol & Gloucs. Arch. Soc. Trans.*, vol. 18 (1893-94).

Clifton (Worcs.): BTC, 1270 (M).

CLITHEROE: WBC, 1409 (F).

CONGLETON: GM, temp. Ed. I; BTC, 1272-c. 1274; WBC, 1430 (F).

COLCHESTER: WBC, 1318 (F); Harrod, H., *Calendar of the Court Rolls of the Borough of Colchester* (1865).

CONWAY: GM, 1284*; BTC, 1284.

COVENTRY: GM, 1267-68*; BTC, 1267. WBC, 1340 (MG), 1406 (CG), 1444 (F); RCHM, i, 100-102; VCH II refers to *Leet Book i*; see also VIII, EG, XII, 226-34 and 641; *Coventry Gild Merchant (1340), EG, XII, p. 226; *Gild of Corpus Christi (lic (1348), EG, XII (b), p. 232; *Gild of Holy Trinity (lic 1364), EG, XII (c), p. 234; EHD, iv, No. 641 (1441); *Craig, H., 'Two Coventry Corpus Christi Plays', *Early English Text Soc.* (extra series), vol. 87 (1902); *Dormer, H. M., 'The Coventry Leet Book', *Early English Text Soc.*, vols. 134, 135, 138, 146 (1907-13); Domer, H. M., 'The Register of the Guild of the Holy Trinity, St Mary, St John the Baptist

(Coventry – continued) –
and St Katherine of Coventry' (Vol. I),
Dugdale Soc., vol. 13 (1935), see also
Templeman below; Fox, L., 'The Coventry
Guilds and Trading Companies with special
reference to the position of women', in
'Essays in Honour of Philip B. Chatwin',
Birm. Arch. Soc. Trans., vol. 78 (1962);
Fretton, W. G., 'The fullers' guild of
Coventry', *Warks. Naturalists' & Arch. Field
Club* (1879); Sharp, T., *The Pageant of the
Company of Sheremen and Taylors, as per-
formed by them on the feast of Corpus
Christi* (1817); Sharp, T., *A Dissertation on
the Pageants or Dramatic Mysteries anciently
performed in Coventry by the Trading Com-
panies of that City* (1825); Sharp, T., 'The
Presentation in the Temple, a Pageant as
originally represented by the Corporation of
Weavers in Coventry', *Abbotsford Club*,
(1836); The Coventry Weavers Play MS. is
now in the possession of the C.R.O.;
Templeman, G., 'The Register of the Guild of
Holy Trinity etc.' (Vol. II), *Dugdale Soc.*,
vol. 19 (1944).
Criccieth (Gwynedd): GM, 1284; BTC, 1284.
DARLINGTON: Dodds, M. H., 'The Bishops
Boroughs', *Arch. Aeliana* (3rd series), vol. 12
(1915).
DARTMOUTH: RCHM, v, 597–606.
Deganwy (Gwynedd): BTC, 1252 (GM, M&F).
DENBIGH: GM, 1333; WBC, 1401 (MG).
DEVIZES: GM, temp. Ed. I*; WBC, 1371
(MG); Kite, E., 'The Guilds Merchant or three
trading companies formerly existing at
Devizes', *Wilts. Arch. & Nat. Hist. Mag.*, vol. 4
(1858), VCH, x, pp. 252–255.
DERBY: GM, 1204*; BBC, 1204; BTC, 1229
(F); Bemrose, H. A., 'The Derby Company of
Mercers', *Derbs. Arch. & Nat. Hist. Soc. Jnl.*,
vol. 15 (1893).
DONCASTER: GM, 1467; WBC, 1505 (F&M).
DORCHESTER: GM, – *; 1485 (M).
DROITWICH: BBC, 1215 (F); WBC, 1330 (F).
Dryslwyn (Carm.): WBC, 1324 (M).
DUNWICH: GM, 1200.
DURHAM: GM, temp. Hen. II; BBC, 1200,
1215.
EAST RETFORD: BTC, 1259* (F); WBC,
1313, 1372, 1449 (F).
EXETER: GM, * ; EG, XVII, 229, 331, 334;
*Gild of Tailors (1466), EG. XVII, p. 299;
*Gild of Cordwainers (ord. 1480), EG, XVII
(b), p. 331; *Gild of Bakers (ord. 1483), EG,
XVII (c), p. 334; Cotton, W., *An Elizabethan
Gild of the City of Exeter* (re Society of
Merchant Adventurers, late 16th c.) (1873);
Cotton, W., 'Some account of the ancient
guilds of the City of Exeter', *Trans. Devon.
Assoc. for the Advancement of Science*, vol. v,
(1872); Orme, N., 'The Kalendar Brethren of
the City of Exeter', *Trans. Devon. Assoc.*,
109 (1977); Rowsell, P. F., 'The Ancient

(Exeter – continued) –
Companies of Exeter', *The Western Antiquary*
(1885).
Farnham: BTC, 1247 (F).
FAVERSHAM: GM.   *
FLINT: GM, 1284; BTC, 1284.
Fordwich (Kent): GM, temp. Hen. II.
Gainsborough (Lincs): GM, temp. Ed. III*.
GATESHEAD: Longstaffe, W. H. D., 'The
Trade Companies of Gateshead', *Gentleman's
Magazine*, vol. 13 (1862); 'Company of Dyers
etc. Admittances 1626–1820, Drapers 1659–
1825 etc.', supp. to *Northern Notes & Queries*
ed. H. R. Leighton (1907).
GLOUCESTER: GM, 1200*; BTC, 1302 (F);
VCH, v, p. 154; Bazeley, W., 'The Gilds of
Gloucester', *Bristol & Gloucs. Arch. Soc.
Trans.*, vol. 13 (1889); Fryer, K. H., 'The
Archives of the City of Gloucester', *Bristol
& Gloucs. Arch. Soc. Trans.*, vol. 1 (1876);
Stevenson, W. H., *Rental of all the houses
in Gloucester in 1455* (1890); Stevenson,
W. H., *Calendar of the Records of the Cor-
poration of Gloucester* (1893).
Godmanchester (Hunts), VCH, ii, p. 295.
Grampound (Cornwall): GM, 1332; WBC, 1333
(MG, F&M).
GRANTHAM: GM, 1462; WBC, 1484 (F&M);
Woolstaplers: Street, B., *Historical Notes
on Grantham* (1857).
GREAT YARMOUTH: GM, 1208*; BBC, 1208;
Mariners' Gild Minutes (1538–87), Simon,
L. R., 'Grimsby Mariners Gild', *Lincolnshire
Historian*, vol. 2 (2) (1955).
GUILDFORD: GM, 1256; WBC, 1346 (F).
GRAVESEND: WBC, 1366 (F&M).
GRIMSBY: WBC, 1318 (F), 1366 (MG).
Harlech (Gwynedd): GM, 1284; BTC, 1284;
WBC, 1513 (M&F).
HARTLEPOOL: GM, 1230*; BTC, 1230*
(GM, F&M).
HAVERFORDWEST: GM, temp. Hen. III;
BTC, 1219–29*.
HEDON: GM, 1348; Park, G. H., *The History
of the Ancient Borough of Hedon etc. . . .*
(1895). Incl. ordinances of the Tailors.
HELSTON: GM, 1201*; BBC, 1201; BTC, 1225–
40, 1260; WBC, 1336 (M&F); Boase, G. C.,
'The Guild of Cordwainers of Helston, Co.
Cornwall', *The Reliquary*, xx (1880). Incl.
ordinances c. 1459.
HENLEY-ON-THAMES: GM, 1300*.
HEREFORD: GM, 1215*; BBC, 1215; BTC,
1227 (G, M&F); Black, W. H. and Hills,
G. M., 'The Hereford Municipal Records and
Customs of Hereford', *Brit. Arch. Assoc. Jnl.*,
vol. 27 (1871); Devlin, J. D., *Helps to Here-
ford History . . . an account of the ancient
Cordwainers' Company of the city etc. . . .*
(1848); Reade, H., 'Some account books . . .
of the Hereford craft gilds', *Woolhope
Naturalists' Field Club* (1924–26).
HERTFORD: WBC, 1345 (M).

HIGH WYCOMBE: GM, 1316*; RCHM, v,
554-65; VCH, iii, p. 121; Greaves, R. W., 'The
First Ledger Book of High Wycombe',
Borough Rec. Soc., Vol. II (1956).

HIGHAM FERRERS: BTC, 1300 (F).

Hope (Powys): GM, 1351; WBC, 1351 (MG).

Horsham (W. Sussex): Cooper, W. D., 'Guild of
St John the Baptist, founded 36 Hen. VI and
chantries in Horsham', *Sussex Arch. Soc.
Collections*, vol. 22 (1870).

HUNTINGDON: VCH, ii, p. 134; BTC, 1252 (F).

HYTHE: BTC, 1261 (F).

IPSWICH: GM, 1200*; BBC, 1200; Fitch, W. S.,
'Notices of the Corpus Christi Guild of
Ipswich', *Suffolk Inst. Arch. Proc.*, vol. 2
(1855).

KENDAL: GM.

Kenfig (Mid-Glam.): GM, 1360*; WBC, 1360.

KING'S LYNN: GM, 1204*; BBC, 1204; BTC,
1305; WBC, 1537 (M&F); EG, XVI-XLVIII,
45-122 (30 Gilds); *Gild of St Anthony
(n.d.), EG, XVI, p. 45; *Gild of St Thomas
of Canterbury (1376), EG, XVII, p. 47; *Gild
of St Leonard (n.d.), EG, XVIII, p. 49;
*Young Scholars' Gild (1383), EG, XIX, p.
51; *The Shipmen's Gild (1368), EG, XX, p.
54; *The Gild of the Nativity of John the
Baptist (n.d.), EG, XXI, p. 58; *Gild of St
Thomas of Canterbury (n.d.), EG, XXII, p.
60; *Gild of St Peter (1329), EG, XXIII,
p. 62, *Gild of the Purification (n.d.), EG,
XXIV, p. 64; *Gild of St Mary (n.d.), EG,
XXV, p. 65; *Gild of St Katherine (n.d.)
EG, XXVI, p. 67; *Gild of St James (n.d.),
EG: XXVII, p. 69; *Gild of St John the
Baptist (1316), EG, XXVIII, p. 71; *Gild of
St George the Martyr (1376), EG, XXIX, p.
74; *Gild of St John the Baptist (1372), EG,
XXX, p. 78; *St Thomas of Canterbury, Lynn
Episcopi (n.d.), EG, XXXI, p. 80; *Gild of the
Holy Cross, Lynn Episcopi (n.d.), EG.
XXXII, p. 83, *Gild of the Conception, Lynn
Episcopi (n.d.), EG, XXXIII, p. 86; *Gild of
the Purification, Lynn Episcopi (1367), EG,
XXXIV, p. 89; *Gild of St Lawrence, Lynn
Episcopi (n.d.), EG, XXXV, p. 91; *Gild of
St Edmund, Lynn Episcopi (n.d.), EG,
XXXVI, p. 94; *Gild of St Nicholas, Lynn
Petri (1359), EG, XXXVII, p. 97; *Gild of
St John the Baptist, West Lynn (1374), EG,
XXXVIII, p. 100; *Gild of St James, North
Lynn (n.d.), EG, XXXIX, p. 103; *Gild of
St Edmund, North Lynn (n.d.), EG, XL, p.
106; *Gild of Candlemas, North Lynn (n.d.),
EG, XLI, p. 108; *Gild of Holy Trinity,
Wiggenhall (n.d.), EG, XLII, p. 110; *Gild of
the Assumption, Wiggenhall (n.d.), EG, XLIII,
p. 111; *Gild of St Peter and St John the
Baptist, Oxborough (1307), EG, XLVIII and
XLIX, pp. 121-2. Also *East Winch*; EG,
XLVII, p. 119*; Richards, W., *The History
of Lynn* . . . (1812); Rye, W., 'The Guilds
of Lynn Regis', *Norfolk Antiq. Misc.*, vol. I

King's Lynn − continued) −
(1873); Taylor, W., *The Antiquities of King's
Lynn, Norfolk* (1844).

KINGSTON-UPON-HULL: GM, − *; BTC,
1299 (M&F); EG, IV, 154-161; *Gild of
Blessed Virgin Mary (1357), EG, IV, p. 154;
*Gild of Corpus Christi (1358), EC, IV (b),
p. 160; *Gild of St John the Baptist (n.d.), EG,
IV (c), p. 161; Lambert, J. M., *Two Thousand
Years of Gild Life* (1891); VCH Yorks (E.R.),
vol. i, pp. 55-59 refers to *Hull Corporation
Records*, BBM 478 at the Guildhall.

KINGSTON-UPON-THAMES: RCHM, iii, 331-3;
BTC, 1256 (G, M&F); WBC, 1556 (F).

Kirkham: GM, 1295; BTC, 1296.

Knowle (Warks.): Bickley, W. B., *Register of the
Guild of Knowle 1451-1535* (1894).

Knutsford (Cheshire): WBC, 1332 (M&F).

LAMPETER: GM, 1332.

LANCASTER: GM, 1337; WBC, 1337 (MG,
M&F); Gild of Holy Trinity and St Leonard
(1377), EG, V, p. 163; Simpson, R., *The
History and Antiquities of the Town of
Lancaster compiled from authentic sources*
(1852).

LAUNCESTON: (as Dunheved): GM, 1231-72*.

LEEDS: Wordell, J., *The Municipal History of
the Borough of Leeds* (1846).

LEICESTER: 'One of the most valuable collec-
tions of municipal records in England . . . the
gild rolls begin with the reign of Richard I . . .'
(Gross), GM, 1107-18*; BBC, 1101-18,
1118-68; RCHM, viii, 403-41; BTC, 1229
(F); Bateson, M., *Records of the Borough of
Leicester 1103-1603* (1899-1905); WBC,
1360, 1473, 1540 (M); *Records of the
Corporation of Leicester* (1956); *Merchant
Gild Roll, 1357*, EHD, iv, No. 614*;
Fosbrooke, T. H. and Skillington, S. H., 'The
Old Town Hall of Leicester', *Leics. Arch.
Soc.*, vol. 13 (1923-24); North, T., *A
Chronicle of the Church of St Martin's in
Leicester* (1866); Skillington, S. H., 'The
Leicester Gild of Tallow Chandlers', *Trans.
Leics. Arch. Soc.*, vol. 15 (1927-28);
Thompson, J., 'On the Archives of the
Borough of Leicester', *Brit. Arch. Assoc.
Trans.*, vols. 70-84 (1846); VCH, iv, p. 14.

LEWES: GM, temp. Stephen*; Turner, E., 'The
ancient merchant guild of Lewes and the
subsequent municipal regulations of the
town'. *Sussex Arch. Soc. Collections*, vol. 21
(1869).

LICHFIELD: GM, − *; WBC, 1387 (MG);
Crofton, H. T., 'Manchester Gilds and the
records of the Lichfield Corvisors (1561-
1870)', *Lancs. & Ches. Antiq. Soc. Trans.*,
vol. 10 (1893); Furnivall, F. J., 'The Gild of
St Mary, Lichfield', *Early English Text
Society* (extra series), vol. 114 (1920);
Russell, W. H., 'The Laws of the Mercers'
Company of Lichfield (1623)', *Roy. Hist.
Soc. Trans.*, N.S., vol. 7 (1893).

Thorpe, H., 'Lichfield: A study of its growth and
function', *Staffs. Rec. Soc.* (1954).
LINCOLN: GM, temp. Hen. II*; BBC, 1157;
WBC, 1409; RCHM, xiv (part viii) 121-58;
EG, VII, 172-185 (7 Gilds); Lambert, J. M.,
'Some old Lincoln gilds', in *Bygone Lincoln-
shire* by Andrews, W. (1891); *Gild of St
Benedict (n.d.), EG, VII, p. 172; *Gild of the
Resurrection of Our Lord (1374), EG, VII
(b), p. 175; *Gild of St Michael-on-the-Hill
(1350), EG, VII (c), p. 176; *Gild of the
Fullers of Lincoln (1297), EG, VII (d), p.
179; *Gild of the Tailors of Lincoln (1328),
EG, VII (c), p. 182; *Gild of the Tylers (or
Poyntours) of Lincoln (1346), EG, VII (d),
p. 184; * Gild of Kyllyngholm (village 3 m.
N.W. of Immingham) (pre-1310), EG, VII
(c), p. 185.
LISKEARD: GM, 1239-40; BTC, 1240 (GM);
1266 (F).
LIVERPOOL: GM, 1229*; BTC 1229; Picton,
J. A., *Selections from the Municipal Archives
of Liverpool from 13th-17th centuries*
(1883).
LLANFYLLIN (Powys): GM. temp. Ed. II;
BTC, post-1286.
Llantrisant (Gwent): GM, 1346*.
LONDON: BBC, 1155-58*; Weavers, 1202*;
Drapers (1438), EHD, iv, No. 639 (1438); Brewers, 1442; EHD, iv, Nos. 634-5; Mercers EHD,
iv, 645 (1463-84). Separate entries are unnecessary here, see bibliographies given in: Unwin,
G., *The Gilds and Companies of London*
(1905; reprinted 1966); J. Toulmin Smith
prints Ordinances of: The Gild of Garlekhith
(1375), EG, I, p. 4; St Katherine's, Aldersgate (n.d.), EG, II, p. 6; SS Fabian and
Sebastian, Aldersgate (n.d.), EG, 111, p. 9.
On Craft gilds and city government, see EHD,
iv, No. 641 (1351-1457): *Report of the City
of London Livery Companies Commission*, in
Parliamentary Papers, Vol. XXXIX (1884);
H. T. Riley (ed.) 'Munimenta Gildhallæ
Londoniensis; Liber Albus, Liber Custumarum
et Liber Horni' in 4 vols. of the *Rolls Series*
(1859-62); Coote, H. C., 'The Ordinances of
some secular gilds of London', *London &
Middx. Arch. Soc. Trans.*, vol. 4 (1871);
Kellet, J. R., 'The breakdown of gild and
corporation control over the handicraft and
retail trade in London', *Economic History
Review* (2nd series), vol. 10 (1958). See
section on Gilds and Companies (London) in
Gross *Bibliography of Municipal History*,
pp. 303-314.
Lostwithiel (Cornwall): GM, 1269; BTC, 1268
(GM, M&F); WBC, 1325 (M).
LOUGHBOROUGH: Fletcher, W. G. D., *Chapters in the History of Loughborough* (1883).
Ludlow (Salop): GM, 1461; WBC, 1552 (M&F),
1604 (F); Gild of the Palmers (1284); EG, IX,
p. 193; Hills, G. M., 'On the ancient company
of stitchment of Ludlow; Their Account Book

(Ludlow — continued) —
(1669) and money-box', *Brit. Arch. Assoc.
Jnl.*, vol. 24, (1868); Jones, L;. 'The antiente
company of smiths and others commonly
called "Hammermen" of Ludlow', *Shrops.
Arch. & Nat. Hist. Soc. Trans.*, vol. 11 (1888);
Sparrow, W. C., 'The Palmers' Guild of
Ludlow', *Shrops. Arch. & Nat. Hist. Soc.
Trans.*, vol. 1 (1878); Sparrow, W. C., 'A
Register of the Palmers' Guild in the reign of
Henry VIII', *Shrops. Arch. & Nat. Hist. Soc.
Trans.*, vol. 7 (1884).
LYDD: WBC, 1494(F).
LYME REGIS: GM, 1284; BTC, 1284; WBC,
1554 (M&F).
MACCLESFIELD: GM, 1261*; BTC, 1261.
MAIDSTONE: Gilbert, W. B., *The Accounts of
the Corpus Christi fraternity and papers relat-
ing to the antiquities of Maidstone* (1865).
MALMESBURY: GM, 1205-22*.
Milborne Port (Som.), WBC, 1397 (M&F).
MARLBOROUGH: GM, 1163; BBC, 1204
(M&F); 1246 (F).
Melcombe Regis (Dorset): WBC, 1314, 1318
(M&F).
MONTGOMERY: GM, 1227; BTC, 1227 (GM
M&F).
MORPETH (Nmbld): BTC, 1239-66* (M).
M&F).
Morpeth (Nmbld): BTC, 1239-66* (M).
NEATH: GM, 1359*; BTC, 1280 (F).
Nevin (Caern.): GM, 1343-76; WBC, 1355
(MG, F&M).
NEWBURY: Money, W., 'Guild of the Cloth-
workers of Newbury', *Brit. Arch. Assoc. Jnl.*
(1896).
Newborough (Angl.): GM, 1303; BTC, 1303.
NEWCASTLE-UNDER-LYME: GM, 1235*;
BTC, 1235; 1281 (F); WBC, 1336, 1438 (F).
NEWCASTLE-UPON-TYNE: GM, 1216*; WBC,
1318, 1490 (F); Boyle, J. R., 'The Gold-
smiths of Newcastle', *Archaeologia Aeliana*,
vol. 16 (1894); Brand, J., *History and
Antiquities of Newcastle upon Tyne* (1789);
Dendy, F. W., 'Extracts from the Records
of the Merchant Adventurers of Newcastle
upon Tyne (1480-1898)', *Surtees Soc.*, vols.
93 and 101 (1895 and 1899); Dendy, F. W.,
'The Struggle between the Merchant and
Craft Gilds in 1515', *Archaeologica Aeliana*,
vol. 16 (1894); Dodds, M. H., 'The Register
of the Freemen of Newcastle upon Tyne',
*Newcastle upon Tyne Records Committee
Pubns*, vol. 3 (1923); Embleton, D., 'The
incorporated company of barber-surgeons and
wax and tallow chandlers of Newcastle upon
Tyne (with extracts from their Minute Books
1616-86)', *Archaeologia Aeliana*, vol. 15
(1891-92).; Walker, J. and Richardson, M.,
*The Armorial Bearings of the several
incorporated companies of Newcastle upon
Tyne with a brief historical account of each
Company* (1824).

NEWPORT (I.o.W.): GM, 1292*.
NEWPORT (Mon.): GM, 1385; WBC, 1385 (MG, F&M).
Newport (Salop): BBC, 1163-66.
Newton (Carm.): GM, 1363*; WBC, 1363 (MG, F&M).
NORTHAMPTON: WBC, 1337, 1495 (F); VCH iii, p. 7 refers to *Liber Custumarum* preserved at Northampton and printed in Markham, C. A. and Cox, J. C., *The Records of the Borough of Northampton* (Northampton Corporation n.d.); Markham, C. A., *Liber Custumarum* (the book of ancient usages and customs from the earliest record to 1448) (1895).
NORWICH: GM, — *; WBC, 1482 (F); EG, IV-XV, 14-42 (11 Gilds); *Gild of St Mary (1360), EG, IV, p. 14; *Gild of St Botolph (1384), EG, V, p. 15; *Gild of St George (1385), EG, VI, p. 17 and p. 443; *Gild of St Christopher (1384), EG, VIII, p. 20; *Gild of Holy Trinity in the Cathedral (1364), EG, IX, p. 25; *The Brotherhood of Barbers (n.d.) EG, X, p. 27; *Gild of Petyers (Furriers) (1376), EG, XI, p. 28; *The Tailors' Gild (1350), EG, XII, p. 33; *The Carpenters' Gild (1375), EG, XIII, p. 37; *The Poor Men's Gild (1380), EG, XIV, p. 40; *The Saddlers' and Spinners' Gild (1385), EG, XV, p. 42; Fitch, R., 'Notice of Brewers' marks and trade regulations in the City of Norwich', *Trans. Norf. & Norw. Arch. Soc.* (1859); Fitch, R., *Norwich pageants: The Grocers' Play* (1856); Grace, M., 'Records of the Gild of St George in Norwich 1389-1547', *Norf. Rec. Soc.*, vol. ix (1937); Hotblack, J. T., 'Norwich Guilds', *Norwich Science Gossip Club* (1911-12); L'Estrange, J. and Rye, W., 'Norfolk Guilds'; *Norfolk Archaeology*, vii, (1872); Mackerell, B., 'An Account of the Company of St George in Norwich in Mackerell's *History of Norwich* (1737)', *Norfolk Archaeology*, iii, 1852; Rye, W., 'Some Norfolk Gild Certificates of 12 Ric. II' *Norfolk Archaeology*, xi (1892); Tingey, J. C., 'Notes on the Craft Gilds of Norwich, with particular reference to the Masons' Lodge', *Quattuor Coronati*, vol. 15 (1902); Norwich Pageants 1449; a list of 12 gilds and their plays EHD, iv, No. 643*.
NOTTINGHAM: GM, c. 1189*; BBC, 1189, 1200; BTC, 1248 (F); WBC, 1378 (F); RCHM, i, 105-6; VCH, ii, p. 272 refers to Stevenson, W. H., *Records of the Borough of Nottingham* (1882-89), Vol. I.
Ormskirk (Lancs.): WBC, 1461 (F).
Orford (Suffolk): GM, 1229; BTC, 1256.
Oswestry (Salop): GM, 1398*; WBC, 1398 (MG).
Overton: GM, 1291-2: BTC, 1292.
OXFORD: GM, temp. Hen. II*; BBC, 1156; c. 1175* (Cordwainers); WBC, 1549 (F); BTC, 1275* (Weavers); Salter, H. E.,

(Oxford − continued) −
'Munimenta Civitatis Oxoniae' (*Oxford Hist. Soc.*, vol. 71 (1917); J. Wilson, 'The Cordwainers and Corveivsors of Oxford', *Arch. Jnl.*, vol. 6 (1849); VCH, IV, pp. 35, 312-27.
PEMBROKE: BBC, 1154-89 (F); 1201* (F).
PETERBOROUGH; Mellows, W. T., *Markets, guilds and fairs of Peterborough* (1909).
Petersfield (Hants.): GM, 1147-73*.
Pevensey (Sussex): BBC, 1207 (F).
PLYMOUTH: GM, 1440; WBC, 1440 (GM, F&M); Burgess, W. H., 'Medieval Guilds in Plymouth', *Trans. Plymouth Inst.*, vol. 15 (1902-15); Rowe, J. B., 'Devonshire Gilds of Plymouth and Totnes', *Devon. Assoc. for the Advancements of Science Trans.*, vol. vi (1873), 'of little value' (Gross).
Plympton (Devon): WBC; 1483 (F).
PONTEFRACT: GM, 1484: RCHM, viii, 169-76.
POOLE: GM, 1568; WBC, 1453 (F&M).
PORTSMOUTH: GM, 1256; BBC, 1194* (F&M); BTC, 1256.
PORT TALBOT (or Aberavon): WBC, 1373 (F).
PRESTON: GM, temp. Hen. III*; BBC, 1189-99 (F); WBC, 1328 (F&M); Abram, W. A., 'The Rolls of burgesses of the gilds merchant of the borough of Preston 1397-1682', *Lancs. & Ches. Rec. Soc.*, vol. ix (1884); Abram, W. A.: *Preston Guild Merchant* (1882); Addison, J., *Extracts from ancient documents in the Archives of Preston* (1842); Clemesha, H. W.. 'The Borough of Preston and its Gild Merchant' in *Historial Essays in Commemoration of the Jubilee of Ovens College*, ed.: T. F. Tout and J. Tait (1902); Dobson W. and Harland, J., *A History of the Preston Guild* (1862); Lingard, J., *The Charters granted to the burgesses of Preston* (1821).
PWLLHELI: GM, 1355; WBC, 1355 (MG, F&M).
QUEENBOROUGH : WBC, 1368 (F&M).
READING: GM, 1253*; BTC, 1254*; WBC, 1510; CG (Clothmaking); *The Gild of Reading (n.d.); EG; XVI, p. 297; Ditchfield, J. H., 'The Guilds of Reading', *The Reliquary*, NS, vol. iv (1890); VCH, ii, p. 198; iii, pp. 66-67.
Rhuddlan (Clwyd): GM, 1278: BTC, 1284; WBC, 1354 (F).
ROCHESTER: GM, 1227*; BTC, 1227: WBC, 1331 (M).
Ruyton (Salop.): GM, 1308-9; WBC, 1309 (MG).
RYE: WBC, 1404 (M).
SAFFROM WALDEN: GM, Hen. IV (?).
ST ALBANS: VCH, iv, pp. 205-8; RCHM, v, 565-8.;
SALISBURY: *Note:* Records at CRO, Trowbridge; GM, 1176*; BTC, 1227 (M&F); RCHM, v, 568-71; VCH, vi, p. 132, 'The Guild Merchant and Craft Guilds before 1612', ref. to *Sarum Corporation Mss Ledgers A & B*; 'The Medieval Guilds of Salisbury',

(Salisbury – continued) –
   Wilts. Arch. & Nat. Hist. Soc., vol. xxix
   (1896); Haskins, C., *The Ancient Trade Guilds
   and Companies of Salisbury* (1912); Rock, D.,
   The Church of our fathers etc. . . . . (1849-53);
   Swayne, H. J. F., 'Gleanings from the archives
   of Salisbury', *Salisbury and Winchester Jnl.*,
   vols 1-30, (1882-1884).
SALTASH: BTC, pre-1246 (F).
SANDWICH: WBC, 1504 (F).
SCARBOROUGH: GM, 1253*; BTC, 1253*
   (G, M&F); VCH Yorkshire (General Volume
   II), p. 553 refers to Hinderwell, T., *History
   and Antiquities of Scarborough* (1798).
SHEFFIELD: Leader, J. D., 'Notes on the
   Cutlers' Companies Accounts', *Assoc. Arch.
   Soc. Reports & Papers*, vol. xii (1874).
SHREWSBURY: GM, 1209*; BBC, 1205 (F);
   BTC, 1227; WBC, 1309 (F); *Gild of Weavers*
   1448, EHD, iv, No. 642*; Cunningham, W.,
   'The Gild Merchant of Shrewsbury (1209-
   10 and 1219-20)', *Trans. Roy. Hist. Soc.*,
   vol. 9 (1895); Drinkwater, C. H., 'Shrewsbury
   trade guilds: The Glovers' Company', *Shropshire Arch. & Nat. Hist. Soc. Trans.*, vol. 10
   (1887); Drinkwater, C. H., 'The Merchant
   Guild of Shrewsbury', *ibid*. (2nd series), vol. 8
   (1896); Drinkwater, C. H., 'Petition of the
   Cordwainers and Drapers 1323-24 and
   1461-62', *ibid*. (2nd series), vol. 6 (1864),
   vol. 8 (1896); Drinkwater, C. H., 'Shrewsbury
   Guild Merchant Rolls of the 14th century',
   ibid. (3rd series), vol. 1 (1901), vol. 2 (1902),
   vol. 3 (1903), vol. 4 (1904); Drinkwater,
   C. H., 'Shrewsbury Guild Merchant Rolls of
   the 14th and 15th centuries', *ibid*. (3rd
   series), vol. 5 (1905); Hibbert, F. A., 'The
   influence and development of English Guilds
   as illustrated by the craft guilds of Shrewsbury', in *Cambridge Historical Essays*, No. 5
   (1891); Leighton, W. A., 'The Guilds of
   Shrewsbury', *Shrops. Arch. & Nat. Hist. Soc.
   Trans.*, vols. 1, 5, 7, 8 (1881-85); Peile, M.,
   'Medieval deeds of the Shrewsbury Drapers'
   Company', *ibid*. (3rd series), vol. 52 (1947-
   48); Pidgeon, H., 'Ancient guilds, trading
   companies and the origins of the Shrewsbury
   Show', *ibid*., vol. 6 (1883).
SOUTHAMPTON: GM, temp. Hen. II*; WBC,
   1496, 1600 (F); Davies, J. S., *A History of
   Southampton* (1883); Platt, C., *Mediaeval
   Southampton: the Port and Trading
   Community* (1973); Bunyard, B. D. M.,
   'The Brokage Book of Southampton I
   (1439-40)'; *Southampton Rec. Soc. Pubns.*,
   (1941), vol. 1; Coleman, O., 'The Brokage
   Book 1443-44', *Southampton Rec. Soc.
   Pubns.*, (1960-61); Smirke, E., 'Ancient
   ordinances of the Gild Merchant of South-
   ampton', *Arch. Jnl.*, vol. 16 (1869); Studer,
   'Port Books of Southampton 1427-30',
   Southampton Rec. Soc., vol. 15 (1913).
SOUTHWOLD: WBC, 1505 (M&F).

STAFFORD: WBC, 1412 (F); Pallister, D. M.,
   'The Boroughs of Medieval Staffordshire',
   North Staffs Journal of Field Studies, vol. 12
   (1972).
STAMFORD: GM, 1462; BTC, 1261 (F); WBC,
   1481 (M&F); *Gild of St Katherine* (1494);
   EG, VIII, p. 187.
Stockton-on-Tees (Cleveland): WBC, 1310
   (M&F).
STRATFORD-UPON-AVON: *Gild of the
   Holy Cross* (n.d.); EG, XI, p. 211; Bloom,
   J. H., *Register of the Gild of Holy Cross, the
   Blessed Mary and St John the Baptist of
   Stratford upon Avon, 1406-1535* (1907);
   Fox, L., *The Borough-town of Stratford
   upon Avon* (1953); Fisher, T., 'The Gilde of
   the Holy Cross etc. at Stratford on Avon',
   Gentleman's Magazine, NS iii, and iv (1835);
   Hardy, W. J., *Calendar of documents of the
   medieval gild of Stratford* (1885).
SUNDERLAND: GM, 1247.
SWANSEA: GM, 1655*.
TAUNTON: Pring, J. H., 'On the age of gilds,
   with a notice of the ancient Guildhall of
   Taunton' (Reprint from *Proc. Soc. Arch. &
   Nat. Hist. Soc.* (1883)).
TEWKESBURY: VCH, viii, pp. 142-3.
TENBY: WBC, 1323 (F).
Thaxted (Essex), Symonds, G. E., 'Thaxted
   and the Cutlers' Guild', *The Reliquary*,
   vol. v (1864).
Tintagel (Cornwall): BTC, 1225-26 (M&F).
TOTNES: BBC, 1199-1216; GM, 1216*;
   RCHM, iii, 341-50; Amery, P. F. S., 'The
   Gild Merchant of Totnes', *Devon Assoc. for
   Advancement of Science Trans.*, vol. xii
   (1880); Rowe, J. B., 'Devonshire Gilds, Ply-
   mouth and Totnes', *Devon. Assoc. for
   Advancement of Science Trans.*, vol. vi
   (1873); Dymond, R., 'Ancient Documents
   relating to the history of Totnes', *Devon.
   Assoc. Trans.*, vol. xxi (1880).
WALLINGFORD: VCH, iii, p. 533; BBC, 1156;
   WBC, 1449, 1558 (F).
WALSALL: GM, 1440*; Religious fraternity,
   Gild of St John the Baptist undertook some
   functions of Gild Merchant; suppressed 1547.
WALTHAM: Holy Cross; VCH Essex, v, p. 171.
WARWICK: WBC, 1413 (F); Cronne, H. A.,
   'The Borough of Warwick in the Middle Ages'
   Dugdale Soc. Occ. Papers, No. 10 (1951).
Wearmouth (Durham): GM, – *; BTC, 1247.
WELLS: BBC, 1201* (F&M).
WELSHPOOL: GM, temp. Ed. I*; BTC, 1241-
   c. 1286.
Wenlock (Salop): GM, 1468.
WEYMOUTH: GM, 1442.
WIGAN: GM, 1246; BTC, 1246; WBC, 1329 (F).
WILTON: GM, temp. Hen. I*; WBC, 1414, 1415
   (F); 1496 (M).
WINCHESTER: GM, temp. Hen. II*; WBC, 1449
   (F&M), anon., *Old Usages of Winchester*
   (n.d.); EG, p. 349.

WINDSOR: GM, 1226--77*; BTC, 1227; WBC, 1466 (F).
WOODSTOCK: GM, 1453*; WBC, 1565 (F&M).
Wootton Bassett (Wilts): WBC, 1571 (F&M).
WORCESTER: GM, 122; EG, IV and II (a), 200-108 and 370; At Guildhall: *The Book of City Ordinances 1467*, Ms *Ordinances of the Glovers 1571-1625; Laws and Ordinances of the Wardens and Fellowship of Glovers, Whittawers, Tanners, Puch-makers, Pursers, Saddlers, Pewterers, Braziers and Hammers; Ordinances of the Glovers temp. Hen. VII; Minutes and Entrance Book of Glovers' Guild; Ordinances of the Carpenters and Joiners.*
At CRO (5955/1-3): *Minutes of the Weavers and Clothiers 1672-1754; a Register of Apprentices of the Weavers 1587; The Order Book of the Clothiers Company (16th century)* and bye-laws; ordinances and accounts of same 1523-1960; leases; *Laws and Regulations of the Worshipful Company of Clothiers (1590)* (1883-84); *Gild of St Nicholas (n.d.), EG, X, p. 200; *Joiners and Carpenters' Gild (n.d.), EG, X, p. 208; *Ordinances of Worcester (1467), EG, II (a), p. 370; Gutch, J. M., 'The Clothiers. Company of Worcester', *Brit. Arch. Assoc. Proc.* (1851); Hooper, J. H., 'The Clothiers' Company at Worcester', *Assoc. Arch. Soc. Reports & Papers*, vol. 15 (1880); Noake, J. 'Ancient Worcester Cordwainers' Company', *Gentleman's Magazine*, vol. 3 (1857); Woof, R., *On the seals and arms of the City of Worcester* (1865).
YORK: GM, 1130-31*; BBC, 1154-48; RCHM, 108-9; WBC, 1312 (MG), 1449, 1502, 1590 (F); *Gild of the Lord's Prayer (n.d.), EG, II, p. 137; *Gild of Corpus Christi (1408), EG, II (b), p. 141. For all known documents re York's Gilds, see Calendar in City Archives, also 'Catalogue of the Gild Records of York' *(Yorks. Archit. & Archaeol. Soc.)* (1949); also York Play list of 1415 in L. Toulmin-Smith's *Plays performed by the Crafts or Mysteries of York* (1944). See for various crafts:
Bakers: Toulmin-Smith, L. 'The bakers of York and their Ancient Ordinary', *Arch. Rev.*, vol. 1 (1888); 'The book of accounts of the Bakers of York', *Arch. Rev.*, vol. 1 (London, 1888); Mill, A. J., 'The York Bakers' Play', *Modern Languages Review*, vol. 30 (1935).
Barber-Surgeons: Furnival, F. J. and P. 'The Ancient Ordinary of Barbers and Surgeons, 1486', *Early English Text Soc.* (extra series), vol. 53 (1888), p. 271; Auden, G. A., *Gild Book of the Barber-Surgeons of York* (published by the Roy. Soc. Medicine, 1928); Bent, J. T., 'Extracts from the Gild-book of the Barber Surgeons of York, 1592-1614', *The Antiquary*, vol. 6 (1882). There are ordinances and extracts relating to the Barber Surgeons in the City Archives from their House Books.

Butchers: Corsair, B. A. and Fitzell, W. L., *The York Butchers' Guild from A.D. 1272* (1975).
Carpenters: There is the original MS and a transcript by F. Hilyard (1741) of the Ordinary of the Carpenters and Joiners in the City Archives.
Bookbinders and Stationers: Gordon Duff, E., 'The Printers, Stationers and Bookbinders of York to 1600', *Bibliographical Soc. Trans.*, vol. 5 (1899).
Curriers: Johnson, B. P., 'The Curriers' Account Books', *Archit. & Archaeol. Soc. Ann. Rept.*, 1951-52.
Drapers: Johnson, B. P., *The Merchant Taylors of York* (1949), Acts and Ordinances.
Fishmongers: Mitchell, C. M., 'The Company of Fishmongers in York', *Yorks. Archit. & Archeol. Soc. Rept.*, 1951-52.
Girdlers: Johnson, B. P., 'The Girdlers' Ordinance Book', *Yorks. Archit. & Archaeol. Soc. Rept.*, 1951-52; Raine, J., 'A volume of English Miscellanies (Documents relating to the craft of girdlers 1428 and of masons and wrights 1417-51)', *Surtees Soc.*, vol. 85 (1890).
Goldsmiths: Fallow, T. M., 'Yorkshire Plate and Goldsmiths', *Archaeol. Jnl.*, vol. 61 (1904); Jackson, C. I., *English Goldsmiths and their marks* (1949).
Hosiers: Johnson, B. P., *The Merchant Taylors of York* (1949).
Mercers and Merchant Adventurers: (see: EHD, iv, 637*, 1430); Sellers, M., 'The York Mercers and Merchant Adventurers' 1356-1917, *Surtees Soc.*, vol. 129 (1918); Kerry, C., 'The Discovery of the Register and chartulary of the Mercers' Company of York (with extracts from those records 1420-1523)', *The Antiquary*, vols. 22, 23 (1890-91); Johnson, B. P., 'The York Residence of the Company of Merchant Adventurers in England', in *Last of the Old Hanse* (published by Yorks. Archit. & Archaeol. Soc., 1949).
Pewterers: Collins, F., 'Register of the Freemen of the City of York, vol. I, 1272-1558', *Surtees Soc.*, vol. 96 (1906); Giles, W., 'The Pewterers Guild of York in the 17th and 18th centuries' (MS notes, City Archives n.d.); Hope, R. C., 'The Pewterers Gild of York', *The Antiquary*, vol. 24, 1891 and *The Reliquary*, N.S., vol. 5 (1891); *Pinners:* Giles, W., 'Sundry Ordinances of the occupation . . . of pinners and wiredrawers of . . . York compiled in 1349 & revised in 1529 with names of apprentices, members . . . down to . . . 1762' (MS copy, City Archives).
Scriveners, Text-writers etc.: Davies, R., *Memoir of the York Press* (1868).
Not included in the 1415 Play-list:
Innholders: Giles, W., 'Extracts from the Civic Records relating to Brewing, ale-tasting,

(*York — (Innholders) — continued*) —
tippling and inn-keeping 1477–1787'.
    Spurriers: Gild Ordinances in City
Archives.
    Marshals and Smiths: Toulmin-Smith, L.,
'Ordinances of the Company of Marshals and
Smiths of York 1409–1443', *The Antiquary*
vol. xi (1885).
    See also: Bartlett, J. N. 'The expansion and
decline of a gild at York in the later Middle
Ages', *Econ. Hist. Rev.* (2nd series), vol. 12
(1959). Palliser, D. V., 'The Trade Gilds of
Tudor York' in *Crisis and Order in English
Towns 1500–1700* by Clark, P. and Slack, P.
(1971). Prestwich, M., 'The Civic Ordinances
of 1301', *British Inst. Hist. Research, Univer-*
sity of York; Borthwick Paper No. 49 (1976).
Scaife, R. H., 'Register of the Guild of Corpus
Christi in the City of York (1408 to the
sixteenth century)', *Surtees Soc.*, vol. 57
(1872). Sayles, G., 'The dissolution of a Gild
at York in 1306', *Engl. Hist. Rev.*, vol. 55
(1940). Raine, A., *Medieval York: A
topographical survey based on original
sources* (1955). Sellers, M., 'York Memo-
randum Book, part i, 1376–1419; part ii,
1388–1493', *Surtees Soc.*, vol. 120 (1912),
and 125 (1915). Toulmin-Smith, L., *The
York Plays performed by the crafts or
mysteries of York on the day of Corpus
Christi in the 15th and 16th centuries*
(1885).

For a light-hearted but more contemporary gazetteer of English medieval towns see 'Some Thirteenth Century English Places and their Associations', printed in *The English Historical Review*, vol. xvi (1901), and reprinted in *English Historical Documents*, Vol. III (No. 230; page 230). The original manuscript is apparently the 'doodling' of an idle traveller who succinctly lists his impressions of 108 towns, such as: Blankets of Blyth, Prostitutes of Charing, Thieves of Grantham, Razors of Leicester, the Crossing of Chelmsford, Skins of Shrewsbury, Rymers (or Reamers) of Worcester, Jousters of Yardley, Soap of Coventry, Beggars of Chichester, Market of Pontefract etc.

CHAPTER SIX

TOWN MAPS AND PLANS c. 1600-1900

THERE WERE FEW if any medieval maps of English towns; the appearance of town plans during the late 16th and early 17th centuries marks an important landmark in the study of urban history and its documents.[1] 'Early maps are of the greatest value for a clear understanding of the development of English towns; a visual picture not only stimulates the imagination, it both clarifies and supplements the documentary evidence'.[2] Town maps conform admirably with the criteria which have guided the selection of those documents most readily available to the local student. Firstly, there is a large store of originals, accessible in local archives and libraries. Secondly, a full series of maps develops for some fortunate towns, from the earliest perspective and bird's-eye-view of Tudor and Stuart times to the first Ordnance Survey plan (of St Helen's in 1843); regular comparisons may be possible. Thirdly, the student has the benefit of extensive national and regional indexes or catalogues, and a comprehensive bibliography which includes many colourful facsimiles of the original maps.

Improvements in mapping techniques and surveying equipment which made the first county maps possible also produced a similar development in town plans. Norwich was the first English city to be surveyed (by Dr. William Cunningham in 1559). At first, many of the earliest town maps appear as separate illustrations in the borders and corners of a county sheet, the most important series being those included in John Speed's *Theatre of the Empire of Great Britain*. County by county, Speed added two, three or four plans of the 'principal towns' of each shire to the corners of his maps, setting a fashion which was to continue for more than 200 years. John Speed was born the son of a Cheshire tailor in 1552. He was given a royal appointment as a surveyor by Queen Elizabeth I, with an office at the Customs House. At first, seeing himself primarily as a national historian and antiquarian, he set out to annotate John Norden's county maps as illustrations to William Camden's historical work *Britannia*, revising and altering the maps rather than surveying anew. (The maps were originally black-and-white, intended to be coloured by the bookseller or purchaser. They are probably more familiar as modern coloured facsimiles, which are available in local art-shops.) Between 1605-10 Speed published the first *Atlas* of the British Isles, based upon the earlier maps of Christopher Saxton (1574-79), and of John Norden (c. 1600-10). Throughout the 17th century county map-makers continually copied and plagiarised the works of Saxton, Norden and Speed, with little if any revision or updating.

Speed's county sheets are usually about 50 cm. wide and 40 cm. deep. His maps are in part pictorial; pallisaded parkland, hillocks, cathedrals and castles being represented by small sketches which give them 'a gay and friendly quality'.[3] The borders and corners of the county maps are bedecked with antiquarian detail, such as coats of arms

131

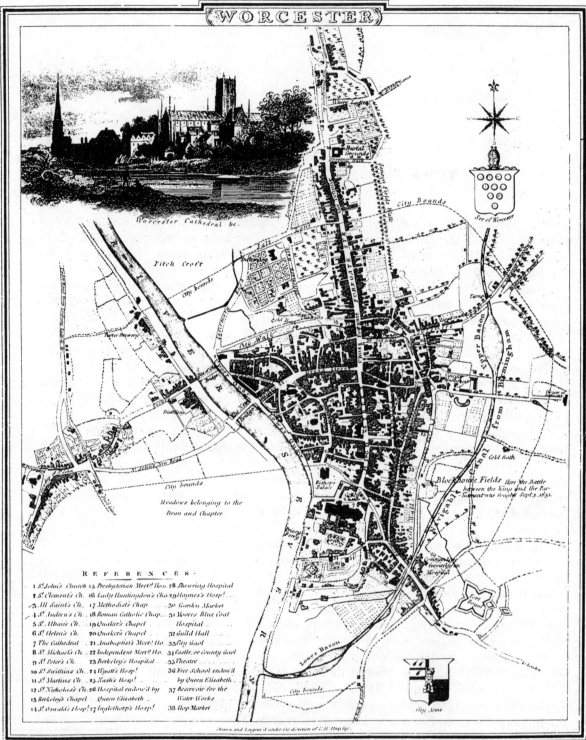

REFERENCES·

1 St John's Church 15 Presbyterian Meetg Ho. 28 Shewring Hospital
2 St Clement's Ch. 16 Lady Huntingdon's Chap. 29 Haynes's Hosp!
3 All Saint's Ch. 17 Methodists Chap 30 Garden Market
4 St Andrew's Ch. 18 Roman Catholic Chap. 31 Moores Blue Coat
5 St Albal's Ch. 19 Quaker's Chapel Hospital
6 St Helen's Ch. 20 Quaker's Chapel 32 Guild Hall
7 The Cathedral 21 Anabaptist's Meetg Ho. 33 City Gaol
8 St Michael's Ch. 22 Independent Meetg Ho. 34 Castle, or County Gaol
9 St Peter's Ch. 23 Berkeley's Hospital 35 Theatre
10 St Swithins Ch. 24 Wyatt's Hosp! 36 Free School endow'd
11 St Martins Ch. 25 Nash's Hosp! by Queen Elizabeth
12 St Nicholas's Ch. 26 Hospital endow'd by 37 Reservoir for the
13 Berkeley's Chapel Queen Elizabeth Water Works
14 St Oswald's Hosp! 27 Inglethorp's Hosp! 38 Hop Market

Worcester in 1808: from J. Roper and G. Young's *British Atlas* (1810).

of the principal baronial families, thumb-nail sketches of historic battlefields, bristling with pikes and pennons, some historical notes and statistics, with the occasional 'portrait'. The map of the county of Monmouth, for example, has Henry V; Warwickshire portrays the bear and rugged staff; Worcestershire shows the battle of Tewkesbury, and Yorkshire has a veritable gallery of pictures of the kings and queens who 'sprang from the royal lines of Yorkshire and Lancashire'. In the *Atlas*, there is usually a numbered index to the places shown on the map, printed on the reverse side of the sheet. Some idea can sometimes be gained as to the relative importance – or even the existence – of different towns as depicted by their symbols on the county sheet, but the main evidence of a few cities' especial prominence are their separate plans, which take up the top right or left-hand corner of each county sheet. Thus we see that, for Speed, *Warwicke* and *Coventree*, but not Birmingham, are Warwickshire's 'principal towns' in 1611. Similarly Worcester (see map, page 134), for the last time in our series of documents, takes its historic place of predominance as the 'county town' of Worcestershire and the most important, as yet, of our three 'sample' towns. In all, 70 English and Welsh towns are surveyed in John Speed's *Theatre* of 1611; 45 of these are his own work. He acknowledges his sources, usually as 'Described by Christopher Saxton, Augmented and Published by John Speed' if not 'Performed by John Speede'. Each of his town maps is rectangular or nearly square, measuring about 15 cm. by 13–20 cm., with a scale, usually of paces, measured off. The scales of different maps vary – their county sheets are about 1 cm. to the mile – from about 200 paces to the inch to somewhat larger.

Elizabethan town plans look back to the towns' medieval origins, as they had existed before maps became fashionable, sometimes just as suburban expansion was becoming extensive. Indeed, the impression we get from most of Speed's town maps is of heavily walled towns, roughly circular in shape. There is a major difference between Worcester, roundly walled, and Birmingham or Dudley which, without town walls, like so many other small towns, straggled in line along the main route through the growing town. The alignment of the medieval walls, the positions of towers and gate-houses, soon to be destroyed or 'slighted' by civil war, and the sites of medieval churches now lost, are especially well-preserved. The main street plan, too, is usually reliable and can easily be transferred to a modern street-map (see illustration pp. 134–135). It is particularly helpful to be able to see the extent to which building was spreading into the suburbs outside the city walls at any time; Worcester, we see, was sending out tentacles of curiously modern 'ribbon development' along all four main approach roads in 1611; new houses line Foregate Street beyond the Gate, over the Severn into 'St Iones', to the north-east towards Lowesmoor and to the south-east via Sidbury (then Sudbury) Street on the present A 44 to Evesham. (Speed's maps fit the small coloured town-plans which are offered in the AA *Book of British Towns* (1979)).

Speed and his contemporaries are never quite sure whether they intend to show a flat ground plan, as most of the streets purport to be, or an oblique perspective, which most of the building plots become. So, the view of any town will vary from vertical to near-vertical and the panoramic picture becomes almost a small-scale 'prospect', which was the fashionable alternative to a town map. Town walls, bridges, castles, churches, individual houses and public buildings, orchards, even market crosses and, occasionally, stocks, pillories and gallows are drawn in detail. The street plan and its building lots are usually lined with token houses in rows which sometimes stand up

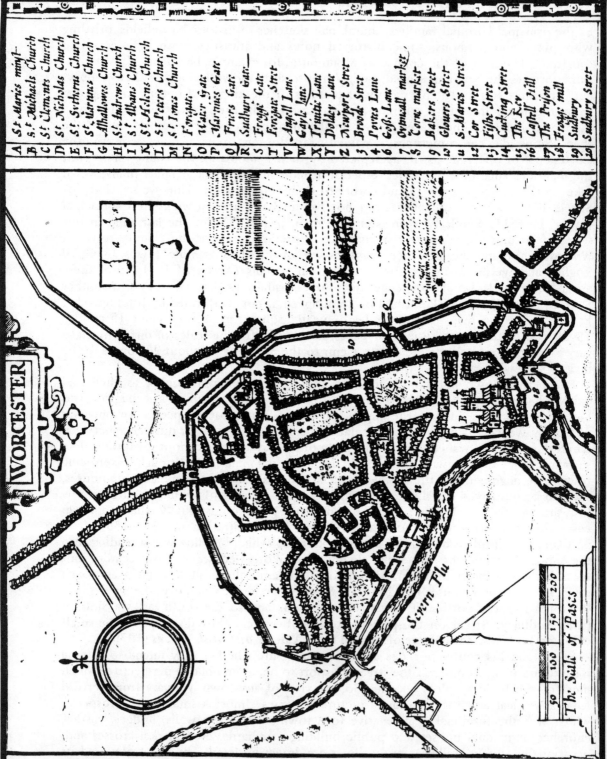

WORCESTER

A St Maries mynſt
B St Michaels Church
C St Clements Church
D St Nicholas Church
E St Sweethens Church
F St Martuns Church
G Alhallowes Church
H St Andrews Church
I St Albans Church
K St Helens Church
L St Peters Church
M St Iwns Church
N Forsgate
O Water Gate
P Martuns Gate
Q Friers Gate
R Sudbury Gate
S Froggs Gate
T Forsgate Strete
V Angell Lane
W Gayle lane
X Trinitie Lane
Y Dolday Lane
Z Newport Strete
3 Brode Strete
4 Powrs Lane
6 Goſe Lane
7 Oxenhall market
8 Corne market
9 Bakers Strete
10 Glowers Strete
11 S Maries Strete
12 Cor Strete
13 Fiſhe Strete
14 Cutting Strete
15 The Key
16 Caſtell Hill
17 The Priſon
18 Froggs mill
19 Sudbury
20 Sudbury Strete

Severn Flu

The Skale of Paces
50 100 150 200

John Speed's marginal map of the city of Worcester, 1610, from a map in the Archives Department of Birmingham Reference Library: actual

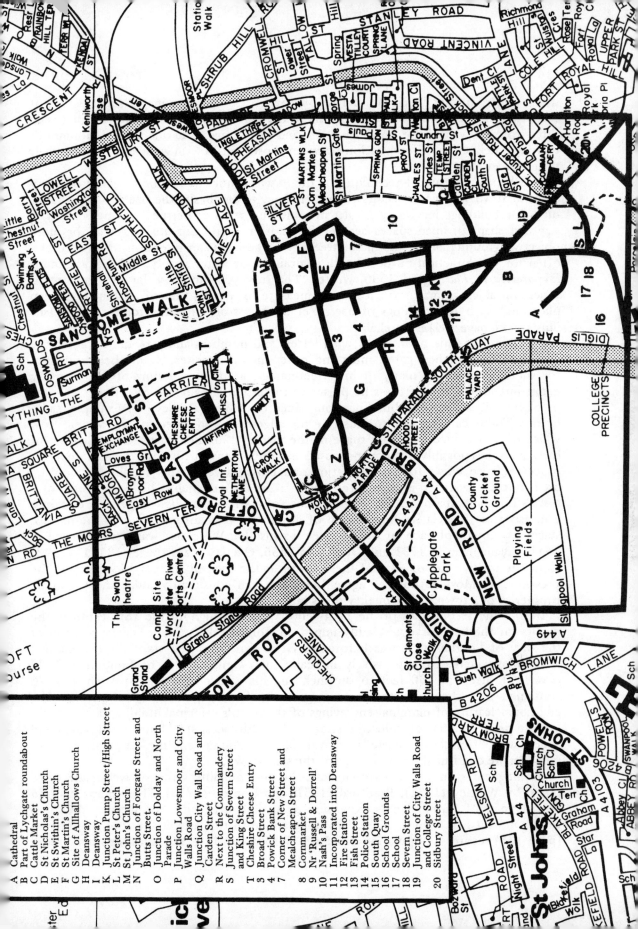

A Cathedral
B Part of Lychgate roundabout
C Cattle Market
D St Nicholas's Church
E St Swithin's Church
F St Martin's Church
G Site of Allhallows Church
H Deansway
I Deansway
K Junction Pump Street/High Street
L St Peter's Church
M St John's Church
N Junction of Foregate Street and Butts Street.
O Junction of Dolday and North Parade
P Junction Lowesmoor and City Walls Road
Q Junction City Wall Road and Carden Street
R Next to the Commandery
S Junction of Severn Street and King Street
T Cheshire Cheese Entry
3 Broad Street
4 Powick Bank Street
7 Corner of New Street and Mealcheapen Street
8 Cornmarket
9 Nr 'Russell & Dorrell'
10 Incorporated into Deansway
11
12 Fire Station
13 Fish Street
14 Police Station
15 South Quay
16 School Grounds
17 School
18 Severn Street
19 Junction of City Walls Road and College Street
20 Sidbury Street

whilst others lie flat in elevation row by row. In some town maps, such as that of Cambridge in 1592, the surveyor seems to draw attention to the difference between three-storey rows and the smaller houses; and sometimes, as in one map of Monmouth there is a deliberate differentiation between those houses with gable-ends or side-walls to the street front.

This happy mixture of techniques is the basis of much academic criticism of many an early town surveyor's accuracy; the tendency to emphasise the size and importance of major buildings inevitably results in some distortion of perspective and scale. The size and shape of open spaces become foreshortened and this quarrels with the more objective ground-plan of the main streets. Yet there was an intention to be accurate, often for very practical purposes such as drainage or water supply. Ralph Agas, in his *Preparative to Platting* of 1596, wrote: 'The surveyor should so lay out the streets, waies and allies, as may serve for a just measure for paving thereof, distance between place and such other things of use'. Yet Speed's scale of paces for Worcester (see illustration, page 134) is unreliable.

Speed indexes his town plans with letters and numbers and provides a key to the main streets, churches, gates, mills and other important sites. He has been criticised for the inaccuracy of many of his street-names, a common failing of 17th-century maps, but in many more cases he preserves the essential evidence of the whereabouts of places, alley-ways and buildings long since destroyed. Dudley, for example, sadly lacks a Tudor cartographer to illustrate the alignment and aspect of the Middle Row which once occupied the inner space of the medieval market-place. The inaccuracy of early maps has possibly been over-stressed and their many virtues overlooked; wherever other evidence exists for corroboration and cross-reference this should certainly be used, but the searcher is fortunate enough if an ancient map is his only source of a town's Elizabethan aspect. The very existence of a street plan before 1700 is certainly a measure of the relative importance of any town. It is an indication of the relative stages of growth of each of our 'model' towns that Worcester was first surveyed in 1611, Birmingham in 1731 and Dudley in 1835. Overlay maps (pages 135, 139, 143) show the relative size of each of these towns at the time of its first survey and in the present day. Most authorities agree that 'one can confidently judge the economic prosperity of a town by the quality of its maps'.[4]

During the second half of the 17th century and throughout the 18th century, the quality of the best surveys steadily improved; John Leake's *Exact Survey* in 1669 of the City of London as it was before the Great Fire set a new standard of accuracy. Many plans increased impressively in scale; John Ogilby's map of London in 1677 covers 21 sheets at 100 feet to the inch and his earlier survey of Ipswich in 1674 contained nine sheets on the same large scale. Eighteenth-century maps offer the additional feature of marginal engravings of the town's principal buildings and contain a great deal of detail of industrial sites, such as furnaces, steel-houses, shipyards and rope-walks. Often they indicate 'land available for building' and these areas of development can be confirmed on later maps of the same town.

Birmingham comes into its own with the best possible series of well-made town plans, by Westley (1731), Bradford (1751) and Hanson (1778). These maps span 75 crucial years of Birmingham's expansion as an industrial city, for Westley describes the town as it had been in 1700. His table, added to the title at the foot of the map (page 138) records a population of 15,032 inhabitants in 1700, a full century before the first national census, these people living in 30 streets, 100 courts and alleys and 2,504 houses. There was one church, dedicated to St Martin, a chapel of St John, a school provided by Edward VI and two Dissenting 'meeting houses'. By 1730, Westley notes in the right-hand table, the population had increased by 8,254 inhabitants; there were 25 new streets, 50 more courts and alleys and 1,215 new houses. There was also another church, St Paul's, a charity school, a market cross and two more meeting houses. Yet more land was marked out 'for building' in the areas of Park Street and Lower Lichfield Street. With the aid of the overlay of Westley's map (page 139) we can trace the growth of the town, generation by generation matching it with modern redevelopment in the city centre.

Many other surveyors associated with particular towns are worthy of special note, such as Millerd, with his perspective map of Bristol, repeatedly revised from 1673 to 1730, at about 93 feet to the centimetre, Cleer, who mapped Norwich in 1696 — a city remarkably well served by map-makers — and John Kip, whose map of Gloucester was printed in 1710. Standards of accurate surveying and mapping continued to improve during the 18th century and a scale of 1:5,000 or even larger is not unusual. Perspective maps and prospects continued to be popular and most major catalogues and indexes of printed maps refer to panoramic views in large numbers, available for many towns, to supplement the street-plans. There are a wealth of published facsimiles which are available from bookshops and second-hand dealers. A useful example is *The British Atlas* of 1810, containing plans of English towns, including Winchester, Carlisle, Bedford and many more which may not have readily accessible maps. These were originally drawn by G. Cole and engraved by J. Roper and reproduced in a facsimile edition in 1970. In his essential handbook, *Maps for the Local Historian: A Guide to the British Sources*, J. B. Harley has a full bibliography which includes some recent facsimiles.

Dudley's earliest maps date from 1835 with the publication of Treasure's survey, though Yates's Map of Staffordshire printed in 1775 at a scale of about 2 miles to 1 inch shows a well discernible, deceptively regular street plan in miniature, with extensive ribbon development along the Wolverhampton road via Gornal. Treasure's map (see illustrations pages 142 and 143) has a pattern of streets whose names fit neatly to the present-day road development, some of which he identifies as turnpike roads, with gates at the four main outgoing routes. He shows few of the industrial features which Bentley's *Directory* lists only five years later. Apart from small workshops, the main undertaking in the centre of the town is represented by three glassworks. We discover that the salubrious distance of the heavy metalworks, mills and furnaces from the centre of Dudley was a virtue of necessity, rather than the result of thoughtful planning. The high saddle of limestone, which was the main feature of the earliest Saxon site, was almost impenetrable to canal throughfare, so that essential limestone, coal and iron ore were kept at a distance from the town for want of cheap transportation such as Birmingham enjoyed. Eventually in 1792 the imaginative solution of a two-mile canal tunnel under the Castle Hill created a link with the Birmingham Canal system. The venture was not as productive as its planners had hoped, as the tunnel was a simple affair, with no towpath and a one-way system. This resulted in the curious and exhausting process of 'legging' which is now a part of local lore beloved by the conservationists of the Black Country Museum. (The boatmen lay on their backs and trod the roof of the tunnel from end to end; this is now an

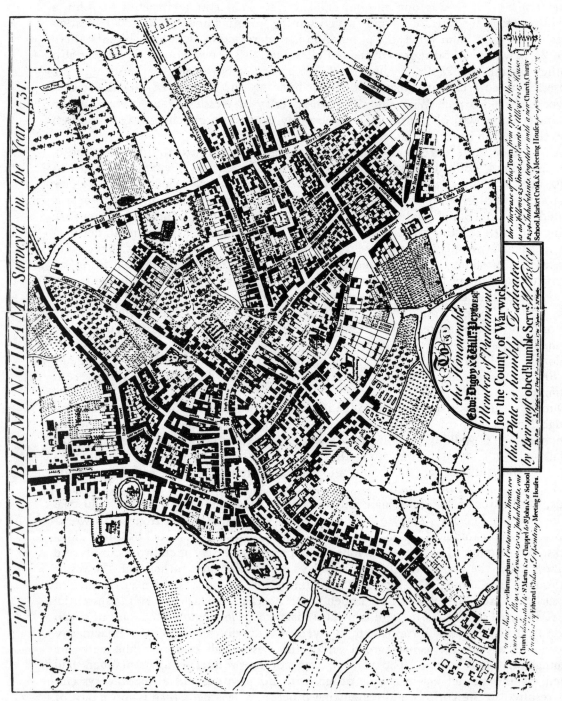

Westley's map of Birmingham, 1731, from the Local Studies Department, Birmingham Reference Library (actual size 11½ in. x 10½ in). Below, Westley's street plan superimposed on the modern city centre (base map by permission of Geographia Ltd.).

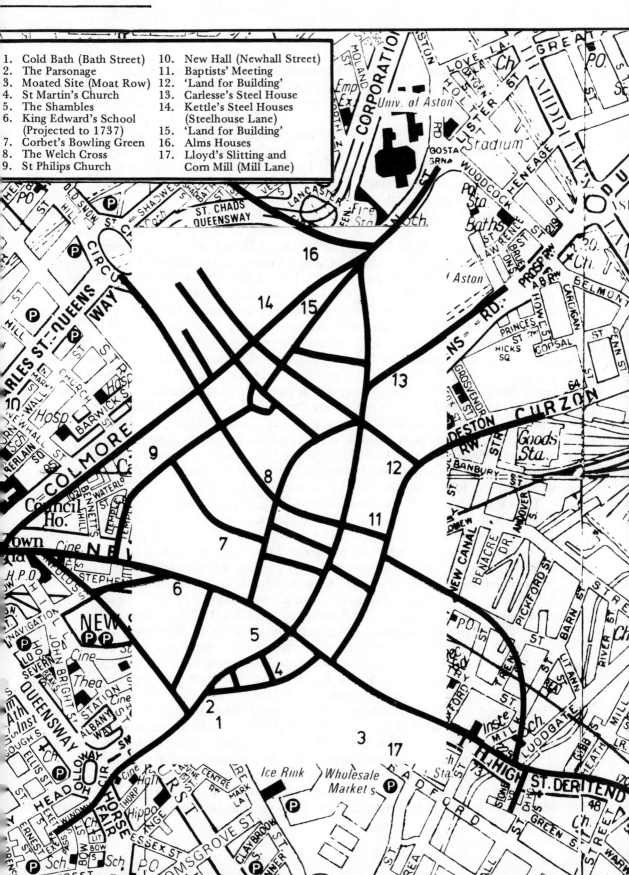

1. Cold Bath (Bath Street)
2. The Parsonage
3. Moated Site (Moat Row)
4. St Martin's Church
5. The Shambles
6. King Edward's School (Projected to 1737)
7. Corbet's Bowling Green
8. The Welch Cross
9. St Philips Church
10. New Hall (Newhall Street)
11. Baptists' Meeting
12. 'Land for Building'
13. Carlesse's Steel House
14. Kettle's Steel Houses (Steelhouse Lane)
15. 'Land for Building'
16. Alms Houses
17. Lloyd's Slitting and Corn Mill (Mill Lane)

enthusiast's pastime). The same inaccessibility would bedevil and delay Dudley's railway age; the Oxford, Worcester and Wolverhampton Railway Company (the O.W. & W., well-known as the 'Old Worse and Worse') did not connect Dudley to the outside industrial world until 1852, again with a single track. The geology of the town site is the reason Dudley never had a canal running through its centre, as Wolverhampton and Birmingham had, nor was there a central railway station. Dudley Port, two miles from town, is a local joke and the Freightline terminal a very recent development. Dudley Station, commemorated by the *Station* Hotel, was farther from the town centre than the Zoo and lasted only from 1850 to 1964.

The absence of central furnaces obviated the fashion of a West End residential housing development upwind of noxious trades. Residences of the ironmasters and glasshouse proprietors could ring the centre of Dudley with halls, greens and houses (see illustration, page 143). This would not long outlast Treasure's map, however. The population in his day had already more than doubled since the first census in 1801, with an increase of 200 houses shown on his map. By 1861 the population would double yet again and the number of houses increase from 4,326 to 8,714. This growth is startlingly evident in William Richards' plan of the borough, surveyed in 1865. The centre of the town has swollen towards the gasworks in St Thomas Ward where Red Hill stood, to the southeast between the New Birmingham Road (now the shortest distance between 30 traffic lights) and the Great Western Railway line in St Edmunds Ward. More significant for the future, however, is the piecemeal growth beyond the town centre, in St James's Ward, where the ancient Russells Hall has become 'Russells Hall Furnaces'; in Woodside Ward, along the railway line at Harts Hill Works and Woodside Works; at Netherton, around several ironworks, and nearer town to the east in St John's Ward at Kates Hill. The spread from town centre into conurbation had begun; places which had been neighbouring hamlets, landed estates, or even small villages, began to be absorbed into the spreading network of the town.

The Ordnance Survey was founded in 1791 and published its first one-inch Map, of Kent, in 1801; the Old Series of 110 one-inch sheets was continually printed between 1805–73. Surveying on the larger scales of 6 inches and 25 inches to the mile began in 1840 and 1853 respectively and maps can be sought in the *Catalogue of Maps and other Publications of the Ordnance Survey*, published from 1862–1924. These precise and detailed records of built-up areas are invaluable to the town historian; even more specific are three series of individual town plans, published between 1843 and 1894 at even larger scales of 1/1056 (50.68 inches to the mile), 1/528 (10 feet to the mile) and 1/500 (10.56 feet to the mile). Both scale and coverage of these maps were immense: for the 1/500 series, all towns with more than 4,000 inhabitants were covered, about 400 towns in all. Liverpool's survey included 304 sheets and even some small market towns run to as many as a dozen. Besides these maps, in 1850 some areas, at their own expense, as a result of the movement towards town improvement initiated by the *First Report of the Commissioners for Inquiring into the State of Large Towns and Populous Districts* in 1844 and the Public Health Act of 1848, had their towns privately surveyed at a scale of 1:528; many of these remained unpublished. 'For work in the densely built-up areas of town centres, the town plans with their often minute topographical detail and ample space for annotation, may be extremely useful.[5]

Dudley, unfortunately, was not included in the 1:528 series of town plans until relatively late; the sheets published in 1883 are the first and only Ordnance Survey edition of a separate plan for the town. The fragment in Chapter 11, p. 291 is chosen to reveal the warren of back-to-back courts and small workshops which were typical of this and other industrial towns of the 19th century. These will be the subject of further investigation in the later Chapter on the Census Returns, in which the same streets are used as illustration. Some long overdue improvements were to some extent provided by 1883 as is evident from the conventional abbreviations for lamps (L) and lamp-posts (LP), manhole covers (MH), water-plugs (WP) and pumps (P) but the courtyard privies have an ominous aspect. Other sheets show schools, chapels and inns, some of which survive and the old Alhambra Theatre which, sadly, does not. Other towns provide earlier surveys from the 1840s to the 1860s; these are listed in the Gazetteer.

We can now compare the nature and extent of the growth of our three very different sample-towns from their various sets of maps. The earlier stages of their growth are shown in the illustrations on pages 135, 139, 143 where the earlier original maps for each town with main landmarks have been overlaid on the modern street plans. In each case too, one or more subsequent surveys have also been outlined to show stages of growth between the originals and the present day. Thus Speed (1610) is outgrown by Roper (1810) in Worcester: Westley's map of Birmingham (1731) is extended by reference to Bradford (1751), Hanson (1785) and Arrowsmith (1834) and Treasure's Dudley (1835) can be compared with Richards' later plan (1865).

What is surprising is that at first the hearts of the two industrial towns, Birmingham and Dudley, were little different in size and shape; each is a rough, irregular triangle, with sides about half a mile long, each straggling outward along its main approach roads. The city of Worcester, already as large as the later towns in 1610 had expanded much less by 1810 and was evidently constricted by the very existence of its ancient walls and gates. A paradoxical result of this confinement is that the smallest and most ancient of the three towns has suffered more rearrangement of its ancient, central streets — in the cathedral precincts, on Friar Street and Dolday — than either of the latecomers. Thus Speed's pattern of streets has been less permanent than that of Westley's later map of Birmingham and the Ringway had obliterated fewer landmarks, streets and place-names than the Deansway.

Obviously each town *was* growing, as the relative population statistics will show, century by century; for the industrial towns, decade by decade. Each town too, has a fairly well-defined area for expansion — none of the three merely spreads out in all directions at once. In Birmingham, there was at first the well-planned development area of New Hall and the elegant squares of St Pauls; at Worcester, in 1610 the city was already spreading beyond Foregate towards the Tithing and St Oswald's and, in the southerly direction across the river into the parish of St John's. In Dudley there was a similar area for overspill in the direction of Kates Hill, Russells Hall and Queens Cross. Yet in every case, the first 18th-century territorial expansion does not really match the increase in population. For a while each town grows 'larger' in terms of inhabitants rather than in terms of new acreage; so that there is for example, little change in new built-up areas of Birmingham between 1735 and 1785, as shown by the maps of Westley, Bradford and Hanson. In each case the squares of New Hall estate are still open for development and outwards towards the village of Aston; though the terraces around Gosta Green are beginning to fill, there are still orchards on New Market Street in 1785 where Westley first showed fields. Not until Arrowsmith's map (1834) has the

DUDLEY CASTLE KEEP.

Treasure's map of Dudley, 1841, from the Archives and Local History Department of Dudley Public Libraries (actual size 18 in. x 25 in.) Opposite: Treasure's street plan superimposed on the modern c (base map by permission of Geographia Ltd.)

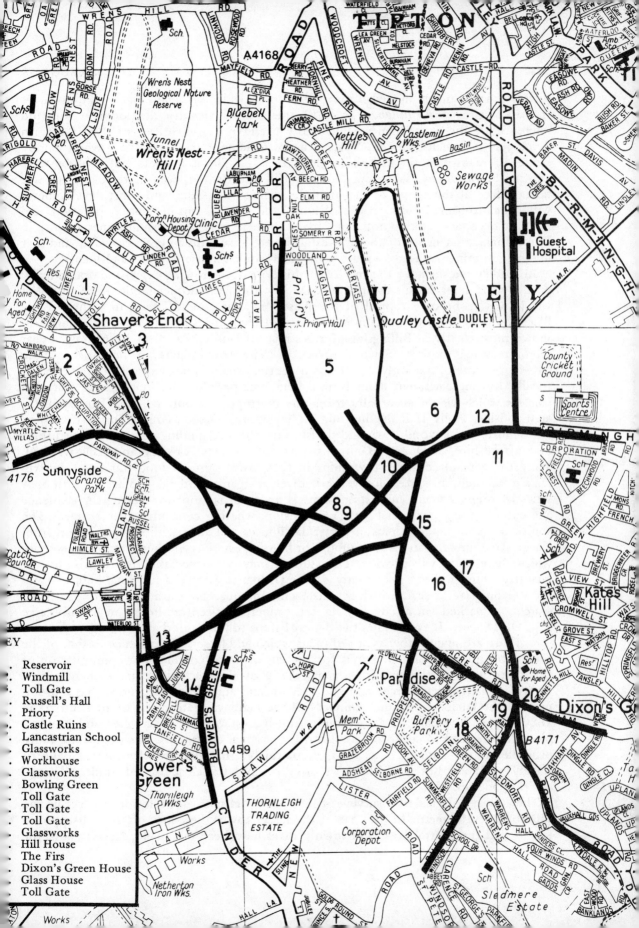

town's encroachment moved outward beyond Westley's frame. Victor Skipp, in his *History of Greater Birmingham to 1830*, traces this concentric development with full reference to the street-names which now preserve the identities of their Georgian developers — Jennens, Gooch, Vyse, Princip, Colemore and Wearman — where family estates were broken up as building lots. In 1780–90, as hamlets and suburbs were growing at Bordesley, Islington, Summer Hill and Ashted, even more re-housing was taking place at the centre of the town, by means of infilling and court development, with 'back-to-backs', 'blind-backs', 'shops' and other forms of 'close population' and multiple occupancy. Skipp notes that by 1836 there were 169 steam-engines at work in Birmingham, that many of the new estates were jerry-built and overcrowded, and that in short 'Birmingham is not a place gentlemen would choose to make a residence'.

In Dudley we shall see the results of this type of in-growing expansion dramatically portrayed in later census returns. Yet Dudley also had another mode of enlargement which was to become typical of the West Midlands connurbation, or rather of the Black Country of which 'Brummagem' is not characteristic. Dudley's difference was shown most clearly in Billingsley Morris's map of Dudley Parish in 1836, only a year after Treasure's more ornamental survey of 'The Town'; Here, in the parish, we see growth beginning, not only at the town centre (which is not extensive), nor concentrically by encroachment as in Birmingham; but peripherally, in all those scattered hamlets which would eventually form one metropolitan borough — in Dudley itself, at Woodside, Holly Hall, Netherton, Dudley Wood, Dixons Green, Darby Hand and Withymore, and beyond town and parish, into the surrounding villages and townships of Staffordshire, at Quarry Bank, Brierley Hill, Sedgley, Coseley and Kingswinford. Many of these places were townships in their own right, of long standing, and will remain as such, fossilized forever, whatever reorganization takes place in future. A series of original maps and estate plans is an essential tool for tracing the sequence and extent of any provincial town's expansion, whether concentric or piecemeal. The ability to discover the origins of particular houses and streets, their assimilation from village street into urban district, suburb or housing estate is another interesting exercise which these maps will provide. The student may often be taken by surprise by the quantity of map sheets — certainly of the Ordnance Survey if not long before — and the startling size of scale which reveals each lamp-post and outhouse. As one satisfied searcher remarked, on discovering his early nineteenth-century house on an early large scale O.S. Sheet: 'It even shows the flight of steps to the front door!'

There are many other types of plans which add large-scale evidence to that of the town map proper. Plans prepared for the enclosure of commons or commutation of tithes are well worth consulting, particularly as their schedules indicate names of owners, tenants, field-names and the uses of land and buildings. Dudley has a useful plan of the enclosure of the remnants of the medieval hunting Chase of Pensnett in 1820. Here, nowadays, is a featureless housing estate, but its avenues and building plots can be seen to conform closely to the original allotments. Such maps are indispensable to the student who feels, despairingly, that his own Pensnett, Speke or Chelmsley Wood has no history to offer beyond the close-packed modern 'semis' and maisonettes.

The almost universal tithe surveys of 1830-40 are indispensable for property-tracing and suburban development. In the case of the larger towns these may often be disappointing, in that the central areas and town centres have been left blank. Nevertheless, the surrounding fields and estates, which provided building land throughout the latter part of the 18th century and the early decades of the 19th century, have explicit detail of ownership, tenancies and land-use. These records are particularly useful in preserving evidence of how an area has changed most, in terms of agriculture or parkland into industrial or suburban uses, or of factory settlements into twilight residential zones. Large-scale plans and estate papers often take over at the outer fringes of the town, where the earlier town maps did not venture, except to indicate a rural setting. Tithe maps, more fully described in *Village Records* (pages 145–157) are usually at a scale of 6 chains to the inch (or about 13 inches to the mile), large enough to identify buildings and trace suburban development very clearly.[6] These maps and their accompanying schedules are most usually found at the Diocesan or County Record Office, though some are housed in borough archives and reference libraries. Birmingham Reference Library, for example, can produce tithe maps of the northern residential areas of Edgbaston and Birmingham Green which clearly show the limits of the build-up streets, the tentacles of earlier industrial extension and the imminent break up of the estates of local gentry for new building land. The extract chosen (see page 146), shows the continuing existence, in 1845, of Boulton and Watt's 18th-century Soho Manufactory and, in the modern key-map, the pool and wharf which are still named, though no longer surrounded by gardens. The related extract from the tithe schedule reads:

LAND OWNERS: Boulton, Matthew
               Piers, Walt.,
OCCUPIERS: Boulton & Watt   241: Part of Soho Manufactory
               Various   244: Gardens
               Thomas Hodgetts and
                 Others   246: Houses and gardens
               In hand   248: Plantation
                                         248a: Part of Hockley Pool
                                         250: Meadow and plantation (Pasture)

The area of Handsworth and Hockley shown on the extract from the map is now largely an industrial wasteland, bordered by a motley collection of houses jumbled together from the 1890s to the 1960s. 'Soho Pool' is a concrete jungle which has never been underwater within living memory. At one end is an industrial estate, the rest is a giant scrapyard criss-crossed with railway lines — the 'Wharf' marked on the modern map is deceptive. A small brook, running sluggishly in a brickbuilt conduit, cuts through Hockley Brook Trading Estate, to which it gives its name, on the line of the brook shown across the Pool in 1845. Soho Works is no more, though the name persists in *Soho Tavern* and the street names.

Today, as you turn off to the right of Soho Road or Soho Hill, there is a choice of Boulton Road, Nineveh Road or Piers Road, which all lead towards Factory Road and the site of the Soho Manufactory. Down Factory Road two small dated (1889) terraces, Cemmaes Place and Dovey Place, probably commemorate immigrant Welsh artisans. Where one turns right into South Road which fringes the site of the Pool, a 20th-century lockmaker's factory has replaced Boulton and Watt's works. (There is however a suspiciously ancient engine-house chimney in the background). Here, rows of houses alternate from once prosperous three-storey Victorian terraces to semi-detached houses of the 1920s. Along the ridge behind the houses are vestiges of ancient trees

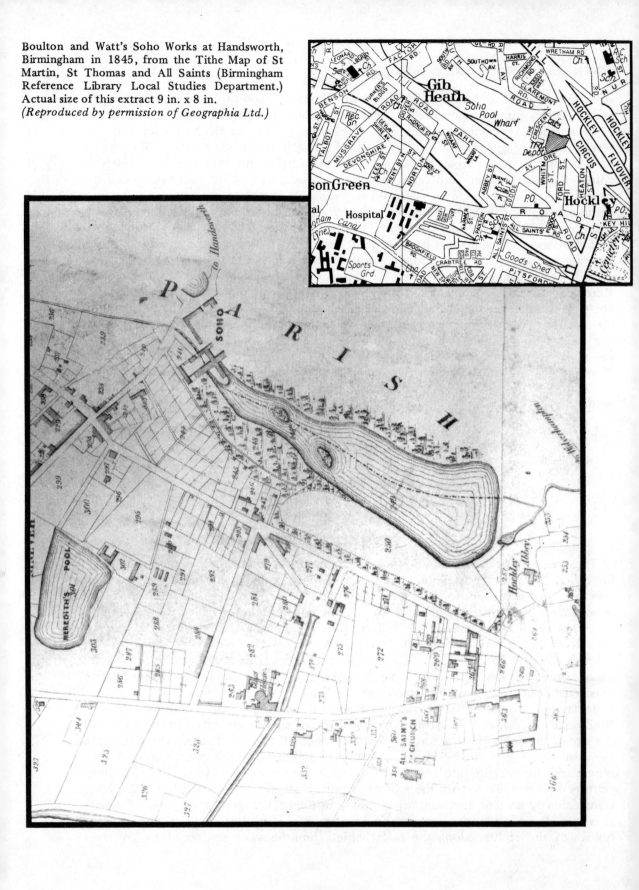

Boulton and Watt's Soho Works at Handsworth, Birmingham in 1845, from the Tithe Map of St Martin, St Thomas and All Saints (Birmingham Reference Library Local Studies Department.) Actual size of this extract 9 in. x 8 in.
(Reproduced by permission of Geographia Ltd.)

and a patch or two of bluebells amongst the debris. 'Industrial Units To Let' range
from aged brick with cobbled entries to concrete blockhouses; their trades are as
varied, ranging from plastics to tools, castings and pressings. It is almost useless to ask
for living memory of these streets and workshops, as no-one seems to have lived there
longer than four years and most are Asiatic; the one knowledgeable resident, according
to the landlord of the *Black Eagle*, 'was buried last week'. The general aspect is,
typically of the Black Country and Birmingham, cheerfully grim; the 'Meadow and
Plantation' (250) is wasteland between the maisonettes; Hockley Abbey is lost under
the looming flyover, the 'Gardens' (244) are submerged between a new 'ten-yard seam'
— of scrapiron. The railway-line, itself now derelict, was evidently the first formative,
intrusive feature after 1845, commemorated by inn-signs: *The Old Engine* and *The
Railway*, which is certainly the most elegant survivor (293) from the Tithe Map. And
all among the ruins and waste, lilac grows and saplings seed themselves.

Another survey of the Soho site, an inset to
Arrowsmith's map of 1834 (from Birming-
ham Reference Library Local Studies
Department; actual size 3⁷/₈ in. x 4 in.)

Another rich source of town maps, collected into one set and available in larger
Reference Libraries, are those which accompany the *Reports of Boundary Commissioners*. These are usually stated to be 'From the Ordnance Survey' or 'Enlarged from
the Ordnance Survey'. Their main value is accessibility to the student at a distance
from the town he is studying — for example one can look up the maps of Cheltenham
or Chatham, Worcester or Bolton in one or two volumes in Birmingham. The scales will
vary from 1-6 inches to the mile, occasionally larger. *The Boundary Commissioners'
Report of 1868*, required by the Representation of the People Act of 1867, surveyed
207 boroughs to discover which ones, whether re-enfranchised or newly represented,
had grown sufficiently to warrant conferring the vote on additional £10 householders

or on other voters. Each town's report states whether the parliamentary and municipal borough are identical in acreage; whether there has been much recent building; and if any of this lies outside the bounds of the existing borough. Populations for 1831 and 1861 are compared, with the nature of their franchise. In Dudley the Commissioners recommended the inclusion of the surrounding areas of Pensnett, Brockmoor and Quarry Bank (an area of 2,500 acres and 5,000 houses) and the districts of Reddall Hill in the parish of Rowley Regis (a further 1,200 acres with 2,400 houses). To Worcester were added 530 more houses in SS Peter, Martin and John's and Birmingham was extended to include the Manor of Aston and Balsall Heath, which covered 1,300 acres, 7,603 houses and 30,500 people. The accompanying maps, which are bound into the *Report*, show in colour the differences, if any, between township and parish boundary, municipal boundary and parliamentary boundary, in 1832 and in 1867.

Most detailed of all town plans are those produced by fire-insurance companies from the end of the 18th century.[7] These reached their highest stage of development from 1885–1896 with the systematic work of Charles E. Goad, who published 73 volumes of plans of the 37 principal towns and cities in the British Isles, including 21 volumes for London alone. These plans are invaluable for their large scale of 40 feet to the inch, and their detail of building use and construction. A simple key indicates whether a house is a dwelling, shop, tenement, office or public-house and the number of storeys and windows is indicated. Building materials are colour-coded to reveal distinctions between brickwork and stone, wooden construction and metal fabric. House-numbers are given and, where an index is available, the names of occupiers will be recorded. Later editions of the plans, made during the 1920s and 1930s, record in their revisions important on-going changes in the central commercial and residential areas of large towns. As Aspinall points out: 'Apart from photographs, these plans are the only record available of the vertical extension of the demolished sections of the central area in the late nineteenth and early twentieth centuries, a dimension which has been largely ignored in historical studies of the morphology of the central business district'.[8] Insurance plans will be found in the local borough library; their availability is noted in this Chapter's Gazetteer.

The source of maps and plans of urban streets and properties is certainly a rich one, well-documented and indexed for the student's use. The British Museum's *Catalogue of Printed Maps, Charts and Plans* in 15 volumes (1967) is the essential starting-point for the student at a distance from his town. This will be available in larger Reference Libraries, and is the basis of our Gazetteer. (It is a fascinating study in its own right, as entries for Ch'en Yung Chi and Chicago occur alongside Cheltenham, Yonkers and Yokohama next to York.) Here we shall certainly find the best-known printed maps of any borough in England and Wales, but local sources will add information on many less familiar regional cartographers and their town plans.

The Gazetteer entry for Dudley (page 154) has been deliberately expanded to include almost all the maps and plans of the town and parts of the town, which are catalogued by the town library's Local History Department. Here there are hundreds of index cards for the outlying parts of the new borough, both suburbs and neighbouring townships. As the Gazetteer shows, the town and its oldest suburbs account for a hundred separate entries. These range from six substantial town-plans proper and several earlier maps of the parish, to industrial sites, including 'water-engines', 'whimsy-engines' and extensive building development surveys of the early 19th-century. Now we see a Market Square where the Middle Row still stood but St James's Road, now a central municipal thoroughfare, did not exist. There are numerous proposals for railways – none of which materialised – for canal extensions, water supply and electric lighting innovations. There is even the sketch-map of a local murder, where X marks the spot.

Many local collections of individual maps, held in libraries at Burnley, Croydon, Darlington, Gateshead, Ilkeston, Liverpool – and so on through the alphabet – have been added to the Gazetteer. Though not to be found in the *British Museum Catalogue*, these references were kindly supplied by borough archivists and librarians in those towns; many more remain to be found by the student on his own ground. Certainly we should not expect to find many manuscript estate plans, which so many local muniment rooms can provide, in the *Catalogue of Printed Maps*, though some enclosure plans and tithe maps are included there. Nor can many of these be contained in the Gazetteer, which is intended as a starting-point for further searching. Several borough libraries and local history collections (such as those in Crosby, Darlington, and Islington) have printed guides to their map-rooms; these are occasionally more informative than those of their county record offices. These catalogues, and some articles in specialised periodicals are also listed in the Gazetteer. Where a county's overall publications may be relevant to several towns, these will be found listed under the county town.

Several county record offices have also produced substantial guides and handlists to their collections of maps and plans. Of these, the outstandingly attractive example is still that of *Maps in the Essex Record Office* (1947–52). Hertfordshire, too, is well-served by catalogues, as also are Buckinghamshire, Warwickshire, Wiltshire, Huntingdonshire and Surrey. The extensive works of Chubb in Wiltshire, Gloucestershire, Somerset and Norfolk, and of Whitaker in Cheshire, Lancashire, Northamptonshire, Northumberland and Yorkshire are also invaluable aids to the student of any towns in those counties. *Village Records* gives a more extensive list of county maps and map-makers. London is particularly fortunate, not only in the large number of specialised guides and other bibliographies about its maps, such as those by R. Hyde (*The Printed Maps of London 1851–1900*) and James Howgego (*Printed Maps of London c. 1553–1850*) but also in the very existence of the London Topographical Society (its Secretary is at Hamilton's, Kilmersdon, in Avon). This society's purpose is 'to assist the study and appreciation of London's history and topography by making available facsimiles of maps, plans and views and by publishing research'. Of the society's 126 publications, more than a third are still in print. (See under LONDON in the Gazetteer). From personal experience this society's representatives could not be more helpful to the enquirer about London's maps.

Enough has been said, in a cursory survey of a rich and attractive field, to show how much more there is to learn from town maps and about them. No Gazetteer can hope to be all-inclusive. Readers will inevitably, one hopes, be able to make their own useful additions to all the starting points mentioned here.

FURTHER READING

Bagley, J. J., 'County Maps and Town Plans', in *Historical Interpretation: vol. II, Sources of English History, 1540 to Present Day* (1971).

Booth, J., *Antique Maps of Wales* (1977).

Harley, J. B., *Maps for the Local Historian: A Guide to the British Sources* (1972).

—— *The Historian's Guide to Ordnance Survey Maps* (1964).

Skelton, R. A., 'Tudor town plans', in *Archaeological Journal*, vol. 108 (1951).

Tooley, R. V., *Maps and Map-Makers* (1970).

GAZETTEER OF TOWN MAPS AND PLANS c. 1600-1900

The main source of information for this list of 325 towns and their maps is *The British Museum Catalogue of Printed Maps, Charts and Plans* (15 vols., 1967). To these have been added any local map which local librarians have drawn attention. Towns mapped by Speed are named in **BOLD CAPITALS**. Scales are given where these are known. Abbreviations used in the gazetteer are as follows:

BA	= J. Roper, The British Atlas (1807)		BC	= Boundary Commission
C	= County map including plan of town		CP	= Canal plan
D	= *Directory* of named town (see Chap. 9)		E	= Estate plan(s)
engr	= engraved by		G	= *Guide* to named town
Gaz	= *Gazetteer* of named town		Ins	= Fire Insurance Plan
P	= *Plan* of named town		PL	= Public library
PM	= Parish map		Pr	= *Prospect* of named town
OS	= Ordnance Survey map of named town		RO	= Record office
repr	= reproduced, reprinted		SM	= Street map
TM	= Tithe map(s)		UD	= Urban district

Note: the entry for Dudley shows the full range of material which can be available for a single town as an example to demonstrate how the bare bones of this Gazetteer can be fleshed out. Other entries are *not* to be regarded as all-inclusive.

ABERGAVENNY: E, Lord Bergavenny
  (3½ and 4 chains: 1in.) 1718; OS 1901.
ABERYSTWYTH: OS (1:528) 1887.
ABINGDON: OS (1:528) 1879; BC, 1868.
ACCRINGTON: OS (1:1056) 1861; OS (1:528)
  1892.
ALDEBURGH: P, (1:2500) 1883; Harbour,
  1601 (1936) 160 yds = 152 mm.
ALTRINCHAM: OS (1:528) 1878.
ANDOVER: E, 1861; BC, 1868; OS
  (1:528); OS (1:500) 1897.
APPLEBY: P, North Hill 1754; OS (1:500)
  1861.
ARUNDEL: Pr, Hollar 1664; BC, 1868;
  Steer, F. W. (ed.), *Cat. Arundel Castle Arch.*
  (W. Sussex County Council, 1968, 1972,
  1976, 1980).
ASHTON-UNDER-LYNE: CP, 1793; Baines
  (Gaz), 1824; OS (1:2500) 1863; BC, 1868;
  OS (1:528) 1894.
AYLESBURY: BC, 1868; OS (1:528) 1870.
BACUP: OS (1:1056) 1852; OS (1:528) 1892.
BANBURY: BC (1:528) 1882; BC, 1868.
BANGOR: Speed 1610; Saxton 1695 (Lea);
  C, Sandby 1776; OS (1:528) 1889.
BARKING: Manorial Plan, Doyley 1815-16; OS
  (1:2500) 1864; (also DAGENHAM) Moll,
  Snr., 'Daggenham Breach' (140 rods = 55 mm)
  1721.
BARNET: OS (1:2500) 1864; (also
  FINCHLEY) E, 'Freehold purchased for the
  members of Finsbury Freehold Land Society'
  1852; 'Moss Hall, as proposed to be laid out
  for building purposes' 1870 (?); OS (1:2500)
  1864; (also HENDON), Crow (100 poles = 45
  mm) 1754; (reduced by Brett-James 1927).
BARNSLEY: OS (1:1056) 1852; OS (1:528)

(Barnsley — continued)
  1889: Municipal Wards (n.s.) 1895.
BARNSTAPLE: OS (1:528) 1889; BC, 1868;
  SM (1 in. = 150 yds) 1895; Sketch-map,
  Sheppard 1908.
BARROW-IN-FURNESS: Kendall P (15 chains
  = 125 mm) 1843; 'Freehold building land'
  1854; OS (1:528) 1874; Municipal Borough
  (Directory), 1875; OS (1:528) 1891; Fowler
  (10 in.: 1 m) 1902.
BASINGSTOKE: OS (1:528) 1874.
BATH: Speed 1610; Gilmore & Savage (660 ft.
  = 63 mm) 1697; Van Hove 1713; Gilmore &
  Savage (36 poles = 148 mm) 1717; Wood,
  1735; Strachey (400 yds = 170 mm); P, 1750,
  1755, 1760; Rocque (200 yds = 58 mm)
  1772; Thorpe & Cole (1 m = 100 mm) 1742;
  P (220 yds = 58 mm) 1772; Hibbart, 1780,
  1783, 1790, 1792; Coffin (220 yds = 25 mm)
  1773; Frederick & Taylor (1:7920) 1780 (?);
  Chantry & Hancock (1000 ft = 65mm), 1793,
  1796, 1801, 1805; Harcourt-Masters, 1795;
  Baly & Tennent, 1800; Day & Masters (20
  chains = 35 mm) 1803; Donne & Godwin,
  1810, 1816, 1825; Meyler & Son (2 furlongs
  = 40 mm) 1811; Gingell & Meyler (G) (½ mile
  = 110 mm) 1842, 1851; Gibbs (½ mile = 85
  mm), 1835, 1858, 1883; Moule & Virtue,
  1837; Hollway, 1848; Cottrell (40 chains =
  125 mm) 1852; BC, 1868; Cottrell & Spack-
  man (*Gibbs New Plan of Bath*) 1870: 'Plan de
  Bathe' (Paris) 1870; OS (1:528) 1885-86;
  Cottrell (12 in.: 1 m) 1898; Goad (Ins) 1902.
  See: Chubb, T. 'A descriptive list of the
  printed maps of Somersetshire 1575-1914'
  (pub. by *Somerset Arch. & Nat. Hist. Soc.*,
  1914).

BATLEY: OS (1:528) 1890; Goad (40 ft:1 in.)
1893 (Ins).
BEAUMARIS: Speed 1610; Saxton 1695; BC,
1868.
BEBINGTON: Griffith & Son (6 in.:1 m), 1890.
BECCLES: OS (1:528) 1884.
BEDFORD: Speed 1610; Jeffreys 1765-67,
1804; Roper (*British Atlas*) 1807; Mercer
(800 ft.:1 in.) 1884; E (10 ft.:1 in.) 1862;
BC, 1868; OS (1:528) 1884.
BERWICK-ON-TWEED: Bergamo (Military), c.
1570, 1572; Johnson 1575; Speed 1610,
1666; Merian (?) 1650 (?); *Carte Nouvelle
d'Ecosse* 1711; Armstrong & Son 1769;
Wood 1822; OS (1:528) 1855; BC, 1868.
See: Whitaker, H. *A descriptive list of the
maps of Northumberland 1576-1900* (1949).
BEVERLEY: OS (1:1056) 1854; BC, 1868; OS
(1:528) 1892.
BEWDLEY: BC, 1868.
BEXLEY: OS (1:2500) 1865; E, 1874, 1876.
(also ERITH) Hollar 1662 (1939); OS
(1:2500) 1865; E (Lesney Park (1874);
Holly Hill House (1889)).
BIRKENHEAD: 'Plan of Birkenhead etc. . . .'
1858; Syers *Ready Reference and Cab Fare
Plan of Birkenhead* 1869; BC, 1868.
BIRMINGHAM: Bickley & Hill (Conjectural),
1553 (1890); Sleigh (Imaginative), 1730
(1923); Westley (10 perches = 18 mm) 1731;
Bradford & Jefferys 1751; Hanson 1778,
1781; Snape 1779 (1884); Pye 1792, 1795;
Kempson 1808, 1819; Beilby, Knott &
Beilby 1824, 1825; Gillies 1822; Drake 1832;
Arrowsmith 1834; Dower 1835; Drake 1835
(?); Henshall and Robbins 1838; Davies 1858;
Granger 1860 (?); Smith and Cornish 1860;
BC, 1868; Davies (Post Office Map) 1 m =
100 mm 1870; Trams, Bus and Railway G
(3 in.:1 m) 1886-87; OS (1:528) 1887;
Goad (Ins) 1889; 'City Map' 1889; 'Plan'
(4 in.:1 m) 1896; Goad (Ins) 1926.
BLACKBURN: D, 1824; OS (1:1056) 1848;
'Map of the Borough and Township' (800
yds. = 185 mm) 1852; BC, 1868; 'Borough of
Blackburn' (12 in.:1 m) 1878-1895; OS
(1:528) 1893. See: *Sources of Local History*
(Blackburn PL 1968).
BLACKPOOL: Heywood 1869; Harding 1878
(?); OS (1:528) 1892.
BLYTH: Plan of the Coal Districts 1851; OS
(1:528) 1861.
BODMIN: BC, 1868; OS (1:528) 1881.
BOLTON: OS (1:1056) 1849; BC, 1868; OS
(1:528) 1891; Brockbank (D), 1897. See:
The Albison and Thompson Collections of
Local Maps and Plans at Bolton Public
Library.
BOSTON: Hall 1741. Armstrong (20 chains =
65 mm) 1779; Bingley & Moule 1837; BC,
1868; OS (1:528) 1889.
BOURNEMOUTH: OS (1:528) 1871; Hankin-
son 1880, 1883, 1887, 1890; Garrett (from

(Bournemouth – continued) –
OS) 586.66 ft.:1 in. 1883; Moore 'The
Penny Map of Bournemouth' 1883; Powell
1883, 1889, 1891; 'Bright's Map of Bourne-
mouth' (3 in.:1 m) 1885; Garrett (*Stevens'
Directory*) 1888; also at 586.66 ft.:1 in.,
1889; Bright & Son's Plan (8 in.:1 m) 1893;
Bacon & Co. (*Stevens' Directory*) 1894-95.
BRADFORD: OS (1:1056) 1852; Dixon 1856;
BC 1868; P (*Smith's Directory*) 400 yds. = 42
mm, 1872; Walker & Virr 1873; Goad (Ins)
1886; OS (1:528) 1891. See (no author's
name) *Bradford in the 19th Century Shown
in Maps* (Bradford Libraries Dept., 1975).
BRECON: Speed 1610; Un-named 1655 (?);
BC, 1868; OS (1:528) 1888.
BRENT: (WEMBLEY) Ward 1910; (WILLES-
DEN) OS (1:2500) 1865.
BRIDGWATER: BC, 1868; OS (1:528) 1887.
BRIDLINGTON: OS (1:1056) 1853; Earnshaw
('Forster's Plan') 9 in.:1 m, 1891; OS
(1:528) 1891.
BRIDPORT: Anon. 'Part of the Borough', c.
18th c.; BC, 1868; OS (1:528) 1888-89.
BRIGHTON: Yeakell & Gardner (engr Whit-
church) 1779; T. Budgen 1788; Marchant
(10 chains = 35 mm) 1809, 1810, 1825;
Sleath (½ mile = 85 mm) 1820, 1830, 1853;
'Map' 1826; Jobbins 1843; Saunders & Son
1841; Rock & Co. 1851; Taylor (D) 40
chains = 40 mm, 1854; BC, 1868; Treacher
1870 (?); Bacon & Co. c. 1875; OS (1:528)
1878; Johnson 1878 (?); Sawyer 1815 (1884);
Gill 1884; Smith & Son (from OS) 4¾ in.:1 m
1894; Goad (Ins) 1898.
BRIGHOUSE: OS (1:528) 1889.
BRISTOL: 'Bristollia' (facsimile, Ricart's 'Plan of
Bristol' 1479) in Gutch's *Bristol*, 1821; Braun
& Hohenbergius 1573-1618, 1660; Speed
1610; Merian (?) 1650 (?); James Millerd
(40 perches = 48 mm) 1670 (reproduced
1818-1922); Rocque (engr Pine) 26 in.:1 m,
1742; and at ½ mile = 6¼ in., 1750; Rocque
1759; Street Plan (Bath ? 1760); Donne (4
furlongs = 75 mm) 1784, 1787; Mathew's P,
1794, 1825; Edwards 1800; Chilcott 1826;
Ashmead & Plumley (engr Turrell) 500 ft. =
65 mm, 1820, 1829, reduced 1833, 1846;
Moule (6 m = 65 mm) 1837; Hall (3 furlongs
= 45 mm) 1840; Landers 'Miniature Pocket
Map' 4 furlongs = 23 mm) 1842; Stansbury
(engr S. Hall) (4 furlongs = 70 mm) 1850;
Lavar's 'New and Improved Map' 1858, 1874;
Trew (5 in.:1 m.) 1876; OS (1:528) 1885; BC
1868; Goad (Ins) 1887, 1921, 1927. See: 'A
Gloucestershire and Bristol Atlas; A selection
of old maps and plans from the 16th to the
19th Centuries'. (*Bristol & Gloucs. Arch. Soc.
1961*). See also; *Guide to the Bristol Archives
Office* (1971). For TM see: Kirby I. M. (ed.)
*Diocese of Bristol: A Catalogue of the records
of the Bishop and Archdeacons and of the
Dean and Chapter* (Bristol Corpn, 1970). For

(*Bristol – continued*) –
Enclosures at Kingswood and Westbury-on-Trym see G, p. 110 and for OS 6 in. and 25 in. (1882–1904), see G, p. 34.
BUCKINGHAM: Speed 1610; Jeffreys 1788; BC, 1868; OS (1:528) 1880. See: Price, U., 'The Maps of Buckinghamshire 1574–1800'. *Records of Buckinghamshire*, No. 15 (1947–51).
BROMLEY: OS (1:2500) 1862; New Road Map of the Parish of Bromley (5 in.:1 m) 1894; Souvenir of Bromley and Neighbourhood 1899; New Map of Croydon, Bromley etc. . . . (4 in.:1 m) 1901; also BECKENHAM: Lane 'Plot of the Manor of Beckenham' 1623; Proudlove (120 perches = 73 mm) 1768; E: Woolsey (6 poles = 94 mm) 1723; Sale, E of John Cator (40 perches = 123 mm) 1777; Sale, Foxgrove Farm (40 perches = 128 mm) 1777; Greame, Lord Gwydir's E (10 chains = 252 mm) 1809 (Kent County Council MS); Eden Park (15 chains = 190 mm) 1864; Beckenham Lodge (15 chains = 120 mm) 1874; Oakwood 1876; Eden Lodge (5 chains = 125 mm) 1878. See: Sister M. Baptist: 'Eighteenth Century Maps and Estate Plans of Bromley, Beckenham and Penge' in *Archaeol. Cantiana*, vol. 81 (1967).
BURNLEY: Jobling (90 yds.:1 in.) 1841; OS (1:1056) 1851: BC, 1868; OS (1:528) 1892.
BURTON ON TRENT: OS (1:528) 1884.
BURY: OS (1:1056) 1849; BC, 1868; OS (1:528) 1891.
BURY ST EDMUNDS: Warren (engr Collins) 20 chains = 150 mm, 1747, 1776; Downing 1740; Payne 1834; BC, 1868; OS (1:500) 1885.
BUXTON: Senior 1631; OS (1:528) 1879; Smith's P (6 in.:1 m) 1886.
CAERNARVON: Speed 1610; Saxton 1695; Humphreys (from 1530?) 1852; BC, 1868; OS (1:528) 1889.
CALNE: repr. Map, Parish of Calne, 1790
. (publ. OS Southampton, 1921).
CAMBRIDGE: Braun and Hohenbergius 1573–1618, 1660; Hammond 1592. Lyne (facsim. Fuller 1840); Speed 1610; Fuller 1634 (facsim. Pricket 1840; facsim. Nichols 1840); Merian (?) 1650 (?); *Illustriorum principumque urbium* 1660 (?); Loggan 1688; Stukeley 1704 (repr 1925); Roper (BA) 1810; Baker's 'New Map' 1830; Dower & Moule (*English Counties Delineated*) 1837; London 'Pictorial Plan' 1844; PMB 1850; BC, 1868; Richard Reynolds Rowe' (20 chains = 190 mm) 1858; Monson (6½ chains =1 in.) 1859; 'Spalding's Plan' by Craig (9 in.:1 m) 1875, 1881, 1887, 1888; OS (1:528) 1886–88. See Clark, J. W. & Gray, A., *Plans of Cambridge 1574–1798* (1921).
CAMDEN: (HAMPSTEAD) Quilley (7 in.:1 m), *Topography and Natural History of Hampstead* by J. J. Park, 1814; OS (1:2500). See LONDON: Sheets II, VII, VIII, XIV, XV,

(*Camden - continued*) –
XVI, 1871; 'Proposed Garden Suburb' (450 ft.:1 in.) 1905; 'Hampstead Tenants' Ltd.: Preliminary sketch plan for proposed development as a Garden Suburb' (1:2500), 1906–7. See: 'Sketch map of the parish of St John, Hampstead' in *London Argus*, No. 46, vol. 2, (1898); (also HOLBORN) 'Plan of St Giles-in-the-Fields. From an original Sketch in the reign of Queen Elizabeth' (in *Literary and Historical Memorials of London* by J. H. Jesse 1847); Cole 1750 (?); Stowe (600 ft. = 65 mm), *A Survey of the Cities of London and Westminster* by J. Stow (6th edn.) 1755. 'Plan of the Parishes . . . of St Giles-in-the-Fields and St George, Bloomsbury' (100 ft. = 1 in.) 1815. Wyld, 'The United Parishes of St Giles and St George 1824, 1828'; Mair 'Plan of the Parishes of St Giles and St George' (180 ft. = 1 in.) 1866; OS (1:2500) LONDON Sheets 24, 25, 26, 34, 35, 1876; Izard 'Plan of St Giles-in-the-Field and St George, Bloomsbury' (180 ft. = 1 in.) 1890. See: *The History of the United Parishes of St. Giles and St George*, by Dobie, R. (1834); (also ST PANCRAS) Cook & Hammond (3 chains = 1 in.) 1800 (1905); Tompson (6 chains = 1 in.) 1804: 'The Terrier book' (ref. in alphabetical order . . . to the Parish of St Pancras) 1804; Davies 'Survey . . . embracing St Pancras and Paddington' (1 m = 220 mm) 1837; Lucas 'Plan of the Borough of St Marylebone, comprising the Parishes of Paddington . . . and St Pancras' (1 mile = 250 mm) 1852; Map of Ward No. 1 1860; OS (1:2500). See LONDON Sheets II, III, VII, VIII, XVI, XVII, XXV, XXXIV, XXV, 1876; Map (½ mile = 120 mm) 1893; Vestry Electric Lighting Map (1000 yds. = 50 mm) 1894. See: 'Sketch Map of St Pancras' in *London Argus*, No. 17, vol. 1 (1897).
CANTERBURY: Braun & Hohenbergius 1573–1618, 1660; Speed 1610, 1666; Merian (?) 1650 (?); Stukeley 1722; P. Lea 1733; Doidge 1752; Andrews & Wren (1200 yds. = 115 mm) 1768; Roper (BA) 1810; Barlow (G) 1815; Collard 1843; Plans of the Municipal Boroughs of England and Wales (1850) (?); BC, 1868; OS (1:528) 1874; Keen's New Map 1876, 1880. See: Hull, F. (ed.) *Catalogue of Estate Maps 1590–1840 in Kent County Archives Office* (1973).
CARDIFF: Speed 1610; Plan of the centre of Cardiff in 1851 (repr 1905); BC, 1868; OS (1:528) 1879; Lewis 1895; Goad (Ins) 1888, 1935.
CARLISLE: Speed 1610; 'P' 1745; Lyson (300 yds. = 85 mm) 1760; Donald 1774; Roper (BA) 1810; OS (1:528) 1866; BC, 1868; Arthur's P. (D) 1880; New Postal Address Map 1880.
CARMARTHEN: Speed 1610; Bowen 1729; BC, 1868; OS (1:528) 1888.

CASTLEFORD: Brierley 1752, E, Mr. W.
Sagar of Catley; OS (1:528) 1890.

CHARD: Plans of the Municipal Boroughs of
England and Wales 1850 (?).

CHATHAM: OS (1:2500) 1866; BC, 1868;
Bacon (G) 1882; see 'An Exact Prospect of
the City of Rochester' by Collins, J., for a
Prospect of Chatham Dock, 1708–13.

CHELMSFORD: Map of 1591 (repr 1945, ERO);
Ogborne, 'Perspective View 1762'; OS
(1:2500) 1876; OS (1:528) 1877; Rowley, N.,
Essex Towns 1540–1640 (ERO pubns., 1970).

CHELSEA: BC, 1868; Pratt, P. (ed.) *Historic
Chelsea in Maps 1700–1894* (1980).

CHELTENHAM: Mitchell 1806; Tovey (engr
Radclyffe) 1825, 1826; Metrett (engr Neale
& Co.) 1834; Darby 1843; BC, 1868; OS
(1:500) 1885; Villar (D) 1890.

CHESTER: Braun & Hohenbergius 1573–1618,
1660; Speed 1610; Hollar (300 paces = 38
mm) 1656; Forbes 1691; de Lavaux 1745;.
Weston (engr Hunter) 1789; Burdett (600
yds. = 80 mm) 1777, 1794; Hunter (G)
600 yds. = 53 mm) 1782; Murray & Stewart
1791; Mutlow 1795; Roper (BA) 1810;
Batenham Jnr. (G) 1819, 1823; Thomas &
Sons 1845 (?); plans of the Municipal
Boroughs of England and Wales 1850 (?);
Pullan (Pictorial Plan) 1851; Bayne (G) 10
chains = 28 mm, 1855; Groombridge & Son
(G) 1860; BC, 1868; OS (1;528) 1879. See
Whitaker, H., 'A Descriptive List of the Maps
of Cheshire', *Chetham Soc.*, N.S. 106 (1942).

CHESTERFIELD: Plans of Municipal Boroughs
1850 (?); OS (1:500) 1877.

COVENTRY: Speed 1610; 'County Map' 1680;
Forbes 1691; Bradford & Jeffreys 1750;
Roper (BA) 1810; BC, 1868; 'Description'
1876; OS (1:528) 1888–89; Goad (Ins) 1897.

CHICHESTER: Speed 1610; Budgen (30 perches
= 30 mm) 1724, 1779; Gardner (engr Yeakell)
1769; Loader (300 yds. = 85 mm) 1812; Plans
of the Municipal Boroughs of England and
Wales 1850 (?); BC, 1868; OS (1:528) 1876.
See: Butler, D. J., *Town Plans of Chichester
1595–1898* (W. Sussex R.O., 1972).

CHIPPENHAM: Powell 1784; Plans of Municipal
Boroughs 1850; BC, 1868; OS (1:528) 1886.

CHIPPING NORTON: Enclosure Map, 1770;
Plans of Municipal Boroughs 1850; OS
(1:2500) 1881.

CHORLEY: OS (1:1056) 1848; OS (1:528)
1890.

CHRISTCHURCH: BC, 1869; OS (1:2500)
1871.

CLEETHORPES: 'Map' 1801; OS (1:1056)
1849; Plans of Municipal Boroughs 1850;
BC, 1868; OS (1:1056) 1886.

CLITHEROE: BC, 1868.

COLCHESTER: Speed 1610, 1662; *Diary and
Plan of Siege* 1648; Witham 1650; Sparrow
1767; Philip Morant 1768; Keymer, late 18th
c.; Chapman & André (40 chains = 132 mm)

(Colchester - continued) –
1771–74, 1777, 1785; Roper (BA) 1810;
Starling 1845; Plans of Municipal Boroughs
1850; BC, 1868; OS (1:528) 1877; Benham
1893; OS, 1873–(rev. 1921).

COLNE: 'Survey of maps of lands . . . (in) . . .
Marsden and Colne belonging to Banastre
Walton', c. 1784; OS (1:1056) 1851; OS
(1:528), 1892.

CONGLETON: Plans of Municipal Boroughs
1850; OS (1:528) 1876.

CONWAY: BC, 1868.

CREWE: OS (1:528) 1876.

CROSBY: See: *Local Maps and Documents in
the Local History Library* (1972); mainly
Liverpool; lists TM 1844; with map of Crosby.

CROYDON: Say 'Plan du bourg de Croydon'
1785; Roberts 'Plan of the Town' (5 chains =
1 in.) 1847; Enclosure, 1793, 1889; Walker
1884; OS (1:2500) 1862; OS (1:2500) 1869;
E: Addiscombe (1862); Woodside (1865);
Streatham Common (1868); Norbury Estate
(1869); Upper Norwood (1870); Croydon
(1888–89).

DARLINGTON: 'Plan: (28 in.: 1 m) 1826; Reed
(6 in.: 1 m) 1829; Dixon (40 in.: 1 m) 1837;
(25 in: 1 m) 1840; Sowerby (6 in.: 1 m)
1842; (40 in.: 1m) 1847; 'Plan' (2½ in.:
1 m) 1856; Lyall (26 in.: 1 m) 1884; 'The
County Borough' (6 in.: 1 m) 1891;
'Extensions and Improvements' (6 in.: 1 m)
1896. PL publishes a *Local History Guide
No. 6* to its collection.

DARTFORD: E: Holmes 1707 (cop. Burdett
1768); OS (1:2500) 1867; E: Baldwyns
(1876); Mount Maseal (1885); Hubbard 1835;
OS (1:528) 1868.

DARTMOUTH: (prob) Townsend 1619 (1950);
BC, 1868; OS (1:528) 1888.

DARWEN: OS (1:528) 1891.

DEAL: OS (1:528) 1873.

DENBIGH: Speed 1610; BC 1868; OS (1:528)
1876.

DERBY: Speed 1610; Saxton & Lea 1699;
Burdett 1791; Moneypenny 1791; Roper(BA)
1810; Board of Health 1852; Bemrose (from
O.S.) 1½ in.: 1 m, 1854, 1876; BC, 1868;
O.S. (1:528) 1883: Kelley (D) 1899.

DEVIZES: May 'Devizes Park' 1654; Dore 1759
(?); BC, 1868; OS (1:528) 1886; see: Chubb,
T., 'A descriptive catalogue of the printed
maps of Wiltshire from 1576 to 1855', *Wilts.
Arch. & Nat. Hist. Soc. Mag.*, No. 37 (1911).

DEWSBURY: Saxton (16 perches = 1 in.) 1600;
OS (1:1056) 1852; BC, 1868; OS (1:528)
1890; Goad (Ins) 1887.

DONCASTER: OS (1:1056) 1852; OS (1:528)
1890; 'Gazette'; (D) 1899.

DORCHESTER: Speed 1610: Donne 1759;
Price 1800 (?); Anon. 1800 (3 in. = 200 ft.)
(corrected 1848); Anon. (1 chain = 1 in.)
1835; BC, 1868; OS (1:528) 1888.

DOVER: Bodenehr 1690–1720; 'Plan of Coast

(Dover — continued) —
  and Port' 1757 (?); Wittington, 'Plan as in the
  Reign of Queen Elizabeth' 1838; Worthington
  (Small & Son) 1844; OS (1: 528) 1861; BC,
  1868; Keen's New Map 1876, 1880; OS
  (1:528) 1881–84.
DROITWICH: BC. 1868; OS (1: 528) 1884.
DUDLEY: Part of Parish, c. 1700 (?); CP and
  proposed extensions: 1775, 1785, 1825,
  1835, 1840, 1841; Colliery plans: College
  (1 chain: 1 in.) 1835; Broad Park (2 chains:
  1 in.) 1838; Old Park (44 yds.: 1 in.) 1870;
  Other industrial sites: Castle Mill (1818); Iron
  works (10 chains: 1 in.); 1839; J. E. Guest's
  Glasshouse, Tower St. (10 ft.: 1 in.)
  1843–44 and fronting Little Castle St.
  (20 ft.: 1 in.) 1843; British Iron Co. (22 yds.:
  1 in.) 1845; Glasshouses 1865; Castle Mill
  works, with 'water-engine' 1866; Building
  developments, house-plots, plans of houses
  and new streets: Eve Hill 1805; Wolverhampton St. (20 ft.: 1½ in.) 1811; adjoining
  Castle Wall (22 ft.: 1 in.) 1820; (10 ft.: 1 in.)
  1821; Plots for sale 1825; Land near Priory
  (20 chains: 1 in.) 1810, (4 chains: 1 in.) 1826,
  'Six Plans' 1826; Lots in Porters Field (1 in
  20 yds) 1827; Dock Lane (2 chains: 1 in)
  1828; Land near Vicarage (2 chains: 1 in);
  1828; Queen St–High St improvement
  (4 chains: 1 in.) 1830; Property in Priory St.
  (11 yds.: 1 in.) 1831; Projected Crescent in
  Priory grounds (2 chains: 1 in.) 1831; Proposed new street Castle St.–Tower St. 1835;
  Middle Row (10 ft.: 1 in.) 1838; Mr. Payton
  and Miss Hughes's Houses in Stone St. and
  High St. (10 ft.: 1¼ in.) 1839: Land near
  Tividale Toll-house, Trindle Rd. (with site of
  a Whimsy-engine; 2 chains: 1 in.) 1840; Proposed houses, Stone St.–High St. 1840;
  Dudley Brewery (2 chains: 1 in.) 1840 (1
  chain: 1 in.) 1852; Property adjoining Griffin
  Inn in Stone St. 1841; Belper Yard, with
  garden-lots (11 yds.: 1 in.) 1844; Land leased
  for Presbyterian Church and schools,
  Wolverhampton St. (11 yds.: 1 in.) 1846–60;
  Potters Field as burial-ground (44 yds.:
  1 in.) 1846; Queen's Cross, for schools
  and burial-ground (2 chains: 1 in.) 1846; St
  John's School, Freebodies (20 ft.: 1 in.) 1846,
  1850; Land adjoining Priory (2 chains: 1 in.)
  1847; Land at the Dock (1 chain: 1 in.)
  1848; Stone St. property (20 ft.: 1 in.)
  1848; Cottage properties, various
  scales 1848: Wolverhampton St. (30 ft.:
  1 in.) 1849-50; Building lots, Constitution
  Hill (1 chain: 1 in.) c. 1852; Downing
  St. (30 ft.: 1 in.) 1852; Castle Crescent
  (22 yds.: 1 in.) 1852; Castle and Downing
  Sts. (1 chain: 2 in.) 1853, 1854; Castle
  Hill (1 chain: 1 in.) 1854; Wolverhampton
  St. (14 ft.: 1 in.) 1858; Part of Town
  Centre (24 in.: 1 m.) c. 1860; Queens Cross
  (44 ft.: 1 in.) 1866: Draft Plan of Blind

(Dudley - continued) —
  Asylum (2 chains: 1 in.) 1869; Encroachments on the property of Mr. Meek made by
  opening windows to overlook gardens, etc.
  situated in Downing St. (8 ft.: 1 in.) 1870;
  Proposed new street (St James's Rd.),
  Parade–Priory St. (44 yds.: 1 in.) 1876;
  Water-supply proposals: (30 chains: 4 in.)
  1826, 1833; Plans of valuable freehold villa
  land situated at St James's Rd. offered for sale
  by auction (41.66 ft.: 1 in.) 1896; Mr.
  Downing's House, Offices, Garden and Fold-
  yard (1 chain: 3 in.) 1821; Scotts Green
  (10 chains: 11 in.) 1820; Old Buffery Estate
  (1 chain: 1 in.) 1852; Electricity supply
  proposals: South Staffs. Electric Lighting
  Co. (200 ft.: 1 in.) 1883; Dudley Corporation
  1896; Dudley, Sedgley and Wolverhampton
  Tramways: 1879, 1881, 1886; Railway
  proposals: 1835-6, 1844; Maps of the
  Parish: 1700, 1786, 1787, 18 ....(5
  chains: 1 in.), 18....(6 chains: 1 in.); 1863
  (44 ft.: 1 in.) 1883; Town Maps: Brettell
  (6 chains: 1 in.) 1824–25; 'Plan of Dudley'
  (2 ft.: 1 m), c. 1830; Craighton (engr J.&C.
  Walker, 3 cm.: 1 m) c. 1830; Treasure (1
  chain: 6 in.) 1835; Morris (220 yds.: 1 in.)
  1836; J.&C. Walker (Bentley's D.) (7 in.: 1 m)
  1839; Richards (12 chains: 1 in) 1865;
  Parliamentary and Municipal Boundaries:
  Possible Parliamentary boundary (1 in.: 1 m)
  1832; Dawson, proposed boundary (2 in.: 1
  m) 1832; Henry James 1867;
  Miscellaneous maps: E. in Dudley and Rowley
  Regis 1798; Lands belonging to Lord Dudley
  (20 chains: 1 in.) 1805; Lands in Dudley and
  Sedgley (2 chains: 1 in.) 1809; Lands in
  Dudley and Tipton (2 chains: 1 in.) 1812;
  Land sold and let by Dudley Canal Co. 1815;
  Road from Turnpike to Wrens Nest (5 chains:
  6 in.) 1819; Himley to Dudley Rd. (8 in.: 1 m)
  1826; OS (1: 2500), 1883, 1884; (1: 500)
  1883.
DUNSTABLE: OS (1: 500) 1880.
DURHAM: Schwytzer 1595; Speed 1610;
  Merian (?) 1650 (?); Forster 1754; Armstrong
  etc. (20 chains = 85 mm) 1768; Roper & Cole
  1804; OS (1: 500) 1861; Ebdy (from OS
  1849) 1865; BC, 1868; Smith & Son
  1893.
EALING: Bassett, The Processional bounds of
  the Parish 1777; OS (1: 2500) 1867; also
  ACTON: OS (1: 2500) 1867.
EASTBOURNE: OS (1: 2500) 1875; OS
  (1: 500) 1877; Fuller 1879; Farncombe
  & Co. (300 yds.: 1 in.) 1890; Johnson (3 in.:
  1 m) 1894; Bartholomew (300 yds.: 1 in.)
  1896; Oakden (10 in.: 1 m) 1900.
EAST RETFORD: BC, 1868; OS (1: 500)
  1885.
ELY: Speed 1610; Merian (?) 1650 (?); OS
  1885–86.
ENFIELD: OS (1: 2500) 1866; Plan of Freehold

(Enfield – continued) –
and Copyhold Estates 1880; Residential area,
Buckskin Hall 1884; Gough Park Estate
(900 ft. = 108 mm) 1888; also EDMONTON:
'Map of the Parish of Edmonton . . . showing
the allotments in the Common Fields and
Common Marshes as divided by Act of Parliament in 1802' (in Wm Robinson's *History
and Antiquities of the Parish of Edmonton*,
1819); Estate map 1837; OS (1:2500) 1867;
Bowes and Palmers Green (15 chains = 83
mm) 1887; Freehold Estates (20 chains = 112
mm) 1887; Eversley, Winchmore Hill 1891.
EPSOM: OS (1:2500) 1868; Ewell, OS
(1:2500) 1867.
EVESHAM: BC, 1868; OS (1:500) 1885.
EXETER: Hooker 1555 (1892); Hohenbergius
1587; Speed 1610; Braun & Hohenbergius
1573-1618; Merian (?) 1650 (?); Izacke
1677; Fairlove & Coles 1709; Nicholls
(1000 ft. = 55 mm) 1723; Rocque 1744;
Donne (40 poles = 59 mm) 1765; Roper &
Hayman 1805; Ackermann 1850 (?); BC,
1868; OS (1:500) 1879; Post Office Direc-
tory (15 chains = 30 mm) 1881; Goad (Ins)
1888-1902; 1927; OS (1:500) 1891. See:
Constable, K. M., 'The Early Printed Maps of
Exeter 1587-1724', *Trans. Dev. Soc.*, 1932.
FALMOUTH: BC, 1868; OS (1:500) 1880;
Post Office Directory, 1895.
FARNWORTH: OS (1:500) 1891: Tillotson
(6 in.:1 m.) 1907.
FAVERSHAM: Jacob 1774: OS (1:2500) 1867;
OS (1:500) 1867.
FLEETWOOR: Port of . . . , 1850.
FLINT: BC, 1868.
FOLKESTONE: East Cliff (1:2500) 1845;
Smirke 1849; OS (1:500) 1873; Keen's
'Watering Places' 1876; Sumner (6½ in.:1 m)
1890.
GATESHEAD: Anon. 1748; Hutton 1770-72;
Beilby 1788; Roper (BA) 1810; Bell (8
chains:1 in.) 1819, (4 chains:1 in.) 1835;
Oliver (10 chains = 83 mm) 1831; Oliver &
Aikman (440 yds. = 55 mm) 1833; 'Plan of
the Borough' 1844; OS (1:500) 1857; BC,
1868; Reid (6 in.:1 m) 1879; OS (1:500)
1896.
GILLINGHAM: Crown Lands in Gillingham
1784; OS (1:2500) 1867.
GLASTONBURY: Hawkes 1844; OS (1 in.:1 m)
1899.
GODALMING: Williams, c. 1830-50; OS
(1:2500) 1872.
GLOSSOP: OS (1:2500) 1880.
GLOUCESTER: Speed 1610; Meriam (?) 1650
(?); Hall & Pinell 1780-82; Roper & Cole
(1805); BC, 1868; OS (1:500) 1885; Goad
(Ins) 1891; Jennings 1900; See: Chubb, T.,
'A Descriptive Catalogue of the Printed Maps
of Gloucestershire 1577-1911', (pub. by
Bristol and Gloucs. Arch Soc., 1913).
GOOLE: Tudor & Tudor (400 ft.:1 in.) 1884;

(Goole – continued) –
OS (1:500) 1891; Ins (400 ft.:1 in.) 1896;
Goad (Ins) 1896.
GOSPORT: Gomme (1320 ft. = 40 mm); OS
(1:500) 1870; OS (1:2500) 1855; Bacon
(6 in.:1 mm) 1890; Holbrook 1895; Portsmouth and Gosport (1 m = 150 mm) 1895.
GRANTHAM: Turner (1:500) 1866; BC, 1868;
OS (1:500) 1887.
GRAVESEND: OS (1:500) 1866; OS (1:2500)
1867; BC, 1868.
GREENWICH: P of the Towns of G. and Deptford 1809; Morris 1834; OS (1,2500) 1874.
See LONDON Sheets 47, 48, 58, 59, 68, 69,
70. Bacon's Map of School Board Districts
(4 in.:1 m) 1879; School Board Districts (6
in.:1 m) 1879; Position of Board Schools etc.
(6 in.:1 m)1892; BC, 1868; also CHARLTON
OS (1:2500) 1874; Eastcombe Park Estate
(1000 ft.:123 mm) 1885; also ELTHAM:
Mayfield Residential Estate 1874; Mottsham
House Residential and Building Estate (2
chains:1 in.) 1883; OS, Lee and Eltham
(1:2500) 1864; also PLUMSTEAD: OS
(1:2500) 1865; OS (1:500) 1866; OS
(Woolwich and Plumstead, 1:528) 1895:
Shrewsbury House Estate (10 chains = 160
mm) 1873; also WOOLWICH: Milton
(Dockyard and part of Town) 1753; Yeakell
(Ordnance Ground) 1810; OS (1:528) 1869;
OS (Woolwich and Plumstead 1:528) 1895;
Bacon (4 in.:1 m) 1901.
GRIMSBY: Armstrong 1778; Faden (Harbour)
1795; Hollingsworth (5 chains:1 in.) 1801;
Smith & Parker 1812; BC, 1868; Goad (Ins)
1896; OS (1:500) 1888; Ins 1896.
GUILDFORD: Richardson (200 yds. = 40 mm)
1739 red. (1944); BC, 1868; OS (1:500)
1871; Hooke (400 ft.:1 in.) 1891. See:
Sharp, H. A., *An Historical Catalogue of
Surrey Maps* (Croydon 1929).
HACKNEY: Starling 1831; Davies (Hackney
Marsh) 1745; Cary 1810; Turner (5 in.:1 m)
1847; Borough of Hackney (3 in.:1 m) D
1872; OS (1:2500); LONDON Sheets XXI,
XXII, XXX, XXXI, XXXII, XL, XLI, XLII,
LI, LII; Bacon's Map of School Board District
(1 m:9³/₈ in.) 1879; School Board District
(6 in.:1 m) 1879; Proportion of population
of East London and Hackney born abroad
1881; Proportion of population . . . born in
other parts of U.K. 1881; Proportion of
population . . . born outside London 1881
(last three in Booth, C., *Labour and Life of
the People* (1889)); Position of Board Schools
etc. (6 in.:1 m) 1892; BC, 1868; also
SHOREDITCH: Anon. (400 ft.:1 in) c. 1720;
Taylor, E at Hogsdon 1770 (1935);
Chassereau (¼ m. = 82 mm) 1798; E in St
Leonards 1832; OS (1:2500); LONDON
Sheets 25, 27, 36, 1875; also STOKE
NEWINGTON; Worgan (E S. of church)
1725; Merrington 1814 (1938); Miller (PM St

(Hackney — continued) —
Mary) 1846; OS (1:2500); LONDON Sheets
44, 45, 55, 56, 66, 1875; 'Sketch Map of
Stoke Newington'; *London Argus*, No. 53,
vol. 3 (1898).

HALIFAX: OS (1:1056) 1852; BC, 1868; OS
(1:500) 1890; Goad (Ins) 1887, 1927.

HAMMERSMITH: Rocque, 'An Exact Survey of
the City's of London, Westminster and the
country near ten miles round', 1754 (1959);
Salter, 'The Hamlet of Hammersmith 1830';
Roberts 1853; (1956); Whitting, P. D., *Some
Notes on a map of the Parish of Hammersmith
in 1853* (1957); OS (1:2500); LONDON
Sheets 22, 23, 31, 32, 40, 41, 51, 52, 1857;
Sketch Map of Hammersmith in *London
Argus*, No. 10, vol. 1, 1897; also FULHAM:
OS (1:2500); LONDON Sheets 41, 52, 53,
63, 64, 1873; Sketch Map of the Parish of
Fulham in *London Argus*, No. 29, vol. 2,
1897.

HARINGEY: HORNSEY: P of Holloway,
Hornsey Rise and Stroud Green (½ mile =
50 mm) 1651 (1930); Rocque's Topogra-
phical Map of the County of Middlesex
(3 m = 150 mm) 1754 (1936); OS (1:2500)
1864; Eleven maps 1828-1881 of Estate of
Harringay Park; Marcham & Marcham, Sketch
Map of the Bp. of London's manor of
Hornsey (1929); also TOTTENHAM:
Robinson, W., *History and Antiquities of
Tottenham*, 1818; OS (1:2500) 1864:
Coleman's Nursery Grounds (laid out in lots)
1810; Duckett's Farm, 1810; Estate of
Finsbury Freehold Land Society, Wood
Green 1853; Moated House Estate (10 chains
= 157 mm) 1870; also WOOD GREEN:
Gunyon, Wood Green U.D. (1:10,560) 1907.

HARTLEPOOL: Dromeslower 1585 (1938);
Laurie 1843; OS (1:500) 1862; OS (1:2500)
1862; BC 1868.

HARWICH: BC 1868; OS (1:500) 1880.

HASTINGS: Iconographical Plan 1810 (?); BC,
1868; OS (1:500) 1876: OS (1 in.:1 m)
1898.

HAVERING: Havering Marsh (64 perches = 55
mm) 1600 (1924); OS (1:2500) 1873; Pyrgo
Park Estate 1867, 1885; Bedfords Estate
1868; Moll, 'Breach in the Levels' 1721;
Bowen (9 m = 125 mm). See: *History of
Essex*, Morant, P. (1768); ROMFORD:
OS (1:2500) 1873; 1874.

HAVERFORDWEST: BC, 1868.

HEDON: Iveson (10 chains: 2½ in.) 1804.

HELSTON: BC, 1868.

HEMEL HEMPSTEAD: OS (1:500) 1879.

HENLEY: OS (1:2500) 1879; OS (1:500)
1879.

HEREFORD: Speed 1610; Taylor 1730, 1786,
1807; Roper & Cole 1806; Jones & Son
(220 yds.:1 in.) 1858; BC, 1868; OS (1:500)
1886.

HERTFORD: Speed 1610; Andrews & Wren

(Hertford — continued) —
1766; BC, 1868; OS (1:500) 1881. See:
Walne, P. A., *A Catalogue of Manuscript
Maps in Hertfordshire R.O.* (1969) and
Hodson, D., *The Printed Maps of Hertford-
shire 1577-1900* (3 vols.) (1969 and 1970).

HEYWOOD: OS (1:1056) 1851; OS (1:500)
1891.

HIGHAM FERRERS: Norden 1591 (in
Speculum Northamtoniæ).

HIGH WYCOMBE: BC, 1868; OS (1:500)
1879.

HILLINGDON: Burgis 'The Panorama';
Uxbridge frontages c. 1800-10; OS (1:2500)
1866; UXBRIDGE: O.S. (1:528) 1866.

HONITON: BC, 1868: P of the Manor (60
chains = 252 mm) 1869.

HOUNSLOW: PM Isleworth 1850: Freehold
estate sale 1851; OS (1:1056) 1873.

HOVE: Treacher 1870 (?); OS (1:2500) 1876.

HUDDERSFIELD: OS (1:1056) 1851; BC,
1868; OS (1:500) 1890; Goad (Ins) 1887;
1936.

HULL: B.Mus.MS (1370)-1560, *Notices Relative
to Hull's Early History*, Frost, C. (1827);
Speed 1610 (1627-1743 repr); Hollar &
Taylor 1640 (600 ft. = 28 mm), Tickell,
J., *History of Hull*, 1783; Vanderpill 1642;
Hollar 1643; Osborne 1668; Fortifications
1681; Durch Danielem Meisnerum etc., 1700;
Gent 1735; Jefferys 1767-71; Bower 1786
(10 chaines = 5 mm); Bower (400 yds. = 95
mm) 1791, 1798; Faden (¼ m. = 55 mm)
1816; Mamtain (440 yds. = 55 mm) 1817;
Smith (600 yds. = 50 mm) 1823; Day 1830;
Moreland 1834; OS (1:1056) 1853, 1855-56;
BC, 1868; Peck & Son (300 yds. = 50 mm)
1873, 1875, 1876; Peck (7 in.:1 m) 1884
(rev. Wellstead 1888); Harland & Son (6 in.:
1 m) 1885, 1898; OS (1:500) 1891-92;
Bartholomew (5½ in.:1 m) 1892; Goad (Ins)
1886-93.

HUNTINGDON: Commissioners of the Duchy of
Lancaster 1514 (1937); Speed 1610; BC,
1868; OS (1:500) 1886. See: Dickinson,
P. G. M., *Maps in the C.R.O., Huntingdon;.*
(1968); and Catalogue of the Local History
Collection (PL, 1950).

HYDE: OS (1:500) 1874.

HYTHE: Hill 1684; Arch. Dept, PL ref. to
'two 17th-c. maps').

ILKESTON: Newman (1 chain:1 in.) 1866;
BC, 1868; Wyld (25 in.:1 m) c. 1880; OS
(1:2500) 1881; OS (1:500) 1881.

IPSWICH: 'A small plan of Ipswiche', n.d.;
Speed 1610; Ogilby 1674-1698; Grove, 1761;
Pennington 1778; Hodgkinson 1783; White
(12 in.:1 m) 1867; BC, 1868; OS (1:500)
1883; 'Street Map' 1883.

ISLINGTON: Warner, 'Survey of the Public
Roads, Lanes and Footpaths', 1735; Baker &
Baker, 'Islington and its Environs' 1793;
Dent (200 ft.:1 in.) 1805-6; 'Roads and

(Islington — continued) —
Footpaths' (Vestry Plan) 1811; 'Sketch Map of the Parish of Islington' in *London Argus*, No. 25, vol. 1, 1897; also FINSBURY: Parish of St James's, Clerkenwell (600 ft. = 48 mm) 1750; Tryer 1805; BC, 1868; OS (1:2500), LONDON Sheets, 26, 27, 35, 36, 1876; Bacon's Map of the School Board District (1 m : 9⅜ in.) 1879; School Board District (6 in.: 1 m) 1879; Positions of Board Schools etc. (6 in.: 1 m) 1892; Horne & Sons, Parishes of St James and St John, 1897; 'Sketch Map of the Parish of St John and St James, Clerkenwell', in *London Argus*, No. 48, vol. 2, 1898; 'Sketch Map of the Parish of St Luke, Middlesex', in *London Argus*, No. 35, vol. 2, 1898. See: *Old Maps and Prints* available repr from Islington PLs (1973).

JARROW: 'Iarro Slike' 1668-69; OS (1:2500) 1857; OS (1:500) 1896.

KEIGHLEY: Jefferys (Maps of Yorkshire) 1775; Greenwood 1817; OS (1:1056) 1852; OS (1:500) 1891.

KENDAL: Speed 1610; 1666; Jefferys (20 chains = 82 mm) 1770; Todd 1787; OS (1:500) 1861; BC, 1868. See: Curwen, J. F., 'The Chorography or a descriptive catalogue of the printed maps of Cumberland and Westmorland'. *Trans. Cumb. & Westm. Antiq. & Arch. Soc.*, N.S., vol. 18 (1918).

KENSINGTON AND CHELSEA: Cary's 'New and Accurate Plan of London and Parts Adjacent' 1810; Messrs. Basset, Christian & Hodskinson (engr. Starling) (½ m. = 173 mm) 1822 (London Topographical Soc.), 1934; Daw (cor. Blore) (1 m = 265 mm) 1852, 1858; OS (1:2500); LONDON Sheets 23, 32, 33, 41, 44, 53, 1873; 'Plan of W. Kensington and District' (210 ft.: 1 in.) 1890; 'Map of the Parish of Kensington: in *London Argus*, No. 5, vol. 1; 1897; BC, 1868.

KETTERING: Eyre/Eayre 1691-1758, n.d., rev. Jefferyes 1779-91; OS (1:500) 1886; see (no author) 'A Walk round Ketterings . . . 1587-1970', Kettering Civ. Soc. (1972).

KIDDERMINSTER: Doharty, Jnr. 1753; BC, 1868; OS (1:500) 1884; Goad (Ins) 1897; 1924.

KING'S LYNN: BC, 1868.

KINGSTON-UPON-HULL: see Horrox, R., *The Changing Plan of Hull 1290-1650* (1978).

KINGSTON-ON-THAMES: Horner 1813; OS (1:2500) 1868.

LAMBETH: Cross 1824; Lee & Parne (Poor Law Commission) 1841; OS (1:2500); LONDON Sheets 44, 55, 65, 66, 75, 76, 85, 88, 89, 90, 1873; School Board District (6 in.: 1 m) 1879; Positions of Board Schools etc. (6 in.: 1 m) 1892; Wards and Parliamentary boundaries (8 in.: 1 m) 1892; E: W. & S. Driver, 'Plan of the North Division of the Manor of Lambeth', 1812 (1933); Portobello House Estate, Lower Norwood (500 ft.: 174 mm) 1876;

(Lambeth — continued) —
Ralegh House and The Lawn, Brixton Hill (300 ft. = 174 mm) 1887; also WANDS-WORTH: Jones Jnr. (½ m. = 120 mm) 1840; OS (1:2500) 1868; 'Sketch Map of the Parish of Streatham' in *London Argus*, No. 59, vol. 3, 1898; 'Sketch Map of the Parish of Wandsworth' in *London Argus*, No. 50, vol. 2, 1898; Metropolitan Boroughs of Wandsworth and Battersea (3⅝ in.: 1 m) 1910. Extensive EP.

LANCASTER: Speed 1610; Braun & Hohenbergius 1573-1618; (repr 1660) Binns 1825; OS (1:1056) 1849; OS (1:500) 1892.

LAUNCESTON: Camden *Brittannia* 1607; Speed 1610, 1666; Alexander, Survey Maps for Local Board of Health 1852.

LEAMINGTON: Messrs Taylor & Hopton 1834; Davidson 1876; OS (1:500) 1887; 'Plan' 1894.

LEEDS: Goad (Ins) 1886; 1902. See: Bonsor & Nichols, 'Printed Maps of Leeds 1711-1900', *Thoresby Soc.*, vol. 47 (1958); Nicholls 1712; 'History of Leeds' 1797; Baines (D) 1817; BC, 1868; OS (1 in.: 1 m) 1896. See: Whitaker, H. *A Descriptive List of the Printed Maps of Yorkshire and the Ridings 1577-1900* (Leeds 1933); and Atkinson, D. H., *Robert Thoresby, the topographer; his town and times* (1885-87).

LEICESTER: Speed 1610; Merian (?) 1650 (?); Stukeley 1722; Prior (500 yds. = 75 mm) 1799, 1804; BC, 1868; OS (1:500) 1886; Goad (Ins) 1888-92.

LEIGH: OS (1:500) 1890.

LEOMINSTER: BC, 1868; OS (1:500) 1886.

LEWES: Budgen 1724, 1779; BC, 1868; OS (1:500) 1875; Fuller (reduced from OS) 1877.

LEWISHAM: OS (1:2500) 1863; E: Sale: Foxgrove Farm (40 perches = 128 mm) 1777; Plaister Lodge (15 chains = 150 mm) 1870; Camps Hill (20 chains = 160 mm) 1879; also DEPTFORD: Evelyn; 'A Map of Deptford 1623', 1750 (50 perches=80 mm); Milton, H.M. Dockyard and part of the Town 1753; Water Supply Map 1809; OS (1:2500); LONDON Sheets 57, 68, 78.

LICHFIELD: Speed 1610, repr 1666; Snape 1781; Yates 1799; Crompton 1862; BC, 1868; 'County of Stafford' 1876; OS (1:500) 1884.

LINCOLN: Speed 1610; Saxton 1695; Stukeley 1722; Marrat 1817 (cor. to 1841, 8 chains: 1 in.); Padley (300 yds = 85 mm) 1842 (cor. to 1868 and 1883); BC, 1868; 'County and City' 1876; OS (1:500) 1887-88.

LISKEARD: BC, 1868; OS (1:2500) 1882.

LIVERPOOL: Chadwick, 'Map of the Streets, Lanes and Alleyways within the Town of Liverpool' (80 yds.: 1 in.) 1725; Eyes 1765, 1768; and 'Plan of Liverpool' (200 yds.: 3 in.) 1769; Perry & Yates (1½ m: 3 in.) 1768; Perry (500 yds. = 100 mm) 1785; Lewis (D) 1790; Conder 1790; 'Plan of the Town with all the Late Improvements' 1790; Palmer

(Liverpool – continued) –
    (500 yds. = 45 mm) 1795; Stuart (1200 ft. =
    55 mm) 1795; Toxteth 1798 (?); Moss (G)
    1801; Horwood 1803; Roper & Cole 1810;
    Troughton 1807; Faden P 1816; Sherwood
    1725 and 1821; Walker & Walker 1823; Gore
    & Son 1825, 1829, 1831; Austen 1834;
    Bennison 1835; Mawdesley & Mawdesley
    1835; Gage (880 yds. = 250 mm) 1836;
    Taylor 1837; Rapkin & Winkles (1000 yds =
    55 mm) 1845; Newlands 1849; Brown, T.,
    Strangers Complete Guide (1850); OS
    (1:1056) 1850 Clarke, B., *British Gazetteer*
    (1852); Hilliar 1851 (?); Fraser's G 1855;
    Howell, c. 1855: 'Syers Ready Reference
    and Cab Fare Plan' 1868; BC, 1868; Philips
    P 1870 (?); Heywood 1870; Philips 'New
    Map' (300 yds.: 1 in.) 1884, 1895; 'Cities
    Series: 1885; 'Pictorial Map' 1885; Philips
    'P' 1890; OS (1: 500) 1890–91: Bartholomew
    (6 in.: 1 m) 1895; 'Diagram' 1899; Goad
    (Ins) 1884–94; 1926. See Speigl, F., *Four
    Centuries of Liverpool 1567–1967* (1967); see
    also CROSBY, Catalogue.
LONDON: Agas 1560–70; Braun & Hohen-
    bergius 1560; Speed 1612; Munster 'Cosmo-
    graphia' 1550; Rocque 1746; See:
    Honeybourne, M. B.: 'Map of London under
    Richard II, from original sources'. (*London
    Top. Soc.* 1960: (all subsequent publications
    by this Society listed as LTS, date)); Holmes,
    M., 'An unrecorded sixteenth century map
    of London', *Archaeologia*, No. 100, 1916.
    Kelly, M., 'Elizabethan London', *Town and
    Country Planning*, No. 33, 1965; Marks, S. P.
    'The Map of Sixteenth Century London' (LTS
    1964); Prockter, A. & Taylor, R., 'The A to
    Z of Elizabethan London' (LTS 1979);
    Hyde, R., 'The A to Z of Georgian London'
    (LTS, 1982); Jones, E. P., 'The Survey of the
    Building Sites in the City of London after the
    Great Fire of 1666' by Mills & Oliver (red.
    facsim. in 5 vols) (LTS 1962–67); Masters,
    B. R., 'The Public Markets of the City of
    London surveyed by William Leybourn in
    1677' (LTS 1974); 'Index to Rocque's Plan
    of the Cities of London and Westminster and
    the Borough of Southwark, 1747' (LTS,
    1968); 'Clothworkers' Company, Survey of
    Properties in 1612 and 1728' (facsim. of 9
    P LTS, 1938–41); 'Seventeenth Century Plans
    of Properties belonging to St Bartholomews
    Hospital (facsim. of 7 plans) (LTS 1950–54);
    'Horwood's Plan of London 1792–99' (32
    sheets) (LTS 1966); 'Langley and Belch's
    New Map of London 1812' in colour (LTS,
    1971). Bull, G. B. G. 'Thomas Milne's Land-
    Use Map of London and Environs in 1800',
    6 sheets (LTS, 1975–76). See also his article
    in *Geog. Jnl.* 122, 1956. Darlington, I. &
    Howgego, J., *The Printed Maps of London
    c. 1553–1850* (1960); Hyde, R., 'Ward Maps
    of the City of London' (London Map

(London – continued) –
    Collectors' series, No. 38, 1967) and 'The
    Printed Maps of London 1851–1900' (Library
    Assoc. Thesis 1970); Jones, E., 'London Life
    in Maps', *Geographical Magazine*, No. 41,
    1968. Later maps include: 'Plan of the
    Metropolitan Boroughs according to the
    Reform Bill 1832'; Crutchley's 'London and
    its Environs' 1834; Stanford's 'Map of
    London and its Suburbs' 1863; 'The Metro-
    politan Boroughs as defined by the Reform
    Bill' (2 in.: 1 m) in Moule, T., 'The English
    Counties Delineated', 1837; BC, 1868; Goad
    (Ins) 1886, 1897, 1899; 'The County of
    London' (OS 1900); Hyde R., 'Mapping
    London's Landlords . . . 1892–1915' (Guildhall
    Studies in L Hist, 1, 1973 and 'Notes on a
    Collection of London Ins Surveys 1794–
    1807'. *J. Soc. Archiv.*, vol. 4 (1971); Olsen,
    D. J. 'The Growth of Victorian London'
    (1976); Dyos, H. J. (intro.) *Collins' Illus-
    trated Atlas of London 1854* (1973).
LOUGHBOROUGH: OS (1:500) 1885.
LOUTH: Armstrong 1778; OS (1:500) 1889.
LOWESTOFT: OS (1:500) 1885.
LLANDOVERY: 'A small town-plan on John
    Ogilby's map of the Presteigne–Carmarthen
    Road' 1675; BC, 1835; TM 1841 (NLW).
LUTON: Cumberland 1842; Davies (3 chains: 1
    in) 1842; Todd 1853; OS (1:500) 1880;
    OS (1:2500) 1881; Goad (Ins) 1895.
LYDD: OS (1:2500) 1873.
LYME REGIS: Wood 1841; BC, 1868.
LYMINGTON, BC, 1868; OS (1:2500) 1868;
    OS (1:500) 1869.
MACCLESFIELD: BC, 1868: OS (1:500)
    1874.
MAIDENHEAD: OS (1:500) 1879.
MAIDSTONE: Brown & Son 1821; Bond, c.
    1860; Railway Map 1863; OS (1:2500) 1867;
    BC, 1868; OS (1:500) 1870; Tootell & Sons
    1884, 1894.
MALDON; BC, 1868; OS (1:500) 1877; OS
    (1:2500) 1875.
MALMESBURY: BC, 1868.
MANCHESTER: 1650 (in Hollingworth, R.,
    History . . . 1839), Casson & Berry 1741 (?),
    1750 (?); Lewis (D) 1788; Laurent 1650 &
    1793; Green (60 yds.: 1 in.) 1787–94; Bancks
    & Thornton 1800 (?); Weimar 1803, 1809;
    Pigot (in Deane & Co.'s D) 1804; Roper (BA)
    1810; Deane & Deane 1808; Pigot (¼ M. = 70
    mm) 1809; Johnson, 1818–19. (160 chains =
    200 mm) 1820; Pigot with recent improve-
    ments) 1825; Walker and Walker 1828, 1840;
    Slater 1850; Thornton (cor. Adshead) 80 in.:
    1 m) 1851; OS (1:1056) 1851; Cornish &
    Cornish 1857; Hale & Roworth (Picture M)
    1857; Syers 'Ready Reference and Cab Fare
    Plan 1868; BC, 1868; Heywood & Sons 1870;
    Slater 1879; OS (1:2500) 1870; Slater 1879;
    OS (1:2500) 1881; Heywood (Picture M)
    1886; Goad (Ins) 1886–1904; 1921.

(Manchester — continued) —
  See: *Maps of Manchester 1650-1848* (facsim.,
  Manchester PL 1970).
MANSFIELD: Sanderson: 'Map of the Country
  twenty miles around Mansfield' (1 in.: 1 m.)
  1836; OS (1:2500) 1878; OS (1:500) 1879.
MARGATE: Edmunds 1821: Perry 1871; OS
  (1:500); 1872: Keen's Watering Places 1876.
MARLBOROUGH; BC, 1868; OS (1 in.:1 m)
  1899.
MERTHYR TYDFIL: BC, 1868.
MERTON: OS (1:2500) 1865; Bacon & Co.
  (1 m = 100 mm) 1909; also MITCHAM,
  OS (1:2500) 1865; also WIMBLEDON,
  Wimbledon Common (War Office) 1861,
  1867; OS (12 in.: 1 m) 1864; OS (1:2500)
  1865; Wimbledon Common (6 in.:1 m)
  1871.
MIDDLETON: *'A Plan of the Lands in the
  Township of Middleton belonging to the late
  Ralph Assheton . . .' 1767; TM: Middleton
  1839; Tonge 1839; Alkrington 1841; OS
  (1:1056) 1851; OS (1:500) 1891.
  (*Available in facsimile from Library).
MONMOUTH: Speed 1610; BC, 1868.
MONTGOMERY: BC, 1868.
MORECAMBE: OS (1:500) 1891.
MORLEY: OS (1:500) 1890.
MORPETH: OS (1:2500) 1862; OS (1:500)
  1866; BC, 1868.
MOSSLEY: OS (1:500) 1892.
NELSON: OS (1:500) 1891.
NEWARK: BC, 1868; OS (1:500) 1885;
  Clampe 'Siege Map' 1646.
NEWBURY: OS (1:500) 1800; OS (1:500)
  1879.
NEWCASTLE-UNDER-LYME: Forbes 1691;
  Hargreaves 1832; Malabar 1861; OS
  (1:2500) 1878; OS (1:500) 1879. See:
  'Newcastle-under-Lyme Maps' (Staffs.
  Education Dept.) contains reproductions of
  maps dated 1691, 1785, 1797, 1832, 1847,
  1861 and 1898.
NEWCASTLE-UPON-TYNE: Speed 1666;
  Corbridge (300 ft. = 76 mm) 1723; Beekman
  (130 paces = 20 mm) 1742; Thompson 1746;
  Armstrong 1769; Hutton 1772; Beilby 1788;
  Roper (BA) 1810; Oliver 1830, 1833, 1844;
  OS; (1:2500) 1861; OS (1:500) 1862; BC,
  1868; Reid ('New Plan') 1879; Goad (Ins)
  1887-1905; Ward (D) 1892; Smith & Son
  1892; OS (1:500) 1896. See: Whitaker, H.,
  *A descriptive list of the maps of Northumber-
  land 1576-1900* (1949).
NEWHAM: as EAST HAM: Neve 1800;
  OS (n.s.) 1864; OS (1:2500); LONDON
  Sheets 12, 13, 20, 21, 29, 30, 38, 39, 47,
  48, 49, and ESSEX Sheet 81, 1874; also
  WEST HAM: Newman (880 ft.: 1 in.) 1883:
  Estridge, Wanstead Flats (15 chains = 354
  mm) 1862; Upton House Residential Estate
  1870; County Borough (6 in.: 1 m) 1900.
NEWPORT (Mon.): Goad (Ins) 1887-1929; 1947.

NEWPORT: (I.o.W.): Speed 1610; Merian (?)
  1650 (?); White (from Speed) 1666; Lea (120
  paces = 18 mm) 1695; Andrews 1775;
  'New . . . Map' 1785; Albin 1795; OS (1:500)
  1865.
NORTHAMPTON: Speed 1610, 1666; Noble &
  Butlin 1746; Roper & Cole (BA) 1810; BC,
  1868; OS (1:500) 1885-86; Goad (Ins) 1888;
  1899; 1946; See: Whitaker, H. A., 'A Descriptive List of the Printed Maps of Northamptonshire 1576-1900', *Northants. Rec. Soc.*, No.
  14, 1948.
NORWICH: Cunningham 1559; Braun & Hohenbergius 1573-1618, 1660; Speed *Atlas* 1610,
  1666; Meridien (?) 1650 (?); Corbridge 1727;
  Hoyle (300 yds. = 27 mm) 1728; Blomefield
  1746; King 1766; Thompson 1779; Smith (D)
  1783; Hochstetter 1789; Roper & Cole (BA)
  1810; Starling 1818-19; BC, 1868; Morant
  1873; Jarrold & Sons 1875; Fletcher & Son
  1876; OS (1:500) 1885; Jarrold (D) 1887.
  See: Bensley, W. T., *Early Maps of Norwich*
  (1889); Goad (Ins) 1894; 1927; Britain, H.,
  *Catalogue of Maps relating to Norwich and
  Norfolk* (1913); Stephen, G. A., *A Descriptive
  List of Norwich Plans 1541-1914* (1928);
  Chubb, T. & Stephen, G. H., *A Descriptive
  List of the Printed Maps of Norfolk 1574-
  1916* (1928).
NOTTINGHAM: Speed's *Atlas* 1610; White
  1677; 'A New Map' 1714; Badder & Peat
  1744; Deering (26⅔ : 1 m) 1751; BC, 1868;
  Stevenson, Bailey & Smith 1871; OS
  (1:500) 1882; Smith & Son (300 yds.: 1 in.)
  1893; Goad (Ins) 1886-93.
NUNEATON: OS (1:500) 1887.
OLDHAM: Butterworth (1 furlong = 83 mm)
  1817; OS (1:1056) 1851; BC, 1868; Worrall
  (12 in.: 1 m) 1875; OS (1:500) 1880; OS
  (1:500) 1892; Clegg 1898.
OXFORD: Agas 1578-88; Agas by Whittlesey
  1728; Hollar 1643; Loggan 1675 (all by
  Oxford Hist. Soc. 1898); Agas 1578-88
  (*Oxford Hist. Soc.*., vol. 38, Nos. 1 and 2,
  1898); Agas 1578 (red. by Skelton 1823)
  Speed 1610; Hollar, Bohem. of Oxford 1643;
  1650; 'Ichonographia' 1648, in Clark, A.
  (ed.); 'Anthony Wood's Survey of the City of
  Oxford 1661-66', *Oxford Hist. Soc.*, vols 1-2
  (1889-90); Loggan 1675 (Overton, H., 1710)
  facsim. in *Oxford Hist. Soc.*, 38, No. 4,
  1898; Schenkii 'Hecatomplis' 1702; Williams
  (1:9750) 1733; Taylor (engr Anderton
  3 chains: 1 in.) 1750, 1789; Rocque (500 yds.
  = 45 mm) 1762; Jefferys (20 chains = 80 mm)
  1768, 1775; Davies etc. (10 chains = 93 mm)
  1797; Roper & Cole (BA) 1808-10; Pearson
  1817; Fisher, 'Dewe's Pictorial Plan' 1850 (?);
  Hoggar 1850; 'Easy Guide' (Shrimpton
  & Shrimpton) 1868; Heywood & Son 1871;
  OS (1:500) 1880; White (Loc. Bd. Dist.) (1 ft.:
  1 m) 1883; Alden & Co. (8 in.:1 m) 1888
  Valters 1891; Bacon (6 in.:1 m) 1896, 1902;

(Oxford — continued) —
Smith & Son (200 yds.: 1 in.) 1900. E:
Grandpoint c. 1500 (OS 1935); Cow Mead
and Swinfell Farm in St Aldates 1726 (OS
1936). See: Salter, H. E., 'Survey of Oxford
1772', *Oxford Hist. Soc.*, vols. 14–20 (1960–
69); Salter, H. E., *Medieval Oxford* (500 ft.
= 122 mm) O.U.P. 1934; Holler, A., 'Old
Plans of Oxford', *Oxford Hist. Soc.*, vol.
38, 1898. (Also numerous maps of col-
leges and their properties.)

PEMBROKE: Speed 1610; Map of Mail Roads
1827.

PENRYN: Boazio (1000 paces = 62 mm) 1597;
(in *Jnl of Roy. Instn. Cornwall* 1889).

PENZANCE: OS: (1:500) 1878.

PETERBOROUGH: Speed 1610, 1666; OS
(1:500) 1886.

PLYMOUTH: Coloured Map. c. 1580 (1939);
also in Tenison, E. M., *Elizabethan England*
(1932); Coloured Map showing Waterworks
built by Sir Francis Drake 1584 (1939);
Coloured Map of fortifications, MS 1591
(1939); also numerous maps of the Dockyards
1736–1790; and charts of the Sound c. 1596–
1954; Hollar (Fortifications, 3 m = 150 mm)
1643; 'Citadel' 1737; Bowen, 1755, 1777,
1795; Donn (40 poles = 55 mm) 1765; Cowl
1778; Cook (½ m. = 50 mm) 1820; Brown
(½ m. = 42 mm) 1830; Cooke (4 furlongs =
65 mm) 1834; Randell (½ m. = 115 mm)
1840, 1875; OS (1:528) 1859; OS: (1:500)
1863; Goad (Ins) 400 yds.: 1 in., 1891.

POOLE: P (100 luggs or poles of 15½ ft. = 113
mm) 1647 (1935); Reekes & Tucker 1751; 'Map
of the Town' 1834 (?); OS (1:500) 1888.

PORTSMOUTH: P temp. Hen. VIII (pre-1540)
Barrell, W. H., 1913 also in *Notes on
the Topography of Portsmouth by
Howell*, (1913); P. Cott. MS. Aug. I, ii,
15 (in *Maritime Enterprise* by Williamson,
J. A., 1913); Adams, c. 1588 (100 ft.: 1 in.)
(1938); Gomme (1320 Eng. ft. = 4 mm)
1668 (in *Notes* . . . etc. 1913); Goubet (cent
toises = 75 mm) 1692. 'Plan of Portsmouth'
1762 (in *Notes* . . . etc. 1913); 'Sketch of
Portsmouth' (5 in.: 1 m) 1823 (in *Notes* . . .
etc. 1913); Charpentier 1850 (?); Maynard
(1 m = 40 mm) 1859; Jarman 1865 (?); 'Ile
de Wight, Portsmouth and Southampton'
1866; OS (1:2500) 1868; Wyld (with the
approaches of a Railway) 1868; OS (1:500)
1870; Curtiss & Sons 1881; Bacon's Map
(6 in.: 1 m) 1890; Charpentier & Co.s 'New
Map' (6 in.: 1 m) 1892, 1893; Holbrook 1895;
Bacon & Co. 1895, 1901. See Hodson, D.,
Maps of Portsmouth before 1801 (City Mus.
Rec. Series No. 4, 1978).

PRESTON: Hulsbergh, 'with the Barricades and
Cannon of the Rebells' 1715; Boyer, 'with the
Batteries and Barricades of the Rebels' 1715;
Shakeshaft (n.d.); OS (1:1056) 1849; OS
(1:500) 1892.

PRESTWICH: Collinson 1887; OS (1:2500)
1880.

PUDSEY: OS (1:500) 1891.

QUEENBOROUGH: MS P of the fortifications
at Qwynborro, c. 1580 (1938); OS (1:2500)
1863.

RADCLIFFE: OS (1:500) 1891.

RAMSGATE: Long, Ames & Mynde (660 ft. =
42 mm) 1736 (in *History of the Antiquities
of the Isle of Thanet* by Lewis, J.); OS
(1:500) 1873; Keen's Watering Places, 1876,
1880; Roscoe (1 m. = 140 mm) in Wilson's D,
1886; 'Margate and Ramsgate' (2 in: 1 sea-
mile) 1894: 'Sketch of Margate' (700 ft.: 1
in.) 1894.

RAWTENSTALL: OS (1:500) 1892.

READING: Speed 1610, 1666; Roque (800 yds.
= 68 mm) 1761; Man & Poole (100 poles =
62 mm), *History of Reading* by Coates, C.
(1802); 'Plan of the Borough' (6 furlongs =
75 mm); *History of the Borough of Reading*
by Man, J. (1816); Weller (½ m. = 50 mm)
1840; OS (1:500) 1879; OS (1:2500) 1881;
Bourne Smith's Street Plan of the Enlarged
Borough of Reading (4 furlongs = 95 mm)
1881; Goad (Ins) 1895, 1929.

REDBRIDGE: As WANSTEAD: Doyley, 'The
Manors of Wanstead, Woodford, Ruckholt
and Alderbrook', 1816; Wanstead from the
TM of 1841 (1850 ?); Noble, The Manor of
Wanstead 1858–69; Stable, Wanstead Park
1859; Wanstead Flats (20 chains = 169 mm)
1860; OS (1:2500) 1864; Mr. Stable's Plan of
the proposed new ecclesiastical District (6 in.:
1 m) 1881; Grove E 1860; Scott Stable,
Wanstead Flats (15 chains = 354 mm) 1862;
Elm Hall, Wanstead 1863; Woodford Park
(Manors of Woodford etc.) from OS (1:2500)
plan, to show grants and enclosures, 1871;
The Grove 1885; also WOODFORD: Peak,
Toms & Mason, 'A Piece of Water near
Woodford Row', 1774; Woodford from the
TM of 1840 (1860?); OS (1:2500) 1864;
also DAGENHAM: Moll, The Late Breach in
the Levels of Havering and Dagenham (140
rodds = 55 mm) 1721; OS (1:2500) 1864;
for manorial lands see WANSTEAD above.
See: *Essex and Dagenham; a Catalogue of
Books, Pamphlets and Maps* (Borough of
Dagenham PL, 1961); and *Dagenham Place-
Names* by O'Leary, J. G. (with repr. of early
maps, 1576–1807) 1958.

RICHMOND-ON-THAMES: Burrell & Richardson, 'Plan of the Royal Manor of Richmond,
otherwise West Sheen' (30 chains = 233 mm)
1771; Jefferys, Plans of the Bridge 1772;
(also plans and views of Royal Palaces, Parks
and Gardens); OS (1:2500) 1868; OS
(1:1056) 1873; Whitby & Scott 1879, E:
Donne House 1865; Cardigan House 1867;
Lansdowne House and Richmond Hill 1868;
also TWICKENHAM: Warren (40 chains =
168 mm) 1846; OS (1:2500) 1865; E: Fulwell

(Richmond-on-Thames – continued) –
Lodge, 1870; Pope's Villa Estate, 1873;
York House, 1873; Meadow Bank, 1875; The
Lodge, 1876; Pope's Garden, 1878; Poulett
Lodge, 1879; Strawberry Hill, 1883. See: *A
Series of Maps of West Middlesex to help in
the teaching of local Geography*. (Geogra-
phical Assn., W. Middx. Branch, 1961); No. 2:
Heston, Isleworth and Twickenham, 1635
(1:10,560); No. 3: Heston, Isleworth and
Twickenham 1800–1816 (1:10,560); also
BARNES: OS (1:2500) 1868.

RIPON: Jefferys 1767–71, 1775, 1800; OS
(1:1056) 1854; OS (1:500) 1891.

ROCHDALE: OS (1:1056) 1851; OS (1:500)
1892.

ROCHESTER: Smith, W. 1588, *History and
Antiquities of Rochester* 1817; Speed 1610,
1666; Merian 1650 (?); Baker, F. 1772,
History and Antiquities . . . (1817); Sale, R.,
ibid.; OS (1:500) 1866; OS (1:2500) 1867;
OS (6 in.: 1 m) 1882. See: *A Collection of
Plans and Views of Rochester 1587–1870* by
Rye, W. B. (1870).

ROMSEY: OS (1:2500) 1867; OS (1:500) 1867.

ROTHERHAM: OS (1:1056) 1853; OS (1:500)
1889.

ROYAL LEAMINGTON SPA: Taylor & Hopton
1834; Davidson 1876; OS (1:500) 1887.

ROYAL TUNBRIDGE WELLS: Bowra (30
chains = 95 mm) 1738; Barrow (showing the
situation of lodging houses, public walks and
everything worthy of notice, 5 chains: 1 in.)
1808; Burton & Rhodes 1828; Rhodes 1838;
Colbran 1850 (?); Joanes, Plan of building
land to be let or sold as part of the Calverley
Estate 1851 (?); Cronk 1863; OS: (1:500)
1867; OS 1874 (?) shows those parts of the
town lying in the County of Sussex; Ward
Boundaries (OS) 1901; E: Beechwood 1864;
Bishops Down Grove 1868; Calverley Grange
1874; Huntleys 1891.

RUGBY: OS (1:500) 1888.

RUTHIN: OS (1:2500) 1875.

RYDE: Ferry Company Plan No. 3 (Parliamentary Papers) 1859; OS (1:500) 1866.

RYE: OS (1:2500) 1874; OS (1:500) 1874;
(also various maps of the Harbour 1717–
1950).

SAFFRON WALDEN: OS (1:2500) 1877;
OS (1:500) 1878.

ST ALBANS: Speed 1610; Algutter (64 in.:
1 m) 1634; Stukeley (*Verulamium Antiquum*)
15 ft. = 90 mm, 1721; Andrews and Wren (10
perches: 1 in.) 1766; Roper and Cole (BA)
1810; Godman and Lambert (100 ft.: 1 in.),
History of the County of Hertford, by
Clutterbuck, R., 1814; Godman & Turrell
1823; St Michael's Parish (1 m = 35 mm)
1841; Hams Wick Estate (3 chains: 1
in.) 1873; OS (1:500) 1879–80; Wilton
1900.

ST AUSTELL: OS (1:500) 1880.

ST HELENS: OS (1:1056) 1849–51; OS
(1:500) 1882.

ST IVES (Cornwall): Jenkyns 1800; Moody
1824; OS: (1:500) 1878; also Plans of the
Bay and Harbour.

ST IVES (Hunts.): Plan of St Ives Bridge, River
and Meadow c. 1800, giving the names of the
owners of various parcels of land. (Hunts.
Map Fund 1940); Plan of the Lordship (6
chains: 1 in.) 1808.

SALE: OS (1:2500) 1877 and 1898.

SALFORD: Maps marked with an asterisk (*)
are available in repr. from Salford Cent. Lib.
Manchester and Salford c. 1650, *Mancunensis*
by Hollingworth, R., 1839*; 'Map of Salford'
1740*; Casson & Berry, n.d.*; Green 1787–
94; Laurent 1793 'A Topographical Plan'
c. 1650 (1793); 'A Plan of Manchester and
Salford' 1800 (?); Von Maasstab (400 yds. =
52 mm) 1803; Pigot (D) 1804; Roper & Cole
(BA) 1810; P 1808; Pigot (¼ m. = 70 mm)
1809; 'Plan von Manchester und Saalford'
1809; P 1825; 'New Plan' 1850 (?); OS
(1:1056) 1851; 'Manchester and Salford'
1857; 'Manchester and Salford with their
Vicinities' 1860 (?). Syers Ready Reference
and Cab Fare Plan of Manchester and Salford
1868; Slater's 'New Plan' (D) 1:233,440, c.
1879; Heywood's Pictorial Map 1866; Smith
& Son (½ m. = 75 mm) 1890, 1896, 1900,
1902, 1910, 1928. Heywood (6 in: 1 m.)
1891; OS (1:500) 1891.

SALISBURY: Speed 1610, 1666; Naish 1751;
Donn (engr Cheevers) 1781; Lucas: Plan of the
City of Salisbury with the Boundaries of the
Borough as laid down by the Reform Act
1833; Clapperton 1857; Brown & Co. (Local
Board of Health) 1857 (?); Botham (Local
Board of Health) 1860; OS (1:500) 1880–81;
Highman 1884; Air-Map (from OS Plans and
Air Photographs, 12 in.: 1 m.) 1919.

SANDWICH: Labelye, 'Map of Lands situated
between Town, Port and Seashore and
between E. Stower and the Road to Deal.
Together with adjacent Ports, the intended
harbour and the New Cutt' 1736; 'Plan of the
Coast with a Plan of the Town and Port',
1757 (?); Andrews (16 perches: 1 in.) 1769;
OS (1:500) 1874. See: *A Series of Historical
Map Studies of the Town and Harbour of
Sandwich, showing changes in the area
between the years 400–1700*, by Fretton,
G. H. (1948–56).

SCARBOROUGH: Vincent (10 chains = 125
mm) 1745; Jefferys, 1767–70, 1775, 1800;
Calver (Admiralty Chart) 1846, 1871; OS
(1:1056) 1852; Bartholomew 1869, 1870;
Smith & Son (8 in.: 1 m) 1892 (?); OS
(1:500) 1892; Foster, G. C. F. in *A
Descriptive Catalogue of the Records in the
Possession of the Corporation of Scarborough*
refers (p. 11, Section D1) to 'Maps and Plans'
1780–1843.

SHAFTESBURY: Upjohn & Woodman (¼ m. =
135 mm) 1799; 'Plan showing the major part
of the town to be sold by auction', 1919.
SHEFFIELD: Gosling (¼ m. = 4¾ in.) 1736;
Fairbank & Jefferys (440 yds. = 85 mm)
1771; Jefferys (in 'County of York') 1771,
1775, 1800; Fairbank & Son (engr Cary,
1 m. = 85 mm) 1795; Fairbank (engr Harris)
(D) (900 yds. = 110 mm) 1797; Smith 1822;
OS (1:1056) 1853; White (6 in.: 1 m.) 1873;
Holmes 'Proposed Improvements' (100 ft.: 1
in.) 1873; OS (1:500) 1890-91; Smith & Sons
(150 yds.: 1 in.) 1894 (?); Bartholomew, J. G.,
Survey Atlas 1903; Goad (Ins) (40 ft.: 1 in.)
1888; 1937.
SHREWSBURY: Speed 1610, 1666; Braun &
Hohenbergius ('300 pases' = 37 mm) 1573-
1618; Rocque (engr Parr) with views of the
Market House, Free School and Castle, 1746;
Williamson & Williamson 1831; Hitchcock,
'Borough . . . as extended and settled by Act
of Parliament, 1832'; Berwick Estate 1876;
OS (1:500) 1882; OS (1:2500) 1882; Tisdale,
1890; OS (6 in.: 1 m) 1878-81 (revised 1901).
See Baugh, R., *Old Maps of Shrewsbury*
(Field Study Council 1973).
SLOUGH: OS (1:500) 1880.
SOLIHULL: PL leaflet on *Local History* (c.
1973 ?) lists: Solihull Village (5¼ in.: 1 m)
pre-1819 Enclosure (in Pemberton, *Solihull
and its Church*), Solihull Village (approx.
10 in.: 1 m) c. 1820; *Solihull Village;
Buildings-by-Age Survey* (1:2500) shows
pre-17th, 18th, 19th and 20th century build-
ings (1959-60).
SOUTHAMPTON: 'Ancient Map c. 1560' (1925);
Speed 1610; Mazell 1771; Milne 1791; Neele
1802; Doswell 1842; Lewis 1843; Wyld (D)
1949, 1850 (?); OS (1:500) 1870; Goad
(Ins) 40 ft.:: 1 in. 1893; Improvement Commissioners (60 in.: 1 m) 33 sheets 1846;
'Plan of Southampton 1846' (Corpn S'ton,
1970); see Welch, E., 'The Earliest Maps of
Southampton', *Cart. Jnl.* No. 2 (1965);
Rogers, W. H., *The Southampton Atlas:
Maps & Plans of Old Southampton 1560-
1905* (portfolio pub. Southampton Rec. Soc.
1907); *Southampton Maps from Elizabethan
Times* (Southampton Corpn., c. 1973 ?); a
portfolio of 24 maps with Introduction.
Three Sheets of OS (approx. 51 in.: 1 m)
1846, covering area of old walled town.
(Southampton Corpn. c. 1973 ?).
SOUTHEND-ON-SEA: OS (6 in.: 1 m) 1863-
73 (rev. 1919-21); 'Plan of Freehold building
land, houses and other property . . . for sale'
(300 yds. = 170 mm) 1869.
SOUTHPORT: OS (1:500) 1891.
SOUTH SHIELDS: OS (1:528) 1861; OS
(1:500) 1896.
SOUTHWARK: Horwood's Plan of London,
Westminster, Southwark and Parts Adjoining
(facsim.) 1792-99. (London Top. Soc. No.

(Southwark — continued) —
106, 1966); 'Southwarick Surry c. 1542' (in
Old Southwark and its People by Rendle, W.
etc. 1878); 'Map of Southwark 1618' (in
LCC Survey of London, vol. xxii, Bankside
1950); 'A Mapp of the Manor or Lordship of
Old Paris Garden, 1627' (LCC Survey etc.);
Capell, 'A Plott of the Counter Prison, the
Kings Arms Tavern and other Buildings and
Tenements at St Margarets Hill in the Bur-
rough of Southwark belonging to the Citie
of London, 1686' (LCC Survey etc.); 'A Plan
of the Chirk Liberty of the Parish of St
Saviours, Southwark, taken by Order of the
Commissioners of Pavements', 1827 (with a
list of the Parish Boundary Marks, 1832) in
Moss, W. G., 'History of the Parochial Church
of St Saviours, Southwark'; North, 'The
Borough Market . . . with adjoining Property
and approaches and the proposed extension
of the Market boundaries 1865 and 1885'
(1893?); Bacon's Map of the School Board
District (1 m = 9⅜ in.) 1879; Map of the
School Board District (6 in.: 1 m) 1879; Map
showing position of Board Schools etc. (6 in.:
m) 1892; E: On East side of Bermondsey St.
(100 ft. = 125 mm) 1835 (1936); in St
James's Parish (100 ft. = 169 mm) 1866.
Also CAMBERWELL: Poole (80 chains =
110 mm) 1834; OS (1:2500); LONDON
Sheets 55, 56, 57, 66, 67, 68, 76, 77, 78,
85, 86, 87, 88, 89, 90, 1875; 'Sketch Map
of the Parish of Camberwell' in *London Argus*
No. 8, vol. 1, 1897.
SOUTHWOLD: Ablett (approx. 1:2500) 1801;
Lenny 1839. (Also in Wake, R., *History of
Southwold and its vicinity*, 1839).
STAFFORD: Speed 1610; Merian (?) 1650
(?); OS (1:500) 1881-82; See: Historical
Sketch-Map of Stafford, by Scrivener, J. T.
(Stafford Borough Council, 1955).
STALYBRIDGE: in OS of ASHTON-UNDER-
LYNE (1:1056) 1852; also OS (1:1056)
1894.
STAMFORD: Speed 1617, 1666; Plan of Naviga-
tions connected with proposed Harbour and
Canal, 1812; Bevan (intended line of Canal)
1810; Knipe 1834; OS (1:500) 1886.
STOCKPORT; OS (1:1056) 1851, 1878; OS
(1:2500) 1876; OS (1:1056) 1895; D (800
yds. = 70 mm) 1899.
STOURBRIDGE: OS (1:500) 1884.
STRATFORD-ON-AVON: Winter 1759;
Saunders 1802; Swanwick c. 1830; Board of
Health (from OS 1:528) 1851; See: Fox, L.,
In Honour of Shakespeare (Jarrold 1972)
p. 60.
STRETFORD: Collinson (6 in.: 1 m) 1887, 1888
(PL also ref. to un-named maps for 1819,
1839 and 1848).
SUDBURY: OS (1:500) 1884.
SUNDERLAND: *Buck and Buck (500 ft.: 1 in.)
c. 1728; Burleigh & Thompson (600 ft.: 1 in.)

(Sunderland – continued) –
1737; *Raine's Eye Plan c. 1790; OS (1:528) 1858. * Facsimiles available.
SUTTON: 'William Robinson: A Plan of Sutton between 1785 and 1815' (Library has facsim. of original at Surrey CRO); Enclosure Maps: Sutton 1815; Cheam 1810; OS (1:2500) 1867; Greatorex (Pile's D) 3000 ft = 130 mm, 1896; E: Morden Park (40 chains = 160 mm); The Grange (100 ft = 49 mm) 1878; also CHEAM: OS (1:2500) 1867; also BEDDINGTON: OS (1:2500) 1868.
SUTTON COLDFIELD: Plan of Four Oak Park (3 chains = 1 in.) 1868.
SWANSEA: OS (1:2500) 1879; OS (1:500) 1879; Wyld (showing Docks, Railways and Tramways, 6 in.: ½ m) 1888; Goad (Ins) 1888–1929.
SWINDON: OS (1:500) 1886.
SWINTON AND PENDLEBURY: OS (1:500) 1891.
TAMWORTH: OS (1:500) 1884.
TAUNTON: Wood 1840; OS (1:500) 1888.
TENBY: Bowen (in A New and Accurate Map of S. Wales) 1729; OS (1:500) 1889.
TENTERDEN: Dawson, 'An Outline Map of the Borough' 1831; Map of Water Undertaking 1898 (both at Kent County Library); OS (1:2500) 1872; Eastweezel and Elmestone Estate . . . Peake Farm, 1861.
TEWKESBURY: OS (1:500) 1885.
THETFORD: Wing, 'A Survey of the Manor of Thetford' 1732 (1937); Martin, 'A Rude Draft showing the Scituation of such dissolved Religious Houses in Thetford as appear by their ruins or I have made out by Authentick abuttalls from Old Deeds' 1779; Browne, 'Map of the Municipal Borough' (3 chains: 1 in.) 1837; OS (1:500) 1883; Wells, Plans of the Estates . . . of Thomas Page' 1843–44.
TIVERTON: OS (1:500) 1889; Hayne House Estate (6 chains: 1 in.) 1864.
TODMORDEN: OS (1:1056) 1852; OS (1:500) 1891.
TORBAY: as TORQUAY: Cockrem (D) 1840 (?), from OS; Croydon's Roy. Lib. 1860 (?), from OS; OS (1:500) 1865; Westley (8 in.: 1 m) 1883 and (12 in.: 1 m) 1883.
TOTNES: OS (1:500) 1888.
TOWER HAMLETS: Beck, 'Various Alterations and Improvements' 1843 (?); BC, 1868; Bacon's Map of the School Board District (1 m = 9⅜ in.) 1879; Map of the School Board District (6 in.: 1 m) 1879; Positions of Board Schools etc. . . .' (6 in.: 1 m) 1892; also BETHNAL GREEN: Gascoyne & Harris 'Actual Survey of the Hamlet of Bethnal Green' (800 yds. = 148 mm) 1703; OS (1:2500); LONDON Sheets 28, 29, 38, 1876; also POPLAR: OS (1:2500) LONDON Sheets 28, 29, 38, 1874; 'Sketch Map of the Parish of Poplar' in *London Argus*, No. 62, vol. 3, 1898; also STEPNEY: 'Copy of a Platt of such

(Tower Hamlets – continued) –
Lands belonging to . . . the Company of Mercers of London, lying within the Parish of Stepney in the Countie of Middlesex' (35 pertches = 100 mm) 1615 (1933); Gascoyne, 'Actual Survey of the Parish of St Dunstan, Stepney, alias Stebunheath' (1320 yds. = 9 in.) 1703; ditto, 'Being one of the ten parishes in the County of Middlesex adjoined to the City of London. Describing exactly the Bounds of the Nine Hamlets in the said Parish' 1703; Gascoyne & Harris, 'Hamlet of Mile End Old Town' (880 yds. = 152 mm) 1703; ditto, with names of land-owners and acreages, 1703; Gascoyne & Harris, 'Hamlet of Lime-House' (A Table of the Names of severall Courts and Alleys, at 35 perches = 75 mm) 1703; Stow (4 furlongs = 2 in.), *Survey of the Cities of London and Westminster*, 1720, 1755; Frazer; 'Correct Ground Plan of the Dreadful Fire at Ratcliff' 1794; OS (1:2500); LONDON Sheets 28, 36, 37, 45, 46, 1876; 'Sketch Map of the Hamlet of Mile End Old Town' in *London Argus*, No. 19, vol. 1, 1897. See: Ravenshill, W., 'Joel Gascoyne's Stepney', *Guildhall Studies in London History*, No. 2, 1977.
TRURO; Boazio, 'The Castelles, Parish Churches, Villages, Gentlemen's Places and Woods' (1 m = 62 mm) 1597 (in *Jnl. of Roy. Instn. of Cornwall*, vol. ix, 1889); OS (1:500) 1896.
TYNEMOUTH: OS (1:2500) 1861; OS: (1:500 with North and South Shields) 1861; OS (1:500) 1896.
WAKEFIELD: 'Motives for making a Navigable Canal from Barnby Bridge by Barnsley to communicate with the Navigable River Calder near Wakefield' (with Map) 1793; 'Plan of Navigations from Wakefield to Ferrybridge', 1826; OS (1:1056) 1851; OS (1:500) 1890.
WALLASEY: TM 1841; P of Birkenhead . . . with parts of the Townships of . . . Wallasey' 1858; 'Syer's Ready Reference and Cab Fare Plan of Birkenhead . . . Wallasey etc.' 1869; OS (1:2500) 1876; Griffith & Son (6 in.: 1 m) 1890.
WALLSEND: OS (1:2500) 1859; OS (1:500) 1896; Willington Estate (20 chains = 85 mm) 1861.
WALSALL: Earl of Bradford's E: (130 yds.: 1 in.) 1763; Snape (80 yds.: 1 in.) 1782; Mason (4 chains: 1 in.) 1824; OS (1:500) 1885–86. See: Dean, K. J. and Liddle, P., *Urban Growth of Walsall 1763–1966* (portfolio pubn. by W. Lib. & Art Gal. Ctee, 1967).
WALTHAM FOREST: 'St John's Ground and the King's Highe Way, 1527'; also CHING-FORD: OS (1:1250) 1870; also WALTHAM-STOW: Forbes, 'Survey of the Manor' 1699; OS (1:2500) 1865.
WANDSWORTH: Lane, 'Survey of Putney' 1636; Rocque's 'Map of the Environs of London 1741–45'; Jones, Jnr. 'Parish of

(Wandsworth − continued) −
Streatham' (½ m = 120 mm) 1840; OS
(1:2500) 1868; 'Sketch Map of the Parish of
Streatham' in *London Argus*, No. 59, vol. 3,
1898; 'Sketch Map of the Parish of Wands-
worth' in *London Argus*, No. 50, vol. 2, 1898;
Metropolitan Boroughs of Wandsworth and
Battersea (3⅝ in.: 1 m) 1910.
WAREHAM: Taylor, 'Worgate Manor Farm and
leasehold estates in Wareham' (10 chains =
23 mm) 1770 (1935).
WARLEY: Repton 1795; Roper 'Plan of the
Hamlet of Smethwick', 1858; 26 Colliery
Plans of the Oldbury area (19th c.).
WARRINGTON: Wallworth & Donbavand 1772;
Hall (6½ in.: 1000 ft.) 1826; Wilkinson (40
chains: 7 in.) 1840; Beaumont, W. (ed.),
'Warrington in 1465; a 19th-c. map as
described in a contemporary rent-roll of the
Legh family' (*Chetham Soc.*, vol. 17, 1849).
WARWICK: Speed 1610; Sheriff (Proposed
canal from Warwick to Braunston), 1793;
Baker (intended canal) 1793 (?); OS (1:500)
1887; 'Plan of Warwick' on Warwickshire
Map (12 in.: 1 m) 1894; *The Town Maps of
Warwick; An Archive Teaching Unit* (County
Mus. 1796).
WATFORD: OS (1:2500) 1873: OS (1:500)
1874.
WELLS: Simes (100 yds. = 53 mm) 1735;
Strachey (1000 yds. = 250 mm) 1736; OS
(1:500) 1886.
WEST BROMWICH: Tipton PM 1789; Wednes-
bury TM (3 chains: 1 in.) 1799: Survey of the
Health of Towns 1853; Survey for the Poor
Law Act (3 chains; 1 in.) 1860 (?); Wood
1837; Enclosure, 1801; Peacock & Cottrell,
Survey in 96 parts (50 in.: 1 m) 1857.
WESTMINSTER: Norden 1593 (facsim. by
London Top. Soc. 1899); Senex (from
Norden) 1723; Speed 1610; Lacy (400 ft. =
185 mm) 'Parish of St Paul Covent Garden
•with part of St Martin in the Fields . . .
belonging to William Earl of Bedford . . . with
Bedford House and the circuit thereof . . .'
1673 (1939); Parish of St James's Westminster
(500 yds. = 40 mm) 1700; Parish of St
George's Hanover Square (600 ft.: 1 in.) 1725
(1880); Mackay, Snr. & Jnr., Parish of St
George's Hanover Square (165 ft.: 1 in.) 1725
(in *The Builder*, vol. 81, 1901); Index to
Rocque's Plan of the Cities of London and
Westminster 1746–47 (London Top. Soc.
1968); Parish of St James's Westminster (500
yds. = 55 mm) (in *Literary and Historical
Memorials of London*, by Jesse, J. H., 1847);
Cole, 'A New and Accurate Plan of the City
of Westminster etc. . . .' 1756, 1775 (in *The
History and Survey of London*, by Maitland,
W. etc.); Morris, ˋSurvey of St George's Parish,
Hanover Square, 1761; Rhodes, Parish of St
James's Westminster, 1770; Waters, Parish of
St Martin in the Fields, 1799. Ward 'Showing

(Westminster − continued) −
the Improvements now in progress at the West
End of London' (1000 ft = 80 mm) 1830;
Saunders, Three Plans to accompany the
results of an Inquiry concerning the extent of
Westminster at various periods' 1835; Cooke,
City and Liberty of Westminster 1847; Plan of
Westminster (1000 ft. = 80 mm) 1850; Beck,
Parish of St Paul, Covent Garden, showing site
of Bedford House and Grounds (from a
Survey by Leybourn in 1686) 1851; BC,
1868; 'Sketch Map of the Parish of St James's
Westminster' in *London Argus*, No. 76, vol. 3,
1898; Bacon's Map of the School Board
District of Westminster (1 m = 9⅜ in.) 1879;
Map of School Board District (6 in.: 1 m)
1879; Map showing Board Schools etc. (6 in.:
1 m) 1892; 'Sketch Map of St George's
Hanover Square' in *London Argus*, No. 12,
vol. 1, 1897; 'Sketch Map of St Martin's in
the Fields' in *London Argus*, No. 27, vol. 2,
1897; Boundaries of St Margaret and St John
the Evangelist, Westminster, in *London Argus*,
No. 23, vol. 1, 1897; also PADDINGTON:
Brasiel (70 perches = 82 mm) 1742; Demesne
lands of Sir John Morshead etc. (40 chains =
167 mm) 1790; Paddington Estate, land for
building leases opposite Hyde Park, 1830;
Gutch 1828; 'Topographical Survey' 1837;
Lucas (½ m = 250 mm) 1842; Dolling (D)
1863; Lucas 1869; OS (1:2500); LONDON
Sheets 24, 33, 1873; 'Sketch Map of
Paddington' in *London Argus*, No. 57, vol. 3,
1898; also ST MARYLEBONE: Prince
'Design of Buildings' (400 ft. = 78 mm) 1719;
Jefferys 'Lord Foley's Lands' 1764; White &
Son 'Improvements proposed on Marylebone
Park Estate' (2000 ft. = 120 mm) 1809;
Davies & Bartlett, M. as defined by Act of
Parliament in 1832 (1 m = 225 mm) 1834,
1837; Lucas (40 chains = 250 mm) 1846,
1849; 'Plan of Borough' 1850; Whitbread
'Elective Wards' 1855; Lucas (½ m = 125
mm) 1869; OS (1:2500); LONDON Sheets
15, 16, 24, 25, 34, 1873; 'Sketch Map of the
Parish of Marylebone' in *London Argus*, No.
33, vol. 2, 1898; Map of the School Board
District (1 m: 9⅜ in.) 1879; Position of
Board Schools etc. (6 in.: 1 m) 1892;
intended Turnpike road 1830; E: Marylebone
and Parrow Hills 1798; Henry Wm. Portman's
Lands 1741. 1780; Duke of Portlands Estate
1789; Marylebone Park Farm Estate 1794.
WESTON SUPER MARE: in Wright's D 1880–
81; also (2000 ft. = 75 mm) 1891–92;
OS (1:500) 1886; Davies Bros. (6 in.: 1 m)
1887.
WEYMOUTH: OS (1:500) 1866.
WHITEHAVEN: Donald (500 yds. = 95 mm)
1774, 1802; Howard 1790; OS (1:500) 1866.
WIDNES: OS (1:500) 1890.
WIGAN: Mather 1827; OS (1:1056) 1848; OS
(1:500) 1890.

WILTON: 'Plan drawn about 1567' (1925);
Within the Walls (Wilton Park) (10 chains =
80 mm) 1828 (1925); OS (1:2500) 1880;
Earl of Pembroke and Montgomery's
Estates in town, 1919.

WINDSOR: Collier (engr Pine) 200 yds. = 57
mm, 1742; Tucker (60 in.: 1 m) 1843; Plan of
the SW of Windsor (1 in. = 135 ft.) 1860 (?);
OS (1:2500) 1869; OS (1:1056) 1870;
Wright's SM 1887; See: *Wenceslaus Hollar
and his View of London and Windsor
in the Seventeenth Century*, by Hind, A. M.
(1922).

WISBECH: OS (1:500) 1887.

WOKINGHAM: OS (1:2500) 1873; OS (1:500)
1874.

WOLVERHAMPTON: Taylor 1750; Bartholomew (from OS) 1870 (?); OS (1:500) 1886.

WORCESTER: Speed 1610; Burnford, 'An
Exact Ground Plot of the City of Worcester
as it stood Fortify'd on 3rd. September,
1651' (in *Boscobel* by Blount, T. etc. 1680,
1725, 1769); Doharty 1741; Young 1779,
1780; Young, G., 1790, Valentine Green,
*History and Antiquities of the City and
Suburbs of Worcester* (1796); Roper & Young
(BA) 1810; Plan of part of the City showing
the proposed Railway 1844; OS (1:500) 1886.

WORKINGTON: OS (1:2500) 1866.

WORKSOP: Kelk 1774; OS 1885.

WORTHING: Phillips 1814; Smith 1877; OS
(1:500) 1874.

YEOVIL: Watts 1831; Borough Boundaries
1854, 1910, 1929; TM 1846; OS (1:500)
1886. ('Other maps', for 1806, 1813, 1842,
1843 at the Borough Library).

YORK: Speed 1610; Braun & Hohenbergius
1573, 1618, 1660; Archer, Capt. J., One of
His Majesties Ingeniors (Table Alphabetik
to know all the Edifises and Remarkable
Places in the Citty) (200 yds. = 42 mm)
1643 (?); Francis Drake (300 yds. = 42 mm)
1736; Cossins (with 16 Views of Houses, 8
on each side and 4 lines of text at the foot)
6 chains = 62 mm, 1784; Chassereau 'Plan
de la Ville et faubourgs de York' (1000 ft. =
92 mm) 1750; Jeffereys 1767–70, 1775,
1800; Gent (300 yds. = 33 mm) 1771; Castle
& Barber (20 chains = 50 mm) 1820; Baines
(1822); Smith 1822; OS (1:1056) 1852;
Monkhouse, Newbald & Steed 1860 (?);
Heywood & Son 1871; Johnson & Tesseyman
(D) 1872; Sessions 'Penny Map' 1879;
Johnson & Co. (3000 ft. = 85 mm) 1886;
OS (1:500) 1891; Bacon's 'Plan' (6 in.: 1
m) 1901.

CHAPTER SEVEN

THE MUNICIPAL BOROUGHS BEFORE 1835

'LOCAL GOVERNMENT', as we know it today, is a recent development. Our present local authorities were the outcome of the Municipal Corporations Act (1835), which created elected town councils, and of the Local Government Act (1888), which introduced county councils and gave county borough status to many of the largest towns. Before those dates, the functions of locally elected councils, assuming responsibilities for the full range of public administration and welfare, did not exist in England and Wales. Although (as we have seen in Chapter Four) there had been medieval and Tudor incorporated boroughs with a 'commonalty' of burgesses, aldermen or freemen, these were privileged groups, acting as the incorporation of vested interests rather than as representative bodies which held themselves responsible to the community at large. Just as gild members, who became aldermen, had combined to restrict and regulate trading, so the corporation of burgesses preserved the right to elect the town's officers, serve on its juries, farm its taxes and, in most cases, to act as justices of the peace and send members to Parliament. The charters of 'liberties' by which these rights were exercised were, in fact, an exclusion of any rights for the majority of the towns' inhabitants. 'Close election' preserved irresponsible local government.

By the end of the 18th century there was a curiously indeterminate number of acknowledged 'municipal' boroughs with recognized corporate status. The exact number, ranging between 250 and 350, is elusive, varying from one authority to another according to their criteria.[1] The Parliamentary Commissioners of 1835 listed a gross total of 284 municipal boroughs in England and Wales, of which 177 were also parliamentary constituencies. (An additional 69 towns were parliamentary but not municipal.) More than a score of the smaller municipal contenders were dismissed by the Commissioners as 'municipal only in name'; many more could produce no charter, some of these relied on ancient 'prescriptive' right, as at Berkeley (Gloucs.), Yeovil (Som.) and Llanelli (Carm.). The total population of a borough might be as few as 68 in Newtown (I.o.W.); many had 'no municipal functions and no municipal revenue'. In 15 boroughs the annual revenue was less than £20 and 17 towns had no revenue at all; only in 19 boroughs was the revenue above £3,000. The average number of qualified 'corporators' or freemen in the most substantial municipalities was less than 5% of their total urban population of 2,028,513 inhabitants.

In some towns, such as Cardigan and Oswestry, the incorporated body was referred to as a 'common council'; in other places, such as Bewdley, Godalming and Gravesend, the borough's authority was nominally vested in 'the inhabitants', but this is misleading to a modern eye. These, as in other towns, were select bodies, whose main functions were to preserve the monopolies of the earlier gilds and to administer the burgesses' corporate lands as an investment for the benefit of the borough's freemen.

Indeed, the restriction of freedom of the borough, by right of birth or expensive purchase, by the exaction of market tolls from other townsmen and their exclusion from trading in the town, created hardship and resentment amongst the ordinary tradesmen and small property-owners of many towns and boroughs. Similarly, though all incorporated boroughs – and many 'private' or 'manorial' townships like Dudley and Birmingham – nominated a mayor, port-reeve and surveyors (Neath, Chard, Beccles), warden and assistants (Louth), high bailiff (Kidderminster), bridgemasters (Maidenhead), jurats (Sandwich, Tenterden), masters (Wells), bailiffs (Tewkesbury, Winchester, Windsor) or capital burgesses (Bideford). These should not be seen as if they were modern town councils. Their functions were almost entirely ceremonial, as were those of the boroughs' officers whom they in turn appointed, the chamberlains, sword-bearers, beadles, coroners and sergeants who appear in many towns.

The city of Worcester is a typical example of an ancient incorporated borough which survived from the Middle Ages into a new industrial era. There, the so-called 'governing body' was a self-electing 'common council' of 72 citizens who elected another body of 48 'capital citizens'; in turn these selected 24 'capital councillors' who chose their own mayor and six aldermen. Only freemen were eligible for election, and freedom of the borough was restricted by right of birth, apprenticeship, or purchase for £20. The city, as we have seen in Chapter Four, claimed its corporate origins in medieval charters of 1189 and 1227 which confirmed the rights of burgesses and gildsmen. As far as the Commission was concerned[2] those charters were irrelevant by the end of the 18th century, conferring only 'exemptions from tolls throughout England and various other privileges and immunities now of no value'. Philip and Mary's further charter of 1544 was recognized as having incorporated the city in the names of its 'Bailiffs and Aldermen, Chamberlains and Citizens', but the corporation's real authority was seen to be that of James I's charter of 1622 which constituted the City and Liberties of Worcester a county of itself, independent of the county of Worcestershire. Many of the towns on our base-list will be found in gazetteers and Municipal Yearbooks to lay claim to their earliest possible charter or ancient 'prescription' when this may not be the true date of their incorporation or recognition by Parliament.

Worcester's chief officers were a Mayor, a Recorder 'learned in the law' and a Town Clerk merely 'skilled in law'; these officers kept the records and managed the legal business of the corporation, assisting the magistrates in the administration of justice. There were also four Auditors, two Chamberlains, two Coroners, ten Surveyors, a Sword-bearer, four Sergeants-at-Mace, five Mayor's Officers, a Water Bailiff and a Coal Weigher, most of whose duties had become obsolete or purely ceremonial. There is no suggestion that these dignitaries and officials were taking large profits from their office. The Town Clerk was paid no stipend but received a modest fee of £3 10s. a year as Clerk of Audit and exacted the usual professional charges for drawing up leases and other legal conveyances. The Sword Bearer received a salary of one guinea a month and was permitted to take various small tolls on some goods sold in the market; these amounted to £50 per annum. The corporation's income came mainly from admission fees and the small nominal rents of unprofitable dwelling-houses from about 470 tenants. The city's total annual revenue was no more than £2,000 and the building of a new market house had left the corporation in debt to a sum of £3,500. Indeed, their situation was so unprofitable by 1822, as to require the loan of £50 from each councillor, and caused the suspension of the Mayor's annual Feast.

As to the normal expenditure of 'local government' in Worcester, by 1831 salaries and wages amounted to £821 a year; furniture, building repairs, ceremonial costume and charitable clothing cost £819. Various charities, such as the Cholera Fund (£21), the Infirmary (£21), the Dispensary (£10 10s.), one year's soup for the poor (£17), the National School (£21), the new Worcester Library (£10) and Worcester Races Fund (£30) accounted for £310 per annum. It was, in these unprofitable circumstances, unfair for the Parliamentary Commissioners of 1835 to draw particular attention to the inescapable fact that, 'upon an annual revenue of £2,000 a year, about £265 is expended upon dinners and wine . . .'. In fact, much of the charitable activity of the corporation was paid for out of the councillors' own pockets.

The borough's judicial function as county court and magistrates' bench is evident in the rôles of its Recorder, the Mayor and the Aldermen as borough magistrates. This was the case in many other incorporated towns. Similarly, the corporation's origins as a gild are as clearly seen in the ancient privileges of its freemen. In Worcester, as elsewhere, these privileges were the exclusive rights of carrying on trade within the city and exemption from small tolls levied in the market. According to the evidence taken by the Commissioners in 1835, the fines to which non-freemen were liable for trading in the town and the high price set upon the purchase of the right to trade operated injuriously, not only on persons starting business with small capital, but also on the owners of houses. These would have been in greater demand to rent had the privileges of trading in the city been exempted from over-charges. The glovers' trade was supposed to have suffered considerable decline in Worcester for this reason, though the Commissioners thought much of this evidence to be exaggerated. Between 1800 and 1831 2,503 freemen were admitted, 1,856 by birth or apprenticeship, only 647 by purchase or gift; the population of the City and its suburbs at that time was 27,000. The sense of medieval custom is heightened by the freemen's surviving privilege of limited right of common over about 20 acres of land.

The position of any corporation in the 18th-century was modified by the survival, or creation, of other independent bodies which either retained, or had recently adopted, certain functions of 'local government'. One can compile a fairly universal list of those functions which had always been recognized by medieval, Tudor, Stuart and Georgian townsmen as essential to decent communal life. This would include the following in its priorities: the assumption of responsibility for law and order by some sort of 'watch and ward'; the maintenance of local courts of justice; the regulation of trade; a high priority on the repair and maintenance of high street, market place and bridges; and a constant preoccupation with the state of the poor. For most of these functions, rates were taken and overseers appointed. Provision of education, the largest single cost of modern local government, was seen as a private matter for church and charity, as was the provision of health services of any sort. It would be an interesting study, in any monastic town, to discover how these provisions and others, such as the hospitality of the abbey's guest-houses, had been made since the dissolution of the monasteries in the 16th century.

When we examine such a list of acknowledged local needs we are immediately aware of the vestiges of many historic authorities other than borough and gild. In non-corporate towns, such as Dudley, often referred to as 'manorial boroughs', the borough court was still administered by the steward of the lord of the manor and dealt with all manner of urban 'nuisances' and market regulations. Chandler, a recent Dudley historian, has commented on a 'state of confusion between the proper scope of manor and borough' which will be found in many another provincial town where the lord's Court Leet regularly acted as borough court.[3] In Dudley, the court's major preoccupations were the state of highways and bridges and their repair; the noisome 'hoosing' (oozing) from private pig-styes and 'necessary houses'; and the regular passing of court orders and fines for the obstruction of the streets by market stalls and 'blocks', by the boiling of blubber, the slaughtering of beasts and swine, and the firing of casks on the pavements. Most significantly, it was the Court Leet which appointed Dudley's Mayor, a standing affront to the town radical, Sam Cook, who protested about this 'illegal' appointment with an equal measure of indignation and derision, which did not, however, cause him to abstain from the annual Mayoral Feast.

Other public services were still the business of the parishes, with their own overseers and guardians, constables and surveyors, appointed for a variety of local purposes. (See *Village Records*, Chapter IV). Primarily concerned in most parishes with the condition of the poor and the collection of a separate rate for their relief, the vestry might at a much later stage find itself assuming responsibility for the electric lighting of the streets of the parish, as at Battersea in 1896 and Bethnal Green in 1899. The parish too, would usually assume some responsibility for road repairs and 'watch and ward'.

By far the most influential factor in diverting the borough corporation's attention from its local municipal responsibility was the additional qualification of borough status, for parliamentary franchise and representation. The politics of 'Eatanswill' were the most corrupting influence upon the attention of the burgesses to local affairs. The Commissioners of 1835 remarked that: 'The election to municipal offices is often a trial of strength between political parties. Instances of systematic bribery for the purpose of securing municipal elections occur at Maidstone, Norwich, Ipswich, Liverpool, Oxford and Hull . . . The most flagrant abuses have arisen from the perversion of municipal privileges to political objects. The Commissioners have generally found that those Corporations which have not possessed the Parliamentary franchise have most faithfully discharged the duties of town government and have acquired, more than the others, the confidence and goodwill of the communities to which they belong . . .'.

Almost half (176) of our base-list boroughs were parliamentary in 1835. Of the 56 'rotten' boroughs totally disenfranchised by the Reform Act of 1832, the majority (such as Bossiney (Cornwall), Wootton Basset (Wilts.) and many more) would not long retain their municipal status; other disenfranchised towns (like Aldeburgh) would remain incorporated, though non-parliamentary, until 1974. Of the 43 towns which received either one or two new parliamentary seats, only a few (such as Kidderminster and Sunderland) were corporate boroughs already, and remained so until the final reorganization; the majority of newly enfranchised towns, mostly in Lancashire, Yorkshire and the industrial Midlands, were not municipal boroughs in 1832. These include Dudley, Birmingham and Wolverhampton and many northern industrial cities. The Commissioners had cited the corporations of Leeds, Lynn and Doncaster as 'turning their attention to municipal duties more sedulously than the majority . . . Among small towns deserving the same character we refer to the corporations of Louth, Bideford, Maidenhead, Beccles, South Molton and Stratford-upon-Avon . . .'. The populations of the English and Welsh municipal boroughs in 1835 ranged from 68 in Newtown (I.o.W.), to 164,175 in Liverpool. The status of every borough, both municipal and parliamentary, as they stood immediately before and after the Municipal Corporations Act of 1835, is given in the Gazetteer at the end of the next Chapter. This includes boroughs which had lost their municipal status before the reorganization of 1974, as well as our base-list.

During the 18th century other means of private enterprise were adopted for a variety of local affairs, separate from any similar provision made by corporation or parish. By 1760 English manufacturing towns were growing into an era of remorselessly expanding population, more effective inter-city communications and booming industrial growth. Thriving trade and industry brought the squalor of overcrowded streets and teeming tenements. The towns' primitive services, of roadways, drainage, market places, factory sites, sewage disposal, water supply and law and order were already strained to breakdown point. Surviving documents constantly remind us of the primitive state of the typical English town at this time; where back-yards were middens; where the main water supply might come from the drainage of a church roof, and a series of sewage-polluted wells; and where back-street furnaces and court-yard forges fought for space with slaughterhouses and piggeries. In Dorchester as late as 1776, it was necessary to forbid the further erection of thatched houses within the borough. Any town's refuse problem, would, as in Dudley, encompass cow-dung, ashes, rotting vegetables, blubber, industrial cinders, abattoir spillage and, in Birmingham as late as 1824, the incessant 'hoosing' of pig-sties, dung-hills and 'bog-houses'.

At the same time the prominent townsmen, manufacturers and merchants, saw inviting prospects opening up with profitable opportunities for further expansion and wealth for the towns and their inhabitants, or at least for themselves. As canals and turnpikes broke open new avenues of trade and communications, the tradesmen looked to their resources. How could each borough be made a more attractive 'place of resort'? It was to meet this challenge that the majority of corporate boroughs, anticipating a new form of town government, established over and above the mayor and corporation, a body of Town Commissioners to regulate their affairs. To this end it was necessary to petition Parliament for a 'private Act'. The example of the similar private enterprise of countless 'turnpike trusts', acting with the authority of private Acts of Parliament was their model. The example was followed again by local canal companies, and by village landowners determined to divide and enclose the common fields for profitable agriculture.

· The impulse of local gentry toward private association for particular ends was very well-marked towards the end of the 18th century. In Dudley, for example, it resulted in an early form of building society, formed in 1779 by its urban shareholders to buy land and build houses for its members. The trustees of this association were prominent townsmen, merchants and professional men, with an interested local builder as their treasurer. A similar group of the same Dudley burgesses formed themselves into a company in 1786, to build their own hotel — the *Dudley Arms* — as a club or assembly rooms for the shareholders paying £50 apiece. As to Dudley education, the same prominent citizens — we shall find them named again and again in the commercial directories (see Chapter Nine) — were active in promoting charitable foundations. The Baylies's Charity School was founded in 1732; its kindly representatives still meet for discussion of generous provision for Dudley youth which the authority cannot afford.

The religious aspect of these Dudley benefactors' philanthropy is seen in the rebuilt parish church of St Edmund's; the Presbyterian Meeting House; a new Methodist

Chapel, described by John Wesley as 'one of the neatest in England'; and chapels for Independents and Baptists.[4] The town was in fact, like so many others we shall find, experiencing a phase of considerable rebuilding and re-facing of timbered houses with neat red brick. On the face of it Dudley was becoming an elegant, prosperous new town, its High Street, as Pearson and Rollason's *Directory* of 1780 will show, the residential centre for surgeons, schoolmaster and attorney, mercer, innkeepers and chandler as well as glassmaker, leatherworkers, brazier, butcher and baker, breeches-maker and weaver. One might imagine, in fact, an elegant 19th-century street, as in the retrospective view of 'Dudley High Street in 1812' (see page 172). Behind this frontage, however, the furnaces smoked, the tenements and courts crawled with people, the gutters ran with blood and grease, and outdoor privies 'hoosed' unchecked. The town was in fact ripe for 'improvement'.

As we have seen, it was not that public-spirited bodies were absent; there were in fact more than enough. Quite apart from the mayor and burgesses there were the Board of Highways; the trustees of the turnpike; the vestry and overseers of the Poor; the Earl of Dudley, who leased the town its market and helped with general improvements; the Court Leet acting as a borough court to prevent 'nuisances'; and the trustees of various charities. To these, in 1791, following the example of scores of other English and Welsh towns, was added a new body of Town Commissioners brought into being by a local Act of Parliament. Such Acts are widespread enough to merit the following Chapter which explains their predominance over other local corporate bodies in the period before the innovation of town councils in 1835 or, for other non-corporate terms like Dudley, a local Board of Health from 1852. The relevant documents are known as Improvement Acts.

It is clear that the Parliamentary Commissioners, who took a prejudiced and partial view of the state of the English and Welsh towns in the age of reform, took some account of Improvement Acts as a sign of any town's civic conscience. Schedule E to the Municipal Corporations Act lists those towns achieving new municipal status which had taken out Improvement Acts. That list is incomplete even for the towns which it includes and, inevitably, takes no account of the scores of 'improved' towns which Parliament had not recognized as new municipal boroughs. Their demise was a foregone conclusion.

The Parliamentary Commissioners' conclusions formed a swingeing attack upon the ancient boroughs, beside which the findings of the Redcliffe–Maud Commission in 1969 pale into significance. Individual towns such as Hedon (founded in 1154, with a population of 1,080 in 1831) were scathingly described: 'The town is small, its appearance is very mean. It contains few or no good houses and there is very little appearance to trade or business . . .'. Small wonder that five ancient towns, Corfe Castle, Dover, Lichfield, Maidstone and New Romney, as well as several of the London Companies, flatly refused to offer any information whatever to the Commission. 'In conclusion', the Commissioners summed up: 'we report to your Majesty that there prevails amongst the inhabitants of the great majority of the incorporated towns a general, and in our opinion a just, dissatisfaction with their municipal institutions, a distrust of the self-elected municipal councils whose powers are subject to no popular control and whose acts and proceedings, being secret, are unchecked by the influence of public opinion. . . . We . . . therefore feel it to be our duty to represent to your Majesty that the existing Municipal Corporations of England and Wales neither possess nor deserve the confidence and respect of your Majesty's subjects and that a thorough reform must be effected before they can become what we humbly submit to your Majesty they might be, useful and efficient instruments of local government.'

Acting promptly upon these recommendations, the Municipal Corporations Act of 1835 reduced the number of recognized borough corporations to 178. These were in future to be governed by a uniform system of councils directly elected by the rate-payers, mayors and aldermen being indirectly elected, as before. The new councils were to take over the functions of the Improvement Commissioners, and all other independent bodies which controlled some aspect of local services were subsequently abolished. Of the 284 boroughs listed by the Commissioners, including 24 which they had described as 'municipal only in name', 106 were not reincorporated by the Act of 1835. The Act annulled the privileges of many small but improved ancient boroughs such as Stockton, Wantage or Fishguard, but failed, as yet, to recognize the municipal pretensions of many more industrial towns which were very thoroughly improved, such as Dudley, Rochdale, Wakefield or Sheffield. Of these 87 more towns (including Dudley and Birmingham) would be officially incorporated before 1882, or by the second Municipal Corporations Act of that year. Thus occurred the first of a long series of local government reorganizations devised by central government. The dates of the incorporation of all the old and new boroughs is noted in the next Gazetteer.

FURTHER READING

Merrewether, H. A. and Stephens, A. J., *The History of the Boroughs and Municipal Corporations of the U.K. from the Earliest to the Present Times* (1972), 3 vols.
Martin, G. H. and McIntyre, S., *Bibliography of British and Irish Municipal History* (1973).

Dudley's Market Hall on Middle Row in 1797; a drawing by Thomas Rowlandson (from an original in Dudley Art Gallery and Museum) actual size 8½ in. x 5½ in.

CHAPTER EIGHT

IMPROVEMENT AND OTHER ACTS 1720-1835

THE ILLUSTRATION (p. 174) illustrates the first page of a so-called 'private' Act of Parliament, passed in 1791 at the petition of a group of Dudley citizens. In 40 pages of Gothick script the Act authorises them to carry out the many improvements which the streets of their town sadly lacked. From the middle of the 18th century such Acts became commonplace for English and Welsh towns. These are often referred to as 'private' Acts to distinguish them from the more general 'public' Statutes of the realm, but the division is sometimes confused in the Acts themselves, so that it is as well to search both indexes of so-called 'public' and 'private' legislation in the several available indexes.

In earlier times, private Acts had dealt only with personal affairs, estates, marriages, divorce and inheritance of private individuals. Indexed separately from the Statutes, they would normally refer to changes of surname, naturalisation of foreign immigrants, care of the mentally infirm or infant heiresses and similar personal matters. The extension by groups of private citizens from about 1750 to 1834, of the procedure to petition the House of Commons in order to gain Parliamentary authority for some course of joint action which would involve the raising of funds, gave a new 'public' significance and scope to what eventually became known, more aptly, as 'public, local and personal acts'; this description is not given until the later years of George III's reign. From the end of the 18th century Parliament's assent was sought for the financing of local turnpike trusts, the enclosure of open fields, the development of canal companies, the laying of railway lines and the introduction of gas-lighting or piped water supply. During the 1760s the bulk of the Acts listed as 'public' which have a local significance deal with the establishment of turnpike roads from town to town; at the same time, the majority of Acts listed as 'private' are those for local enclosures (see *Village Records*, Chapter V). During the later years of George II's reign a new kind of local Act becomes more numerous amongst the turnpike Acts; these are later indexed under the heading 'Paving and Improvement of Towns' or as 'Improvement Acts'. Until about 1800 these are listed with the turnpike measures, that is as if 'public'; indeed, the final clause of any such Act will usually be found to assert that the Act 'shall be deemed, adjudged and taken to be a Publick Act'. Eventually, they will appear amongst the new contents of 'Public, local and Personal Acts'.

Strictly speaking, an index should list for reference all public Statutes with arabic numerals to number their individual Chapters or separate Acts, e.g.: 2 Geo II, c. 70. Footnote and other references will refer to the *Index of Local and Personal Acts* as, e.g.: 2 Geo IV, c. lxx, a different Act from the first example. For the sake of space and clarity this Chapter's Gazetteer uses arabic numerals in every case, as it is

ANNO TRICESIMO PRIMO

Georgii III. Regis.

****

CAP. LXXIX.

An Act for better paving, cleanfing, lighting, watching, and otherwife improving the Town of *Dudley*, in the County of *Worcefter*, and for better fupplying the faid Town with Water.

HEREAS the Streets and other Preamble. publick Paſſages and Places within the Town of Dudley, in the County of Worceſter, are not properly paved, lighted, cleanſed, or watched, and are ſubject to various Incroachments, Obſtructions, Nuiſances, and Annoyances, and are in ſome Parts narrow and incommodious for Paſſengers and Carriages; and the ſaid Town is not properly ſupplied with Water: And whereas it would be of great Benefit and Convenience to the Inhabitants of the ſaid Town, and to all Perſons

30 X 2 reſorting

The first page of Dudley's Improvement Act of 31 Geo. III (1791) from the Archives and Local History Dept. of Dudley Public Libraries (actual size 7¼ in. x 12 in.).

advisable to check both sets of Acts for Paving and Improvement. The majority of earlier Acts will be found to be public, the majority of later Acts are local and personal. Note too, that the date of any Act is always given by reference to the king's *regnal year*. This will run irregularly from reign to reign, across one or more calendar years. For example, George I's regnal years begin in August, George II's in June and George III's in October. Thus, the calendar years of each reign will be, for example, 1714-15, 1727-28 and 1760-61 etc. Adding the number of years of the Statute to the earliest year of any reign will give an approximate date for most Acts, within one year. Thus, 26 Geo III is 1785 from 25th October to December 30th, but 1786 for the rest of the regnal year. Useful tables of every year of each monarch's reign will be found in the *Handbook of British Chronology*, ed. by Powicke, F. M. and Fryde, E. B., 2nd edn., 1961. These tables will give a more accurate reading than our Gazetteer, which is approximate. The Acts themselves, their contents and much of their actual text, will be found in the bulky volumes of *Statutes at Large* stored in the larger reference libraries. Individual local Acts relevant to particular places will be found in separate collections in smaller borough libraries.

As in the case of Dudley, such local Acts were widely sought by interested bodies of residents in provincial towns who were prepared to act as town commissioners, possibly for a limited period, to achieve certain well-defined objectives. Their public works programme would almost always include a standard provision for paving, lighting, cleansing and watching the streets of the town. This would include levelling, resurfacing and draining the streets; it could imply the demolition of some obstructive buildings, the widening of the thoroughfare, and even the opening up of new streets. These were to be furnished with oil lamps (later gaslight), street-signs and house-numbers. The work would usually involve attention to drainage, sanitary conditions and refuse disposal; sewage is rarely specifically mentioned, except in a few rare cases such as Southwark in 1771 or the City of London in 1793. Frequently, as at Chester (1761), special provision is made for a fire brigade and a fresh water supply is often required, sometimes as the subject of a separate Act, as in Knaresborough (1763). The licensing of playhouses, though a somewhat different matter, will also be found amongst the local Acts, as for Newcastle (1786). Otherwise, for the basic essential improvements, one town's Act will be found to be very much like any other.

In general terms, the prevention of the 'Various Enroachments, Obstructions, Nuisances and Annoyances' on most High Streets reveals a multitude of anti-social practices which the Acts bring luridly to light in town after town. A typical town's Improvement Act, like Dudley's, will deal most specifically with the paving of the streets, variously referred to as 'footways, lanes, passages, crossways, alleys, squares, public places and carriage ways'; a distinction is usually made between the roadway and the pavement. Specifications will be made for downspouts on buildings for the drainage of rainwater; the widening of narrow alleys; demolition of derelict buildings, and the removal of other obstructions such as prominent bay-windows, referred to as 'bulk-windows', projecting shop-signs, and other impedimenta (such as unofficial market stalls, 'blocks', counters, sheds, penthouses, fences and out-houses). Hazards such as open cellar steps and 'dung-holes' were also to be dealt with. Conservationists might feel that this was a period when our towns became less 'picturesque'.

The Dudley Act makes it clear that the new Commissioners were well aware of the magnitude of their task in taking up and remaking the streets of their town:

IX. And be it further enacted, That the said Commissioners are hereby authorised and impowered, from
Time to Time, to cause all or any of the present or
future Pavements in the several Streets and other
publick Passages and Places already or hereafter to be
made in the said Town, as well the Carriage Ways
as the Foot Ways, to be taken up, and the said Streets,
Passages, and Places, or any of them, to be new paved,
relaid, repaired, raised, lowered, altered, cleansed, lighted,
and watched, and all Annoyances, Obstructions, Nuisances, and Incroachments to be removed therefrom,

Commissioners impowered to cause the Streets to be paved, &c.

The Act continues to picture for us the ornate but inconvenient clutter of eighteenth-
century street furniture. It refers to the individual house-holder's responsibility to
remove any such projections which might 'obstruct the free passage along the Carriage
or Foot Ways of any of the said streets . . .' and to replace them with flat facia boards
and functional down-spouts:

and all Sign Irons, Sign Posts, and other Posts,
Sheds, Pent Houses, Spouts, Gutters, Steps, Window
Shutters, Rails, Pales, Palisadoes, Porches, Bulks,
Shew Glasses, and Shew Boards, and other Encroachments, Projections, and Annoyances belonging, or which
hereafter shall belong, to such respective Houses and Buildings, and which obstruct the free Passage along the Carriage
or Foot Ways of any of the said Streets and publick Passages and Places, to be removed, altered, or reformed,

Street-cleaning was initially the responsibility of individual householders and shopkeepers. Frontages and side-streets were to be swept at least two days a week, before
10 in the morning, as announced by the Commissioners from week to week. The 'Dirt
and Soil arising' from the various workshops and outhouses was expected to include
rotting vegetables, offal, cow-dung, grease, coals and ashes; though the new regulations
were intended to bring about a measure of control over insanitary habits, public
slaughtering, scalding of hides, dumping of building rubbish and the waste products
of the more noxious trades. It is sometimes difficult to remember that we are envisag-
ing a relatively recent period of town history when, as late as 1773, in industrial
Birmingham, an Improvement Act was necessary so that 'swine and cattle shall not
be suffered to wander in the streets' a prohibition that it was necessary to repeat in
a later Act of 1828. With an almost medieval sense of *laissez-faire*, identical offences
are prohibited in the same towns by Act after Act, as if totally disregarded from
generation to generation. The precautions envisaged by the Dudley Act in 1791 give a

graphic picture of the state of an 18th-century shopping street, where the passer-by might encounter any imaginable occurrence from the slaughtering of a cow, the bleeding of a stuck pig, the scalding of barrels or the rolling of giant casks along the footpath, the shoeing of a horse, the lighting of bonfires, the setting off of fireworks or decapitation by a swinging sheaf of iron rods. This is how the Act envisages some of those 'Annoyances' which might have been expected to cause distress to the more sedate inhabitants of Dudley:

To prevent
Annoyances

XVIII. And be it further enacted, That if any Person shall run, drive, carry, or place on any of the said Foot Ways (other than such as shall be made across any of the said Carriage Ways) any Wheel, Sledge, Wheelbarrow, Hand-barrow, Truck, or Carriage, or shall roll any Cask for the Space of Forty Yards, or wilfully ride, drive, lead, place, or expose to Sale any Horse or other Beast or Cattle on any of the said Foot Ways (other than as aforesaid), or shall, within any of the said Streets, or other publick Passages or Places, kill, slaughter, singe, scald, dress, or cut up any Beast, Swine, or other Cattle, or hoop, cleanse, scald, or fire any Cask,

| every Person offending in any of the Cases aforesaid shall, for every such Offence, forfeit and pay the Sum of Five Shillings; and if any Person shall cause any Bull or other Beast to be baited within the said Town, in the Manner called Bull-baiting, or Bear-baiting, every such Person shall, for every such Offence, forfeit and pay the Sum of Forty Shillings.

Refuse collection was to be the responsibility of the Town Commissioners and their appointed scavenger, whose weekly passage by cart, announced 'by Bell, loud voice or otherwise . . .' to collect the accumulated heaps of 'Ashes, Rubbish, Dust, Dirt and Filth (except any Filth from any Privy or Necessary House) . . .' is vividly described. There would still be alleyways too narrow for the refuse-carts to reach, and the scavengers would be held culpable, on penalty of a fine, for any neglect or refusal to collect legitimate rubbish. One is reminded of the very up-to-date suburban conflict with council 'bin-men' who flatly refuse to accept any garden rubbish:

Scavenger's
Duty

XV. And be it further enacted, That the Person or Persons to be employed as Scavenger or Scavengers in pursuance of this Act shall come Once in every Week, and at such other Times as the said Commissioners shall ap-

point, with a Cart oʒ Carts, oʒ other Conveniencies, into
the several Streets and other publick Paſſages and Places
within the said Town, where ſuch Cart oʒ Carts, oʒ other
Conveniencies can paſs, and at oʒ befoʒe his oʒ their
Approach, by Bell, loud Voice, oʒ otherwiſe, ſhall give
Notice to the Inhabitants of his oʒ their coming.

The lamps to be provided for street-lighting in 1791 were described in detail, with
penalties for vandalism or negligence. Gaslight was introduced to English streets about
1803 in Chester, Doncaster and King's Lynn, at first referred to as 'oil-gas' light. In
Dudley, lamp irons or lamp posts were to be fixed 'into, upon or against the Walls or
Palisadoes of any of the Houses, Tenements or Buildings within the said Town' with
as many lamps and reflectors as the Commissioners found necessary. The fines fixed
as penalties for interference with the Commissioners' arrangements were high, for 'if
any Person shall wilfully break, throw down, take away or spoil or damage any of
the Lamps or Reflectors . . . (he) . . . shall pay any Sum not exceeding Forty Shillings',
plus the cost of making good any damage or loss. It is a very satisfying sense of
detection which can be felt when we find these very posts and lamp-irons marked
precisely in place on the earliest Ordnance Survey large-scale maps of a town (see
Chapter Six, page 143) and, map in hand, search out hopefully any of the buildings to
which one was affixed, in case any survive.

Though most towns' Acts refer generally to the improvement of the streets, some
will mention specific roads in the town. In Aldgate, for example, in 1771, the
Improvement Act, 11 Geo III, c. 23 was 'for paving and regulating Rosemary Lane from
the Parish of St Botolph Aldgate to Cable Street, also the said Cable Street, the footpath in Back Lane, part of the precinct of Well Close, the Street leading from
Nightingale Lane to Ratcliffe Cross, Butcher Row and Brook Street and the several
Streets, Lanes and Passages opening into the same . . .'.

A curious feature of these Acts is that the local Commissioners appear to
assume full responsibility for defining the bounds of their town to the satisfaction
of later Boundary Commissioners and are capable, as at Dudley, of re-defining
and expanding the bounds, if necessary at a later date. This will usually apply only
to 'town' as opposed to 'foreign' or 'parish' within a larger surrounding boundary;
similarly, the municipal and parliamentary bounds of the borough must often
be distinguished. A particular area of the town is often specified, separating in
medieval fashion the town 'within the walls' from the later growth outside the gates
(Canterbury 1787) or 'without the walls but within the Liberties' (Newcastle-on-Tyne
1812). This was a period when township was being established and defined, as well as
improved.

Opportunities for cross-reference, adding details of people and places from different
documents, are now arising, to give us a clear picture of many towns, their tradesmen
and residents. To the details of the Improvement Acts we can add the visual evidence
and topography of the town maps (Chapter Six), the identification of townsmen
named as Commissioners by means of the Commercial Directories (Chapter Nine) and,

finally, the house-to-house enumeration of the Census (Chapter Eleven). For a town as large as Birmingham the evidence becomes especially graphic.

Birmingham applied for eight main Improvement Acts, each extending the powers of the last, from 1768 to 1828; we see how conveniently the descriptions of the streets to be widened and improved can be matched with an almost exactly contemporary series of town maps, for example Bradford's (1751), Hanson's (1778) and Arrowsmith's (1834), for a 'before-and-after' comparison (see illustrations pages 191–193). It is significant to note how each successive Act extends its powers over more streets, for each Act provides a schedule of buildings to be taken down 'in pursuance of this Act'. The first Act (in 1768) required only eleven houses or 'tenements' to be demolished, most of them at the entrance to New Street; these are carefully measured; 234 feet of frontages, with their dimensions clearly identifiable. Also to be demolished were the upper 'roundabout house' (the first of St Martin's 'close' to go) and a 30 ft. by 15 ft. building fronting the Corn Market, its side towards the passage leading into St Martin's churchyard. The last house was in the occupation of one Francis Moules, who does not seem to have been important enough to find a place in Sketchley's *Directory of Tradesmen* in 1770 — presumably his livelihood had gone with his premises.

As four years passed, the Birmingham Commissioners discovered that the 1768 Act had proved insufficient 'though considerable improvement has been made in the execution of the said Act . . . Because a navigation canal has lately been made up to the said town of Birmingham a much greater number of carts and carriages are now used there than formerly in conveying goods and merchandise . . .'. Six more streets were affected by the new Act of 1772; six tenements and a blacksmith's shed were marked down in Moor Street, as well as six tenements, part of a close and 3 perches of land 'next to the road at the end of New Street' to make the road 60 ft. wide; four houses in Bull Lane, a tenement and enough land from Messrs. Duncombe and Co. to make the road by the side of St Philip's Church 30 ft. wide; another piece of land belonging to the same firm in Mount Pleasant in order to make the road 48 ft. wide; and a small tenement of James Onions in Smallbrook Street. Neither Duncombe nor James Onions can be found in Sketchley's *Directory* two years *before* their premises were demolished.

By 1801 the Commissioners' powers were again inadequate; 59 more 'messuages or tenements' in seven more streets between Dale End and St Martin's were listed for demolition. The Welsh Cross at the lower end of Bull Street, at its junction with Dale End, was to be removed; the Market Place widened; and the remaining parts of the Shambles was to be taken down, with seven more of St Martin's 'roundabout houses'. When the upper end of St Martin's Lane was widened, a tenement called the 'Engine House' was to be demolished. All the owners and occupiers of these premises are named in the schedule, but the properties are not as carefully measured as before.

In 1812 new powers to regulate the town's police force and its markets were entrusted to 'the same Commissioners'. Their first general measures (the usual prohibitions of projections, 'bulk-sashes' and open cellar steps and the requirement of rainwater spouts and gutters) reiterate the earlier regulations. It is startling, at this early decade of the 19th century, to find that prohibition of thatched houses was still necessary in Birmingham. Birmingham's 'Industrial Revolution' is clearly defined by the same Act's restrictions on pig-styes, dung-hills, wandering cattle and thatched houses alongside its requirement that steam-engines must be so designed as 'to consume their

9° GEORGII IV. *Cap*.liv.   1217

OWNERS.	OCCUPIERS.	DESCRIPTION.
*James Walmsley - -	Richard Bromwich - -	House and Appurtenances.
Ditto - -	Ann Mills - - -	Ditto.
Ditto - -	Joseph Smith - -	Ditto.
Ditto - -	Thomas Kesterton - -	Ditto.
Ditto - -	John Massingham - -	Ditto.
Ditto - -	Margaret Greenhill - -	Ditto.
Ditto - -	Samuel Hall -	Two Houses, Shops, and **Ap**-purtenances.
George Birch - -	Charles Dicken - -	Malthouse and Appurtenances.
Ditto - -	John Warner - -	House and Appurtenances.
Ditto - -	Elizabeth Turner - -	Ditto.
Ditto - -	William Wheal - -	Ditto.
Ditto - -	Mary Ingram - - -	Ditto.

Nelson Square.

Matthew Mills - -	Mary Hemming - - -	House.
Ditto - -	Hannah Horton - - -	Ditto.
Ditto - -	John Maddox - - -	Ditto.

Gullett.

Trustees and Executors of the late Edward Millward - - -	Mary Fletcher - - -	House and Appurtenances.
	Mary King - - - -	Ditto.

New Street.

John Hart, Lessee of W. P. Inge, Esquire -	Elizabeth George - -	House, Stable, Brewhouse, and Outbuildings.
William Ashburner, as Lessee to W. P. Inge, Esq. - -	Richard Harvey - - -	House and Appurtenances.
William Jones, Lessee to Governors of Free School - - -	William Jones and others	Rooms and Shops, or House and Appurtenances.
	John Benjamin - - -	House and Appurtenances.

Worcester Street.

James Onions, as Lessee to Free School - -	James Onions - - -	House.
	Thomas Deakin - - -	Ditto.

Edgbaston Street.

James Onions, as Lessee to Free School - -	Joseph Deakin - - -	Ditto.

Worcester Street.

Elizabeth Vowles, Lessee to W. P. Inge, Esquire	Elizabeth Vowles - -	House and Outbuildings.
Ditto - - -	William Tanner - - -	Ditto.
Ditto - - -	John Bagnall - - -	Ditto.
Ditto - - -	Hannah Smith - - -	Shops.
Ditto - - -	William Johnson - - -	Ditto.

[*Local*.]   14 *F*

* Continuation of Stafford Street.

Part of the Improvement Schedule for Birmingham, 1828, from 9 Geo. IV, c. 54,
Birmingham Reference Library, Local Studies Dept., actual size 6¾ in. x 12 in.

own smoke'. The Bull Ring was to be the new Market Place; the Beast Market was to be removed from Dale End and the entrance of New Street to the enclosure of the Moat House, where buildings were taken down in order to make an open space. New streets built by any private developer were to be of a minimum width of 42 ft. (many of the surviving streets of Birmingham still conform to this width); the Commissioners appointed surveyors to fix a building level, pave the gutters on each side of the new road and charge the ground tenants according to the breadth of their frontages. The street itself was to be paved by the owners. The 1812 Act has no further schedule of demolitions.

The last Act of this series was passed in 1828 and extends the Commissioners' activities more widely yet; taking in for widening and improvement some streets on the west side of St Philip's parish, which had been newly built within the half century since Hanson's 1785 map. The 11 page tabulated schedule to this Improvement Act (see illustration, page 180) comprises more than 350 properties for demolition in 34 Birmingham streets. They were mostly in the area between New Street and Edgbaston Street, but for the first time attention was turned to a group of northerly streets (now submerged beneath the great Masshouse roundabout). Many of the premises due for demolition in 1828 were slaughterhouses — there were 14 in Rann's Yard alone — piggeries, stables and outhouses; a machine house is listed at Snow Hill, dye-houses in St Martin's Lane and a tobacco warehouse in Moat Lane. As the printed schedule shows, the names of owners, occupiers and businesses can be traced in the contemporary directories.

Worcester City's chief preoccupation at this time was with the re-siting of its vital bridge over the Severn. (See the map on page 132). A toll-gate was to be erected on the western side of the bridge and the Improvement Act (passed in 1769) lists the scale of charges, which range from 5d. for 20 oxen, cows or meat cattle, or 2½d. for 20 calves, sheep or lambs, to 1s. 0d. for 'any coach, berlin, chariot, chaise, calash, hearse, litter or caravan drawn by six or more horses', or 6d. for 'any waggon, wain or wheel carriage drawn by six horses or other cattle' and 1½d. for 'every sledge or dray without wheels, drawn by three or more horses'. As well as the tolls, a contribution of £10 a year was to be paid by the Corporation towards the upkeep of the bridge. No house or building was to be erected on the new bridge, a prohibition and change of style which is also found in Leeds in 1760, when a similar Act ordered 'the removal of houses which straiten and obstruct the passage to and over the said bridge . . .'. Though four more 'paving and improving' Acts were passed for Worcester between 1770 and 1823, it is evident that the City was not under the same industrial pressure as Dudley and Birmingham; its needs, as the tolls show, were mainly those of an agricultural market town. Indeed, just as Speed's town map of 1610 (see above) is the last of the series of early documents which show the city in a leading position, so the Improvement Acts are the first documents which show the growing industrial towns taking the lead.

Responsibility for improvement was not invariably vested in a new body of Commissioners. We have seen the Corporation of Worcester involved in bridge-building; occasionally a private individual, as lord of the manor, might act. At Taunton in 1788 Sir Benjamin Hammett was empowered to build a new street. Very rarely, as at Kensington in 1789, the vestry was to act. The problem of fund-raising to pay for improvement was always pressing; frequent reference is made to rates to be raised or tolls to be taken. In London lotteries were sometimes organized by authority of the Acts, to fund the building of bridges, as at Westminster in 1738. The close connection of local rates and poor relief is often evident; for a short period during 1775–80 the dubious practice arose, again in London, of raiding the Orphans' Funds. In 1778 this sort of loan raised £4,000 in Southwark and £9,000 in Spitalfields to pay for public works. Otherwise, the most usual provision was the sale of Corporation property, as at Hereford in 1774, where the Corporation were prime movers in the improvement of the market. Rate-collection was an expensive item in itself, when handbills had to be printed, space taken in local newspapers, rate-collectors paid and legal costs defrayed. Dudley's were not the only town rates which were continually in arrears.

The scope of so many Improvement Commissions' work was immense. Our Gazetteer lists more than 800 Improvement Acts for 300 different places, ranging in size from London squares to cathedral cities, small market towns and thriving industrial areas. The local Commissioners' improvements could encompass the building of a town gaol, lighting the streets, building bridges, opening up new streets, organizing a fire brigade or police force, rebuilding a market hall, creating a pleasure garden or maintaining the Roman baths. Pump Rooms, Exchanges, Moot Halls and Court Houses were all part of this Georgian rebuilding programme.

It is impossible to date the beginning of this movement towards urban public works precisely. Chichester, Ipswich and Newark hark back to the precedents of Elizabethan statutes; Bristol cites *11 Wm III*, and Liverpool refers to an Act of Queen Anne's Parliament. As to 18th-century Improvement Acts in their more familiar widespread form, for 'paving, cleansing, lighting and watching' the streets, Norwich (1726) or Beverley (1727) might claim to be the first towns outside London to have turned to improvement. Several seaports had taken out local Acts even earlier in George I's reign (as, for example, Dover (1723)), but these were more concerned with the quayside than with the streets of the town. Some towns, such as Tiverton and Blandford, paid the penalty for picturesque half-timber and thatch; both towns were forced to seek Acts in 1737 'for better and more easily rebuilding after the late dreadful fire there'.

A graph (page 183) shows the wide distribution of these local Acts from the earliest Georgian years to the reign of William IV and the Municipal Corporations Act of 1835. It is interesting to note where any town appears – or fails to appear – on this time-scale of urban development, for, as in the case of town maps, provincial newspapers and commercial directories, their incidence is a 'barometer reading' of any town's growth, prosperity and aspirations to future status.

The Gazetteer to this Chapter reveals the extent of these Improvement Acts, so widespread over England and Wales. Of the 284 boroughs which were incorporated before 1835, 178 would be re-incorporated by the Municipal Corporations Act of that year. Of those, 105 had taken out improvement Acts between 1727 (Canterbury) and 1834 (Chippenham). More than 300 other Acts were passed on behalf of towns like Dudley, Manchester, Wolverhampton, Ramsgate, Taunton, Barnsley and Bolton. They are particularly thick on the ground in the non-municipal parishes around London which are now parts of Southwark, Camden and Tower Hamlets, or, as an Act of 1776 describes them, in the 'villages of Camberwell and Peckham . . .'. Birmingham, as we have seen, was improved by eight Acts before its incorporation in 1838.

DISTRIBUTION OF IMPROVEMENT ACTS

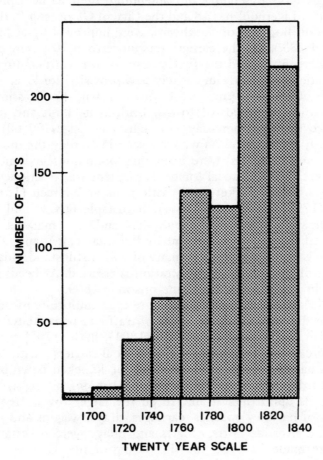

George I   1714 - 1727
George II 1727 - 1760
George III 1760 - 1820

Smaller towns, boroughs and non-boroughs alike, also petitioned Parliament for private Acts. Chudleigh in Devon sought powers to rebuild the town and prevent the further dangers of fire in 1808; Fishguard (Dyfed), opened a new market in 1834 and Frome (Som.) sought to 'enlighten' its streets in 1810. Cirencester (Gloucs.) in 1825, Melksham (Wilts.) in 1816, Stony Stratford (Bucks.) in 1801, Tetbury (Gloucs.) in 1817 and Wantage (Berks.) in 1828, are only a few examples of this widespread non-municipal movement. Even small villages like Ombersley (Worcs.) in 1814 and Potterne (Wilts.) in 1824 might seek private Acts, though these usually deal with relief of the poor or the erection of a new workhouse rather than a more urban style of 'improvement'. Generally speaking, the vast mass of local Acts on the Statute Books occur much later, during Queen Victoria's reign; the majority of earlier Georgian Acts are for towns which were already boroughs or would soon aspire to that status. Some towns applied for several Acts, 'extending and amending' their earlier applications. Bristol has at least 17 Acts, Liverpool has 18 and the City of Gloucester 9; the parishes which make up the London Borough of Southwark were improved by at least 37 local Acts between 1725 and 1835. Of the earlier Acts more than 70% were passed in the last quarter of the 18th century and the first quarter of the 19th century, just before the Municipal Corporations Act made an entirely new provision for local government.

The wide range of activities proposed by many towns' Commissioners gives a vivid picture of the state of hundreds of towns. Bridges are built and rebuilt on a scale reminiscent of the earliest Domesday boroughs (see pages 59–60). The town as a market is constantly to the fore. As we have seen in Dudley the dung and bloodbath of 'Beast Market and Shambles' were becoming 'obnoxious' nuisances in the centres of thriving commercial or industrial towns. Parliament was petitioned for the removal of Butchers' Rows, swine markets and cattle pens at Wisbech (1810), King's Lynn (1803), Newark (1798), Gloucester (1764), Barnstaple (1811) and Bridport (1785); and at Bristol, a new site was sought for the hay and straw markets. The status of the market town is confirmed at the same time by the enlargement and rebuilding of many elegant Market Halls and Moot Houses, many of which still stand today. In other cities the judicial aspect of the town's administration is asserted. At Leeds it was considered appropriate to build a new Court House and prison in 1809.

Just as the Acts' descriptive phrases conjure up a multitude of narrow streets and alleyways, so their descriptions of the types of traffic to be regulated are richly varied. These include sedan chairmen at Weymouth (1801), Bath (1793) and Chester (1762). At Bath too, there were 'basket-women' and 'coal-carriers', with 'water-carriers' at Hull. In Dudley's narrow streets residents could be knocked down by sledges, wheelbarrows, trucks, carriages, rolling casks or porters running by night, bearing unlighted bundles of iron rods upon their heads. In all the larger towns frequent reference is made to the hire of hackney coaches, carriages, drays, wagons and watermen. In the seaports and inland riverside ports, wharfs and quays were necessary. At Sandwich, arrangements were made in 1787 for the paving of the 'Common Quay belonging to the said town'. In London, the Improvement Acts are particularly detailed for individual parishes, streets and squares, and more numerous than in the provinces. Westminster alone produced more than 100 individual Acts, from Bayswater to the Strand and Regent's Square. A particularly attractive feature of the London and Westminster improvements is their concern for style as well as function. This applies particularly to the enclosing and paving of several famous squares, where, as early as 1726, an Act was sought 'to enable the present and future inhabitants of St James's Square to make a rate on themselves for raising money sufficient to clean, adorn and beautify the said Square and continue the same in repair . . .'.

Most Improvement Acts will take up more sheets of close print with complex legal safeguards of qualifications, fines, distraints, raising of capital by loans, definitions of rateable value and legitimate exemptions than will be devoted to graphic detail of social conditions. The Dudley Act in 1791 enrolled as Town Commissioners every person resident in the town, who paid rent of £20 a year, owned property of that value in his own or his wife's right, or possessed a personal estate valued at £800. The Birmingham Commissioners' qualifications were slightly different, being related to a Poor Law assessment of not less than £15 per annum and a personal estate of £1,000.

Unlike Dudley, Birmingham's first Act of 1768 lists the names of the first 50 Commissioners alphabetically. They were all prominent men, identifiable from Sketchley's *Directory* of 1770, including several medical practitioners and apothecaries, presumably as authorities on matters of public health. Otherwise, the following are all familiar names from any aspect of Birmingham's history of that time. Their names are taken from the Act, their addresses and trades are found in the *Directory*: John Baskerville, Printer, Easy Hill; William John Banner, Button-maker, 33 Steelhouse Lane; Samuel Bradburne, Ironmonger, 16 The Square; Thomas Bingham, Plate and Brass Nut-cracker maker, 54 Steelhouse Lane; John Cope, Druggist, 40 High Street ; Thomas Faulconbridge, Merchant, 11 New Hall Street; Samuel Garbett, Merchant, 11 New Hall Street; John Kettle, Merchant and Steel Convertor, 50 New Street; Sampson Lloyd, Sen. and Jnr., Merchants, 46 Edgbaston Street; John Oseland, Steel Converter, 3 The Square; Thomas Pemberton, Jeweller, 15 Snow Hill; Thomas Russell, Merchant, 50 Digbeth; Richard Rabone, Buckle Maker, 2 New Hall Street; and William Walsingham, Gun and Pistol Maker, 51 Park Street.

In towns such as Dudley, where the Improvement Act does not name the Commissioners, it is necessary to seek the Commission's Minute Book, which lists its members. It would be an interesting exercise to match those names against the owners of demolished properties, in order to discover whether the prominent citizens were more improvers than improved-upon. The Commissioners appointed in Dudley undertook to meet 'from time to time' at the sign of the *Dudley Arms*, the 'establishment's' assembly rooms and social club, depending upon a quorum of five members. Any later meeting of a larger number could revoke any measure passed before by an inadequately attended meeting, a dangerous clause. The Commissioners defrayed their own expenses and were debarred from any office or contract arising from their actions. They were empowered to appoint such 'Officers' as they found to be necessary, more particularly a clerk, a treasurer, surveyors, assessors of properties' values and rate collectors, as well as employees such as watchmen, scavengers, lamplighters and carters. Much of the work to be done was contracted out and all possible by-products, especially the 'muck' from the streets, were sold to the highest bidder. Legal costs were high and in more than one unfortunate case fell within appeal to the Statutes of Limitations, which meant that an individual citizen who had taken action on behalf of the Commission was left to pay the main costs of an Act out of his own pocket. Buildings listed for demolition raised handsome prices as compensation to the owners and costly litigation was always imminent. In the last resort many an urban Hampden flatly refused to carry out the Commissioners' orders.

There was no democratic principle involved in this type of premature 'local government'; the whole procedure is a typical 18th-century amalgam of private interest, philanthropy, jobbery and *laissez-faire* mixed up with an undeniable impulse towards public-spirited and a sense of responsibility which is usually unfairly denied to the Commissioners of most towns by their local historians. These gentlemen are too often dismissed as ineffectual, if not downright corrupt, with too little reference to the magnitude of their tasks and the novelty of their concept. It goes without saying that any group of Commissioners must have been conscious of opportunities for private advantage in town improvement. Paradoxically, as the wealthiest rate-payers, their main interest was as likely to become the pegging of as a low a rate as a limited amount of activity would demand — an attitude shared by many a metropolitan district council.

Occasionally they saw their function as jealous preservation of yet another form of private monopoly. In this role it is a shock to find that even a self-advertised radical like Dudley's Sam Cook would resist competition from any form of private association, effectively blocking the appeal to further essential Acts to 'amend and extend' their powers – and the rates – for as vital a matter as a healthy water supply in a cholera-ridden town. Some Improvement Acts must be interpreted as pious statements of intention rather than as definite and final arrangements. Certainly repeated prohibitions of the same sorts of anti-social behaviour and the constant need to extend inadequate powers must be checked against actual achievement, as revealed by town maps and official reports. The most important provision of all from the local student's point of view, is the requirement of an adequate record of the Commissioners' proceedings. In the Dudley Improvement Act, for instance, we can read: 'VI. And be it further enacted, That fair and regular Entries shall be made, in a Book to be provided for that Purposes, of all the Acts, Order, and Proceedings . . .'. The provision of a Minute Book for recording attendances and decisions of a Town's Commissioners adds an additional source of documentary evidence to the local archives. In Dudley, the Commissioners' Minute Books survive from 1791 to 1851, when a local Board of Health took over their responsibility for public welfare. The Minute Books record a sad history of irregular meetings and inadequate attendance, and are invariably cited as evidence of the Commissioners' failure to act responsibly. A specimen page of their 'fair and regular Entries' is illustrated on page 187. In some towns it will be possible to confirm the activities and attitudes of the Commissioners from reports in contemporary newspapers, as a Wolverhampton historian has done to good effect.[1] The author proves that press reports may show the Minutes to be incomplete records of the business of the Commissioners' meetings. Wolverhampton named 125 Commissioners!

The Dudley Commissioners' Minute Book, stored at the Borough Library, records a typical annual round of activity – and inactivity. The names of the original Commissioners are listed, with later replacements, almost all with the laconic annotation 'Dead' in later handwriting. Fortunately, the origins of the Improvement Commission coincide with the publication of several Dudley directories, so that the names of the prominent citizens who took office can be checked against their trades and addresses, as listed by Pearson and Rollason in 1781, by Bailey in 1784, in the *Universal British Directory* for 1793 and so on, for as long as the Commission lasts. Here we find Joseph Hodgetts, nail manufacturer; Edward Dixon, hop merchant and banker; Thomas Badger, nail and chain-maker; William Fellows, attorney; Joseph Amphlett, another ironmonger; Thomas Wainwright, surgeon; and others – tallow chandlers, mercers, tea-dealers, grocers, maltsters, mercers and booksellers. It brings these men to life again to see their flourishing signatures, week by week.

It is certainly true, as critics of the Commissioners invariably point out, that attendance was sporadic and meetings regularly postponed for want of a quorum. In the first half-year after the Dudley Act took effect there were ten meetings, of which four were abortive. In the second year, of 20 meetings only 6 were adjourned for want of members. By 1793–94, the number of sessions dropped from 16 to only 7 in the year – there were no meetings from May to September in 1794 – of which almost every other one was unproductive. From January to May 1793 the first six monthly meetings had no quorum. As the Minutes illustrated show, the Dudley Commissioners' range of activities was at a fairly basic level of lighting streets and organizing the

At a Meeting of the Commissioners of the before named Act of Parliament held at the Dudley's Arms Inn in Dudley this 15th day of November 1816 pursuant to the last Adjournment

We appoint Mr Wainwright Chairman of this Meeting.

A Requisition addressed to our Clerk was laid before us at this Meeting to take into consideration the propriety of establishing a Watch in this Town during the Winter.

We order that four men be employed for the above purpose and that they be required to enter upon their duty each Night at half past ten o'Clock, and continue on duty till five o'Clock in the Morning; and we authorize Mr Richard Moore and Mr Edward Guest to select and appoint proper Persons as Watchmen at such Wages as they shall agree upon finding each of them a Blue Flannel Great Coat —

Thomas Wainwright

Jos Dalton

Richd Moore

Booth Hodgetts

J. Robinson

Thos Badger

Edwd Guest.

Extract from the minutes of a meeting of Dudley's Commissioners, 15 November, 1816, from the Archives and Local Hist. Dept., Dudley Public Libraries, (each page 8 in. x 13 in.).

watchmen in their blue flannel greatcoats. Their meetings deal far less with the compulsory purchase of buildings to be demolished than was the case in the neighbouring town of Wolverhampton; the Dudley Commissioners were more concerned with un-muzzled dogs and un-numbered houses.

The main weakness of any body of Town Commissioners would inevitably be their continual inability to raise adequate funds for the costly compulsory purchases which were usually envisaged. This was a far more onerous burden than the original vestry commitments to unwilling 'voluntary' labour and obsolete statute-service. (See *Village Records*, Chapter IV). Dudley's Improvement Act laid down a scale of rates for this purpose:

(that is to say), all Perſons who ſhall occupy any ſuch Houſes, Granaries, Malt Houſes, Glaſs Houſes, or other Buildings, Yards, Gardens, and Lands as aforeſaid, under the yearly Value of Five Pounds, ſhall be rated and aſſeſſed at any Sum not exceeding One Shilling in the Pound of ſuch Annual Value; and that all Perſons who ſhall occupy any ſuch Houſes, Granaries, Malt Houſes, Glaſs Houſes, or other Buildings, Yards, Gardens, and Lands as aforeſaid, of the yearly Value of Five Pounds, or upwards, ſhall be rated and aſſeſſed at any Sum not exceeding Two Shillings in the Pound of ſuch Annual Value;

At 1s. or 2s. in the £1 Dudley's rates were higher than those fixed for Birmingham, which ranged on a sliding scale from 2d. in the £1 for property valued at £6–£10 per annum to 8d. for that worth £25. By 1812, Birmingham's rates rose no higher than 9d. to 1s. 6d. Even so, the total annual income from Dudley's rate was pathetically small for all that was required to be done, rising very little above the starting figure of £200 a year from 1793 to 1813. Even this amount was continually in arrears, despite the incentive offered to the collector of 6d. for himself of every £1 he collected. A meeting on 25th January 1804 found that Mr. Thomas Bate, the Rate Collector (a saddler by trade according to a directory), '. . . is now a considerable sum of money in arrear, and upon Application to him for payment he has neglected so to do. We therefore nominate and appoint Mr. William Roberts Collector in the Room and Stead of the said Thomas Bate and order that Notice of such appointment be given in all the places of Public Worship in this Town on the ensuing Sunday. We direct that our Clerk apply to Mr. Bate for the immediate Liquidation of his Account and in case the same is not paid or a satisfactory Security given on or before the 26th Day of January Inst., that legal Measures be taken for the Recovery thereof . . .'. The Commissioners soon decided to auction the rates to the highest bidder, usually at a sum of about £230 a year, to collect at whatever profit the speculator could make.

Meanwhile, the Pig Market was moved to the upper part of Castle Street; the houses in the main streets were numbered and the names of those streets were painted 'in large letters against the sides of the buildings in some conspicuous parts thereof ...'. 'Bulk' windows and building rubble were moved, at the owners' cost and no charge to the rates. It is, presumably, of some credit to the Commissioners that, before Dudley was ever incorporated, before the organization of a local Board of Health, Bentley could describe the town in his *Directory* of 1840 as an attractive 'place of resort': 'The streets are spacious, kept in excellent repair and at night well lighted with gas and the exterior appearance of the shops and houses in the principal streets and their interior replenishments show them to be of a spacious and substantial order ...'. By that time, the population of Dudley had tripled since 1791, to a total of 31,232 inhabitants. The rates had risen to £855 a year — and remained largely unpaid.

Directories, we must remember, represent publicity and public relations and must be carefully matched with other sources of information. Less flattering to the booming town are the dry, impartial Reports of various Government Inspectors, decade by decade. A fundamental problem left unsolved by the powerless Dudley Commissioners, was that of the town's inadequate and polluted water supply. Throughout the early 19th century successive plans were projected, maps made, reservoirs nominated, feeders planned, without a final solution. There was never sufficient water — from the church roofs, the contaminated wells, even the drainage water baled out from the mines in buckets by the women of the town. Not until the formation of the Dudley Waterworks Company in 1834 was the way opened to eventual takeover by the South Staffordshire Company, which survives today as a member of the Severn-Trent Water Authority. It takes only a cursory view of the present supply network — from neighbouring wells at Kinver, Ashwood and Prestwood, from the River Severn at Stourport, and the regulation of the river itself by reservoirs at Llanidloes — to appreciate what a losing battle the Commissioners of 1791 had committed themselves to.

In 1830, the price of foul water was cholera; in 1871 it was typhus. The medical Inspectors of the state of Dudley's health were less flattering than Bentley; their statistics are appalling. In 1852, William Lee, a superintending Inspector reporting to the General Board of Health,[2] noted that when the average age of death in England and Wales was 29.4 years, 41.4 in rural Worcestershire, and with London's inhabitants surviving to an average 29 years of age, Dudley's mortality bill was pegged at 16.7 years. Lee concluded that 'In no other part of England and Wales is the work of human extermination effected in so short a time as in the District surrounding Dudley and in no part of that District is the time so short as in the parish of Dudley. So far as the duration of life there is concerned, Dudley is the most unhealthy place in the country ...'. And, 'spacious' though the main streets might be, Dr. Lee's description of the rest of the industrial town is devastating: 'The whole of the mining part of the town' he reported, 'has the appearance of a place that has been terribly shaken by earthquakes ...'. There was, as one reliable local history measures it, one mile of drains for 36 miles of Dudley streets.[3] In 1832 the first cases of cholera were promptly followed by 600 deaths.

A later Report on the sanitary condition of the town in 1871 reveals how little real progress was being made against the rising tide of teeming humanity.[4] Dudley was by then an incorporated borough with a population of more than 40,000 people in 10,000 houses. 'In many parts of Dudley', Thorne, the compiler of the Report, writes, 'the houses may be seen grouped together regardless of plan, almost all available space being covered either by the dwellings themselves or by blocks and rows of nail shops, in such a way as to render proper ventilation impossible. The majority of the yards are dirty, neglected and unpaved. In their interiors, many of the houses are extremely filthy, being neglected by both landlord and tenant. The sleeping accommodation is in many instances peculiarly revolting, overcrowding in bedrooms being carried on to the extent of giving each person less than 90 cubic feet of space'. (The present Dudley Council's Housing Department's codes of practice would estimate about 5 to 6 times that amount of space per person in a modern council-house bedroom). Thorne's description of a court in Birmingham Street is a sad postscript to the well-intentioned efforts of 18th-century Town Commissioners to combat the 'nuisances' of 1791. This court 'presented the usual filthy appearance found in the poorer parts of the town. Refuse and ashes were lying about, and a large neglected midden shared in the task of polluting the atmosphere. In one cottage the family consisted of eight persons; seven had the fever and the eighth was apparently sickening of the same disease. They all slept in one room, a dilapidated window in the second bedroom rendering it uninhabitable . . .'. This was the town which, in 1856 had removed its medical officer of health as 'a useless and unnecessary Officer'.

The Town Commissioners' insoluble problem was, in fact, not nuisance, annoyance or unlighted streets, but the sickly congestion caused by an uncontrollable population growth. We must therefore turn our attention in a later Chapter to the main documents on population in the 19th century, the national censuses.

FURTHER READING

Chalklin, C. W., *The Provincial Towns of Georgian England 1740-1829* (1979).
Martin, E. W., *Where London Ends; English Provincial Life after 1750* (1957).
Morgan, P. & Clark, P., *Towns and Townspeople 1500–1780* (1977).
Roper, J. S., *Dudley: The Town in the Eighteenth Century* (Dudley Public Libraries Transcripts, No. 12, 1968).
Skipp, V., *A History of Greater Birmingham down to 1830* (1980).
Sutcliffe, A. (ed.), *The Rise of Modern Urban Planning* (1980).

These maps all come from Birmingham Reference Library, Local Studies Department. Each extract represents the same area of approximately 534 x 410 yards.

From 'The Plan of Birmingham Survey'd in the Year 1731' by William Westley. Full size of Westley's map, 11½ in. x 10½ in. at 10 perches: 7/16 in. or approx. 126 yds.: 1 in. Original size of extract 4¼ in. x 3¼ in. This map shows the market area. N.B. Westley's map is unusually orientated.

From 'A Plan of Birmingham Surveyed in MDCCL [1750] by Samuel Bradford . . .'. Full size of Bradford's map 32½ in. x 26 in. at 10 chains: 3½ in. or approx. 63 yds.: 1 in. Original size of extract 7½ in. x 6 in. Predating the first Improvement Act, this shows the Shambles, the Old Cross, the Swine Market and St Martin's 'Roundabout'.

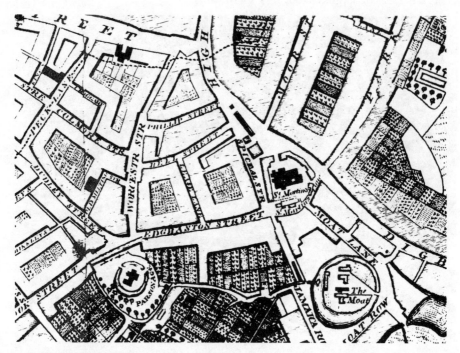

From 'A Plan of Birmingham Surveyed by Thos. Hanson in 1785'. Full size of Hanson's map 14 in. x 12 in. at 10 chains: 1⅜ in. or approx. 160 yds.: 1 in. Original size of extract 3 in. x 1¾ in. The 1768 Improvement Act had little effect; the Moat House and the Parsonage survive. Hanson's unshaded buildings give a misleading 'park' effect.

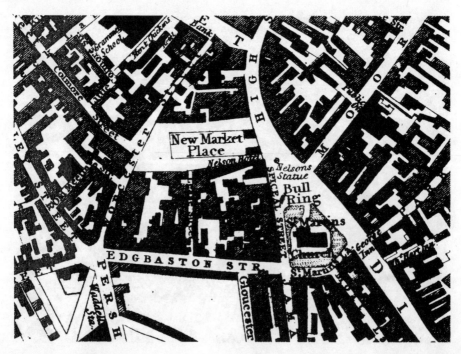

From 'A New Plan of Birmingham . . . by . . . J. Arrowsmith' (1834). Full size of Arrowsmith's map 27 in. x 22 in. at ½ mile: 3½ in. or approx. 250 yds.: 1 in. Orig. size of extract 2¼ in. x 1½ in. The effects of a series of Improvement Acts are now evident. Note the new Market Place and the clearance of the Bull Ring and Roundabout houses. The Old Cross has been replaced by a statue of Nelson and the Moat House by Smithfield Market.

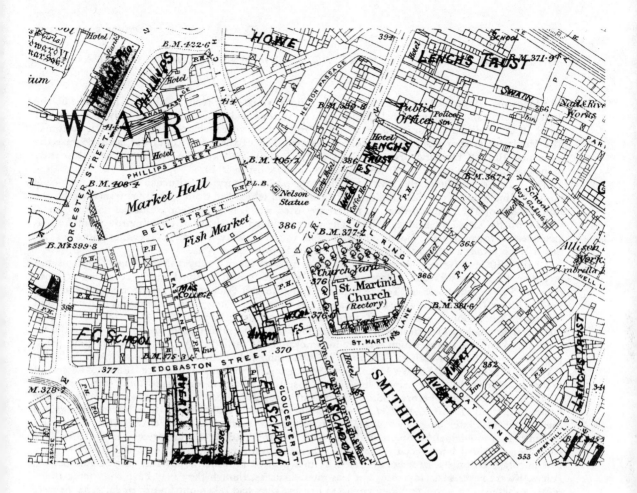

From Ordnance Survey Warwickshire Sheet XIV 5, surveyed in 1888: full size of the O.S. sheet 39 in. x 27 in. at 1/2500 being 25.344 inches to a statute mile or approximately 64½ yds.: 1 in. Original size of extract 6½ in. x 5 in. Note the new Market Hall and Fish Market and the increased width of most main streets. Streets shown here which had been designated for 'enlargement' in various Acts include Edgbaston Street, Worcester Street, Philip Street, Digbeth, Moat Lane, St Martin's Lane, Bell Street, New Street, Colmore Street, Bull Ring, Park Street and Jamaica Row. This copy was taken from a sheet with additional coloured shading and annotation to show freehold properties by the City Surveyor's Office in 1892. Note the Lench Trust's property (see Chapter Five).

GAZETTEER OF IMPROVEMENT ACTS AND MUNICIPAL INCORPORATIONS

The following Gazetteer lists 284 municipal boroughs which were recognized at least in name by the Parliamentary Commissioners of 1835, though they described 24 as 'municipal only in name' and listed 18 as 'manorial corporations' governed by royal and baronial charters or 'prescriptive customs'. The Municipal Corporations Act of 1835 reinstated 178 of these towns but did not recognize the remaining 106. Of the survivors, four (Bridgnorth, Ludlow, Stockton and Wenlock), later lost their municipal status, the others comprise about half our base-list in 1974.

The Gazetteer includes 69 towns which were parliamentary constituencies but not municipal boroughs, including those like Dudley and Birmingham which had been recently enfranchised by the Reform Act of 1832. In addition, 40 towns are listed which were neither municipal nor parliamentary boroughs (e.g., Trowbridge, Wilts.). These are included by virtue of their Improvement Acts, as examples of towns which, though not municipal in status, were nevertheless seeking improvement; this is by no means a complete list of non-municipal Improvement Acts.

Of the 830 Improvement Acts listed, the majority were taken out by 143 municipal boroughs, not including those parishes and villages which are now contained in the London boroughs of Westminster, Southwark, Camden, Tower Hamlets, Islington and Hackney etc.; these are numerous. We see that those towns which were boroughs in 1834 were more likely than other towns to have sought 'improvements', though exactly half their number had never applied for Acts when other non-municipal towns had. The following key describes the conventions used to describe the different types of town: All towns which were re-incorporated by the 1835 Act are named in **bold print**, (e.g.: **Wenlock**). Those which survived until 1974 as municipal or county boroughs are listed in **BOLD CAPITALS** (e.g.: **ABERYSTWYTH**). Towns which had been boroughs before 1835 but were not re-incorporated in 1835 are printed in *italics*. Those towns given in *lower-case italics* (e.g.: *Aberavon (Glam.)*) were boroughs before 1835 but were not recognized by the Act, nor at a later date. Those names printed in *ITALIC CAPITALS* were old boroughs not recognized in 1835, but which regained their status at a later date (e.g.: *ALDEBURGH*). Towns listed in ROMAN CAPITALS, though not recognized as municipal boroughs in 1835, were incorporated later and survived until 1974; they have been included here because they had taken out Improvement Acts (e.g.: DUDLEY) or were Parliamentary boroughs, later incorporated. Names printed in roman lower case (e.g.: Gainsborough (Lincs.)) were never officially recognized as municipalities, though they may have considered themselves to be 'private' boroughs; they are listed because they had taken out Improvement Acts, or were parliamentary constituencies, with or without 'improvements'. The names of counties are not given for any 1974 borough (in roman capitals) which is normally included in the base-list; counties as they were in 1835 are given for the less familiar towns not usually included. Boroughs which are normally on the base-list but are not included in this Gazetteer, had no municipal or parliamentary status in 1835 and have not, as yet, disclosed any Improvement Act to the author.

Abbreviations relating to towns:

Co. = a city which is also a county of its own.
M. = municipal status recognized by the Parliamentary Commissioners and reaffirmed by the Municipal Corporations Act.
M. = pre-1835 borough not reincorporated by the Act.
(M) = town which the Parliamentary Commissioners described as 'Municipal only in name'.
* = inserted before the place-name indicates town which the Commissioners described as Manorial Corporation.
P = Parliamentary borough in 1835.
(P) = borough which had been *completely* disenfranchised by the Reform Act of 1832.
P* = borough which had been enfranchised by the Reform Act.
Dates: The first date given in *italics* immediately after the place-name is that of the 'governing charter' recognized by the Commissioners; this is usually a later date than that of the earliest charter claimed by the town in most Gazetteers and Year Books, which is the second date given after the town's designation (M. P. etc.). Where there is a *single* date as (1869) or (1179), this *either* means the Commissioners did not include it, *or* that the charter was granted after 1835.
(*p*) = in place of the first date indicates the Commissioners' decision that a town was considered an incorporated borough 'by prescriptive customs'. This may be stated in some cases where the town gives a charter.

(nc) = similarly indicates that the Commissioners did not find, or approve any charter. The towns' governing charters are tabulated in vol. 7 of the Commissioners' Reports (pages 261–264); there are several omissions in this Table.

Population: The populations of those towns which were *not* incorporated by the Act of 1835 are given; their average is about 1,500 inhabitants per town, ranging from 68 in Newtown, Isle of Wight, to 5,000 at Alnwick (Nmbld.). Wherever a town was a parliamentary and municipal borough, any difference in each population is indicated by m and p with the population figures.

Sources: All the above data are taken from: *The First Report of the Commissioners on Municipal Corporations of 1835*, and are mostly tabulated in vols. 2 and 7. The report is published in the Irish University Press series of *British Parliamentary Papers* (1969). Reference should also be made to the tabulated schedules appended to the *Municipal Corporations Act* itself, in *Statutes at Large: 5-6 Wm IV, c. 76.* To seek out any town's Improvement Act inadvertently omitted from this Gazetteer, refer to the following Indexes: Bramwell, G., *Index to the Private Acts, 1727-1834; an Analytical Table* (1835); Vardon, T., *Index to the Private Acts, 1798-1839*; or, more usually available on open reference shelves: *Index to Local and Personal Acts, 1801-1949* (H.M.S.O. 1949). Failing these Indexes, the student must resort to a more laborious search of the large printed volumes of *The Statutes at Large* available, for example, at Birmingham Reference Library. Each volume comprises two to four years of Parliamentary Acts with some of their texts, and a useful chronological contents list at the beginning. Later volumes, of the Acts of George III also have a 'copious Index' in alphabetical order of subjects at the end of each volume which will list Acts under *Paving and Improvement* and, sporadically, by names of places. Fortunately, most reference libraries offer an 'internal' printed index to relevant local Acts which refer either to the borough itself, or to its locality. Thus in Birmingham Reference Library the *Miscellaneous Local and Private Acts (Staffs., Warwicks. and Worcs.)*, refers, not only to Birmingham, but also to other towns, such as Redditch, Kidderminster, Stafford etc. Similarly, even smaller town libraries often hold copies of the full text of particular Acts, as in the case of the *Dudley Improvement Act, 1791* used in the Chapter, which is available for reference at Dudley Public Library.

Abbreviations of Details of Improvements

Am   = Amending, extending and explaining earlier Acts.
B   = Special building regulations, e.g.: prohibiting thatch.
BG   = Provision for a burial-ground.
Bo   = Definition of the boundaries of the Commissioners' authority.
Br   = Building and rebuilding bridges.
C   = Cleansing streets, scavenging and refuse collection.
CH   = Building, rebuilding or demolishing a Court House (also refers to Town Hall, Sessions House, Moot Hall, etc.). See also MH.
F   = Provision of fire-engines, firemen etc.
G   = Town Gaol to be built or rebuilt.
Gas = H.M.S.O. *Index to Local and Personal Acts* lists all early lighting under *Gas*, including some surprisingly early examples before 1814, usually taken as the earliest date for street gas-lighting. See the same *Index* for later references to *Electric Lighting, Tramways* etc.
I:LG = Reference to the same *Index* of Acts 1801-1949 includes all Improvement Acts under *Improvement and Loc. Govt.* a quick but inadequate ref. to the real content of these Acts.
L   = Lighting streets by oil or gas-light.
MH   = Market House demolished, re-sited or re-built.
Misc = Miscellaneous and unusual provisions, e.g.: 'Protection of the Roman Baths' at Bath and enlargement of the Pump Rooms.
Mk   = Market regulations or change of a market's site.
N   = Removal and prevention of nuisances, annoyances, obstructions.
NS   = Opening up new streets.
Nav. = In seaports, harbours or river-basins; regulations for navigation.
P   = Paving streets (usually includes drainage).
PH   = License for a play-house.
Po   = Organization of a police force (see also W).
Poor = Provision for poor-law relief or labour.
Q   = Regulations for quays, wharves, docks or piers in ports and harbours.
S   = Sale of land or other means of defraying costs or raising funds.
Sew = Sewage disposal.
Tr   = Regulation of transport within the town, e.g.: Hackney carriages, porters, etc.
W   = Watching by day or night.
Wd   = Widening streets or approaches to a new bridge.
Wtr = Provision of water supply.

GAZETTEER OF IMPROVEMENT ACTS AND MUNICIPAL INCORPORATIONS

Aberavon (Glam.): (*p*); M. P.; (1372); (Pop. m
573, p 2,350).

ABERGAVENNY: (1542?); 34 Geo III, c. 106
(1794) I:LG; 55 Geo III, c. 24 (1815) I:LG.

ABERYSTWYTH: (*p*); M. P. (1227); 5-6 Wm IV,
c. 46 (1835) I:Wtr.

ABINGDON: (*1556*); M. P. (1556); 34 Geo III,
c. 89 (1794) P:C:L:W:N.

Adpar (Card.): P.

ALDEBURGH: (*1636*). M. (P); (Pop. 1,538).

Almwch (Angs.): P.

Alnwick (Nmbld.): (*p*); M. (Pop. 5,000).

ALTRINCHAM: (temp. Ed I) (M); (Ed I &
1937).

ANDOVER: (*1600*); M. P. (1157); 55 Geo III,
c. 43; (1815) P:C:L:N.

APPLEBY: (*p*); M. (P) (1179); (Pop. 1,233).

ARUNDEL: (*p*); M. P. (1586); 6 Geo II, c. 12
(1825) Q; 25 Geo III, c. 90 (1785) P:C:L:N.

Ashburton (Devon): P.

ASHTON-UNDER-LYNE: (*nc*); M. P*; (1847);
(Pop. m 'not stated', p 14,673); 7-8 Geo IV
c. 77 (1827) I:LG; 9 Geo IV, c. 42 (1828)
I:LG.

Axbridge (Som.): (*1600*); M. (1600); (Pop. 998).

AYLESBURY: P. (1882).

Bala (Merioneth): (*nc*); (M); (Pop. 2,359).

BANBURY: (*1714-15*); M.P.; 6 Geo IV, c. 130
(1825) P:C:L:W:I.

BANGOR: (*nc*); M. P. (?   and 1883); (Pop.
m 'none'; p 4,000).

BARNSLEY: (1869); 3 Geo IV, c. 25 (1882)
I:LG.

BARNSTAPLE: (*1610*); M. P. (930); 51 Geo III,
c. 154 (1811) P:I:Mk.

BASINGSTOKE: (*1641*); M. (1392); 55 Geo III,
c. 7 (1814) P:C:W:Wd:I.

BATH: (*1590*);|M. P. (1590); 30 Geo II, c. 65
(1757) C:L:P:Tr; 6 Geo III, c. 70 (1765) Mk:
Wd:P:C:L:W:I:N:Wtr; 8 Geo III, c. 10 (1767)
PH; 29 Geo III, c. 73 (1789) Baths: Pump
Room:Wd; 33 Geo III, c. 89 (1793) P:C:W:N:
Po:Tr; 41 Geo III, c. 126 (1801) P:C:L:W:
N:Po; 6 Geo IV, c. 74 (1825) Am:(P:C:L:W).

BEAUMARIS: (*1562);* M. P. (1294).

BECCLES: (*1664*);|M. – (1584); 36 Geo III,
c. 51 (1796) P:C:L:I.

BEDFORD: (*1604*); M. P. (1166); 43 Geo III,
c. 128 (1803) I:Br; 50 Geo III, c. 82 (1810)
Am.

Berkeley (Gloucs.) (*p*); M. – (Pop. 900).

BERWICK-UPON-TWEED: (*1604*); M. P. Co.;
(1302); 40 Geo III, c. 25 (1800) L:Q:Br:
P:N.

BEVERLEY: (*1685*); M. P. (1573); 13 Geo I,
c. 4 (1727) C; 48 Geo III, c. 87 (1808) Am:
(L:W:I).

BEWDLEY: (*1605*); M. P. (1462).

BIDEFORD: (*1618*); M. – (1573).

BIRKENHEAD: – – (1877); 3-4 Wm IV, c. 68
(1834) I:LG.

BIRMINGHAM: – P* (1838); 8-9 Geo III, c. 83
(1768) Wd:I:C:L:N.; 13 Geo III, c. 36 (1773)
Am:(Wd:I:C:L:N); 41 Geo III, c. 39 (1801)
Am:(Wd:I:C:L:N); 52 Geo III, c. 113 (1812)
Po: Mk; 9 Geo IV, c. 54 (1828) P:L:W:C:Wd;
Bordesley and Deritend: 28 Geo III, c. 70
(1788) I:LG; 31 Geo III, c. 17 (1791) C:L:W:
N:Tr; Aston: 10 Geo IV, c. 6 (1829) I:LG.

Bishop's Castle (Salop): (*1617*); M. (P) (1618);
(Pop. 1,729).

BLACKBURN: – P* (1851); 43 Geo III, c. 39
(1803) I:LG.

BLANDFORD FORUM: (*1605*); M. – (1605);
5 Geo II, c. 16 (1732) B:F.

BODMIN: (*1798*); M. P. (1798); 55 Geo III,
c. 85 (1815) Mk; 6-7 Wm IV, c. 12 (1836)
I:LG.

BOLTON: – P* (1838); 57 Geo III, c. 59 (1817)
I:LG; 11 Geo IV, c. 46 (1830) I:LG.

Bossiney (Cornwall): (*p*); (M) (P); (Pop. 330).

BOSTON: (*1545*); M. P. (1545); 16 Geo III
c. 25 (1776) L:W:N; 32 Geo III, c. 80 (1792)
P:C:I; 46 Geo III, cc. 40, 41 (1806) Am:
(L:W:N).

BRACKLEY: (*1687*); (M) (P) (1687).

BRADFORD: – P* (1847); 43 Geo III, c. 90
(1803) A:LG.

Brading (Hants): (*1547*) (M) (1547); (Pop.
2,000).

Bradninch (Devon): (*1605*); M – (1605);
(Pop. 1,524).

BRECON: (*1555*); M. P. (1412); 16 Geo III,
c. 56 (1776) Wtr:P:C:I:L:Wd.

Bridgnorth: (Salop)' (*1426*); M. P. (1426).

BRIDGWATER: (*1683*); M. P. (1200); 19 Geo
III, c. 36 (1779) MH:P:C:L:W; 7 Geo IV, c. 7
(1826) MH:Mk:P:C:L:W.

BRIDPORT; (*1666*); M. P. (1253); 8 Geo I,
c. 11 (1772) Q; 25 Geo III, c. 91 (1785)
MH:CH:Mk:P:C:L:W:N:B.

BRIGHTON: – P* (1854); 13 Geo III, c. 34
(1773) P:L:C:N:Mk:Nav.; 50 Geo III,
c. 38 (1810) I:LG; 6 Geo IV, c. 179 (1825)
I:LG.

BRISTOL: (*1709*); M. P. Co. (1188); 11 Wm III,
c. 23 (1699) Nav:C:P:L; 8 Geo I, c. 5 (1722)
Exchange; 22 Geo II, c. 20 (1749) Am:(Nav:
C:P:L):Tr:Mk; 28 Geo II, c. 32 (1755) W;
29 Geo II, c. 47 (1756) Am: (W); 33 Geo II,
c. 52 (1760) Br:Wd:Am; 6 Geo III, c. 34
(1766) Am:(P:C:L:W:I); 8-9 Geo III, c. 66
(1769) Hospital; 14 Geo III, c. 55 (1774)
Wd:BG; 26 Geo III, c. 111 (1786) Am:
(Br:Wd); 28 Geo III, c. 65 (1788) N:Tr:Q:W:
Nav; 28 Geo III, c. 66 (1788) B; 28 Geo III,
c. 67 (1788) Wd:CH:Records; 46 Geo III, c.
26 (1806) Am:(P:C:L); 2 Geo IV, c. 89
(1821) L:W:Poor; 3 Geo IV, c. 4 (1822) Poor:
Am:(P:C:L); Clifton: 5 Geo IV, c. 79 (1824)
I:LG.

BUCKINGHAM: M.P. (*1553*); (1553).

BURNLEY: — — (1861); 59 Geo III, c. 34
(1819) I:LG.
BURTON-ON-TRENT: (*nc*); (M); (Pop. 4,399);
(1878); 19 Geo III, c. 39 (1799) P:C:L:N
BURY: — P* (1876).
BURY ST EDMUNDS: (*1668*); M. P. (1606);
21 Geo II, c. 21 (1748) Poor:P; 51 Geo III,
c. 9 (1811) P:C:L:W:I; 1 Geo IV, c. 61
(1820) Am:(P:C:L:W:I).
Caergwrle (Flints.): (*nc*); M. P. (1351); (Pop.
m. 402; p. 402).
CAERNARFON: (*1558*); M. P. (1558).
**Caerwys (Flints.)*: (*1408*); M. P. (1408); (Pop.
m 500, p. 500).
CALNE: (*p*); M. P. (1565).
CAMBRIDGE: (*1631*); M. P. (1207); 7 Geo III,
c. 99 (1767) Hospital; 28 Geo III, c. 64
(1788) P:C:L:N:Wd; 34 Geo III, c. 104
(1794) Am:(P:C:L:N:Wd).
CAMDEN: — —: Bloomsbury: 34 Geo III c. 96
(1794) P:C:L:W; 39–40 Geo III, cc. 1, 50
(1800) (Russell Square) I; 46 Geo III, c. 134
(1806) (St Giles-in-Fields) I:LG; 47 Geo III,
c. 38 (1807) I:LG; 59 Geo III, c. 73 (1819)
I:LG; 11 Geo IV, c. 10 (1830) I:LG. Cal-
thorpe Estate: 54 Geo III, c. 128 (Gray's Inn
Lane) (1804) I:LG. Camden Town: 3 Geo
IV c. 82 (1822) I:LG. Clerkenwell: 11 Geo
III, c. 33 (1771) P:C:L:W:N; 14 Geo III, c. 24
(1774) P:L:W:Wd; 17 Geo III, c. 63 (1777)
Am:(P:L:W:N):C:Wd; 10 Geo IV, c. 101
(1829) I:LG. Hampstead: 15 Geo III, c. 58
(1775) L:W. Harrison Estate: 50 Geo III,
c. 170 (1810) I:LG. Holborn: 10 Geo II, c.
25 (1737) W; 6 Geo III, c. 100 (1766) Poor:
C:L:W; 39 Geo III, c. 41 (1799) W; 47 Geo
III, c. 38 (1807) I:LG; 59 Geo III, c. 119
(1819) I:LG; 6 Geo IV, c. 175 (1825) I:LG;
2–3 Wm IV, c. 66 (1832) I:LG. Kentish
Town: 55 Geo III, c. 194 (1815) I:LG; 57
Geo III, c. 14 (1817) I:LG; 7–8 Geo IV,
c. 45 (1827) I:LG. Lincoln's Inn Fields:
8 Geo II, c. 26 (1735) C. Red Lion Square:
10 Geo II, c. 15 (1724) P:W:C; 46 Geo III,
c. 76 (1806) I:LG. St Pancras: 29 Geo III,
c. 71 (1789) P:L:C:W:N; 31 Geo III, c. 18
(1791) Am:(P:L:C:W:N); 37 Geo III, c. 80
(1797) P:C:L:W; 39–40 Geo III, c. 89 (1800)
I; 41 Geo III, c. 131 (1801) I:LG; 43 Geo
III, c. 139 (1803) I:LG; 48 Geo III, c. 86
(1808) I:LG; 49 Geo III, c. 49 (1809) P:C:
L:W; 50 Geo III, cc. 147, 170 (1810) I:LG;
51 Geo III, c. 155 (1811) I:LG; 52 Geo III,
c. 74 (1812) I:LG; 53 Geo III, c. 62 (1813)
I:LG; 54 Geo III, c. 155 (1814) I:LG; 55 Geo
III, cc. 25, 58 (1815) I:LG; 56 Geo III, c. 82
(1816) I:LG; 57 Geo III, c. 14 (1817) I:LG;
3 Geo IV, cc. 81, 82 (1822) I:LG; 5 Geo IV,
c. 70 (1824) I:LG; 7–8 Geo IV, c. 45 (1827)
I:LG. Somers Town: 3 Geo IV, c. 81 (1823)
I:LG. Southampton Estate: 41 Geo III, c.131
(1801) I:LG; 43 Geo III, c. 139 (1803) I:LG;
55 Geo III, c. 25 (1815) I: LG.

Camelford (Cornwall): (*1669*); M (P): (Pop.
597).
CANTERBURY: (*1604*); M. P. Co. (1448)
1 Geo II, c. 20 (1727) Poor:L; 27 Geo III
c. 14 (1787) P:C:L:W:N; 3, 4, 5 and 6 Geo
IV (1822–26) I:LG.
CARDIFF: (*1600*); M. P. (1608); 14 Geo III,
c. 7 (1774) P:C:L:N; 5–6 Wm IV, c. 51
(1835) I:LG.
CARDIGAN: (*p*); M. P. (1230).
CARLISLE: (*1637*); M. P. (1158) 44 Geo III,
c. 58 (1804) L:P:I; 7–8 Geo IV, c. 86 (1827)
W:I.
CARMARTHEN: (*1761*); M. P. Co. (1313); 45
Geo III, c. 3 (1803) I:LG.
**Castle Rising (Norf.)*: (*p*); M. (P); (Pop. 887).
Cefn Llys (Radnor.): — P.
CHARD: (*p*); M. — (1570).
CHATHAM: — P* (1891); 12 Geo III, c. 18
(1772) P:C:W:L:N; 16 Geo III, c. 58 (1776)
Am:(P:C:W:L:N).
CHELMSFORD: — — (1888); 29 Geo III, c. 44
(1789) P:C:L:W:N; 3 Geo IV, c. 59 (1822)
I:LG.
CHELTENHAM: — P* (1876); 26 Geo III, c. 116
(1786) P:C:L:B:N; 46 Geo III, c. 117 (1806)
I:LG; 1–2 Geo IV, c. 121 (1821) I:LG; 3–4
Wm IV, c. 21 (1833) I:LG.
CHESTER: (*1506*); M. P. Co. (1506); 2 Geo III,
c. 45 (1762) P:C:L:W:F:Tr; 17 Geo III, c. 14
(1777) PH; 28 Geo III, c. 82 (1788) Am:(W:
L:C):N:Po; 43 Geo III, c. 47 (1803) I:Tr.
CHESTERFIELD: (*1598*); M. — (1598); 6 Geo
IV, c. 77 (1825) I:LG.
CHICHESTER: (*1685*); M. P. (1685); 25 Geo II,
c. 99 (1752) Poor:L; 31 Geo III, c. 63 (1791)
P:C:N; 47 Geo III, c. 68 (1807) I:LG; 1–2
Geo IV, c. 68 (1821) L:W.
CHIPPENHAM: (*1554*); M. P. (1554); 4 Wm IV,
c. 47 (1834) L:C:W:P:I.
CHIPPING NORTON: (*1606*); M. — (1606).
**Chipping Sodbury (Gloucs.)*: (*p*); (M) (1693);
(Pop. 1,306).
CHRISTCHURCH: (*nc*); M. P. (p) and (1886).
Cirencester (Wilts.): — P.
CLITHEROE: (*p*); M. P. (1147).
Clun (Salop): (*temp. Ed. II*): M —; (Pop. 930).
Cockermouth (Cumb.): — P.
COLCHESTER: M. P. (1189); 51 Geo III, c. 43
(1811) I:LG.
CONGLETON: (*1625*); M. — (1272).
CONWY: (*1547*); M. P. (1284).
Corfe Castle (Dorset): M. (P) (*nc*); (Pop. 960).
COVENTRY: (*1622*); M. P. Co. (1345); 3 Geo
III, c. 41 (1763) P:C:L:N:Wtr; 8 Geo III,
c. 40 (1768) G; 30 Geo III, c. 77 (1790)
P:C:W:N:L:Wtr; 54 Geo III, c. 45 (1814)
I:LG; 1–2 Geo IV, c. 1 (1821) I:LG:Gas.
Cowbridge (Glam.): (*1681*); M.P. (1693); (Pop.
m 1,097, p. 1,097).
Criccieth (Caern.): (*nc*) M. P.; (Pop. 500).
Crickhowell (Brecon.): (*p*) (M); (Pop. 1,061).
Cricklade (Wilts.): — P.

CROYDON: — —; 46 Geo III, c. 130 (1806)
L:LG; 10 Geo IV, c. 73 (1830) I:LG.
DARLINGTON: — — (1867); 4 Geo IV, c. 3
(1823) L:C:W:I.
DARTFORD: — — (1933); 54 Geo III, c. 108
(1814) I:LG.
DARTMOUTH: (1605); M. P. (1341); 55 Geo
III, c. 28 (1815) MH:P:L:Wd:I.
DAVENTRY: (1576); M. — (1595); 46 Geo III,
c. 118 (1806) P:C:L:W:Mk:CH.
DEAL: (1699); M. — (1699); 31 Geo III, c. 64
(1791) P:C:N; 36 Geo III, c. 45 (1796)
Am:(P:C:N); 52 Geo III, c. 73 (1812) P:C:L:
W:N.
DENBIGH: (1662): M. P. (1290).
DERBY; (1682); M. P. (1154); 28 Geo III, c. 64
(1788) Br; 32 Geo III, c. 78 (1792) P:C:L:I:S;
6 Geo IV, c. 132 (1825) P:I.
Devonport (Devon): — P.
DEVIZES: (1639); M. P. (1605); 21 Geo III,
c. 36 (1781) I:C:L:W:N; 6 Geo IV, c. 162
(1825) P:L:C:W:I:N.
*Dinas Mwdw (Merion.): (M) — (nc).
DONCASTER: (1664); M. — (1194); 43 Geo III,
c. 147 (1803) Am:(L:W:I:N).
DORCHESTER: (1629); M. P. (1324); 16 Geo
III, c. 27 (1776) P:C:L:W:N:B; 4 Wm IV
(22 May) (1833) P:C:L:W:I.
DOVER: (nc: refused to submit records); M. P.
(1278); 9 Geo I, c. 30 (1723) Q; 10 Geo I, c.
7 (1724) Am:(Q); 31 Geo II, c. 8 (1758) Am:
(Q); 18 Geo III, c. 76 (1778) P:C:L:W:N;
50 Geo III, c. 26 (1810) Am:(P:C:L:W:N); 7
Geo IV, c. 5 (1826) I:LG; 11 Geo IV, c. 117
(1830) I:LG.
DROITWICH: (1624); M. P. (1215); 28 Geo II,
c. 48 (1755) Wd:P.
DUDLEY: — P* (1865); 31 Geo III, c. 70
(1791) P:C:W:L:N:Wtr.
DUKINFIELD: — — (1899); 6 Geo IV, c. 67
(1825) I:LG.
Dunmow (Essex): (1597); (M) — (1597); (Pop.
2,462).
Dunwich (Suff.): (1694); M. (P) (1694); (Pop.
232).
DURHAM: (1780); M. P. (1602); 30 Geo III,
c. 67 (1790) P:C:L:W:I:N:Wd:Mk; 3 Geo
IV, c. 26 (1822) I:LG.
*Dursley (Gloucs.): (p); (M) — ; (Pop. 3,266).
EALING: — — ; 7 Geo III, c. 72 (1767) Wd:I.
EAST RETFORD: (1607); M. P. (1246).
EVESHAM: (1606); M. P. (1604); 3 Geo IV,
c. 67 (1822) P:C:W:I:Br:S.
EXETER: (1627); M. P. Co. (1156); 1 Geo III,
c. 28 (1761) L; 46 Geo III, c. 39 (1806)
Am:(I:L):W; 50 Geo III, c. 146 (1810)
P:L:C:W:I; 2-3 Wm IV, c. 108 (1832) P:L:
W:C:I.
EYE: (1697); M. P. (1206).
FALMOUTH: (1661); M. P. (1661).
Farnham (Surrey): (nc): (M); (Pop. 3,142).
FAVERSHAM: (1545); M. — (1252); 28 Geo
III, c. 69 (1768) P:C:L:W:N.

Finsbury (Mx): — P*; see Islington.
Fishguard (Pembs): M. P. (nc); (Pop. m 750,
p 1,600); 4-5 Wm IV, c. 66 (1834) Mk.
FLINT: (1337); M. P. (1284); 53 Geo III, c. 49
(1813) I: LG.
FOLKESTONE: (1668); M. — (1313); 36 Geo
III, c. 109 (1796) P:C:N.
Fordwich (Kent): (p); M. — ; (Pop. 487).
Fowey (Cornwall): (nc); (M) — ; (Pop. 1,767).
Frome (Som.): — P*.
Gainsborough (Lincs): — — ; 8-9 Geo III, c. 21
(1769) P:C:L:W:S; 27 Geo III, c. 15 (1787)
Br.
Garstang (Lancs.): (1679) M. — ; (Pop. 929).
GATESHEAD: (p); M. P* (nc) and (1835);
54 Geo III, c. 109 (1814) C:L:I.
GLASTONBURY: (1705); M. — (1705); 51 Geo
III, c. 173 (1811) P:I.
GLOUCESTER: (1672); M. P. Co. (1483);
14 Geo II, c. 11 (1741) Wtr; 23 Geo II, c. 15
(1750) B:Wd:Mk; 4 Geo III, c. 60 (1764)
Poor:L; 17 Geo III, c. 68 (1777) Br:P:C:N;
21 Geo III, c. 74 (1781) G:Am:(Poor):L:
P; 1-2 Geo IV, c. 22 (1821) Mk:W:I; 2-3
Wm IV, c. 89 (1833) I:LG; 4 Wm IV, c. 44
(1834) I:LG; 59 Geo III, c. 69 (1819) Gas.
GODALMING: (1666); M. — (1575); 51 Geo
III, c. 172 (1811) Mk; 54 Geo III, c. 20
(1814) Gas; 6 Geo IV, c. 177 (1825) P:L:
W:I; 9 Geo IV, c. 14 (1828) Mk.
GODMANCHESTER: (1605); M. — (1605).
GOSPORT: — — (1922); 3 Geo III, c. 55
(1822) P:N.
Grampound (Cornwall): (nc) (M); (Pop. 715).
GRANTHAM: (1613); M. P. (1463); 27 Geo
III, c. 61 (1787) CH.
GRAVESEND: (1631); M. — ; (1562); 13 Geo
III, c. 15 (1773) P:C:L:N; 56 Geo III, c. 77
(1816) Am:(P:C:L:N):Poor; 3 Geo IV, c. 51
(1822) P:C:L:W:I:N.
GRIMSBY: (1688); M. P. (1201).
GREAT YARMOUTH: M. P. (1208); 9 Geo I,
c. 10 (1722) Q; 23 Geo II, c. 6 (1750) Q:
Nav:F; 50 Geo III, c. 23 (1810) P:L:C:W:N:I.
GREENWICH: — P*; 33 Geo III, c. 11 (1760) B;
4 Geo IV, c. 70 (1823) I:LG; 9 Geo IV, c. 43
(1828) I:LG; 11 Geo IV, c. 48 (1830) I:LG.
Woolwich: 47 Geo III, c. 43 (1807) I:LG.
GUILDFORD: (1337); M. P. (1257); 32 Geo II,
c. 58 (1759) W:L; 52 Geo III, c. 51 (1812)
P:C:I.
HACKNEY: — — : Blackwell: 53 Geo III, c. 84
(1813) I:LG. Newington: 52 Geo III, c. 111
(1812) I:LG; 54 Geo III, c. 113 (1814) I:LG;
3 Geo IV, c. 112 (1822) I:LG; 7 Geo IV, c. 35
(1826) I:LG; 7-8 Geo IV, c. 39 (1827) I:LG;
11 Geo IV, c. 45 (1830) I:LG. Shoreditch:
20-23 Geo II, c. 21 (1750) P:C:L:W; 8 Geo
III, c. 33 (1768) Wd:P:N; 16 Geo III, c. 60
(1776) Am:(W:P:N); 25 Geo III, c. 96 (1785)
Am:(Wd:P:N).
HALIFAX: — P* (1848); 2 Geo III, c. 40 (1762)
Wtr; 8 Geo III, c. 44 (1768) Am:(Wtr):P:C:

(Halifax — continued) —
L:N; 9 Geo IV, c. 90 (1828) I:LG.
HAMMERSMITH: — — ; Fulham: 12 Geo I,
c. 36 (1726) Br; 12 Geo I, c. 37 (1726) P.
HARINGEY: — — ; Highgate: 15 Geo III, c.
43 (1775) L:W.
Harlech (Merion.): (M) *(nc);* (Pop. 658).
HARTLEPOOL: (1593) M — (1201); (Pop.
1,330); 53 Geo III, c. 35 (1813) I:LG.
HARWICH: *(1605);* M. P. (1603); 59 Geo III,
c. 118 (1819) P:C:L:W:Wtr.
HASTINGS: *(1668);* M. P. (1588); 29 Geo III,
c. 27 (1789) P:C:L:N; 1 Geo IV, c. 12 (1820)
I:LG. St Leonards: 2 Wm IV, c. 45 (1832)
P:C:L:W:I; 2 Wm IV, c. 91 (1832) P:L:W:
C:I:Mk:Wtr.
HAVERFORDWEST: *(1610);* M. P. Co. (1479);
5-6 Wm IV, c. 73 (1835) I:LG.
HAVERING: as Romford; 59 Geo III, c. 75
(1819) I:LG.
Hay (Brecon): (M) *(nc);* (Pop. 1,709).
HEDON: (1565); M. (P) (1154); (Pop. 1,080).
HELSTON: *(1774);* M. P. (1201).
HENLEY-ON-THAMES: (1723); M. — (1526);
(Pop. 2,800); 6 Geo IV, c. 174 (1825).
HEREFORD: *(1597);* M. P. (1189); 14 Geo III,
c. 38 (1774) P:C:L:N:S:Poor; 56 Geo III,
c. 23 (1816) Am:Mk:I.
HERTFORD: *(1680);* M. P. (1555); 8 Geo III,
c. 58 (1768) MH; 28 Geo III, c. 75 (1788)
P:C:L:W:M; 9 Geo IV, c. 38 (1828) Am:
(P:I).
HIGHAM FERRERS: (1555); M. (P) (1251);
(Pop. 975).
HIGH WYCOMBE: *(1663);* (as Cheping
Wycombe); M. P. (1237); 53 Geo III, c. 164
(1813) Wd:C:W:L:I:N.
HILLINGDON: as Uxbridge: — — ; 46 Geo III,
c. 60 (1806) I:LG.
Holt (Denbs.): (1563); M. P. (1563); (Pop.
m 1,015, p 1,015).
Holyhead (Angs.): — P.
Holywell (Flints.): — P.
HONITON: — P; 30 Geo III, c. 25 (1790) P:I.
Horsham (Sussex): — P.
HOVE: — — (1898); 11 Geo IV, c. 16 (1830)
I:LG.
HUDDERSFIELD: — P* (1868); 1 Geo IV, c. 43
(1820) I:LG.
HUNTINGDON: *(1630);* M. P. (1630); 25 Geo
III, c. 9 (1785) P:C:L:N; see also separately,
Godmanchester.
HYTHE: *(1575);* M. P. (1575); 38 Geo III,
c. 16 (1798) P:C:L:W:N.
Ilchester (Som.): (1557); M. (P) (1557); (Pop.
965).
IPSWICH: *(1200);* M. P. (1200); 13 Eliz. I, c. 24
(1571) P; 33 Geo III, c. 92 (1793) P:C:L:I:N;
37 Geo III, c. 44 (1797) Am:(P:C:L:I:N); 55
Geo III, c. 26 (1815) Am:(P:C:L:I:N):W;
1-2 Geo IV, c. 104 (1820) Am:(P:L:I).
ISLINGTON: — — ; Charterhouse Square; 16
Geo II, c. 6 (1743) P:W:C:I. Finsbury: 31

(Islington (Finsbury) — continued) —
Geo III, c. 90 (1791) P:L:W:C:N; 35 Geo
III, c. 45 (1795) Am:(P:L:W:C:N); 46 Geo
III, c. 219 (1806) I:LG; 5 Geo IV, c. 125
(1824) I:LG. Goswell Street: 20 Geo III, c. 48
(1780) P:L:W:C:N. Hampton Court: 23 Geo
II, c. 37 (1750) Br. St Luke's Old Street: 50
Geo III, c. 149 (1810) I:LG. St Mary's: 12
Geo III, c. 17 (1772) L:W.
KEIGHLEY: — — (1882); 5 Geo IV, c. 123
(1824) I:LG.
KENDAL: *(1684);* M. P* (1575).
KENSINGTON AND CHELSEA: — — ;
Kensington: 12 Geo I, c. 37 (1726) P; 29
Geo II, c. 63 (1756) Poor:P:C; 35 Geo III,
c. 74 (1795) P:L:W:N; 43 Geo III, c. 10
(1803) I:LG; 59 Geo III, c. 120 (1819)
I:LG; 5 Geo IV, c. 108 (1824) I:LG.
Brompton Square: 5 Geo IV, c. 108 (1824)
I:LG. Chelsea: 6 Geo III, c. 66 (1766) Br;
30 Geo III, c. 76 (1790) P:I; 42 Geo III,
c. 89 (1802) Mk; 43 Geo III, c. 134 (1803)
Mk; 45 Geo III, c. 102 (1805) I:LG; 46 Geo
III, c. 32 (1806) I:LG; 47 Geo III, c. 68
(1807) I:LG; 56 Geo III, c. 21 (1816) I:LG;
57 Geo III, cc. 1, 40 (1817) I:LG; 1-2 Geo
IV, c. 62 (1821) I:LG; 5 Geo IV, c. 147
(1824) I:LG; 7 Geo IV, c. 58 (1826) I:LG
1-2 Wm IV, cc. 1, 76 (1831) I:LG; 4-5 Wm
IV, c. 58 (1834) I:LG.
Kenfig (Glam.): (p); M. P.; (Pop. m 486,
p 275).
KIDDERMINSTER: *(1827);* M. P* (1636);
33 Geo II, c. 50 (1760) Wd:P:MH; 53 Geo III,
c. 83 (1813) P:C:L:W:I.
Kidwelly (Carm.): (1618); M. — ; (Pop. 1,435).
Kilgerran (Pembs.): (p); (M) — ; (Pop. 879).
KING'S LYNN: *(1524);* M. P. (1204); 43 Geo
III, c. 37 (1803) P:C:L:W:I:N:Mk; 46 Geo
III, c. 21 (1806) I:LG.
KINGSTON-UPON-HULL: *(1443);* M. P. Co.
(1440); 28 Geo II, c. 27 (1755) Am:(Poor):
P:C:L:N; 2 Geo III, c. 76 (1762) Am:(C:
L:N); 4 Geo III, c. 74 (1764) Am:(C:L:N);
8-9 Geo III, c. 17 (1769) PH; 23 Geo III,
c. 55 (1783) G:Tr:BG:L:B:N:Q; 35 Geo
III, c. 46 (1795) NS; 41 Geo III, c. 30 (1801)
P:C:L:W:I:N:Tr; 50 Geo III, c. 41 (1810)
W:C:L:I:N.
KINGSTON-UPON-THAMES: *(1628);* M. —
(1628); 13 Geo III, c. 61 (1773) L:N:I; 48
Geo III, c. 134 (1808) CH:MH.
Knaresborough (Yorks.): — P; 4 Geo III, c. 93
(1764) Wtr.
Knighton (Radnor.): — P.
Knucklas (Radnor.): — P.
LAMBETH; — P*; 52 Geo III, cc. 112, 197
(1812) I:LG; 3 Geo IV, c. 112 (1822) I:LG;
7 Geo IV, cc. 35, 46 (1826) I:LG; 10 Geo IV,
c. 129 (1829) I:LG. Clapham: 52 Geo III,
c. 112 (1812) I:LG.
*LAMPETER: (1814) M. P. (1814); (Pop. m
1,000, p 1,000).

LANCASTER: *(1820)*; M. P. (1193); 5 Geo IV,
  c. 66 (1824) L:C:W:P:I.
Langport Eastover (Som.): *(1617)*; M. — ; (Pop.
  1,245).
Laugharne (Carm.): *(1300)*; M. — ; (Pop. 1,423).
LAUNCESTON: *(1555)*; M. P. (1199).
LEEDS: *(1661)*; M. P* (1626); 28 Geo II, c. 4
  (1755) L:P; 33 Geo II, c. 54 (1760) Br:B:Wd;
  30 Geo III, c. 68 (1790) Wtr:L:C:N; 49 Geo
  III, c. 122 (1809) Am:(Wtr:L:C:N):CH:G:
  Wd; 55 Geo III, c. 42 (1815) Am:(CH:G):
  Po:W; 5 Geo IV, c. 124 (1824) I:LG.
LEICESTER: *(1587)*; M. P. (1589); 1–2 Geo IV,
  c. 3 (1821) Gas.
LEOMINSTER: *(1554)*; M. P. (1554); 48 Geo
  III, c. 148 (1808) P:I.
LEWES: — P (1881); 46 Geo III, c. 48 (1806)
  I:LG; 9 Geo IV, cc. 27, 29 (1808) I:LG.
LICHFIELD: *(1623)*; M. P. Co. (1594); 46 Geo
  III, c. 42 (1806) P:C:L:W:I; 55 Geo III, cc.
  27, 29 (1815) I:LG.
LINCOLN: *(1628)*; M. P. Co. (1154); 31 Geo
  III, c. 80 (1791) P:L:W:N; 9 Geo IV, c. 27
  (1828) P:L:W:I:Po.
LISKEARD: *(1587)*; M. P. (1240).
LIVERPOOL: *(1695)*; M. P. (1207); 8 Anne, c. 8
  (1709) Q; 3 Geo I, c. 1 (1717) Am:(Q); 11
  Geo II, c. 32 (1738) Q; 21 Geo II, c. 24
  (1748) B:C:L:W; 2 Geo III, c. 68 (1762)
  B:BG:P:Tr; 26 Geo III, c. 12 (1786) Wd:Wtr:
  M: Mk:Tr; 28 Geo III, c. 13 (1788) Am: (L:
  C:W:N); 39 Geo III, c. 36 (1799) Wtr; 42 Geo
  III, c. 80 (1802) Tr: Wd; 58 Geo III, c. 66
  (1818) Gas; 59 Geo III, c. 9 (1819) Mk; 1 Geo
  IV, c. 13 (1820) Am:(Wd:P:L:N); 4 Geo IV,
  c. 39 (1823) 'Oil Gas'; 6 Geo IV, c. 75 (1825)
  I:LG; 7 Geo IV, c. 57 (1826) Wd:N:F; 11
  Geo IV, c. 15 (1830) P:Sew:Bo; 4–5 Wm IV,
  c. 1 (1835) 'Oil Gas'; 5–6 Wm IV, c. 54
  (1836) I:LG.
LLANDOVERY: *(Ric III)*; M. — (1485).
LLANELLI: *(p)*; M. P.; (Pop. m 4;173, p 4,250)
  and (1913); 47 Geo III, c. 107 (1807) I:LG.
Llanfyllin (Mont.): *(nc)*; M. P.; (Pop. m 1,836,
  p 1,100).
Llangefni (Angs): — P.
LLANIDLOES: *(nc)*; M. P. (1280).
Llantrisant (Glam.): *(p)*; (M) P; (Pop. m 956.
  p 956).
LONDON: (not incl. in Commrs.' Rep. or 1835
  Act); M. P. Co.; City: 10 Geo II, c. 22 (1737)
  W:P:C:Sew; 18 Geo II, c. 33 (1745) Tr; 17
  Geo II, c. 29 (1744) L; 24 Geo II, c. 10
  (1751) B: F; 30 Geo II, c. 22 (1757) Tr; 6
  Geo III, c. 26 (1766) P:C:L:N; 6 Geo III, c.
  27 (1766) Am:W:I; 7 Geo III, c. 37 (1767)
  Br:P; 8 Geo III, c. 21 (1768) Am:(P:C:L:N);
  33 Geo III, c. 75 (1793) Sew:P:C:L:N.
  Aldgate: 47 Geo III, c. 38 (1807) I:LG; 52
  Geo III, c. 72 (1812) I:LG; 53 Geo III, c. 72
  (1813) I:LG; 54 Geo III, c. 214 (1814) I:LG;
  56 Geo III, c. 45 (1816) I:LG. Aldersgate:
  18 Geo III, c. 73 (1778) P; 55 Geo III, c. 96

(London (Aldersgate) — continued) —
  (1815) I:LG. Bank: 39–40 Geo III, c. 89
  (1800) I:LG. Billingsgate; 42 Geo III, c. 87
  (1802) Mk. Blackfriars Bridge: 52 Geo III,
  c. 183 (1812) I:LG. Cheapside: 55 Geo III,
  c. 91 (1815) I:LG. Fleet Street: 29 Geo III,
  c. 38 (1789) Wd. Foster Lane: 55 Geo III,
  c. 91 (1815) I:LG. London Bridge: 31 Geo
  II, c. 20 (1758) Br; 4 Geo IV, cc. 35, 46
  (1823) I:LG; 7 Geo IV, c. 40 (1826) I:LG;
  7–8 Geo IV, c. 30 (1827) I:LG; 10 Geo IV,
  c. 136 (1829) I:LG; 11 Geo IV, c. 64
  (1830) I:LG; 1 Wm IV, c. 3 (1830) I:LG;
  2–3 Wm IV, c. 23 (1832) I:LG; 4–5 Wm IV,
  c. 13 (1834) I:LG. Minories; 33 Geo III, c. 82
  (1793) P:C:L:W. Moorfields: 18 Geo III,
  c. 71 (1778) Wd:CH; 52 Geo III, c. 210
  (1812) I:LG. New Bridge Street: 35 Geo III,
  c. 131 (1795) P:L:W:Br:Wd. St Bartholomew
  the Great: 28 Geo II, c. 37 (1755) L:C:W;
  9 Geo III, c. 23 (1769) L:C:W:P:N. St
  Botolph: 7 Geo III, c. 23 (1767) Br:P; 8–9
  Geo III, c. 22 (1769) P:C:L:W:N; 11 Geo
  III, c. 23 (1771) I:LG. St George-in-the-East:
  46 Geo III, c. 77 (1806) I:LG. St Katherine:
  47 Geo III, c. 38 (1807) I:LG; 54 Geo III,
  cc. 214, 220 (1814) I:LG; 55 Geo III, c. 68
  (1815) I:LG. St Luke: 50 Geo III, c. 149
  (1810) I:LG. St Martin-le-Grand: 55 Geo III,
  c. 91 (1815) I:LG. Snow Hill: 42 Geo III, c.
  73 (1802) I:LG; 44 Geo III, c. 27 (1804)
  I:LG; 49 Geo III, c. 82 (1809) I:LG; 51 Geo
  III, c. 131 (1811) I:LG. Temple Bar: 38 Geo
  III, c. 61 (1798) Wd; 39–40 Geo III, c. 42
  (1800) Wd; 44 Geo III, c. 27 (1804) I:LG;
  49 Geo III, c. 82 (1809) I:LG; 51 Geo III, c.
  203 (1811) I:LG. Tower Hill: 37 Geo III,
  c. 87 (1797) P:L:W:C:N.
Looe, East (Corn.): *(1685)*; M. (P); (Pop. 865).
Looe, West (Corn.): *(1574)*; M. (P); (Pop. 593).
Lostwithiel (Corn.): *(1753)*; M. (P): (Pop.
  1,074).
Loughor (Glam.): *(p)*; M. P.; (Pop. m 665, p.
  665).
LOUTH: *(1551)*; M. — (1551); 6 Geo IV, c. 129
  (1825) P:L:W:C:I.
LOWESTOFT: — — (1885); 50 Geo III, c. 42
  (1810) I:LG.
Ludlow (Salop): *(1461)*; M. P.: 29 Geo II, c. 59
  (1756) Wd:P:MH; 33 Geo III, c. 25 (1793)
  P:L:W:I.
LYDD: *(p)*; M. — (1885); (Pop. 1,357).
LYME REGIS: *(p)*; M. P. (1284).
LYMINGTON: *(p)*; M. P. (1150).
MACCLESFIELD: *(1684)*; M. P* (1281); 54
  Geo III, c. 23 (1814) L:W:Po; 6 Geo IV, c.
  96 (1825) L:W:I:Po; 11 Geo IV, c. 124
  (1830) Wtr.
Machynlleth (Mont.): M. P.; (Pop. m 'none',
  p 3,795).
MAIDENHEAD: *(1685)*; M. — (1582).
MAIDSTONE: *(1748)*; M. P. (1549); 31 Geo III,
  c. 62 (1791) Wd:I:P:C:L:N:Wtr; 42 Geo III,

Plympton, Earl (Devon.): (*1692*); M. (P); (Pop. 1,015).

PONTEFRACT: (*1685*); M. P. (1194); 50 Geo III, c. 40 (1810) P:I:Wtr.

POOLE: (*1568*); M. P. Co. (1248); 29 Geo II, c. 10 (1765) Q:W:L:B.

PORTSMOUTH: (*1627*); M. P. (1194); 31 Geo II, c. 39 (1758) B; 8 Geo III, c. 62 (1768) P:C:N:Wd; 16 Geo III, c. 59 (1776) L:W: Am:(P:C:N:Wd); 32 Geo III, c. 59 (1792) P:C:W:I:N; 7 Geo IV, c. 64 (1826) L:P:W: Am:(P etc.).

Presteigne (Radnor): (*nc*); M. P.; (Pop. m 1,629, p 1,700).

PRESTON: (*1684*); M. P. (1179); 24 Geo II, c. 36 (1751) Br; 55 Geo III, c. 22 (1815) L:W:P:C:I:F.

PWLLHELI: (*nc*); (M) P. (1355).

QUEENBOROUGH: (*1626*); M. (P) (1626 and 1885); (Pop. 786).

Radnor, New (Radnor.): (*1739*); M. P.; (Pop. m 2,501, p 2,501).

RAMSGATE: – – (*1884*); 22 Geo II, c. 40 (1749) Q; 25 Geo III, c. 34 (1785) P:C:L: W:N:MH:Mk; 36 Geo III, c. 43 (1796) Am: (P:C); 5 Geo IV, c. 75 (1824) I:LG; 7–8 Geo IV, c. 106 (1827) I:LG.

READING: (*1638*); M. P. (1253); 25 Geo III, c. 85 (1785) P:L:C:W:N; 7 Geo IV, c. 56 (1826) P:C:L:W:I.

REIGATE: – P.

Rhayader (Radnor): – P.

*Rhuddlan (Flints.): (*1284*); M. P.: (Pop. m 2,500, p 2,500).

RICHMOND: (*1669*); M. P. (1093); 6 Geo III, c. 72 (1766) Poor:P:C:L:W:N.

RIPON: (*1622*); M. P. (886).

ROCHDALE: – P* (1856); 3 Geo IV, c. 58 (1822) I:LG; 4 Geo IV, c. 36 (1823) I:LG; 6 Geo IV, c. 128 (1825) I:LG.

ROCHESTER: (*1629*); M. P. (1189); 9 Geo III, c. 32 (1769) P:C:L:W; also Strood: 52 Geo III, c. 37 (1812) Poor.

*Romford (Essex): (*1465*); M. –; (Pop. 6,812); 59 Geo III, c. 75 (1819) I:LG.

Romney Marsh (Kent): (*1605*); M. –; (Pop. 7,500).

ROMSEY: (*1698*); M. – (1607); 50 Geo III, c. 141 (1810) I:LG.

Ross (Herefs.): – –; 11 Geo IV, c. 43 (1830) I:LG.

*RUTHIN: (*1508*); M. P. (1508).

Ruyton (Salop.): (*1309*); M. –; (Pop. 933).

RYDE: – – ; (1868); 10 Geo IV, c. 39 (1829) I:LG.

RYE: (*p*); M. P. (1289); 7 Geo I, c. 9 (1721) Q; 9 Geo I, c. 30 (1723) Q; 10 Geo I, c. 7 (1724) Am:(Q).

SAFFRON WALDEN: (*nc*); M. – (1513).

ST ALBANS: (*1640*); M. P. (1553); 44 Geo III, c. 8 (1804) P:C:L:W:I.

St Asaph (Flints.): – P.

St Clears (Carm.): (*p*); M. –; (Pop. 1,083).

St David's (Pembs.): (*nc*); (M) –; (Pop. 1,025).

ST IVES: (*1685*); M. P. (1639).

SALFORD: – P* (1835); 5 Geo III, c. 50 (1765) C:L:F:N; 32 Geo III, c. 69 (1792) C:L:W:Wd; 11 Geo IV, c. 8 (1830) I:LG.

SALISBURY: (*1611*); M. P. (1227); 10 Geo II, c. 6 (1737) P:L:W; 39–40 Geo III, c. 53 (1800) CH:G; 55 Geo III, c. 23 (1815) I:LG.

SALTASH: (*1774*); M. (P) (1774 and 1885); (Pop. 1,637).

SANDWICH: (*p*); M. P. (1226); 22 Geo II, c. 40 (1749) Q; 28 Geo II, c. 55 (1755) Br; 27 Geo III, c. 67 (1787) P:C:L:W:N:Q:Br:Nav; 55 Geo III, c. 23 (1815) Am:(P:L:W); 10 Geo IV, c. 105 (1829) I:LG.

SCARBOROUGH: (*1356*); M. P. (1181); 5 Geo II, c. 11 (1732) Q; 41 Geo III, c. 94 (1801) P:I:Tr; 45 Geo III, c. 94 (1805) I:LG.

Seaford (Sussex): (*1543*); M. (P); (Pop. 1,098).

SHAFTESBURY: (*1665*); M. P. (1604).

SHEFFIELD: – P* (1843); 58 Geo III, c. 54 (1818) I:LG; 7–8 Geo IV, c. 58 (1827) I:LG.

Shelton (Staffs.): – – ; 6 Geo IV, c. 73 (1825) I; 9 Geo IV, c. 28 (1828) I.

Shepperton: – – ; 20 Geo II, c. 22 (1780) Br.

Shoreham (Sussex): – P.

SHREWSBURY: (*1638*); M. P. (1447); 29 Geo II, c. 78 (1756) P:C:L:W; 1–2 Geo IV, c. 58 (1821) Am:(P:L:W).

SOUTHAMPTON: (*1640*); M. P. Co. (1447); 20 Geo II, c. 15 (1747) Wtr. Portsea: 4 Geo III, c. 92 (1764) P:N; 10 Geo III, c. 25 (1770) P:C:N:Wd:L:W. Portsea: 32 Geo III, c. 103 (1792) P:C:Wd:N; 50 Geo III, c. 169 (1810) Am:(P:C:L:W).

South Molton (Devon): M. – (*1590*).

SOUTH SHIELDS: – P* (1550); 7 Geo III, c. 28 (1767) Mk:S; 28 Geo III, c. 15 (1788) Wtr; 10 Geo IV, c. 40 (1829) I:LG. North Shields: 26 Geo III, c. 110 (1786) Wtr.

SOUTHWARK: – P, as 'Southwark' only: 28 Geo II, cc. 9, 23 (1755) Mk; 30 Geo II, c. 31 (1757) Am:(Mk); 6 Geo III, c. 24 (1766) P:C:L:W:N; 7 Geo III, c. 37 (1767) Br:G:P; 7 Geo III, c. 37 (1767) NS; 11 Geo III, c. 17 (1771) Am:(P:Sew); 14 Geo III, c. 75 (1774) Poor: Wd; 17 Geo III, c. 23 (1777) L:W; 18 Geo III, c. 51 (1778) P; 26 Geo III, c. 120 (1786) P:C:L:W:N:NS; 28 Geo III, c. 68 (1788) P:C:L:W:Wd; 44 Geo III, c. 86 (1804) I:LG; 52 Geo III, c. 14 (1812) I:LG; 10 Geo IV, c. 34 (1829) Mk. Bermondsey: 25 Geo III, c. 23 (1785) P:C:L:W:N; 43 Geo III, c. 137 (1803) I:LG; 52 Geo III, c. 111 (1812) I:LG; 55 Geo III, c. 76 (1815) I:LG; 59 Geo III, c. 21 (1819) I:LG; 3 Geo IV, c. 112 (1822) I:LG; 4 Geo IV, c. 91 (1823) I:LG; 4–5 Geo IV, c. 95 (1834) I:LG. Camberwell: 16 Geo III, c. 26 (1776) L:W; 27 Geo III, c. 52 (1787) L:W; 54 Geo III, c. 213 (1814) I:LG. Christchurch (Surrey): 31 Geo III, c. 61

(Southwark (Christchurch) − continued) −
(1791) P:C:L:W:Wd:I:N; 33 Geo III, c. 90
(1793) NS; 51 Geo III, c. 32 (1811) I:LG; 57
Geo III, c. 48 (1817) I:LG; 3 Geo IV, c. 112
(1822) I:LG. Peckham: 54 Geo III, c. 213
(1814) I:LG. Rotherhithe: 23 Geo III, c. 31
(1783) P:C:L:W:N. St George the Martyr: 52
Geo III, c. 111 (1812) I:LG; 3 Geo IV, c. 112
(1822) I:LG; 4 Geo IV, c. 34 (1823) Mk; 11
Geo IV, c. 45 (1830) I:LG. St John's: 23
Geo II, c. 18 (1750) L:W.
SOUTHWOLD: *(1689)*; M. − (1489).
STAFFORD: *(1827)*; M. P. (1206); 11 Geo IV,
c. 44 (1830) P:L:W:C:I.
STALYBRIDGE: − − (1857); 9 Geo IV, c. 26
(1828) I:LG.
STAMFORD: *(1685)*; M. P. (1461); 4 Geo IV,
c. 101 (1823) Gas.
*STOCKPORT: ('ancient charter with no date');
M. P* (1220); 7 Geo IV, c. 118 (1826)
L:C:W:I:Po.
Stockton (Durham): *(p)*; M. −; 1 Geo IV, c. 62
(1820) L:C:I.
STOKE-ON-TRENT: − P* (1910); 6 Geo IV. c.
73 (1825) I:LG.
Stony Stratford (Bucks.): − − ; 41 Geo III, c.
130 (1801) Gas.
STOURBRIDGE: − − (1914); 25 Geo II, c. 47
(1785) Mk:Wd; 31 Geo III, c. 70 (1791)
L:C:W:N; 6 Geo IV, c. 19 (1825) I:LG.
STRATFORD-ON-AVON: *(1664)*; M. − (1553).
Stroud (Gloucs.): − P*.
SUDBURY: M. P. (1554); 6 Geo IV, c. 70
(1825) I:LG.
SUNDERLAND: *(1634)*; M. P* (1634); 3 Geo I,
c. 3 (1717) Q; 50 Geo III, c. 25 (1810) L:W:
C:P:N; 50 Geo III, c. 27 (1810) P:W:C:Mk:
MH:I:W; 7 Geo IV, c. 120 (1826) P:L:W:C:I:
Mk.
SUTTON COLDFIELD: (1664); M. − (1676);
(Pop. 3,684).
SWANSEA: *(p)*; M. P. (1169); 14 Geo III, c. 27
(1774) Mk; 49 Geo III, c. 79 (1809) P:C:L:
W:N.
TAMWORTH: *(1664)*; M. P. (1560).
TAUNTON: − P (1660); 8−9 Geo III, c. 44
(1769) MH:Mk:C:L:N; 28 Geo III, c. 79
(1788) NS; 49 Geo III, c. 84 (1809) I:LG;
57 Geo III, c. 65 (1817) I:LG.
Tavistock (Devon.): − P.
TENBY: ('numerous'; *p*); M. P. (1402).
TENTERDEN: *(1600)*; M. − (1600).
TEWKESBURY: *(1698)*; M. P. (1574); 26 Geo
III, c. 17 (1786) P:C:L:W:N:Tr:Wd.
THETFORD: *(1693)*; M. P. (1573).
Thirsk (Yorks.): − P.
Thornbury (Gloucs.): (p); (M) −; (pop. 1,500).
TIVERTON: *(1725)*; M. P. (1615) 5 Geo II,
c. 14 (1732) B:F; 34 Geo III, c. 52 (1794)
P:I; 3 Geo IV, c. 60 (1822) Am:(P.I.L); 6
Geo IV, c. 139 (1825) I:LG.
TORBAY (as Torquay): − − (1968); 6 Wm
IV, cc. 45, 108 (1835) I:LG.

TORRINGTON ('several'): M. − (1554).
TOTNES: *(1596)*; M. P. (1206).
TOWER HAMLETS (Mx.): − P*; Bethnal
Green: 24 Geo II, c. 26 (St Matthew) (1751)
C:L:W; 33 Geo III, c. 88 (1793) P:N; 53 Geo
III, c. 113 (1813) I:LG. Christchurch (Mx.):
11 Geo II, c. 35 (1725) L:W; 28 Geo III, c. 60
(1788) Am:(P:C:L:W:N). Goodmans Fields:
18 Geo III, c. 50 (1778) Wd. Limehouse: 54
Geo III, c. 194 (1814) I:LG. Mile End, Old
Town: 17 Geo III, c. 66 (1777) W; 1−2 Geo
IV, c. 72 (1821) I:LG. Mile End, New Town:
20 Geo III, c. 66 (1780) P:C:L:W:N. Norton
Folgate: 32 Geo II, c. 49 (1759) L:C:W; 18
Geo III, c. 77 (1778) P:N; 50 Geo III, c. 5
(1810) I:LG. Poplar: 53 Geo III, c. 84 (1813)
I:LG. Ratcliffe: 29 Geo II, c. 87 (1756)
W:L:P:C; 22 Geo III, c. 87 (1782) P:N; 50
Geo III, c. 83 (1810). Shadwell: 29 Geo II,
c. 87 (1756) W:L:P:C; 15 Geo III, c. 54
(1775) P:N; 50 Geo III, c. 208 (1810) I:LG.
Spitalfields: 18 Geo III, c. 78 (1778) Wd:S;
22 Geo III, c. 43 (1782) Wd. Tower of
London: 29 Geo II, c. 87 (1756) W:L:P:C; 14
Geo III, c. 30 (1774) Poor:P:C:L:W:N.
Wapping: 29 Geo II, c. 87 (1756) W:L:P:C;
11 Geo III, c. 21 (1771) P:N:Wd; 17 Geo III,
c. 22 (1777) P; 22 Geo III, c. 86 (1782) Am:
(P); 52 Geo III, c. 75 (1812) I:LG. White-
chapel: 3 Geo III, c. 53 (1763) Poor:C:L:W:
S; 11 Geo III, cc. 12, 15 (1771) P:N; 18 Geo
III, c. 37 (1778) Wd:I:N; 23 Geo III, c. 91
(1783) P:N; 46 Geo III, c. 89 (1806) I:LG.
Tregony (Corn.): (1622); M. (P); (Pop. 1,127).
Trowbridge (Wilts.): − − ; 39 Geo III, c. 61
(1769) P:C:L:N.
TRURO: *(1589)*; M. P. (1589); 30 Geo III, c.
62 (1790) P:C:L:Wd:N:Tr; 5−6 Wm IV, c.
100 (1835) I:LG.
TYNEMOUTH: − P* (1849).
Usk (Mon.): (p); (M) P.; (Pop. m 1,160, p. 1,250).
Uxbridge (Mx.): − −; see Hillingdon.
WAKEFIELD: − P* (1848); 11 Geo III, c. 44
(1771) P:C:N:Wd; 36 Geo III, c. 50 (1796)
L:W:C:N; 3 Geo IV, c. 7 (1822) I:LG.
WALLINGFORD: *(1663)*; M. P. (1155); 35 Geo
III, c. 75 (1795) P:C:L:W:I:N.
WALSALL: *(1627)*; M. P* (1159); 5 Geo IV, c.
68 (1824) P:L:W:C:Wd:I.
WANDSWORTH: − −: Battersea: 6 Geo III, c.
66 (1766) Br; 52 Geo III, c. 112 (1812)
I:LG.
Wantage (Berks.): − −; 9 Geo IV, c. 90 (1828) L.
Ware (Kent): − −; 51 Geo III, c. 8 (1811) L.
WAREHAM (temp. Anne): M. P. (1211 and
1886); 3 Geo III, c. 54 (1763) B.
WARRINGTON: − P* (1847); 53 Geo III, c.
118 (1813) I:LG; 3 Geo IV, c. 7 (1822) Gas.
WARWICK: *(1693)*; M. P. (1545) 28 Geo III,
c. 9 (1788) Br; 3 Geo IV, c. 29 (1822) Gas.
Weobley (Herefs.): (nc); (M) (P); (Pop. 506).
WELLS: *(1589)*; M. P. (1201); 19 Geo III, c. 31
(1779) CH:Mk; 1−2 Geo IV, c. 12 (1821)

(Wells − continued) −
  I:P:C:L:W:N; 2 Wm IV, c. 37 (1831) L.
Wenlock (Salop): *(1631)*; M. P.: 29 Geo II, c. 60
  (1756) Wd:P:MH.
Westbury (Wilts.): *(p)*; M. P.; (Pop. m 800, p
  7,324).
WELSHPOOL: *(1615)*; M. P. (1615).
WESTMINSTER: − P; 2 Geo II, c. 11 (1729)
  P:C; 9 Geo II, c. 29 (1736) Br; 18 Geo II
  c. 33 (1745) Tr; 23 Geo II, c. 14 (1750) Mk;
  29 Geo II, c. 25 (1756) Po; 30 Geo II, c. 22
  (1757) Tr; 31 Geo II, c. 17 (1758) Po; 31 Geo
  II, c. 25 (1758) Mk; 31 Geo II, c. 27 (1758)
  Mk; 2 Geo III, c. 21 (1762) P:C:L:N; 2 Geo
  III, c. 58 (1762) Poor:C:BG; 3 Geo III, c. 23
  (1763) Am:(P:C:L:N); 4 Geo III, c. 39 (1764)
  Am:(P:C:L:N); 4 Geo III, c. 55 (1764) W; 5
  Geo III, c. 13 (1765) P:C:L; 5 Geo III, c. 50
  (1765) P:C:L:I; 30 Geo III, c. 53 (1790)
  P:C:L:N; 39 Geo III, c. 82 (1799) I; 44 Geo
  III, c. 61 (1804) I:LG; 45 Geo III, c. 115
  (1805) I:LG; 46 Geo III, c. 137 (1806) Sew;
  47 Geo III, c. 7 (1807) Sew; 50 Geo III, cc.
  28, 119 (1810) Sew:I:LG; 52 Geo III, c. 48
  (1812) Sew; 54 Geo III, c. 154 (1814) I:LG;
  1−2 Geo IV, c. 45 (1821) I:LG; 7 Geo IV,
  c. 78 (1826) I:LG; 7−8 Geo IV, c. 33 (1827)
  I:LG. Bayswater: 4−5 Geo III, c. 96 (1834)
  Sew. Bryanston Square: 54 Geo III, c. 5
  (1814) I:LG. Charing Cross: 29 Geo II, c. 38
  (1756) Br:Wd; 53 Geo III, c. 121 (1813)
  I:LG; 56 Geo III, c. 128 (1816) I:LG; 7 Geo
  IV, c. 77 (1826) I:LG; 9 Geo IV, c. 70 (1828)
  I:LG; 10 Geo IV, c. 61 (1829) I:LG.
  Cockspur Street: 30 Geo II, c. 34 (1757)
  Br:Wd. Covent Garden: 9 Geo II, c. 13 (1736)
  W; 23 Geo III, c. 42 (1783) P:C:L:N; 42 Geo
  III, c. 19 (1802) Mk; 53 Geo III, c. 71 (1813)
  Mk; 9 Geo IV, c. 113 (1828) Mk; 10 Geo
  IV, c. 68 (1829) I:LG. Deans Yard: 28 Geo
  II, c. 54 (1755) B. Dorset Square: 54 Geo III,
  c. 6 (1814) I:LG. Grosvenor Square: 14 Geo
  III, cc. 52, 90 (1774) P:C:L:W; 5−6 Wm IV,
  c. 43 (1835) I:LG. Golden Square: 24 Geo II,
  c. 27 (1784) P:L:I; 7−8 Geo IV, c. 44 (1827)
  I:LG. Grosvenor Place: 7 Geo IV, c. 58
  (1826) I:LG; 4−5 Wm IV, c. 58 (1834) I:LG.
  Haymarket: 39 Geo III, c. 74 (1799) NS.
  Lincoln's Inn Fields: 8 Geo II, c. 26 (1735)
  I:LG. Manchester Square: 29 Geo III, c. 5
  (1789) I:LG. Middle Row: 17 Geo III, c. 38
  (1807) I:LG; 59 Geo III, c. 119 (1819) I:LG.
  Millbank Row: 57 Geo III, c. 54 (1817)
  I:LG. Paddington: 5 Geo IV, c. 126 (1824)
  I:LG. Piccadilly: 15 Geo III, c. 57 (1775)
  I:LG. Privy Gardens: 5 Geo IV, cc. 58, 100
  (1824) I:LG; 6 Geo IV, c. 38 (1825) I:LG;
  9 Geo IV, c. 64 (1828) I:LG; 2−3 Wm IV, c. 56
  (1832) I:LG. Regent's Park: 3 Geo IV, c. 58
  (1822) I:LG; 5 Geo IV, c. 100 (1824) I:LG;
  6 Geo IV, c. 38 (1825) I:LG; 9 Geo IV, c. 64
  (1828) I:LG; 2−3 Wm IV, c. 56 (1832) I:LG.
  Savoy Precinct: 5−6 Wm IV, c. 18 (1835)

(Westminster (Savoy Precinct) − continued)
  I:LG. St Anne's: 9 Geo II, c. 19 (1736) W.
  St Clement Danes: 23 Geo III, c. 89 (1783)
  P:C:L:N; 49 Geo III, c. 113 (1809) I:LG.
  St George's-Fields: 50 Geo III, c. 191 (1810)
  I:LG; 52 Geo III, c. 211 (1812) I:LG. St
  George's, Hanover Square: 25 Geo II, c. 97
  (1752) Poor:C:P; 21 Geo III, c. 84 (1781)
  P:C:L:N; 7 Geo IV, cc. 58, 121 (1826) I:LG;
  7−8 Geo IV, c. 33 (1827) I:LG; 1−2 Wm IV,
  c. 50 (1831) I:LG; 53 Geo III, c. 38 (1813)
  I:LG. St James and St George: 8 Geo II, c. 15
  (1735) W. St James's: 59 Geo III, c. 23
  (1819) I:LG; 7−8 Geo IV, c. 44 (1827) I:LG.
  St James's Square: 12 Geo I, c. 25 (1726) I.
  St Margaret's: 11 Geo II, c. 25 (1738) Br.
  St Margaret and St John Evangelist: 9 Geo II,
  c. 17 (1736) W; 23 Geo II, c. 23 (1752) Poor:
  C:P; 6 Geo IV, c. 134 (1825) I:LG; 5−6 Wm
  IV, c. 18 (1835) I:LG. St Martin-le-Grand:
  8−9 Geo III, c. 13 (1769) P:C:L:W:N; 11 Geo
  III. c. 22 (1771) Am:(P:C:L); 55 Geo III, c.
  91 (1815) I:LG. St Martin's-in-the-Fields: 9
  Geo II, c. 8 (1736) W; 23 Geo II, c. 35 (1750)
  B. (York Buildings); 29 Geo II, c. 90 (1756)
  Poor:C:W; 23 Geo III, c. 90 (1783) P:C:L:N.
  St Marylebone: 29 Geo II, c. 53 (1756)
  W:C:L:P; 8 Geo III, c. 46 (1768) Am:W:C:L:
  P; 10 Geo III, c. 23 (1770) P:C:L; 13 Geo III,
  c. 48 (1773) Am:(W:P:C:L); 35 Geo III, c. 3
  (1795) W:Poor; 46 Geo III, c. 90 (1806)
  I:LG; 53 Geo III, cc. 62, 63, 121 (1813)
  I:LG. (Montague Square): 54 Geo III, c. 7
  (1814) I:LG; 56 Geo III, c. 128 (1816)
  I:LG. (Portman Square): 4 Geo IV, c. 4
  (1823) I:LG; 3 Geo IV, c. 84 (1822) I:LG;
  7 Geo IV, c. 77 (1826) I:LG; 9 Geo IV, c. 70
  (1828) I:LG; 10 Geo IV, c. 61 (1829) I:LG.
  Strand: 7 Geo IV, c. 77 (1826) I:LG; 9 Geo
  IV, c. 70 (1828) I:LG; 10 Geo IV, c. 61
  (1829) I:LG. Temple Bar: 39−40 Geo III,
  c. 42 (1800) Wd:I. Tothill Fields: 6 Geo IV,
  c. 134 (1825) I:LG.
WEYMOUTH AND MELCOMBE REGIS:
  (1804); M. P. (1280); 16 Geo III, c. 57 (1776)
  P:C:L:W:N; 50 Geo III, c. 187 (1801) C:L:W:
  N:Tr:Mk:Q; 37 Geo III, c. 129 (1797) Wtr.
Whitby (Yorks.): − P*; 23 Geo II, c. 39 (1750)
  Q; 29 Geo III, c. 12 (1789) P:C:L:W:Wd:N:
  Tr:Br.
WHITEHAVEN: − P*; 46 Geo III, c. 115 (1806)
  I:LG; 56 Geo III, c. 44 (1816) I:LG; 58 Geo
  III, c. 15 (1818) I:LG.
*Wickwar (Gloucs.): *(p)*; (M) −; (Pop. 927).
WIGAN: M. P. (1246); 4 Geo III, c. 75 (1764)
  I:LG.
WILTON: *(1662)*; M. P. (1100); (Pop. m 1,550,
  p. 7,444).
Winchelsea (Sussex): *(p)*; M. (P); (Pop. 772).
WINCHESTER: *(1588)*; M. P. (1155); 11 Geo
  III, c. 9 (1771) P:C:L:W:N:Wd; 41 Geo III,
  c. 132 (1801) I:LG; 48 Geo III, c. 2 (1808)
  Am:(P:C:L:W:N).

WINDSOR: *(1664)*; M. P. (1277); 9 Geo II, c. 15 (1723) Br; 9 Geo III, c. 10 (1769) P:C: L:W:N:Wd; 47 Geo III, c. 8 (1807) I:LG.

WISBECH: *(1669)*; M. – (1549); 50 Geo III, III, c. 206 (1810) Mk:P:C:L:W:M:Nav.

*Wiston (Pembs.): (M) P. (*nc*); (Pop. m 745, p 745).

WOLVERHAMPTON: – P* (1848); 17 Geo III, c. 25 (1777) Wd:C:L:B:N:Tr; 54 Geo III, c. 106 (1814) I:LG; 1 Geo IV, c. 8 (1820) Gas. Bilston: 5 Geo IV, c. 51 (1824) I:LG.

WOODSTOCK: (1664) M. P.

Wootton Bassett (Wilts.): (*p*); M. (P); (Pop. 1,520).

WORCESTER: *(1622)*; M. P. Co. (1189); 8–9 Geo III, c. 84 (1769) Br; 10 Geo III, c. 22 (1770) Wtr:P:L:N; 11 Geo III, c. 13 (1771) Am:(Wtr:P:L:N); 20 Geo III, c. 21 (1780) Am:(Wtr:P:L:N); 4 Geo IV, c. 69 (1823)

(Worcester – continued) – Wtr:P:L:W:I.

WORTHING: – – (1890); 43 Geo III, c. 59 (1803) I:LG; 49 Geo III, c. 114 (1809) I:LG; 1–2 Geo IV, c. 59 (1821) I:LG.

*Wotton-under-Edge (Gloucs.): (*p*); (M) (P); (Pop. 804).

WREXHAM: – P (1157).

Yarmouth (Hants.): *(1610)*; M. (P); (Pop. 586).

YEOVIL: (*p*); M. – (1854); 11 Geo IV, c. 116 (1830) I:LG.

YORK: *(1664)*; M. P. Co. (1160); 3 Geo III, c. 48 (1763) C:L:N:Tr; 8–9 Geo III, c. 17 (1769) PH; 49 Geo III, c. 126 (1809) I:LG; 50 Geo III, c. 86 (1810) I:LG; 55 Geo III, c. 71 (1815) I:LG; 6 Geo IV, c. 127 (1825) P:L:W:I:Po; 3–4 Wm IV, c. 62 (1833) Mk: Am:(P:L:W:L).

CHAPTER NINE

COMMERCIAL DIRECTORIES 1763–1900

THE DIRECTORIES described in Chapter V of *Village Records*, which give a vivid picture of the commercial and social life of villages and market towns during the 18th and 19th centuries, are equally revealing of the development of municipal boroughs during the same period. When their evidence is combined with that of the earlier town plans, contemporary newspapers and later census returns, we find a wealth of sources to draw upon and many practical openings for the local searcher. Each of these sources extends and supplements the others and the information which each provides will develop instantaneous pictures of the changes which were taking place in the life, work and management of most towns during their most formative period. Pieced together like a jigsaw puzzle, a vivid picture emerges of industrial growth and booming prosperity; or perhaps, in less well-situated towns, of stagnation and eventual decline.

The first London directory was printed for Samuel Lee in 1677 and sold at his shop in Lombard Street, near Popes Head Alley, and by Daniel Major at the 'Flying Horse' in Fleet Street. It provided 'A Collection of the names of the Merchants living in and about the City of London.' Later publication of provincial directories matches the period between the extension of a network of canals from town to town (from 1770 to 1848) and the ensuing 'railway mania' of the 1830s and 40s. The extension of the Birmingham Canal to join the Staffordshire and Worcestershire Canal in 1772 gave the Midlands access to Bristol. In 1777, the Grand Trunk Canal made connections with Liverpool and Hull and the Warwick and Birmingham Canal extended further links to London in 1799. Sketchley's earliest directories of Birmingham were published from 1763 to 1767. Similarly, if we ponder a reason for the rash of Birmingham directories printed in the single year 1823 — eight in all — we may remind ourselves that this was the year of the foundation of the London-to-Birmingham Railway Company, which opened its line to Euston in 1838. Meanwhile, James Pigot, a Manchester printer, extended his publication of directories to cover towns all over England, opened his offices in London, and employed an agent in Paris. Merchants all over Europe were provided with details of suppliers and customers in every major English town and a multitude of country markets. *The Universal British Directory* (published in five volumes) as early as 1793 listed 'The Inhabitants of London, Westminster and Borough of Southwark and of all the Cities, Towns and Principal Villages in England and Wales', together with 'An Historical Detail of the Antiquities, Curiosities, Trade, Polity, and Manufactures of each City, Town and Village'. Inclusion in the *Universal Directory* is a useful indication of the relative importance of any English or Welsh town of moderate size at the close of the 18th century.

The pages which illustrate typical samples of directories (see illustrations pages 208–209) are chosen to show the different formats we may expect to find when we take these useful volumes from the shelf of reference library or record office. The most widely ranging are the *Universal Directory* alphabetically arranged, town by town, and Holden's *Annual Directory* (1816) which lists '480 separate towns in England, Ireland, Scotland and Wales'. There are also regional editions such as Bailey's *Western and Midland Directory* (1783). Even more widespread are the county directories of later date, which list substantial villages and market towns, both large and small, as shown in *Village Records*, from the village of Chaddesley Corbett to the city of Worcester. Individual entries in these large-scale works will be relatively short, especially in earlier editions. Usually for a town of Dudley's size with '2,000 families' an early directory includes from 30 to 200 residents, with a rudimentary separation of 'Gentry, Clergy, Law, Physic and Traders' in separate lists with some additional details of coach services, postal deliveries and principal hotels. In earlier directories the exact address of each resident may not be given and all sorts of trades will be listed together.

It is a measure of any provincial town's size, prosperity and general importance when a publisher chooses to give it an entire volume. This is the type of directory which is listed in the Gazetteer at the end of this Chapter. In less prosperous cases we shall still find regular entries in the appropriate county or 'universal' directories; some of these will be substantial, extending to four or five closely printed pages, though for the smallest towns a brief general list of the principal residents and tradesmen may suffice. In each type of directory the arrangement of data will differ from publisher to publisher. In the earliest examples available from the second half of the 18th century, a general list of names is usual, indexed alphabetically by surnames and giving the occupation and street-address of each resident. Pearson and Rollason's entry for Dudley in 1780 is an early example of this type of directory (see illustration page 208), 75 tradesmen are listed, with additional entries for a schoolmaster, an attorney, three surgeons, an auctioneer and the innkeepers of the *Sun* and *Old Bush*, both in the High Street. The one unspecified resident, Gilbert Fownes, may be the only entry of a private resident or 'gentleman' for the whole town. General lists of this type require selective searching in order to collect the groups of tradesmen or crafts, or the occupants of the same street. Later directories, as they become more extensive, adopt other modes of listing residents, in addition to a general alphabetical index Some provide a second list reclassified by occupations, as shown in the illustration (page 209) of Sketchley's *Directory of Birmingham* for 1770. As the extract shows, Sketchley heads each list of craftsmen with an enthusiastic description of the various processes involved in their manufacture. Later 'Post Office' directories also list residents and tradesmen street by street, with houses, shops and other premises numbered and intersections of adjoining streets, arcades and alleys indicated. Street directories are invaluable, in the absence of an earlier town plan, in pinpointing vanished streets long gone under the bulldozers' tracks. A typical example of a street directory is Kelly's *Worcestershire Directory* for 1896, which shows the Elgar family's music shop in High Street, Worcester.

For all sorts of directories, the most effective single reference book is Jane E. Norton's *Guide to the national and provincial directories of England and Wales, excluding London, published before 1856*, published by the Royal Historical Society in 1968. This can be augmented locally by reference to library and record offices' handlists

A LIST of the INHABITANTS
OF
DUDLEY.

A

ABBIS, Joseph, cordwainer, High street
    Abbis, John, ditto, ditto
Amphlett, Joseph, ironmonger, ditto
Arch, John, bleacher, Priory
Afton, Sarah, Swan inn, High street

B.

BADDELEY, William surgeon, High street
    Balton, Richard, grocer and chandler, ditto
Bannifter, Jof. baker, ditto
Banton, James, weaver, ditto
Barlow, widow, ditto ditto
Bate, Thomas, fadler, ditto
Bate, Benjamin, maltfter, Hampton ftreet
Bathew, John, mercer, High ftreet
Bennet and fons, ironmongers, New ftreet
Benfon, Jofeph, dyer, Hampton ftreet
Blews, Lewis, padlock maker, High ftreet
Bourn, Jof. grocer and chandler, High ftreet
Bourn, Myles, mercer, ditto
Bradney, Samuel, currier, Hall ftreet
Brinton, Stephen, butcher, High ftreet
Bunn, Richard, maltmill and bellows maker, ditto

CADDICK,

Hughes, Wm. baker, Queen ftreet
Hughes, Benj. mercer and ftationer, High ftreet

J.

JACKSON, Thomas, fchoolmafter, High ftreet
    Jackson, James, maltfter, Fifher's ftreet
Johnfon, Jofeph, butcher, Hall ftreet
Jones, George, mafon, ditto

L.

LAUGHER and Hancox, ironmongers, High
    ftreet

M.

MASON, Benjamin, breeches maker, ditto
    Maxwell, Charles, maltfter, High ftreet
Mills, ——, brazier, ditto
Moore, Jofeph, cordwainer, ditto
Moore, James, horfe dealer, ditto

Onions, John, grocer, Hall ftreet

P.

PACKWOOD, John, hinge maker, High ftreet
    Parkes, Wm. brufh maker, ditto
Penn, Philip, Hall ftreet
Penn, Bate, grocer, High ftreet
Penn, Wm. glafs maker, Hall ftreet
Peters, Enoch, draper, High ftreet
Powell, Stephen, plumber and glazier

R.

RAYBOLD and Bourn, milliners, High ftreet
    Read, Emanuel, nailor's toolmaker, Bannifter ftreet
Richards, Thos. attorney, New ftreet
Rollinfon, Jofeph, bag weaver, Hampton ftreet

SANSOM,

C.

CADDICK, John, Old bufh, High ftreet
    Chambers, John, patten ring maker, Hampton ft.
Creighton, George, mercer, High ftreet

D.

DIXON and fon, cyder and hop merchants, New ft.
    Dixon and fon, patten ring makers, High ftreet
Dudley, Wm. grocer and chandler, ditto
Dunton, George, cordwainer, ditto
Dunton, John, ditto, ditto

F.

FAWKES, Daniel, weaver, Hampton ftreet
    Fellows, Benjamin, whitefmith, ditto
Finch and Parfons, ironmongers, ditto
Finch, John, failcloth maker, ditto
Fownes, Gilbert, High ftreet

G.

GORTON, Richard, butcher, High ftreet
    Green, Jonathan, glafs maker, Dixon's green
Greenfield, Daniel, ironmonger, High ftreet
Gregory, Wm. hatter, ditto

H.

HANCOX, Edward, currier, High ftreet
    Hancox, Jof. baker and maltfter, ditto
Hancox, John, cooper, ditto
Hancox, widow, malfter, ditto
Harper, Richard, whitefmith, New ftreet
Hartill and Dudley, thread makers, Queen ftreet
Hawkes, Abraham, glafs maker, High ftreet
Hawkes, Thos. butcher, ditto
Hodgetts, widow and fons, ironmongers, ditto
Homer, widow, malfter, ditto

Hughes,

S.

SANSOM, James, haberdafher, Hall ftreet
    Saunders, John, furgeon, High ftreet
Seager, Thomas, attorney, ditto
Shaw, Read, furgeon, ditto
Smith, Samuel, auctioneer, New church yard
Stokes, Jofeph, baker, Queen ftreet

T.

TAYLOR, Samuel, baker and maltfter, Hampton ft.
    Thompfon, Jofeph, glazier, High ftreet

W.

WAINWRIGHT, Jofeph, furgeon, High ftreet
    Wilkinfon, Edward, lockfmith, Peas ftreet
Wilkinfon, Charles, glazier, High ftreet
Woolley, Thos. horfe lock maker, Peas ftreet
Woolley, Benjamin, factor, Caftle foot
Woolley, Richard, horfe and gate lock maker, ditto
Wright, widow and fon, vice makers, Hall ftreet

O   A LIST

B R A S S   F O U N D E R S.

*These ingenious Artists make an infinite Variety of Articles,
as Sconces, Cabinet Handles, Escutcheons, Hinges, Cloak
Pins, &c. &c. and this is the only Place for Merchants and
Others, to be provided upon the best Terms.*

BACHE William,   ——   No 28. Bell Street.
Berry David, and Pocket Book Clasp Maker, No 18.
New Meeting Street.
Boyce and Radcliffe, and Ironmongers, No 12. Free-
man Street.
Botton John,   ——   No 16. Lichfield Street.
Cave John,   — —   No 27. New Hinkleys.
Clare Thomas,   —-   No 96. Lichfield Street.
Clarke John,   ——   No 28. Holloway Head.
Gregory John,   — —   No 68. Chapel Row.
Harcourt John,   ——   No 11. Coleshill Street.
Haywood James,   --   No 12. Catharine Street.
Heely Samuel, and Factor,   No 8. Freeman Street.
Hervey and Pemberton, Coach and Cabinet, No 6.
Exeter Row.
Hidson Durant,   ——   No 25. Church Street.
Hurst and Co.   — —   No 15. Paradise Row.
zon John,   ——   no Number, Coleshill Street.
Lowe William,   — —   No 56. Moor Street.
Marston John,   — —   No 2. Paradise Row.
Parker Samuel,   — —   No 110. Snow Hill.
Radcliffe John,   ——   No 96. Moor Street.
Raven George, and Silverer and Tinner, No 60. Cha-
pel Row.
Shephard John,   no Number, Smallbrook Street.
Smith and Cocks,   —   No 9. Colemore Row.
Smith Thomas,   — —   No 2. Exeter Row.
Smith Timothy, and Factor,   No 4. Park Street.
Swaine James,   — —   No 21. Chapel Row.
Tovey William,   — --   No 30. Park Street.
Tranter William,   ——   No 7. Paradise Row.
Underhill Thomas,   —   No 17. Lichfield Street.
Underhill John, and Cabinet Maker, No 58. Park Street.
Webster

Webster and Parkes,   —   No 5. Brickiln Lane.
Wilmot Matthew,   —   No 5. New Meeting Street.
Wootton Richard, and Powder Flask Top, No 63.
Coleshill Street.
Yates William, and Cock Founder, No 9. High Street.

B R A Z I E R S.

BIRCH George, and Son,   No 140. Digbeth.
Blunt Joseph,   ——   No 31. High Street.
Durnall Edward, Founder and Ironmonger, No 30.
Bull Street.
Durnall Elizabeth,   ——   No 49. High Street.
Fearon Joseph,   — —   No 134. Digbeth.
Freeman George,   —   No 11. Edgbaston Street.
Mercer Robert, and Tinman,   No 80. Digbeth.
Pidgeon James,   — —   No 119. Ditto.
Stringer Mary,   — —   No 99. Bull Street.
Wells Edward, and Tinman,   No 48. High Street.

B R U S H   M A K E R S.

BELCHER James, and Dealer in Hops, No 51. Edg-
baston Street.
Bissell Thomas,   — —   No 104. Digbeth.
Boswell John,   — —   No 16. Park Street.
Conway Thomas,   — —   No 2. Moor Street.
Cooper Joseph,   — —   No 76. Bull Street.
Hodgets William,   — --   No 21. Dale End.
Holt Richard,   — —   No 41. Bull Street.
Paton Joseph,   No 12. London Prentice Street.
Robinson Thomas,   ——   No 21. Bull Street.
Woodcock John, and Wool-Comber, No 12. Spiceal
Street.

B 2   BUCKLE-

The entry for Dudley from Pearson and Rollason's *Birmingham, Wolverhampton, Walsall,
Dudley, Bilston and Willenhall Directory* (1780) from the Local Studies Department, Birmingham
Reference Library.

Above: Extract from *The New Triennial Directory of Birmingham* (1818), by R. Wrightson (from a
facsimile edition, Newcastle-upon-Tyne, 1969).

of their own holdings. A particularly valuable example is D. F. and S. Radmore's *Guide to the Directories of the West Midlands*, published by the Library Association in 1971. This lists all available West Midland directories chronologically, and analyses the content of each volume, giving the number of pages allocated to commercial lists, street guides, introductory description, maps and coach timetables and indicating the whereabouts of each directory in various local libraries. A similar guide has been produced for Staffordshire by N. E. Merry and D. R. Beard; most reference libraries can produce their own substantial handlists. About one-third of the list of municipal boroughs — more than 120 in all — have individual directories as well as the usual entries in their county or regional volume. Several towns have as many as five, or even a dozen successive directories to themselves at regular dates from the turn of the 18th century to 1900. Although the national publishers such as Kelly have continued to publish Post Office directories down to the present day we are concerned only with those issued before the end of the 19th century; later directories will, of course bring a local study up-to-date.

If we take account of all the entries for one town of moderate size, like Dudley, including shorter ones in county, regional and 'universal' directories, besides the town's single complete volume — *Bentley's Directory* of 1841 — we can assemble at least 30 references between 1770 and 1881, when *Blocksidge's Almanacks* began to make their regular annual appearances which continued until 1952. By way of contrast, Birmingham had at least 30 different publications devoted to it, some printed for five or six successive years, between 1763 and 1854. In fact, Birmingham can boast the earliest of the separate town directories, run close by *Gore's Directory* of Liverpool, which appeared in 1766. Though by no means as numerous as local newspapers, directories are a similar barometer of their prosperity and expansion. They will often signal a particular year or period of years as being especially significant in the development of a town. See, for instance, the particular importance of the year 1823 for Derby, or 1836 in West Bromwich.

In addition to their lists of residents and occupations, directories are a mine of additional information, often derivative but sometimes unique. From the earliest issues they included official information about the town's corporation, its officers, churches, schools, bankers and other public offices, postal services and hotel accommodation. Most are inevitably concerned with particulars of transport and communication from town to town, with extensive details of the arrivals and departures of stage and mail coaches, as well as particulars of coastal vessels, steamships, canal barges, trows, wherries, waggons, carriers, hackney carriages, fly-gigs and public omnibuses (when these were available) with the names and addresses of principal coaching inns, wharfs and staging posts. Finally, they may include the earliest railway timetables, which reveal surprisingly little difference from the modern inter-city journey times, with considerably more stopping services from town to town. Many directories, even the brief entries in the great *General Directories* of Pigot, include for even the smallest towns, a general historical and descriptive survey. This usually gives statistics of population, the town's civic status and parliamentary representation, as well as the principal trades and occupations, with much antiquarian detail and description of the chief buildings. As early as 1770, a generation before the first national census, Sketchley ends his *Directory of Birmingham* with 'An Account of the Number of Houses and the Inhabitants, Male and Female, in the Town of Birmingham &c.' He lists

135 streets, with 6,025 houses entered street by street, and 30,804 inhabitants, in almost equal proportions, male and female. This continues the information given by the earlier mapmakers, Westley in 1731 and Bradford in 1750. (See Chapter Six).

It is fortunate for the student, not only that original directories can often be bought from antiquarian bookdealers, but also that their format lends itself readily to modern lithographic processes. Thus they are often available for purchase and home study. In the gazetteer as many of these reproductions as possible are especially noted. For the purposes of our 'model' of Birmingham, we can take Wrightson's *New Triennial Directory* for 1818 which was reprinted in 1969. This useful source lists 6,000 residents, mainly tradesmen, and abstracts, 1,285 of the 50 principal tradesmen, from awl-makers to wire-drawers. This trades-list includes professional people such as agents and attorneys, but unfortunately omits a classification of grocers, tavern-keepers and other retailers who can be found in the general index of surnames. Also, like many town directories, as opposed to county versions, the 'gentry' are barely included nor even identified to permit comparison of their relative strength in town and countryside.

It is important to check the extent of any directory's proportionate coverage of the town's population. At the time of Wrightson's publication in 1818 the census return for Birmingham gives a total population approaching 100,000; the directory accounts for only 6% of all townsmen, a fairly typical coverage for a single-town volume at that time. The earliest editions are scantier; Pearson and Rollason's *Directory of Dudley* in 1781 lists only 87 inhabitants and Bailey includes only 34 tradesmen for the same town. These are 'general' or 'universal' gazetteers however; when Dudley aspired to a complete directory in 1841, the editor, Joseph Bentley, listed 1,850 inhabitants and re-classified 1,311 of these under 114 different crafts. Once again this represents 6% of the 1841 census return of 31,232 inhabitants of Dudley. Like Wrightson, Bentley lists no gentry; instead Dudley's top people are coal masters and iron masters, with a passing reference to 'Lord Ward, the Lord of the Manor' in a general introduction.

Directories are often an additional source of town maps; Bentley's *Directory* is embellished with the 'New Plan of Dudley' which is a useful record of the extensions of the town's building since Treasure surveyed the town in 1835. Similarly, several Worcester directories for 1800-1820 can be matched with the *Plan of Worcester* first engraved by J. Roper in 1810 (see page 132). The Birmingham directories of Sketchley complement the early maps of Westley (1731) and Bradford (1750) to create revealing distribution maps of the town's principal industries at a formative period.

Looking forward from the earliest directories for any town we can often anticipate the first census returns for at least one generation before 1801. Only when a full street population survey is added to a partial 'Index of Residents and Tradesmen', as in the case of Sketchley's *Directory of Birmingham* (1770), can we be fairly certain of the total population of any directory's town. It is possible, however, with any alphabetical directory, however incomplete, to compare all the listed residents of a particular street with the names and premises recorded in the later census returns. Pearson and Rollason list 46 tradesmen in Dudley High Street in 1780, more than half their total entries. The street houses several leather-workers, a currier and three cordwainers; there is also a weaver and one glassmaker, otherwise the heaviest industry in the High Street is the brazier. Apart from other workshops making hinges, bellows, locks and brushes, most occupants are retailers. There are four mercers, three grocers, a butcher, baker, milliner and draper; the street is also something of a professional centre, housing the directory's full complement of three surgeons, a schoolmaster and an attorney.

Directories certainly cannot be used statistically. They are, as we have seen, a partial and incomplete source of information, selective of certain trades and occupations which were of particular interest to the publishers and their commercial buyers. They require constant cross-reference to more reliable registers, such as a town's Rate Books and the official census returns. They do, however, contain some information which may be unique for any town. For example, directories name streets which may remain anonymous on earlier maps and which have long since disappeared. They keep a register, however incomplete, of townsmen who might otherwise go unrecorded, particularly for the years 1760–1800, and for these they give occupations and trades. Early town maps may show the street plan but only rarely do they indicate the nature of a building's occupation – Westley's indication of Lloyd's Slitting and Corn Mills and Kettle's and Carless's Steel Houses in central Birmingham is exceptional. There is no sign of the hives of industry which thronged Great Charles Street, Charlotte Street and Colmore Row; only Sketchley's *Directory* shows us these. Directories are useful indicators of trends and changes – their very choice of trades as important is significant. Nowhere else are we likely to learn of the changes in fashion which put 56 Birmingham peruke-makers, who were recorded by Sketchley in 1770, out of business by the time that Pigot's *Directory* of 1818 was published; while for the same period, and beyond, into Pigot's 1842 edition, stays and staymakers continued to thrive.

We must remember that directories only ennumerate occupations; they give no indication of the scale or quality of a trade or industry. That some were well-established is evident from the familiar names which appear at an early date; Baskerville was a Birmingham printer in 1770; John Cadbury roasting coffee and selling cocoa in 1841, Lea and Perrins as Worcester chemists about to immortalise themselves and the city in sauce; Pickford's the local carriers and W. H. Smith a Birmingham stationer – every manufacturing town can produce their own parallels. However, Pigot's Worcester entry of only three 'porcelain manufacturers' gives no indication of the quality and reputation of Worcester ware. Similarly, Bentley's total of 71 ironfounders and 12 chainmakers is too few to represent Dudley's 10% of heavy metal industries; on the other hand 70 boot and shoemakers bulk too large as 49% of the town's retail tradesmen. If we select directories for different years and different towns by the same publisher, we can make some comparisons. We may end up with a true picture only of what directory publishers considered important at a given time, but their criteria may at least remain the same from town to town. In general, directories were prejudiced in favour of manufacturing and retail trades; *Village Records* (pages 167–169) noted the disproportionate lack of attention to agriculture.

Publishers provided the sort of information their customers were looking for but some were more careless than others. James Pigot admits in his prefaces the difficulties of ensuring accuracy; he refers to the dangers of spoken evidence, possibly mispronounced, which results in spelling errors; he mentions the problems of rewriting from draft to draft and the unreliability of some of his sources. Nevertheless, it is evident that Pigot took great pride in constant revision and up-dating of new editions and was prepared to do his best to ensure accuracy. As for the most recent results of industrial growth and urban expansion, we can use for comparison a modern town plan and the 'Yellow Pages' of the local telephone directory. These reveal the up-to-date aspects of a town and unearth the vestiges of earlier industrial workshops and tenements, often surprising us with the extent of the survival of old industrial sites in modern settings. Bearing in mind the statistical limitations of the directories' overall view, what can we learn of the early industrial commercial development of our three West Midlands towns? Taken as samples only, directories are best used to compare one town with another.

The first point to emerge is the remarkable diversity of activity in all three towns. Birmingham is the paramount example of industrial versatility, the 'hardware village' and 'toyshop of Europe'. Metal foundries are still in evidence at the very centre of the town, but iron is giving way to brass and steel and the numbers of platers, stampers, white-metal dealers and braziers steadily increases from 1770 to 1841. Numerically greater, however, is the multitude of metal goods now produced which is illustrated by numerous directory entries. See for instance, Wrightson's 1818 description of the manufactory of Thomas Whitfield: 'brazier, iron-plate worker and frying-pan maker, manufacturer of upright iron tinned tea kettles, sea boilers, saucepans, pots, stewpans, fish kettles, cinder sifters, dust pans, coffee roasters, coal scoops and hods, Rumford, cottage and perpetual ovens, ship and cabinet stoves, stove-piping, cocks, ladles, skimmers, flesh forks, braziers for airing rooms, water buckets, steak pans, cow and ships' bells, Dutch smoothing irons, stage lamps and various other articles in the above line of business'.

One of the most characteristic features of the booming city's trade from the end of the 18th century was the concept of the 'toy'. Birmingham's 'toys' were trinkets of all sorts, made for an adult market; no sooner was a new process discovered — in the plating and stamping of metal, the cutting of glass, or the shaping of tortoiseshell — than the Birmingham workshops employed it to manufacture 'toys'. Sketchley describes the versatility of these 'artists': 'TOY MAKERS: An infinite Variety of Articles that come under this Denomination are made here, and it would be endless to attempt to give an account of the whole, but for the information of Strangers, we shall here Observe that these Articles are divided into several Branches, such as the Gold and Silver TOY MAKERS who make Trinkets, Seals, Tweezers, . . . Inkstands &c &c. The Tortoise TOY MAKER makes a beautiful Variety of the above and other Articles; as does also the Steel, who make Cork Screws, Buckles, . . . Sugar Nippers, &c. and almost all of these are likewise made in various Metals, and for Cheapness, Beauty and Elegance, no Place in the World can vie with them.' Pigot lists 308 small manufacturers of 'toys' in Birmingham in 1818 and 456 in 1841. As to quality, *Nuttall's Standard Dictionary* (1891) has the last word: '*Brummagem*, of tinsel quality, sham. Birmingham, as pronounced, as celebrated for its plated and cheap ware'.

'Toys' apart, Birmingham workshops made almost everything — brushes, straw hats, saddlery, ordnance for the Army, nails (as in Dudley), japanned ware (as in Wolverhampton), whips and china ware (as in Worcester). There are gas-fitting manufacturers, 322 boot and shoe-makers, cork-cutters, needle makers, organ builders, ropewalkers, locksmiths, gunsmiths, whitesmiths and steam-engine works. Nothing was too large or too small, from iron-built boats and boilers to pins, pencils and pocket books. No part of the town was immune from the smoke and noise of manufacture. As the distribution maps show, the very centre of the city was a hive of workshops from Great Charles Street to the High Street, from Digbeth to Colmore Row. No sooner was an elegant 18th-century building estate completed than it swarmed with furnaces and forges or

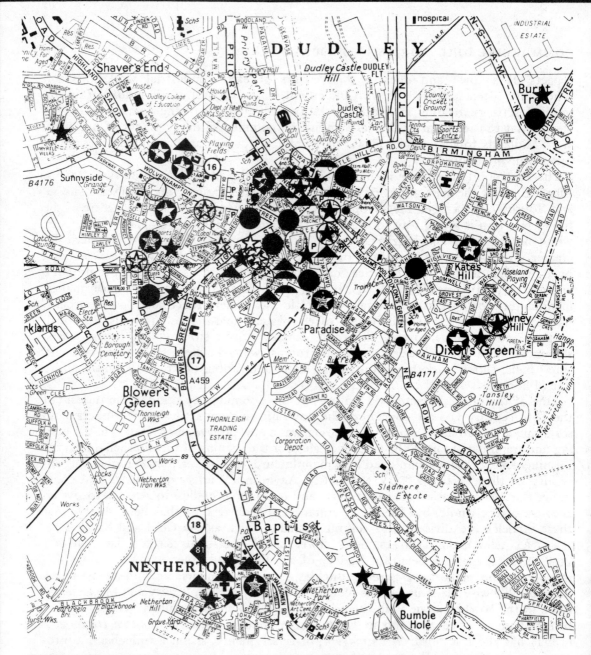

DUDLEY'S INDUSTRIES IN 1840 : From Bentley's Directory

A few of the heavier manufactures given in Bentley's Directory are indicated, though the congestion of trades in the central area of the town makes only an approximate distribution possible. The following trades are shown:

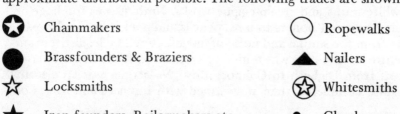

- ✪ Chainmakers
- ● Brassfounders & Braziers
- ☆ Locksmiths
- ★ Iron founders, Boilermakers etc.
- ◗ Vice-makers
- ◯ Ropewalks
- ▲ Nailers
- ✪ Whitesmiths
- • Glasshouses

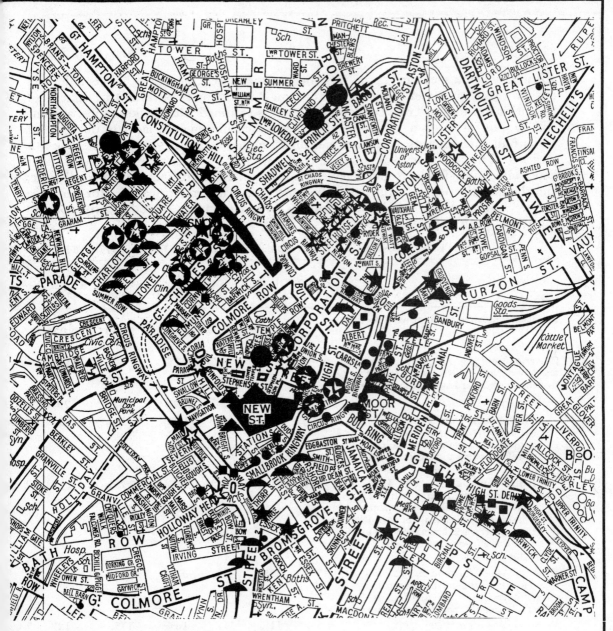

BIRMINGHAM'S INDUSTRIES 1770 - 1818

The symbols show the distribution of iron and brass foundries as given in *Sketchley's Directory of 1770* and those additional foundries and some other manufacturers indicated in *Wrightson's Directory of 1818*.

Key:-

■ Iron foundries in 1770
▲ Iron foundries in 1818
● Brass foundries in 1770
◗ Brass foundries in 1818

● Gunsmiths
☆ Locksmiths
★ Toolmakers

The following trades in 1818 only:-

▲ Jewellers and Gilt toys
★ Silversmiths

A few samples only are given to show the general areas of distribution.

was in-filled with sheds and shops. By contrast, Dudley kept most of its heavier industries out of the High Street, with Netherton and Withymoor as an industrial annexe of foundries and forges. True, Dudley's backstreets swarmed with bucket-shops, as some still do, but there was a 'centre' to the town which Birmingham lacks to this day, for all its Bull Ring flyovers. Worcester had almost no heavy industry at all; its decline to a position of market town was about to begin. We find 12 braziers and tinplate workers here, with 3 iron-founders and 4 nailers, but the mainstay of the town is retail trade, and the manufacture of leatherwork and porcelain. The directory entries for our three 'model' towns can be tabulated as follows with a summary of the county position previously given in *Village Records*:

TABLE OF OCCUPATIONS AS GIVEN IN COMMERCIAL DIRECTORIES, 1770–1841

	BIRMINGHAM 1770	1841	DUDLEY 1780	1841	WORCS. 1840	WORCS. COUNTY 1840
Population as listed in the town directory of that date	1,668	9,322	139	1,311	2,010	13,718
OCCUPATIONS						
I. *Agricultural*, e.g. Farmers, corn, hop and hay dealers; millers, cattle and horse dealers; market gardeners and seedsmen.	—	1%	4%	2%	3%	20%
II. *Industry and Crafts*	53%	45%	42%	29%	26%	29%
(i) *Heavy metalwork*, e.g.: Iron-founders; rollers; forges; brass-founders; chainmakers; nailers, boiler-makers and steam engine works; casters; platers.	(10%)	(10%)	(6%)	(10%)	(3%)	(10%)
(ii) *Miscellaneous crafts*, e.g.: Tool-makers; 'toy' makers: gold and silversmiths; building trades, glass-making; textiles; makers of brushes; japanned ware; hatmakers; lock-smiths; gun-smiths; umbrellas; clockmakers.	(34%)	(35%)	(36%)	(19%)	(23%)	(19%)
III. *Retail shops for food and clothing*, e.g.: Taverns; butchers; bakers; malt-sters; grocers; merchants and factors; drapers; hosiers; ironmongers; fishmongers.	42%	43%	43%	53%	54%	39%
IV. *Miscellaneous, services*, e.g.: Teachers; officials; carriers. auctioneers; accountants; agents; surgeons; bankers; hairdressers.	5%	11%	11%	16%	17%	12%

Bentley's *Directory* (1840) is of particular interest for its well-written introduction. This gives a graphic picture of 19th-century Dudley which will not be found in other sources; it is particularly helpful in outlining the town's government and the efficacy of recent reforms, at a time before the *Dudley Weekly Times* takes up the narrative (see pages 231–234). 'Dudley is governed by a Mayor, bailiff and constables, who are annually appointed at the Court Leet, held by the steward of Lord Ward, the Lord of the Manor. The town is paved, cleansed, lighted, watched, and otherwise improved, by commissioners appointed under an Act obtained in 1791; who annually levy a rate, and hold occasional meetings for carrying into effect the provisions of the said Act.

In 1840 nine day and night police were appointed for the suppression of crime, by the commissioners. The cell in which the police place prisoners for temporary safety, is at the workhouse, in Tower-street; and when any cases require it, the magistrates hold a petty sessions during the week, besides the sessions every Monday ... The town is generally orderly and peaceful (if drunken brawls are excepted) but during the political demonstrations of July, 1839, considerable excitement existed among the people; ... The streets are spacious, kept in excellent repair and at night well lighted with gas, and the exterior appearance of the shops and houses in the principal streets, and their interior replenishments, shew them to be of superior and substantial order. The leading streets always present a scene of animation, but on Saturday and Monday they are almost impassable, from being in such a crowded state; and in passing along the less frequented parts of the town, the sound of the hammer and anvil ring in the ear at every step ...'.

An attractive bonus of the directories is the wealth of advertising matter which many of them offer. Used with a facsimile reprint of any Victorian shoppers' price-list, such as *Harrod's 1895 Catalogue (Victorian Shopping)* (1972), the full range of Dudley and Birmingham's 'curious Manufacture' is confirmed, page after page. All the wealth of plated 'toys' is advertised in the directories' pages and priced in the catalogues. Here are the Brass Fire-tongs, with Copper Twist, at 10s. 6d. the set; the Dudley Aneroid Barometer in carved Oak Frame at £1 10s.; and the full Birmingham Oak Tool Chest No. 3, containing 20 woodworker's standard tools for 17s. 6d. For further comparisons and a comment upon modern inflation, there are the same items available in your local antique shop ...

There are other, more substantial, survivals of the towns whose people and trades are listed in the directories. In Birmingham, the manufactures themselves have been remarkably persistent, despite the advances of technology and an increasing diversity of lighter 'plastic' trades. The 'Yellow Pages' show that there are still brass-founders in New Bartholomew Street and Brass House Passage, toolmakers in Livery Street and Vyse Street, and wireworkers and weavers at King Edward Place and Charles Henry Street. The heaviest trades of all, the ironfounders and casters have moved outward in the conurbation to Tipton, Willenhall, Brierley Hill and Wolverhampton; one of the last survivors, in New Bartholomew Street, left the city centre only recently. Silversmiths and manufacturing jewellers still abound in large numbers, many in the very streets they used in 1818, when Wrightson published his directory. Camden Street, Frederick Street and Newhall Street are still the centres of this trade. Gunsmiths have been permanent residents in Bath Street, like locksmiths in Factory Road and Soho Hill.

Some of the original tradesmen's names are still familiar. The type-face which immortalised John Baskerville is fashionable again and the site of his house is now an imposing civic building. W. & T. Avery, 'Manufacturers of Scales, Money Scales etc.' who were listed in 1818 are still at a Digbeth Road address, and John Cadbury's cocoa and chocolate shop at the coffee roasters in Bull Street has certainly prospered. Even more tenacious are the names of the streets and their alignment, so that in many cases, despite roundabouts and flyovers, the street plans of Westley, and Sketchley's addresses can come to life again in the student's hands. In spite of the bulldozers and the planners, countless backstreet sites remain a little longer for the industrial archaeologist's investigation. Commercial directories are one of the most easily accessible sources to identify them.

FURTHER READING

Duggan, E. P., 'Industrialisation and the Development of Urban Business Communities; Research Problems, Sources and Techniques', *Loc. Hist.*, vol. 11, No. 8 (1975).

Page, D., 'Sources for Urban History (8): Commercial Directories and Market Towns', *Loc. Hist.*, vol. 11, No. 2 (1974).

Richards, P. H., 'Sources for Urban History (2): The Growth of Towns, A Study in Methodology', *Loc. Hist.*, vol. 9, No. 4 (1970).

Shaw, G., 'The Content and reliability of nineteenth-century trade Directories', *Loc. Hist.*, vol. 13, No. 4 (1978).

Timmins, G., 'Measuring Industrial growth from trade Directories', *Loc. Hist.*, vol. 13, No. 6 (1979).

Tupling, G., *Lancashire Directories, 1684–1957* (1976).

Wilde, P., 'The Use of Business Directories in comparing the industrial structure of towns (Macclesfield, Congleton and Leek)', *Loc. Hist.*, vol. 12, Nos. 3 and 4 (1976).

GAZETTEER OF COMMERCIAL DIRECTORIES FOR TOWNS: 1763–1900

There can be no substitute for Jane E. Norton's *Guide to the national and provincial directories of England and Wales, excluding London, published before 1856* (1950). This *Guide* gives full details of national directories and is then arranged by counties with the separate town directories for each county appended. The content of each volume is classified according to the type of list (general, commercial, trades and streets etc.), with details of those which contain maps. The location of copies of directories in the main public libraries is given as well as those in the British Museum and other national libraries. In this Gazetteer only the author, publisher and date of main directories are given; the majority of entries are intended to be *town* volumes only but some county directories have been referred to wherever the local librarians have drawn particular attention to these. Special reference is also made to the *Universal British Directory* (shown as UBD, 1793–98), to one of Holden's *Triennial Directories* (published in 1816 and shown here as H) and to Pigot's *National Directory* for 1818 (shown as P). These are given to include some early examples of towns which might otherwise have no separate entry. The extent of any town's entry cannot be guaranteed, many will be brief, or only passing reference, but are worth checking as a starting point. The *Universal British Directory* is very elusive so that the references to it here are due to the unfailing patience of the staff of the Guildhall Library in London, who will supply photocopy extracts. Borough Reference Libraries and Local History Departments are the most rewarding places to seek out these and other directories; local archives will undoubtedly offer additional references too numerous to be included here. See, for example, the extended entry for DUDLEY which shows how many references can be found for a town of moderate size, if every type of entry and directory is considered. After entries for county towns references to county directories with useful entries for that town and possibly others are given: CD = County Directories.

ABERGAVENNY: UBD ii, 7, 1793.
ABERYSTWYTH: Williams, S. 1816; H.
ABINGDON: UBD ii, 10, 1793; H; Kelly (Oxon) 1889.
ALTRINCHAM: UBD ii, 33, 1793; Balshaw, C. 1855.
ANDOVER: UBD ii, 47, 1793.
APPLEBY: UBD ii, 52, 1793; H.
ARUNDEL: UBD ii, 55, 1793; H.
ASHTON-UNDER-LYNE: P; Morris & Co. 1874; see also Pigot's and Slater's Directories for Manchester and District.
AYLESBURY: UBD ii, 79, 1793; H.
BANBURY: UBD ii, 253, 1793; H; Rusher, J. G. 1832-55; Potts 1842, 1852; Webster 1872

BANGOR: UBD ii, 258, 1793; H.
BARNET: UBD ii, 271, 1793.
BARNSLEY: UBD ii, 259, 1793; H; P.
BARNSTAPLE: UBD ii, 313, 1793; H.
BASINGSTOKE: UBD ii, 315, 1793.
BATH: Gye, W. 1792; UBD ii, 86, 1793; Robbins 1800; Browne, J. 1805, 1809; Wood G. & Cunningham, G. 1812; H; Gye, H. 1819; Keene, Jn & Jas 1824, 1826, 1827, 1829; Binns, A. E. 1833; Silverthorne, H. 1833, 1837, 1841, 1846; Wood, G. 1837; Clark, C. 1849, 1850; Erith, F. N. 1850; Vivian, S. 1852. See (no author) *Guides, Directories & Newspapers in the Ref. Lib.* (Bath Mun. Lib. 1966).
BATLEY: Smith, F. 1878.

BEAUMARIS: UBD ii, 341, 1793.
BECCLES: UBD Appx.
BEDFORD: (Bedfordshire: Henington, J. F.
  1785; Hyatt, B. 1785); UBD ii, 319,
  1793; H.
BEVERLEY: UBD ii, 459; H.
BERWICK-UPON-TWEED: UBD ii, 281, 1793;
  Lockhead, W. 1806; H.
BEWDLEY: UBD ii, 464, 1793; H.
BIDEFORD: UBD ii, 435, 1793; H.
BIRKENHEAD: Mortimer & Harwood 1843;
  Osborne, W. 1843; Pinkney, R. 1851.
BIRMINGHAM: Sketchley, J. 1763, 1764,
  1767; Sketchley, J. & Adams, O. 1770;
  Pearson, T. A. & Rollason, 1777, 1780,
  1781, 1785, 1787, 1788; Swinney, M.
  1773, 1774, 1776, 1777, 1783; Pye, C.
  1785, 1787, 1788, 1791, 1797, 1800; Ward,
  J. 1792, 1798; UBD ii, 201, 1793; Pearson,
  T. A. 1777; Swinney, M. & Hawkins 1800;
  Bisset, J. 1800, 1808; Chapman 1800, 1801,
  1803, 1805, 1808; Thomas, L. & Wrightson,
  R. 1808, 1812, 1815; Wrightson, R. 1815-
  31; H; P; Cooper, W. 1823; Thomson, L.
  1823; Ward & Price 1823; Wood, T. 1823;
  Hodgetts 1823; Butterworth, J. 1823; Belcher,
  J. 1823; Beilby, Knott & Beilby 1828-30;
  Pigot, J. 1829, 1830, 1842; Wrightson, R. &
  Webb, W. 1833-47; Robson, W. 1839;
  Beilby, J. H. 1842, 1852; Post Office
  Directory 1845; Blurton, J. 1849; White, F.
  1849; Slater, I. 1852; Howe, W. 1853;
  Joesbury 1853; Wrightson, R. & Bell, J.
  1854.
BLACKBURN: UBD Appx, 1798; H; P; Oakey,
  H. 1852; 'Peter Whittle' 1852. See Black-
  burn Library Handlist.
BLANDFORD FORUM: UBD ii, 304, 1793;
  H. (See also Pigot's Directory for Dorset
  1823-24).
BOLTON: Holden, W. 1805-7, 1816. P;
  Wardle, M. & Wilkinson, T. 1829; Holden,
  R. M. 1848; Mackie, A. 1849.
BOURNEMOUTH: Stevens, 1888, 1894-95.
BRACKLEY: UBD ii, 348, 1793.
BRADFORD: UBD ii, 346, 1793; H; P;
  Ibbotson 1845, 1850; Smith, 1872.
BRECON: UBD ii, 404, 1793; H.
BRENT: UBD ii, 403.
BRIDGWATER: UBD ii, 356, 1793; H.
BRIDLINGTON: UBD ii, 361, 1793; H.
BRIDPORT: UBD ii, 364, 1793; H. (CD:
  Pigot 1823-24; Kelly 1848-1939; Harrod
  & Co. 1865; Mercer & Croller 1871).
BRIGHTON: UBD ii, 369 (as Brighthelmstone)
  1793; Cobbey, E. 1799, 1800; Lee, W. & A.
  1799, 1800; Button, J. V. 1805; Baxter, J.
  1805, 1822, 1824; H; Boore, T. H. 1822;
  Sicklemore, R. 1822; Christopherson, C.
  1832; Swaysland, T. A. & Gill, J. 1832,
  1833; Burn 1833, 1845; Leppard, W. 1839,
  1843, 1845; Clarke, B. c. 1845; Mason,
  W. H. c. 1845; Folthorpe, R. 1848, 1850,

(Brighton — continued) —
  1852, 1854; Stewart & Murray 1848;
  Taylor, W. J. 1854.
BRISTOL: Sketchley, J. 1775; Becket, J. B.
  1785; Browne, A. 1785; Bulgin, W. 1785;
  Lloyd, J. 1785; Norton, J. 1785; Shiercliff,
  E. 1785; Thorbran, J. 1785; Bailey, W.
  1787; Routh, W. 1787; Browne, W. 1792;
  Reed, J. 1792; UBD ii, 117, 1793; Mills, T.
  1795; Mathews, E. 1805-11; Mathews, J.
  1812-33; H; Evans, J. 1816, 1817;
  Mathews, M. 1834-55; Hunt, E. & Co.
  1848; Scammell, W. 1852, 1853.
BUCKINGHAM: UBD ii, 393, 1793; H. (CD:
  Musson & Craven 1853; Stevenson & Co.
  1853).
BROMLEY: UBD ii, 380, 1793; Wilson, T.
  1797; Hamilton, J. 1799.
BURNLEY: UBD ii, 408; H; P; Worral 1872;
  Barret, P. & Co. 1879, 1883, 1887, 1890,
  1893, 1896 etc.
BURTON-ON-TRENT: UBD ii, 413, 1793; H.
BURY: UBD ii, 443, 1793; P; Heap, J. 1850.
BUXTON: UBD ii, 446, 1793. (See White's
  Derbyshire Directories).
CALNE: UBD, ii, 595, 1793; H.
CAMDEN: UBD ii, 539, 1793.
CAMBRIDGE: UBD ii, 481, 1793; H; Bailey's
  British Directory 1784; Spalding 1878-
  1940. (CD: Gardner, R. 1851).
CANTERBURY: UBD ii, 498, 1793; H. (CD:
  Finch, W. 1803; Wake 1803; Robins, J.
  1831, 1833; Hinton, I. T. 1831; Stapleton &
  Co. 1838; Fry, T. 1840; Bagshaw, S. 1847;
  Ridge, 6, 1847; Williams, J. 1849, 1850).
CARDIFF: UBD ii, 638, 1793; Bird, J. 1796;
  Ridd, T. 1813; H; Bird, W. 1829; Ewen, J.
  1855; Jones, W. 1855; Wakeford, C. 1855.
CARDIGAN: UBD ii, 756, 1793; H.
CARLISLE: Smith, L. 1792; UBD ii, 625
  1793; Henderson, A. 1810; H; Steel, J.
  1837; Lowes, H. 1840; Tait, J. 1840.
CHARD: UBD ii, 546, 1792.
CHATHAM: Public Library refers to 'a list of
  residents in Chatham, Rochester and Stroud,
  taken from an old Gazetteer of 1702-1802'.
  See also UBD ii, 653, 1793 and H.
CHELMSFORD: UBD ii, 511, 1793; H.
CHELTENHAM: UBD ii, 549, 1793; Shenton,
  J. 1800, 1802; Davies, H. 1837-55; Simpkin
  & Co. 1837; Paine, W. & Co. 1839; Weller,
  T. E. 1839; Fordham, A. T. 1842; Harper,
  S. C. 1843, 1844, 1853; Rowe, G. 1845;
  Rowe & Norman 1845; Edwards, R. 1848-
  55; Villar's Map in Directory of 1890 (?);
  Roe, G. *Illustrated Cheltenham Guide 1850*
  (repr. 1970).
CHESTER: Broster, P. 1787, 1795, 1796, 1797,
  Poole, J. 1792; UBD ii, 692, 1793; Bulkeley
  1795, 1796, 1797; H; P; Parry & Son, 1840
  (CD: Broster, P. 1781, 1782, 1783; Cowdroy
  1789; Williams, J. 1845; Williams, J. Snr.
  1846; Bagshaw, S. 1850; Ridge, G. 1850).

CHESTERFIELD: UBD ii, 672, 1793; H; P; Wood 1868-1964.

CHICHESTER: UBD ii, 601, 1793; Seagrave, J. 1804; H. (CD: Pigot 1839; Kelly 1855 etc.).

CHIPPENHAM: UBD ii, 590, 1793; H.

CHIPPING NORTON: UBD ii, 556, 1793; H.

CHORLEY: UBD ii, 667; H; P; Robinson 1835.

CHRISTCHURCH: UBD ii, 558; 1793; H.

CLITHEROE: UBD ii, 659, 1793.

COLCHESTER: UBD ii, 517, 1793; H; Kelly 1845-1937; Benham & Co. 1898-1965. (See also Pigot's Directory of Essex 1835).

COLNE: H; P.

CONGLETON: UBD ii, 575, 1793; H; P.

CONWAY: H.

COVENTRY: UBD ii, 613, 1793; H; P; Lascelles & Co. 1850; Lewin, D. 1850.

CROYDON: UBD ii, 610, 1793; Gray, J. 1851, 1853; Gray, J. & Warren 1855.

DARLINGTON: UBD, ii, 758, 1793; H; Kelly 1885, 1887; Parson & White 1827-28; Cook, W. J. 1901-2. (See Public Library's *Local History Guide No. 2*).

DARTFORD: UBD ii, 760, 1793; H; Perry, A. 1863.

DAVENTRY: UBD ii, 771, 1793; H.

DEAL: UBD ii, 817, 1793; H.

DENBIGH: UBD Appx 1798; H.

DERBY: UBD ii, 879, 1793; H; P; Bathew, T. 1823; Brewer 1823; Wilkins, G. 1823; Glover, S. 1843, 1849, 1850; Mozley, H. 1843; Rowbottom, S. 1849, 1850. (CD: Glover, S. 1829; Mozley, H. 1829; Bagshaw, S. 1846; Saxton, W. 1846; Freebody 1852; Richardson & Son 1852).

DEVIZES: UBD ii, 777, 1793; H.

DEWSBURY: P; Smith, F. 1878.

DONCASTER: H; P.

DORCHESTER: UBD ii, 910, 1793; H.

DOVER: UBD ii, 785, 1793; H.

DROITWICH: UBD ii, 889, 1793; H.

DUDLEY: Appears in: Sketchley & Adams 1770; Pearson & Rollason 1780, 1781; Bailey's Western & Midland Directory 1783; Bailey's British Directory 1784; UBD ii, 913, 1793; Holden's Triennial Directory 1805, 1809, 1811, 1816; Pigot's Commercial Directory 1818; Lewis's Worcestershire Directory 1820; Pigot's London and Provincial New Commercial Directory 1822; Ward & Price's New Birmingham Directory 1823; Wrightson's Triennial Directory of Birmingham 1823, 1825; Pigot 1828; Pigot's Directory of Birmingham 1829; Pigot's Directory of Birmingham, Worcester & Environs 1830; Pigot's National Directory 1835; Robson's Birmingham and Sheffield Directory 1839, 1840; Bentley 1840; Pigot's National Directory 1841; Post Office Directory of Birmingham, Warwickshire and part of Staffordshire 1845; White's Birmingham Directory 1849; Slater's

(Dudley — continued) —
National Directory 1850; Melville 1852; Blocksidge (Almanack) 1881-1952.

DURHAM: UBD ii, 856, 1793; White, T. 1845; Walker, G., Jnr. 1846-55. (CD: Baines, E. 1827; Hagar & Co. 1851).

EASTBOURNE: UBD iii, 32, 1798; Gowland, T. S. 1872.

EAST RETFORD: UBD iv, 354, 1798; H.

ELLESMERE PORT: UBD Appx.

ELY: UBD iii, 41; H.

ENFIELD: UBD iii, 80, 1798 (also Edmonton UBD iii, 78).

EPSOM AND EWELL: (Epsom) UBD iii, 47, 1798; Robson 1839; Andrews, L. W. & Sons 1895-99; (Ewell) UBD iii, 58, 1798.

EVESHAM: UBD iii, 51, 1798; H; Bentley 1840.

EXETER: UBD iii, 1, 1798; Trewman 1807; Trewman & Son 1816; H; Trewman & Co. 1825-33; Besley, T. & H. 1828, 1831; Trewman, R. J. 1834-55; Besley, H. 1845, 1847, 1853, 1854.

EYE: UBD: Appx.

FALMOUTH: UBD iii, 96, 1798; Trathan, J. 1815; H; Philp, J. 1827.

FAVERSHAM: UBD iii, 104, 1798; H.

FLINT: UBD iii, 113, 1798.

FOLKESTONE: UBD iii, 116, 1798; H.

GATESHEAD: Whitehead, W. 1782, 1783, 1784.

GILLINGHAM: UBD ii, 408, 1793.

GLASTONBURY: UBD iii, 156, 1798.

GLOUCESTER: UBD iii, 186, 1798; Raikes, R. 1802; Rudge, T. 1802; Holden 1816; Lewis 1841; Hunt & Co. 1847; Jefferies, C. T. 1853; Scammell, W. 1853. (CD: Gell, R. & Bradshaw 1820; Roberts, J. 1820; Hunt, E. & Co. 1847, 1849).

GODALMING: H; Chennell, T. 1868: Craddock, H. T. 1876.

GODMANCHESTER: UBD iii, 154, 1798.

GRANTHAM: UBD iii, 158, 1798; H; Cook 1897.

GRAVESEND: Holden 1811; Johnston, J. 1842, 1845; Hall 1853.

GREENWICH: UBD iii, 165, 1798.

GRIMSBY: UBD iii, 180, 1798; Houlston & Stoneman 1852; Tesseyman, W. 1852.

GUILDFORD: UBD iii, 197, 1798.

HACKNEY: Turner, C. 1843.

HALIFAX: UBD iii, 319, 1798; H; P; Walker, J. U. 1845; Burton, D. 1850.

HAMMERSMITH: UBD iii, 454, 1798.

HARROGATE: UBD iii, 519, 1798.

HARROW: Crossley, J. S. 1850; Smith, T. 1850; Wright, W. N. 1850.

HARTLEPOOL: UBD iii, 235; 1798; H; Kelly 1895.

HARWICH: UBD iii, 239, 1798; H.

HASTINGS: UBD iii, 305; H; Longman, Hurst & Co. 1820; Powell, P. M. 1820; Smith, T. 1850.

HAVERFORDWEST: UBD iii, 245, 1798; H.
HEMEL HEMPSTEAD: UBD iii, 254, 1798.
HENLEY-ON-THAMES: UBD iii, 365; H.
HEREFORD: UBD iii, 220, 1798; H; Hunt &
Co. 1847. (CD: Lascelles & Co. 1851; Swan
Bros. 1851).
HERTFORD: UBD iii, 369, 1798; H. (CD:
Williams, J. 1850).
HIGH WYCOMBE: UBD iii, 263, 1798; H.
HILLINGDON: Lake, W. (Uxbridge) 1840.
HONITON: UBD iii, 388, 1798.
HUDDERSFIELD: UBD iii, 295, 1798; H; P;
Rider, J. 1845; Williams, J. 1845; Charlton,
R. J. 1850; Roebuck, D. I. 1850.
HUNTINGDON: UBD iii, 313, 1798; H. (CD:
Hatfield, J. 1854; Craven & Co. 1855).
HYDE: UBD iii, 444, 1798.
HYTHE: UBD iii, 275; H.
IPSWICH: UBD iii, 419, 1798; H.
ISLINGTON: UBD iii, 433, 1798; Trounce,
T. 1851.
KENDAL: UBD iii, 469, 1798; H.
KEIGHLEY: Holden 1816; Craven, A. 1884
(includes Bingley & Skipton). See also
Baines, E. (York) 1823 and White, W.
(W. Riding) 1837, 1847, 1853, 1861.
KETTERING: UBD iii, 478, 1798; H.
KENSINGTON AND CHELSEA: (Chelsea)
UBD ii, 747, 1798.
KIDDERMINSTER: UBD iii, 501, 1798; H;
P; Lewis 1820; Howard 1840; Bentley 1840;
Broadfield 1889.
KINGSTON-UPON-HULL: UBD iii, 325, 1798;
Battle, R. G. 1791, 1792, 1803, 1806, 1810,
1814, 1818, 1821. Gray, A. 1792; Innes, D.
1792; Rawson, J. & W. 1791; Clayton, T.
1803; Cowley 1803; Rawson, W. 1806,
1814; Carroll, M. W. 1810; H; Topping, T.
& Rawson, W. 1818; P; Topping, T. 1821;
Baines, E. 1826; Parson, W. & White, W.
1826; Craggs, J. Jnr. 1835; Lee, G. 1835;
Noble, J. 1838; Purdon, W. 1839; Stephen-
son, W. 1842, 1848; Freebody, 1851;
Pulleyn, J. 1851.
KINGSTON-UPON-THAMES: UBD iii, 490,
1798; H.
LANCASTER: UBD iii, 618, 1798; H; P.
LAUNCESTON: H.
LEEDS: Wright, G. 1797, 1798; Wright T.
1797, 1798; Binns, J. & Brown, G. 1800;
Wilson, G. 1807; Baines, E. 1809, 1817,
1826, 1827; Robinson, M. 1809; H; Parson,
W. 1817, 1826, 1827; P; Baines, E. &
Newsome 1834, 1839; Haigh, T. 1839;
Williams, J., Snr. 1845; Wilson, C. A. 1845;
Charlton, R. J. 1847; Baines, E. & Sons
1845; Charlton, R. J. & Archdeacon, W.
1849; Green, T. W. 1849; Slade, W. Jnr. &
Roebuck, D. 1851; White 1853; White, W.:
*Dir. of Leeds & the Clothing District of
Yorkshire* (repr. 1968).
LEICESTER: UBD iii, 585, 1798; Weston, R.
1794; Fowler J. 1815; H; P; Combe T. &

(Leicester – continued) –
Son 1827; Cook, T. 1843.
LEIGH: UBD iii, 739, 1798; H.
LEOMINSTER: UBD iii, 542, 1798; H.
LEWES: UBD iii, 745, 1798.
LICHFIELD: Parson & Bradshaw 1818; Egging-
ton (*Household Almanack and Year book*)
1875, 1877, 1879, 1881; Lomax (*Red Book
Almanack*) 1893, 1895, 1899, 1901–15).
LINCOLN: UBD iii, 549, 1798; H; Victor &
Baker 1843. (CD: Baines, E. 1826; Parson,
W. 1826; White, W. 1842; Hagar & Co. 1849;
Stevenson & Co. 1849).
LISKEARD: UBD iii, 743, 1798.
LIVERPOOL: Gore, J. 1766–1803; Nevett, W.
1766, 1767, 1769, 1781; Bailey, W. 1787;
Wosencroft, C. 1790; UBD iii, 635, 1798;
Schofield, J. and Schofield, T. 1800; Wood-
ward, C. 1804, 1805; Lang, J. 1804, 1805;
Gore, J. 1805–55; H; P; Picken, A. 1827;
Syers, R. 1830; Robinson, G. & J. 1830;
Marples, D. 1830; Robson, W. 1840; Pigot, J.
& Slater, I. 1843; Williams, J. Snr. 1846;
Macorquodale, G. 1848.
LLANELLY: H.
LLANIDLOES: H.
LONDON: See: Goss, C. W. F. *The London
Directories 1677–1855* (1932).
LOUGHBOROUGH: UBD iii, 576, 1798; H.
LOUTH: UBD iii, 579, 1798; H.
LOWESTOFT: UBD iii, 572.
LYDD: UBD iii, 583.
LYME REGIS: UBD iii, 278, 1798; H.
LYMINGTON: UBD iii, 734, 1798; H.
MACCLESFIELD: UBD iii, 894, 1798; H;
Corry, J. 1817; Ferguson, J. 1817; Leigh,
J. 1817; Parson, W. 1817; P; Plant, J. &
Gregory, T. 1825; Varey, D: 1825.
MAIDSTONE: UBD iii, 868, 1798; H; Smith,
J. 1839; Phippen, J. 1850; West, W. 1850;
Monckton, W. 1854.
MALDON: UBD iii, 877, 1798.
MANCHESTER: Baldwin, R. 1772; Raffald,
E. 1772, 1773, 1781; Harrop, J. 1773,
1781; Holme, E. 1788; Radford, J. 1788;
Scholes, J. 1794, 1797; Sowler, T. & R.
1794, 1797; UBD iii, 766, 1798; Bancks,
G. 1800, 1802; Dean, R. & W. 1804, 1808,
1811, 1813; Pigot, J. 1811, 1813; Wardle,
M. 1811; Pigot, J. & Dean, R. W. 1815,
1817, 1819, 1821, 1824; H; P; Wardle, M. &
Wilkinson, T. 1828, 1829; Pigot, J. & Son
1829, 1830, 1832, 1833, 1836, 1838;
Butterworth, J. 1822, Pigot, J. & Slater, I.
1840, 1841, 1843; Slater, I. 1843; Ireland,
A. 1855.
MANSFIELD: UBD iii, 881, 1798; H; Linney,
J. 1872.
MARGATE: UBD iii, 900, 1798; Holden 1811,
1816; Pigot (Kent) 1823; Robins, *Watering
Places* (1833).
MARLBOROUGH: H.
MERTHYR TYDFIL: H.

MIDDLETON: See: Leigh, J. (*Lancashire*)
1818.
MONMOUTH: UBD iii, 925, 1798; H. (CD:
Lascelles & Co. 1852).
MONTGOMERY: UBD iii, 929, 1798; H.
MORECAMBE AND HEYSHAM: Mannex,
P. & Co. 1866
MORPETH: H.
NEWARK: H; UBD iv, 56, 1798.
NEWBURY: H; UBD iv, 77, 1798.
NEWCASTLE-UNDER-LYME: UBD iv, 100,
1798; Parson & Bradshaw 1818; Allbut
1822; Bayley, J. 1836; Cottrill, I. 1836,
1839; Hyde & Crewe 1839; Ingamells, J.
1871; Bayley, T. 1874. (See also *Octo-
centenary Guide* published by Newcastle
Public Library, 1973, Section B).
NEWCASTLE-UPON-TYNE: UBD iii, 929,
iv, 20, 1798; Angus, T. 1778, 1787;
Whitehead, W. 1778, 1782, 1787, 1790;
Lawson 1782; Akenhead, D. 1790; Angus,
M. 1795; Hilton, W. 1795; Mitchell, J. 1801;
Mackenzie & Dent 1811; H; P; Humble,
Francis 1824; Humble, Stephen 1824;
Hodgson, T. & J. 1833; Ihler, A. 1833;
Richardson, M. A. 1838, 1839; Blackwell &
Co. 1844; Williams, J. 1844.
NEWPORT (I.o.W.): UBD iii, 403, 1798; H.
NEWPORT (Mon.): H; Christophers, W.
1847; Kelly, W. 1848; Scott, J. M. &
Morris, D. 1847.
NORTHAMPTON: UBD iv, 84, 1798; H;
Phillips, T. 1853. (CD: Gardner, R. 1849;
Whellan, W. 1849).
NORWICH: Chase, W. 1783; UBD iv, 3, 1798;
Bacon, R. M. 1803; Berry, C. 1810; Adlard
& Palmer 1852. Jarrold & Sons 1843
(CD: Blurton, E. 1854).
NOTTINGHAM: UBD iv, 44, 1798; Willoughby,
E. 1799; H; P; Dearden 1834; Glover 1825,
1844. (CD: White, W. 1832; White, F. & J.
1844; Blurton, J. 1844, 1853; Whittaker &
Co. 1849; White, F. 1853).
OKEHAMPTON: UBD iv, 170, 1798; H.
OLDHAM: H; Butterworth, J. 1817; Clarke, J.
1817; P; Worrall, 1871, 1875, 1880.
OXFORD: UBD iv, 112, 1798; H; Vincent, J.
1835; Hunt 1846. (CD: Hunt, E. & Co.
1846; Gardner, R. 1852).
PEMBROKE: UBD iv, 209; H.
PENRYN: UBD iv, 258, 1798; H.
PENZANCE; UBD iv, 282, 1798; H.
PETERBOROUGH: UBD iv, 187, 1798; H.
PLYMOUTH: UBD iv, 261, 1798; M'Creery, J.
1812; Rees & Curtis 1812; Woolcombe, H.
1812; Rowe, S. 1814; H; Nettleton, E. 1822;
Taperell, N. 1822; Johns, J. 1823; Longman,
Hurst & Co. 1823; Byers, W. 1830; Brindley,
R. 1830; Thomas, J. 1836; Flintoff, G.
1844; Stevens, J. 1835; Williams, J. 1847;
Battenbury, L. E. G. 1847; Brendon, F.
1852, 1853.
PONTEFRACT: H.

POOLE: UBD iv, 230, 1798; H.
PORTSMOUTH: UBD iv, 193, 1798; H.
PRESTON: UBD iv, 249, 1798; 'Peter Whittle'
(ps) 1821; Wilcockson, I. 1821; Mannex,
P. J. & Co. 1851; H; Johnson, W. B. 1851.
(CD: Tupling, G. *Lancashire Directories
1684–1957* (1968)).
PUDSEY: UBD ii, 441, iv, 761, 1798.
PWLLHELI: H.
RAMSGATE: H; Wilson, S. R. 1886.
READING: UBD iv, 301, 1798; H.
REDBRIDGE: Horniman, R. 1828; Ingall,
C. 1837.
RICHMOND: H; Darnhill, J. 1824, 1825;
Evans, J. 1824, 1825; Spencer, T. 1871,
1875.
RICHMOND-ON-THAMES: UBD iv, 292,
1798.
RIPON: UBD iv, 312, 1798; H.
ROCHDALE: UBD iv, 357, 1798; H; P; Evans,
T. J. 1820; Butterworth, J. 1820.
ROCHESTER: UBD iv, 357, 1798; H; Cox,
W. H. 1838; Wright, I. G. 1838.
ROTHERHAM: UBD iv, 361, 1798; H; P.
ROYAL LEAMINGTON SPA: Bissett 1814;
Moncrieff 1829, 1830, 1833, 1837;
Merridew, J. 1829, 1830, 1833, 1837.
Fairfax, J. 1832, 1833, 1834, 1835, 1838;
Beck 1842, 1845; Williams, J. 1846;
Dewhirst 1849.
ROYAL TUNBRIDGE WELLS: Sprange, J.
1808; Stapley, W. 1845; Colbran, J. 1849,
1850.
RUGBY: H.
RYDE (I.o.W.): Gabell & Co. 1846.
RYE: UBD iv, 346, 1798.
SAFFRON WALDEN: H.
ST IVES (Cornwall): UBD iv, 369, 1798.
ST IVES (Hunts.): UBD iv, 371, 1798.
SALISBURY: UBD iv, 543, 1798; H.
SANDWICH: UBD iv, 376, 1798; H.
SCARBOROUGH: UBD iv, 381, 1798; H;
Storry, T. 1846.
SHAFTESBURY: UBD iv, 390, 1798; H.
SHEFFIELD: Wilkie 1774; Sketchley, T.
1774; Gales, J. & Martin, D. 1787;
Robinson, G. & J. 1787; UBD iv, 395, 1798;
Robinson, J. 1797; H; Todd, W. 1817; P;
Gell, R. and Bennett, R. 1821; Bacon,
H. A. 1821; Brownell, W. 1817; Varey, D.
1825; Blackwell, J. 1828; White, W. 1833,
1841, 1845, 1849; Rogers, H. & T. 1841;
Kelly, F. 1854.
SHREWSBURY: Minshull, T. 1786, 1793,
1797, 1803, 1804; Pryse 1786; UBD iv, 413,
1798; Hodges, J. 1803 and 1804; H;
(CD: Tibnam & Co. 1828: Bagshaw, S.
1851; Harrison, S. 1851).
SLOUGH: UBD iv, 793, 1798.
SOUTHAMPTON; UBD iv, 452; Cunningham,
A. 1803, 1811; H; Fletcher & Son 1834,
1836; Cooper, W. 1843, 1845, 1847;
Fletcher, Forbes & Fletcher 1843, 1845;

(Southampton — continued) —
Forbes & Knibb 1847, 1849, 1851; Rayner,
C. & J. 1849; Williams, E. D. 1849, 1851,
1853, 1855; Forbes & Marshall 1853, 1855.
SOUTHPORT: Glazebrook, T. K. 1826;
Haddock, J. & J. 1826; Rivington, C. & J.
1826. 'Peter Whittle' (ps) 1831, 1836;
Whittaker & Co. 1836; Whittle, P. & H.
1836; Hall, A. & Co. 1848; Johnson, R.
1848; Robinson, F. 1848; Poore, J. 1849;
Alsop, W. 1832; 'S.J.' 1849.
SOUTH SHIELDS: UBD iv, 517, 1798.
STAFFORD: UBD iv, 436, 1798; H; Parson &
Bradshaw 1818; Williams 1846. (CD: Allbut,
J. & Son 1802; Chester & Mort 1810; Leigh,
J. 1818; Allbut, T. 1822). See: Merry, N. E.
& Beard, D. R. *Staffordshire Directories; a
Union List of Directories relating to the
Geographical County of Staffordshire*
(1966). C.D: Parson & Bradshaw 1818.
STALYBRIDGE: UBD iv, 442, 1798.
STAMFORD: UBD iv, 442, 1798; H.
STOCKPORT: UBD iv, 475, 1798; H; P.
STOKE-ON-TRENT: UBD iv, 109, 1798; P;
Keates 1873-74; 1875-76, 1879.
STOURBRIDGE: UBD iv, 493, 1798; H; P;
Bentley 1840; 'Almanack' 1885-1917.
STRATFORD-ON-AVON: UBD iv, 534, 1798.
SUDBURY: UBD iv, 506, 1798.
SUNDERLAND: UBD iv, 519, 1798; H;
Kelly 1896.
SUTTON: Robson 1839; Morgan, J. 1864;
Church 1872; Holt 1890-96; Pile 1896-
1938.
SUTTON COLDFIELD: UBD iv, 541, 1798.
SWANSEA: UBD iv, 520, 1798; Morris, Z. B.
1802; H; Mathews, M. 1830.
SWINDON: H.
TAMWORTH: UBD iv, 576, 1798; H.
P.
TAUNTON: UBD iv, 583, 1798; H.
TENBY: H.
TENTERDEN: UBD iv, 590, 1798.
TEWKESBURY: UBD iv, 593, 1798; H.
THETFORD: UBD iv, 602, 1798.
TIVERTON: UBD iv, 617, 1798; H.
TORBAY: (Torquay) Blewitt, O. 1832;
Cockrem 1832; Simpkin & Marshall 1832.
TOTNES: H.
TRURO: H.
WAKEFIELD: UBD iv, 654, 1798; H; P.
WALLINGFORD: UBD iv, 662, 1798; H;
Webster 1869, 1872.
WALSALL: Sketchley 1767, 1779; Pearson &
Rollason 1780, 1781; UBD iv, 665, 1798;
Pearce, T. 1813; Thomson, Lewis & Wright-
son, 1813; H; Parson & Bradshaw 1818; P.

WAREHAM: UBD iv, 712, 1798.
WARRINGTON: H; P; Worral 1871.
WARWICK: UBD iv, 690, 1798; Sharpe 1817,
1822. (CD: Blurton, J. 1850; Beilby, J. H.
1852; Harrisons 1855).
WATFORD: UBD iv, 697, 1798.
WELLS: UBD iv, 713, 1798; H.
WELSHPOOL: UBD iv, 707, 1798; H.
WEST BROMWICH: UBD iv, 706, 1798;
Baldwin & Cradock 1836; Davies, T. 1836;
Reeves, J. 1836.
WESTON-SUPER-MARE: Wright, J. 1880-81.
WEYMOUTH: UBD iv, 723, 1798; H; Kay, G.
1816, 1827; Benson, B. 1828; Commin, J.
1828.
WHITEHAVEN: UBD iv, 746, 1798; H.
WHITLEY BAY: UBD iv, 870, 1798.
WIGAN: UBD iv, 755; H; P.
WILTON: UBD iv, 566, 762, 1798.
WINCHESTER: UBD iv, 877, 1798; H;
Gilmour, G. & H. 1854.
WINDSOR: UBD iv, 775, 1798.
WISBECH: UBD iv, 800, 1798; H.
WOLVERHAMPTOM: Sketchley 1767, 1770;
Pearson & Rollason 1780, 1781; UBD iv,
810, 1798; H; P; Smart, J. 1827; Bridgen, J.
1833, 1838, 1847; Williams, G. 1849;
Melville, F. R. 1851; Stanley, J. 1851;
Hinde, A. 1902. See Roper, J. S., *Trades &
Professions in Wolverhampton, 1802* (Loc.
Hist. Pamp. No. 3, 1970).
WOODSTOCK: UBD iv, 823, 1798; Webster
1872, 1889-99.
WORCESTER: Tunnicliff 1788; Grundy, J. 1788,
1790, 1792, 1794, 1797; UBD iv, 1798,
836; H; Pigot 1830, 1835; 'Guide' 1837;
Stratford, T. 1837; Haywood 1840; Bentley
1840; Hunt & Co. 1847; Stanley, J. 1851;
Littlebury 1882, 1885, 1896; Deighton
1882, 1905-18. (CD: Eaton, T. 1820;
Bentley, J. 1840, 1841; Bull & Turner
1840, 1841; Heming, J. 1820; Lascelles &
Co. 1851; Lewis, S. 1820).
WORKINGTON: UBD iv, 832, 1798; H.
WORKSOP: H. (CD: Pigot, 1830).
WORTHING: UBD iv, 580, 1798; Jones,
N. W. 1811; Mackcoull, J. 1811; Phillips,
J. 1849, 1850; Whittaker & Co. 1849,
1850.
WREXHAM: H; P; Crocker, 1881.
YARMOUTH (Great): H.
YEOVIL: UBD iv, 959, 1798; H.
YORK: Ward, A. 1787; UBD iv, 950, 1798;
H; P; Smith, W. H. 1843; Williams & Co.
1843. (CD: Baines, E. 1823, 1830; see also
Bailey's *Northern Directory* 1781).

CHAPTER TEN

PROVINCIAL NEWSPAPERS FROM 1690

THERE IS NO source of local history as evocative of the atmosphere of any 19th-century town as its local newspaper. There is certainly no contemporary document more redolent of local identity and municipal pride. Though perhaps offered to guests with some slighting comment on 'the local rag', its continuing circulation is better evidence of the paper's real popularity, as is the well-established habit of sending copies regularly to relatives abroad or removed to less fortunate towns. A remarkable number of local newspapers have been published during the past 300 years and a considerable number still survive. Nor are they all taken over by the large national press combines; a significant number still maintain themselves to be 'independent' and truly 'local'. Nothing else as vigorous as these countless *Reporters, Gazettes* and *Observers* offers such explicit statements of the aspirations and attitudes of Georgian and Victorian townspeople. They reveal the political views, not only of their owners but of prominent citizens and the man-in-the-street. Their very titles set the local scene and its principal activity, as the *North Shields and Northumberland Advertiser and Agricultural, Shipping and Commercial Journal* gives a comprehensive picture of Tyneside in 1831–2.

If we include, not only the 'hard news' papers and political news-sheets, but also some of the theatrical programmes, fashionable reviews and visitors' lists, the religious magazines and specialist papers on hobbies, or local scientific and literary journals, a well-rounded picture of urban and suburban life over two full centuries can be compiled. In our Gazetteer, however, precedence has been given to the large number of actual *newspapers*, particularly those associated with particular towns by name. In general, most of the *Temperance Advocates, Racing Specials, Fur and Feather Fanciers* and *Evening Football Echoes* have been omitted. Yet a few of the more significant or curious of these specialised publications have also been added. Thus Cardiff has its *Shipping Gazette* (1869-1911), and Plymouth its *Emigrants' Penny Magazine* (1850-1) and an occasional *Prices Current* or *Suburban Property Review* has been considered relevant. Nor have the minority publications of the cities been entirely omitted; the Jewish community of Leeds and the Catholic and Welsh folk of Liverpool are represented, as are a few *Congregational Monthlies* and some long-standing school magazines which may be of vital importance to the family historian. Seaside resorts and spas were particularly enthusiastic producers of *Visitors' Lists* and *Amusement Guides* — Brighton at least 50 works of this type from 1822 — and a few of them will also be found in the Gazetteer.

Every possible aspect of the new and thriving towns of 19th-century England and Wales is here. These numerous publications give a lively, many-faceted picture of the life of Victorian provincial towns. We are reminded of the strong theatrical tradition of Liverpool, the cosmopolitan atmosphere of Cardiff, the industries of Rochdale and the West Riding, and the ecclesiastical importance of Lichfield and Lincoln. Provincial newspapers are as old, if not a little older, than the London press. The first London daily paper, the *Daily Courant*, was published in 1702; several provincial cities lay claim to an earlier weekly paper. The *Norwich Post*, later the *Gazette*, was first issued in 1701, *Berrow's Worcester Journal*, which is still published weekly, begun its circulation as the *Worcester Post Man* in 1690 and the *Stamford Mercury*, also surviving, lays a similar claim to 1695. The oldest surviving newspaper of all, the *London Gazette*, was first published as the *Oxford Gazette* before it was transferred to the capital in 1665. The *Gazette* was but one of a series of Royalist *Mercuries* which had opposed the Parliamentary rebels from the King's stronghold in Oxford. In all there were in 1982 21 local newspapers which originated in the years from 1690 to 1775. There are more than 400 *surviving* provincial newspapers which began publication before 1900 and more than half of these pre-date the Local Government Act of 1888. Our Gazetteer shows that at the height of municipal growth in the provinces, it was by no means unusual for a town like Wolverhampton or Huddersfield to see the weekly publication of four or five local newspapers.

Many smaller towns, including some which were never boroughs, supported their own local press throughout the 19th century. Thus we find the market town of Ludlow in Shropshire issuing four newspapers between 1840 and 1912, and townships of un-remarkable size such as Shifnal in the same county (present population 5,000) combining to circulate the *Advertiser* with the neighbouring small towns of Oakengates, Ironbridge and Madeley at the turn of the century. Hundreds of these local papers were ephemeral, perhaps lasting for no more than a dozen issues, but they were not all short-lived; there are in fact at least 60 non-chartered towns which currently publish a local newspaper which is usually of at least a century's standing. These include places like Shepton Mallet (pop. 5,910) in Somerset, with its *Journal* from 1854, and Dursley in Gloucestershire (pop. 5,500) which has published the *Gazette* since 1878.

The coverage of provincial newspapers from the end of the 17th century – and certainly for the past 150 years – is widespread across the country. Of our basic list of 375 municipal and county boroughs, only six have no recorded newspaper at any time; they are Hedon, Higham Ferrers, Kidwelly, Llandovery, Lydd and Ruthin. Three other boroughs (Bebington, New Romney and Tenterden) published no newspapers before 1936. For the rest, the average number of newspapers and periodicals is about 10 per town, with Liverpool boasting a grand total of at least 146 before 1920. In all, our Gazetteer lists more than 450 productive towns, and nearly 4,000 different titles.

Certain limitations impose themselves upon a search for local journals; as always, we are dependent upon the availability and comprehensiveness of catalogues. These are in the case of newspapers relatively easily available in a central location, and relatively far-reaching as well; but they are incomplete, and remote from the localities they record. The major aid in the compilation of the Gazetteer was the *British Museum's Tercentenary Handlist of English and Welsh Newspapers, Magazines and Reviews* first published in 1920 and re-issued as a facsimile reprint in 1966. This is available in many reference libraries and catalogues the actual holdings of the British Museum in 1920. The Museum's collection comprised all periodicals deposited since the Copyright Act of 1842 plus two great 17th and 18th-century private collections. The *Handlist* states that it is 'believed to be practically exhaustive as regards the 17th and 19th centuries. The 18th-century list, however, is far from complete'. No conjectural dates are used and we are reminded that the *Handlist* refers not to the full continuous existence of every newspaper, but only to the dates of copies *actually held* in the Museum. These give numbers of the issues held, so that given a perpetual calendar and the assumption of an unbroken run, an estimate can be made backward from the earliest date held to the calculated date of issue No. 1. This is the cause of many disputes over origins and the reason why the date given as the first issue in current *Press Guides* is often the editor's calculation and different from the Museum's recorded first date. The *Handlist* is arranged chronologically but indexed alphabetically.

In 1932 the Newspaper Repository built in 1903 at Colindale, north of London, became the Newspaper Library. It survived extensive bomb-damage in 1940 to become part of the British Library, separated from the British Museum in 1973. The Library contains 500,000 volumes and parcels of periodicals and 90,000 reels of microfilm, occupying approximately 20 miles of shelving. There is a very helpful information service and excellent facilities for students who should, however, write in advance of a planned visit for details of how to obtain a Reader's Ticket, enclosing a stamped addressed envelope. The printed *Catalogue of the Newspaper Library* (in 9 volumes) is arranged both by titles (alphabetically) (volumes 5–8) and by place-name (alphabetically) in the earlier volumes. *Volume 1* deals with London, *Volume 2* with the British Isles and *Volumes 3–4* with overseas publications. This *Catalogue* was produced in 1975 and is thus more up-to-date than the *Tercentenary Handlist*; it is also better arranged for reference by towns as each place's total collection from first to last is arranged under a single heading. Again, this is a catalogue of actual holdings, without conjectural dating. Unfortunately, this *Catalogue* appears to be available only in large city reference libraries such as Birmingham and Worcester.

Additional reference can be made to two annual *Press Guides* which are currently available in almost every reference library. These are *Benn's Press Directory* and *Willing's Press Guide*. These list, alphabetically, each town's current newspapers and periodicals with data on year of origin and earlier titles; they do not, of course, list issues no longer in print but could be searched year by year from 1975 to trace losses from the *Newspaper Library Catalogue*. Thus, we have three main reference points for our Gazetteer, 1920, 1975 and the year in which it was compiled, 1981–2. No newspaper of which publication began after 1920 is listed. If a Batley newspaper is concealed in the index of the *Handlist* under a title other than *The Batley . . .* , as for example *The Thunderer*, it will have escaped notice, but would have been found under 'Batley' in the 1975 Catalogue.

A final source of information is available in the collections and catalogues of each local public library or town archives. Newspapers are essentially library material; we shall not expect to find them collected, apart from a few strays, in county record offices. Fortunately many town libraries have indexed collections of their earliest newspapers and, occasionally, those of neighbouring towns. Many libraries have kindly provided information and lists for addition to this Gazetteer; these sometimes reveal hidden newspapers unknown to the nationally-printed catalogues. Gloucester City Library, for example, records the existence of the *Gloucester Gazette* (1792–6). Halifax Public Library has the *Journal* (1801–11) and *Reformer* (1847–8); and Hull Library lists the *Courant* (1796–99). None of them are contained in the Newspaper

Library *Catalogue*. Similarly, local libraries often indicate earlier copies than those held at the British Library. Thus it is expedient to refer cautiously to numbers and dates, never to assert that any town 'has had no early newspaper'; in every case we must add 'as far as the available catalogues show . . .'. Local memory at Llandovery may know better.

Most of our major towns were incorporated boroughs long before they published their first newspaper. Others began publication about ten years before an Act of Parliament gave them borough status. Of the chartered cities and towns of our base-list more than 200 (almost 60%) have at least one current newspaper with origins in, or before, the 19th century. The graph reveals the time-span of local newspaper publication

DATE OF THE PUBLICATION OF EACH TOWN'S FIRST NEWSPAPER

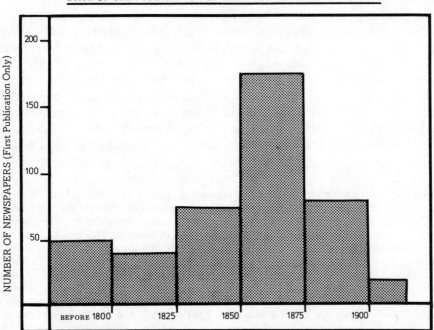

and demonstrates the immense proliferation of the local press between the Municipal Corporations Act of 1835 and the creation of county boroughs in 1888. The graph shows that about 50 of the chartered boroughs of our base-list had published their first newspaper before 1800. Of these, several are outstanding, in that their earliest titles are still in current circulation; for example the *Stamford Mercury* (1715) and the *Gloucester Journal* (1722).

Most newspapers were shorter-lived. Amalgamations, reorganization under new titles and successive changes of circulation were commonplace. Often, as in the case of the *Kendal Mercury*, the changes are repeatedly rung, here on different combinations of 'Westmorland, Kendal, Advertiser, Mercury and Times', as many as six times between 1829 and 1920. Repeatedly a pair of neighbouring towns, such as Prescot and St Helens (Lancs) or Pendlebury and Swinton (Lancs) vie for precedence and alternate 'top-billing' on their banners. Newspaper titles give an interesting insight into the interplay of relationships between county-town and county. Many towns, particularly the industrial cities and new boroughs of the North and Midlands, maintain their independence. Their newspapers bear the name of their town, and no other. From *Telegraph* (1852) to *Telephone* (1904) Barnsley's newspapers are only *Barnsley* and Bolton's never mention Lancashire. In the south-east, we see a different picture; there, newspapers begin in the towns but are often 'taken over' by a new circulation, with a county title: Kent in particular can show many examples of this trend. Most Aylesbury newspapers too are for Buckinghamshire; Hertford sustains no independent journal of its own; and Winchester's only surviving paper is the *Hampshire Chronicle and Courier*. If, as seems apparent in the metropolitan counties, the ability to found and to sustain the circulation of a town newspaper is a barometer of municipal pride and independence, then the urban atmospheric pressure in some counties was low.

There is no doubt that the Victorian provincial town saw its claim to municipal status and its pride in the local newspaper in the same light. The *Dudley Herald* was founded in 1866, one year after the town's incorporation. Its shorter-lived predecessor, the *Dudley Weekly Times*, was in no doubt either of the power of the press or the importance of the town. In its first issue of 20 December 1856, the editor saw the primary function of the newspaper as a medium of advertising, 'to facilitate business transactions . . . Dudley taking as it does, its stand as one of the first manufacturing towns in England'. The *Weekly Times*' intention, therefore, was ' . . . to place Dudley on an equal footing with other towns of its class . . .'. The editorial continued:

> 'No agency of modern times vests such an influence upon public opinion or operates as powerfully upon the minds and habits of the people as the public press. Never perhaps was this influence more strenuously or more widely extended than at the present time. The slightest ruffle in the sea of politics, the smallest wavering in the scale of markets and the least convulsion in the social world is immediately chronicled by hundreds of newspapers and commented on by writers as varied in ability as they are diversified in opinion. This intelligence and these comments are immediately circulated with amazing rapidity through the length and breadth of the land, finding access to the workshop of the artisan, the counting house of the merchant, the study of the learned, the cottage of the poor and the mansion of the great. Now indeed we have newspapers in abundance and of all varieties, from the stately daily journal down to the smallest weekly chronicle. . . . It is not only important that the great national events should be chronicled and commented upon, but also that those which are of local character and of more local interest must be recorded and this can only be done by the local press. Every place has interests of its own and matters of moment peculiar to itself. . . . Our columns are open to any person or persons who may reasonably consider themselves unjustly treated and we shall always be ready to insert any suggestions for local reform or the exposure of local abuses. Our leading principle will be to serve the interests of our town and district and if, by exposing such an abuse, we lead to a useful reform, we shall be happy to think we have been of some use in our day and generation . . .'.

Crusading or reforming zeal was a constant feature of the local presses, occasionally negated by an equal desire to appear impartial and offer objective facts. In Leeds we find *The Gutter News (A Journal to Expose Immorality)* in 1885; and the *Portsmouth Borough Reporter* of 1841 was sub-titled *Exposer of Abuses and Advocate of Reform*. Several diverse origins of the provincial newspaper were, from their inception, influential on their format and content and indeed some of these persist to the present day.

Originating in the 16th century as nameless, handwritten newsletters, or the work of a country gentleman's London or overseas 'Intelligencer', the content of the earliest newspapers *was* that of news, the affairs and events of foreign Courts and the 'relations' of great events. Often they took the form of ballads or broadsheets. Political and religious argument was another contemporary aspect of the *corantoes* which first appeared as handwritten political tracts or religious pamphlets, later as *diurnals* or daily news-books. From the start government took an obstructive view of public circulation of such opinions; information was seen as a royal prerogative. For this reason, the earliest printed English broadsheets were smuggled into the country from Holland. Such breaches of the royal restrictions on publication were a Star Chamber matter; printers and publishers were liable to corporal punishment, their works subject to constant suppression. Governments of all shades of political opinion, Royalist and Puritan, Whigs and Tories, were equally opposed to any freedom of the press. At first this was invariably assumed to refer to the London presses, which were limited in number by means of licensing and the passing of restrictive Printing Acts. When, in 1695 these lapsed, being unworkable, a series of punitive Stamp Acts controlled the activities of London and provincial printers.

From 1712 to 1855 a series of Acts levied prohibitive duty on newsprint, rising from ½d. a sheet in 1712 to 4d. in 1815. This added a tax equivalent to a present-day £2 to the cost of producing each copy of a newspaper, to which were added other charges for advertisements and the cost of postage from town to town. All paper for the printing presses was brought ready-stamped from London, making the emergence of the provincial press expensive, though relatively free from supervision and punishment. The determination of journalists to publish news and opinion in spite of penalties, even at some stages despite the absence of much real news, had a profoundly formative effect upon the familiar form and content of our local newspapers. The regulations were repeatedly evaded by means of paying the same duty per sheet on larger pages and smaller print. At first both London and provincial newsmen aimed at a weekly issue, with several different newspapers appearing on successive days of the week. In the provinces editors and printers adopted the simple method of reprinting items brought by the first and fastest post from the London papers. The collection and distribution of news was a hazardous business employing pony express 'post-boys' who braved floods, blizzards, footpads and rival gangs to bring the news in time to beat their employers' competitors.

In the country, several news-sheets were founded in different towns by the same men. Some of these were patent medicine salesmen who used their news-sheets as advertising media. The combination of quacks and hacks accounts for another prominent feature of early newspapers; many an otherwise dull chronicle of insignificant events is enlivened for the local historian by the dramatic quality of its advertisements. The following examples, for instance, appeared in no. 6163 of the *Newcastle Courant* on 22 November 1794:

'SOLD, WHOLESALE and RETAIL, by HALL & ELLIOT, in Pilgrim Street, Newcastle, The most incomparable and never-failing CHYMICAL DROPS; Being a speedy cure for coughs, colds, asthmas, phthisicks, wheezing, shortness of breath, and all sorts of consumptions. Their virtues vastly exceed any thing that was ever published, or ever known in the whole universe'.

'The following singular case is another remarkable Instance of the superior Efficacy of SPILSBURY'S ANTISCORBUTIC DROPS: Elizabeth Elston of Folkingham, in the County of Lincoln, was afflicted near twenty years with a violent scorbutic humour in one of her legs; during which period she was, at different times, under the care of several eminent members of the Faculty but never received any benefit. By the advice of a neighbour, she was prevailed upon to try *Spilsbury's Anti-Scorbutic Drops*, and purchased a bottle of Messrs. Ward & Son in March 1793; she continued to take them regularly, when two pieces of the bone were fortunately extracted. These curious substances being removed, it began gradually to heal, and to her great joy and surprise became apparently well'.

These advertisements and others — for antiquarian books, 'Best Crown Timber, lately imported from Memel' and 'A Quantity of Madeira Wine, to be sold by auction' — are typical of a four-page paper of which only the fourth is devoted to news.

Other 18th-century examples will include numerous notices of meetings of the trustees of various local turnpike roads, and police advertisements of rewards for the apprehension of forgers, felons and fugitives. There will also be theatre bills — the *Newcastle Courant* was publicising 'A Favourite New Comedy, written by R. Cumberland Esq., called THE JEW, to which will be added a Musical Farce called THE WATERMAN, at the Theatre Royal (which Mrs. Cookson will honor with her patronage on December 8th.)'. Notices of bankruptcy are frequent, as are sales of shops, farms and businesses. Advertisements of this sort continue to be a staple content of most local newspapers into the 19th century, though by the 1850s in town newspapers such as the *Dudley Times* they have become rather more mundane 'shopping guides' to the local ironmongers, linen drapers and furniture emporiums. By this time notices of railway stock for sale and prospective inter-city lines have replaced turnpike notices and coach time-tables, though inns, musical evenings and theatres are still popular.

We can, throughout the course of the 18th and 19th centuries, read the local reactions to all great events, both national and international. The *Weekly Worcester Journal* of 16 July 1742 offers 'the most Material Occurrences. Foreign and Domestic' amongst, or after the usual notices of stolen geldings and escaped apprentices. Foreign news from the courts of Europe and the plantations of Virginia is usually fully and factually reported. The *Weekly Worcester Journal* in 1741-2 for example, carries news from Hamburg of the surrender of Prague: 'the troops are in motion in the dominions of Hamburg and Hessia to make a camp . . .' and from Frankfurt, there was news of the King of Prussia's accession to the Treaty of Breslau. At the Hague a resolution for putting 45,000 men of the Republic's troops into a state of readiness to march had been proposed by the States General. From Prague came 'a genuine letter from an officer of distinction in the French Army who wrote "We are here in a hard situation, a superior enemy at the gates and none but enemies within. M. de Bellisle arrived from Dresden on 15th., to our great joy . . ."'. From the early campaigns of revolutionary France, through the Napoleonic Wars and the Peninsular campaign, to the victories of Trafalgar and Waterloo, country gentlemen and shopkeepers of Worcester were kept regularly informed by the *Weekly Journal*. So, in the local press, the boundaries of 'local history' are vastly widened.

Each of our three West Midland models has its flourishing and characteristic presses, and demonstrates the circulation of papers typical of each type of town. Worcester, a county-town and ancient city, was first in the field in 1690, and is one of several to claim 'Britain's oldest newspaper'. The *Post Man* and its successors, still current in the present-day as *Berrow's Worcester Journal* is very much the landed, aristocratic intelligencer. Birmingham, beginning publication of nearly 100 different successive papers with *Aris's Birmingham Gazette* in 1741, is typical of many industrial cities. Of its lengthy chain of titles, the *Post* (1857), the *Evening Mail* (1870) and the

Sunday Mercury (1918) are still flourishing. The former county borough of Dudley is equally typical of the mid-19th century aspirant to municipal rank, supporting 14 successive publications of *Times, News, Guardian, Mercury, Chronicle and Gazette*, from 1856 to 1887 and beyond. Of these the present *Dudley Herald* is a vociferous survivor.

Typical of the later newspapers of the heavily industrial boroughs are the *Birmingham Journal* of 1832 and the *Dudley Herald* of 1867. Here, rather than in the ancient cathedral city, we see that the real issues of the 19th century urban press reform and town government. The *Birmingham Journal* gives a lively picture of the struggle for the first Reform Bill's passing and of the remarkable part played by the city in that struggle. According to the *Journal*, victory was almost entirely due to Birmingham's organization of its neighbouring townships in political unions; to Birmingham's reforming leader, Thomas Attwood; to their peaceable but gigantic demonstrations; and, by implication, to the constant pressure of the *Birmingham Journal*. On 18 May, 1832, the newspaper's second edition – 'Express from London' – announced triumphantly: 'The cause is at last triumphant and our prophecy of last week is fulfilled. Lord Grey is recalled to office and the Reform Bill will be immediately passed . . . Men of Birmingham! All England gives you, and your great leader Thomas Attwood, the credit of having been one of the principal instruments of effecting the great triumph of giving liberty to Great Britain and Ireland and of frustrating a most atrocious and deep-laid conspiracy against the liberties of the world. We believe that the proceedings in Birmingham on Wednesday and the sending of our Deputation to London have effected incalculable good . . . The Ten Days of British Revolution delivered us from bondage and the domination of borough-mongers.' Heading the newspaper's list of new Parliamentary constituencies to be formed in accordance with reform is Birmingham, with two members of parliament (of whom Thomas Attwood would be one). Wolverhampton was also to have two new MPs, Dudley, Kidderminster and Walsall one each.

Dudley, as we have seen, came relatively late to the full flood of local newspaper publication and its first newspapers reflect the sense of identity of press and borough government. The *Dudley Times* was the town's first weekly newspaper. Its front page is tabulated with typical advertisements, for Gomer's Family Repository, Hutching's Wholesale and Retail Bookseller, Stationer and Music Seller, Wilson's Cheap Drapery and Millinery Establishment (with black silk bonnets at 1s. 10d. each and Victoria Lawn for children's funerals at 4½d. a yard). There is to be a 'Free and Easy' at the 'Fox and Dogs' in the Market Place, where the celebrated vocalist Mr. J. Francis will 'preside at the pianoforte and sing some of the popular songs of the day'; stereoscopes were on sale at Buck's the chemist in the High Street with views at 9d. to 8s. 6d. each and viewers from 1s. 6d. to 25s. There is entertainment at the Garrick Club, lectures at the Mechanics' Institute and the Lancastrian Schoolroom and a public meeting about income tax. The town was much concerned with taxes at this time; income tax, 7d. in the pound in 1855, had risen to 1s. 4d. in the previous year and threatened to go higher 'even though promised to be reduced when peace [in the Crimea] was signed'. The *Dudley Times* is adamant: 'If they cannot carry on the government at their present rate of expenditure, let them do as other people do – retrench. The necessities of life are dear, men with incomes of £150 a year cannot afford to pay an Income Tax under present circumstances. They have to make a

THE
Worcester Post-Man;

Containing the Heads of all the remarkable Occurrences both Foreign and Domestick.

Semper Eadem

Worcester-Arms

From *Friday*, January 26, to *Friday* February 2. 1711.

Saturday's and *Monday's* Post.

From Dyer's *Letter, and other Intelligence.*

A Flanders *and* Holland *Mails brings the following Advices.*

Constantinople. Decemb. 26.

THE Grand Seignior sent a Capigi to Mitelene to fetch the Head of Ali Bashaw, formerly Grand Vizier, because there were Proofs of his secret Intelligence with the Muscovites: But he escap'd with his Guards and the Dizdar or Governor of the Castle, and 'twas believ'd he has got into Muscovy.

Vienna, Jan. 21. Our Court has lately receiv'd certain Advice, That an Ambassador will be speedily sent hither from Turkey, to assure the Emperor, that the Sultan will inviolably observe the Peace.

Paris, Jan. 30 'Tis reported here, That the Duke of Noailles has writ to the King, that he's afraid he must raise the Siege of Gironne.

They write from Madrid, That King Philip is at Saragossa with the Queen and Prince. His Army which continues in the Neighbourhood, could not advance to Catalonia, by reason of the bad Weather. Count Staremberg has left Balaguer, and gone for Barcelona. He had

pointed for that Service, shall march by the end of this Month.

London, Jan. 25. Yesterday the Lords proceeded upon the Affair of Spain, and after a long Debate came to this Resolution, *viz.* That *my* Lord Galloway's giving the Post of Honour to the Portuguese, after they had past their own Confines, and were marched into Spain, was against the Hon. of the Imperial Crown of *Great Britain*: The House divided upon that Resolution, Yeas 64, Noes 44. The Plea that was made for his Lordship was, that the Portugueze are a stubborn and humersom People, and if his Lordship had not comply'd with them in that particular, he should not have prevail'd with them to have marched into Spain. The Convocation met yesterday according to their last Adjournment, when the Right Honourable the Lord Dartmouth one of the principal Secretaries of State, brought down and presented to his Grace the Archbishop of Canterbury, in a handsom Speech, the Royal Licence under the Broad Seal ith-powering them to sit and proceed on Business, which Speech his Grace answer'd with another, after which both Houses unanimously agreed in an Address of Thanks to Her Majesty, and adjourn'd to Friday, when they are

The Dudley Weekly Times

AND SOUTH STAFFORDSHIRE & EAST WORCESTERSHIRE ADVERTISER.

PUBLISHED EVERY SATURDAY MORNING BY WILLIAM COLLINS, CASTLE STREET, TO WHOM ALL COMMUNICATIONS MUST BE ADDRESSED.

VOL. I.
No. 1.

SATURDAY, DECEMBER 20, 1856.

PRICE 1½D.
BY POST 2½D.

From the Newspaper Library, British Library, actual size of page 22½ in. x 17 in.

decent appearance, to educate their children, to bring up and maintain their families. They cannot pay 1s. 4d. in the pound to the tax collector'.

Foreign news was also available to the Dudley townsfolk. We find accounts of insurrection in the slave states of Kentucky and Tennessee, and Russian preparations of an army of 40,000 men on the borders of Persia. The Russians appear to be contemplating an expedition into Turkestan and the Prussians are preparing for war with an enlisted army of 135,000 men. Nearer Dudley, there had been yet another pit explosion, this time at Kingswinford; Lord Lyttleton had lectured at the Mechanics' Institute on 'The Colonies of Great Britain'; and there was to be a Railway Supplement in the next edition. For the prurient, there was the 'curious case of the alleged abduction of a governess from the house of a clergyman in Bath, by one John Webb Roche, a gentleman of fortune'. The Dudley Petty sessions recorded a dreary litany of felonies and assaults and the offences heard at Worcester Assizes were very largely presented from Dudley. The *Times'* explanation was that Dudley 'is very thickly peopled . . . the inhabitants could not be held under that control which gentlemen by their influence could exercise in the agricultural parts of the county'.

By the time the *Dudley Herald* was first published in 1866, Dudley was a year old as a municipal borough. A typical issue of 1867 is mainly concerned with the possibility of strikes and the question of 'public education'. There had been a meeting of the South Staffordshire Educational Association in Wolverhampton, to debate whether the educational provisions of the Factory Act might be introduced 'into a district such as this?' The *Herald* was not optimistic: 'Notwithstanding the many gigantic attempts that have hitherto been made to elevate and refine the tastes of the people, notwithstanding the schools aided by the Government or those supported by the efforts of various religious denominations or endowed by private charity, throughout the country, gross, deep, dark, lamentable ignorance prevails amongst the lower classes . . . How are the expenses necessarily attendant upon a compulsory Act to be defrayed? We should think that a district Education Rate would be the fairest and easiest way of meeting it. Possibly many will object to further rates, the existing ones being so very high; we admit that they are high. But what is the reason? Is it not that a large proportion of our goals and workhouses are filled through causes preventable by education? . . . '

There can be no doubt that times were hard in Dudley in 1867. Regular weekly meetings of the Board of Guardians are fully reported in the *Herald*, recording 630 people in the workhouse (compared with 581 in the previous year). In one week 21 had been admitted, 2 born and 1 died; 20 were discharged and £268 had been spent in outdoor relief. Vagrants given relief totalled 74; there had been a weekly attendance of 127 at the workhouse school, and 38 youths were receiving industrial training. The overseers were in debt and their tradesmen unpaid. An interesting case was reported at this particular meeting, of a Coseley doctor's complaint that the relieving officer had refused to sign his prescription of wine for a pauper patient suffering from erysipelas, who 'required plenty of stimulants'. The doctor complained that the particular officer frequently refused or failed to sign such 'orders'. He was reminded that a private doctor could not 'order' foods such as meat, milk, porter or other articles of diet for his poor patients, only recommend.

Another report described the reopening of a soup-kitchen in the market place 'when the distress and wretchedness which have so long been rife in the borough of Dudley

have been multiplied and intensified by the recent inclemency of the weather';
500 were being turned away each day after nearly as many had already been supplied.
The *Herald* refers to the 'well-known depression existing in the district, in the manufacture of Wolverhampton japanned ware, the Willenhall lock trade, amongst the
Wednesbury tube-makers, the Darlaston nuts-and-bolts, screws and other ironworks,
the Bilston tray and tin-plate workers and the chain-makers of Dudley', all of whom
were finding fewer and fewer contracts to fill. Only the nailers of Sedgley and its
adjoining hamlets were 'moderately employed'. Colonial demand was subsiding and the
demand from India was 'quiet'. The editor foresaw that the 'disturbed political state
of the United States will interrupt the flow of orders to this and other manufacturing districts'.

In the face of such depression, philanthropy was at work, for another report
described the Earl of Dudley's gift to the borough of a massive fountain of red and
grey granite and Portland stone, 'the most important and elegant work of its kind we
have yet seen.' This still stands, a fine specimen, in Dudley market place just as the
Herald describes it, with figures of Agriculture and Mining, lions' heads discharging
water and two basins filled by dolphin-figures. Further decorated with seahorses,
surmounted by Industry and Commerce, and finished off with two nude children
holding scrolls with appropriate mottoes, the fountain is a fitting memorial to the
original borough.

The reporting of Dudley's municipal affairs *par excellence*, however, is without
doubt the *Herald*'s monthly account of council meetings. These offer an invaluable
insight into the scope and nature of Victorian municipal government in a town of this
size. It appears that the more things have changed in local government, the more they
have remained the same. There is a small-scale informality about the business of the
council which is still vaguely familiar. In 1867 there were four chief officers of the
new council, some of them co-opted from private practice. These were the town clerk;
the borough surveyor (who resigned at the beginning of 1867 to continue with his own
business); the borough treasurer (and rate collectors); and the inspector of nuisances.
There was also a redundant Cattle Plague Inspector who according to the outspoken
Dudley councillors 'was the best-paid officer under the Corporation, while he did least
work and gave a great deal of dissatisfaction'. Early retirement not being available at
that time, they recommended an outright reduction of his salary.

There was a Finance Committee of the council which also met as a local Board of
Health, and the council also received reports from other committees, such as the
Street and Gas Committee. (They had recently met the directors of the private gas
company 'who did not feel justified in making any further reduction in their prices
at the present time.') The Watch Committee was responsible for the payment of the
borough force, but the council had recently called for the attendance of the Chief
Constable of Worcestershire to answer questions referring to the latest 'consolidation'
of the borough police (reputed to have carried out their responsibility to the full
satisfaction of the council) and the county (which was believed to be expensively
incapable of understanding the town's real needs). The Chief Constable was hectored
with the rude good humour that is still so typical of local council meetings in these
parts. The Inspector of Nuisances and Lodging Houses (with a monthly budget of £40)
was able to report that the sanitary state of the town was 'most satisfactory and
that there was no increase in contagious disease'. The burgesses had, since the terrible

cholera epidemic of the 1830s, built three great churches as prophylactic measures against the contagious results of sin; these, apparently, had some effect; £480 a year would certainly not have gone as far.

The Borough Treasurer's accounts were invariably fraught with the difficulties of actually collecting the rates due to him. The townspeople paid, or not, much as the mood took them. Council business included the Town Clerk's salary, problems of defective drainage in Withymore, the question of the duties and salary of the borough surveyor, and, repeatedly, the vexed question of a site for the town's cattle market, which the Earl of Dudley refused to countenance anywhere near the centre. The signing of cheques for the payment of the principal officers' monthly accounts concluded the business of every meeting, each being left with a normal credit balance of £3 to £20 in hand. We are reminded of a time when local government not only covered its own costs from a modest rate, but even made a margin of profit — if it could only collect the money due.

Thus we see that from their inception, local newspapers have combined ingredients familiar to us all today — news both local and foreign, advertisements, sex and violence, crime, features and nine-day wonders, literary reviews and scientific or pseudo-scientific articles, even on some occasions the inclusion of serialised fiction and 'part-works'. The national press was capable of line-drawn illustration as early as the 1840s; the provincial press was not equipped for pictures until fifteen or twenty years later. In the 1850s and 60s a few titles do include the *Illustrated* claim. They do not, however, appear to have been particularly popular, for although several early *Illustrateds* survive, as in the *Bridport Illustrated News* (founded 1855), many more were short-lived.

Altogether the provincial press has a remarkable record and offers an invaluable historical source. The general standard of reporting is impressive, though occasionally torn between the objective and the sensational, the crusade and the temptation of easy circulation. Frequently, however, the local newspaper is impartial and sedulously avoids the temptation to imitate the national press too slavishly in party line or pin-ups. Each is, presumably, reconciled to the certainty that it cannot please all its readers at once, yet must maintain a healthy circulation if it is to survive. The incidence of losses is revealing, as the 1914–18 war, the 1933 depression, the 1939–45 war and the post-war economics of the 1950s took their successive toll on title after title. Those which do survive — and they are numerous — are convincing evidence of 'township'; in some cases, such as Manchester's *Guardian* and Leeds' *Yorkshire Post*, local patriotism achieves a high national prestige. Whether the local newspaper, as evidence of the municipal identity, will fail to survive the additional pressures of boundary changes and amalgamation of one town with another, or their assimilation into a district, is an interesting conjecture. The pressures of economic change will probably be more decisive than those of local politics and borough reorganization. It may well be that only the 'local rag' can preserve an otherwise lost identity for what was once a host of municipal boroughs, each with its own charter as well as its own newspaper.

FURTHER READING

Boyce, G., *Newspaper History from the Seventeenth Century to the Present Day* (1978).
Cranfield, G. A., *The Development of the Provincial Newspaper 1700–1760* (1962).
—— *A Handlist of English Newspapers and Periodicals 1700–1760* (1952).
Frank, J., *The Beginnings of the English Newspaper 1620–1660* (1961).

Lucas, P., 'Sources for Urban History (9): Local Newspapers', *Loc. Hist.*, vol. 11, No. 6, May 1975.

MacMahon, K. A., 'Local History and the Newspaper', *Amat. Hist.*, vol. 5, No. 7, 1961.

Mellor, R. R., 'History from Newspapers', *Amat. Hist.*, vol. 2, No. 4, 1955.

Morsley, C., *News from the English Countryside 1750-1850* (1979).

Read, D., 'North of England Newspapers (1700-1900) and their value to Historians', *Proc. Leeds Phil. Soc.*, vol. viii, pt. 3, 1957.

Read, D., *Press and People 1790-1815: Opinion in Three English Cities* (1971).

Salmon, L. M., *The Newspaper and the Historian* (1923).

Wiles, R. McK., *Freshest Advices: Early Provincial Newspapers in England* (1965).

See also the *Bibliography of British Newspapers* published by the British Library Reference Division (1978-82 and continuing). The volumes to appear so far cover Wiltshire, Kent, Durham and Northumberland.

GAZETTEER OF ENGLISH AND WELSH NEWSPAPERS 1690-1981

The main source is the *Tercentenary Handlist of English and Welsh Newspapers, Magazines and Reviews* held in the British Museum in 1920 (first published in that year, facsimile reprint 1966). The *Handlist*'s chronological entries, which give all the newspapers published everywhere in the country for each year, have here been rearranged under towns to give individual chronological accounts. These entries have been updated from the *Catalogue of the Newspaper Library* (vols. 1 and 2, published 1975). Newspapers still published (that is, which were still published in 1981, the chosen finishing date), have been verified from the current editions of *Benn's Press Directory* and *Willing's Press Guide*. As a general rule, the Gazetteer includes only those newspapers in the various catalogues which include the name of one or more towns in their titles, and newspapers which do not conform to this format may have escaped notice. The *Handlist* and the *Catalogue* often disagree on the final date of papers which the *Handlist* described as 'in progress' in 1920; according to the *Catalogue* many of these ceased publication before 1920, usually between 1914 and 1918. This may be due to the British Museum having ceased to take in many newspapers during the First World War. In these cases, both suggested end-dates are given, as for instance 1916 (1920). Whenever a date is given in brackets – for instance (1975) – this indicates the last *verified* reference; some newspapers may have continued after that date. The full address of the Newspaper Library is: The British Library, Newspaper Library, Colindale Avenue, London NW9 5HE (01-200 5515). It is opposite Colindale Underground Station, and admission is by British Library reader's ticket (see page 226 above).

Supplementary information about early newspapers came from two sources. The first of these was the *British Union Catalogue* (1970), found at only the largest reference libraries, a 'record of the periodicals of the world from the 17th century to the present day in whatever language and on whatever subject, represented permanently in British libraries'. Unfortunately this *Catalogue* – although it includes information from various provincial libraries as well as the British Library – excludes newspapers published after 1799 for the most part.

The second source of supplementary information was that supplied by local libraries. Such entries are preceded by the indication '!'. It should be noted that extra newspapers whose existence is unknown to the *Handlist and Catalogue* can be discovered in this way.

An asterisk '*' before the name of a newspaper refers the reader to a named library given at the end of the entry which holds one or more copies, either in original form or on microfilm (MF). In many cases, it is likely that others newspapers which do not have asterisks may also be seen locally: consult your library for further information. Many of them publish useful guides or lists on their newspaper holdings, or even of newspaper holdings in the area. A few of the most useful are listed in this Gazetteer, but this list should not be regarded as being all-inclusive.

Abbreviations

'as'   =   a change of title

'with' = amalgamation with another newspaper.

– before any title, as in '– Express',

    =   town name, as in 'Abingdon'.

BL   =   Borough Library.

CL   =   Central Library.

CRO   =   County Record Office.

L   =   Library.

MF   =   microfilm of newspaper named. available.

NC   =   complete run of newspaper named not avail.

PL   =   Public Library.

RL   =   Reference Library.

*   copy available in named library.

!   the following information comes from local libraries.

† town so marked had a functioning local newspaper in 1981. Note: the final date in each case normally means the discontinuation of a publication in that year, but if marked thus: (1981), the newspaper concerned was still a going concern when this Gazetteer was compiled.

Towns in lower case (e.g. Alton) were not listed in our baselist, but have a surviving newspaper (these, and other small towns not listed, may also have earlier series).

GAZETTEER OF ENGLISH AND WELSH
PROVINCIAL NEWSPAPERS 1690-1981

Aberavon: see PORT TALBOT.

†ABERGAVENNY: — Herald 1855-6; — Chronicle 1871-(1981); — Echo 1897; — Mail 1904-14.

ABERYSTWYTH; Yr Oes 1853; Yr Wasg 1854-5; — Times 1868-70; — Observer 1869-(1920); Cardigan Bay Visitor 1889-1905 as — Dispatch 1905-(1920); Welsh Gazette 1903-(1920).

†ABINGDON: — Herald 1868-1910 as North Berks. Herald 1910-(1981); — News 1878-79; — Express 1887-8; Abingdonian 1890-(1920); — Free Press 1902-16.

ACCRINGTON: — Free Press 1858-60; — Guardian 1861-63; — Observer and Times 1866-(1981); — Reporter 1868; — Times 1868-92 with — Observer; — Herald 1870; — Gazette 1881-1927; — Echo 1884-7; — Advertiser 1889-1915 (1920); — Star 1894-95; — Express 1903-4.

Acton: see EALING.

ALDEBURGH: — Times 1900-12; — Post 1914.

†ALDERSHOT: — Military Gazette 1859-(1920); — Camp Times 1870; — and Farnham Observer 1872-3; — Camp Gazette 1880-1 with Hampshire and Surrey Times; May's — Camp Gazette 1869-95; — News 1894-(1981); — Guardian 1897; — Review 1898-99.

†Alton: — Gazette 1885-(1981).

APPLEBY: — Recorder 1869; — and Kirkby Herald 1874; — Chronicle 1886.

†ARUNDEL: West Sussex Advertiser 1853-(1981) (as West Sussex Gazette and South of England Advertiser).

†Ashbourne: — News Telegraph 1895-(1981).

†ASHTON-UNDER-Lyne: *— Reporter 1855-1889 — and Dukinfield Herald 1889-(1981); — Standard 1860-83; * — News 1868-74; Earlstown Guardian 1880-90 as — Golborne, Haydock and Makerfield Guardian 1890-(1920); *— Herald 1887-1936.

*! Manchester CL. Incomplete series of the Herald; Reporter (1855-1973) & Weekly Herald (1910); all MF.

Aston: see BIRMINGHAM..

*AYLESBURY: *Bucks. Herald 1792-(1981); — News Advertiser and Aylesbury News 1836-(1981); Bucks. Chronicle 1840 and 1848-72. — Independent 1868; Bucks. Standard 1859-(1981); Bucks. County Chronicle 1867-74; Spade and Whip 1871; Reporter 1882-1906; Bucks. Examiner 1889-(1981). *Aylesbury BL.

BACUP: — and Rossendale News 1863-1901 with Haslingden Gazette 1901-1926; * — Times 1865-1965; — Chronicle 1902-65 with Rossendale Free Press; Rossendale Free Press 1889-1920; — Express 1895-(1920); — Watchman 1876; — Echo 1898-(1920).

(Bacup — continued) —
    * Bacup BL, MF.

Balham & Tooting: See WANDSWORTH.

†BANBURY: — Guardian 1843-(1981); — Advertiser 1855-1975; — Herald 1861-69 with Oxfordshire Weekly News; — Beacon; 1868-1905; Evening News 1877; — Telegraph 1893-95.

†BANGOR: North Wales Chronicle 1808-(1981) (with Flintshire Observer 1855, Holyhead Chronicle 1905); North Wales Gazette 1822-7 and 1850; Cymro 1848-66; Cronicl Cymru 1866-72; Y Wynllan 1872-(1920); Llais Y Wlad 1874-84; Gwalia 1881-6; — Observer 1883-(1920); Y Cronicl 1890-(1920); Glorianydd 1891-(1920); — Herald 1907-8; Yr Ymwelydd 1913-(1920).

BARKING: — and East Ham Advertiser 1888-9 with East Ham Standard; — and East Ham Standard 1895-1902; — and Beckton Star 1900-1; — Gazette 1909-10; — Chronicle 1910-(1920).

†BARNET: — Gazette 1856-61; — Press 1859-(1981); — Herald 1890; — Times and Finchley Telegraph 1890-1907; — Mercury 1898-1899 (1920); — Courier 1909-10. Also: EDGWARE; — Reporter, Stanmore and Elstree Chronicle 1890-4. FINCHLEY: — Telegraph and Barnet Times 1892-6 (1920); Free Press 1895 with — Press; Guardian 1902-5; — Press 1903-(1981); — Recorder 1906; — Mail 1912-5; HENDON: — Times 1875-(1981) (as — and Finchley Times with Golders Green and Stanmore Times); — Courier 1887; — Arrow 1889 with — Courier; — Advertiser 1894-1922.

†BARNSLEY: — Telegraph 1852; — Times 1855-82 as — Independent 1883-1939; — Record 1858-66; — Chronicle 1858-(1981); — Herald 1860-66; — Echo 1869-74; — Sporting News 1894-1902 as — Daily Argus 1902-3; — Express 1903-4 as — Telephone 1904-20. See BRADFORD also.

†BARNSTAPLE: North Devon Journal-Herald 1824-(1981); North Devon Magazine 1824; Syles — Herald 1826; County and North Devon Advertiser 1832-48; — Looker-On 1847; — Times 1851; Western Standard 1852; Illustrated — and Bideford Times 1855 — as North Devon Advertiser 1855-1910; — Times 1859-61 as North Devon Times 1861-65; Devonshire Chronicle 1861-62; — Times 1861-1908; — Messenger 1870-3; North Devon Herald 1870-1941; North Devon Journal 1870-1941 as — Herald-Journal 1941-(81). See Smith, L., *Devon Newspapers; A Finding-List* (Standing Conf. Conf. Devon Hist., 1973).

†BARROW-IN-FURNESS: — Herald 1863–
1914; — Advertiser 1868–70 with — Pilot;
* — Times 1868–85 with — News; — Pilot
1871–7 with Herald; — Daily News 1875;
* — News 1881–(1981); Ulverston News
1883; — Daily Telegram 1892; — Evening
Echo 1894–8; — Evening Mail 1898–(1975);
* — Guardian 1912–1947.
    * Barrow-in-Furness BL: NC.
BARRY: — and Cadoxton Journal 1889–91;
— Dock News 1892–1925 as — and District
News 1925–75; — Herald 1896–1962 with —
and District News.
†BASINGSTOKE: Hampshire and Berkshire
Gazette and Basingstoke Journal 1878–
1970 as — Weekend Gazette 1970–(1981);
— Standard 1882–5; Hampshire Observer
and — News 1903–16.
†BATH: — Miscellany 1740; * — Journal
1744–58; — Advertiser 1755–7 as Chronicle
1760–(1981); Boddeley's — Journal 1756;
Farley's — Journal 1756; * — and Bristol
Chronicle 1770; — Journal 1766–1803 * as
Keene's — Journal 1825–1916; Salmon's
Mercury 1777–81; — Chronicle 1784–9; —
Herald 1793–1862 with — Express 1862–75;
Omnium Gatherum 1814; — Theatrical
Review 1822–4; — and Cheltenham Gazette
1825–97 with — Herald; — and Bristol
Magazine 1832–32; — Guardian 1834–9;
Somerset Constitutional and — Post 1837–
40; — and Bristol Luminary 1837; Penny
Figaro 1838–9; Protestant 1838–40; Phono-
graphic Journal 1842–4; — and Clifton
Looker-on 1849; — Magazine 1853; —
Express 1855–75 as — Herald 1876–1925;
—Free Press 1858; — Times 1858; West
Somerset Free Press 1860–(1981); — Obser-
ver 1876–1960; Argus Evening Telegraph
1875–6 as Evening Argus and — Argus 1876–
1900 with Daily Chronicle: — Argus 1876–
97 as Weekly Argus 1897–1911 with —
Chronicle; Evening Chronicle 1877–83 as
Daily Chronicle 1883–(1981); — Pictorial
1889–97; — and County Weekly News 1892–
3; — and County Graphic 1896–1904;
Somerset Guardian and Radstock Observer
1898–1902 with Somerset Standard.
    * Bristol CL holds sets of Bath and
Bristol Chronicle (1770) and Bath Journal
(1744–58).
†BATLEY: * Reporter 1869–1959 with — News;
— Free Press 1870; — * News and Yorkshire
Woollen District Advertiser 1879–1949 as
— News 1949–1981; * — News 1883–1959
as — News and Reporter; * — Examiner
1893–5 with Dewsbury District News; —
Free Press 1903–20. See also DEWSBURY.
    * Batley PL and Huddersfield CL,
originals and MF.
Battersea: see WANDSWORTH.
BEAUMARIS: — Visitor 1857–88.
BEBINGTON: None listed before — News

(Bebington — continued) —
    1936–56, as — News and Advertiser
    1965–(1981).
BECCLES: — Weekly News 1858–67 as East
Suffolk Gazette 1867–1926; — Record
1896–9 as North Suffolk Advertiser 1899–
1902.
Beckenham: see BROMLEY.
†BEDFORD: — Beacon 1837–8; — Mercury
and Huntingdon Express 1837–57 as
Bedfordshire Mercury 1857–1912 with —
Bedford and County Record; — Standard
1843 and 1848; — Times 1845–72 as
Bedfordshire Times 1872–1981; — News
1845; — Notes 1856–7; Bedfordshire
Independent 1857–9 with — Times; County
Chronicle 1867–74; — Record 1874–(1981);
— and Bedfordshire Herald 1878–87 with
Luton Times; — Bee 1879; Bedfordshire
Standard 1883–1939 with Times; — Daily
Circular 1903–39 with — Record; — and
District Evening News 1907–9; — Guardian
1908–10.
†Belper: — News 1896–1981.
Bermondsey: see SOUTHWARK.
†BERWICK ON TWEED: — Advertiser 1825–
(1981); — and Kelso Warder 1835–58 as —
Warder 1858–84 as Border Counties' Gazette
and Agriculturist 1884–5 as Border Counties'
Gazette and Berwick Warder 1885–98;
Illustrated — Journal 1855 as — Journal
1855–1928 as — Journal and Northumber-
land News 1928–57 with — Advertiser;
— News and General Advertiser 1869–1957
as Berwickshire News and Berwickshire
Advertiser 1957–(1981); — Gazette and
County Guardian 1885–95; — Times 1899–
1900.
†BEVERLEY: — Weekly Recorder 1855–1921;
— Guardian 1856–(1981); — Express 1857–8;
— Echo 1885–1903; — Independent 1888–
1911; — and East Riding Telegraph 1895–
1903 with — Guardian.
BEWDLEY: The Sun; The Kidderminster,
Bewdley, Stourport and District Family
Journal 1877–1900.
BEXHILL: — Chronicle 1887–1930; Illustrated
Visitors' List 1896–1900 (1920); — Calendar
1896–98; — Observer 1896–00; — Daily
News 1901; Kursaal 1903–4 as — Chronicle
1904–7.
†BEXLEY: — etc. Observer 1867–(1981); —
Times 1905–18. Also: ERITH: — Observer
1867–(1981); — Times 1883–1919; —
Chronicle 1898–1918 with — Observer.
†Bicester: — Advertiser 1879–1981.
†BIDEFORD: — Advertiser or — and North
Devon Gazette 1854–(1981); Illustrated
Barnstaple and — Times 1855 as North
Devon Advertiser 1855–1910; North Devon
and East Cornwall Gazette 1856 as —
Weekly Gazette 1856–1909 (1920); —
Visitors' List 1877.

†Biggleswade: – Chronicle 1891-(1981).
Bilston: see WOLVERHAMPTON.
†BIRKENHEAD: Prophetic Herald 1845-50;
– Advertiser 1853-60 as – and Cheshire
Advertiser 1861-1940; Guardian 1855;
Weekly Times 1858-59; – Guardian 1861-6
and 1869; Composite 1870; – and Cheshire
Guardian 1875; – News 1878-(1981); –
Times 1879-80; Daily Albion 1885-7;
– Times 1885-7; Weekly Albion 1886-7;
Hoylake News and Advertiser 1888-(1981);
– Magazine 1889-(1920); – Town Crier
1898-9; Robinson's – Monthly Coming
Events 1899-1905; Rockferry District
Herald as – and Wirral Herald 1905-9.
†BIRMINGHAM: Aris's – Gazette 1741-72
and 1888 with – Daily Gazette; – Register
1764-65; Swinney's – and Stafford
Chronicle 1791-1827; – Commercial
Herald 1809; Searchlight 1817; – Argus
1818; Comet 1819-20; Theatrical Looker-
on 1822-3; – Chronicle 1823-5; Theatrical
John Bull 1824; – Journal 1825-69 with
– Daily Post; Oscotian 1828-29; Monthly
Argus and Public Censor 1829-31; Midland
Reporter and – Herald 1831 with – Journal;
– Advertiser 1833-48; Herald 1836-8 as
Midland Counties Herald 1838-1933;
Midland Monitor 1841-43 with – Journal;
Midland Observer 1844; – Pilot 1844-6;
Watson's – Weekly Diary 1847; – Mercury
1848-58 with Weekly Press; Midlands
County Express 1851; Midlands Metropoli-
tan Magazine 1852-53; Midlands Counties
Illustrated News 1855; Daily Mercury 1855-
7; Daily Press 1855-8; James Baines's Times
1856; Weekly Press 1857-58; *Daily Post
1857-(1981); Saturday Evening Post 1857-
69 as Weekly Post 1869-1960; Midland
Advertiser 1858-60 as – Times 1860-1;
Daily Free Press 1860; – Town News 1862;
Daily Gazette 1862-1904 as Gazette and
Express 1904-1912; The Third Member for
– 1868; District News 1869; Dail Mail
1871-1917 (1920); Morning News 1871-6;
Monthly Messenger 1872-3; *Evening Mail
1870-(1981); Weekly News 1875-6;
Evening News 1875-6; – Examiner 1876;
Liberal Review 1880; Daily Globe 1880;
Weekly Review 1884; – Graphic 1884-
1913; Suburban Times 1884-1901; Weekly
Mercury 1884-(1981) or Sunday Mercury
1884-(1981); Daily Times 1885-90; – and
Midland Counties Trade Journal 1886;
Workman's Times 1890; – Leader 1890;
Citizen 1891-2; – Daily Argus 1891-1902;
– Gazette 1891-2; – Comet 1893-7; Our
City 1896-99; Magazine 1897-1904; – Echo
1898-1915 (1920); Sunday Mail 1899-1916;
Magnet 1901-5; Midland Gazette 1901-14
with – Daily Gazette; – Evening Despatch
1902-63; – Citizen 1904; – City Press
1904. Also: ASTON: Chronicle 1875-80 as

(*Birmingham – continued*) –
– and – Chronicle 1880-97; – Times 1884-
1901; – Weekly News 1891-2 as – and East
– News 1892-1906 (1920). EDGBASTON:
– Advertiser 1874-5; Edgbastonia 1881-
95; – Society Journal 1894. HANDS-
WORTH: – and Smethwich Free Press
1885-88; – News 1888-1901; – Chronicle
1889-1911; – Herald 1891 as North –
News 1891-92 as – Herald 1892-1930
with – News. HARBORNE: – Herald 1877-
1901; - Times 1885-7 with – Herald; –
– Weekly News 1891 as – and West – News
1892-1906. MOSELEY: – and Balsall Heath
News 1882 as – News 1892-00; – and
King's Heath Journal 1892-95. YARDLEY:
– News Letter 1895. KNOWLE: – Journal
1893-1901. See Briggs, A., 'Press & Public in
Early 19th century Birmingham' (*Dugdale Soc.
Occ. Papers*, No. 8, 1949); *Birmingham RL.
†BLACKBURN: * – Mail 1793-1829 and
1824-43; Gazette 1832-40; *Alfred 1832-
35; * – Standard 1835-93 as Weekly Standard and Express 1893-1909; – Mercury
1843-46; *Weekly Times 1855-71 as –
Times 1871-(1981); * – Patriot 1859-73;
– News 1860; – Gossip 1865; – Echo 1880-
1; *Northern Daily Telegraph 1886-(1981);
*Lancashire Evening Express 1887-99; –
Evening Express 1887-95 as Daily Express
and Standard 1895-99; – Weekly Express
1888 with – Standard; – Labour Journal
1898-1907; * Weekly Telegraph 1899-
1923; * – Daily Star 1902-3; * – Gazette
1905-11; Weekly News 1914.
    * Blackburn PL: Standard, Times and
Northern Daily Telegraph MF. See *Sources
of Local History* (1968, PL).
†BLACKPOOL: – Visitor 1868 as Visitor and
Advertiser 1869; – Times 1870-1933; – News
1873; Herald 1874-(1981); – Gazette 1874-
1975 – as Herald 1975-(1981); Daily Programme
1887; – Graphic 1889; – Programme 1893-
4 as – Visitor 1894-1900; – Amusements
1894-1900; Advertiser 1895; – Echo 1896-
98; – and South Shore Weekly 1899-1907 as
Weekly Standard 1907-17; – Journal 1900-
5; – Pilot 1903; – Magazine 1910-(1920).
BLANDFORD FORUM: Ringwood, – and
Wimborne Telegram 1862-69; Express 1869-
95; Telegram 1874-86; – Weekly News
1885-94; Gazette 1903 with Gillingham
Gazette.
    See *Dorset Newspapers* (Weymouth CL
1972).
†BLYTH: Morpeth and – Echo 1870-1 as –
Echo 1871-2; Illustrated Weekly News
1874-94 as – Bi-Weekly News 1894-1900
as – News 1900-74 as News Post 1974-
(1981); Examiner 1888-94.
BODMIN: – Post 1900-1909; – Guardian and
Cornwall County Chronicle 1901. (See
Cornish Guardian).

†BOLTON: * – Herald 1813; * – Chronicle 1823-31 and 1831-1917; – Express and Lancashire Advertiser 1823-6; Voice of Truth 1832; * – Free Press 1835-47 as – Times 1848; – Advertiser 1848-1900; – Guardian 1853; *Monthly Advertiser 1853-4; *Mercury 1853-4; Mackey's – Advertiser 1854-9 and 1868-92; Winterbourne's Advertiser 1854; Bowton Loominary 1855-60; *Spectator 1857-8; * – Examiner 1859-61; * – Guardian 1859 and 1865-93 with Weekly Journal; *Evening News 1867 and 1868-(1981); – Morning News 1870; – Journal and Guardian or Weekly Journal 1871-1973; – Daily Chronicle 1873-1907; * – Evening Guardian 1873 and 1874-93 with – Evening News; – Express 1888-99; Trotter 1891-3; * – Star 1891; – and District Independent Labour Party Pioneer 1894-5; * – Evening Echo 1894; Boltonian 1899-(1981); Citizen 1913-4.

*Bolton PL: Chronicle, Evening News and Weekly Journal, MF.

†BOOTLE: * – Times 1867-(1981); Waterloo Times 1879-1963; Waterloo Crosby and Seaforth Magazine 1886 as – Seaforth etc. Magazine 1886-87 as West Lancashire Magazine 1887-9; – Advertiser 1891-3.

*! Bootle PL holds Times from 1878, MF. Liverpool CL holds late (1960s) series of Herald and Times.

†BOSTON: – Gazette 1811-32 and 1860-93; – Advertiser 1812-13; Lincolnshire Herald 1829-32; * – Lincoln and Louth Herald 1832-53 as Lincolnshire Herald 1854-94; Smith's Lincolnshire Estate Register 1850; – Guardian 1854-1958; – Spa Journal 1873-79 as – Spa News 1879-(1981); Independent 1879-1912 with Lincolnshire Standard; – Daily Telegraph 1898; – and Lincolnshire Standard 1912-5 as Lincolnshire Standard 1915-(1981).

*! Grimsby PL has Boston Gazette and Lincs. Advertiser (MF various 1811-32); Boston, Lincoln and Louth Herald (MF 1832-5).

†BOURNEMOUTH: – Times 1858-(1981); Visitors' Directory 1868-1919 as – Times and Directory 1919-56 as – Times 1956-(1981); – and Christchurch Standard 1868; Wimborne Journal 1869-72 as Dorset Free Press 1874-5 as – Observer 1875-1901 with Observer and Chronicle for Hampshire and Dorset; – Chronicle 1872-6 with – Observer; Dorset Free Press 1874-5; – Observer 1875-1901 with Observer and Chronicle for Hampshire and Dorset; – Advertiser 1879-81; Observer and Chronicle 1881-1909; Guardian 1883-1928; Gazette 1889-90; Weekly News 1890-2; Students' Association Gazette 1891-6; – and Boscombe Amusements 1894-1930; –

(*Bournemouth – continued*) – Daily Echo 1900-(1981); – Graphic 1902-14 (1920); Free Press 1911.

See *Dorset Newspapers* (Weymouth CL 1972). Several of the Bournemouth newspapers listed are held at Poole CL.

BRACKLEY: – Observer and Northamptonshire Advertiser 1869-1901.

Bracknell: see WOKINGHAM.

†BRADFORD: – Instructive and Entertaining Miscellany 1818; and Wakefield Chronicle 1825-26; and Huddersfield Courier 1825-8; British Labourer's Protector and Factory Child's Friend 1832-3; – Observer 1834-1901 as Yorkshire Daily Observer 1901-9; – Herald 1842; – Gazette 1847; – Times 1854; – Advertiser 1855-90; – Review 1858-70; – News 1861-3 as Keighley News 1863-(1981); Bradfordian 1860-1; – Telegraph 1863-64; – Times 1865-71; Social Reformer 1867-8; Daily Telegraph 1868-(1981); – Daily Review 1869-70; Observer Budget 1869-77 as – Observer Budget 1877-1911 as Yorkshire Observer Budget 1911-00; – Weekly Telegraph 1869-(1981); – Weekly Mail 1871-74; – Daily Times 1871; Yorkshire Magazine 1871-4; – Evening Mail 1871-5; Chronicle 1872-82 as Daily Chronicle and Mail 1882-83; Shipley and Saltaire Times 1876-1905 as Shipley Times and Express 1905-(81); – Antiquary 1880-(1920); – Times 1880-83; – Debater 1881; – Citizen 1884-90 as Leeds Saturday Journal 1887-1907; Eastern Star 1888; – Mercury 1890-1900; – Labour Journal 1892; – Ha'porth 1892-93; – Local Stock and Share List 1892-93; – Daily Argus 1892-1925 with – Telegraph; – Labour Echo 1898-90; Bradford 1895-6; – Chamber of Trades Journal 1906-75 as Journal of – Chamber of Trade 1965-6; – Socialist Vanguard 1908-20; – Pioneer 1913-36; – Weekly War Album 1914-5.

Bradford PL issues a Local Studies Leaflet No. 5 which lists the L's newspaper holdings. These include sets for Keighley, Bingley, Scarborough, York, Barnsley, Cleckheaton, Edinburgh, Halifax, Hull, Leeds, Morley, Richmond and Whitby.

BRECON: Silurian or South Wales General Advertiser 1838-55; – Journal 1855-67; – Reporter 1863-67; – County Times 1866-1933; – Free Press 1883-85 as Brecknock Beacon 1885-96 with – County Times.

†BRENT: see WILLESDEN: – and Brent Chronicle 1877-(1981) with – Mercury; – and Kilburn Chronicle 1877-1964; – Advertiser 1884; – Herald 1884-93 as – Times 1893-4; Stanmore Observer 1895-1906 as – Observer 1901-3; – Citizen 1903-65 as – Mercury 1965-(1981); – Call 1913-18 (1920). Also: WEMBLEY:

(Brent — continued) —
— and District Recorder 1911-5 (1920).
Brentford: see HOUNSLOW.
†Bridgnorth: — Journal 1854-(1981).
†BRIDGWATER: — and Somerset Herald 1831;
— Times 1845-61; — Mercury 1857-9 as
Western Counties Herald 1859-63 as
Somerset County Gazette 1863-(1981);
Somersetshireman and Leader 1857; —
Standard 1861-70; — Mercury 1863-1975;
Sydenham Gazette 1872-85; — Gazette
1874-85 with Independent.
†BRIDLINGTON: — and Quay News 1855-8;
— Quay Mercury 1858-68; — Quay
Observer 1859-99; Free Press 1859-(1981);
— and Quay Gazette 1874-1914; — and Quay
Advertiser 1896-7; — and Quay Chronicle
1897-(1981).
†BRIDPORT: Illustrated — News 1855-(1981);
— Beaminster and Lyme Regis Telegraph
1866 with Western Chronicle; — Monthly
Review 1892.
    See *Dorset Newspapers* (Weymouth CL
1972) Editions of Bridport News (1910) are
held at Bridport PL.
†BRIGHOUSE: — and Rastrick Chronicle
1859-64; — News 1870-1911 with —
Observer; — and Rastrick Gazette 1874-99;
— Echo 1887-(1981); — Free Press 1898-
1941; — Observer 1912-5.
†BRIGHTON: Gleaner 1822-3; Evangelical
Gleaner 1923-4; — Herald 1825-1971;
— Gazette 1825-(1981); — Guardian 1827-
1901; — Co-operator 1828-30; — Patriot
1835-9; — Dramatic Miscellany 1838; —
Examiner 1853-96; — School Journal 1850-
1; — Times 1853 and 1863; — Pulpit
1853-61; — Paper 1854; — Chronicle 1859;
Quarterly Magazine 1857; Fashionable
Arrival List 1858-65; — Chronicle 1859;
Sussex Mercury 1859-60; The Hurst Johnian
1859-60; Contemplator 1864; Election
Reporter 1864; — Magazine 1864; Fashionable Visitors' List 1865-78 as — Standard
1878-1953; Treacher's Brighton Record
1867-1905; West Sussex Halfpenny Times
1867-1905; — Daily News 1868-80;
Courier of Fashion 1871-2; Sussex
Daily News 1872-1956; Telegraph
1864-5; Revue Anglo-Francaise
1872-7; London and — Magazine
1874-5; — Illustrated Weekly
1874; — Free Press 1874-5; — Observer
1876-9; — and Sussex Daily Post 1876-85;
Brightonian 1880-4; — Argus 1880-96 as
— Evening Argus 1896-(1981); — etc.
Advertiser 1880-1925; Sussex Evening
Times 1880-(1920); — Society 1887-1927; —
and Hove Entertainment Chronicle 1891-
4; — Morning Argus 1897-1926; — Amusements 1903;.— Life 1912-(1920); — and Hove
Graphic 1914-6; Mid-Sussex Times 1881-
(1981).

†BRISTOL: — Post Boy 1704; Sam Farley's
— Post Man 1715; Weekly Mercury 1716;
*Farley's — Newspaper 1725-32; *Oracle
and County Intelligencer 1743-9; * —
Weekly Intelligencer 1749-59; *Bonner and
Middleton's — Journal 1774-91; * —
Gazette 1771-1872; *Felix Farley's —
Journal 1776-1853 with — Times; —
Constitutional Chronicle 1780-2; — and
Bath Magazine 1780-2; *Sarah Farley's —
Journal 1782-5; Fenley and Sheppard's B
Journal 1804; * — Mirror 1805-64; —
Mercury 1806-1901 as — Daily Mercury
1901-9; — Memorialist 1816-23; * —
Observer 1819-23; — Mirror (previously
Bonner and Middleton's — Gazette) 1819-
64; Monthly Blowing Heart's Ease 1822;
The Thespian 1823; The Visitor 1823;
*Bristolian 1827-9; — Herald 1829;
Chronicle of — 1829-30; Job Nott 1831-3;
*Liberal 1831-2; Policeman 1836; —
Advocate 1836-7; — Standard 1839-42;
*Times and Bath Advocate 1839-53 as
— Times and Felix Farley's — Journal 1853-
64 as Daily — Times 1865-84 as * — Times
and Mirror 1865-(1920); — Magazine 1841;
Great Western Advertiser 1844-7 as —
Weekly News 1847; Sealey's Western Miscel-
lany 1845; — Monthly Advertiser 1846-7;
— Examiner 1850-1; Clifton Directory
1850-1 as *Clifton Chronicle 1851-1921;
— Guardian 1855 and 1902-(1920); — Tele-
graph 1855-6; * — Advertiser 1856; —
Magazine 1857-58; Western Daily Press
1858-(1981); — Observer 1859-1962; —
News 1864; Daily Post 1860-78 with —
Mercury; — News 1864; — Commercial
Register 1864 as — Record 1864-5; —
Review 1869; — News 1870; — Draught
Player 1872-4; — Daily Advertiser 1874;
— Advertiser Evening Telegram 1875-6;
— Evening News 1877-1932; — Household
News 1880 as Gazette 1880-2 with Somer-
set County Gazette; — Review 1882; —
Magpie 1882-1911 with — Express; —
Weekly Chronicle 1888-9; * — Guardian
1897-1935; — Evening Press 1899-1900;
— and North Somerset Review 1900; — and
Clifton Amusements 1900-3; — Echo 1901-
9; — Weekly Mercury 1902-9 with — Weekly
Western Post; — Evening Times 1904-32;
Bedminster, Knowle and Brislington Record
1909-10; — as South Bristol Free Press
1910-31; East Bristol Election Labour
Herald 1910; — Express 1911-15; North
Somerset Gazette 1912-1935; Bristolian
and Clifton Social World 1913-4 with
Bristol and the War; — and the War 1914-6.
    * Bristol CL has a typescript list of
newspaper volume locations, including MF
and listing Bath and Gloucester papers
marked * in their Gazetteers.
†Bromsgrove: — Messenger 1860-(1981).

†BROMLEY: — Magazine 1845; — Record 1858-1913; — Telegraph 1868-1913; — Journal 1869-1912 with South-Eastern Gazette; Sidcup and District Times 1884-97 as — and District Times 1898-(1981); — Independent 1889; Chronicle 1891-1921; — Advertiser 1895-6; — Local Guide 1903-44; West Kent District Times 1905-27. Also: BECKENHAM: — Journal 1876-(1981); — and Penge Advertiser 1888-(1981). CHISLEHURST: — Times 1881-(1981).

†BUCKINGHAM: Bucks. Beds. and Herts. Chronicle 1827-9; Midland Progressionist 1848; — Advertiser 1854-(1981); Bucks. Free Press 1856-(1981); — Express 1865-1915 (1920); Bucks. Examiner 1889-(1981); Bucks. Advertiser 1914-(1981).

†Burnham-on-Sea: — Gazette 1864-(1981).

†BURNLEY: *— Advertiser 1853-80 with — Express; *—Free Press 1863-74 as *—Gazette 1864-1914 with — News; Padiham Advertiser 1876; — Express 1877-(1981); Mid-Weekly Gazette 1884-7; — Radical 1887; — Socialist 1893-1914; — News 1902; *— News 1912-33;—Pioneer 1914-7*Burnley PL.

†BURTON-ON-TRENT: — Times 1855-74; — Weekly News 1856-90 with — News and Standard; — Chronicle 1860-1957; High Peak News 1870-1959; — Express 1874 79; — Standard 1880-7 with — Weekly News; — and Derby Gazette 1881-7 (1920); — Independent 1893; — Guardian 1894-1914; — Mail 1898-(1981); — Observer 1898-1916 as — Observer and S. Derbs. Weekly Mail 1916-67 as — Observer and Chronicle 1957-(1981).

†BURY: Provincial Spectator 1821; — Observer 1850; — Chronicle 1853; * — Times 1855-(1981); *— Guardian 1857-1935; East Lancashire Echo 1874-92; — Borough Advertiser 1905-9; — Visitor 1908-28; — and Rossendale Historical Review 1909; — Observer 1909-12. * Bury PL.

†BURY ST EDMUNDS: Suffolk Mercury or St Edmundsbury Post 1717; * — and Norwich Post 1793-1931 with Bury Free Press; — Gazette 1822; Suffolk Herald 1827-8 as Bury and Suffolk Herald 1828-49 with Bury and Norwich Post; — and Suffolk Press 1832-3; — and Suffolk Farmers' Journal 1844-45; — Free Press and West Suffolk Observer 1855-(1981); — and Suffolk Standard 1869-87; East Anglian Echo 1869-70; — and West Suffolk Advertiser 1886-1907; — and West Suffolk Journal 1886-90.

* Norfolk County Library (Norwich Division) holds sets of several East Anglian newspapers, fully listed for the reader in typescript. These include the Bury and Norwich Post (1793-1849).

†BUXTON: * — Herald 1842-1951; * — Advertiser 1855-1951; — and Matlock Times

(Buxton — continued) —
1870-2; — Fashionable Visitors' List 1872; High Peak Reporter 1875-(1981); Matlock, — and Tideswell Advertiser 1877-80 as High Peak Advertiser 1881-1937; High Peak Daily News 1880; Bates's — Observer 1882-3; — Chronicle 1888-1905; High Peak Herald 1909-14.

! *Buxton PL holds originals of — Advertiser and Herald from 1880.

CAERNARVON: — Herald 1831-88; Y Seren Obleddol 1835; Papyr Newydd Cymraeg 1836-87; — and Denbigh Herald 1836-1900; Cylchgrawn Rhyddid 1841-2; Amaethydd 1845-6; Humphrey's General Advertiser 1852-3; Herald Cymraeg 1855-(1920); Y Llenor 1860-8; Golud Y Oes 1863; North Wales Press 1871-2; North Wales Express 1877-84 as North Wales Observer 1884-1937; Chwarelwr Cymreig 1893-1902; Papur Pawb 1893-1956; Cymru 1893-(1920); Y Llusern 1893-(1920).

CALNE: — Chronicle 1876-8 with North Wilts. Herald; — and Chippenham Express 1907.

Camberwell: see SOUTHWARK.

†CAMBRIDGE: — Independent Chronicle 1744-(1981); — Journal 1746; * — Chronicle and Journal 1770-1924; — Intelligencer 1793-1800 (1920); — Chronicle 1829; The Snob 1829 as Gownsman 1829-30; — Quarterly Review 1833-4; — University Magazine 1835; — Guardian 1838; — General Advertiser 1839 as Advertiser 1839-50 as New — Advertiser 1850; Town Magazine 1840-3; University Magazine 1840-3; — Express 1868-1909; — University Reporter 1870-(1920); Cambridgeshire Times 1872-(1981); Tatler 1877; — Review 1879-(1920); — Examiner 1881-92; — Meteor 1882; University Magazine 1886; — Daily News 1888-1962 as — News 1962-9 as — Evening News 1969-(1981); Weekly News 1889-(1920); — Observer 1892-93; — Gazette 1898-1900; Weekly Gazette 1899-1908; — Independent 1910-1925; — Magazine 1912-(1920).

! Bradford PL holds copies of the Cambridge Intelligencer (1795 and 1796). *Cambridge BL holds files of — Chronicle and Journal (1770-1924) also on MF; CRO also has these MF.

†Cannock: — Advertiser with Courier 1878-(1981).

†CAMDEN: — and St Pancras Chronicle 1857-(1981); — and Kentish Towns Gazette 1866-82. Also: HAMPSTEAD: — and Highgate Express 1872-(1981); St John's Wood and South — Advertiser 1883-1906 as — and St John's Wood Advertiser 1906-13 (1920); — Record 1889-1918 as — and Highgate Record and Chronicle 1918-63 as Camden, — and Highgate Record and Chronicle 1963-75 with Hackney Gazette. HOLBORN:

(Camden (Holborn) – continued) –
— Journal 1858–73; — Guardian 1876–
(1981); — Notes and Comments 1885; —
and West Central News 1891; — Monthly
Magazine 1903–4..ST PANCRAS: —
Reporter 1857–69; — and Holborn Times
1858–61; — News 1859–66; North Londoner
1869–74; — Guardian 1874–1925; — Press
1885; — Star 1894–6; Londoner 1896–7;
Peoples Advertiser 1899–1900; — Chronicle
1900–63.

†CANTERBURY: Kent Express and — Newsletter 1729–69; Kentish Gazette 1768–
(1981); Kentish Weekly Post or — Journal
1768–1838; Genius of Kent 1792–5; Kentish
Herald 1802–3 as Kent Herald 1824–(1975);
Kent County Herald 1808–10; The Whim
1810–1; Man of Kent 1818–9; Kentish
Observer 1832–(1981); British Lion 1833;
— Magazine 1834–5; Penny Sunday Reader
1835–41; Weekly Journal and Farm Gazette
1836–1900; Kentish Times and Corn-Law
Advocate 1840 with — Journal; — News
1855 as East Kent Times 1855–65 with
Kentish Chronicle; Journal of Kent General
Reform Association 1854; Kentish Times
1857–8; Kentish Times 1859–60; Kentish
Chronicle and — Weekly 1859–1902 (1920);
Kentish Standard 1866–8; East Kent Inde-
pendent 1867–70 with Kentish Chronicle;
Goulder's — Chronicle 1869–70 as —
Chronicle 1870–1 with Kentish Chronicle;
East Kent Times and — News 1871; —
Times 1884–6 with Kentish Gazette.

†CARDIFF: Greal Y Bedyddwyr 1827–36;
Glamorgan, Monmouth and Brecon Gazette
1833–44 as — and Merthyr Guardian 1845–
74 with South Wales Weekly Telegraph of
Newport; Ystorfa Y Bedyddwyr 1838;
Y Bedyddwyr 1849–59; Yr Agolygydd
1851–3; — and Merthyr Advertiser 1850–1;
— Times 1857–1928; — and Advertiser
1858–9; — Mercury 1861–2; — News 1864;
— Standard 1864–5; — Chronicle 1866–8;
Western Mail 1869–(1981); Shipping etc.
Gazette 1869–1911; Weekly Mail 1870–
1957; South Wales Coal Iron and Freight
Statistics 1872–4; — Examiner 1873–4 with
South Wales Evening Telegram; — Indepen-
dent 1875; Darlunydd 1876–9; — Free
Press 1876–84 with West of England
Observer: Principality 1880; The Red
Dragon 1882–7; Y Geninen 1883–(1920);
— Evening Mail 1884–5; — and South Wales
Whip 1886–8; — Evening Express 1887–
1930; Freight Gazette 1888; — Advertiser
1891–4; South Wales Labour Times 1893;
Monthly Stock and Shares List 1893–4;
Bibliography of Wales 1903–(1920); Figaro
1901–3; — etc. Journal of Commerce 1904–
35; In and Around — 1905; The Welsh
Review 1906–7; — Citizen 1911; Weekly
Post 1913–4.

Carisbrooke; see NEWPORT (I.o.W.)

†CARLISLE: Northern Observer 1824; Patriot
1831–1910; — Journal 1831–1968; Border
Herald of Temperance 1839; Whitridge's
Northern Miscellany 1845–6; — Advertiser
1854; — Examiner 1857–70 with — Express;
— Express 1861–70 as Express and Examiner
1870–1913 with — Journal; — Standard
1868; — etc. Cumberland News 1883–1910;
— Evening Journal 1885–1913; Carliol
1891–(1920); Cumberland News 1910–
(1981); Cumberland Evening Mail 1915;
Weekly Citizen 1915.

†CARDIGAN: — Herald 1869–73; — and Tivy
Side Advertiser 1870–(1981); — Observer
1876–98; — and Merioneth Herald 1885–
(1920); — Bay Visitor 1889–1905 as
Aberystwyth Dispatch 1905–(1920); County
Times 1897–1907 with Aberystwyth
Observer.

†CARMARTHEN: Trysorfa Gwybodaeth 1770;
— Journal 1810–(1981); Y Brud a Sylwydd
1828; Welshman 1829–(1981); Udgorn
Seion 1849–55; Seren Cymru 1851–1900;
Gwron Cymreig 1851–60; Welsh Calvinist
Methodist Record 1852–54; — Weekly
Reporter 1860–(1920); Y Cyfaill Eglwisig
1867–(1920); — Times 1875; — Express
1876–8; Carmarthenshire Notes 1889–91.

†CASTLEFORD: — Chronicle and Knottingley
Advertiser 1858–62; Illustrated — Guardian
1859 as Guardian 1859–60; — Star 1869–82;
— Normanton and Whitwood Herald 1872;
— Gazette 1872–1902; — Free Press 1875–
76; * Pontefract and — Express 1880–
(1981); — Telegraph 1892–1900; Pontefract
and — Weekly Herald 1892–1900 with
Pontefract Advertiser; — Stalwart 1906–10.
　* Castleford PL, Pontefract and Castleford Express from 1880 to the present, MF.

†CHARD: — Union Gazette 1840–1 with
Sherborne Journal; Newland's Weekly Star
1859–83; — and Ilminster News 1874–
(1981); — etc. Weekly Advertiser 1883–5
with Yeovil and — Chronicle.

†Chatteris: — Advertiser 1872–(1981).

†CHATHAM: — and Rochester Standard 1835
with West Kent Guardian; The Liberal 1835;
Rochester, Chatham and Gillingham Journal
1854 as Rochester etc. Journal and
Standard; Taylor's Monthly Record of
Passing Events 1857; * — News 1859–85 as
Rochester News 1885–(1981); — Gazette
1868–69; * — Observer 1870–1968.
　* ! — Chatham PL, Chatham Observer
(1872–1968), — Standard (1947 to present)
and — News (1880–1892) and from 1946.

†Cheadle: — and Tean Times 1896–(1981).

Cheam: see SUTTON.

†CHELMSFORD: Essex Chronicle 1764–
(1981); — and Colchester Chronicle 1768–71
as — Chronicle 1771–1884 as Essex County
Chronicle 1884–1900; — Gazette 1824–5;

(Chelmsford — continued) –
Essex and Suffolk Press 1832 with Essex
Independent; Essex Weekly News 1862–
(1981); South Essex Independent 1862–69
as Essex Independent 1869–1920; The
Essex Review 1892–(1920).
Chelsea: see KENSINGTON and
WANDSWORTH.
†CHELTENHAM: — Chronicle and Gloucs.
Advertiser 1810–49 as Chronicle and Parish
Register and General Advertiser etc. 1850–
87 as — Chronicle 1887–1900 as — Chronicle
and Gloucs. Graphic 1901–(1981); —
Journal 1827–68; Gloucester and — Herald
1827–8; — Looker-on 1833–1920; — Free
Press 1834–1908 with — Examiner; —
Examiner 1839–1913; — Parish Register
1849 with — Chronicle: — Observer 1855;
— Mercury 1855–1903; — Penny Times
1855; — Times 1860–82; — Herald 1862;
— Express 1866–88; — News 1867; —
Telegraph 1868–77; Gloucestershire Echo
1873–(1981); Evening Express Telegram
1874–82; Working Men's College Magazine
1884–85; Indicator 1888–89; — Chronicle
Supplement 1901–42.
†Cheshunt: — and Waltham Telegraph 1863–
(1981).
†CHESTER: Adams' Weekly Courant 1739–
92 as — Courant and Anglo-Welsh Gazette
1825–31 as — Courant and Advertiser for
North Wales 1831–(1981); — Chronicle 1775–
(1981); The Pleasing Entertainer 1814; —
Guardian 1822; — Gleaner 1824; Y Drysorfa
1831–(1920); Y Gwladgarwr 1833–41; —
Gazette 1836–40; Farmers' Herald 1843–
1913 (1920); Cheshire Observer 1854–
(1981); — Record 1857–8 with Guardian;
County Guardian 1868–1956; County Gazette
1861; Cheshire News 1866–7 as Chester News
and Cheshire Guardian 1868–1956; Cheshire
Sheaf 1880–(1920); — Daily Guardian
1884–85.
†CHESTERFIELD: Derbyshire Courier 1831–
1922; Derbyshire and — Reporter 1831–
1930; North Derbyshire Chronicle and —
Advertiser 1836–9 as Derbyshire Chronicle
1839–42 with Derbyshire and — Reporter;
Derbyshire Times and — Herald 1854–
(1981); Derbyshire and — Express 1862–64
as Hatton's Derbyshire News 1864–6 with
Ilkeston Pioneer; — and District Free Press
1890–93.
†CHICHESTER: * Sussex Chronicle and —
Advertiser 1803; — Magazine 1838; West
Sussex Gazette 1852–(1981); — Journal
1860–4; — Express 1863–1902; — Courier
1869; * Mason and Wilmhurst's — Advertiser 1869; Bognor Regis Observer 1872–
(1981); — Advertiser 1878; — Observer
1887–(1981); West Sussex County Chronicle
1887–90 with Portsmouth Times.
    * Chichester PL Sussex Chronicle and

(Chichester — continued) –
Chichester Advertiser from 1803.
CHIPPENHAM: — Journal 1841; — Chronicle
1876–82; Calne and — Express 1907.
CHIPPING NORTON: see Oxfordshire Weekly
News 1869–1928.
Chislehurst: see BROMLEY.
†CHORLEY: — Standard 1864–1908 as — and
District Weekly News 1908–(1920); —
Guardian 1871–(1981).
†CHRISTCHURCH: — Times 1858–(1981); —
News and Bournemouth Chronicle 1872–
76 with Bournemouth Observer; — Guardian
1883–5 with Bournemouth Guardian.
Clapham: see LAMBETH.
Cleckheaton: see SPENBOROUGH.
CLEETHORPES: — and District Gazette
1886–7.
Clerkenwell: see ISLINGTON.
†CLITHEROE: — Times 1890–(1920) — with
Advertiser 1895–(1981); Gazette 1907–9.
†COLCHESTER: — Weekly Journal 1736;
Pilborough's — Journal 1739; — * Gazette
1814–37 as Essex and Suffolk Times 1837–
41; Evening Gazette 1814–(1981); Sickle
1828 as — Courier 1828–9; Essex Standard
1831–92 as Essex County Standard 1892–
(1981); Essex Independent 1832–3 with
* — Gazette 1836–69; Essex Telegraph
1858–1908 as Essex County Telegraph
1908–51; Essex Magazine 1862; — Mercury
1868–1901; Essex Times and Journal 1870
as — Times 1870–2 as Essex Journal 1872–6
with East Anglian Daily Times; Chronicle
1876–92; — Gazette 1877–1970; — News
1887–9; — Journal 1888–9.
    * ! Colchester PL holds a *File of Bound
    Newspapers* in stock, including series —
Gazette, — and Essex Independent, —
Mercury and Essex Express and Pilborough's
Colchester Journal for 1793. Mercury also
MF.
†COLNE: — and Nelson Guardian 1863–69; —
and Burnley Times 1867–8; * — and Nelson
Times 1874–(1981); — and Nelson Pioneer
1882–90; — Observer 1901–6; * — Valley
Guardian 1903–76.
    * Colne PL, Colne and Nelson Times
    from 1875; originals of Colne Valley
    Guardian (1903–76) at Huddersfield CL.
COLWYN BAY: — Gazette 1884–91 with
Abergele and Pensarn Visitor; — Visitor
1889–93; — and Welsh Coast Pioneer 1898–
1964; What's News? Pa Newydd? 1899 with
Weekly News; Halfpenny Herald 1900–
(1920); — Sentinel 1913–6.
†CONGLETON: — Advertiser 1856–76; — and
Macclesfield Mercury 1858–95 with —
Chronicle; — Guardian 1868; — Guardian
1890–1956; — Chronicle 1893–(1981).
CONWAY: * North Wales Weekly News 1889–
1902 as Colwyn Bay Weekly News 1902–4
as North Wales Weekly News 1905–(1920);

(Conway – continued) –
Deganwy Sentinel 1915 as – Sentinel 1915
with North Wales Standard.
†COVENTRY: * Jopson's – Mercury 1741-87
as – Mercury 1787-1823 as * – Standard
1836-1969; – Herald 1824-63 as – Herald
and Free Press 1863-1940; – Observer
1827-30 with – Herald; – Advertiser 1852;
– Times 1855-1914; with – Herald; Free
Press 1858-63 with – Herald; – Observer
1858; – Examiner 1859; – Liberal 1868;
– Independent 1873-88 as – Mercury
1888-1909; Athletic Reporter 1885-1911
as – Reporter 1911 with – Herald; Midland
Daily Telegraph 1891-1941 – as * Evening
Telegraph 1941-(81); Cycle Maker 1897;
* – etc. Graphic 1911-21.
      * Coventry CL, a few copies of Joplin's
Coventry Mercury, the Standard and
Evening Telegraph, MF.
COWBRIDGE: Bridgend, Cowbridge and
Maesteg Times 1859-60.
Cradley Heath; see STOURBRIDGE.
†CREWE: – Guardian 1869-1965; – and
Nantwich Chronicle 1875-(1981); – and
Nantwich Observer 1908-32. See Chaloner,
W. H., *The Social & Economic Hist. of
Crewe 1780-1923* (1950).
†CROSBY: Waterloo – and Seaforth Magazine
1886-90; Waterloo and – Herald 1895-
(1981).
†CROYDON: The Satchel 1831; Chapman's
Miscellany 1843; * Chronicle 1855-1912;
Weekly Standard 1859-87 as Bucks. Stan-
dard 1887-(1981); – Times 1861-1967;
– Observer 1863-1904; – Journal 1863-
1902; Surrey News 1869-93; * – Advertiser
1869-(1981); – Express 1878-1919 with
– Advertiser; – Review 1880-95; – Echo
1887-9; – Star 1889-92; – Standard 1891-
2; – and County Pictorial 1903-6; Citizen
1904-9; – Daily Argus 1905 as Surrey
Daily Argus 1905-8 with Surrey Morning
Echo; Surrey Morning Echo 1908-10;
Surrey Evening Echo 1908-10; – Penge,
Annerley and Norwood Telephone 1912.
      * Croydon PL, Chronicle and Advertiser
for 1869-71 and 1874 to date.
Darlaston: see WOLVERHAMPTON.
†DARLINGTON: * – and Stockton Times
1847-(1981); Teesdale Mercury 1854-(1981);
Northern Express 1855-6; Aycliffe
Chronicle 1857-(1981); Telegram 1858;
* Mercury 1864-72 with – and Stockton
Times; * Northern Echo 1870-(1981);
Ironworkers' Journal 1874-1916; North
Star 1882-1924; – Evening Echo 1884-5;
– Evening Star 1892; – Advertiser 1905;
Northern Dispatch 1914-(1975).
      * Darlington PL, all MF. Also typescript
Local History Guide (No. 4 of a series)
published by the L's Local History Depart-
ment, 1971. This lists a number of other

(Darlington – continued) –
towns' newspapers held at Darlington, e.g.:
Durham, Kendal, Newcastle and York, with
a number of useful Histories of individual
papers, e.g.: The Comet or Darlington
Observer (Manuscript), Darlington and
Stockton Times (*Centenary Handbook
1847-1947*), Darlington and Stockton Times
(issue of 2 October 1937).
†DARTFORD: * – Chronicle 1869-(1981);
– Express 1875-1918 (1920); – Times
1885-7 with – and West Kent Advertiser;
– and West Kent Advertiser 1889-1938; –
Gazette 1903; – Bexley and Crayford Mail
1906-7; Gravesend and – Reporter 1856-
(1981).
      * Dartford PL, Dartford Chronicle
(1869-1970), MF.
†DARTMOUTH: – Chronicle 1869-(1981).
† DARWEN: – News 1876-1971; – Post
1885-99 as – Gazette 1899-1921; –
Advertiser 1893-(1981); Monthly Leader
1896.
†DAVENTRY; – Express 1869-(1981); –
Spectator 1869-76 with Northamptonshire
Guardian; Midland Times and – Gazette
1877-8.
†Dawlish: – Gazette 1897-(1981).
†DEAL: – Walmer and Sandwich Telegram
1858-95 as Kentish Telegram 1895-1918
(1920); – Mercury 1865-(1981); East Kent
Mercury 1865-(1981); – Chronicle and
Dover Gazette 1874-1900; – News 1877-
78; – Walmer and Sandwich Chronicle
1879-90; – Paper and Waltham News 1893-
1942.
DENBIGH: – Journal 1853-54; Banner
Cymru 1857-59 as Naber ac Amserau
Cymru 1859-(1920); Mold and – Chronicle
1869-70; – Free Press 1882-1957; North
Wales Times 1895-1957.
Deptford; see GREENWICH and LEWISHAM.
†DERBY: Post Man 1720; – Mercury 1788-
1933; Anti-Slavery Magazine 1824; – and
Chesterfield Reporter 1831-1930; Derby-
shire Advertiser 1846-(1981); Derbyshire
Times and Chesterfield Herald 1854-(1981);
Illustrated Derbyshire Chronicle 1855-73;
– Telegraph 1855-69; – Exchange Gazette
1860 as Daily Gazette 1860-5 as Derby and
Derbyshire Gazette 1866-99; British Coal
and Iron Trades Advertiser 1871-4; –
Evening Telegraph 1879-(1981) (incorporat-
ing – Daily Telegraph and – Daily Express);
– Daily Telegraph 1879-82 with Evening
Telegraph; – etc. Evening Gazette 1879-84;
Chronicle 1881; – Daily Express 1884-
1932 with – Evening Telegraph; Morning
Post 1885-7; – Weekly Express 1885; Ram
1892; – Comet 1893-4; Derbyshire Tele-
phone 1898-1901 with Belper News; Weekly
Observer 1903; Free Press 1904; Derbyshire
Herald 1907-8.

†DEVIZES: — and Wiltshire Gazette 1824–
(1981); Wiltshire Independent 1836–76 as
Wiltshire Times 1876–1981; — Miscellany
1852; — Advertiser 1858–76 as — and
Wiltshire Advertiser 1877–1933; Herald
1869–70.

Devonport: see PLYMOUTH.

†DEWSBURY: — and Batley Herald and
Heckmondwike and Ossett Advertiser 1854–
5; — and Batley Herald 1855; * — Reporter
1858–(1981); — Chronicle 1869–95 with
District News; Cleckheaton and Spenborough Guardian 1967–(1981);
Examiner 1870; Heckmondwike Herald
1877–(1981); — and Batley Standard 1884–
5; * — District News 1891–1959; — Batley
and District Social Democrat 1907–9;
* — Free Press 1915–7.
      * Batley PL, also Huddersfield CL.

†DONCASTER: — Nottingham and Lincoln
Gazette (1786) 1828–1881 as — Gazette
1881–(1981); — etc. Times 1833; — etc.
Chronicle 1836–1963; — Reporter 1867–
90; — Free Press 1868–90; — News 1872;
— Express 1898; — Argus 1898–1900;
— Weekly News 1899–1900; — Borough
Advertiser 1906–9.

DORCHESTER: Dorset County Chronicle
1829–1957; Dorset and Somerset Reporter
1854; Dorset Express and Agricultural
Gazette 1855–6 — as Dorset County Express
1856–86 with Western Chronicle of Yeovil;
Weymouth, Portland and — Telegram 1866–
86 as — Telegram 1886–1901 as — Telegram 1901–4 as — Mail 1904–27.
      See *Dorset Newspapers* (Weymouth CL
1972). ! Gazette at both Dorchester PL and
Weymouth CL (MF).

†Dorking: — Advertiser 1887–(1981).

†DOVER: — Telegraph 1833–1927; —
Chronicle 1835–79 as — and County
Chronicle 1880–1927; — Warden 1858–9;
— Express 1858–(1981); — Independent
1860–5; Cinque Ports Pilot 1860–7; —
Times 1863–4; — News 1866–79 as South
Coast Echo 1879; — Morning Chronicle
1868; — Standard 1871–(1920); — Times
1887–90; — Observer 1895–1905 as — Times
1905–14 (1920).

Dovercourt: see HARWICH.

DROITWICH: Bromsgrove and — Weekly
Messenger 1860–1962; Bromsgrove, Redditch and — News 1871; — Guardian 1883–
1930.

†DUDLEY: * — Weekly Times 1856–8; * —
News 1857; * — and Midland Counties
Express 1857–8 with — Times; * — Times
1858; Midland Magazine 1861–2; — Herald
and Oldbury Guardian 1866–(1981); — and
* East Worcester Gazette 1869; * — Guardian 1869–75 — with Herald; — Times
1872; * — and District News 1880–5; —
Chronicle 1885–1935 with Herald;

(Dudley — continued) –
      * — Mercury 1887–90 with County
Express. Also: BRIERLEY HILL:
      * — Advertiser 1856–7 as Advertiser 1857–
1907 as County Advertiser for Staffs. and
Worcs. 1907–25 as County Advertiser and
Herald for Staffs. and Worcs. 1925–66; The
County Express, Brierley Hill, Stourbridge,
Kidderminster and Dudley News 1867–70
and 1873–85 as Stourbridge, Brierley Hill
and County Express for Worcs. and Staffs.
1885–91 as County Express for Worcs. and
Staffs. 1891–(1981).
      * Dudley Local History L has typescript
list of holdings, all MF. Smethwick PL has
all newspapers indicated here, also has
Brierly Hill Advertiser, 1856–74.

DUKINFIELD: Ashton, Stalybridge and —
Elector 1868; Stalybridge and — Standard
1869–1900; — Herald 1890–1901.

Dulwich: see SOUTHWARK.

†DUNSTABLE: — Reformer 1856–7; —
Chronicle 1856–60; * — Borough Gazette
1865–(1981); Weekly Reporter and —
Advertiser 1878 as Weekly Reporter and
Leighton Buzzard Advertiser 1878–84 as
Leighton Buzzard Advertiser 1884–1905
(1920) with Luton Reporter.
      * Dunstable PL has no newspaper collec-
tions, recommends ref. to Gazette local
offices.

†DURHAM: The Pamphlet or Northern
Scourge 1817; * — Chronicle 1823–1930;
* County Advertiser 1823–30 as * —
Advertiser 1830–43 as — County Advertiser
1855–(1981); Northern Messenger 1859;
— City and County News 1870–2; — City
News 1887.
      * ! Sunderland RL has copies of —
Chronicle and Sunderland Times (1832),
— County Advertiser (1815–30). —
Chronicle (1841), Sunderland and Durham
County Herald (1838–80) and Sunderland
and Durham Gazette (1831). Durham
Chronicle, 26 Oct. 1832, Durham County
Advertiser (various 1817–74) in Darlington
PL.

†Dursley; — Gazette 1878–(1981).

Dymchurch: see NEW ROMNEY.

EALING: * — Illustrated Magazine and General
Advertiser 1858–9 as — Post 1863; Middlesex County Times 1863–(1981); — Register
1877; — Gazette 1898–1923; — Guardian
1898–1900. * — Illustrated Magazine and
General Advertiser 1858–9 as * — Parish
Magazine and Monthly Advertiser for Ealing,
Acton, Hanwell and Brentford 1860–3 as
* — Post and General Advertiser for Ealing
etc. 1863–6 as * Middlesex County Times
1866–1941 as * Middlesex County Times
and West Middlesex Gazette 1942–74 as
* Ealing Gazette 1974–(1981); — Gazette
1898–1923 as West Middlesex Gazette

(Ealing — continued) —
1923–41 as Middlesex County Times and
West Middlesex Gazette 1941–(1975). Also:
†ACTON: – Press 1870–1; * – Gazette
1871–(1981); – Press 1898–1900 with
County of Middlesex Independent; –
Express 1900–11 as Chiswick Express
1911–8 (1920); – and Chiswick District
Post 1911–25; SOUTHALL: * – News
1885–88.
    * Ealing CL, originals and MF. These
date, with the Ealing Illustrated Magazine,
from 1858.
†Easingwold: – Advertiser 1892–(1981).
†EASTBOURNE: * – Gazette 1859–(1981);
– Express 1863–1902; * – Chronicle
1866–1951; – Standard 1868–70; –
News 1870; Eastbournian 1870–(1920);
– Fashionable Arrival List 1875–80 with
Courier: –Standard 1875–80; – Courier
1877–87 as – Echo 1887; Illustrated
Visitors' List 1877–1911; – Scorpion
1883–92; Cliftonian 1884–5; Review
1885–90; – Observer 1885–90 and 1892–
1902; – and Sussex Society 1899–1909;
– Amusements 1901; – Pictorial 1903–
(1920). – Programme 1908–17 (1920);
– Illustrated 1914.
    * Eastbourne PL.
†East Grinstead: – Observer 1881–(1981).
†EASTLEIGH: – Weekly News and Gazette
1892–1901 as Weekly News and Hants
Gazette 1901–(1981).
†EAST RETFORD: – Advertiser 1854–9;
– and Bassetlaw Gazette 1858–9; Worksop
etc. News 1867–1968 as Gainsborough
News; Retford, Worksop, Isle of Axholme
and Gainsborough News 1867–(1920); –
and Gainsborough Times 1869–(1981);
– and Worksop Herald 1889–1929.
†ECCLES: – Advertiser 1869–1908; – and
Patricroft Journal 1874–(1981); – Division
News 1889–90; Navvy's Guide 1891.
Edgbaston: see BIRMINGHAM.
Edgware: see BARNET.
Edmonton: see ENFIELD and HARINGEY.
Egham: see STAINES and EGHAM.
ELLESMERE PORT: – Advertiser 1915–76.
Eltham: see GREENWICH.
†ELY: Soham Advertiser 1872–(1981); –
Standard 1875–(1981); – Chronicle 1878–
(1881); – Weekly Guardian 1889–1910 as
Cambridgeshire Weekly News: – Gazette
1898–1903 as Cambridgeshire Independent
Press 1903–1925.
†ENFIELD: Meyer's – Observer 1874–(1981);
– Express 1888–9; – District News 1894–5;
– Illustrated Magazine 1898; – Chronicle
1898–1904; – Free Press 1902; – Tatler
1905. Also: EDMONTON: – and Totten-
ham Weekly Guardian 1884–1906.
†Epworth: – Bells 1873–(1981).
†EPSOM AND EWELL: Epsom Advocate

(Epsom and Ewell — continued) —
1856–7; Epsomian 1870; Epsom Herald
1881–3; Epsom District Times 1901–17
(1920); Epsom Observer 1901–8 with
– Advertiser; – Guardian 1909; * – Adver-
tiser 1910–73; * – Herald 1945–(1981).
    * ! Epsom and Ewell BL has Advertiser
(1910 to date), also Epsom and Ewell
Advertiser 1869–(1974); Epsom and Ewell
Weekly Post (1906–8) formerly Mid-Surrey
Weekly Post 1904–6 as Epsom and Ewell
Guardian 1908–9; Epsom Ormonde 1920.
Erith: see BEXLEY.
Eton: see WINDSOR.
†EVESHAM: – Journal 1860–(1981); Vale of
– News 1869–73; – Standard 1888–1961.
Ewell: see EPSOM AND EWELL.
†EXETER: Joe Buss's Exeter Post Boy 1711;
– Mercury 1714; Protestant Mercury or
Exeter Post Boy 1715; – Mercury 1716;
– Mercury 1721–2; Fairley's Exeter Journal
1726; Trewman's Exeter Flying Post 1804–
1917; Alfred etc. 1815–31 as Exeter
Independent 1831 with Western Luminary;
Trewman's Exeter Flying Post 1827 with
Saturday edition of Evening Post of Exeter;
Besley's Exeter News 1827 as Devonshire
Chronicle 1827–53; Woolmer's Exeter and
Plymouth Gazette 1827–1903 as Devon
and Exeter Gazette 1903–(1981); Exeter
Weekly Times 1827–8 as Western Times
1829–(1981); Devonshire Agricultural
Magazine 1834; Featherstone's Exeter Times
1836–7; Parthenon 1847–8 as Western
Miscellany 1849–50; – Journal 1856–61
as Devon Weekly Times; Devon Weekly
Times 1861–1904; Plymouth Gazette Daily
Telegram 1863–85; – Express and Echo
1864–(1981) as Devon Evening Express
Exmouth Journal; – Evening Express of
Devon Weekly Times 1866–(1975); –
Weekly Marvel 1869; – Evening Post 1885–
1902 (1920); – Evening Post Daily
and Weekly 1885–1902 with Trewman's
Exeter Flying Post; – Evening Gazette
1885; – Day by Day 1911–4.
†EYE: Suffolk Mercury (Eye and Framlingham
edition) 1971–(1981).
†FALMOUTH: – Packet 1829–48; Packet and
Cornish Herald 1829–48; Cornubian 1830–7
with Express; – Express and Colonial
Journal 1838– 46 with Royal Cornwall
Gazette of Truro; Cornwall Weekly Times
1847; Lake's – Packet and Cornwall
Advertiser 1858–(1981); – Weekly Times
1861–94 as Penryn Times 1894–6 as Cornish
Echo 1896–1952; News Slip 1880–1902.
†FARNWORTH: – Observer 1868–73 with
– Journal 1873–(1981); – Express 1890–1;
– Chronicle 1906–17 (1920).
†Farnham: – Herald 1892–(1981).
†FAVERSHAM: – Gazette 1855–7; – Mercury
etc. 1860–1938 as – Times and Mercury

(Faversham — continued) —
and North-East Kent Journal 1939-72 as —
Times and—Gazette 1972-(1981);—Institute
etc., Monthly 1862-(1920); — Express
1870-1; — News 1883-(1981); — and North-
East Kent Advertiser 1903-10.
Finchley: see BARNET.
Finsbury: see ISLINGTON.
†FLEETWOOD: * — Chronicle 1845-(1981); —
Express 1882-1921.
    * Fleetwood BL copies of the Fleetwood
Chronicle from 1877-1974, later years also
MF.
FLINT: Flintshire Observer 1857-1916; —
County Chronicle 1866-7; Flintshire News
1909-13 with — Observer.
FOLKESTONE: — Chronicle 1855-1906; —
Observer 1860-70 with Kentish Express; —
Express 1868-1940; Visitors' List 1870 as
Borough Gazette 1870-1; — Free Press
1875-6; — News 1876-90; Holbein's
Visitors' List 1884-91 as Visitors' List
1891-9 with Hythe Reporter; — Advertiser
1884-7 with — Chronicle; — Argus 1889-91;
— Herald 1891-(1981); — Telegraph 1898-
1908; — Amusements Guide 1901; —
Society Times 1902.
†Formby: — Times 1895-(1981).
Framlingham: see EYE.
Fulham: see HAMMERSMITH.
†Gainsborough: — News 1883-(1981); and see
EAST RETFORD.
GATESHEAD: — Observer 1837-86; — and
Tyneside Echo 1879-88; — Guardian 1895-
1900.
    ! Gateshead BL, in 1974 had about 80
volumes of local newspapers including
Newcastle editions 1744-1834, also holds
originals Gateshead Observer (1837-43) with
the years 1837-86 MF.
GILLINGHAM: — Monthly 1893; — Gazette
1903-4 as Three Shires Advertiser 1904-24;
— Times 1909.
†GLASTONBURY: — Chronicle 1859-(1981);
Central Somerset Gazette 1861-(1981);
— Monthly 1893.
GLOSSOP: Lister's — Advertiser 1854; —
Record 1859-71; — Times 1869-1901 with
Derbyshire Times; Dale Chronicle 1871-81;
North Derbyshire and North Cheshire
Advertiser 1872-1901 as North Cheshire
and North Derbyshire Advertiser 1901-23;
High Peak Chronicle 1906-37.
†GLOUCESTER: * — Journal 1722-(1981); *—
Gazette 1792-6; *— and Cheltenham Herald
1802-23 and 1826-8, 1827-8; — Mercury
1828-9; — Chronicle 1833-(1920); Lucy
and Co.'s Prices Current 1854-5; Philpots
and Co.'s Corn Circular 1854-5; — Times
1855-6; — Free Press 1885 as * Mercury 1856-
94 with — Journal; City of — Guardian
1859; City and County News 1863; — News
1870-2 as * Standard 1872-1902; —

(Gloucester — continued) —
Gloucestershire Echo 1873-(1981); —
* Citizen 1877-(1975); — Times 1888-9;
Magpie 1891-2; Household News 1911-2.
    * Bristol CL, 3 volumes of — Journal
(1728-1836), all others Gloucester PL.
GODALMING: Guildford and — Weekly
Press 1912-38.
†GOOLE: — Times 1853-4; Howden and —
Chronicle 1855; — Weekly Times 1869-94
as — Times 1894-(1981); Marshland and
Howden Gazette 1870-3; Howdenshire
Gazette 1873-(1975); — Telegraph 1875-9;
— Saturday Journal 1889-1941; — Weekly
Herald 1891-1901; Wednesday Journal
1893-1913 (1920); — Free Press 1894-5.
GOSPORT: — Times 1866-7; — County
Journal 1905-13; and see PORTSMOUTH.
†GRANTHAM: * — Journal 1855-(1981);
— Times 1859-60; — Wesleyan Messenger
1872-3; — Post 1882-3; — Times 1884-
1902; — Chronicle 1886; — and Stamford
Guardian 1873-4; — Young Men's Magazine
1893; — Advertiser 1902-6 (1920).
    * Grantham PL, Grantham Journal from
1854, not including 1902-9.
†GRAVESEND: — and Milton Journal 1835-7;
Kentish Standard 1842; — Free Press 1855-
90; — Reporter 1856-64; — and Dartford
Reporter 1864-(1981); — Journal 1864-92
with — Standard; — and Dartford Miscellany
1871-90; — Argus 1882-5; — and Northfleet
Standard 1892-1915 (1920).
†GREAT YARMOUTH: * Norwich, — and
Lynn Courier 1818-23; The Blue Dwarf
1820; — Advertiser 1853-4; Norfolk and
Suffolk Monthly Advertiser 1854; — Free
Press 1855-7 as Independent 1857-1940;
— Standard 1857; — Weekly News 1858 as
Norfolk Standard 1858-9 as — Standard
1859-60; — Chronicle 1863-91; — etc.
Constitutionalist 1869-72 as — Advertiser
1896-1901 with — Mercury; — Free Lance
1870-1; — Critic 1872; — and Lowestoft
Dove 1874; — and Lowestoft Era 1874;
— Mercury 1880-(1981); — and Gorleston
Times 1880-1923; — Comet 1893; * —
Weekly Standard 1906-26.
    * Norfolk County Library hold, at
Norwich CL copies of — Weekly Standard
for 1906 and Norwich, Yarmouth and Lynn
Courier (1818-23).
†GREENWICH: South-East London and
Kentish Mercury 1833-(1981); * — Wool-
wich and Deptford Gazette 1834-9 with
Kentish Mercury; — Woolwich, Deptford
and West Kent Guardian 1834-5 with West
Kent Guardian; — Woolwich and Deptford
Patriot 1837-8; *Kentish Independent
1843-1967; — and West Kent Observer
1853-4; — Free Press 1855-65; Borough of
— Free Press 1857; — and Deptford
Chronicle 1869-85 with Deptford Observer;

(Greenwich – continued) –
— Good Templar 1875-6; — Observer 1879-89 with Kentish Mail; — and Deptford Echo 1888-9. Also: WOOLWICH: — Advertiser 1839-40 as — Gazette 1840-1 with Kentish Mercury; — Gazette 1869-1903 as Borough of — Gazette 1903-9 as — Gazette and Plumstead News 1909-39 as Mid-Weekly Gazette 1939-40; — Echo 1887-9; — Herald 1896-(1920); Borough of — Labour Journal 1901-4; Borough of — Gazette 1903-(1920); Borough of — Pioneer 1904-6 as — Pioneer and Labour Journal 1906-(1920). Also: Eltham: — Times 1881-(1981).
* Greenwich PL, MF Gazette and Kentish Independent and bound volumes of latter from 1901.
GRIMSBY: * — Gazette 1853-5; — and North Lincs. Advertiser 1854-61 as Grimsby Independent 1861-6 as — Advertiser 1866-7; — Guardian 1854-67; etc. Advertiser 1854-77; * — Independent 1858-60; * — Free Press 1860-8; — Herald 1863-81; — Gazette 1866-1920; — Times 1869; * — News 1874-1957. * — Observer 1874-1904; — Express 1878-91 with Hull Daily News; — Weekly Express 1883-98; — Echo 1884-5; — Times 1884-5; Independent 1892-7; Grimbo Joco 1895; — Times 1898-1916 (1920); * — Post 1899-1900; — New Free Press 1899-1900; — Daily News 1910-5; — and Cleethorpes Amusement Programme 1914; *Illustrated Weekly 1908-12; * — and County Times 1908-12.
* Grimsby PL has typescript list of 22 local newspapers for the town, held as bound volumes and in most cases as MF. Also holdings for Hull, Lincoln, Stamford, Louth and Rutland.
†GUILDFORD: County Herald and Weekly Advertiser for Surrey 1818-73; — Times 1855-(1981); West Surrey Times 1855-1920; West Surrey Express 1862; — Chronicle 1863; — News 1863; — Observer 1863-4 with Surrey Gazette; — Journal 1863-1902; Surrey Advertiser 1864-(1981) — Gazette and North London Advertiser 1864-(1981); West Surrey County Chronicle 1870-1; — Free Press 1900-12 as — and Godalming Weekly Press 1912-3 as Surrey Weekly Press 1913-38.
†HACKNEY: — Magazine 1833-8; — Journal 1842; — Observer 1857-69 as — Express 1869-1903 as — Observer 1903-15 (1920); — Magazine 1858; — and Kingsland Times 1862-3; East London and — Advertiser 1866-(1981); — and Kingsland Gazette 1869-1926 as Hackney Gazette and North London Advertiser 1926-(1981); — Times 1869-72; — Guardian 1874-5; — Standard 1877-1907 (1920); Carriage Guardian 1884-95; — Mercury 1885-1906; Hackney (Typescript) 1892; — and Clapton Free Press

(Hackney – continued) –
1894; — Carriage and Hackney Cab Gazette 1908-9; — Telegraph 1909; Borough of — Standard and North London Herald 1909-10. Also: SHOREDITCH: — Herald 1852; — Observer 1857-1915 (1920); — Advertiser 1860-9; — Citizen 1889 with East Central Times; — Guardian 1894-6 as Eastern Post; — Mail 1906-10.
HALESOWEN: Cradley Heath Reporter 1864 as — Observer 1864-6 as Stourbridge Observer 1866-88; see also STOURBRIDGE.
Halesworth: See SOUTHWOLD.
†HALIFAX: * — Advertiser 1759-60; * — Journal 1801-11; * — Commercial Chronicle 1829-30; * — and Huddersfield Express 1831-41; * — Guardian 1832-1921 with — Evening Courier; — Reformer 1847-8; * — Courier 1853-(1981); — Observer 1862; — Times 1872-95; — Mercury 1890-5; — Evening Courier 1892-(1981); — Local Opinion 1892-3 as — Comet 1893-1904; — Daily Guardian 1906-21 with Evening Courier; etc. Labour News 1909; * — Naturalist 1896-1904. * Halifax PL.
* Bradford PL has Halifax Journal (1801-9), Huddersfield CL has Advertiser; Huddersfield Express; and Guardian, all MF.
HAMMERSMITH: — Advertiser 1861-6; — Express 1889-90 as — Express and West London Gazette; — Socialist Record 1891-3; Hammerer 1894; — Searchlight 1900; — Weekly Express 1905-7; — Home Chronicle 1913-5. Also: † FULHAM: — Magazine 1885-6; — Chronicle 1888-(1981); — and Walham Green News 1889-1904; — Observer 1893-1913 with West London Observer; — Frolic 1894; — Argus 1901; — and West Kensington Gazette 1914-6.
Hampstead: see CAMDEN.
Handsworth: see BIRMINGHAM.
Harborne: see BIRMINGHAM.
HARINGEY: — Hornsey and Finsbury Park Express 1899-1900; — Hornsey and Wood Green Telegraph 1901-2. Also: †HORNSEY: — Hornet 1866-8; — and Finsbury Park Journal 1881-(1981); — and Middlesex Messenger 1888-9; — Hawkeye 1897. †TOTTENHAM: — and Edmonton Advertiser 1855-80; — and Edmonton Weekly Herald 1861-(1981); — Observer 1875-9; — Free Press 1888; — and Stamford Hill Times 1890-1905; — and Wood Green Star 1891-6 with Middlesex Mail; — Advertiser 1909-10. †WOOD GREEN: Wood Green Weekly Herald 1861-(1981); — Gazette 1889; — Mercury 1899 with North London Mercury.
†HARROGATE: — Advertiser 1836-(1981); — Weekly Gazette 1837-41; — Herald 1847-(1981); Wetherby News 1857-(1981); Knaresborough Post 1863-(1981); Pateley Bridge Herald 1863-(1981); — Gazette 1873-9

(Harrogate – continued) –
as – News 1879-90 with Wetherby News;
– Comet 1893; – Visitor 1894-1900; and
Claro Times 1903-20; – Star 1908-17
(1920).
†HARROW: – Herald 1863-1914; – Gazette
1869-(1981); – Press 1892-7; Wealdstone,
– and Wembley Observer 1895-(1981).
†HARTLEPOOL: – Advertiser 1850-1; – Free
Press 1855-72; West Hartlepool Guardian
1855; Stockton and – Mercury 1855-65 as
South Durham and Cleveland Mercury
1865-1906 with South Durham and Auck-
land Chronicle of Darlington; South Durham
Herald 1866-91; Northern Evening Mail
1878-83 as Northern Daily Mail 1883-
(1981); Northern Guardian 1891-1902;
– Weekly Journal 1901-9; – Daily Shipping
List 1904-16; – Borough Advertiser 1913-6.
†HARWICH: – Penny Newsman 1870-(1920);
– and Dovercourt Observer 1871-81; – and
Dovercourt Free Press 1884-1906; – and
Dovercourt Standard 1906-(1981).
†Haslemere: – Herald 1892-(1981).
HASLINGDEN: – Chronicle 1867-72; – and
Rossendale Gazette 1882 as Bacup, –
and Rossendale Gazette 1882-3 as – and
Rossendale Gazette 1883-7 with Bacup
and Rossendale News; Guardian 1890-1965;
– Gazette 1901-26.
†HASTINGS: – and Cinque Ports Iris 1830-1;
– and St Leonards Journal 1835; Cinque
Ports Chronicle 1838-40; – etc. Record
1848-1905; – and St Helens News and East-
bourne Record 1848-1905; – and St
Leonards Gazette 1856-96; – and St
Leonards Times 1857-8 and 1877-99 with
– Weekly Mail; Osborne's Directory and
Fashionable Advertiser for – 1859-63 as –
and St Leonards Advertiser 1863-1918
(1920); – and St Leonards Chronicle 1863-
1904; – and St Leonards Observer 1866-
(1981); – and St Leonards Independent
1873-91 as – and Bexhill Independent
1891-1917 (1920); – and St Leonards
Fashionable Guardian 1875-8; – etc.
Amusements 1876-1903; – etc. Times
1877-99 with – Weekly Mail; – and St
Leonards World 1878; – Evening Journal
1889-90; – St Leonards and Bexhill
Amusements 1896-1903; – and St Leonards
Weekly Mail 1898-1911; – and St Leonards
Standard 1899.
†HAVERING: see ROMFORD: – Times 1912-
(1940) as Hornchurch, Dagenham and –
Times 1940-5 as Hornchurch, Dagenham,
Brentwood and – Times 1945-68 as Haver-
ing and – Express 1968-74 as Havering
Express and – Times 1974-7 as – and
Hornchurch Express and – Times 1977
as – Express 1977-(1981).
HAVERFORDWEST: Pembrokeshire Herald
1844-1924; The Principality 1847-50; –

(Haverfordwest – continued) –
and Milford Haven Telegraph 1854-1937;
Potters Electric News 1855-69 with
Pembrokeshire Herald; Potters Newspaper
1871-2.
†Haverhill: – Echo 1888-(1981).
†Hebden Bridge: – Times 1881-(1981).
(HEDON): None listed.
HELSTON: – Grammar School Magazine
1852; – Advertiser 1910-18 (1920).
†HEMEL HEMPSTEAD: Bucks. and Middlesex
Advertiser 1854-(1975) as Middlesex
Advertiser and Gazette; – Gazette 1858-99
as Herts. Hemel Hempstead Gazette and
West Herts. Advertiser 1899-(1981);
Inspector 1884-5; – Advertiser 1895-1901;
– Reporter 1901.
Hendon: see BARNET.
†HENLEY-ON-THAMES: – Advertiser 1870-
1908; – Free Press 1885-92 as Standard
1892-(1981); – Chronicle 1904 with
Oxford Chronicle.
†HEREFORD: British Chronicle and Pugh's
Hereford Journal 1773-92 as – Journal
1793-1925; – Independent 1824-6; –
Times 1833-(1981); – County Press 1837-
40; The Pioneer 1839-40; – Chronicle
1858-60; – Weekly News 1860-3 and 1882;
– Express 1864-5; – Mercury 1864-1925;
– Weekly Marvel 1869-1904; – Evening
News 1882; – Market Express 1884.
†HERTFORD: – Scrutator 1820-1; Hert-
fordian 1822; – Mercury 1825-8 as
Hertford, Huntingdon, Bedford etc. Mercury
1828-33 with Essex Mercury; Ware Patriot
as – and Ware Patriot 1833-4 as Radical
Reformer 1834-5; County Press for Hertfordshire 1834-57 with – Mercury:
Reformer for Hertfordshire 1836-43 as
Hertfordshire Mercury 1872-(1981); Hertfordshire Guardian 1852-1901; Hertford-
shire Telegram 1861; Hertfordshire News
1861-2; Observer 1861-(1981); Hertfordshire County Chronicle 1867-71; Hertfordshire Standard 1869-70; – Record 1883-92;
– Chronicle 1893-96; Hertfordshire Mail
1903.
+Hexham: – Courant 1864-(1981).
Heysham; see MORECAMBE and HEYSHAM.
†HEYWOOD: Illustrated – Advertiser 1855-
(1981); – Guardian 1870-1; – Standard
1878-82; – and District Free Press 1889-
90; – News 1892-1924.
(HIGHAM FERRERS): None listed.
†HIGH WYCOMBE: – and South Bucks
Monthly Advertiser 1854-5; – Free Press
1856-62; South Bucks Free Press 1856-
(1981); Illustrated Wycombe Independent
1859; – Guardian 1863-5; – Telegraph
1874-8; South Bucks Standard 1890-
1914; – Mail 1898-9.
†HILLINGDON: see UXBRIDGE; Middlesex
Advertiser and Gazette 1840-(1981); – Times

(Hillingdon (Uxbridge) – continued) –
1857; – Times 1869–72; – Marvel
1873–7; – Gazette 1883; – Review 1899–
(1920).
†Hinckley: – Times 1889–(1981).
Holborn: see CAMDEN.
Holloway: see ISLINGTON.
HONITON: – Weekly News 1878–9; –
Gazette 1883–4.
†Horley: – Advertiser 1898–(1981).
†Horncastle: – News 1885–(1981).
Hornchurch: see HAVERING.
Hornsey: see HARINGEY.
†HOUNSLOW: *Middlesex Chronicle (for
Hounslow, Brentford, Staines, etc.) 1858–
(1981); – and Brentford Independent
1877–9 with Middlesex Mercury; –
Advertiser 1881; – Independent 1883–4;
Brentford and Chiswick Times 1895–
1981.
    * Hounslow PL, MF from 1900.
HOVE: – Passing Notes 1880–1 as – Courier
and West Brighton Era 1881–2; – Gazette
and Sussex Recorder 1896–1925; – Echo
1897–1903 with – Gazette.
†HUDDERSFIELD: *Voice of the West Riding
1833–4; * – Chronicle 1850–1915 (1920);
* – and Holmfirth Examiner 1851–60 as
– Examiner 1861–(1981); – Observer
1867–71 as – Weekly News 1871–1904;
– Times 1869–79; – Daily Chronicle 1871–
1915 (1920); – Daily Examiner 1871–
(1981); – Echo 1886–7; – Ha'porth 1891–3
as – Comet 1893–4; Northern World Municipal World and Guardians Gazette 1904–5;
– Worker 1905–22; – District Advertiser
1913–7 (1920).
    * Huddersfield CL ! Bradford PL lists
holdings of Bradford and Huddersfield
Courier (1825–8). Kirklees Libraries and
Museums Service Local Studies and Archives
Dept. has handlist, Local Studies, listing
newspapers for Batley, Cleckheaton, Colne,
Dewsbury, Halifax, Leeds, Spenborough.
Hungerford: see MARLBOROUGH.
†HUNTINGDON: – etc. Gazette 1818–9 as
Cambridge Independent Press 1819–81 as
Cambridge Independent Press and University
Herald 1881–(1920); – Cambridge and
Bedfordshire Weekly Journal 1825–8;
Huntingdonshire Post 1869–(1981); Hunts.
County Chronicle 1870–3; Hunts. Guardian
1870–93 with Hunts. Post; Hunts. County
News 1886–1926.
†HYDE: *North Cheshire Herald 1853; – and
Glossop News 1856–8 as North Cheshire
Herald 1860–(1981); – and Denton
Chronicle 1873–84; – Telegraph 1891;
* – Reporter and Telegraph 1895–1933.
    * ! Hyde PL North Cheshire Herald
(1889–1933), Hyde Reporter and Telegraph
(1895–1933), North Cheshire and Hyde
Reporter (1934–1974).

HYTHE: – and Sandgate Gazette 1869–70 as
South Kent Gazette 1870–1; – and Sandgate Advertiser 1884–1940; * – Reporter
1890–1928; – Monthly Seaside Register
1904–6.
    * Hythe PL, Hythe Reporter for 1892,
1916 and 1917.
†ILKESTON: * – Pioneer 1853–1967; –
News 1857–8; – Leader 1861–3; – and
Erewash Valley Telegraph 1868–79;
* – Advertiser 1881–(1981); – Journal
1896–1900.
    * Ilkeston BL, originals Ilkeston Pioneer
(1853–1967), Ilkeston Advertiser (1922–
1974); also MF Advertiser (1881–1921).
†Ilkley: – Gazette 1861–(1981).
†IPSWICH: – Magazine 1799; * – Journal
1720–1886 as Daily – Journal 1886–87 as
Weekly – Journal 1887 as – Daily Journal
1887–8 as Weekly Journal 1888 as –
Journal 1888–1902; – Gazette 1733–7;
Suffolk Chronicle 1801–10 as – Mercury
1810–(1981); – Gospel Herald 1835–86;
Suffolk Literary Chronicle 1837–8; Suffolk
Express 1839–40; East Anglian Circular
1839–58; – Express 1839–74 as East
Anglian Daily Times 1874–(1981); Phono-
graph Press 1845–6; Suffolk and Essex
Free Press 1855–(1981); East Suffolk
Mercury 1858–62 as Suffolk Mercury
1862–76 as Suffolk Times 1876–99; Suffolk
Examiner 1866; – Times 1866–74 with
East Anglian Daily Times; – Free Lance
1870–1; – Free Press 1874–86 as Eastern
Counties Gazette 1886–9; Star of the East
1892–3 as Evening Star 1893–(1981); –
Observer 1906–9; – Independent 1908–11.
    * Colchester PL, – Express (1839, 1843
and 1846–52), – Journal (from 1739)
Journal also MF.
†ISLINGTON: – Gazette 1828; – Hornsey,
Highgate and Kentish Town Family Newspaper 1855; * – Gazette 1856–(1981);
– Times 1857–84; *Holloway Press 1872–83
as North London Press and as Holloway
and – Journal; – News 1877–1919 (1920);
– Press 1883; – Guardian 1884; – Post
1899–00; – Herald 1987–8; – Mercury
1902–3; – Labour Arrow 1906; – Guardian
1914. Also: FINSBURY: – Magazine
1863–4; – Free Press 1868–9; – Conservative 1874–5; – Park and North London
Advertiser 1880 as North London Advertiser; The Clerkenwell Chronicle 1884–6 as
The Weekly News and Clerkenwell Chronicle
1886–7 as The Weekly News and Chronicle
1888–1900 as The Finsbury Weekly News
and Chronicle 1900–4 as The Finsbury
Weekly News and Clerkenwell Chronicle
1904–75 with The Hackney Gazette; Independent 1885; – Times 1886–7; Finsbury
1900; – Herald 1903.
    * Islington PL has MF Gazette (1856),

(Islington – continued) –
Holloway Press (from 1872). Finsbury PL
has MF Finsbury Weekly News (1856–1904
and 1955-60). There is a large collection of
newspapers cuttings held by the Islington
Libraries. See *A Guide to the Local History
Collection of Islington Libraries* (1968).
JARROW: – Chronicle 1870-1; – Guardian
1872-1913; Express 1873-1920; – Labour
Herald 1906-7.
†KEIGHLEY: The Monthly Teacher 1829-31;
* – etc. Saturday Observer 1842-3; – News
1855; – Advertiser and Airedale Courant
1855-6; – and Howarth Argus 1855; –
Mercury 1856-7; * – News 1862-(1981);
– Visitor 1866; – Daily Telegraph 1870-1;
– Wharfedale and Airedale Observer 1871-
(1981); * – Herald 1873-1911; – and
Airedale Tatler 1883-85; – Echo 1894-96;
– Labour Journal 1894-1902; * – Chronicle
1905-9 with – News.
   * Bradford PL has Keighley Advertiser
and Airedale Courant (1855-6). Keighley
and Haworth Argus (1842), Keighley Labour
Journal 1894-1902, Keighley News
(1862-5) and Keighley Visitor (1866).
* Keighley PL, News, Herald and Chronicle,
originals and MF. See BRADFORD also.
†KENDAL: * – Weekly Mercury 1735; Westmorland Gazette and – Advertiser 1818-
(1981); Westmorland Advertiser and –
Chronicle 1829-34 as – Mercury and
Westmorland Advertiser 1834-40 as –
Mercury and Northern Advertiser 1841-80
as – Mercury and Times 1880-1913 as
Westmorland Mercury and Times 1913-
7 (1920); – Times 1864-80 with – Mercury
and Times; – Courier 1873-4; Westmorland
Journal 1875-80; – and County News
1887-99. – Notebook 1888. A facsimile
edition of the Kendal Weekly Mercury for
3 May 1735 was included with the Jubilee
Issue of 24 June 1887. See also
DARLINGTON.
†KENSINGTON: – Spectator 1852; –
Chronicle 1859; – and Chelsea News 1865-9;
– News and West London Times 1869-
1975; South – News and Chelsea Post
1869-(1981); – and Hammersmith
Recorder 1875; – Park Record 1875; –
Argus 1878-9; – Express 1886-1921;
– Review 1886; – Weekly Advertiser
1888-90 with – Society; – Society 1890-6;
– News and Post 1890-(1981); Kensington
1901. Also: CHELSEA: – Gazette 1822;
West London Observer 1855-(1981); –
News 1857-(1981); – and Pimlico Advertiser
1860-66; – Magazine 1861; Pimlico and –
News 1865-9; – Courier 1871; – Times
1873-5; – Herald 1884 with West London
Standard: Pick and Shovel 1900.
KETTERING: – News 1878-90; – Guardian
1882-1923; – Observer 1882-90 with

(Kettering – continued) –
– Leader; – Leader 1890-1959; – Comet
1893-4; – Evening News 1896-8; with
Northampton Daily Reporter; – Weekly
Gazette 1902; – News 1908-9.
†Keswick: – Reminder 1896-(1981).
†KIDDERMINSTER: – Messenger 1836-8 as
Ten Towns Messenger 1838-49; – Times
1867-(1981); – and Worcestershire Telegraph
1869; – Shuttle 1870-(1981); – News
1875-85; – Sun 1877-1900; – News
1900-11.
(KIDWELLY): None listed.
KING'S LYNN: * – and Wisbech Packet 1801-2;
– Weekly Journal 1870-4 as – Journal
1875-90.
   * Lynn PL; sets of the Norwich, Yarmouth
and Lynn Courier (1818-23) are available in
the Local Studies Department of Norwich
Central Library, also early newspapers for
Diss, Cromer and Wymondham.
†KINGSTON-UPON-HULL; – Courant 1746-9;
* – Advertiser 1799-1867; – Packet 1800-86;
Humber Mercury 1805-6; – and Lincoln
Chronicle 1807 as Lincoln and Hull 1807-10;
Rockingham and Hull Weekly Advertiser
1808-28 as Hull, Rockingham, Yorkshire
and Lincoln Gazette 1828-44; East Riding
etc. Panorama 1812; – Portfolio 1831-3;
– Express 1833-1912; – etc. Observer
1834-41; – Literary Wreath 1838-9; East
Counties Herald 1838-61 as Hull and East
Counties Herald 1861-84 with Hull News; –
Literary and Philosophical Miscellany
1843-5; – News 1852-84 as * – Daily News
1884-1923 as – Evening News 1923-30;
Whiting's Free Press 1853-60; – Free Press
1853-60; Yorks. and Lincs. Advertiser
1853-69; Illustrated Hull Mercury 1855-6;
– Times 1855; – Express 1855; – Times
1857-(1981); Eastern Weekly News 1864-6;
Eastern Evening News 1864-7; Eastern
Morning News 1864-1929; – and East
Riding Congregational Magazine 1867-75;
– Morning Telegraph 1869-80; – News
Evening War Bulletin 1870; – Evening
News 1870-6; – Sun 1875; Turf Herald
1875-7; – Express 1876-91 with – Daily
News; – Review 1882; – and East Riding
Critic 1883-94; – News Supplement 1883-
1929; – Quarterly 1884-5; – Daily Mail
1885-(1981); – Illustrated Journal 1887-8;
– Arrow 1888-9; – Globe 1888-90; –
Workman's Times 1890; – Comet 1873;
– Grimsby etc. Free Programme 1894-
1900; – and East Yorkshire Times 1897-
1924 as – and Yorkshire Times 1924-74 as
– Times 1974-(1981); Kingston Mercury
1903; – Monthly Labour Journal 1904-18
(1920); East Hull Free Press 1905-13;
East Yorkshire Gazette 1906-7 as – Topics
1907-14 as – Weekly Echo 1914-(1920);
West Hull Advertiser and Weekly Post 1910.

(Kingston-upon-Hull – continued) –
* Grimsby PL has incomplete bound
volumes of Hull Advertiser for 1852–55,
complete for 1857–9. See BRADFORD also.
†KINGSTON-ON-THAMES: Seeley's Kingston
Miscellany 1841–2; Surrey Comet 1854–
(1981); – and Surbiton News 1882–1900
(1920); Surrey Reformer 1886 as – and
Richmond Express 1886–94 with Middlesex
and Surrey Express; and Surbiton Guardian
1900–7 (1920).
Knowle: see BIRMINGHAM.
†Knutsford: – Guardian 1860–(1981).
†LAMBETH: – Gazette 1853–5 with South
London Gazette; – and Southwark Advertiser 1855 with South London News; South
London Press 1865–(1981); Clapham and
Lambeth News 1868–(1981); – Parliament
1882; – Post 1883–91 with South London
Mail; – Times 1887–9 with –Post; – Times
1900. Also: WANDSWORTH: – and
Battersea Standard 1871–2; – Borough
News 1885–(1981); – and Putney Observer
1887–1904; – and Battersea Trade Adver-
tiser 1890; – Gazette 1899–1900; – News-
letter 1912–6; STREATHAM: – News
1891–(1981).
LAMPETER: Y Brython Cymreig 1892–
1901; Y Llan A'r Dywysogaeth 1899–
1919; Y Cardi 1902–3.
†LANCASTER: – Gazetteer 1801–3 as Gazette
1803–94; – Companion 1835; – Guardian
1837–1920 with Observer; – Observer
1860–(1981); – Weekly News 1872; –
Examiner 1873–5; – Standard 1893–1909;
– Press 1905.
LAUNCESTON: – Journal 1784; Light from
the West 1832–41; The Reformer 1832; The
Guardian 1832; – Examiner 1844; – Weekly
News 1866–1931.
†Leatherhead: – Advertiser 1887–(1981).
†LEEDS: * – Mercury 1720–1939 with
Yorkshire Post; * – Intelligencer 1754–
1866 as Yorkshire Post 1866–(1981); –
Correspondent 1815–22; Blanketeer 1819;
– Domestic Miscellany 1819; – Literary
Observer 1819; – Independent 1821;
Leodensian 1827–8 and 1845–6; – Patriot
and Yorkshire Advertiser 1829–33; – Half-
penny Magazine 1832; * – Times 1833–
1901 with – Mercury Weekly Supplement;
– Spectator 1838–9; – Repository 1839–
40; – New Moral World 1840; – Wednesday
Journal 1841; – Conservative Journal 1842;
– Mercury Weekly Supplement 1844–1905
(1920); – Peoples' Guardian 1845; Ben
Ridding's Aerial 1852; – Express 1857–67
as – Evening and Weekly Express 1867–
1901; * – Telegraph 1864; * Monthly Illustrated Journal 1868–70; – Critic 1873;
– Daily News 1873–1905 as Yorkshire
Evening News 1905–63; Yorkshire Independent 1875–81; * Monthly Record of

(Leeds – continued) –
Current Events 1875–6; Yorkshire Weekly
Post 1882–1937; – Weekly Draught Player
1882; The Gutter News (A Journal to
Expose Immorality) 1885; – Varieties
Herald 1885; * – Saturday Journal 1887–
1907; – Evening Post 1890–(1981); South
and West – Echo 1890–5; – Labour Chronicle
1893; * – Hospital Magazine 1893–
1965; – Express etc. Tissue 1894–9; – and
Suburbs 1894; – Stock Exchange Daily
Share List 1903; – Budget 1906–11; * –
Town Topics 1909–11; New – News 1912–3
as North Leeds News 1913–58; * – and
District Weekly Citizen 1911–(1981).
   * ! Bradford PL holds sets of Leeds
Intelligencer (1778–1863) and various numbers of Mercury, Patriot, Times and Wednesday Journal. Sets of Leeds Mercury
(1738–1850), MF available, Huddersfield
CL, Local Studies Department. Leeds CL
has no handlist of newspaper holdings; but
does have a large card-catalogue. Among
many others, early, but incomplete, sets of
the Intelligencer and Mercury are available
at the Library.
†Leek: – Post and Times 1870–(1981).
†LEICESTER: – Journal 1775–(1920); Leics.
Herald 1827–8 as Leicester Herald 1828–42;
– Chronicle 1827–1915 as Illustrated –
Chronicle 1915–(1981); – Conservative
Standard 1835 as – and Derby Conserva-
tive Standard 1836–7; – Corporation and
Parochial Reformer 1835–6; Leics. Mercury
1836–64 as Leics. Chronicle; Paynes' – and
Midland Counties Advertiser 1842–50 as –
Midland Counties Advertiser 1851 as –
Advertiser 1851–(1981); – Magazine 1849;
Leics. Monument 1850; – New Monthly
1853–4; Midland Counties Historical
Collector 1855–6; – Guardian 1857–76;
– News 1857; Midland Workman 1861–2;
– News 1857; – Express 1861–4 with
Leics. Advertiser; – Mail 1865–70 with –
Weekly Express; – Daily Mail 1869–70
with – Weekly Express; – Daily Mail 1869–
70 with – Weekly Express; – Daily Post
1872–1921; Evening Post 1874; – Daily
Mercury 1874–(1981); – Evening News
1875–8; – Echo 1883–4; – Evening Stan-
dard 1885–6; – Era 1889; – Light 1890;
– Daily Express 1892–9; – Evening News
1903–5; – Pioneer 1905–28; – Evening
Times 1905–6 (1920); – Mail 1910–31 as
– Evening Mail 1931–63 with Mercury.
See Temple Patterson, E., *Radical Leicester*
(1954).
†LEIGH: – Monthly Magazine 1845; –
Reporter 1852–(1981); – Chronicle 1855–
1963 as – Reporter and South Lancs Advertiser 1964–75; – Weekly Journal 1874–
(1981); – Times 1875 with – Weekly
Journal; – Express 1898–9; – Observer

(Leigh – continued) –
1898-9; Westcliff and – Express 1904–
(1981); – -on-Sea Recorder 1908-10.
†LEOMINSTER: – and Bromyard News
1880-(1981); – Standard 1913-4.
†LEWES: Sussex Weekly Advertiser 1773–
1804 as Sussex Advertiser 1825-1904; The
Provincial Magazine 1818; Gleaner's Portfolio 1819; Surrey Standard 1835-1902
with Sussex Express; Sussex Agricultural
Express 1837-(1975); Sussex Express and
South-Eastern Advertiser, now Sussex
Express and County Herald 1837-(1981);
– Times 1855-63 and East Sussex News
1863-1941; Surrey Gazette 1863-1904.
LEWISHAM: – Times 1870; West Kent Courier
1880-3 as – and Blackheath Courier 1884-7
with – Gazette; – and West Kent News
1881-5; – Opinion and Lee Observer
1884-5; – Gazette 1885-1914 with –
Journal; – Opinion 1888-9; – Free Press
1890-92; – Independent 1892-1900 as
– Borough News 1901-(1920); – and Lee
Herald 1894-6; Journal 1902-(1920). Also:
DEPTFORD: – Chronicle 1895-8;
Chronicle 1907.
†LICHFIELD: – Mercury 1815-33; * –
Mercury 1830-3 and 1877-(1981); Stafford-
shire Examiner 1836-42; – Advertiser
1865-6; – City and County Recorder 1869;
– City Times 1877-8 with – Herald; –
Herald 1883-97; – South Staffordshire
Times 1911-5.
    * Lichfield PL, Lichfield Mercury, from
1899.
†LINCOLN: * – Stamford and Rutland
Mercury 1793-1910; Boston Gazette and
– Advertiser 1811-32; – Herald 1829-32
as *Boston, – and Louth Herald (1832-5);
Lincolnshire Chronicle 1833-(1981);
Lincolnshire Independent 1832; – Gazette
1835 as Boston and Newark Gazette or
Tuesday Gazette 1836-41; – Standard
1836-46 as – and Lincolnshire Standard
1847-8; – Advertiser 1844; Lincolnshire
Advertiser 1846-50; Lincolnshire Free Press
1847-(1981); Lincolnshire Times 1847-57
as Lincolnshire Notes and North Midland
Times 1851-61 with Lincolnshire Chronicle;
– Times 1856-(1981); Lincolnshire Penny
News; 1857-9 with Lincolnshire Guardian;
– Gazette 1859-1924; – Journal 1861;
– Standard 1862-9; – Journal 1869-74;
– Leader 1869-1929; Lincolnshire Echo
1899-(1981); – Visitor 1911-4.
    * Grimsby PL has Lincoln, Rutland and
Stamford Mercury (1802-1921) and MF
1793-1910; Boston, Lincoln and Louth
Herald (1832-5), MF.
†LISKEARD: – Gazette 1855-74 as Western
Herald 1874-89; Cornish Times 1857-
(1981); – Weekly Mercury 1898-1910
with Western Weekly Mercury of Plymouth;

(Liskeard – continued) –
Cornish Leader 1904-14 with Cornish
Guardian.
†LIVERPOOL: – Courant 1712; – Chronicle
and Marine Gazetteer 1757-9; – General
Advertiser 1765-77 as * Gore's General
Advertiser 1777-1876; Williamson's – Ad-
vertiser 1766; – Chronicle 1767-8 and
1825-68; – Weekly Magazine 1774; General
Weekly Magazine 1794; * Billinge's – Adver-
tiser 1794-1802; – Trade List 1798-1800;
* – Chronicle and Commercial Advertiser
1804-7; – Dramatic Censor 1806; –
Courier 1808-1929; – Mercury 1811-1904
with – Daily Post; – Corrector or Dramatic
Intelligencer 1816; – Freeman 1816; * –
Magazine 1816; * – Magazine and General
Provincial Miscellany 1816; – Monthly
Magazine 1817; – Gleaner 1817; The Quiz
1818; The Kaleidoscope 1818-31; – Im-
perial Magazine 1819-34; – Christian
Reflector 1820-9; The Bee 1820-1;
– Academic 1821; – Hermes 1822; Myer's
Mercantile Advertiser 1822-38 as – Mercan-
tile Gazette 1838-75; Saturday's Advertiser
1823-33; * Billinge's – Advertiser 1823-8 as
– Times 1829-56; Liver 1824-5 and 1893-
4; Nepenthes 1825; – Commercial
Chronicle 1825-8; – Teachers' Magazine
1826; – Dramatic Speculum 1826; Philan-
thropist 1826; – Repository 1826; –
Journal of Commerce 1826-(1981);
Lancashire Literary Museum 1827-8; The
Albion 1827-8 as Weekly Albion; Herald
of Truth 1828; – Chronicle 1828-68; Le
Panorama 1829; Ladies' Magazine or
Lancashire Witch 1829; * – Journal 1830-4;
– Examiner 1832; – Dramatic Journal
1832; The Parnassus 1832; – Comet or
Fairley's Liverpool Observer 1832; Lancashire Omnibus 1832; – Standard 1832-56;
– Spectator 1832; The Pioneer or Trade
Union Magazine 1833; – Dramatic Censor
1834; Brittania: Jones's Manchester, Liver-
pool etc. Advertiser 1834-8; Paul Pry in –
1834; Horoscope 1834; Brazen Head 1834;
Ould Paddy Kelly's Ghost 1835; Dicky Sam,
the Lancashire Herald 1835; Leporello in –
1835; – Literary Journal 1835; Thespian
Register 1836; Temperance Advocate 1836;
Y Pregethwr 1836; Lancashire Conservative
1836; – Companion 1836-7; * – Mail 1836-
81; – Satirist 1836; – Telegraph 1836-8
with – Chronicle; – Mercantile Gazette
1838-75; Monthly Magazine 1838-9; –
Politician 1838; Teetotal Times 1838-9; –
Free Press 1837; Stock and Share List 1839;
* – Weekly Mercury 1839-1915; – Steam
Packet Circular 1840; – European and
General Commercial Intelligencer 1841-2;
Willmer's American Newsletter 1842-5;
Willmer and Smith's European Times 1843-
68; – Prices Current and Mercantile List

(Liverpool – continued) –
1845; – Health of Towns Advocate 1845-6;
Lloyd's – Railway Times 1845; – Dramatic
Argus 1846; – Weekly News and General
Commercial Advertiser 1846-7; – Tele-
graph and Shipping Gazette 1846-80 as
– Shipping Telegraph 1880-9 with –
Journal of Commerce; * – Express 1847;
– Lion 1847-8; Willmer's European Mail
1847-9; – Burgesses. etc. Magazine 1851;
– General Review 1853; North of England
Advertiser 1853-4 as – and Manchester
News 1854; Northern Daily Times 1853-7
as Northern Times 1857-60 as – Daily
Times 1860-1; – Prices Current 1854-5;
Blessig Braun's Prices Current 1854; Photo-
graphic Journal 1854-60 as British Journal
of Photography 1860-(1920); Pattinson and
Clarke's Prices Current 1854; * – Daily Post
1855-79 as – Daily Post 1879-(1981);
Greenwood's Weekly Herald 1855-1915
(1920); – Weekly Mercury 1855-(1920); –
Herald 1855-6; – Daily Mail 1857; –
Australian Gazette 1858-9; Willmer's –
Morning News 1859; – Morning News
1861; – Literary Gazette 1861; –
Reformer 1866; – Weekly Courier 1867-
1925; – Liberal Review 1869-82 as –
Review 1883-4 as – Liberal Freeman
1904-6 as – Freeman 1906; * – Daily Albion
1873-87; – Evening Express 1873-1958;
– Town Crier 1874-5; Weekly List of
Cotton Ships at Sea 1875; – Critic 1876-7;
* The Argus 1876-80; – Weekly News 1878-
(1981); – Weekly Post 1878-1940; –
Lantern 1878-82; – Gazette and Bootle
Advertiser 1879-80; – Echo 1879-(1981);
* Wasp, 1880-2; Toxteth Observer 1881-3;
West Derby and Wavertree Times 1881-92;
Garston and Toxteth Times 1881; South –
Times 1883-5; – Evening Times 1883-4 as
– and Bootle Evening Times 1884-94;
Liverpudlian 1885; – Halfpenny Weekly
1885-90; – Link 1886; – Citizen 1887-91;
Bootle and Walton Free Press 1887; Garston
and Woolton Reporter 1888-(1920); Corn
Trade News 1888-95 as Broomhall's Corn
Trade News 1895-1968; – Programme
1888-9 as – Reformer 1889-92; – Monthly
Magazine 1889; * – Athletic and Dramatic
News 1890-1; – Miscellany 1890; – Maga-
zine 1890; – Commercial World 1893;
Young Wales 1893; – Weekly Courier 1891-
1903; – Daily Commercial Report 1897-
(1920); – Free Press 1898; * General Adver-
tiser for – and Surrounding District 1902-3;
– Entertainment and Pleasure Programme
1903-4 as Smith's – Weekly 1904-(1920);
– Opinion 1906. * Liverpool RL.
(LLANDOVERY): None listed.
†LLANELLI: Y Diwigiwr 1836-(1920); –
Advertiser 1848; Y Tywysydd A'r Gymraes
1852-(1920); Y Beiraiad 1859-73; –

(Llanelli – continued) –
Guardian 1869-1953; South Wales Press
and Carmarthen Advertiser 1869-1934;
Cerddor Y Cymry 1883-94; Y Cylchgrawn
1891-3; – Press 1894-6; Seren Ysgol Sul
1895-(1920); – Star 1909-(1981); –
Argus 1911-31.
LLANIDLOES: Yr Eurgrawn Weslaidd 1809-
55; Y Athraw 1836-44; Y Winllan 1848-
(1920); Radnorshire Observer 1869-76;
Montgomeryshire Echo 1888-1912.
†LOUGHBOROUGH: – Telegraph 1837 as
Leicestershire etc. Telegraph 1837-9; –
Monitor 1859-1977; with – News; –
News 1861-70 with – Monitor; – Advertiser 1872-84; – Home News 1876
with – Advertiser; – Herald 1880-1920;
with Monitor; – Examiner 1895-1903
with Notts. Weekly Express; – Echo 1913-
(1981); – Weekly Times 1913-(1920) 1915.
    ! Loughborough PL holds a large collec-
tion of newspapers.
LOUTH: * Boston, Lincoln and – Herald
1832-5; – and North Lincs. Advertiser
1859-1957; – Gazette 1866-70; – Echo
1872-4 as Lincs. Echo 1874-88; – Times
1873 as – and North Lincs. News 1897-
1912; – Herald 1894-9; – Record of
Events 1916-(1920).
    * Grimsby PL has MF copies of Boston,
Lincoln and Louth Herald (1832-35).
†LOWESTOFT: – Advertiser 1853; The East
Anglian 1858-(1920); Eastern Times 1869-
71 as – News 1871-95; – Mercury 1871-6;
– Observer 1870-5 with – News: East Coast
Visitor 1871; – Magazine 1872-93; –
Weekly Journal 1873-(1981) (as Journal
and Mercury); * – etc. Standard 1882-1904;
– Weekly Press 1886-1918 with Norfolk
News. See also GREAT YARMOUTH.
    * Lowestoft PL.
†Ludlow: – Standard 1840; – Advertiser 1855-
69; as – and Tenbury Advertiser 1869-
(1981); – Herald 1875-6; – & Church
Stretton Chronicle 1910-12.
†LUTON: – Recorder 1855-9; – Times
1855-93 as Bedfordshire Advertiser 1894-
1916; Hitchin Gazette 1859-(1981); –
Gazette 1869; – Reporter 1874-1924; –
Advertiser 1877 with – Times; * – News
1891-(1981); – Observer 1897-1900 (1920);
– Herald 1909-10; Bedfordshire and Herts
Saturday Telegraph 1914-71.
    * Luton PL has copies of – News from
1891 and 'other local newspapers'.
(LYDD): None listed.
†LYME REGIS: – Mirror with Bridport News
1913-(1981). See *Dorset Newspapers*
Weymouth CL 1972).
LYMINGTON: – etc. Chronicle 1857-1935
(various titles); Bright's – Courier 1866-9;
– Protestant 1866-7; – Observer 1875-81
with Observer & Chronicle of Bournemouth.

LYTHAM ST ANNES: – Times 1870–(1920);
Lytham and St Annes Visitor 1896–9;
– Standard 1905–52.
†MACCLESFIELD: The Nondescript 1805; –
Courier 1825–7 as – Courier and Herald
1828–(1981); – Herald 1825–7 with –
Courier; – Weekly Observer 1858–71; –
Advertiser 1868–(1981); – Guardian 1873–8
with – Chronicle; – Free Press 1874; –
Chronicle 1877–1906 with – Times; – Times
1898–(1920); – Leader 1906–8; Wednesday's
Courier 1906–14.
†MAIDENHEAD: – Advertiser 1869–(1981);
– Courier 1891–3; – Times 1895–1900;
– Argus 1900–4; – Chronicle 1911–39.
†MAIDSTONE: – Mercury 1725; – Journal
1737; – Telegraph 1787; – Journal 1787–
1853 as – and Kentish Journal 1853–1912
with South-Eastern Gazette; – Gazette
1830–51 as South-Eastern Gazette 1852–
(1920); – Independent 1855; Kentish
Express 1855–(1981); Kent News and
Advertiser 1857 as Thanet and Kent News
1857–8; Kent Messenger 1859–(1981); –
Telegraph 1859–71 with Kent Messenger;
Essex Examiner 1869–72; Essex Observer
1871–3; Middlesex County Journal 1871;
Sussex Labourers' Herald 1874–5 with Kent
Messenger; Kent and Sussex Times 1875–87
as Kent Times 1887–1912; – and Kent
County Standard 1875–1912 with South-
Eastern Gazette; – Chronicle 1888–9; –
Gazette 1902–4.
MALDON: – Express 1872–1939; – and Hey
Bridge Gazette 1898–1900; – Magpie 1901;
– Local Guide 1902–3; – Advertiser
1910–6.
†Malvern: – Gazette 1898–(1981).
†MALMESBURY: Wiltshire and Gloucs.
Standard 1837–(1981); – Journal 1871.
†MANCHESTER: – Weekly Journal 1722–5;
– Magazine 1737–60; *Adams' Weekly
Courant 1751–8; * – Mercury 1752–1830;
*Whitworth's – Magazine 1755–6; * Ander-
ton's – Chronicle and Universal Advertiser
1762; * Prescott's – Journal 1771–81;
Wheeler's – Chronicle or Advertiser 1781–
1842 with * – Chronicle; Cowdrey's –
Gazette and Weekly Advertiser 1796–1824
as – Gazette 1824–7; – Townsman 1803–6;
– Argus or Theatrical Observer 1804–5; –
Mail 1805; *British Volunteer and –
Express 1805–22; Wheeler's – Guardian
1806–34 as – Chronicle 1839–43 with
Advertiser: *Aston's – Commercial Advertiser 1809–26; – Magazine 1815–6; The
Prompter 1815–6; – Political Register
1817; The Courier or – Advertiser 1817–9
as Saturday's – Courier; * – Spectator
1818, 1849–51 and 1856–8; * – Observer
1818–22 with Wooler's British Gazette
1819–23; – Patriot 1819–20; Wooler's
British Gazette 1819–23; Wardle's –

(Manchester – continued) –
Observer 1819–23; * – Guardian 1821–
(1981); The Scrapbook 1822; *Iris 1822–3;
* – Advertiser 1825; *Times and Gazette
1828–48; Voice of the People 1831; * –
and Salford Advertiser 1831–48 with –
Times; – Herald and Wednesday's Commer-
cial Advertiser 1831–6; Lancashire Co-
operator 1831; * Courier 1825–1916; –
Advertiser 1833–41 and 1854–60; – Herald
of the Rights of Industry 1834; Brittania:
Jones's – and Liverpool Advertiser 1834–8;
– Gospel Standard 1837–(1920); – Journal
1838–9; *Northern Star 1838–52; * –
Chronicle and Salford Standard 1839–42;
Anti-Corn Laws Circular 1839–41 as * –
Anti-Bread Tax Circular 1841–3; * – Times
and Lancashire Examiner 1841–4; * Jewish
Chronicle 1841–1974; Bradshaw's – Journal
1841–3; * – Herald 1841; – Herald and
North of England Journal 1843; Burns'
Commercial Glance 1845; – Argus 1845;
* – Examiner 1846–94 with – Umpire;
– Dramatic and Musical Review 1846–7;
– Express 1847; – News 1848; * – Times
1848; – Spectator 1849–51; Coffin's
Botanical Journal 1849–59; The Champion
1849–50; * – Weekly Advertiser 1853–61;
Mandley's – Trade Circular 1854; – Prices
Current of Cotton and Woollen Goods
1854; – Teachers' Journal 1854–5; Burns'
Monthly Colonial Circular 1854; – Alliance
1854–5 as *Alliance Weekly News 1855–61
as Alliance News 1861–(1981) –; War Express
and Daily Advertiser as – Express 1854–6;
– Spectator 1856–58; – Weekly Guardian
1860 as – Weekly Express 1869–3; – Review
1860–1 with – Express; * – City News
1864–1963; – Weekly Times 1863–1922; –
Cricketers' News 1867; – Evening News
1868–(1981); – Weekly News 1869–71;
* – Critic 1871–8 as Reform Gazette
1878–9; Co-operative News 1871–(1981);
– Advertiser 1873; – Gazette 1873–74; * –
Evening Mail 1874–1916 with Weekly
Times; – Liverpool and Northern Counties
Advertiser 1873; City Lantern 1875–81;
City Jackdaw 1875–80; * – Weekly Post
1875–87; – Congregational Magazine
1879–97; – Chronicle 1880 – with Middleton Guardian; The Ship Canal Gazette 1882–
3; *Cotton Factory Times 1885–1937;
Sunday Chronicle 1885–1955. *South –
Gazette 1885–8; Saturday Halfpenny 1888;
Riley's Ardwick Advertiser 1888–93; Com-
mercial Gazette 1888–1975; – Citizen
1888–93. – Faces and Places 1889–1906;
South – Chronicle 1889–7; – South District
Advertiser 1891–1943; * – Clarion 1891–
1934; – Journal of Commerce 1894–1900;
– Mercury 1895–6; * – Evening Chronicle
1897–1963; Catholic Herald 1898; – Shipping Telegraph 1897; – and Salford Sentinel

(Manchester – continued) –
1898-1903; – Daily Mail 1900; – Daily
Dispatch 1900; Illustrated Weekly 1903;
Suburban Advertiser 1904; – Graphic
1904; – and Suburban Illustrated Property
List 1905-13; – and District Property
Circular 1905-7 (1920); – and District
Property Market Values 1905–(1920); –
Programme 1907-34; – Jewish Telegraph
1908; –Catholic Herald 1908; Nachtrichten
1910-2; – Weekly Citizen 1910-2; – Daily
Citizen 1912; – Weekly Press 1914; * –
Jewish Guardian 1919-21.

   * ! Blackburn PL, MF Manchester Magazine (1737-60). Bury PL, MF Manchester
Mercury (1752–1926). Manchester City L
has typescript index to its large collection
of local newspapers, both originals and MF.
Includes sets for Ashton-under-Lyne, Salford
and Stockport. Has many Manchester
newspapers not listed at British Library.
MANSFIELD: * – Reporter 1858-1956 with
   * – and North Notts Chronicle Advertiser;
   – and Southwell Monthly Messenger 1872;
   * – and North Notts Advertiser 1873-1952;
   * – Chronicle 1895-1952 with – Advertiser.
   * ! Mansfield PL, MF Reporter (1858-
1950). Advertiser (1871-1952), Chronicle
(1895-1952) and Mansfield and North
Notts Chronicle Advertiser (1952-71).
†MARGATE: Genius of Kent 1792-5; Thanet
Magazine 1817; East Kent Gazette 1855-
1981; Thanet Guardian 1866-1920; Keble's
– and Ramsgate Gazette 1870-1909 as –
Ramsgate and Isle of Thanet Gazette 1909-
(1981); Perry's – and Ramsgate News 1871;
– and Ramsgate News 1877-8; Westgate-
on-Sea Chronicle 1882-5; Thanet Weekly
Telegraph 1885; Thanet Free Press as – and
Ramsgate Chronicle 1887-8 as Thanet
Chronicle 1888-9; Thanet Journal 1904-9.
†MARLBOROUGH: – Times   1859-(1981); – and
Hungerford Express 1860-3; Marlburian 1865;
– Journal 1873-7; Marlburian 1884; Wilt-
shire Opinion 1902-14; Wiltshire, Berkshire
and Hampshire Counties Paper 1901-48.
Melcombe Regis: see WEYMOUTH AND
   MELCOMBE REGIS.
†Melton Mowbray: – Times 1859-(1981).
†MERTHYR TYDFIL: South Wales Reporter
1837; – and Cardiff Chronicle 1837; Udgorn
Cymru 1842; – Telegraph 1858-81; – and
Aberdare Times 1858-9; – Star 1859-72;
– Express 1864-(1975); Fellten Y 1868-76;
Y Tyst A'r Dydd 1871-(1981); – Times
1871-3; Western Observer 1872; – Work-
man's Advocate 1873-5; Amddiffnydd Y
Gweithiwr 1874-5; Star of the West 1876;
Llusera Y Llan 1880; Y Cenad Hedd 1886-
(1920); Dowlas and Merthyr Times 1891-9;
Cronicl Cenadol 1897-1907; Y Ffon A'r
Ffynon 1913-(1920); South Wales Worker
1913-4; Pioneer 1913-22.

MERTON: see MITCHAM: and Tooting Mercury 1913-20. Also WIMBLEDON: –
Courier 1880-2; – Times 1889-90; –
Advertiser 1889; – Chronicle 1889; –
Gazette 1892-(1920); – News 1894–
(1981); – Property Advertiser 1894; – Post
1896-8 with South-Western Comet; – Free
Press 1904-5; – Park etc. Newsletter 1911-2
with Putney Newsletter; – Express 1913-4.
MIDDLETON: * – Advertiser and Chronicle
1853; * – Albion 1857-95; * – and Tonge
Advertiser 1866; – Advertiser 1871-2; * –
and Tonge Advertiser and Heywood Black-
ley and Prestwich Gazette 1871.
   * Middleton PL, originals and MF.
†Millom: – News 1884–(1981).
†Mirfield: – Reporter 1881–(1981).
†MONMOUTH: – Merlin 1829-91; – Beacon
1837-(1981); – Advertiser 1840-1 with
Merthyr Guardian; – Gazette 1849-52;
Glamorgan and Brecon Herald 1853-1903
with South Wales Weekly Argus; – Chronicle
1865; – Telegraph 1869; – Chronicle 1875-
84 with West of England Observer; – Free
Press 1876-7; – Telegraph 1885; – County
Times 1905; Daily Post 1908-10; – Evening
Post 1908-22; Weekly Post 1908-22.
MONTGOMERY: Newtown and Welshpool
Express 1869-76 as Montgomery Express
1870-(1920); – Echo 1888-1912; County
Times 1893-(1920).
†MORECAMBE AND HEYSHAM: * – Visitor
1874-1981; – Times 1881-(1981); –
Telegraph 1899-1901. * Morecambe PL.
†MORLEY: – Reporter 1868-75; * – News
and Gildersome Advertiser 1870; * –
Observer 1871-(1981).
   * Bradford PL, some copies News and
Advertiser; Observer.
†MORPETH: – Monthly Herald 1854-(1981);
Northumberland and – Gazette 1854-
(1981); – and Blyth Echo 1870-1 as Blyth
Echo 1871-2; Northumberland County
Standard 1872.
Moseley: see BIRMINGHAM.
†MOSSLEY: Saddleworth and – Standard
1878-1900; - and Saddleworth Reporter
1878-(1981); – and Saddleworth Herald
1899-1901 with Ashton-under-Lyne
Herald.
NEATH: – Times 1880; – Gazette 1889-1911
as Mid-Glamorgan Herald 1911-4 with
Swansea Herald: – News 1910-2 with
County Standard; Mid-Glamorgan Observer
1911 with – News; – and County Standard
1912-4; Vale of – Advertiser 1914.
†NELSON: – and Colne Express 1887-1900;
– Chronicle 1890-1904 as – Leader 1904-
(1981); – Advertiser 1892.
†NEWARK * – Herald 1791-2; – Times 1830
as Lincoln and – Times 1831 with West
Stamford News; – Magnet 1832; – Observer
1832; – Bee 1838-9; – Times 1839-41;

(Newark – continued) –
    South Notts Advertiser 1854; – Advertiser
    1859-(1981); – Herald 1873-1960.
    * Bradford PL, one copy, 1793.
†NEWBURY: – Journal 1855-6; – Berkshire
    Journal of Agriculture and Commerce 1855
    as – Telegraph 1855-6; – Journal 1855-6;
    – Weekly News 1867-(1981); – Advertiser
    1880-1; – Express 1886-9; – and District
    Free Press 1907-9; – Chronicle 1910-39.
NEWCASTLE-UNDER-LYME: Staffordshire
    Gazette 1813 as Staffs. and – Advertiser
    1814 as * – Journal 1855-56 as Staffs.
    Times 1874-82; – and Pottery Gazette
    1818-34; Staffordshire Daily Times 1875;
    * – Guardian 1881-1909; – * Free Press
    1882-1908.
        * ! Newcastle-under-Lyme PL: MF
    Newcastle Journal, Newcastle Guardian,
    Newcastle-under-Lyme Free Press; originals
    Staffordshire Sentinel from 1854; collection
    local history newspaper cuttings (18th–19th
    centuries); other newspapers also (publishes
    guide). Newcastle Borough Museum: Free
    Press (1888); Hanley RL: Staffordshire
    Advertiser from 1795.
†NEWCASTLE-UPON-TYNE: * – Courant
    1724-5 as Weekly Courant 1884-1902 as
    Weekly Courant and Journal 1902-10; * –
    Journal 1739-76 and 1832-60 as Daily
    Journal 1861-1915 as – Daily Journal and
    Courant 1915-24 as – Daily Journal,
    North Star and Courant 1924-39 as –
    Journal and Northern Mail 1939-58 as The
    Journal 1958-(1981); – General Magazine
    1747-60; * – Chronicle or General Weekly
    Advertiser 1764; – Chronicle 1768-1864;
    * – Advertiser 1780: Protestant Packet or
    British Monitor 1780-1; – Weekly Magazine
    1776; – Magazine 1785-6; – Advertiser
    1800-14; Tyne Mercury 1802-46 with –
    Guardian; Northumberland and – Monthly
    1818-19; – Magazine 1820-1; Fisher's
    Garland 1821-31; – Selector 1827-28;
    Northern John Bull 1829-31; Aurora
    Borealis (Society of Friends) 1833; – Press
    1833-4; Northern Liberator 1837-40 as
    Northern Liberator and Champion 1840;
    Great Northern Advertiser 1840-3 as
    Northern Advertiser 1843-8; English Non-
    Intrusionist 1843; Anti-Monopolist Religious
    and Political 1844-5; – Register 1843-4;
    Peace Advocate and Correspondent 1846; –
    Guardian 1846-72 with North of England
    Advertiser; The Slave 1851-6; Brown's
    Export List 1853-84; S. M. and N. Lotinga's
    List of Freights Outward 1854; Northern
    Tribune and Reasoner 1854-5; – Messenger
    1855-7; * – Daily Chronicle 1858-61 as
    Daily Chronicle 1862-1939; Guardian
    1858-9; Northern Evening Express 1866-
    86; – Daily Telegraph 1869-70 as –
    Morning Telegraph 1870-71 as – Evening

(Newcastle-upon-Tyne – continued) –
    Telegraph 1871; – Evening Courant 1870-4
    with Daily Courant; North of England
    Farmer 1870-6 with – Courant; – Tele-
    graph 1870-1; Northern Weekly Leader
    1885-1919 (1920); – Evening Chronicle
    1885-(1981); – Evening News 1893-9;
    Tyneside 1894-5; – Weekly News 1898-
    9; – Morning Mail 1898-1901; Northern
    Mail 1901-(1920); – Evening Mail 1903-5;
    Mid-Tyne Link 1904-6; Northern Democrat
    1906-12; Northern Weekly Record 1909-
    10; Illustrated Chronicle 1910-25; Northern
    Graphic 1910-11; – Evening Mail 1910-7
    (1920).
        * ! Darlington PL; Advertiser (1780-95);
    Chronicle (1764 and 1774); Courant (1769
    and 1780); Daily Chronicle (1874);
    Journal (facsimile of 1771 issue). See also
    GATESHEAD.
†NEWHAM: EAST HAM: – Express 1892-3;
    – Echo 1895-1941; and Barking Free Press
    1903-4; – and West Ham Mercury 1909-10;
    – Mail 1913-32. Also: WEST HAM: The
    Stratford Express, East London and South
    Essex Advertiser etc. 1866-87 as Borough of
    West Ham and Stratford Express 1887-94 as
    Borough of West Ham, East Ham and
    Stratford Express 1894-1945 as Borough of
    West Ham, East Ham, Barking and Stratford
    Express 1945-64 as Newham, Barking and
    Stratford Express 1964-8 as Stratford and
    Newham Express 1968-(1981); – Review
    1886; – Guardian 1888-1902; – Herald
    1892-99 with South Essex Mail; – Times
    1849-99; Citizen 1899-1900; Borough of
    West Ham and South Essex Mail 1902-12 as
    West Ham and South Essex Mail 1912-28.
Newington: see SOUTHWARK.
†Newmarket: – Journal 1872-(1981).
†NEWPORT (I.o.W.): Isle of Wight Mercury
    with – Advertiser 1853-(1981); Isle of
    Wight Chronicle 1866-(1981); Carisbrooke
    Magazine 1880-91; – Echo 1884-5; Isle of
    Wight County Press 1884-(1981); – Times
    1898-1905 as Isle of Wight Journal 1905-
    20; Isle of Wight Leader 1906-9; Island Star
    1910-20. See also Yarmouth (I.o.W.).
†NEWPORT (Mon.): Monmouthshire Merlin
    1829-91; – Glamorgan and Brecon Herald
    1853-1902 as South Wales Times with
    South Wales Weekly Argus; – Gazette
    1857-8 as – Weekly Gazette 1870-2 as
    South Wales Weekly Telegram 1872-91;
    South Wales Times 1857-61; – Reformer
    and South Wales Times 1861-2; – Free
    Press 1869-74 as Monmouth Valleys
    Reporter 1874; – Evening Telegram 1870 as
    South Wales Evening Telegram 1870-91; –
    Weekly Mail 1879-80; South Wales Argus
    1892-(1981); – Skits 1894; – and Mon-
    mouth Evening Telegraph 1903; Monmouth
    County Times 1905; Monmouth Daily

(Newport, Mon. – continued) –
Post 1908–10; Monmouth Evening Post
1908–22; Monmouth Weekly Post 1908–22.
NEW ROMNEY: None listed before Dym-
church and – Post 1937–9.
†NORTHAMPTON: – Mercury 1720–(1981);
– Miscellany 1721; – County Press 1808–
11; – Free Press 1831-3 as – and Leaming-
ton Free Press 1833-4; – Herald 1831–
1931; – Chronicle 1836-7 with – Beacon;
– Citizen 1845; – Advertiser 1855;
Northants Penny News 1856-7; Northants
Free Press 1856-7 as South Midlands Free
Press 1858-60 as Midlands Free Press 1860-
1917 (1920); – Express 1860-4; – Albion
1873-4; The Radical 1874; Northants
Guardian 1876-90; – Evening Mail 1880-1;
– Evening Herald 1880-1 as Daily Chronicle
1881-1931 with – Echo; – Daily Reporter
1880-1908 as – Daily Echo 1908-(1981);
Weekly Reporter 1881-5 with Northants
Guardian; Northants Notes and Queries
1884-96; – Evening Telegraph 1897-(1981);
– Comet 1903; – Independent 1905–
(1981); Northants and Hunts. Gazette
1913-23.
†Northwich: – Guardian 1860-(1981).
†NORWICH: * – Post 1708 as * – Postman
1709; * – Gazette 1709-33, 1761-64 and
1771-(1920); – Weekly Packet or Courant
1714; * Weekly Mercury or Protestant
Packet 1721; * – Mercury 1725-(1981);
Iris 1803-4; Roope's Weekly Letters 1810;
– Yarmouth and Lynn Courier 1818-23;
Norfolk Yeoman's Gazette 1823; *Bury
and Norwich Post 1826-1931; – Theatrical
Observer 1827; – Enigmatic Repository
1828: East Anglian 1830-3 with Bury and
– Post; – Magazine 1835; – Searcher 1839;
Norfolk and – Weekly Satirist 1839; –
Gazette 1840-5; – and Norfolk Times
1841-2; – Protestant Herald 1841-2;
Norfolk and – Monitor and Police Gazette
1840-5; – Advertising Sheet 1842; – Rail-
way Gazette 1844; – and Norfolk Railway
Advertiser 1844; Norfolk News 1845-1918
as Norfolk News and Weekly Press 1919-49
as Norfolk News and Norwich Mercury
1949-55 as Norfolk News, Norwich Mercury
and Journal 1955-61 as Norwich Mercury,
Norfolk News and Journal 1962-(1981);
Railway Gazette 1854-5; – Weekly Express
1855-6; Norfolk Rifle 1860; Green's
Monthly – Illustrated Journal 1861; Norfolk
Times 1862; * – Spectator 1862-64; * –
Argus 1863-93 with Norfolk Weekly
Standard; Diss Express 1864-(1981);
Peoples' Weekly Journal 1864-1922; –
Telegraph 1867; – Dispatch 1867 as Nor-
folk Herald 1867-76 as Norfolk Conservative
Advocate 1876; – Penny Magazine 1870;
Eastern Daily Journal 1870-1; * Eastern
Counties Daily Press 1870-1 as Eastern

(Norwich – continued) –
Daily Press 1871-(1981); East Coast Mail
1872; – Herald 1876 as – Express 1876-7;
Norfolk Mail 1876-86; Norfolk Echo 1880;
Norfolk Globe 1880; Nórfolk Daily Stan-
dard 1887-1905; – Union Magazine 1890-
(1920); Norfolk Military Gazette 1896;
* Eastern Star 1891-2; – Budget 1893-5;
Norfolk Military Gazette 1896; * Eastern
Morning Gazette 1902-4; * Eastern Evening
News 1882-(1981); – Free Press 1908-10.
    * Norwich Divisional Library's Local
Studies Department holds a large selection
of Norwich, Norfolk and East Anglian news-
papers, including issues for Bury St
Edmunds, Lowestoft, Diss and Cromer;
many also MF. Has summary handlist.
See also: *Periodicals and Sets relating to
British History in Norfolk and Suffolk
Libraries; A Finding List* (1970) and
*Periodicals in Libraries of the Norwich Area
1979-80: A Finding List*, both produced
by the University of East Anglia.
†NOTTINGHAM: – Post 1711; * – Mercury
1715; Cresswell and Burbage's – Journal
1783-87 as – Journal 1787-1887 with
– Daily Express; – Review 1809-70
with – Daily Express: – Gazette 1813-15;
– Opinion 1818; and Newark Mercury
1827-41 as – Mercury 1841-52; Protestant
Tracts 1846-7; Notts. Guardian 1846-1969;
Midland Sporting Chronicle 1852-4; Notts.
Advertiser 1854-60 with Free Press;
Stevenson's Special Express 1856; Charivari
1856; Community's Journal 1857; – Telegraph 1857-63; Universal Magazine etc.
1858; Whitehead's Exchange Gazette 1859;
– Free Press 1859-60; News of the Day
1860; – Daily Express 1860-1953; –
Magazine 1861-2; – Daily Guardian 1861-
1905 as – Guardian 1905-53 as Guardian
Journal 1953-73; Advertising Post 1864-5;
The Pupil Teacher 1876-81; – Evening Post
1878-(1981); – and Derby Home Reader
1881; Weekly Journal 1884-7 with Weekly
Express; Figaro 1885; – Evening Mail 1885-
6; – Evening News 1885-1963; Nottingham-
shire Weekly Express 1886-1922; Notts. Free
Press 1887-(1981); – Argus 1894-8 as – City
News 1898-1900; – Amusements 1899; South
– Gazette 1901-3 as – Chronicle 1903 as
South – and Notts. Gazette 1908-11; – Midday
Post 1904; Notts. Herald 1907-34; – and
Notts. Echo. 1908. * Nottingham CL.
NUNEATON: * – Chronicle 1868-(1920); –
Advertiser 1868-1943; – and Attleborough
News 1874; – Times 1875-8; * – Observer
1877-(1981); – and District Record
1907-8; – Star 1911-2 (1920); * Midland
Counties Tribune 1914-57.
    * ! Nuneaton PL; MF Chronicle (1868-
1956); Observer (1877-1973); Midland
Counties Tribune (1914-1957); Evening

(Nuneaton – continued) –
Tribune (1957-1973). Also originals of latter.
†OKEHAMPTON: – Gazette and Advertiser 1913; – Post 1921-45 as – Post and Launceston Weekly 1945-(1981).
†OLDHAM: – Reformer 1854; – Advertiser 1854-60; – Free Press 1854; – Chronicle 1854-(1981); – Standard 1859-1947; – Telegraph 1859 with – Advertiser; – Times 1860-3; – Express 1867-70; – Ensign 1868; – Evening Express 1869-89; – Wesleyan Herald 1872; Northern Times 1877-80 as – Evening Standard 1880-2 as – Daily Standard 1882-1928; – Evening Chronicle 1880-(1981); – Express 1880-9; – Operative 1884-5; – Advertiser 1889-91; – Worker 1904; – Weekly Times 1915-6.
†Ormskirk: – Advertiser 1853-(1981).
†Orpington: – Times 1881-(1981).
†OSSETT: – Observer 1864-(1981).
†OXFORD: Jackson's – Journal 1753-1928; – Gazette and Reading Mercury 1753-67 as Reading Mercury 1767-1960; – Mercury and Midland Counties Chronicle 1795; – City Herald 1806-8; – Review or Literary Censor 1807-8; Farrago 1816; Il Vagabondo 1816; Oxonian 1817; Undergraduate 1819; – Miscellany 1820; University and City Herald 1830 as City and County Herald 1831-52 as University Herald 1852-92; University Magazine 1834; – Conservative 1834-5; – City and County Chronicle 1837-42 as – Chronicle and Reading Gazette 1842-5 as – Chronicle and Berks. and Bucks. Gazette 1846-1929; – Farmers' Gazette 1843-4; – Magazine 1845; Oxonian 1847; – Protestant Magazine 1847-8; Halls Oxonian Advertiser 1853-6; – Critic 1857; Illustrated Oxfordshire Telegraph 1858-94; – Free Press 1858; – Flying Post 1859; – Times 1862-(1981); – University Gazette 1870-(1981); – Messenger 1873-7; Guardian 1884-92; – Review 1885; – Echo 1898-1900; – Telegraph 1900-3; – Herald 1907; Oxfordshire Advertiser 1908-9; – Chronicle 1913-29; Fortnightly 1913-4; Review 1919.
Paddington: see WESTMINSTER.
PEMBROKE: – Dock Chronicle 1860 – with Tenby and – Dock Observer; Pembrokeshire Advertiser 1871-5; – Dock and Tenby Gazette 1874-1920; – Dock Journal 1901-7; – Dock Weekly Post 1904-5; – Dock etc. News in a Nutshell 1912.
Pendlebury: see SWINTON AND PENDLEBURY.
PENRYN: Falmouth and – Weekly Times and General Advertiser 1861-1952; Commercial Shipping and General Advertiser for West Cornwall 1862-1912 as – Falmouth Advertiser 1912-35.

†PENZANCE: – Gazette 1839-58; – Journal 1847-50; Cornish Telegraph 1851-1915 with Cornishman; – Congregational Magazine 1875-8; Cornishman 1878-(1981).
†PETERBOROUGH: – Monthly Advertiser 1846; – Herald 1850; – Advertiser 1854-5 as Weekly News 1855-8 as – Advertiser 1858-(1981); The News Magazine 1864-5; – Times 1865-74; – and Hunts. Standard 1872-(1981); – Express 1884-1917 (1920); – Evening News 1896-1911; – Citizen 1903-46.
Pimlico: see KENSINGTON.
†PLYMOUTH: – Weekly Journal or General Post 1718-25; The Selector 1809; The Magnet or – Monthly Magazine 1822-3; Royal Devonport Chronicle and – Chronicle 1827-63 with Western Weekly News; Philo-Damnonian 1830; Devonport and Stonehouse Herald 1831-76; – and Devonport Weekly Journal 1831-63 with Western Daily Mercury; South Devon Monthly Museum 1833-6; – etc. News 1836-7 with Western Herald; West of England Conservative 1836-52 as Western Courier 1852-4; – Times 1842-8; Emigrants' Penny Magazine 1850-1; – Mail 1852-61; Rendle's Prices Current 1854-5; Daily Western Mercury 1860 as Western Daily Mercury 1860-1921; Western Morning News 1860-(1981); Western Weekly News 1861-1939; Mid-Devon Advertiser 1863-(1981); Western Counties Daily Herald 1868-9; Western Daily Standard 1870; Thunderbolt 1871-2; Weekly Times 1873 as West of England Advertiser 1873-4 as Bristol and West of England Advertiser 1874-6; Western Counties Herald and – Advertiser 1874-6; – Evening Mercury 1877; Weekly Mercury 1879-1921; The Socialist 1895; Western Evening Herald 1895-(1981).
†PONTEFRACT: The Yorkshireman 1833-7; – Telegraph 1857-1902; Copley's – Advertiser 1858-9 as – Advertiser 1859-1900; as – and Castleford Advertiser 1900-18 as – Advertiser 1920-37; – Chronicle 1860-1 with Wakefield Journal; – and Castleford Express 1880-(1981); – and Castleford Weekly Herald 1892-1900 with – Advertiser; – etc. Business Guide 1914-56.
†POOLE: – and Dorset Weekly Herald 1846-95 as – Parkstone and East Dorset Herald 1895-(1981); – Guardian 1883-5 with Western Chronicle of Yeovil; – Telegram 1886 with Telegram of Yeovil; – Sun 1908-9.
†PORTSMOUTH: – Gazette 1793-1802; – Telegraph 1799 as Motley's Telegraph and Hampshire Telegraph 1802-(1981); – Chronicle 1802-3 and 1861; – Portsea and Gosport Journal 1803-4; – and Chichester Advertiser 1805; Hampshire Courier 1810 with Hampshire Chronicle of Winchester;

(Portsmouth – continued) –
— Portsea and Gosport Literary and
Scientific Register 1823; — Portsea and
Gosport Herald 1829–35 with Hampshire
Advertiser; — etc. Free Press 1839; — Portsea
and Gosport Pioneer 1839; — etc. Free
Register 1841; Borough Reporter, Exposer
of Abuses and Advocate of Reform 1841;
Hampshire and West Sussex Standard
1841–3 with Hampshire Advertiser of
Southampton; Hampshire Guardian 1846; —
Portsea and Isle of Wight Advocate 1848;
— etc. Register 1841; — Times 1850–1928;
Guardian 1851–6 and 1861–8; — Chronicle
1861; — Observer 1870–1; The News 1877–
(1981); Evening News 1878–1959; Curtis
and Son's Monthly Shipping List 1880–94;
Chat 1884–1921; — and Southsea Amuse-
ments 1894–5; — Guardian 1895–6; —
Telegraph 1899; — Free Press 1900: — North
End Advertiser 1901; What on in — ? 1913;
— Daily Post 1913.
PORT TALBOT: Mid-Glamorgan Observer,
Aberavon Advertizer and — Times 1911
with Neath News; Aberavon and — News
1919–20.
    ! Port Talbot PL has late (1937) editions
of the — Guardian and Glamorgan Gazette;
also several South Wales editions for General
Strike of 1926.
Prescot: see ST HELENS.
†PRESTON: — Pilot 1831–88; — Chronicle
1831–93 with — Guardian; — Observer
1837–40; — Temperance Advocate 1837;
Livesey's Moral Reformer 1838–9; Pollard's
— Advertiser 1840–1; The Struggle (Corn
Laws) 1842–6; — Magazine 1843; —
Guardian 1844–1964; — Standard 1855–6;
— Herald 1855–1964; — Daily Guardian
1870; — Evening News 1870–1; — Commer-
cial Travellers' Review 1874–5; Lancashire
Evening Post 1886–92 as Lancashire Daily
Post 1892–(1981); — Monthly Circular
1895–1915 (1920); — Weekly News 1914;
Lancashire Daily Herald 1916.
PRESTWICH: — and Failsworth News 1890–1;
— District etc. Times 1904.
†PUDSEY: — and Stanningley News 1872–
(1981); — District Advertiser 1889–1932;
Echo 1896–1905 (1920).
PWLLHELI: — Chronicle 1889–93.
†QUEENBOROUGH: Sheerness Guardian 1858
with Sheerness Times as Sheerness Guardian
1868–(1981).
†RADCLIFFE: * — Express 1888–1902; —
Guardian 1899; — Guardian 1910; * —
Times 1899–(1981).
    * Radcliffe PL, both from 1899.
†RAMSGATE: Thanet Advertiser 1859–
1955; Kent Coast Times 1866–96 as
East Kent Times 1896–(1981); Pullen's
Kent Argus 1873–1924. See also
MARGATE.

†RAWTENSTALL: — Free Press 1883–5 as
Rossendale Free Press 1885–(1981).
READING: — Mercury 1723; — Mercury and
Oxford Gazette 1777–8; Berkshire
Chronicle 1829–1967; — Herald 1868–70;
Berkshire Telegraph 1869–73; — with
Reading Observer; — Observer 1873–1924;
— Express 1879–84; — Standard 1887–
1965; — and County Times 1909–10; —
Journal 1912–3.
†REDBRIDGE: as ILFORD: — Recorder 1889–
(1981); — and Redbridge Post 1894 with Essex
Guardian 1898–(1981); — Leader 1899–1900;
— and Manor Park News 1900–1; — and Seven
King's Mercury 1901–2; — Express 1901–2;
— Gazette 1904–20; — Graphic 1912.
Also: WANSTEAD: — Mail 1900–3 with
Woodford Mail; — Bugle 1907–(1920).
WOODFORD: — Times 1869–1970; — Mail
1897–1907; — and District Advertiser
1906–55.
†Redditch: — Indicator 1859–(1981).
Redhill: see REIGATE.
REIGATE: Surrey Guardian 1857; — and
Redhill Journal 1863–1902 with Sussex
Express; Redhill and — Express 1873–5;
— and Redhill Gazette 1907–13; Redhill
and — Chronicle 1909–12.
RHONDDA: — Chronicle 1884–98; — Gazette
1889–91; — Post 1898–9; — Leader 1899–
1921.
RICHMOND (Yorks.): — Weekly News 1855–6
as * — and Ripon Chronicle 1856–94; —
Telegraph 1873–6 with York Herald.
    * Bradford PL, odd copies Richmond and
Ripon Chronicle for 1873 and 1877.
†RICHMOND-ON-THAMES: — Observer and
Surrey Chronicle 1851; — News 1864–5; —
Pioneer 1870; — and Twickenham Times
1873–(1981); — News 1879 with Mid-
Surrey Times; — Herald 1855–(1981);
Thames Valley Times 1886–(1975); —
Express 1890–2; — Society 1896; — News
1902–3; — and Twickenham Conservative
Gazette 1908–9; — and Twickenham Home
Journal 1912–31. Also: TWICKENHAM:
— Observer 1869; — Advertiser 1909–10; —
Gazette 1911–4.
†Ripley: — News 1889–(1981) (as— Times).
†RIPON: The Liberal 1836; Bedale and —
Times 1858–1914 with — Gazette; —
Gazette 1868–(1920) with — Observer; —
and Richmond Chronicle 1870–94; —
Observer 1889–(1981); — Advertiser 1911–
22.
†ROCHDALE: — Sentinel 1853–5; — Weekly
Banner 1855; — Standard 1855–7; *Observer
1856–(1981); — Pilot 1857–71 with —
Times; — Spectator 1866–8; * — Times
1871–1924; — Star 1888–99; — Labour
News 1896–1900; — Advertiser 1902–3; —
Free Press 1903–4.
    * Rochdale PL, originals and MF.

ROCHESTER: — Gazette 1830-5 as Chatham and Stroud Gazette 1835-68; — and Chatham Miscellany 1855-6 as Taylor's Monthly Record 1857; — and Chatham Journal 1857-1947 as Chatham Standard 1947-(1975); — and Chatham Times 1889-92 with — Journal; — and Chatham Standard 1892-1908. See CHATHAM.

†ROMSEY: — Railway Chronicle 1850-96 as * — Advertiser 1897-(1981); Register 1859-94; Standard 1883-4.

　　* ! Hampshire County Libraries publish *A Romsey Bibliography* (1972); this adds other newspapers (Hampshire Chronicle, 1772; Romsey Advertiser, 1850; Southern Evening Echo) but lists no library holdings. Advises enquire newspaper offices, Winchester, Romsey and Southampton.

Rossendale: see HASLINGTON.

†ROTHERHAM: — Journal 1857-61; — Advertiser 1858-(1981); — Guardian 1877; South Yorkshire Times 1877-(1981); — Express 1887; — Free Press 1894; — Express 1896-1920; — Weekly News 1899-1900; — Evening Echo 1906-8. See also SHEFFIELD.

†ROYAL LEAMINGTON SPA; * — Courier 1828-(1981); * — Press 1834-5 as — Chronicle 1835-59; — Looker-on 1843; — Advertiser 1849-1904; — Magnet 1849-50; — Observer 1850; County Mirror 1856; — Mercury 1856-7; — Chronicle 1865-97 as — Warwick, Rugby and County Chronicle 1897-1956; — Monthly Record 1865-6; — News 1882-1900; — Journal 1887; — Illustrated Visitors' Guide 1890-1; * — Daily Circular 1869-1919 as * — and District Morning News 1919-(1981).

　　* Leamington Spa PL.

†ROYAL TUNBRIDGE WELLS: The Sphinx 1835; The Phoenix 1835-6; — Gazette 1855-92 as Counties Gazette 1892-3 as — Gazette 1983-(1920); — News 1855; Kent Times 1857-62; — Weekly Express 1863-94; — Telegraph 1863-1905; — Journal 1863-1904; — Chronicle 1863-9; The Tonbridgian 1865-(1920); — and Tonbridge Weekly 1865-1902; Kent Pioneer 1866; — Standard 1866-85 and 1911-2; — Free Press 1871-(1975); Kent Courier as — Kent and Sussex Courier 1872-(1981); Fashionable Visitor 1875; — Advertiser 1882-(1981); — and Sevenoaks Standard 1892-1912 — with South-East Gazette; Municipal Post 1902-3; — Society 1908-9; Gazette and Pictorial News 1909-17 (1920).

†RUGBY: — Advertiser 1850-(1981); — Recorder 1857-8; — Gazette 1858-76; as Midland Times 1876-1906 with — News; New Rugbeian 1860-1; — Review 1896; — News 1898-1908; — Register 1898-9; — Review 1905; — Observer 1911-39; — and Kineton Advertiser 1913-43.

Runcorn: see WIDNES.

(RUTHIN): None listed.

†RYDE: — Visitor 1839-41; Isle of Wight Observer 1845-6 and 1852-1922; Isle of Wight Mercury 1855-(1981) as Examiner 1860-1; Isle of Wight Express 1861-3; Isle of Wight Times 1862-(1975); — News 1870-9 as — and Isle of Wight News 1880-1900; Ventilator 1872; — Pilot 1873-4; Isle of Wight County Press 1884-(1981); Isle of Wight Evening Times 1895; — Visitors' Companion 1904.

RYE: — and Hastings Advocate 1827; — Chronicle 1859-61 as South-Eastern Advertiser 1861-1917 (1920); — Telegram 1865-7 with Kentish Express of Ashford; — Free Press 1870-1; East Sussex and Weald of Kent Mercury 1871.

SAFFRON WALDEN: — Weekly News 1889-1900; — Gazette 1891-5; — Critic 1905.

†ST ALBANS: — Times 1858-65 as Herts. Advertiser 1866-(1981); — Dial 1858; — Herald 1863-4; Henfry's Journal 1864; Clock Tower 1895-8 as — Gazette 1898-1909; — Post 1906-11 as Herts. Post 1911-3.

ST AUSTELL AND FOWEY: Cornish Engine Reporter 1847-8; — Gazette 1868-9; — Weekly News 1869-95; — Star 1889-1915 (1920); — Gazette 1895-7 with — Star.

†ST HELENS: — News and Advertiser 1869-1940; — as Newspaper etc. 1940-(1981); Prescot Reporter 1869-77 as — Prescot Reporter 1877-9 as Prescot Reporter 1879-(1981); — Standard 1869-77 with Prescot Reporter; — Examiner and Prescot Weekly News 1879-1924; Newton Reporter and Guardian 1880-(1981); — Free Press 1907-12.

†ST IVES (Cornwall): — Penny Post 1878; — Weekly Summary 1898-1918 with Cornishman; Western Echo 1901-57 with Times (1918).

ST IVES (Hunts.): — Post 1718; — Postboy or Loyal Packet 1718-9; — and Hunts. Gazette 1857-9 as Eastern Counties Gazette 1859-60 as Hunts. News 1860-74; — Hunts. and Cambs. Examiner 1863-(1920); — Chronicle 1889-1901; — Courier 1896.

St Leonards: see HASTINGS.

St Marylebone: see WESTMINSTER.

St Pancras: see CAMDEN.

Saddleworth: see MOSSLEY.

†SALE: * — and Stretford Guardian 1879-(1981);

　　* Sale PL, MF from 1926.

†SALFORD: * — Weekly News 1859-89; * — Chronicle 1869-1916; Pendleton Reporter 1879 as *Salford City Reporter 1879-(1981); *Salford County Telephone 1889-92; — Times 1905-7 (1920).

　　* Salford City L: Manchester Guardian 1821-1971 originals, 1972 onwards MF; Salford Weekly News 1859-88, Salford Chronicle 1868-1910 originals; Salford

(Salford – continued) –
Reporter 1899 onwards MF. Manchester
City L: Reporter 1886 onwards; County
Telephone 1889-92; Salford Weekly News
1867-89. See also Frankland, T., *Salford in
Print (1862-1924)* (Salford Loc. Hist. Soc.,
1975).

†SALISBURY: – Postman 1715; – Journal or
Weekly Advertiser 1744-5; – and Win-
chester Journal 1824-(1981); Wiltshire
Standard 1833; – and Wiltshire Herald
1833-52 with Wiltshire County Mirror;
Western Literary Advertiser 1841; Wiltshire
County Mirror 1852-1911 with Wiltshire
News of Trowbridge; Wiltshire County
Telegraph 1863-9; – Examiner 1867-8;
– Times 1868-(1981); – Standard 1869-
70; South Wiltshire Express 1873-7 with
Wiltshire County Mirror.

SALTASH: – Gazette 1905-41.

Sandgate: see HYTHE.

SANDWICH: – Express 1870-1; – Paper
1893-5 as – News 1895-1900; – Advertiser
1904-27.

†SCARBOROUGH: – Repository 1824; The
Burgess 1836; – Herald 1836-46; – etc.
Chronicle 1836-7; * – Gazette 1845-1922;
– Record 1845-46; *Illustrated – Mercury
1855-(1981); – Times 1855-69; – Advertiser 1857; – Herald 1862-4; – Express
1865-83; – Watchman 1868; – Post 1876-
1909 (1920); – Illustrated Visitors' List
1883-5; * – Evening News 1886-(1981);
– Pictorial 1913-16.
    * Scarborough PL: originals, incomplete,
of Scarborough Gazette 1847 onwards;
Evening News and Mercury from 1933 (pre-
1933 MF). Scarborough Town Hall, some
copies of Scarborough Gazette (1859,
1861), Mercury (1860-1), Scarborough
Times (1860-1): see Forster, G. C. F., *A
Descriptive Catalogue of the Records of the
Corporation* (1968). See also Bradford PL.

SCUNTHORPE: Brigg Express 1898 (July-
October); – News 1900-1; – News 1908-10;
– Advertiser 1910.

†Selby: – Times 1860-(1981).

Sevenoaks: see ROYAL TUNBRIDGE WELLS.

SHAFTESBURY: – Gazette 1870-6; –
Monthly 1893; – Magazine 1895; –
Gazette 1903.

Sheerness: see QUEENBOROUGH.

†SHEFFIELD: – Weekly Journal or Doncaster
Flying Post 1754-6; – Weekly Register or
Doncaster Flying Post 1855-6 with –
Weekly Journal; *Public Advertiser or
Universal Weekly Chronicle 1761-93; –
Register or Yorks. Derbs. and Notts. Univer-
sal Advertiser 1787-94; * – Courant 1793-
97; *Iris or – Advertiser 1807 as * – Iris
1828-56; – Mercury 1808-12 as – Mercury
and Hallamshire Advertiser 1826-48 with
– Times; * – Independent and Commercial

(Sheffield – continued) –
Register 1819-1938 with – Telegraph;
– Parlour Fireside 1824; Yorks. and Derbs.
Magazine 1824; – Theatrical Examiner
1825; – Comet 1828-35; – Independent
1828-39 as – and Rotherham Independent
1839-1901 with Daily Independent; Local
Register 1830-72; Figaro in – 1833;
Pearce's – Magazine 1833; – Monthly
Reporter 1835; The Witness 1835-36; * –
Chronicle 1837-38; – Patriot 1838-41; The
Tocsin 1840; * – Times 1846-74; * –
Advertiser 1852-8; * – Examiner 1854-5;
*Morning's News 1855; * – Daily Tele-
graph 1855-(1981); * – Daily News 1856-
62; * – Free Press 1857; * – Argus 1858-61
with – Times; – Christian Herald 1858-61;
* – Evening Argus 1858; – Daily Argus
1859; Weekly Supplement to – Daily
Telegraph 1862-83 as – Weekly Telegraph
1883-1951; * – and Rotherham Weekly
Advertiser 1861; South Yorks. Advertiser
1866; – Monthly Messenger 1872; * – Post
1873-87; – Daily Mail 1855; * – Evening
Star and Daily Times 1874; – and Rother-
ham Monthly 1874-5; – Portrait Gallery
1874-7; – Weekly Independent 1884-1920;
– Weekly Echo 1885-7 as Yorks. Free Press
1887; * – Evening Telegraph 1887-8 as
* – Evening Telegraph and Star 1898-
(1981); – Week 1888-1902 as – Weekly
News 1902-22; * Morning and Weekly
Guardian 1888-9; – Anarchist 1894-96;
– City Chronicle 1896-7; – Miscellany
1896-7; – Guardian 1906-16; – Evening
Mail 1908-9; – Guide 1909; Picture
Paper 1911.
    * Sheffield City L holds as marked.
Also has reference list giving much informa-
tion on individual newspapers and their
history.

†Shepton Mallet: – Journal 1854-1981.

Sherborne: see YEOVIL.

Shoreditch: see HACKNEY.

†SHREWSBURY: – Chronicle 1773-(1981);
Salopian Magazine 1815-7; Salopian Journal
1822-43; – News and Cambrian Reporter
1838-44; Shropshire and North Wales
Standard 1839; Shropshire Mercury 1840
with Ten Towns Messenger of Kidder-
minster; Shropshire Conservative 1840-61;
Salopian Budget 1841 as –Salopian Tele-
graph 1841-4; Salopian Phoenix 1842;
Eddowe's – Journal 1843-91; Salopian
Advertiser 1852-5; Newport and South
Shropshire Journal 1854-(1981); – Register
1855-9; Salopian Journal 1861-2; Shrop-
shire and Montgomery Times 1863-6; –
Free Press 1865-81; Salopian 1871;
Salopian Monthly Illustrated Journal 1875-
80; Shropshire Post 1881-93; Shropshire
Guardian 1881-91; Shropshire Notes and
Queries 1885-90; Shropshire Evening News

(Shrewsbury – continued) –
1885–90; Outlook 1911; – Commercial and Literary Circular 1915–55.

†Sidcup: – Times 1881–(1981).

†SLOUGH: – Chronicle 1871–2; – etc. Observer 1883–(1981); – Herald 1890–1; – Journal 1908; – Chronicle 1912–39.

Southall: see EALING.

SOUTHAMPTON: Hampshire Advertiser 1829–1940; Isle of Wight Mercury 1830; – Argus 1831; Hampshire Independent 1836–1923; Royal Mail Packet 1847; – Advocate 1847; – Chronicle 1848; – Examiner 1854; – Free Press 1856–7; – Examiner 1858; – Examiner 1860; Hampshire Examiner 1860 with – Times; – Times 1860–1925; – Observer 1867–1906 as News and Views 1906–7; Southern Evening Echo 1888–(1981); – Amusements 1895–1912 with – and District Pictorial; – and District Pictorial 1912–20; What's On in – ? 1909–34.

*   Southampton Central RL holds most newspapers listed; others at offices of the Southern Evening Echo.

†South Molton: – Gazette 1870–1981.

†SOUTHEND-ON-SEA: – Standard 1868–(1981); – Observer 1880–1947; Independent 1894–95; – Echo 1894–1908 (1920); – Argus 1898; – Telegraph 1900–71; – Weekly Chronicle of Events 1902–3; – Monthly Guide 1906–(1920); – and Westcliff Graphic 1907–18 (1920); – Borough Recorder 1908–10.

†SOUTHPORT: – Visiter [*sic*] and General Advertiser 1844–(1981); – Free Press 1853–4; – Advertiser 1857–58; Independent 1861–72 as – News 1872–5 as – Daily News 1875–7 as Liverpool and – Daily News 1877–81; – Critic 1878–82; – Echo 1879–80; – Gazette 1881–2; – Guardian 1882–1959; – News 1881–5 as – Standard 1885–99; – Hornet 1886–7; – Journal 1904–59; – Weekly News 1905–8 with – Journal; – Welcome 1915–6.

Southsea: see PORTSMOUTH.

†SOUTH SHIELDS: Northumberland Advertiser 1831–4; Port of Tyne Pilot 1839–42; Tyne Courier 1842; North and South Shields Gazette 1849–84 as South Shields Daily Gazette 1884–(1981); – Advocate 1855–7 as Shields Advertiser 1857–8; Tynesmouth Guardian 1861; Shields Daily News 1864–(1920); The Shield 1870; Shields Daily Standard 1880–1; Shields and Tynemouth Argus 1881–2; Shields Morning Mail 1899–1901; Tyneside Weekly News 1908–9; Northern Observer 1911.

SOUTHWARK: – Sentinel 1832; Borough of – News 1868 as – News, Lambeth Times and Surrey Advertiser 1869; – Mercury 1879–81; – Recorder 1882–1933; – Standard 1884–91 with London Mail;

(Southwark – continued) –
– and Newington Parish Parliament 1888 as Southgate, Newington and Bermondsey Ratepayers' Chronicle 1889–94. Also: BERMONDSEY: – Review 1855–87; – and Rotherham Advertiser 1868–82 as Southwark Recorder 1882–1933. CAMBERWELL: – and Peckham Times 1870–4 with South London Observer; – Peckham and Dulwich Express 1871–5; – News 1876–80 with South London Gazette; – Herald 1896; – Advertiser 1896–9; – Gazette 1908–10; – Borough Advertiser 1910–20; – etc. Mirror 1911. DULWICH: – Chronicle 1904–7; – Post 1909–10; – and Forest Hill Mail 1915.

†SOUTHWOLD: Halesworth Times and – Mercury 1885–(1981).

†Spalding: – Guardian 1881–(1981).

†SPENBOROUGH: Cleckheaton Advertiser and Tradesman's Circular 1847–87 as Spen Valley Times 1887–95 as Cleckheaton Advertiser and Spen Valley Times 1895–1916 as Cleckheaton Advertiser and Spenborough Times 1916–39 with Cleckheaton and Spenborough Guardian; Cleckheaton Guardian and Liversidge, Gomershal, Scholes and District Recorder 1874–85 as Cleckheaton Guardian and Spen Valley News 1895–1915 as Cleckheaton and Spenborough Guardian 1915–55 as Spenborough Guardian 1955–(1981).

STAFFORD: * Staffordshire Advertiser 1795–(1973); * – Mercury 1814–5; Staffordshire Gazette 1831–2 and 1839–42; – County Herald 1831–2; – Mercury 1863; – Chronicle 1877–1955 with – Advertiser; Staffordshire Courier 1890–1. * Stafford PL.

†Staines and Egham: – News 1893–(1981). See also HOUNSLOW.

STALYBRIDGE: – and Dukinfield Standard 1869–1900; – News 1874; – Reporter 1874–(1975); – Examiner 1875–6; – Advertiser 1880.

†STAMFORD: – Mercury 1715–6 as Howgrave's – Mercury 1733–(1981); Drakard's – News 1809–34 with Lincoln Gazette; – Fireside Magazine 1819; Champion of the East 1830; – Lincoln and Newark Times 1832 with – News: –Bee or – Herald and County Chronicle 1833 as – Bee 1833; Lincs. Chronicle 1833–61; – Mirror 1836–7; Sharre's Agricultural Companion 1846–7; Lincs. Express 1862–4; – Wesleyan Messenger 1872; – Guardian 1873 as Grantham and – Guardian 1873–4 as – and Rutland Guardian 1875–1918 (1920); Rutland Post 1885–95.

! Grimsby RL, Lincoln, Rutland and Stamford Mercury (1802–1921); MF 1793–1910.

Stanningley: see PUDSEY.

†STOCKPORT: * — Advertiser 1822–(1981);
North Cheshire Reformer 1836–9 as —
Chronicle 1840–2 as Macclesfield — and
Congleton Chronicle 1842–48; — Mercury
1847–51; Smith's Advertising Gazette 1853
as Smith's — Gazette 1853–5; — Free Press
1854; — News 1855 as — and Cheshire News
1855–76 as Cheshire County News 1876–
1912; — Guardian 1857; — Albion 1871;
— Chronicle 1874–6; — Evening Star 1877–
8; — Guardian 1878; — Echo 1883–9 as
Cheshire Echo 1889–(1920); — Free Press
1884; — County Borough Express 1889–
(1981); — Chronicle 1891–1906; — Times
1893–4; District Express 1895–(1981); —
Record 1910–(1920); — Independent 1894.
     * Manchester City Library, MF from
1822, The Stockport Advertiser.
Stockton: see HARTLEPOOL.
†STOKE-ON-TRENT: — Monthly Narrative
1852; Staffordshire Potteries Telegraph
1852–5; Potteries Free Press 1853;
Staffordshire Weekly Sentinel 1854–(1981);
Potteries Times 1854; — Evening Sentinel
1873–(1981).
†STOURBRIDGE: * — Times, East Worcester-
shire and South Staffs. Herald 1861–2; * —
Mercury 1862–9; Cradley Heath and Stour-
bridge Observer as — Observer Cradley
Heath, Halesowen and District Chronicle
1864–66 as — Observer, Cradley Heath,
Halesowen and District Chronicle 1866–
88; * — Sun 1884–5; Stourbridge, Brierley
Hill and County Express for Worcs. and
Staffs. 1885–91 as County Express for
Worcs. and Staffs. 1891–(1981).
     * Dudley Central RL, MF Mercury
(1862–9), Sun (1834–5), Times (1861–2).
†STRATFORD-ON-AVON: * — Shipston and
Alcester Journal 1750–3. Theatrical Review
1827–8; * — Herald 1866–(1981); * —
Chronicle 1866–85; — News 1901–2.
     * The Shakespeare Birthplace Trust has
— Journal (1750–3), — Chronicle 1861–85
and Herald (1860–1974).
Streatham: see LAMBETH.
STRETFORD: — Examiner 1879–80 with
Warrington Examiner; — Division Chronicle
1889–95; — Division Advertiser 1891–1942.
†SUDBURY: — Free Press 1855 as West
Suffolk and North Essex Free Press 1855–6
as Suffolk and Essex Free Press 1865–
(1981); Suffolk and Essex News 1857–9 as
Essex and Suffolk News 1857–1921; —
Express 1871–2; — Herald 1904.
†SUNDERLAND: — Literary Miscellany 1815;
* — and Durham General Shipping Gazette
1831; * — Herald 1831–1902 as * — Daily
Post 1902–(1920); * — Beacon 1838–9 as
Northern Times 1839–43; — Mirror 1839;
* — Times 1844–76 as Weekly Times 1876–
80; — News 1851–5; — and Hartlepool
General Review 1853; Hartley and Co.'s

(Sunderland — continued) —
Glass Tariff Newspaper 1853; — Examiner
1852–4; — Advertiser 1854; Christian
Freeman 1856–(1920); — Daily News 1857;
* — Telegram 1858; — Weekly News 1865–8;
— Daily Shipping News 1865–1913; —
Sentinel 1867–9; — Evening Chronicle
1870–1; * — Daily Echo 1873–(1981); —
Daily Times 1876–8 with Daily Echo; —
Weekly Times 1876–80; * — Daily Post
1876–81; — with Daily Herald; * — Daily
Herald 1880–1; * — Weekly Echo and
Times 1881–1913; — Socialist 1894; —
Citizen 1897–99; — Morning Mail 1898–
1901; — Weekly News 1898–9; * —
Daily Mail 1898–9; Sunday Morning
Mail 1899–1901.
     * Sunderland RL has 30 Sunderland,
Durham and Teesside newspapers.
Surbiton: see KINGSTON-ON-THAMES.
†SUTTON: — Journal 1863–1902; * — and
Cheam Advertiser 1869–(1981); * — Herald
1878–(1981) with — Times; Wallington and
Carlshalton Herald 1881–97 with Surrey
County Herald of Carlshalton; — and Cheam
Weekly Record 1909–11; — Guardian 1910;
Weekly Post 1907.
     * ! Sutton PL has originals Advertiser
(1897–1909); Herald (1897–1909); Weekly
Post (1907); and MF Herald and Advertiser
(1878–1885).
†SUTTON COLDFIELD: * — News 1870–84
with Warwickshire Herald; — Times 1883–
1901; — and Eardington Mercury 1875–1905
with Lichfield Mercury; — and Eardington
Chronicle 1896; * — News 1900–(1981).
†SWANSEA: Y Cylchgrawn 1815–93; Seren
1818–56; Llenad Yr Oes 1827–30; — Journal
1843–5; — and Glamorgan Herald 1847–90
with Herald of Wales; — and Neath Advertiser 1849–52; — Journal 1852; — and South
Wales Advertising Journal 1855–90 as South
Wales Radical 1890 as South Wales Liberal
1890–3 as — Journal 1893–1902; Shipping
Gazette 1859–61; — Mercury 1860–3 with
South Wales and Glamorgan Herald; South
Wales Herald 1864; South Wales Critic
1869–88; — Daily Shipping Record 1888 as
— Gazette 1888–1913; Welsh Industrial
Times 1888–91; South Wales Daily Post
1893–1932 as South Wales Evening Post
1932–(1981); * — and South Walian 1896–
1906; — Daily Industrial World 1897;
Stock Exchange Weekly Official Price List
1905–11; Llais Llafur (The Voice of
Labour) 1905–71.
†SWINDON: Cirencester and — Express 1851–2
with Wilts. and Gloucs. Standard; — Advertiser 1854–1956; North Wilts. Herald 1861–
1941; New — Observer 1866; New — Express
1876–80; — News 1890; Evening — Advertiser 1898–(1981); — Borough Press 1906–
15 (1920); — Daily Echo 1908.

†SWINTON AND PENDLEBURY: Mex-
borough, — and Neath Record 1865;
*Pendlebury and Swinton Journal 1872–
1904 as Swinton and Pendlebury Journal
1904–(1981); — Times 1875-1901.

    * Swinton and Pendlebury Local Studies
Library has Eccles and Patricroft Journal MF
1874–1933, and originals/MF for 1933 onwards. This newspaper is identical with
Pendlebury and Swinton Journal for 1874–
1933. See Singleton, F., *Tillotson's 1850-
1950: A Centenary of a Family Business*
(1950) for history of this newspaper. See
also *Newspapers first published before 1900
in Lancs., Cheshire & Isle of Man* (Library
Association 1964).

†TAMWORTH: — Herald 1868–(1981); —
Advertiser 1869-72; — Miners' Examiner
1873 as * — Examiner 1874-6; — Mercury
1878-1957; — Chronicle 1884; — Advertiser
1884-1913; — Times 1892-7; — Times
1905-12.

†TAUNTON: — Courier 1810–1936; Sher-
borne, Dorchester and — Journal 1829–86
with Western Chronicle; Somerset County
Gazette 1836–(1981); Somerset County
Herald 1834–1964; Illustrated Western News
1855 as Western News 1855–(1920); —
Gazette 1857-65; — Chronicle 1860 as
Somerset Chronicle 1860-2; West Somerset
Chronicle 1865; Western Herald 1866-7 as
Western Counties Herald 1867-8; Webb's
Advertising News 1868 as Webb's Weekly
News 1869-9 as — Sun 1875-8; — Weekly
Advertiser 1868-9; Somerset County
Chronicle 1874; — Gazette 1875; — Echo
1887-1933; Somerset Express 1887-1933;
— Mail 1894–1923.

†Tavistock: — Gazette 1857–(1981).

†TEESSIDE: Evening Gazette (Middlesbrough)
1869–(1981); Tees Daily Shipping List
1887-1916 (1920); — Weekly Herald 1904–
29.

†Tenbury Wells: — Advertiser 1870–(1981).
See LUDLOW.

TENBY: — and Pembrokeshire Chronicle
1846-7; — List of Visitors 1853 as —
Observer 1853–(1920); Tenby 1869-74 as
— Times 1874-6; — Chronicle 1877; —
Telephone 1879-85 as Pembrokeshire Times
1885-1918 (1920); — and County News
1893-1919 (1920).

TENTERDEN: None listed before — News
1938.

TEWKESBURY: — Monthly Advertiser 1846;
— Weekly Record 1855-1921; — Herald
1857; — Register 1858-1967; — Mail
1904-14.

†THETFORD: — and Walton Times
1880–(1981); — Weekly Post 1905-16
(1920).

†Thurrock: — Gazette 1884–(1981).

Tipton: see WEST BROMWICH.

†TIVERTON: — Gazette 1858–(1981);
— Times 1869-84 with Western Times of
Exeter; — News 1875-6 as Devon and
Somerset Weekly News 1876–(1981).

TODMORDEN: — Times 1862-9; — Weekly
Advertiser 1862-1934; — and District
News 1869-1934; — Echo 1887-9; —
Herald 1900-12.

Tonbridge: see ROYAL TUNBRIDGE WELLS.

TORBAY: as TORQUAY — and Tor
Directory 1846-52 as * — Directory
1853-1949; * — Chronicle 1849-65;
Wreford's Visitors' Guide 1849; — Times
1869–(1975); — Family Times 1879-80;
— Press 1905-6 (1920); Torbay News and
Dartmouth Gazette 1911-22; — Times
1912–(1975).

    * Torbay PL holds Torbay Directory,
Torbay Chronicle.

TORRINGTON: — Weekly News 1909-11
with Western Express.

†TOTNES: Kingsbridge Gazette and South
Devon Advertiser 1854–(1981); — Times
1869–(1981); Western Guardian 1882-1967
with — Times.

Tottenham: see HARINGEY.

†TOWER HAMLETS: — Mail 1857-58;
Bethnal Green Times 1862-69; — Express
1869-76; Bethnal Green Chronicle 1873-
74 with East London Standard: Bethnal
Green News 1894-95.

†TRURO: Royal Cornwall Gazette 1811–
(1981); West Briton and Cornwall Advertiser 1811–(1975); Cornish Guardian 1834-
35 and 1901–(1981); Cornish Weekly News
1858-77 with Royal Cornwall Gazette;
Cornwall County News 1909-18 with
Royal Cornwall Gazette.

Twickenham: see RICHMOND-ON-
THAMES.

TYNEMOUTH: Northumberland Advertiser
and Agricultural, Shipping and Commercial
Journal 1831-2 as Northumberland Advertiser and North and South Shields Gazette
of Agriculture, Shipping and Commerce
1832-34; Port of Tyne Pilot and Counties
of Durham and Northumberland Courier
1839-44 as The Tyne Pilot 1841-2; North
and South Shields Gazette and Northumberland and Durham Advertiser 1849-63;
North and South Shields Gazette 1855-84;
— Guardian and North and South Shields
Advertiser 1861; — Gazette and Visitors'
Register for Tynemouth, Whitley and
Cullercoats 1870-1; Shields Daily News
1870-1933 as Shields News 1933-7 as
Shields Evening News 1838-59 with
Shields Gazette and Shipping Telegraph;
Shields and — Argus 1881-2; — Sentinel
1895-8 as Borough of — Sentinel 1899-
1900; — Weekly News 1908-9; see also
SOUTH SHIELDS.

†Uttoxeter: — Advertiser 1882–(1981).

†WAKEFIELD: — and Halifax Journal 1828–
33 as — and Dewsbury Journal 1833–4; West
Riding Herald 1835–8 as — Journal 1838–72
as — and West Riding Herald 1872–1913;
— and West Riding Examiner 1849–52 with
— Journal; — Advertiser 1851; — Express
1852–(1981); — Press 1860–1902; —
Guardian 1866–7; Normanton Free Press
1872–6; — Wesleyan Messenger 1872–3; —
Free Press 1880–3; Normanton Guardian
1880–3; — Echo 1882–1906; — Evening
Press 1883–5; — Correspondent 1886;
— Evening Herald 1889–90; — Saturday
Night 1889–91; — Sentinel 1899–1901;
Normanton Echo 1904–20; Normanton
Gazette 1905–7; — Advertiser 1906–25;
The Cycle Car 1912.
　　* Bradford PL holds copies of Bradford
and Wakefield Chronicle (1825–6).
†WALLASEY: — Standard 1886–7 with
Birkenhead Times; * — and Wirral Chronicle
1888–1957; New Brighton and — Times
1894–1900; * — News 1899–(1981); —
Property Register 1911–2; — Observer
1916.
　　* Wallasey CL has originals Wallasey
News from 1899 and incomplete series of
Chronicle.
WALLINGFORD: — Chronicle 1868–70 with
Abingdon Herald; — Times 1888.
WALLSEND: — Herald 1901–9 as — Herald
and Advertiser 1909–13.
WALSALL: — Courier 1853; * — Free Press
1856–1903 with — Observer; — Guardian
1856–69; — Herald 1861–2; * — Observer
1862; * — Advertiser 1862–1915; * — News
1865–72; — Observer 1869–9; — Spectator
1874–5; — Illustrated Journal 1895–1915
(1920); * — Recorder 1906; * — Pioneer
1916–22; * — Times 1925–54.
　　* Walsall CL holds originals as indicated;
the Observer is on MF.
†WALTHAM FOREST: — Abbey and Cheshunt
Weekly Telegraph 1863–(1981) (as Cheshunt
and — Telegraph); Walthamstow and —
Guardian 1870–(1981); — Abbey Times
1893–4.
†WANDSWORTH: — and Battersea District
Times 1870–90 as Battersea News 1905–
(1981); — and Battersea Standard 1871–2; —
Tooting, and Putney Wesleyan Advocate
1872; — and Putney Observer 1887–1904;
— and Battersea Trade Advertiser 1890;
— Gazette 1899–1900; * — Boro' News
1900–(1981); — Newsletter (formerly
Wimbledon Park and Southfields News-
letter). Also: BALHAM AND TOOTING:
— News 1878–(1981); BATTERSEA: — and
Chelsea News 1866–9; — and Wandsworth
Observer 1873–5; — News 1895; — Beacon
1900–1; — Mercury 1901–4; — Chronicle
1903–4; — Borough News 1912–1965 as
Battersea News 1965–(1981).

(Wandsworth — continued) —
　　* Wandsworth BL has Wandsworth
Borough News from 1884 to date.
Wanstead: see REDBRIDGE.
WAREHAM: — Corfe Castle etc. Advertiser
1870; Tribbett's — Advertiser 1880–9; —
and Swanage Guardian 1885; — Guardian
1885.
†WARLEY: *Oldbury Weekly News 1880–1967
as Warley Weekly News with Smethwick
Telephone; *Smethwick Telephone 1884–
(1975) as Warley News Telephone 1967–(1981)
now News Telephone; Handsworth and
Smethwick Free Press 1885–8; Smethwick
Globe 1895 with Midland Sun; Smethwick
Advertiser 1909.
　　* Smethwick CL has MF of Smethwick
Telephone.
†WARRINGTON: *Eyre's Weekly Journal
1756; Butterfly 1827; * — Borough Press
1851–2; * — Guardian 1853–(1981); —
Intelligencer 1853; Independent 1855; —
Standard 1858–62 with — Advertiser; —
Times 1859 with — Standard; — Chronicle
1861; * — Advertiser 1862–89; — Weekly
Mail 1868–9; — Mail 1869; * — Examiner
1869–78 as — and Mid-Cheshire Examiner
1879–1957; Mid-Cheshire Examiner 1870–
78; — Evening Post 1877–80; — Weekly
Post 1880; Earlstown and Newton Examiner
1882–(1920); — Observer 1889–1914; —
— Daily Guardian 1891–1903; Wednesday's
Observer 1893–5; — Times 1902–4; —
Review 1904–21.
　　* Warrington PL, originals and MF as
marked.
† Warminster: — Journal 1881–(1981).
†WARWICK: * — and Warwickshire Advertiser
1806–(1981); * Warwickshire Chronicle
1826-7 and 1867–9 with Royal Leamington
Chronicle; Warwickshire Times 1838;
Warwickshire Antiquarian Magazine 1859–
75; — and Leamington Times 1869–1918
(1920). * Warwick PL.
†WATFORD: — Observer 1863–(1981) with
West Herts. Observer; — Times and Budget
1883–7; — Times 1871; — and West Herts.
Post 1887–1916 as — Post and Echo 1916–
70; — Advertiser 1889–92 with — Times;
— Times 1891–7; — Leader 1893–7; —
News 1899; — Magnet 1902; — News Letter
1907–20; — Herald 1908–12.
Wednesbury: see WEST BROMWICH.
†Wellington: — Weekly News 1860–(1981).
†WELLS: * — Journal 1851–(1981); * —
Guardian 1859–60; Monthly Review 1893.
　　* Wells PL has MF as indicated.
WELSHPOOL: Montgomery County Times and
Shropshire and Mid-Wales Advertiser 1893–
1952 as County Times 1952–69.
Wembley: see BRENT AND HARROW.
WEST BROMWICH: * — Weekly Times 1867–
68; — Reporter 1869; — Wesleyan Record

(West Bromwich — continued) —
1871–3; * Midland Free Press 1875–1933;
* — Weekly News 1878; * — Echo 1879;
* — and Oldbury Chronicle 1896–(1975).
Also: WEDNESBURY: — and West Brom-
wich Advertiser 1869–72 — as Midland
Advertiser 1872–1916 as Midland Adver-
tiser and Wednesbury Herald 1916–24
as Midland Advertiser, Wednesbury Boro'
News and Darlaston Chronicle 1924–66 as
Wednesbury News, Midland Advertiser and
Herald 1966–72 as Wednesbury Borough
News 1972–4 with Midland Chronicle; —
Times 1872; — Examiner 1874–5 with
Midland Examiner; — Free Press 1884–7;
— Watchman 1885; — Leader 1898–1908
(1920); Borough of Wednesbury Herald
1876–1916 with Midlands Advertiser.
TIPTON: — and Great Bridge Times 1889.
   * ! West Bromwich PL has copies indi-
cated, from 1857 onwards. Also holds
Weekly Times (1867) and Echo (1879).
Westcliff: see LEIGH AND SOUTHEND-
ON-SEA.
West Ham: see NEWHAM.
†WESTMINSTER: — Journal 1742–1808; —
Magazine 1773–85; — Journal 1805–10;
Weekly News 1856; — and Pimlico News
1857–(1981); — and Covent Garden
Journal 1861; — News 1863–4; — Times
1863–6; — Gazette 1869–79; — Chronicle
1870–5; — and Chelsea News 1879–85; —
and Lambeth Gazette 1881–91; — Times
1885–96; — Work 1890–4; — Gazette 1893–
1928; Popular 1893–(1920); Westminster
1896–8; — Mail 1900–18 (1920); — Observer
1902–4; Westminster 1902–6; — Express
1904–16 (1920); — Record 1916–39. Also:
PADDINGTON: — News 1859–61; —
Advertiser 1861–6; — Times 1870–1918;
— Kensington and Bayswater Chronicle
1873–1949; — Star 1879–80; — and West
London Mercury 1889–(1981); — Weekly
Register 1893–5 with W Gazette; Weston's
Gazette and — Weekly Register 1895–
1939. ST MARYLEBONE: — Journal 1837;
— Mercury 1857–69 as Borough of —
Mercury 1869–(1981); Kilburn Times with
— Times and St Pancras Gazette 1868–
(1981); — Newspaper 1869–73; — Messenger
1885–6; Independent 1885–6; Borough of —
Times 1885; — Gazette 1894–5; — Star
1904–5; — News 1912–4; — Record and
West London News 1914–71.
†WESTON-SUPER-MARE: — Mercury 1843–
(1981); Westonian 1844–7 as — and Somer-
set Mercury 1847–8; — Gazette 1845–
(1920); Brown's Weston Visitor 1847–8; —
Directory 1858; — Chronicle 1860–1; —
Star 1900.
WEYMOUTH AND MELCOMBE REGIS:
   * Southern Times 1852–1954; — Journal
1854–6; as — Guardian 1866–84 as — and

(Weymouth, etc. — continued) —
Dorset Post 1884–6 as Dorset County Post
1886–8 as Southern Star 1888–93 with
Telegram; — Portland and Dorchester
Telegram 1866–1904 as Dorchester Mail
1904–32; Dorset Leader 1867; Yeomanry
and Visitors' Guide 1890–2; — Directory
1892–1914; — and Portland Standard
1906–27.
   * Weymouth PL; see *Dorset Newspapers*
(Weymouth CL 1972) which lists holdings in
Dorset libraries, County Museum, Poole CL
and Weymouth CL. This is valuable for all
Dorset towns.
†Whitby: — Gazette 1854–(1981).
†WHITEHAVEN: — Herald 1831–78 with
West Cumberland Guardian; — News 1852–
(1981); — Messenger 1855–9 as — Times
1859–67; — Budget 1872. — Guardian
1875–8 with West Cumberland Guardian;
West Cumberland Guardian 1878–80 with
— Free Press; — Free Press 1879–1918
(1920).
WHITLEY BAY: — Express and Coast Adver-
tiser 1908; — Seaside Chronicle 1910–57.
†Whitstable: — Times 1864–(1981).
†WIDNES; Runcorn Observer 1860–8 with
Runcorn Guardian; Runcorn and —
Guardian 1862–(1981); Runcorn and —
Examiner 1870–6 as — Examiner 1876–
(1975); — Guardian 1876–1956; — Weekly
News 1878–(1981); Runcorn Chronicle
1902–3 as — and Runcorn Chronicle 1903–
18 (1920); Runcorn Leader 1905.
†WIGAN: — Gazette 1836–42; — Times 1849–
53; *Observer 1853–(1981); * — Examiner
1853–1961; Monthly Advertiser 1854; —
Monthly News 1854; — Sunday School
Magazine 1860–2; — Courier 1866–7 with
— Examiner; — Times 1892; — Catholic
Herald 1894–1934.
Willenhall: see WOLVERHAMPTON.
Wimbledon: see MERTON.
†WINCHESTER: Hampshire Chronicle and
Courier 1816–(1981); — Hampshire and
West of England Magazine 1828; Hampshire
Mirror 1846; — Observer 1855; — Standard
1864–5; Hampshire County Chronicle 1867–
74; — Herald 1870–3 as Hampshire Herald
1873–9; — Observer 1877–86 as Hampshire
Observer 1886–1957; — Review 1880.
See Lewis, R., and J., *Publishing & Printing
in Winchester 1830–1880* (1980).
†WINDSOR: — and Eton Press 1816–(1981);
— and Eton Journal 1839–41 with Bucks.
Herald of Aylesbury; Royal Standard
1861–4 as Berkshire Standard 1864–5;
— and Eton News 1866–7; — and Eton
Herald 1868–74; — Advertiser 1871–2;
— Gazette 1874–95 as — Chronicle 1895–
1906; Royal Press 1874–6; — Chronicle
1910–39.
†Winsford: — Guardian 1877–(1981).

†WISBECH: — Gazette 1838; — Advertiser
1846–86 as Isle of Ely and — Advertiser
1877–1962; Godard's — Albion
and Railway Advertiser 1850; —
Journal 1854; — Chronicle 1858-90; East
Anglian News 1859-60; — Mirror 1869;
Constitutional Gazette 1873-1943;
— Daily Telegraph 1877; South Lincs.
Mirror 1877; — Telegraph 1880-4; — Mart
Advertiser 1888-(1920); — Standard 1888-
(1981); North Cambs. News and North
Cambs. Echo (formerly — Chronicle)
1890-1903.

†Witney: — Gazette 1882-(1981).

†Woking: — News and Mail 1894-(1981).

†WOKINGHAM: — Record 1891; — and
Bracknell Free Press 1903-4 with Berkshire
Chronicle; — and Bracknell Gazette 1903-5
as East Berkshire and Berkshire Gazette
1906-27 as — Gazette 1927-30 as — Times
1930-(1981); — Chronicle 1912-39.

†WOLVERHAMPTON: — Chronicle 1789-93;
* — Courier 1818; — Chronicle 1829-1900;
* — Political Magazine 1831; — Eagle and
Stafford Courier 1848-9; — Herald 1851-59
with — Journal; — Municipal Guardian 1852;
— Journal 1853-72; Spirit of the Times
1859-68 as — Advertiser 1868-9; Midland
Counties Saturday Express 1861-6; Midland
Mercury 1866; *Midland Counties Express
1867-1930 as Midland Counties Express and
— Chronicle 1931-47 as — Chronicle and
Midland Counties Express 1947-(1981);
Monthly Messenger 1872; — Daily News
1874-5; — Times 1874-9; Weekly News
1874-5; Midland Counties Evening Express
1874-84 as — Evening Express and Star
1884-9 as Express and Star 1889-(1981);
Midland Examiner and — Times 1877-9;
Daily Midland Echo 1877-9; Lantern 1879;
*Evening Star 1880-4 with Evening Express;
Staffordshire Herald 1882; Magpie 1882-7;
*Midland Evening News 1884-(1920); Mid-
land Weekly News 1884-1915; Midland
Wednesday News 1884-1908; Metcalfe's
Musical Express 1885-90; * — Comet
1893-6; — Journal 1902-9. Also: BILSTON:
— Herald 1871 as Midland Weekly Herald
1904-6; — Mercury 1875-7 with — Herald;
— Observer 1887-93. DARLASTON:
— Weekly Times 1882-7 with Midland
Weekly Herald. WILLENHALL: — Magazine
1863; — Reporter 1885 with Midland
Weekly Herald.
    * Wolverhampton Central RL has
originals as indicated, with Express and
Star (1894-1932) on MF. Wolverhampton
Polytechnic has MF Spirit of the Times
(1859-68). Dudley BL has MF Wolver-
hampton Chronicle (1830-66). See also
Hardcastle, J. B.: *History of the Wolver-
hampton Chronicle* (1893).

Woodbridge: — Reporter 1859-(1981);

Woodford: see REDBRIDGE.

Wood Green: see HARINGEY.

Woolwich: see GREENWICH.

WOODSTOCK: — and Charlbury Messenger
(a religious magazine) 1875-6.

†WORCESTER: * — Post Man 1690-1712-3;
as — Post or Western Journal, 1722-5;
*Weekly — Journal 1725-48; as — Journal
1748-53; as * Berrow's — Journal 1753-
(1981); * — Herald 1794-1930; Worcester-
shire Miscellany 1829-31; * Worcestershire
Guardian 1834-46; *Worcestershire
Chronicle 1838-1930; — and Malvern
Record 1857-8; *Worcestershire Advertiser 1865-1937; — News 1861-9 with
— Advertiser; — Evening Post 1877-83 as
Worcestershire Echo 1883-1930; — Daily
Times 1880-(1975); *Worcestershire Echo
1883-1929; Worcestershire Sauce 1887-9;
— Stock and Share List 1893-5; Worcestershire Standard 1897-1928; — Malvern and
District Weekly 1907-9 as — City Post 1909.
    *Worcester RL has some originals
Worcester Herald (1794–1927); MF Journal
from 1742 and MF other papers, as indi-
cated. Berrow's Worcester Journal at
publishers' offices, Worcester.

WORKINGTON: — Times 1857-8 with —
News: — Gazette 1857-8; — Reporter
1865-7; Solway Pilot 1870 as — Free Press
1870-93; — Standard 1881-2; — News
1883-1918 (1920); — Weekly Mail 1886-7;
— Observer 1887-8; — Advertiser 1881-99;
— Star 1888-1967; — Guardian 1891-9; —
Sun 1901-2.

†WORKSOP: — Advertiser 1873-4; as —
Bassetlaw and County Express 1874; * —
Guardian 1896-(1981); — Standard 1908.
    * Worksop PL, complete series of
Guardian from 1899, MF.

†WORTHING: — Monthly Record 1853-5;
— Express 1863-1902; — Visitors' List
1867-9; — Intelligencer 1867-1901; —
Arrival List 1869; Sussex Coast Mercury
1870-1903 as — Mercury 1903-19 (1920);
— Gazette 1889-(1981); — Times 1900-1;
— Observer 1901-16 (1920); Western
Gazette 1911 as — Advertiser 1911-2 as
County Gazette 1912-4.

WREXHAM: Y Wenynen 1836; Y Hyfforddwr
1852-3; * — Weekly Advertiser 1854-
1958; Wrexhamite 1855-6 as — Telegraph
1857-63 as Denbigh and Flintshire Telegraph 1863-7; — Monthly Herald 1858-61;
Y Eisteddfod 1864-65; Cerddor Cymreic
1868-76; * — Guardian 1869-79 as North
Wales Guardian 1879-1925. Illustrated —
Argus 1884-1916 (1920); Yr Ymwellydd
Misol (1903-1920); — Journal 1913-17
(1920); * — Leader 1920.
    * Wrexham PL has originals as
indicated.

Yardley: see BIRMINGHAM.

Yarmouth (I.o.W.): Freshwater, Totland
and — Advertiser 1904-15 (1920).
†YEOVIL: Western Gazette 1736-(1981);
*Sherborne Mercury 1740-1867; — Times
1847-71 with Flying Post of Sherborne;
Pulman's Weekly News 1857-(1981);
Kingdon's Sherborne News 1858-62; —
Telegram 1861-5; Western Chronicle
1886-1931; — Magazine 1900; — Leader
1904-24.
†YORK: — Mercury 1719-24; — Journal 1724-
25; Protestant York Courant 1749; *York-
shire Post 1754-(1981); *Chronicle 1772;
Yorkshire Freeholder 1780; Yorkshire
Magazine 1786; * — Courant 1798-1848
with — Herald; * — Herald 1790-1889;
—'Chronicle 1817-40; Yorkshire Observer
1822-3; *Yorkshire Gazette 1823-(1981);
— Electors' Guide 1826; Yorkshireman
1834-58 with — Herald; — Times 1847-71
with Western Flying Post; Fairburn's —
Monthly Advertiser 1849; Farmer's Friend
and Freeman's Journal 1850-5 with — Free
Press; — and Northern Express 1851; —

(York — continued) —
News and Advertiser 1853-(1981); Yorkshire Advertiser 1859-69; — News 1867;
Yorkshire Express 1868-70; Yorkshire News
1868; Yorkshire Telegraph 1869-76 with
— Herald; Yorkshire Evening Press 1882-
(1981); Yorkshire Daily Chronicle 1888-93;
*Yorkshire Chronicle 1869-1914; — Comet
1893-4; — Sentinel 1894-8; — Monthly
1894; Yorkshire Weekly Herald 1902-16;
— Daily Labour News 1906; — Star
1910-58.
    * ! Bradford PL has York Herald (1790-
1853) and other York shire editions. Darlington PL has Chronicle and General Advertiser
(1778); Courant (1811); Herald and General
Advertiser (1816-20); Yorkshire Gazette
(1825); Yorkshire Post (1906). See also
Gibb, M. A., and Beckwith, F., *The Yorkshire Post: Two Centuries* (1954); Read, D.,
'North of England Newspapers and their
value to historians (c. 1700-1900)' (*Leeds
Philosophical and Literary Society Proceedings*, vol. 8, 1900).

CHAPTER ELEVEN

THE NATIONAL CENSUSES 1801-1901

THE WORD 'CENSUS', from the Latin *censeo* — 'I estimate', originated in the Roman citizen's obligation to declare to two *censors* the names and ages of himself and his wife, together with the number of their children and slaves. In due course the censors also demanded a statement of the citizen's debts and the names of his creditors. Government's intention to number its people and investigate their private lives stems from the State's insatiable need of soldiers and revenue; it is as old as government itself. There are several Biblical references (Numbers 1: 1-3; 3: 42-47; and II Samuel 24: 1-17; Luke 2: 1) to Hebrew and Roman censuses. Several more recent documents of English local history were censuses of a sort. Domesday (Chapter Three) is an early example of an almost nationwide government survey, though it deals primarily with land tenure and in some counties numbers cattle as well as people. Lay Subsidy Rolls, ratebooks, poll books, burgess lists and school registers also preserve partial forms of enrolment. Most of these early returns, however, set out to record a special class of people — manorial tenants, taxpayers, voters, pupils or some other section of a community. We are misled if we assume that we have studied an entire population from a single available record when hundreds have gone unrecorded because they did not qualify for inclusion. From medieval times more comprehensive rolls and registers of population are found among the ecclesiastical archives; a late example is the Register of the See of Canterbury, taken in 1676. Throughout the 18th century, there were many local surveys which might properly be described as small scale censuses. More than 130 such records are known, mostly in urban areas, though few of the originals survive.[1] Enrolments of ratepayers and householders are recorded at Cambridge in 1728, and for many other towns; some of these are listed in this Chapter's Gazetteer.

In an earlier Chapter (pages 131-165), we saw how many an 18th-century mapmaker, like Westley in Birmingham in 1731, would tabulate the numbers of houses and inhabitants, street by street, as a useful guide to his map. Of our sample towns, Dudley was not systematically recorded before 1801, though its population was estimated as 5,000 in 1750 and 8,000 in 1775. Birmingham in 1750 returned a roll of 23,688; by 1770 this had increased to 30,804. The City of Worcester listed only 1,100 of its residents in 1770 with an estimated population of ten times that number. Early directories (Chapter Nine) also include population statistics for each town listed, but these are more usually the findings of a decennial census after 1801.

In 1750 these estimates listed 20 towns of 10-50,000 inhabitants. London alone accounted for half the English urban population and 30 other towns varied in size from 5-10,000 inhabitants. In 1775 town dwellers numbered 25% of the nation and by 1801 the proportion had risen to more than one-third. The overcrowded state of most towns was notorious, giving rise to sensational predictions by Malthus, who envisaged only the social dangers of unceasing increase. As yet however, these observations were no more than informed guesswork. As late as 1822, when three national census returns had been tabulated, men like the writer William Cobbett could confidently assert that 'all observation and reason is against the fact' (of population increase). He did not believe the census returns: 'As to the Parliamentary returns, what need we say more than this: they assert that the population of Great Britain has increased from ten to fourteen million in the last twenty years. That is enough! A man that can suck that in will believe, literally believe, that the moon is made of green cheese'.

Other nations were ahead of Britain in census-taking. Quebec claims the earliest census on a national scale, in 1665. Sweden was enrolled in 1749 and the United States in 1790. A five-yearly census of Great Britain, proposed in 1753, was violently rejected by Parliament, who saw the proposal as an intrusion leading to undesirably effective and increased taxation. There was angry talk of horseponds and horsewhips. By 1800, however, the threat of renewed Napoleonic war was seized by Pitt as inescapable justification for new measures. The gloomy predictions of Malthus, an abortive French invasion of Fishguard and a disastrous crop failure all added to the sense of national emergency (which invariably extends the power of government irreversibly). The results were the Census Act of 1800 and, in the same year, the organization of the Ordnance Survey. Income tax, at 2s. in the £, was already established in 1799; like the census, it had come to stay.

The first British census then took place in 1801 and has continued as a regular decennial event down to 1981, with the sole omission of 1941, and the first quinquennial census took place in 1966. The first four censuses, from 1801 to 1831, set out only to take an overall total of householders, classified by sex with broad categories of occupation, but taking no names. A facsimile of the first enumeration form is shown below (page 274). This simple numerical total made further verification or cross-checking virtually impossible. All the statistical information from these and later censuses down to 1981 became the basis of statistical *Abstracts* and regular *Parliamentary Reports* which are available as printed volumes in the larger reference libraries. An invaluable guide to the whole corpus of post-census publication was given in an out-of-print Stationery Office pamphlet (*70/561/2*) which may be found in the larger libraries but is otherwise elusive. This is L. M. Feery's *Guide to the Official Sources No. 2: Census Reports of Great Britain 1801–1931* which was published for the Interdepartmental Committee on Social and Economic Research and makes useful observations on the relative accuracy of the various returns. More recently published by the Stationery Office, and still available, is the *Guide to Census Reports, Great Britain 1801–1966* (H.M.S.O. 1977), which is 'a detailed guide to the social and demographic information in the abstracts and tables'. This refers to relevant tables and sections of the reports but does not reprint them.

Abstracts of population are of incomparable value to the social historian for the measurement of any town's growth during the 19th century and for comparing the progress of one town or region with another. Fortunately, in many counties this information is more readily accessible than by reference to official abstracts. The tables of population are published in most *Victoria County Histories* and are reproduced in the Gazetteer to this Chapter. They tabulate census totals parish by parish

FORM OF ANSWERS BY THE OVERSEERS, &c. IN ENGLAND,

To the Questions contained in the Schedule to an Act, intituled, *An Act for taking an Account of the Population of Great Britain, and of the Increase or Diminution thereof.*

County, &c.	Hundred, &c.	City, Town, &c.	Parish, &c.	QUESTION 1 HOUSES — Inhabited	QUESTION 1 HOUSES — By how many Families occupied	QUESTION 1 HOUSES — Uninhabited	QUESTION 2 PERSONS, including Children of whatever Age — Males	QUESTION 2 — Females	Total of PERSONS in Answer to Question 2	QUESTION 3 OCCUPATIONS — Persons chiefly employed in Agriculture	QUESTION 3 — Persons chiefly employed in Trade, Manufactures or Handicraft	QUESTION 3 — All other Persons not comprised in the Two preceding Classes	TOTAL of PERSONS. N.B. This Column must correspond with the Total of Persons in Answer to Question 2

N.B.—*If any Family occupies Two or more Houses in different Parishes, Townships, or Places, the Individuals belonging to such Family are to be numbered only in those Parishes, Townships, or Places where they severally happen to be at the Time of taking the Account.*

REMARKS, in Explanation of the Matters stated in Answer to the preceding Questions.

1st Question.
2nd Question.
3rd Question.

ATTESTATION on Oath (*or* Affirmation) by the OVERSEERS or substantial Householders in ENGLAND

I, *A.B.* One of the Overseers (*or* a substantial Householder) of the Parish, Township, &c. of   in the County of   do swear (*or* affirm), That the above Return contains, to the best of my Knowledge and Belief, a full and true Answer to the Questions contained in the Schedule to an Act, intituled, *An Act for taking an Account of the Population of Great Britain, and of the Increase or Diminution thereof.*

The above-mentioned *A.B.* was sworn (*or* affirmed) before us the Justices of the Peace in and for the   of   this   Day of

C.D. and E.F.

The 'Form of Answers' for the first national census in 1801, from 41 Geo. III c. 15, 'An Act for taking an account of the population of Great Britain, etc' reproduced by permission of Birmingham Reference Library, Social Science Department. Actual size 8x11 inches.

from 1801 to 1901. Some *County Histories* more recently published extend the
series further, as in the case of Kent (to 1921), Cheshire and Wiltshire (both to 1951)
and Leicestershire (to 1971).

In attempting to make any sort of comparison from these tables it is vital to
recognize their essential basis of the 'ancient parish'. The first censuses were taken by
means of the local machinery of the Poor Law, as a house-to-house enquiry carried
out by each parish's Overseers and supplemented by information provided by the
incumbent from the parish registers. The resulting tables of baptisms, burials and
marriages from 1700–1800 returned by the clergy were separately entered with the
Abstracts. The overseers' tallies were sent to the justices of the peace and passed to
the Clerks of the House of Commons by the clerks of the peace and town clerks. In
tabulating the first 11 censuses the earlier *Victoria County Histories* take as a base-line
the county and its parishes as they stood in 1841. This can lead the unwary into some
confusion, as the boundaries of individual towns and parishes change from decade
to decade. Fortunately, the tables are annotated to indicate those parts of any parish
which lay in different hundreds or even in a separate county, as is the case in Burton-
on-Trent (Staffordshire and Derbyshire) and Rochdale (part in Lancashire, part in
Yorkshire). In these cases different parts of the parish will appear in two *County
Histories*, if both are published.

Even more likely to be mislaid are those towns, some of which are now very
substantial places, which were not at first entered under their modern name as
'township', 'hamlet' or 'chapelry', but are concealed within a less familiar parish. This
is particularly the case for many Lancashire towns. These must be traced to their
parishes with the help of a county record office's index. For example: 'Bacup was in
the township of Newchurch in Rossendale in the ancient parish of Whalley; Burnley
township and Nelson were also in Whalley; Heywood was in Bury, Mossley in Ashton-
under-Lyne, Swinton-with-Pendlebury in Eccles, Southport in North Meols, Morecambe in the township of Poulton-le-Sands and the parish of Lancaster. St Helens was
in the township of Windle and the parish of Prescot and Rawtenstall was in the parish
of Whalley'.[2]

Confusion is worse confounded in the study of a large city if we are unable to make
a firm enough definition of the town 'then' or 'now' or, even less firmly, 'the present
town as it was then'. This may involve a complex process, either of dismantling a
present-day metropolis into its earlier component parishes, perhaps with sole attention
to the 'township', or as it is frequently described the 'chapelry' or, conversely, putting
together the mosaic of earlier dependent parishes to make up the modern conglome-
rate. Middlesex and Surrey are peculiar examples of counties once containing scores
of parishes which need careful identification if we are to build up the present-day
London boroughs which they enlarged. This the Gazetteer attempts to do. *Victoria
County History* tables can be helpful in revealing the *potential* size of a modern city
as it was in 1841, with its future suburbs grouped around the township.

Manchester City, as tabulated in the *Victoria County History for Lancashire* (pages
343–4 and 349) is an eminent example of the problems of determining the total population of any city. In 1841 Manchester parish was divided between Salford Hundred,
Manchester Town and Salford Township — the last to be added to Manchester City's
total at our peril! In the first two divisions were listed 30 townships, hamlets and
chapelries. Of these, some such as Blackley, Didsbury, Gorton, Moss Side, Openshaw,

Harpurhey and Manchester Township can properly be considered as part of the present city. Twelve others, for example Broughton, Denton, Droylsden and Failsworth, are still separate from the city, though within Greater Manchester County. The local historian is probably well advised to play safe and refer only to the original 'Manchester Township' in making comparisons from such a table, though this will tend to minimise the growth of the town. Happy is the searcher who deals with a borough which never changed its boundaries. Otherwise, as Professor Beresford warns us: 'to ignore boundary changes of this kind, would, of course, bedevil the evidence'.[3] Yet, the difficulties, often the impossibility, of comparing like with like at different decades should not be underestimated.

The most recently published *Victoria County Histories* such as Cheshire, and more particularly Leicestershire, set out to unravel these problems for the searcher by arranging their population tables from decade to decade so as to show successive changes in each place. As a town grows or is amalgamated, from ancient parish to urban district, to municipal borough and county borough, each is given a new line of entry, instead of endeavouring to maintain a common base-line. This untangles the knots of concealed and combined identities, but also reveals the full complexity of some towns' growth. Many topographical problems are unwittingly concealed by the earlier format, particularly in counties where the multiple identity of parishes and townships is unfamiliar to the reader. The H.M.S.O. *Guide to Census Reports* already mentioned (page 273) gives a useful table (pages 270-1 of the *Guide*), which shows the principal areas recognized by successive censuses. These include: ancient counties, 1801-1901; wapentakes, hundreds and ancient parishes, 1801-1881; boroughs, 1801-41; tithings, chapelries, townships and hamlets, 1801-61; registration districts and sub-districts, 1841-1966; municipal boroughs, 1851-1916; county boroughs, 1861-1966; metropolitan boroughs, 1881-1966; urban districts, 1881-1966; civil parishes, 1871-1961; conurbations, from 1961; and 'New Towns', from 1951.

The first census volume (for 1801) simply tabulates 'town, township, parish, or village'. In 1811 the census abstracts carefully identified 'boroughs' and this distinction was preserved until 1841, when the difference between 'parish' and 'borough' was irrevocably confused. The most recent censuses of 1971 and 1981 have published their reports in separate volumes for the reorganized counties, the 1971 reports giving the counties twice, before and after reorganisation. Reliable maps, particularly those prepared for 19th-century Boundary Commissioners, or an index to parishes, are essential aids for the searching-out of an unfamiliar town, especially in the case of the labyrinth of reorganized London boroughs and the more recent metropolitan districts 'then and now'.

A town's population will grow or decline for various reasons. Genuine increases, within the same geographic boundary, must be due either to additional surviving births as a result of increased fertility, beneficent food conditions, shelter, hygiene and improved natal care, or to longer survival at all ages. A diminishing death-rate, as a result of better conditions, will give the same net effect. Immigration of newcomers into the same area may produce an increase, accompanied by additional housing newly built within the town's boundaries or by overcrowding of existing accommodation. Conversely, a genuine decline in population will be traced to fewer births, more deaths or emigration. Sometimes the two trends of life-span and migration will work contrarily, one masking the other, so that it is not unusual to find a town's population increasing as the number of births falls, because of continuing immigration of adults. Similarly the population may continue to increase after the *rate* of increase in births begins to fall.

Birmingham's population changes have been closely analysed by reference beyond the census to the *Annual Reports of the Registrar General on Births, Deaths and Marriages*.[4] The population's steady increase from 1851 to 1861 and its decline during the next decade is matched with an intricate balancing of natural increase in births with migration to and from the city. We see the *rate* of natural increase falling as actual *numbers* of births increase, with migration as the final, decisive influence on the nett total of inhabitants. Immigration increases the population of Birmingham from 1851 to 1861, and emigration diminishes it from 1881 to 1891. Death rate and 'crude mortality rate' tended to improve, though infant mortality was erratic, reaching a peak of 183 per 1,000 in 1865–9. The 'crude fertility rate' continually declined but desertion of the central areas of the city was due to other social factors. As housing was demolished to make room for railway development, movement outward was encouraged by the 'pull' of employment in new factories and housing on new estates in the outer areas of Aston and later, Northfield.[5]

A totally different type of population change is the result of boundary extension by local government reorganization of one sort or another, so that people on the outskirts of the original town are included in its nominal population. Thus Dudley appears to have increased its population 32-fold since 1901, not from natural increase in Dudley itself, which is declining, but by encroachment upon surrounding areas, which were part of southwest Staffordshire before 1967, or independent Worcestershire boroughs, Halesowen and Stourbridge, before 1974.

Before the most recent boundary changes town plans grew larger as boroughs extended their suburbs and 'dedicated streets' into neighbouring parishes throughout the 18th and 19th centuries. As a result, the population of the outer fringes will be seen to grow at a more rapid rate than the inner cities, to the logical present-day conclusion of actual decline, if not decay, in the central areas as a result of demolition of the hearts of the towns to clear slums, build office blocks, extend shopping precincts or lay down 'ringways'. Such destruction of accommodation, combined with the pull of suburban housing estates, lightweight factory development and more available commuter traffic makes the 'town centre' a silent Sunday desert. We have see this sort of 'improvement' beginning in central Birmingham with the Improvement Acts of 1769 to 1791 (between pages 185–186).

The graph (over page) shows the comparative rate of growth of our three Midland towns. The population of Dudley at last exceeds that of the ancient City of Worcester in 1841, but makes its most dramatic expansion in the 20th century. The last columns of the Gazetteer indicate the difference between the new geography of many reorganized towns between 1961 and 1981, as well as the more natural increase, or decline, of some of them. It is almost impossible to compare the growth of Birmingham after 1821 with the other two Midland towns; its population barely fits any manageable graph. Only after the reorganization of 1974 does Dudley become remotely comparable, as a smaller metropolitan district of the new West Midlands county.

There are many interesting ways in which some towns' populations were enhanced or depleted at successive census years, which have been noted by the compilers of the

| | 1801 | 1831 | 1861 | 1891 | -- | 1961 | 1971-4 |
| DUDLEY | | | | | | | |

| | 1801 | 1831 | 1861 | 1891 | -- | 1961 | 1971-4 |
| WORCESTER | | | | | | | |

| | 1801 | 1831 | 1861 | 1891 | -- | 1961 | 1971-4 |
| BIRMINGHAM | | | | | | | |

Key : 10,000 People.

100,000 People.

Population growth during the 19th and 20th centuries in three cities.

Abstracts from the 'Remarks in Explanation of the Matters Stated' by the enumerators. The population of Woolwich, for instance, was augmented in 1841 by 1,165 convicts caged in hulks on the river, as was also that of Portsea in 1811 and 1821. At Blackburn, an increase of nearly 7,000 between 1811 and 1821 was partly attributed to the successful innovation of vaccination. We see the extension of Monks Coppenhall into the vast railway centre of Crewe, with its population increase from 203 (1841) to 17,810 in 1871. The decline of the silk trade in Macclesfield is indicated by a fall of population in 1861; in the same year, Hyde's cotton mills caused an expansion. Fluctuations in Durham's numbers invariably reflect expansion or contractions of the coal industry. Meanwhile at Sale, Bebington and other villages on Wirral and in Cheshire, commuters' villas mushroomed during the second half of the 19th century, to house merchants, clerks and warehousemen, who could now travel into Liverpool and Manchester by train.

The building of a workhouse, a military barracks, a hospital, a prison, or even a large boarding-school, can produce increased numbers. From 1841 the encampment of gangs of railway navvies, several hundred strong, their families billetted on the outskirts of town, is a commonplace reason for an increase. Conversely, tragic losses from cholera and typhus are often well-marked, as in Dudley during the 1830s, 1850s and 1870s. Throughout the 'Hungry Forties and Fifties', and indeed for the rest of the 19th century, emigration to the United States, Canada and Australia would be a constant cause of depletion. Yet agricultural depression at home, or the failure of rustic cloth-mills and cottage industries were as likely to swell the numbers of people living in towns, with country-born domestic servants, or soldiers in barracks. Census returns, particularly after 1851, when the place of origin of every member of each household is recorded, are primary sources for the study of population mobility, whether it be caused by the immigration of Welsh miners, Irish navvies or house servants from rural Shropshire. Some *Victoria County Histories* list all the explanatory notes of special circumstances affecting population in the county from decade to decade; Wiltshire is an excellent example of this.

The original schedules compiled by the local investigators are no longer available for the rudimentary censuses of 1801 to 1831. These were officially destroyed in 1904, but a few 'strays' escaped destruction as drafts or copies never sent on by the enumerator; some of them have found their way into local archives. These are carefully recorded by J. S. W. Gibson in his *Directory of Local Holdings* where we find references to the survival of originals from 1801 at Bromley, Leeds, Hampstead and Guildford, a few from 1821-31 at Walthamstow, Poplar and Leyton and at Tenterden for 1831.[6] With the census of 1841 the records take on a new dimension when not only are the final results of the enumeration available as *Abstracts*, but the original drafts of the schedules also survive. These reflect a more sophisticated form of enquiry and a more thoroughly organized machinery for the collection of data than is produced in the *Abstracts* of 1801-31 or the *Victoria County History* population tables.

Whig legislation after the reform of Parliament in 1832 brought about far-reaching improvements. A new Poor Law Amendment Act established local Poor Law Unions in 1834, and the General Registry Act of 1836 introduced compulsory civil registration of births and deaths. This created an army of registrars to supervise registration districts, which usually corresponded with the area of the Poor Law Unions. The Municipal Corporations Act of 1835 set up an urban machinery for the supervision of public health and welfare; the new town wards were usually equated with the registration sub-districts; bureaucracy was finding its feet and taking confident steps towards a more exact routine for enquiry. A new set of enumeration forms survive *en masse* and change very little from 1851 to the end of the century, providing a basis for enquiry into the social conditions of Victorian towns and domestic lives of the people.

A significant feature of the 1841 Census which, though well-known, goes singularly unremarked, is that in that year, for the first time, census forms were distributed to houses for the individual householder to complete and return to the visiting enumerator on the due date. It is some small measure of the nation's general standards of literacy that as many as 35,000 local enumerators of no special professional or clerical status, could be found to interpret and write up so many complex forms and carry out the task. By and large, with some unfortunate lapses by less able enumerators, the returns are legibly written, at best in impeccable copperplate, reasonably well-spelt by modern standards, and revealing a considerable amount of general, social and geographical knowledge. It is always interesting to check the name of the enumerator entered at the beginning of his return, and, if possible, discover him and his family living in their own street, and learn his occupation. The commercial directories further identify a sufficiency of well-educated professional men and shopkeepers who were used to book-keeping, who could be called upon for enumeration duties in Dudley in 1851.

Much more striking is the fact that in 1841, 30 years before compulsory elementary education was introduced, the majority of the population could be expected (albeit with the enumerator's help, and, at the last resort, his completion of the form) to read, understand and complete so complicated a questionnaire. According to the introduction to the printed Report on the 1841 Census 'the Householders' Schedules contributed in no small degree to the accuracy of the returns . . . '. It is impossible to discover what happened to the original forms, which were presumably destroyed by the enumerators on completion of their Schedules or sent on with the enumeration books. The Public Record Office offers no information on them but it would be surprising if, like the original enumerators' returns of 1801, no 'strays' have survived in local archives. These would be a rich fund of insight into the literacy, attitudes, comprehension and co-operative efforts of any ordinary Victorian street. Most historians assume too readily that the poorer householders surrendered their forms *en masse* and unanswered, for the better educated enumerator to complete. Either the Government could assume that most forms delivered to householders would be completed by them, or it had knowingly set the local enumerator an impossible one-day task.

Unusual insight is given into the experiences of a Hertfordshire enumerator in 1871 as he set off, 'a leathern bag slung across the left shoulder, an ominous-looking blue book in the left hand, which was also filled with suspicious-looking papers, and a lead pencil in the right hand . . . '. This was uncovered through the kind offices of Mr. Jeremy Gibson, referring me to the *Family History News and Digest* (Spring 1982) which in its turn offers the reference to the local magazine *Hertfordshire People* (No. 13). Here we find a facsimile reprint from the *Herts Advertiser and St Albans Times* (27 May 1871) of 'The Experiences of an Enumerator', who comments on 'the difficulty with which many persons were made to understand the object of the work and the nature of the information required; they roundly abused the government for resorting to such means to obtain information as to what income-tax they ought to pay!' Many enumerators came to regret undertaking the task; one volunteer was terrified by his contact with 'a female nursing a child with a well-developed form of small-pox'. The writer comments on the misspelling of some of the names 'which were very ludicrous and puzzling' and quotes many extensive answers given, such as '. . . better known as Cast-Iron Jack; lodger; unmarried, N.B. not my fault; iron-monger's assistant and a good hand at mixing tacks; born at —: mother says that I am a Luny but I don't think I am . . .'. Jack died within the fortnight. Some gave incomplete information. One couple recorded their ages, 50 and 51 as 500 and 501; the youngest member of the family was often entered simply as 'baby', occasionally 'unmarried'. Sometimes the 'afflictions column', intended for the deaf-and-dumb, blind or mentally ill, was filled with minor ailments, or the fortunate statement 'all healthy'. One old lady offered her occupation as 'inability' explaining at length that she was dependent upon parish relief. Allowing for heavy Victorian humour and an anecdotal approach, it is still evident that the enumerator expected most house-holders to offer their information to him *in writing*, that there was a tendency for them to write too much rather than too little, and that totally illegible returns are not typical even of 'deprived' areas.

The 1841 returns are also mistakenly underrated as being less comprehensive than later versions of the census; streets were named but houses were rarely numbered, though a separate count was made of houses 'inhabited', 'uninhabited' and 'building'. Names were now entered, by surname, one forename and other initials. The sexes were separated in columns for the entry of their ages, which were rounded off to the nearest five years. Houses were separated by a fairly distinct individual entry, with the street name repeated house by house. Nevertheless, families tend to run on without adequate spacing, so that it is sometimes difficult to recognize the enumerator's intention as to multiple occupancy.

The printed report on the 1841 census gives a breakdown of all the occupations of each county, each with a sample selection of figures from two or three main towns. In Worcestershire, these are Dudley, Worcester and Kidderminster; in Warwickshire, Birmingham is separately analysed. The places of birth of the inhabitants of each county are also tabulated. From now on the bulk of the analytical tables will begin to outnumber the basic enumeration of the counties.

The enumerators' local schedules now record descriptions of occupations; abbre-viations such as CM for coal-miner (or chain-maker?) and SM for stone miner are usual and can cause conjecture. It is difficult to say in 1841 whether a particular enumerator is interpreting his brief as being to record 'employment of head of household', 'all employed males' or 'all employed men and women'. In Dudley in 1841, the number of women recorded as employed is suspiciously low if we anticipate the accepted generalization about Victorian enslavement of women and children. In 1841 Eliza Robinson aged 15, Mary Braznall (40), another of the same name aged 15 and 'Jasey' Jones (15) are the only females in downtown Fisher Street who are employed in industry; they are all nailers. This apparent female underemployment continues in later Dudley censuses. We find the occasional shoebinder (Eliza Richard, 24) but nail-bag weaving is the main industrial occupation of Dudley women in the latter half of the century. Most women are described as washerwomen, mangle-women, publicans, shopkeepers, dressmakers, governesses and, amongst the youngest, 'general house servants' aged from 11 to 16. In Fisher Street in 1851, we find an aged pedlar — Amelia Thomas aged 72 — and a hawker, Elizabeth Price aged 46. On the outskirts of the town at Quarry Bank, we see a fortune-teller, 'Broseley Moll', a gypsy woman aged 50, living with a scissors-grinder known as 'Broseley Will'. They had three daughters aged 10 to 15 but alleged that their names were 'not known'. Children are rarely given as employed, particularly in 1841, so that one begins to wonder whether considerations of income tax did not lead to concealment of family income, or whether families preferred to pretend that wife and children were not compelled to work by need. Occupation is certainly not as clearly stated in 1841 as it was to be in 1851 and later returns. A wry observation of Victorian morality is seen in the fact that many women had no objection to describing themselves frankly as 'prostitutes' — it was the chauvinism of the enumerator which compelled him to translate this in most cases as 'woman of independent means'.

A greater failing of the 1841 schedule is that relationships within the household are not stated, whereas from 1851 all occupants are associated in a special column as 'Related to the Head of the Family'. Then the association is extended as far as Lodger or Visitor, as well as Servant or Apprentice. In 1841 the relationships from house to house are left to conjecture and, though it may be reasonable to deduce a probable family structure from the surnames and ages given, this will not be infallible. For example, in the following entry from Dudley's Fisher Street in 1841 we have: 'Edward Duffey, 50, CM [? Chain-maker] ; Ann Duffey, 35; Sarah Braznall, 60; Jacey Jones, 15, Nailer; Mary Braznall, 15, Nailer'. Ann may be Edward's younger wife — she is too old to be his daughter — but she might be his unmarried sister, or niece, or a sister-in-law whose husband was not at home. Sarah Braznall is perhaps Edward's mother-in-law and Mary Braznall a niece, but they might be unrelated lodgers or relics of Ann's earlier marriage to a Braznall. Unfortunately, Duffey does not appear in any later, more explicit census of the street where these problems might have been resolved.

Many historians criticise this census because of these problems which result from this ambiguous way of listing households, and anyone concerned with genealogy or family history must approach this record with caution. At best, the 1841 household lists give us an informed lead into the more reliable parish registers. For most purposes, however, the normal run of relationships is fairly obvious, so that the explanation of a more typical Fisher Street family — 'John Lilley, 38; Lydia Lilley, 35; Sarah Lilley, 12, John Lilley, 10; Mary Lilley, 4; and James Marr, 40' — is almost certainly that of man and wife with three children and a lodger; a reasonable assumption which is born out by reference to the 1851 census where these relationships are clearly stated.

From 1851 the 'Relationship' column contains the abbreviations H (Head), W (Wife), S (Son), D (Daughter), L (Lodger) and V (Visitor). Relationships such as Mother, Aunt, Sister-in-law, Servant and Apprentice were usually entered as fully as a narrow column would permit. Some enumerators lose the thread of relationship in a large household, particularly if an additional family, say that of the Head's brother, is at home but not entered as a separate household (which strictly speaking, might have been more correct, with the brother as a new Head). In such cases the enumerator may stray from the relationship of the Head to those of his brother, entering a second set of 'Wife', 'Son' and 'Daughter' instead of maintaining the strict relationship of 'Sister-in-Law', 'Nephew' and 'Niece'. Relationships also become ambiguous if the

Parish or Township of *Dudley* — Ecclesiastical District of *St Edmunds* — City or Borough of *Dudley* — Town of *Dudley*

No of House, Schedule	Name of Street, Place, or Road, and Name or No. of House	Name and Surname of each Person who abode in the house, on the Night of the 30th March, 1851	Relation to Head of Family	Condition	Age of Males	Age of Females	Rank, Profession, or Occupation	Where Born	
97	continued	Thomas Darrel	son		15		Coal Mason (son?)	Worcester Sh Dudley	✓
		Joseph Brazuell	son			15	do	do	
		John Ambrose	son		13		do	do	
		Emanuel do	son		1		do	do	
98	Fisher street	William Jones	Head	Wid	80		retired Crate Quaker	do	✓
		Ann do	Sour	Un		51	Housekeeper	do	
99	Fisher street	John Tilley	Head	Mar	57		Miner	do	✓
		Lydia do	Wife	Mar		51		do	
		William Maff	son in law	Mar	24		Stone Miner	do	
		Jacob Wm Maff	son	Un				do	
		John Lilley	Lo-r	Un	20		Basket Maker	do	
		Mary do	daughter	Un		11	Scholar	do	
100	Fisher street	Richd Jones	Head	Mar	22		Coal Miner	do	✓
		Sarah do	Wife	Mar		22		do	
		Richard do	son		1		Infant	do	

Total of Persons ... 10 – 5

Total Houses	1	3	U — 3 —

Households of Fisher Street, Dudley, from the 1851 census: reproduced by permission of the Public Record Office. Page from an enumerator's book, ref. no. HO107/2033, actual size 14x8 inches.

Head is temporarily away from home; a woman's name entered as 'Head — Married' raises more doubt than the same woman's name entered as 'Head — Widow'. Rarely does an enumerator lapse into completely uninformative terms such as 'Relation' or 'Friend' though we might prefer a better definition, if there was one, of the visitors. The occasional transposition of occupation into the 'Relationship' column is misleading and we should beware of the Victorian convention of 'mother-in-law' for 'stepmother' (*vide* Sam Weller). The rare entry of 'Child at Nurse' may be unfamiliar at first sight and some marital relationships do not bear very close examination.

The 'Occupation' column supplies a mass of material for analysis of the economic structure of any town, its streets and households. Empty factories and warehouses are mentioned incidentally as landmarks, if at all, but the location of family work-shops, businesses and smallholdings can be plotted and the incidence of agriculture, commerce, retail trade, industry, crafts and the professional and service classes can be calculated. As to the nature of 'family business' or occupation of the household, even when these are clearly stated from 1851, extending to every employee in the family, it is open to question whether all are employed in the same house, in the family forge, nail-shop or weaving-shed or whether young sons, nephews, nieces and brothers-in-law do not go out to another place of work. Presumably if the relationship of 'Apprentice' or 'Servant' to the Head of the household is clearly stated, then these must work with him but occasionally when a domestic servant is also a blood relation — daughter, sister or niece — we may assume that she goes out to work. This explains the unexpected but prevalent appearance of servants in artisan households. From 1851 enumerators were required to add to the occupation of 'Farmer' the acreage of his farm and number of men employed, and to any workshop owner or shopkeeper his number of employees. Thus entries such as 'Ironmaster employing 5 men and a boy' and 'Farmer of 250 acres employing 3 men' became usual, though sporadic. These details of farms and industrial sites prompt cross-references to the tithe awards and plans of *c.* 1841 which will usually confirm and map the holding and its labourers' cottages (see *Village Records*, Chapter Five).

In 1841 the final column entered with 'Y' or 'N' referred to the birthplace of each individual, as 'Yes' or 'No' to the question 'Whether born in the same County' (but unfortunately not 'Whether born in the same Parish or Town'). The data is no more precise than that, except in cases of those born in Scotland, Ireland or Foreign Parts (S, I or F are entered). From 1851 onward the county, village or town of each birth-place is given and though misplacing in the wrong county occasionally occurs, the origins of each resident are usually clear. They will lead family historians to many a distant parish register. The 'Where Born column' is also a quarry of implied informa-tion about population mobility, immigration, movement from countryside to town and other matters of family history. For example:

No.:	Name	Rel.:	Mar.:	Age.:	Occupation:	Where Born:
20:	William Stainforth	H	M	48	Cutler	Yorkshire
	Mary „ „	W	M	38		Dudley
	Randolph „	S	U	18	Cutler	Wolverhampton
	William Burton	Stepson	U	17	Coalminer	Dudley
	Henry „	Stepson	U	11	Scholar	Dudley
	Hannah „	Stepdtr.		8	Scholar	Dudley

This entry for Stone Street, Dudley, in 1861 indicates some probabilities about the Yorkshireman William Stainforth and his marriages, with his earlier period of residence in Wolverhampton, the possible date of removal to Dudley and above all the complexity of his children's ages. Presumably Randolph is Mary's stepson by William's first marriage about 20 years before, but whether this took place in Yorkshire, Wolverhampton, or somewhere entirely different, we cannot tell. The young Burtons are children of Mary's previous marriage which ended within the past nine years, probably in Dudley. As to the date of William and Mary's marriage to each other and the movements which brought them together from Yorkshire to Wolverhampton and Dudley, we have only a rough outline to build on.

The importance of enumerator's schedules to the local historian and demographer has been sufficiently evident to local historians, since their first release in 1941. The gross totals printed in the *Abstracts* and *Reports*, are useful large-scale reference points which indicate main population trends, but are not open to closer examination or to cross-reference from one variable factor to another. For example, only by reference to the internal data of the schedules can Welsh miners be separated from the rest, artisan's children who were scholars to be numbered separately, or domestic servants born in Shropshire counted. Totals for different parishes and their numbers to the acre can be compared from the *Abstracts*; only the enumerators' returns will provide the evidence which makes it possible to compare street with street and house with house.

The main limitation of this sort of analysis arises from the fact that returns were made as statements of the *de facto* occupany of each house *only on the single day when the census was taken*. We can expect no insight into what had happened to the family in the years before the census day, nor even the day before. There will be no information about those temporarily or permanently absent from the house, except in the occasional enumerator's 'aside'. We know nothing of children who had been born and died or left home in the intervals before or between each census. We cannot be sure whether William Stainforth's marriage to Mary Burton was a second, third or fourth venture, nor whether older children of his first marriage had gone away to marry or to work. We cannot tell whether Randolph was born during a holiday in Wolverhampton, or during a period of more prolonged residence. Nor does the census return enlighten us as to whether the cutler's trade was followed by father and son in the house, or elsewhere, and we cannot tell whether Randolph worked with his father, or for another master. Some of these doubts may be removed by reference to other documentary sources such as parish registers, commercial directories and tithe awards. Many problems will be solved if we can trace the same family from one census to another, bearing in mind that a great deal can happen, unrecorded, to any family during a ten-year interval. The census returns cannot provide us with all the facts we need.

Nevertheless, questions which clamour for attention from the availability of such a mine of information on the Victorian social scene are innumerable. The groups of entries under 'Name', 'Relation' and 'Marital Condition' columns indicate the size of each family and its structure. We might expect to discover the incidence of nuclear or extended families, the provision for dependent relatives, widows, orphans and other dependents such as servants and apprentices. 'Lodgers' and 'Boarders' — often clearly differentiated — will include journeymen and employees living with their master and his family. The 'Relationship' column gives some indication of provision for unmarried sons, daughters, brothers and sisters, with occasional illegitimate children of unmarried sisters or daughters, and orphaned grandchildren and nephews. The question of multiple occupancy of houses, whether sublet, or occupied as lodging houses or 'rookeries', is raised by the distinction between 'House' and 'Household', though the enumerators' returns are often ambiguous on these points. The 'Age' column adds another dimension to family structure; we might expect to reach some conclusions about the relative ages of man and wife and intervals between the births of their children. Ages at marriage and childbirth can be calculated or conjectured, and the ages at which children appear to leave school, gain employment and leave home are reasonably explicit. Life-expectation and provision for older relatives is evident with occasional mention of 'Retirement', and an increasing number of 'Annuitants' and 'Fund-holders'.

We are at the mercy of human fallibility, the consistency of the enumerator, the possibility of exaggeration of status, the failure of recollection, inaccuracies of age and birthplace. We are especially dependent upon the enumerator's skill; untidy or illegible handwriting can cause a great deal of uncertainty, though most returns are legible. More frustrating is the clerk's habit of checking off entries with the slash of a pen-stroke, line by line, often deleting essential initials or figures. Fortunately, each household's entry will contain a number of possible cross-checks, as for example the separate columns for males' and females' ages, which indicate whether we are endeavouring to decipher a girl's name or a boy's and, usually, a descending order of children's ages, so that X9 between a clear 21 and 17 is probably 19.

The reader is more likely to experience difficulties which arise from ambiguous entries than from illegible ones. The preliminary 'Instructions to the Enumerator' set out at the opening of each new schedule are well worth reading, though these will sometimes leave our questions — and presumably those of the baffled enumerator — unanswered. The exact distinction between 'House' and 'Household' is indefinite, as is the precise interpretation of 'Family' where the exact status of 'Head' is sometimes in doubt. The exact meaning of 'Lodger', 'Boarder', 'Visitor' and 'Servant' is doubtful in some households, so that the difference between nuclear and extended family, household and business is sometimes blurred.

More subtle problems of interpretation emerge as we attempt to move from facts to value-judgements. Our view of Victorian society becomes more subjective as we read more census returns. Accepted generalizations offered by textbooks may become confused by the evidence. Many of the necessary hypotheses for interpretation depend on imprecise terms such as 'poverty', 'class', 'overcrowding', 'servant', 'household' and 'family', to say nothing of 'standards' or 'change'. In any of these cases it is misleading to interpret the records in the modern sense of such terms, or by reference to only one source of data. The record of a large number of people in a house does not indicate overcrowding unless we know the number of rooms and their floor area — facts not included in the census. The working conditions of Victorian servants or the educational standards of Victorian scholars should not be estimated by reference only to Dickens's Marchioness or Wackford Squeers . We cannot equate large families with 'poverty' unless we know the total income of the family and its expenses. 'Hardship' is not a matter of conjecture.

An amusing example of confusion of modern and Victorian viewpoints was seen in the case of an enterprising young Dudley headmaster, who, having acquired a brand new microprocessor, and the Teachers' Centre bank of encoded census returns, had his primary school pupils run a lively investigation into standards of living in Victorian Dudley. Predictably, the computer offered the startling conclusion that 'In 1851 more children below the present statutory school age of 5 years were "scholars" in Dudley than are in the town's nursery schools in 1981'. The publicity given by an avid local press to this inflammatory statement did not endear the possibilities of computer studies to the local education committee. It was an interesting example of the infinite possibilities of confusion between modern assumptions and the realities of the Victorian social scene. Neither party in the dispute was really able to match the terms 'scholar' (1851) with 'nursery school pupil' (1981); the difference in educational tradition and aspiration is immense. More evidence than the census returns provide would be required to make any sort of adequate comparison. Modern administrators would rightly assume that the statistical basis of the census material is questionable. It is certainly surprising when reading many census returns from 1841 to 1861, to note the frequency of 'scholars' from 3 to 13; doubts arise when the lower age level drops (rarely) to 1 year old or when reference is made to 'Scholar at Home'. As to the number of weekly attendances, hours spent at school, the teacher–pupil ratio, teachers' qualifications, the curriculum, cost to parents, nature of discipline and activities or standards set and achieved, other records must be sought to answer these and other questions; not least the recollections published by survivors of the Victorian schoolroom. These were not within the view of the census enumerators.

The modern sociologist's preoccupation with 'class' is also foreign to the census records, so that it is all the more remarkable how inaptly modern analysts of census data attempt to force the inhabitants of Victorian streets into the straitjacket of the present-day Registrar General's *Classification of Occupations*. That way confusion will arise on the basis that Class IV occupations *should not* have servants, or children at school or wives who do not make chain. Victorian behaviour patterns do not match those of our uneasy 'class' structure. If we continue to make modern assumptions we shall frequently be surprised that so many 'lower-class' people had servants living-in, that the term 'unemployed' is rarely used before the Census of 1881, that longevity and infant survival are not unusual. We have been conditioned to a sensational view of Victorian town-life. In searching the streets of 19th-century Dudley, if we set aside the plethora of sensational reports on a minority of the townsfolk and their dwellings, we cannot escape the impression, from thousands of entries that some of these assumptions have remained too long unchallenged. For modern schoolchildren there is no Victorian middle-class, everyone was aggressively rich or desperately poor. They have no knowledge of Mr. Pooter's many inexpensive comforts, nor of the beneficent effects of domestic service upon the upbringing of so many of our great-great-grandmothers and their own children. We have been led to expect to find squalid 'rookeries'; high infant mortality, low expectation of life and a surfeit of human misery. These expectations are not substantiated by the life-style of the inhabitants of the courts and alleys of Dudley from 1841 to 1881, or, at least, they are not evident in the census returns.

Our sense of excitement in the ability to 'repopulate' the long-gone streets and houses is a special gift of the census returns. At last the archives available for the study of any 19th-century town come together in rewarding combinations. To the census returns, house by house, can be added the pages of the commercial directories,

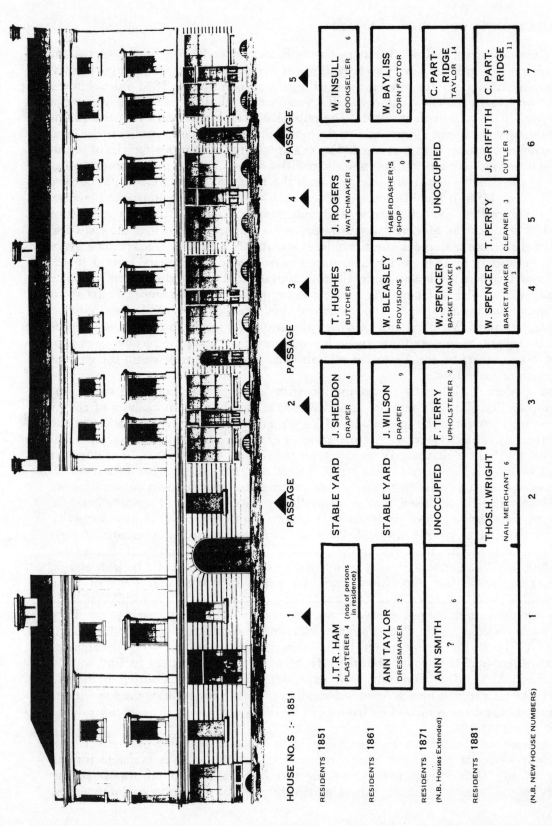

The inhabitants of 1-5 (later 1-7) Stone Street, Dudley, 1841-1881 using information from census microfilms in the Archives and Local History Department of Dudley Public Libraries.

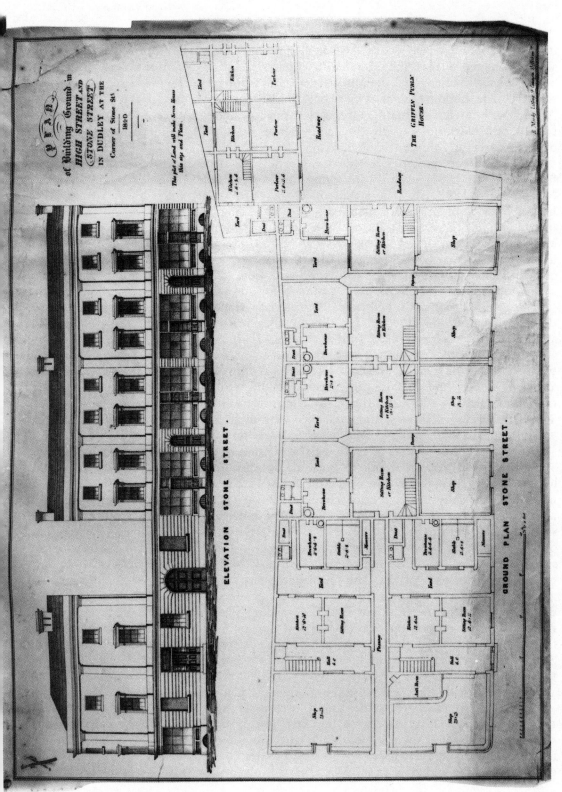

Plan and elevation of Mr. Bagott's houses at 1-5 Stone Street, Dudley, 1840. Reproduced by permission of the Archives and Local History Department of Dudley Public Libraries (ref. 1732/1739c). Actual size 24x18 inches, scale 1/8 inch:1 foot.

shop by shop, the volumes of parish registers, family by family and the town's rate-books and newspapers. To set the scene, there is the groundfloor detail of large scale Ordnance Survey maps, revealing cellar steps, 'bulk windows' and lamp-posts. Some houses have escaped demolition and may be imaginatively restored by reference to large-scale building plans which occasionally survive amongst the local archives. Armed with such first-hand material we can populate a street, its houses, shops, taverns and workshops, with the living people of a past century. Such is the case of Stone Street in Dudley.

The local library provides, as well as microfilm and street-indexes for all the censuses from 1841 to 1881, usefully matching directories, such as Bentley's for 1840 and Melville's for 1852; also, best find of all, a set of plans and elevations of six new houses built – or originally planned – for a Mr. Bagott on a site leased by the Earl of Dudley in 1840. This Bagott was possibly John, a tailor with a shop in the Market Place, according to Bentley's *Directory*. His houses filled a building plot on a corner, with two house-fronts on High Street and four more behind them at right-angles, facing Stone Street. The buildings were three-storied, each with shop, sitting-room and kitchen on the ground floor, drawing room and parlour on the first floor, and four attic bedrooms. By modern standards all the rooms were large, the drawing room 20 ft. x 16 ft., the downstairs sitting room 18 ft. x 15 ft. 6 in. and the bedrooms from 10-17 ft. x 8 ft. 6 in.–15 ft. 3 in. There were roomy cellars, with 'under-kitchens', store-rooms and an outside yard for every house, each with a two-seat privy, or 'petty', brewhouse and refuse bunker. The two High Street houses also had stables and manure-pits. Access to the yards was by three 4 ft. passages, one from High Street, the other two from Stone Street, between houses 2–3 and 4–5. The elevations show a simple façade with arched doorways to the passages and a pair of square shop windows flanking each house-door. (See pages 288–289).

The site of these houses is clearly defined by the High Street corner at one end and the 'Griffin', which is still in business, at the other, separated from the newer houses by a right-angled roadway. Public houses are invaluable reference points to old maps and especially in the census schedules, as we can count houses from one pub to another and discover which side of the street the enumerator is checking. (The other side may lie in another part of his circuit.). Earlier census returns will not name an inn, only the landlord, as 'victualler', but a contemporary *Directory* will usually list every sizeable hotel, public-house and beerseller, so that the houses of the census's victuallers can be traced in each street. The Ordnance Survey 1:528 map of Dudley in 1883 gives a clear plan of Stone Street, carefully placing every doorstep. A significant difference between the O.S. map and the builder's plans of 1840 is the disappearance of the passage between the two High Street houses and the second passage on Stone Street – the other is clearly marked. Two additional houses have appeared on Stone Street by 1883, one filling the space which had been the stable yard of No. 1, the other where the second Stone Street passage used to be; the layout of the back-yards is also slightly different from those originally planned. (See page 288.)

Mr. Bagott's houses still stand today, preserving many of the features surveyed in the 19th century. Both blocks of building have been refaced with imitation stone, similar to the fashion specified by Mr. Bagott's builder in 1840. This modern face-lift has covered two upper windows with new pilasters of cement but the spacing of the other upstairs windows is exactly as shown in the elevation. The lintel on the last

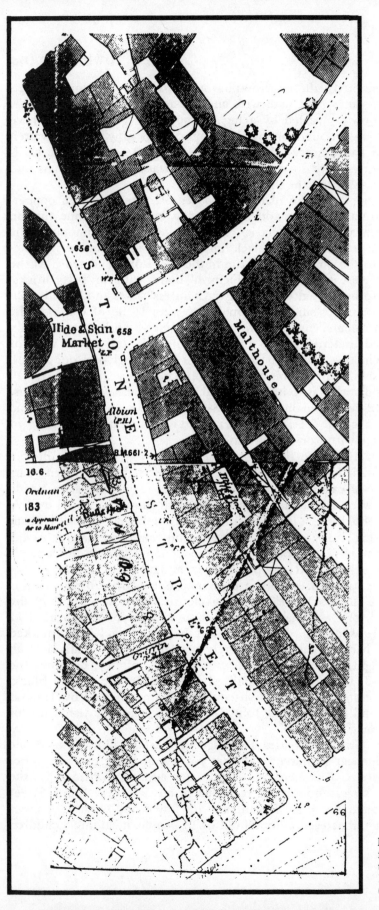

Map of Stone Street, Dudley, in 1883, from Ordnance Survey sheet for Worcestershire I 16.1/LXVII 16.1 (1883). Scale 10.56 feet: 1 mile or 41.66 feet: 1 inch (1:500).

window on Stone Street (marked with an arrow) has survived alone and almost intact, as has the chimney on the same gable end, with another added on the front corner. The pitch of the roof is now concealed by a high parapet; the ground floors have been gutted to form four large modern shops. The upper floors now house a warren of stockrooms, offices and hairdressers: At the rear, as far as one can see, the yards and some of the outbuildings have survived as outdoor lavatories, stockrooms and litter bins, with access to the backs of the shops.

Exact specifications accompanied the plans, five pages of closely written copperplate script. Separate instructions were addressed to the bricklayer, stone mason, plasterer, carpenter and joiner, plumber, glazier, slater, painter and ironmonger. The brick building was to be faced with the best black lime, 'jointed and coloured to represent stone, the mouldings to the cornices to be run in the best Roman cement'. At the gable ends the best bricks were to be laid in 'Flemish' bond, with no 'sutty bricks' allowed. The houses were to be roofed with 'Bangor Countess' slates and leaded, 6 lb. to the foot. Door frames, window sills and shop floors were to be of old oak, the roof rafters and purlins of 'Memel' or 'Riga' fir. All the joiner's work must use only the 'best and well-seasoned materials'. The outer window sills and lintels were of 'Gornal' stone, the shop-windows glazed in the brightest 'Crown' glass. Door hinges, mortice-locks, shutters, sashes and columns for the shop windows were to be crafted in iron and brass. All woodwork was to have two coats of oil paint, three outdoors. The houses were connected to the main sewer in Stone Street; each brewhouse had a soft-water cistern of 231 cubic feet; the cellars, 'petties' and outhouses were of hard blue brick, whitewashed, with iron-barred windows.

Turning to the census of 1841, we find that these houses were not yet built; the enumerator begins at the 'Griffin' after leaving the corner of High Street. Ten years later, all are occupied and we can trace changes of occupier from decade to decade until 1881. In 1851 there were, as planned, five houses with shops, occupied by five families. The smallest household was a married couple and the largest that of William Insull the bookseller, with his family of six. The population graph (see page 278) has shown that the period from 1841 to 1861 was a time of rapid growth in Dudley's population with an increase of one-third in population, from 31,232 to 44,975.

The appearance of two extra houses on the O.S. map is explained by the census returns of 1871 and 1881. In 1861 the additional houses did not exist; only the original five were occupied, one as a haberdasher's shop without residents. In 1871 seven houses are recorded, as on the 1883 map, but Nos. 2, 5 and 6 are marked 'uninhabited', presumably because they were barely completed. Ten years later all are inhabited; Thomas Wright, a nail merchant, with a family of five, occupies the newly remodelled Nos. 1–3. including the rebuilt stable-yard. In the second block, houses 5 and 6 (the enumerator now gives house-numbers) are occupied by Thomas Perry, a cleaner, his wife and nephew, and John Griffiths, a general cutler, with his wife Selina and their baby daughter, Sarah.

At No. 7, next to the 'Griffin', Charles Partridge (a master tailor), shared the distinction with William Spencer (a basket-maker at No. 4) of being the only other resident recorded in two consecutive censuses at the same address. Partridge has the further distinction of the largest household recorded in any of these Stone Street houses, which usually accommodated small families with few if any servants. Charles Partridge, at 32 years of age, mustered a household of 14 people, including 8 children aged from 2 months to 13 years, two younger brothers from Devon (where Charles was born), a sister-in-law as a shop assistant, and a solitary domestic servant, Jane Walker aged 16. Charles's brother, John, was also a tailor, probably employed in the family business. By 1881 the Partridge family was reduced to eleven people. The baby, Rupert, ominously, is no longer recorded though all the other children were still at home. Charles's eldest daughter Matilda was a certificated teacher aged 23, her brother Frederick aged 17 a pupil teacher. An older boy, Charles had taken up his father's trade and uncle John the tailor was still living with the family, though the younger Uncle George and the shop-assistant aunt do not appear in the return of 1881. The family still employed only one servant, an older woman of 27.

The Partridge household is the only case in which we shall be able to refer at all confidently to a 'crowded' house. When we turn later to the less salubrious back-to-back houses of Fisher Street, with many families as large or larger than Charles Partridge's — though few with such a rapid birth-rate — we have no comparable evidence before 1891 of the number and size of rooms to each house. At No. 7 Stone Street the two babies possibly slept in their parents' large bedroom, leaving an attic bedroom for three boys aged 5 to 10, another for three girls aged 3 to 13, a third for the two unmarried uncles. This left another small attic for the 43-year-old aunt Isabella Ayling, either by herself or sharing with the 16-year-old servant. Otherwise, Jane Walker slept in the basement in true Dickensian fashion. There is no doubt that Mr. Bagott's houses set out to be the 'upper end' of Stone Street, being larger houses with small families and aspirations to a 'higher class of trade' than the publicans, pork butchers and potato-salesmen who occupied the lower end of the Street below the 'Griffin', where families were usually 7 to 12 in number. In the newer houses we find dressmakers, a watchmaker, a haberdasher, a corn factor and a bookseller, more than one tailor, an upholsterer and a nail merchant.

For 50 years the character of the street remained much the same, although in 1861 and 1871 several houses lay unoccupied. Lower down the street, No. 11 was a pork butcher's shop for at least 30 years as two competitors went out of business. At No. 10, Arthur Timmins, a young bed and mattress maker ('employed 4 men and a boy') in 1861, prospered as a furniture dealer, occupying the house and shop next door and then selling the enlarged business to Sarah Crump, who appears as a furniture dealer at the same premises in 1881. Only at the outset in 1851 were the 13 houses of Stone Street's left-hand side occupied by exactly 13 households; by 1881 15 houses are kept by 12 families. There was no tradition of multiple occupancy of houses by several large families, rather the reverse, with small families taking over the occupation of an additional house next door.

As soon as we begin to make cross-references, from house to house, from street to street and from census to census, with the use of a large number of schedules, access to a computer becomes almost essential. However it is possible to read and annotate many hundreds of entries with no more complex aids than a pocket calculator and a simple card index, or alphabetically divided notebook. In this way we can analyse the nature of a single street or trace three or four families from decade to decade. In Fisher Street, Dudley, for example, with its elegantly named 'Packwood Square' which later became, more bluntly, 'Nos. 1 and 2 Courts', we find families who remain in Fisher Street, growing steadily older (though in the case of some of the ladies

Fisher Street, Dudley, 1883, from Ordnance Survey Worcs./Staffs. sheet I.16.1 LXVII 16.1 and sheet I.16.1/LXVII 16.1 (1883). Scale 10.56 feet: 1mile or 41.66 feet: 1 inch (1:500).

becoming a little younger at each census). There were, for instance, the Clarkes and the Morrises, the Lilleys and the Vanes.

In 1841 Elizabeth Clarke, aged 40, and her 13-year-old son Joseph, who was a miner, lived together in what was later known as No. 5, One Court, in Fisher Street. Ten years later the enumerator records that Elizabeth, now a more accurate 56, is a widow and lodging-house keeper with three lodgers and no son at home. In 1861, with his mother (now an optimistic 60) as 'housekeeper', Joseph is at home again, still a miner; there are no lodgers. By 1871 there is no record of Elizabeth, but Joseph Clarke is 42 and married to Sarah, 12 years younger than himself. In the last available return for 1881 Joseph still occupies his mother's house but is now an 'annuitant', with a different wife, Matilda, a 41-year-old laundress from Netherton. There are two boarders, an unmarried, unemployed young man, John Tucker aged 20 and Alice Tucker, a 'scholar' of 6 years old.

A similar family history can be gleaned for John Morris coal-miner, who lived at No. 8 Fisher Street from the age of 30 to 70. John too was twice married; his second marriage was to a neighbour in the same street, Mary Braznall, a nailer who was younger than himself. As a widow with a four-year-old son in 1841, Mary had kept a full house of lodgers, including an old lady of 70 and five children named Marsh, aged from 5 to 15. John brought up his stepson with his own four children, Eliza, Thomas, John and Emmanuel, a baby of 5 months in 1841. His three sons became miners like their father and their stepmother is described as a 'nailer' until the age of 64. By 1871 John Morris had prospered; he now describes himself as a coal-seller. Mary his wife is now 74 and all his children have left home except the youngest unmarried son, Emanuel, now aged 27. In the last census, John and Mary Morris are no more; the house is kept by Emanuel now aged 39, with Sarah his wife. He is described as a 'carter'; his daughter Hannah born in Dudley and presumably in the same house, is a 'scholar' of 8 and there is a 'general servant', Mary Collier, aged 18. John Lilley, a shoemaker of Fisher Street, who retired at 78 with lodgers to look after him, is another who brought up three children to marry and live in the same house for 50 years. Fanny Vanes, like Mary Braznall, moved across the road as mother-in-law to Thomas Hillman, a leather-seller. By 1861 she is described as a 'proprietor of houses' and had brought her son Robert Ward Vanes and his son Benjamin aged 5 to live in her daughter Lucy's house which also accommodated a 'maidservant', Priscilla Thompson, aged 16.

It is evident that a complex structure of family tenancies was established in Fisher Street over a long period of years; that there is inter-marriage from house to house and that sons and daughters take over their parents' tenancies both before and after their deaths. There is a complicated system of lodging as a mode of social welfare, caring for the very young and the elderly. Some lodgers were apprentices to the Head of the household and some of the girls possibly paid for their accommodation in domestic service. There is no doubt that if all cross-references could be matched and compared with relevant parish registers of baptisms, burials and marriages — of which a comprehensive printed set is published for Dudley — then this network of social interdependence would become more apparent. We might discover the antecedents of the laundress from Netherton, the stepmother from farther down the road, the lodger from a different parish and the whole extended family of a widower's three marriages. From a small sample and simple 'eye-ball' cross-checking we can only expect to gain a subjective *impression* of a street or two. Yet those impressions are persistent. Fisher Street later became notorious as one of the least salubrious areas of central Dudley and was eventually demolished to make room for a bus terminus and shopping precinct. The impression in the 19th century remains one of respectable people caring for each other and in several cases prospering by a lifetime of hard work.

The number of houses in Fisher Street remains constant over the half-century; two more were 'building' in 1841 but were never added to the total for the street, unless two others were demolished at the same time. By 1871–81 there was a significant number of houses uninhabited. The number of inhabitants tends to fluctuate from census to census, usually being slightly less than the ratio of 5.2 per house recorded by Dr. Ballard in 1874 (see below, pages 298–300). The number of households or families is equal to the number of houses, though several lodgers are not counted as separate families by the enumerators, being usually single men or women. The ratio of men to women also fluctuates from house to house. In some cases a widowed housekeeper like Mary Braznall looks after a houseful of male lodgers, in other cases a male 'head' supports a houseful of womenfolk. Most of the people of Fisher Street, from beginning to end of the half-century, were born and bred in Dudley and, as we have seen, many of them actually in Fisher Street. A simple 'manual' count produces the following table:

Places of Birth of Fisher Street residents, 1841–1881

	Total	Per house	Dudley	Same county*	Other counties & other towns	'Foreign'
1841	233	5.0	—	72%	27%	2 only
1851	246	5.2	68%	12%	18%	2%
1861	210	4.5	64%	17%	14%	5%
1871	170	4.8	61%	17%	14%	5%
1881	196	5.0	70%	16%	13%	2%

* Dudley's unusual 'extra-county' geographical position means that this column includes adjacent areas of Staffordshire and Worcestershire.

In Fisher Street the majority of newcomers usually arrived from the neighbouring villages of Staffordshire and Worcestershire, such as Sedgley, Kingswinford and Gornal which are now part of the metropolitan borough, or from nearby towns such as Wolverhampton, West Bromwich, Rowley Regis and Tipton. Even those who came from farther afield usually came from counties not far away, many from Shropshire and Herefordshire. Only in 1861 do we find a significant number of Irish lodgers; genuine immigration, from other countries is usually about 2% — the two foreigners in 1841 came from Prussia, a wife and her daughter.

Like microfilm, the microprocessor has been the most effective key to open up the vast storehouse of census documents. The sheer *number* of entries and the countless *combinations* of the data is an ideal task for the most up-to-date retrieval equipment. Until recently only large-scale organizations such as universities and local education authorities could offer students and searchers access to 'main-frame' computers; the present attractive advertisement of cheap microprocesses for home use will revolutionize this situation, to the advantage of the lone home-student. The potential uses of computers and their peculiar affinity with census data has been well remarked by scholars. Computer skills form an essential part of an interesting Open University

Course for History students and there has been a great deal of scholarly work on the demography of particular towns.

When we begin to study census returns we are at the mercy of the enumerator, his efficiency, his literacy and his consistent interpretation of the mass of data he collects. When we turn to the computer we are at the mercy of the programmers and their codes. Fortunately, thanks to the influence of the Schools Council, there has been some movement towards standardised thesauruses of codes giving places of birth and occupation. Arcane 'languages' have given place to plain words and the cheapness of microprocessors has released the student from the monopoly of the 'main frame'. Nevertheless, experience suggests that it may be many years yet before any town has a reliable and consistent base, a set of adequate samples, range of years, common language and compatible equipment. Too often, the very area we most require is not yet encoded or banked, the very hypothesis we need to test is not yet programmed. Frequent changes in available models with different storage or printing systems cause constant rewriting of existing codes and programmes. This laborious process, which sometimes drives the student in despair back to the small-scale 'manual' analysis is thankfully, improving rapidly.

However, the comprehensive print-out of a large sample can in itself be a daunting source of information for 'manual' counting and analysis. An unforseen lesson for the uninitiated is the strict discipline which the computer exercises over inexpert questions and hypotheses. The machine teaches us to discard questions of 'rich and poor', 'old and young', 'Class I and Class IV' or 'master and man'. There is a welcome similarity about the discipline of the programme and that of the original document. We must beware of questions which are trivial, like the happy discovery that the girls' names Elizabeth and Sarah are most popular in Dudley in 1851, or, more correctly 'show the highest frequencies of 65 and 61 on 1,294 records'. Equally time-consuming to no real effect are the painstaking conclusions that, for example the upper classes tended to live in the more salubrious areas of the town, or that the poor have fewer servants than the rich. The computer will perform two vital, slightly different tasks for us. Firstly, it can count innumerable facts very quickly indeed, working out totals, averages and percentages. For example, from a 'hit-count' of 4,648 in central Dudley in 1851 the *Enquiry Analysis on Occupations* first separates 550 juvenile 'scholars' (12%) and adds to these 311 (6.6%) of young workers aged 7 to 16. The scholars are 42% of the age-group now of statutory school-age, the potential schoolchildren employed were 24%; it would require a more precise breakdown of the year-groups to discover whether most of the 'scholars' were younger than 13 and most of the employed children were older than 13. Nearly 10% of urban Dudley's townsfolk were occupied in agricultural trades and occupations; a larger proportion, 18%, were iron-workers and miners. Of womenfolk, about 25% were in some sort of employment, two-thirds of them were unmarried girls. For comparison with Fisher Street's immigrants, we find an identical proportion (68%) born in Dudley town. Of the newcomers, fewer of the Fisher Street inhabitants were born out of England than was usual over all Dudley (10%), and fewer were born in the same county; more of Fisher Street's immigrants came from major towns and distant counties than was the case for the town as a whole(7%).

The other task which a computer can perform is more demanding than its use as an adding machine. This is the correlation of one variable factor with another. For

Quarry Bank, once on the outskirts of the town, now an integral part of the borough, a programme of correlations has been devised which is particularly useful for analysing the structure of households and families. There were 254 houses in Quarry Bank and 260 households, a similar absence of multiple occupancy to the state of Fisher Street. Taking as the nuclear family only father, mother and children, an inexpensive microprocessor can now tabulate the following analysis of 'family plus other occupants':

Family = Household	65%	Family + 4	2%
Family + 1	20%	Family + 5	1%
Family + 2	6%	Family + 6	0%
Family + 3	6%	Family + 7	1 only

There were 33 houses (13%) with only 1-2 occupants, and 59 families as small (23%). Larger households included 52 families of 7-9 (20%) and 23 houses with 9-12 occupants (9%). Obviously, the structure of small families with large numbers of supernumeraries and large families with many additional occupants, etc., could be calculated but an equally interesting analysis is the simple count of relationships to heads of household in Quarry Bank. This gives:

Relationships	Male	Female	Total	Percentage
Heads	229	28	257	20%
Wives	—	212	212	16%
Sons and daughters	324	332	646	50%
Extended family	51	47	98	8%
Servants	2	10	12	1%
Apprentices	5	1	6	0.5%
Lodgers and Visitors	32	28	60	5.5%

These figures are much the same as for Fisher Street in Dudley, with almost complete employment in nail and chain making, iron puddling and similar heavy industry. At least one of the chainshops was still in production within the past ten years at Quarry Bank.

The lifetime of all these Black Country folk spans a period when official reports on their social condition were at their most sensational. These accounts of unredeemed squalor are inescapable evidence, of a type which the census enumerators were not asked to provide, of the unacceptable face of Victorian town life. Their main failing in Dudley is that they are not as geographically precise as the enumeration schedules, nor do they offer much statistical evidence, except in terms of mortality. Their statements about the filthy state of the houses and streets of Dudley in the 1870s are woefully explicit. In 1874 Dr. Ballard confirmed in horrendous detail the earlier findings of his colleague Dr. Thorne in 1871.[7] Thorne had referred to 'The unwholesome condition of cottage property upon limited areas, the overcrowding of houses with inhabitants, the dirtiness of their yards and courts . . .'. He spoke of the unwholesome condition of the supply of well-water, the prevalence of pig-keeping in town and the almost total failure of the sewage system. Nothing had improved in the three years since Thorne's report. Throughout both doctors' reports special reference is continually made to the unhealthy condition of Netherton and Woodside, as being the town's disaster areas, but they add that 'the unwholesome conditions prevailed in them similar to those observed in the town of Dudley itself'. One historian has described such towns as insensate man-heaps.[8]

The wards in which we have studied Stone Street and Fisher Street stood relatively high on Ballard's list of prevailing conditions – his chief criterion of 'wholesomeness' is a higher proportion of women than men in any area. Yet Birmingham Street, which joins Fisher Street, is singled out as inadequately improved: 'One woman showed me where an ashpit on other property at the rear of her house drained into her pantry. At this part, the drainage from courts at the rear pass by superficial conduits under the houses into the street channel. I saw instances there where these conduits were choked up with filth and very offensive . . .'. Elsewhere, 'in a lodging-house called *Elephant and Castle* in Bond Street, filthy to the last degree, I found a cellar dwelling illegally occupied and in an outbuilding at the rear, persons living in a room over a large and stinking privy from which nothing separated the occupants but the floorboards. In December of last year this outbuilding was reported to the Council by its Medical Officer of Health as "unfit for human habitation" but it is still permitted to be occupied'.

There is a puzzling difference between the apparent nature of Bond Street and its inhabitants, as revealed by the bare bones of the 1871 census returns and Dr. Ballard's lurid scenario. A careful search of the enumeration schedules reveals no lodging-house in Bond Street either by the name of *Elephant and Castle* or otherwise; indeed, there is no inn or public house of that name in the Dudley Directory of that date. No head of household is listed as 'lodging-house keeper', nor for that matter are there many lodgers in the houses. There is no apparent multiple occupancy of houses, though there are, ominously, 14 uninhabited in a street where there are more than 50 inhabited houses, including three courts. There is a suspicious reference to six houses 'at the back of No. 47'. These were inhabited by six families described as: Thomas Anstey, a labourer with three small children; James Stone (an unmarried mine-sinker, aged 43) with a general servant, Lucy King, aged 32; two childless couples; a nailmaker and chainmaker with their wives; and a widow called Bridget McCann who was a hawker, aged 50, who lived with her son. Could these people have been living in the cellar and outhouse condemned by Dr. Ballard, though each dwelling is enumerated as an 'inhabited house'?

The rest of Bond Street in 1871 housed retired folk, small tradesmen, working women and one or two prosperous manufacturers. We find, for example, a general dealer, Charles Stringer, aged 64, living with Elizabeth his wife, his son who was an iron merchant, a lady's maid and a general servant. There was also a chain and pump manufacturer employing 10 men and 10 boys and a fender-maker employing 17 men, 4 boys and 4 females. Other residents included a tailoress, a pawnbroker, a small shopkeeper so-called, a grocer's widow, the landlord of the *Hope and Anchor* with his staff and family and the local lamplighter. Other than 'the back of No. 47' the nearest we see to a lodging-house is that of David Morgan, a carpenter, with three theatrical boarders. These were John O'Dowd, 'chemist and comedian' born in County Cork, aged 28, James Pickles a 'musician' aged 63 and his wife, Elizabeth, a 'comedienne' of 59. Are we to believe that these people were prepared to put up with shit in the living-room and not have moved away?

Nevertheless, everywhere in the town Ballard draws attention to the lack of any improvement in 'unwholesome structural arrangements of privies and ashpits', an accumulation of horse and pig dung, blood and offal in slaughterhouse refuse pits, with a few houses 'so dirty as to be injurious to health'. A pump in Newhall Street gave water that was 'turbid and offensive — in fact sewage water, yet, unless the inhabitants of the houses beg or steal water they have none other to drink . . .'. The nuisances of pig-keeping, blubber-boiling, smoking forges and flooded privies are positively medieval in their total disregard of public health. The Georgian Improvement Acts might never have been.

The results of this disgusting situation were, inevitably, epidemics and high mortality.[9] In 1870 it was scarlet fever, whooping cough and 'fever'; in 1871 it was measles and 'fever'; in 1872 it was smallpox, scarlet fever and whooping cough; in 1873 it was scarlet fever and 'year by year there has been a large fatality from diarrhœal affections . . . The Sanitary Authority might have largely prevented [this], had it duly exercised the powers with which it had been carefully invested for this very purpose by the legislature, but which . . . it has neglected to exercise'. Dudley's death-rate was indeed shocking. In 1872 there were 436 deaths per 1,000; the present rate is 11. In 1872 the infant mortality rate was 220 per thousand, at present it is 10.7, against a national average of 11.7. 450 babies died in Dudley during 1872. Little Rupert Partridge at No. 7 Stone Street must have been one of them.

The steady decline in Dudley's infant mortality rate — not long ago a matter of concern to the press — is an instructive example of the merits of local reorganization. If we turn to the Annual Reports of the Medical Officers of Health for the original county borough in 1965 and 1973, before the successive extension of the new borough's boundaries, we find the death rate beginning its steady decline. In 1965 'old' Dudley's infant mortality rate was 24.4 per 1,000 (nationally 19.0); in 1970, 20 per 1,000 (nationally 18.50); in 1973 12.6 (nationally 12.1) and in 1981 10.7 (nationally 11.7). This clearly demonstrates either the value of seventeen years' medical progress or the statistical benefits of extending a small town's boundaries into the surrounding countryside.

It is crystal clear that Ballard's report is a swingeing attack upon the negligence of Dudley's urban sanitary authority — the mayor and corporation. We are not dealing here with the tyranny of a master-class or rich employers; most of Dudley's 'masters' were small men like Charles Partridge, Joseph Clarke and John Morris. Landlords presumably had much to answer for on the condition of houses which were not always built to the high standards demanded by Mr. Bagott in High Street. 'Throughout the Borough of Dudley the labouring classes of the population, the class for whom low-rented dwellings are provided, greatly predominate'. Nor can we condemn the 'shiftlessness' of the 'poor and labouring classes', whose worst offence appears to have been the keeping of pigs in the courtyards, rather as council-house tenants of the 1930s were reputed to keep coal in the bath. The people of Dudley were at the mercy of the mayor and corporation, and no amount of family stability could preserve them from dirt, disease and death.

Ballard roundly accuses the council: 'No steps whatever have been taken by the Council, the Sanitary Committee or the Inspector of Nuisances to enforce these notices' (of conditions injurious to health). The Inspector of Nuisances was known to be 'both incompetent and negligent'. Yet, 'neither the Committee nor the Council thought it necessary to stir in those matters. They were forgetful of the fact that the responsibility in respect of nuisances had been laid by the Legislature upon themselves and that they are not relieved of it merely by appointing a paid officer to act in their name ...'. As to the regular recommendations of the borough's Medical Officer of Health, 'in certain important matters they passed unheeded'. The Council 'has not taken a single step to carry the Artisans and Labourers Dwelling Act into operation ...'; 'there is no Smoke Inspector ...' and the permanent hospital, 'alleged to have been provided' had in fact been closed.

As to refuse and nightsoil collection: 'The neglect of them by the Town Council has been most flagrant and I can only speak of it in the strongest terms of reprobation. Privies are to be seen in all parts, and especially in the poorer parts, loaded to the top of the seat with excrement, so loaded that the inhabitants of cottages can use the privies no longer and are compelled in some instances to ease themselves upon the surface of the ground, or throw themselves upon the charity of some less unfortunate neighbour'. 'The Council appears in this and in other matters to have regarded the entry of a minute adopting a recommendation of its Committee as equivalent to the performance of the act recommended'. 'In a filthy Borough and a filthy and neglected town these preventable diseases selected in each ward as the spots where they were most fatal, those spots which were the most neglected and the most filthy ...'. To Ballard his recommendations were 'a painful task'. More painful still was his realization — the bane of local government officers and inspectors at any time — that 'I can express little hope that they will be carried into effect by the Town Council of Dudley'.

It is not until 1891 that the census abstracts can offer any information on the overcrowding of houses, for not until that year was the number of rooms per house recorded and analysed, and, as if by modern computer programme, tabulated into different house-sizes. Every previous census had afforded a simple calculation of the average number of persons in each household. That year's census tables analysed the range of 'tenements with less than 5 rooms'. There were 6,908 of these, 75% of all the houses in Dudley. There were 83 tenements of only two rooms which each housed families of 8–12 people and another 380 houses which accommodated the same numbers in 2–3 rooms. In all, these 380 houses accommodated 3,190 people in 1,056 rooms, that is about 3 persons to a room. We are speaking here of 7% of Dudley's population. The town certainly had more small houses than most other comparable places; Wolverhampton had 50% of houses with fewer than 5 rooms and Birmingham 60%. Urban Cheltenham had only 34% of such small houses, urban Worcester 45% though rural Clun, in Shropshire was nearer 60%. Chelsea at that time was nearer Dudley, with 70% of houses less than 5 rooms. If we are curious about the present-day comparison with single 'bed-sits' and 'flatlets' we learn from the similar tables of the 1971 Census (a 1% sample only) that in England as a whole there are now 2.9 persons and 4.8 rooms per household, fewer than one person per room on the overall average. The proportion of houses with fewer than 5 rooms was 28% in 1971, as compared with Dudley's 75% in 1891.

It seems evident that the apparent contrast between the respectable stability suggested by the census returns and the more lurid pictures painted by the social reformers reflects a town in transition, at the breaking-point of its public services, with a great deal of derelict housing and no amenities for normal domestic life. Otherwise, we may be forced to ask how true was Dr. Ballard's picture of the town, not only as a whole, but even in its working-class areas? Was the doctor selective in his use of evidence? Were some of his informants prompted to exaggerate their hardships?

Were his descriptions of the houses deliberately sensational and were his motives to any extent political, in opposition to a hard-pressed council? As a perceptive nine-year-old once said of the factory reports of Robert Horne in 1841: 'If he goes on asking this sort of question in this sort of way he will always get this sort of answer . . .'. Yet, time and again, the appalling Dudley death-rate bears out Ballard's worst judgements on the Victorian town.

If we return to the census returns, and to the City of Worcester in 1851, we shall find yet more examples of the most culpable aspects of Victorian society. The enumeration of the streets of the town reflects prosperity and domestic stability, even more so than the Dudley returns. We are aware from the shops and households of the Worcester businessmen of a large and prosperous market town, at least on Foregate Street and the Cross. There, for instance, we find goldsmiths — William Manning, born in Thetford, employing his son and two assistants; William Hobbs, auctioneer and surveyor employing three sons as clerks, and another two and their sisters as surveyors, with two 'assistants' who were his brother and niece. There is Eleanor Parry, china and glass merchant, selling products of the numerous china potters, plate makers, porcelain painters and burnishers who occupy the backstreets of the city. On Foregate Street is John William Scott, a draper employing ten assistants, a book-keeper, two apprentices and a house porter. The shopping streets are crowded with the offices of veterinary surgeons, vendors of books, land agents, auctioneers, singing-masters and piano dealers.

We are reminded that this is an ancient cathedral city. In College Green we find the house of Edward Winnington, canon of the Cathedral, with a son of 30 on half-pay from the Navy, his house staffed by butler, cook, housekeeper and two maids. Living in the West End of the Cathedral was another canon, John Fortescue with a wife and four children aged 3 to 7, all 'scholars at home', looked after by a nurse, cook, laundry maid, kitchen-maid, housemaid and groom. Here was also George Wyke the sexton, William Done the cathedral organist and music-master and Octavus Fox, M.A., 'a clergyman not having care of souls' being instead the Head Master of Worcester Grammar School. There is the Deanery, where John Peel, born in Bury, Lancashire, was Dean, living with his wife and sister-in-law, accommodating a butler and under-butler, footman, two grooms, two ladies' maids, two kitchen maids, two housemaids and an under-coachman. The picture so far is pure Trollope.

Any sentimental view of a complacent Victorian scene is dispelled, however, when we turn to the Union Workhouse and the County Gaol. At the Infirmary and the Trinity Almshouses, the superficial picture of a caring society is preserved. The Infirmary patients, 109 in all, are mostly young and middle-aged, with a large number of children and adolescents; their occupations, apart from 'scholars' and errand-boys, are mainly those of labourers, glovers and 'gloveresses', servants, boatmen and the occasional carpet-weaver and staymaker. The Almshouses, like Fisher Street in Dudley, show concern for the elderly by younger relatives and lodgers. Elizabeth Jones aged 70, formerly a charwoman, keeps a lodger, aged 53, to look after her and Mary Sammons has her grand-daughter aged ten, Sarah Glover's daughter, aged 33, shares her almshouse, and one married couple, a cordwainer and his wife, were in their 50s. In the Workhouse and the Gaol, the picture is stark and inescapable.

There were 243 paupers resident in Worcester Union's workhouse in 1851; many of them were in their 70s and 80s. Men and women are listed separately; the special form for an institution generally differs from the normal household schedule in that it has a different heading to the 'relationship' column. Here, the relationship is 'to the institution' as 'pauper' or 'prisoner'; or as a member of the staff. (This is not invariably the case in smaller towns; Dudley's workhouse is included on the normal schedule for Tower Street, flanked by ordinary householders.) More than 80 of the Worcester inmates had no occupation in 1851; of the rest, the large majority of the women and a few men had been occupied in leatherwork, particularly gloving. Analysis of the occupations of workhouse inmates at any time is a useful indicator of those trades which were depressed. Only a dozen inmates had been employed in agriculture; the largest occupation for women was, equally, gloving or domestic service. Amongst this human flotsam were a schoolmaster and a governess, a musician, an equestrian, a painter, a beggar and four poor souls 'of imbecile mind'. The worst of Victorian society is still to come, for listed amongst the 'males and females' without other distinction were 64 children aged from two months to 14 years, the largest age-group about six to eleven. They too have their trades – the 'beggar' turns out to be a ten-year-old. There is a 'gloveress' of 13, John Roberts a tailor of 10, Thomas Hopkins a shoe-maker of the same age and Margaret Angelenetta, a house-servant aged 13. Worse still are the infants and babes-in-arms, one Frederick Ball only 12 months old and 'born in the County Prison'. There are six other little boys, the youngest Thomas Clarke aged 4, the oldest Thomas Nash aged 10, 'born in the Workhouse', as were also six girls, aged from three months (Mary Ann Bovey) and 'under two months' (twin girls, Fanny and Elizabeth Dooley) to the gloveress and housemaid, who were each aged 13. At the County Gaol the position was, if anything worse, at least for adolescents. There we find James Judge, 'a collier'; Mary Ann Fuller and Louisa Stamp, both nailers; all three came from Dudley. James Judge was 15 years old. There were others younger still – James Leighton a 'field labourer' from Leigh in Worcestershire was 11, George Wilkes a 'boatman' born in Gloucester was 13 and Matilda Jennings was a 'shoebinder' of 13. We could turn to the contemporary local newspapers (listed after Chapter Ten) to discover what crimes had been considered heinous enough for this.

In many towns, both large and small, we can also use the enumerators' returns to reveal the home life of our local worthies, eminent men of politics, letters and the arts. In Birmingham, for instance, it is an easy matter, having first consulted the alphabetical list of residents given in *Kelly's Post Office Directory* to discover the 1871 address of Joseph Chamberlain, the city's most illustrious Liberal politician. At the new Central Library (in Chamberlain Square) we trace the house at 'Southborne' in Augustus Road at Edgbaston and, from the microfilm we find the following family listed at that address:

Joseph Chamberlain	Head:	M:	34:	Town Councillor,	Member of the Sch. Bd.
				Wire-drawer	Born: Camberwell, Surrey
Florence „	Wife:	M:	23:		Born: Birmingham
Beatrice M.„	Daughter:		8:	Scholar	Born: Edgbaston
Joseph A. „	Son:		7:	Scholar	Born: Edgbaston
Arthur N. „	Son:		2:		Born: Edgbaston
Ann Blackwell	Servant:	U:	34:	Cook	Born: Llanidloes
Emma Shingley	Servant:	U:	24:	House-servant	Born: Essex
Eliz. Hadden	Servant:	U:	25:	Nurse	Born: Leics.
Eliza Siviter	Servant:	U:	26:	Under-nurse	Born: Halesowen, Worcs.

It is interesting to reflect that, though at this time Joseph Chamberlain was yet to become mayor of the city and its member of parliament, the house on Augusrus Road was already the home of two future Colonial Secretaries, a Foreign Secretary, a Chancellor of the Exchequer and a Prime Minister, as well as of two mayors of Birmingham. The sons of Joseph's two tragic marriages — Florence was his second wife who would die soon after the birth of a fifth child four years later — were both to be known by their second Christian names, Austen and Neville.

In the end we are left with the ultimate Benthamite question about the elaborate machinery of the census since 1801: 'What was the use of it?' What, if any, were the beneficial effects of so close a scrutiny, decade by decade, of the domestic arrangements of so many people? The predictable answer is 'social welfare' but the eight censuses taken from 1801 to 1871 do not appear to have had much effect upon government's ability to improve the lot of the people of Dudley as Dr. Ballard saw it in 1874. Significantly, it is another doctor, writing in the *British Medical Journal*, who assumes that 'every government department must now look to the census as an essential part of the statistical foundation of its work. Especially perhaps, this is true of the Ministries of Health and Labour — and of the Treasury'.[10] Regular census returns in fact have made a heyday for statisticians and bureaucrats, with little lasting benefit to the Health Service, nor to full employment.

Presumably, the knowledge of the private lives of its citizens, and the power which knowledge brings, has armed the government with a mass of official publications as reference material for more White Papers. Presumably too, this helps the management of government departments and establishes a pecking order in the scattering of funds. As to whether this knowledge has also improved the performance of government in its social policies, or helped to reverse the more undesirable social trends since 1801, that is debatable. Social engineering and political gerrymandering are certainly more feasible as a result of regular censuses. It would, of course, be naïve to expect census-taking alone to prevent unemployment or remedy social problems by itself, but what other effects has it had?

Certainly, the number of questions has proliferated. In 1801 there were six; the 1971 census form was a booklet of 36 different demands for information. Information required by the modern 'censors' has included: the number of rooms in the house and the former occupation of retired persons (1891); the duration of previous marriages and the fertility of women (1911); the extent of unemployment (1931); the sharing of accommodation (1951); the number of kitchens, sculleries, cars and garages (1966); of baths, showers and flush 'toilets' (1971); the number of Welshmen speaking Welsh in Wales (1971); children's 'O' and 'A' level results (1971) and adults' higher scientific and technological qualifications (1966); the type of tenure of each householder (1961) and his mode of transport to work (1966). These and other questions are neatly tabulated in order of their date of introduction in the *Guide to Census Reports, Great Britain 1801-1966* (H.M.S.O. 1977). It is a significant turning point for the student of the abstracts when the number of volumes containing tables and analysis begins to bulk larger than the basic returns. Only two basic tables are contained in the single bulky volume of the 1801 report, that giving county population returns by parish, township and town and the tabulation of baptisms and burials; those for 1971 take up 262 separate volumes.

It is fascinating to note how the census-takers run along behind those very problems which have outdistanced the power of government to solve. Thus, the breakdown of the public transport system, the choking of the roadways with private motor-cars, the appalling unemployment of one depression after another, schools' failure to provide an adequate basis for science and technology, a rise in the birth-rate or its decline, all are confirmed, too late, by these statistics. Apparently the best which any government can do is to *enumerate* the social factors which add up to the decay of the inner cities and *list* the miseries imposed upon the decent people of Fisher Street in 1871 or of Brixton and Toxteth in 1981. No social problem since 1801 has been solved half as effectively as the needs of the state to exact taxation, marshal voting areas and mobilize the people in arms. Otherwise, perhaps the most productive use of the 19th-century census returns rests with the work of the impartial social historian and the searcher after local history.

Fortunately for the student, these records are readily accessible in record offices and libraries. The main source for originals is the Public Record Office (P.R.O.). At the time of writing there are facilities for reading the census returns on microfilm without the requirement of a reader's ticket, or the payment of any fee, at the Old Land Registry building in Portugal Street, London, W.2. (However, since various schemes are under discussion for the removal of the returns to another P.R.O. building, students intending to pay a visit for this purpose should telephone in advance to ascertain the current situation). The P.R.O. will undertake limited searches, and issue a leaflet detailing the services they offer, but the widespread availability of microfilm copies of the enumerators' schedules should make these unnecessary for most students. It is heartening to find at a time of financial stringency how many local record offices and libraries keep up-to-date census returns for their town and county, even including the most recently available ones for 1881. These are in constant use in reading rooms — evidently the most popular family record of all time.

The general availability of this revolutionary aid to census studies is comprehensively listed, county by county, by J. S. W. Gibson in *Census Returns (1841–1881) on Microfilm: A Directory to Local Holdings* which includes references to photocopies and transcripts available.[11] Some towns' microfilms lie scattered in several neighbouring counties, as well as in their own record office. They are also found in county libraries, town archives and college libraries, so that the *Directory* is invaluable to the student who cannot easily travel to the county record office. Censuses of various Leicestershire parishes, for instance, can be found in eleven different libraries, as far afield as Burton-on-Trent, Loughborough, Birmingham, Derby and Nottingham University, as well as at Northampton, Stafford and Leicester county record offices. In most cases the record office holds microfilm of the historic county's censuses from 1841–1881; each town also has its own copies. Most libraries produce indexes relating local streets to their enumeration district numbers. Dudley, for example, has an excellent set of indexes for 1841–81; many county record offices, too, can provide a comprehensive index to parishes on microfilm. Worcestershire, though it has as yet no overall county index, has the complete set of microfilms and a useful index to the streets of Worcester City. Some town libraries even provide an index of surnames in the censuses. The P.R.O. offers street indexes for some towns; these are listed by Beresford and Gibson and are marked with an asterisk in the Gazetteer to this Chapter; microfilm can be ordered by the serious searcher from the P.R.O. From the normal 35 mm reel there will be 12 frames to a foot with an average of 3 to 4 normal-sized households on each frame. Microfilm can be projected by an ordinary filmstrip projector and does not require a special micro-reading machine, provided that the film is not allowed to become too hot. Photocopies can be ordered from the P.R.O. if the enumeration district and parish are known, or if there is a street index.

Some county record offices will carry out searches on behalf of students. Most public librarians and archivists will remind the reader that, being Crown copyright, photocopies cannot be taken from the P.R.O. microfilm. Some archives, however, as at Stafford, are equipped with reader-printers and have an arrangement by which instantaneous copies can be made for the student.

In any case, armed with a notebook, or pad of computer coding sheets and a reel of enumerators' schedules on the micro-reader, any searcher can amass a wealth of information about the homes of Victorian townsmen within a few hours. Allowing for occasional human error, the exaggeration of a lifetime's work by an over-ambitious title, forgetfulness of exact age or confusion as to birthplace, these records are incomparable. Generally speaking, from thousands of entries we gain an impression of modest people obediently and ingenuously offering their domestic secrets for the statisticians' benefit. Some must disclose their illegitimate 'nephew', others admit to being paupers; a few are cruelly marked as 'idiot'. Many more quietly prosper. As to whether they were content, no computer programme can find that answer.

FURTHER READING

The Public Record Office has a leaflet obtainable by post, entitled *Censuses of Population 1841–1881* which is an adequate brief guide to these documents.

Armstrong, W. A., 'The interpretation of the Census Enumerators' Books for Victorian towns' in *The Study of Urban History* (ed.: H. J. Dyos) (1968).

Barke, M., 'Census enumeration books and the local historian', *Loc. Hist.*, vol. 10 (5) 1972.

Beresford, M. W., 'The unprinted census returns of 1851 and 1861 for England and Wales', *Loc. Hist.*, vol. 5 (8), 1963.

Drake. M., *Historical Demography: Problems and Projects* (1974).

Dyos, H. J. and Baker, A. B. M., 'The possibilities of computerising census data' in *The Study of Urban History* (ed.: H. J. Dyos) (1968).

Fell, C., *The Eighteenth Century Religious Census: A Select Bibliograph of Materials relating to England and Wales* (Wesley Hist. Soc., 1979).

Gibson, J. and Chapman, C., *Census Indexes and Indexing* (Fed. Fam. Hist. Soc., 1981).

Glass, D. V., *The Development of Population Statistics* (1973).

Gwynne, T. and Sill, M., 'Census enumeration books: A study of mid-nineteenth century immigration', *Loc. Hist.*, vol. 12 (2) (1976).

Henstock, A., 'House Repopulation from the Census Returns of 1841 and 1851', *Loc. Population Stud.*, No. 10 (1973).

Laslett, P., 'The history of population and social structure', *Int. Soc. Sci. Rev.*, No. 589 (1969).

Law, C. M., 'Local censuses in the 18th century', *Population Stud.*, No. 23 (1969).

—— 'The growth of urban population in England and Wales', *Inst. Brit. Geog. Trans.*, vol. 41 (1967).

—— 'Sources for urban history (6): A short bibliography of eighteenth century urban population history', *Loc. Hist.*, vol. 10 (3) (1974).

Lawton, R., *Census and Social Structure: An Interpretative Guide to the Nineteenth Century Censuses for England and Wales* (1978).

Mills, D. R., 'The technique of house repopulation: Experience from a Cambridgeshire village', *Loc. Hist.*, vol. 13 (2) (1978).

Mitchison, Rosalind: *British Population Change since 1860* (1977).

Rushton, P., 'Anomalies as evidence in nineteenth century censuses', *Loc. Hist.*, vol. 13 (8) (1979).

Smith, R., 'Demography in the nineteenth century: an introduction to the local historian', *Loc. Hist.*, vol. 9 (8) (1970).

Spencer, K. M., 'Sources for industrial history (4); Census enumeration schedules', *Loc. Hist.*, vol. 11 (3) (1974).

Taylor, A. J., 'The taking of the census 1801–1951', *Brit. Med. Jnl.*, 7 April, 1951.

GAZETTEER OF URBAN POPULATION 1801–1974

The following table of towns' population is taken either from the original printed abstracts, in which case the figures are given in normal print (e.g.: 10,016) or from the *Victoria County History* tables, in *italic* numbers (e.g.: *57,312*). In some cases where there appears to be a discrepancy between these two sets of numbers (as under ABINGDON), both versions are given, bracketed together, wherever they coincide the abstracts' figure is printed. Any difference will usually be due to a different interpretation of the geographic area of township or parish, as described on pages 275–276, and should in any case be carefully checked, particularly wherever there appears to be a significant anomaly in a town's rate of growth. The census abstracts are by no means consistent in their definitions of the same places from decade to decade. An asterisk after the place-name (e.g.: ASHTON-UNDER-LYNE*) indicates the availability of a P.R.O. street-index for that town. The pre-1801 column indicates the existence of an early local census or estimate of population, as given by C. M. Law in 'Some notes on the urban population of England and Wales in the 18th century' in *Local Historian*, vol. 10 (3), 1974, to which further reference should be made.

Tables of population are printed in the *Victoria County Histories* of all English counties except Cornwall, Cumberland, Devon, Herefordshire, Monmouthshire, Norfolk, Northamptonshire, Northumberland and Westmorland. Those tables which are been published are found in the following volumes:

Bedfordshire, Vol. II	Berkshire, Vol. II
Buckinghamshire, Vol. II	Cambridgeshire, Vol. II
Cheshire, Vol. II	Derbyshire, Vol. II
Dorset, Vol. II	Durham, Vol. II
Essex, Vol. II	Gloucestershire, Vol. II
Hampshire, Vol. V	Hertfordshire, Vol. IV
Huntingdonshire, Vol. II	Kent, Vol. III
Lancashire, Vol. II	Leicestershire, Vol. III
Lincolnshire, Vol. II	Middlesex, Vol. II
Nottinghamshire, Vol. II	Oxfordshire, Vol. II
Rutland, Vol. I	Shropshire, Vol. II
Somerset, Vol. II	Staffordshire, Vol. I
Suffolk, Vol. I	Surrey, Vol. IV
Sussex, Vol. II	Warwickshire, Vol. II
Wiltshire, Vol. IV	Worcestershire, Vol. IV
Yorkshire (General Volumes), Vol. III.	

Place-names listed in **bold print** (e.g.: **ABERGAVENNY**) are towns which were already incorporated boroughs before the first national census. Other towns in normal type (e.g.: ACCRINGTON) have their population figure given in **bold numerals** in the decade during which they gained incorporation. The remainder are those towns which were not incorporated before 1901; those are listed in *italics* (e.g.: *ALDERSHOT*) and the date of their incorporation is entered between the columns for 1901–1961 or 1971 as required. The population figures for 1961 are taken from the *Index of Place Names (A–K and L–Z)* published by the General Register Office (H.M.S.O. 1965) which confirms the description of each town at that date, as MB (metropolitan borough), CB (county borough) or UD (urban district) at that date and is a convenient gazetteer, being alphabetically arranged for England and Wales, not county by county. For 1971 the easiest reference is to *Census 1971 England and Wales; Preliminary Report* (H.M.S.O. 1971). Here, *Table 4: Population 1951–1971* notes successive changes of boundaries and place-names. More convenient — and more up-to-date — is the *Index of Place-Names (A–K and L–Z)* for that census (H.M.S.O. 1977). This takes into account the boundary revisions of 1972–74, listing the districts which were not in fact effective at the time of the 1971 census. Thus, the 1961 figures are given for the last census before the London Borough reorganizations and the 1971–77 figures record the effects of the more widespread boundary changes. The preliminary figures for 1981 were given previously in the Gazetteer to Chapter One (pages 1–27) and are available in the *Preliminary Report: Census 1981* (Office of Population Censuses and Surveys 1981). Unfortunately, these preliminary figures, which are quoted by Almanacks such as *Whitaker* for the several years which now elapse between census and full publication, are usually considerably different in many towns from the final analysis; this may result in discrepancies between one published population figure and another.

The 1981 *Preliminary Report* gives comparative figures for 1961, 1971 and 1981; this is also the case in several of the earlier printed abstracts and reports. This reduces the amount of reference otherwise required from volume to volume in each decade. For example, the report for 1831 tabulates the totals for 1801–1831 inclusive and calculates each county's percentage increases over that period. The 1841 Report has comparative tables (for 74 towns only) from 1801–1841. The Report for 1871 tabulates the figures for 1861 and 1871 and distinguishes between municipal and parliamentary boroughs. The report for 1891 has summary tables arranges alphabetically, indicating the nature of each local authority, whether UD, MB, etc. and gives comparative figures for 1881 and 1891. The table also notes boundary changes since 1881; these are marked (**B**) in this Gazetteer's 1891 column. The 1901 census report is in some ways the most useful starting point to tabulate any town's population, as the whole of Britain is listed alphabetically, not by counties, from Abbas Bradford to Zoyland St Mary, with a statement of all the different authorities with the same place-names; indicating also CB, MB and Met B as distinct from the wider-spread parliamentary boroughs, ecclesiastical parishes, civil parishes and urban districts. Most of the reports from 1841 give extensive analyses of the distribution of age-groups, occupations, places of birth and in some cases, e.g. 1891, maps.

ABBREVIATIONS

The abbreviations in the final column are those descriptions used in the Census Reports of 1971 and 1981: (Loc) = Location; (Par) = Parish; (Com) = Community; (LB) = London Borough; (D) = District. The use of such terms indicates how low the status of many former boroughs has now become.

'District' populations (e.g. of Chichester District, Barnsley District), which will differ from populations of old boroughs, are listed in the Gazetteer to Chapter One.

A note on London Boroughs

Before 1889, parishes in London and its environs were also within the counties of Middlesex, Surrey, Kent or Essex. These original descriptions are given with each London place-name in the first column of the Gazetteer. By the Local Government Act of 1888 the metropolis became the separate County of London and by the London Government Act of 1899 this county was divided into 28 metropolitan boroughs; these are listed in the 1961 column. The London Government Act of 1963 combined the L.C.C. with the entire county of Middlesex, parts of Surrey, Kent, Essex and Hertfordshire, to form Greater London, which now includes the City of London and 32 London Boroughs. These are identified in the last column of the Gazetteer. Dates of those municipal or county boroughs which had been incorporated before 1963 are noted before the 1961 column, which also adds their status as (MB) or (CB); urban districts (UD) are also shown here. See the *Guide to Local Administrative Units of England 1: Southern England* by F. A. Youngs (Royal Hist Soc. 1969) for successive changes in these and other towns.

TOWN	Pre-1801	1801	1811	1821	1831	1841	1851
ABERGAVENNY, Mon		2,573	2,815	3,388	3,940	4,657	4,797
ABERYSTWYTH, Card		1,758	2,264	3,556	4,128	4,916	5,231
ABINGDON (1), Berks	1750:3,000	(4,683)	(5,173)	(5,456)	(5,617)	(6,149)	(6,848
	1775:3,600	(4,356)	(4,801)	(5,137)	(5,259)	(5,585)	(5,954
ACCRINGTON (2), Lancs		3,077	3,266	5,370	6,283	8,719	10,374
ALDEBURGH, E.Suff		804	1,066	1,212	1,341	1,557	1,627
ALDERSHOT (3), Hants		494	498	525	665	685	875
ALTRINCHAM (4), Ches		1,692	2,032	2,302	2,708	3,399	4,488
ANDOVER, Hants		3,304	3,295	4,123	4,748	4,941	5,178
APPLEBY (5), Westm		1,631	2,160	2,616	2,723	2,519	2,709
ARUNDEL, W.Suss		1,855	2,188	2,511	2,803	2,624	2,748
ASHTON-u-LYNE, Lancs		15,632	19,052	25,967	33,597	46,304	(56,959
							(30,676
AYLESBURY, Bucks	1706–21:2,250	3,186	3,447	4,400	5,021	5,429	6,081
BACUP (6), Lancs		5,046	6,930	8,557	9,196	11,668	16,915
BANBURY, Oxon	1750:2,500	2,755	2,841	3,396	3,737	3,751	4,026
	1775:3,000						
BANGOR, Caern		1,770	2,383	3,579	4,751	7,232	6,338
BARKING (7), Essex		3,906	5,543	6,374	8,036	8,718	9,888
Also: *Dagenham, Essex*		1,057	1,488	1,864	2,118	2,294	2,494
BARNET (8), Herts		1,258	1,579	1,755	2,369	2,485	2,380
Also: *East Barnet, Herts*		353	406	507	547	598	663
Friern Barnet, Msx		423	487	534	615	849	974
Finchley, Msx		1,503	1,292	2,349	3,210	3,664	4,120
Hadley, Msx		584	718	926	979	945	1,003
*Hendon, Msx**		1,955	2,589	3,100	3,110	3,327	3,333
BARNSLEY, Yorks (WR)*		3,606	5,014	8,248	10,333	12,370	13,43
BARNSTAPLE, Devon	1709:2,500	3,748	4,019	5,079	6,840	7,902	11,37
	1779:3,200						
BARROW-in-FURNESS, Lancs		—	—	—	—	—	—
BARRY, Glam		70	62	67	72	104	74
BASINGSTOKE (9). Hants		2,589	2,656	3,165	3,581	4,066	4,26
BATH, Som*	1750:9,000	27,686	31,496	36,811	38,063	38,304	(52,240
	1775:20,500						(39,10
BATLEY, Yorks (WR)		2,574	2,975	3,717	4,841	7,076	9,30
BEAUMARIS, Angsy		1,576	1,810	2,205	2,497	2,701	2,59
BEBINGTON (10), Ches		1,026	1,206	1,678	2,193	5,008	10,01
BECCLES, E.Suff		2,788	2,979	3,493	3,862	4,086	4,39
BEDFORD, Beds	1706–21:3,130	3,984	4,605	5,859	6,959	9,178	11,69
	1788–92:3,380						
BERWICK-u-TWEED, Nmbd	1750:4,000	7,187	7,746	8,723	8,920	8,484	15,09
	1775:5,500						
BEVERLEY, Yorks	1750:3,600	6,001	6,731	7,503	8,302	8,671	8,91
	1775:4,400						
BEWDLEY, Worcs	1773:3,442	3,671	3,454	3,725	3,908	3,400	3,12
BEXHILL, E.Suss		1,091	1,627	1,907	1,827	1,822	2,02
BEXLEY, Kent		1,441	1,774	2,311	(3,026)	(3,955)	(4,49
					(1,533)	(2,082)	(2,23
Also: *Crayford*		1,210	1,553	1,866	2,022	2,408	2,93
Erith		969	1,119	1,363	1,533	2,082	2,23
Sidcup — as part of Foots Cray parish							
BIDEFORD, Devon	1750:2,500	2,987	3,244	4,053	4,846	5,211	5,77
	1775:3,000						
BIRKENHEAD (11), Ches*		110	105	200	2,569	8,223	24,28
BIRMINGHAM (12), Warks,*	1750:23,688	73,670	85,753	106,722	(146,980)	(190,542)	(232,84
Worcs, Staffs					(174,378)	(228,640)	(294,12

1861	1871	1881	1891	1901	......	1961	1971-77
5,801	6,318	6,941	7,743	7,795		9,624 (MB)	9,401 (Com)
5,641	6,898	7,088	6,725	8,014		10,427 (MB)	10,688 (Com)
(6,700)	(6,943)	(7,019)	(6,773)	6,689		14,287 (MB)	18,610 (Par)
(5,680)	(5,805)	(6,755)	(6,557)				
17,688	21,788	31,435	38,603	43,122		39,018 (MB)	36,894 (Loc)
1,721	1,990	2,106	2,159	2,405		3,007 (MB)	3,180 (Par)
16,720	21,682	20,155	25,595	30,974	(UD 1922)	31,225 (MB)	33,390 (Loc)
6,628	8,478	11,250	12,440	16,831	(UD 1937)	41,222 (MB)	40,787 (Loc)
5,221	5,501	5,653	5,852	6,509		16,985 (MB)	25,881 (Loc)
2,844	1,680	1,855	1,776	1,764		1,755 (MB)	1,890 (Par)
2,498	2,956	2,748	2,644	2,739		2,617 (MB)	2,990 (Par)
(66,801)	(64,558)	(75,310)	(80,991)	(86,001)		50,154 (MB)	48,952 (Loc)
(34,886)	(32,020)	(37,040)	(40,463)	(43,890)			
6,168	6,962	7,795	8,680	9,099	(UD)	27,923 (MB)	40,569 (Loc)
24,413	26,823	25,034	23,498	22,505		17,308 (MB)	15,118 (Loc)
4,059	4,106	12,072	12,768	12,968		21,004 (MB)	29,387 (Loc)
10,662	10,825	9,005	9,892	11,269		13,993 (C:MB)	14,558 (Com)
10,996	12,523	16,848	25,214	(62,781)	(1931)	72,282 (MB)	153,870 (LB)
				(21,547)	(UD)		
2,708	2,879	3,411	4,324	6,091	(1938)	108,363 (MB)	(Loc)
2,989	3,375	4,095	5,496	7,876	(UD)	27,846 (UD)	305,700 (LB)
851	2,925	3,992	5,128	6,839		40,641 (UD)	(Loc)
3,344	4,347	6,424	9,173	11,566		28,813 (UD)	(Loc)
4,937	7,146	11,191	16,647	22,126	(1932)	69,311 (MB)	(Loc)
1,053	978	1,160	1,294	1,389			(Loc)
4,544	6,972	10,484	15,843	22,450	(1932)	151,500 (MB)	(Loc)
17,885	23,021	29,790	35,427	41,086		74,704 (CB)	75,395 (D)
10,743	11,636	12,284	13,058	14,137		15,944 (MB)	17,317 (Par)
—	18,245	47,259	51,712 (B)	57,586		64,927 (CB)	64,034 (D)
87	112	494	13,278	27,030	(UD 1939)	42,084 (MB)	41,681 (Com)
4,654	5,574	(6,806)	(8,213)(B)	9,510		25,980 (MB)	52,587 (D)
		(6,681)	(7,960)				
(52,528)	(52,542)	(51,814)	(51,844)	(49,839)		80,901 (C:CB)	84,670* (D)
(37,362)	(36,266)	(34,383)	(33,379)	(31,215)			
14,173	20,868	27,505	28,719	30,321		39,639 (MB)	42,006 (Loc)
2,558	2,234	2,239	2,202	2,326		1,962 (MB)	2,102 (Com)
15,105	23,725	(8,722)	(9,588)	(9,938)	(UD 1937)	52,814 (MB)	61,582 (Loc)
4,266	4,818	5,721	6,669	6,898		7,332 (MB)	8,015 (Par)
13,413	16,849	19,533	28,023	35,144		63,334 (MB)	73,229 (D)
13,265	13,231	13,998	13,377	13,437		12,178 (MB)	11,647 (D)
9,654	10,218	11,425	12,539	13,183		16,031 (MB)	17,132 (D)
2,905	3,018	(3,088)	(2,876)	(2,866)		5,041 (MB)	7,237 (Par)
		(3,259)	(3,048)	(3,027)			
2,011	2,051	2,333	5,089	12,110	(UD 1902)	28,941 (MB)	32,898 (Loc)
(4,944)	(6,448)	8,793	10,605	12,918	(UD 1937)	89,550 (MB)	216,400 (LB)
(4,143)	(8,289)						
3,103	3,887	4,347	5,268	6,572		31,287 (UD)	(Loc)
4,143	8,289	9,812	13,414	25,296		45,026 (MB)	(Loc)
						86,892 (UD)	(Loc)
						As Chiselhurst & Sidcup UD	
5,742	6,953	6,512	7,831	8,754		10,498 (MB)	11,802 (Par)
33,212	42,891	84,006	99,857 (B)	110,915		141,813 (CB)	137,852 (Loc)
(296,076)	(343,696)	(436,971)	(478,113)(B)	(522,204)		1,107,187 (C:CB)	1,014,670 (D)
(391,071)	(483,785)	(602,079)	(679,450)	(744,973)			

TOWN	Pre--1801	1801	1811	1821	1831	1841	1851
BLACKBURN, Lancs*	1750:4,000 1775:6,000	11,980	15,083	21,940	27,091	36,629	46,536
BLACKPOOL (13), Lancs		473	580	749	943	1,968	2,564
BLANDFORD FORUM, Dorset		2,326	2,425	2,643	3,109	3,349	(3,948) (2,504)
BLYTH, Nmbd		1,170	1,522	1,805	1,769	1,921	2,060
BODMIN, Cornwall		1,951	2,050	2,902	3,375	4,205	4,327
BOLTON, Lancs*	1773:5,339	12,549	17,070	22,037	28,297	33,610	61,171
BOOTLE, Lancs		537	610	808	1,133	1,902	4,106
BOSTON, Lincs	1709:3,008 1767:3,470 1778:5,476	5.926	8,180	10,373	11,240	12,648	14,733
BOURNEMOUTH (14), Hants		—	—	—	—	905	1,330
BRACKLEY (15), Nthants		1,495	1,580	1,851	2,107	2,121	2,157
BRADFORD (16), Yorks* (WR)		6,393	7,767	13,064	23,233	34,560	103,778
BRECON, Brecon (or Brecknock)		2,576	3,196	4,193	5,026	5,701	5,673
BRENT							
As: _Wembley, Msx_	In Harrow	—	—	—	—	—	—
Willesden, Msx		751	1,169	1,413	1,876	2,930	2,939
BRIDGWATER, Som	1750:2,800 1775:3,200	3,634	4,911	6,155	7,807	10,450	(10,965 (10,317
BRIDLINGTON, Yorks (ER)	1750:2,000 1775:2,800	3,130	3,741	4,275	4,792	5,162	5,839
BRIDPORT, Dorset		3,117	3,567	3,742	4,242	4,787	4,653
BRIGHOUSE (17), Yorks (WR)		2,879	3,357	3,936	4,977	5,421	6,091
BRIGHTON (18), E.Suss*	1739:4,500 1794:5,669	7,339	12,012	24,429	40,634	46,661	65,569
BRISTOL (19), Glos*	1750:50,000 1775:55,000	63,645	76,433	87,779	103,886	122,296	137,328
BROMLEY, Kent*		2,700	2,965	3,147	4,002	4,325	4,127
Beckenham:		955	1,093	1,180	1,288	1,608	1,688
Chislehurst:		1,217	1,450	1,586	1,820	1,792	2,088
Orpington:		693	727	754	842	907	1,203
Penge: (Hamlet)		—	—	228	229	270	1,169
BUCKINGHAM, Bucks		2,605	2,978	3,465	3,610	4,054	4,020
BURNLEY, Lancs*		3,305	4,368	6,378	7,551	10,699	14,706
BURTON-u-TRENT (20), Staffs*	1750:2,500 1775:2,800 1789:3,479	3,679	3,979	4,114	4,399	4,863	6,374
BURY (21), Lancs*		(23,300) (7,072)	(29,917) (8,762)	(34,355) (10,583)	(47,627) (15,086)	(62,125) (20,710)	(70,143 (25,484
BURY ST EDMUNDS, W.Suff*	1757:5,819 1775:7,135	7,655	7,986	10,029	11,436	12,538	13,900
BUXTON, Derbs		760	934	1,036	1,211	1,569	1,991
CAERNARFON (22), Caern*		3,626	4,595	5,788	7,642	8,001	8,674
CALNE, Wilts		3,767	3,547	4,612	4,876	5,128	5,118
CAMBRIDGE (23), Cambs	1728:6,422 1744:9,868	10,085	11,108	14,142	20,917	24,453	27,815
CAMDEN, Msx		—	—	—	—	—	—
Also: _Clerkenwell, Msx *_		23,396	30,537	39,105	47,634	56,756	64,778
Hampstead, Msx *		4,343	5,483	7,263	8,588	10,093	11,980
Holborn, Msx *		29,986	31,454	35,762	37,079	38,790	40,846
Bloomsbury, Msx *		36,502	48,536	51,793	52,907	54,292	54,214
St Pancras, Msx		31,779	46,333	71,838	103,548	129,735	166,956
CANTERBURY, Kent	1770:9,000	9,642	10,237	12,779	13,679	15,435	(14,526 (18,398
CARDIFF, Glam*		1,870	2,457	3,521	6,187	10,007	18,351

1861	1871	1881	1891	1901	.....	1961	1971-77
63,126	76,339	(91,958)	(104,342)	(108,865)		106,242 (CB)	101,806 (D)
		(104,014)	(120,640)	(127,626)			
3,907	7,092	(14,229)	(28,846)	(47,348)		153,186 (CB)	151,860 (D)
		(12,711)	(21,624)	(38,079)			
(3,900)	(4,052)	(3,791)	(4,014)	3,850		3,566 (MB)	3,647 (Par)
(1,521)	(1,536)	(3,753)	(3,974)	—		—	—
2,901	2,918	2,831	3,728 (B)	5,472	(UD 1922)	35,921 (MB)	34,653 (Loc)
4,466	4,672	5,061	5,151	5,353		6,214 (MB)	9,207 (Par)
70,395	82,854	105,414	115,002	168,215		160,789 (CB)	154,199 (D)
6,414	16,247	27,374	49,217 (B)	58,556		82,773 (CB)	74,294 (Loc)
14,712	15,756	14,941	14,593	15,667		24,915 (MB)	26,025 (D)
2,488	6,034	18,607	37,781 (B)	47,003		154,296 (CB)	153,869 (D)
2,239	2,154	2,476	2,591	2,467		3,208 (MB)	4,480 (Par)
106,218	145,827	194,495	216,361 (B)	279,767		295,922 (C:CB)	294,177 (D)
5,235	5,845	6,372	5,794	5,741		5,766 (MB)	6,304 (Com:D)
						—	280,657 (LB)
—	—	—	—	—	(1937)	124,843 (MB)	(Loc)
3,879	15,869	27,453	61,057	114,852	(1933)	170,835 (MB)	(Loc)
(12,120)	(12,636)	(12,704)	(13,246)	(14,900)		25,600 (MB)	26,642 (Loc)
(11,320)	(12,101)	(12,007)	(12,436)	(15,209)			
5,775	6,203	8,343	8,916	12,482		26,023 (MB)	26,776 (Loc)
4,645	4,643	3,936	3,768	3,053		6,530 (MB)	6,369 (Par)
7,340	9,871	12,660	15,571	17,073		30,804 (MB)	34,141 (Loc)
77,693	90,011	(107,546)	(115,873)	(123,478)		163,159 (CB)	161,351 (D)
		(99,091)	(102,716)	(102,320)			
154,093	182,524	206,874	221,578	328,945		437,048 (Co.C.CB)	426,657 (D)
5,505	10,674	15,154	21,684	24,625	(UD 1903)	68,252 (MB)	306,680 (LB)
2,124	6,090	13,045	20,707	26,331	193	77,290 (MB)	(Loc)
2,287	3,313	.5,341	6,443	7,417		86,892 (UD)	(Loc)
					As Chiselhurst & Sidcup UD (see Bexley)		
1,727	2,371	3,050	4,099	4,259		80,293 (UD)	(Loc)
5,015	13,202	18,650	20,375	22,465		25,743 (UD)	(Loc)
3,849	3,703	3,585	3,364	3,152		4,379 (MB)	5,076 (Par)
(19,971)	(21,501)	(28,744)	(39,550)	(44,045)		80,599 (CB)	76,513 (D)
(28,700)	(31,608)	(63,339)	(87,016)	(97,043)			
9,534	9,450	9,348	8,212	7,370		50,751 (CB)	50,201 (Loc)
(80,558)	(85,906)	(99,494)	(102,103)	(102,687)		60,149 (CB	67,849 (D)
(37,563)	(41,517)	(54,717)	(57,212)	(58,029)			
13,318	14,928	16,111	16,630	16,255		21,179 (MB)	25,661 (Loc)
1,877	2,451	6,025	7,540	10,181	(UD 1917)	19,155 (MB)	20,324 (Loc)
8,512	9,370	10,258	9,894	9,760		9,055 (MB)	9,260 (Com)
5,098	5,256	5,194	5,518	5,344		6,754 (MB)	9,688 (Par)
26,361	30,058	35,363	36,983	38,379		95,527 (C.MB)	98,840 (D)
—	—	—	*Camden Town* Loc in St Pancras Met.B.				203,640 (LB)
65,681	65,380	69,076	66,216	64,077	Loc in Finsbury Met.B		(Loc)
19,106	32,281	45,452	68,416	82,329		98,844 (Met.B)	(Loc)
39,399	39,400	32,854	30,734	27,079		22,008 (Met.B)	(Loc)
54,076	53,556	45,382	39,782	34,534	Loc in Holborn Met.B		(Loc)
198,788	221,465	236,258	234,379	234,912		124,855 (Met.B)	(Loc)
(17,027)	(16,904)	(17,401)	(18,503) (B)	(19,798)		30,415 (Co.C.CB)	33,176 (D)
(21,324)	(20,961)	(21,848)	(23,062)	(24,899)			
32,954	39,675	82,761	128,915	164,333		256,582 (C.CB)	279,111 (D)

TOWN	Pre-1801	1801	1811	1821	1831	1841	1851
CARDIGAN, Card		1,911	2,129	2,397	2,795	2,925	3,876
CARLISLE, Cumb	1763:4,158	10,221	12,531	15,476	20,006	23,012	26,310
	1780:6,229						
	1787:2,677						
	1796:8,716						
CARMARTHEN, Carm;	1750:4,000	5,548	7,275	8,906	9,995	9,526	10,524
	1775:4,700;						
CASTLEFORD, Yorks (WR);		793	890	1,022	1,141	1,414	2,150
CHARD (24), Som;		2,784	2,932	3,106	*5,141*	*5,788*	*(5,297*
							(2,291
CHATHAM, Kent		*10,505*	*12,652*	*15,268*	*16,990*	19,470	22,399
CHELMSFORD, Essex	1738:2,151	*3,755*	*4,649*	*4,994*	*5,435*	6,789	7,796
	1770:2,800						
CHELTENHAM, Glos*		3,076	8,325	13,396	22,942	*31,411*	*35,051*
CHESTER (25), Ches*	1722:11,000	15,052	16,140	19,949	21,344	23,115	27,776
	1774:14,713						
CHESTERFIELD, Derbs*	1783:3,335	4,267	4,476	5,077	5,077	5,775	7,101
	1791:3,987						
CHICHESTER, W.Suss.	1739:4,500	4,752	6,425	*7,362*	*8,356*	*8,512*	*(8,647*
	1755:4,600						*(8,622*
CHIPPENHAM, Wilts		3,366	3,410	*3,506*	*4,333*	*5,438*	*(6,706*
							(1,707
CHIPPING NORTON (26), Oxon		*2,200*	*2,331*	*2,640*	*2,637*	*3,031*	*(3,368*
							(2,932
CHORLEY, Lancs		4,516	5,182	7,315	9,282	13,139	12,684
CHRISTCHURCH, Hants		*3,773*	*4,149*	*4,644*	*5,344*	*5,994*	*6,256*
CLEETHORPES (27), Lincs		284	375	406	497	803	839
CLITHEROE, Lancs		*1,368*	*1,767*	*3,213*	*5,213*	*6,765*	*7,244*
COLCHESTER, Essex	1738:2,151	11,520	12,544	14,016	16,167	17,790	19,443
	1770:2,800						
COLNE, Lancs		3,626	5,336	7,274	*8,080*	*8,615*	*8,987*
COLWYN BAY (28), Denb.							
CONGLETON (28(a)), Ches	1722:2,250	*3,861*	*4,616*	*6,405*	*9,352*	9,222	*10,520*
	1789:3,000						
CONWY, Caern		889	1,053	1,105	1,245	1,358	2,105
COVENTRY (29), Warw*	1749:12,817	*(21,187)*	*(23,352)*	*(28,811)*	*(37,154)*	*(41,101)*	*(47,965*
	1775:14,500	*(16,034)*	*(17,923)*	*(21,242)*	*(26,070)*	*(30,743)*	*(36,308*
CREWE (30), Ches		*121*	*114*	*146*	*148*	*203*	*4,571*
CROSBY (31), Lancs		*742*	*852*	*1,033*	*1,615*	*2,340*	*2,810*
CROYDON, Surrey*	1750:3,000	5,743	7,801	9,254	*12,447*	16,712	20,343
	1783:4,000						
Coulsdon: Surrey		*420*	*440*	*516*	*630*	*1,041*	*713*
Purley: Surrey							
DARLINGTON (32), Durham	1750:2,500	*5,349*	*5,820*	*6,551*	*9,417*	*11,877*	*12,453*
	1767:3,295						
DARTFORD, Kent		*2,406*	*3,177*	*3,593*	*4,715*	*5,619*	*6,224*
DARTMOUTH, Devon		—	—	—	—	—	*4,508*
DARWEN (33), Lancs		*5,233*	*6,216*	*8,949*	*9,639*	*12,425*	*15,223*
DAVENTRY, Nthants		*2,582*	*2,758*	*3,326*	*3,646*	*4,177*	*4,430*
DEAL, Kent	1750:2,500	*5,420*	*7,351*	*6,811*	*7,268*	*6,688*	*7,067*
	1775:3,000						
DENBIGH, Denb.		2,391	2,714	3,195	3,786	5,238	*5,498*
DERBY, Derbs*	1712:4,000	10,832	13,043	17,423	23,607	32,741	40,609
	1750:6,250						
	1788:8,563						
DEVIZES, Wilts	1750:2,800	*3,574*	*3,750*	*4,208*	*4,562*	*4,631*	*6,554*
	1775:3,100						
DEWSBURY, Yorks (WR)*	1775:3,000	*4,566*	*5,059*	*6,380*	*8,272*	*10,600*	*14,049*

1861	1871	1881	1891	1901	.....	1961	1971–77	
3,543	3,535	3,669	3,449	3,510		3,789 (MB)	3,810	(D)
29,417	31,074	36,585	39,176 (B)	45,480		71,101 (C.CB)	71,582	(D)
9,993	10,499	10,414	10,264	10,025		13,247 (MB)	13,081	(D)
3,876	6,268	10,530	14,143	17,386	(UD 1955)	40,350 (MB)		
(5,316)	*(5,636)*	*(5,682)*	*(6,075)*	*(6,318)*		5,779 (MB)		
(2,276)	*(2,400)*	*(2,411)*	*(3,575)*	*(4,437)*				
25,183	*26,661*	*26,889*	31,901	*37,302*		48,784 (MB)	57,153	(Loc)
8,407	*9,318*	9,885	11,111	12,627		49,908 (MB)	58,194	(D)
39,693	*41,923*	43,972	42,914	44,805		72,154 (MB)	74,356	(D)
31,110	35,275	36,794	37,105 (B)	38,309		59,268 (Co.C.CB)	62,911	(D)
9,836	11,426	19,835	22,009	27,185		67,858 (MB)	70,169	(D)
(8,884)	*(8,205)*	*(8,569)*	*(7,887)*	*(8,934)*		20,124 (C.MB)	20,649	(D)
(8,059)	(7,850)	(8,149)	(7,830)	(12,244)				
(6,999)	*(6,589)*	*(11,039)*	*(10,010)*	*(10,677)*		17,543 (MB)	18,696	(Loc)
(1,603)	(1,387)	(4,495)	4,618)	5,074)				
(3,510)	*(4,092)*	*(4,607)*	*(4,564)*	*(4,130)*		4,245 (MB)	4,763	(Par)
(3,137)	(3,640)	(4,167)	(4,222)	(3,780)				
15,013	16,864	19,478	23,087	26,852		31,315 (MB)	31,659	(D)
7,042	*9,475*	*12,965*	25,957	32,941		26,336 (MB)	31,463	(D)
1,230	1,768	2,840	4,306	12,578	(UD 1936)	32,700 (MB)	35,837	(D)
7,000	8,217	10,192	10,828	11,414		12,158 (MB)	13,194	(Par)
23,815	26,345	28,379	34,559	38,373		65,080 (MB)	76,531	(D)
7,906	8,633	10,313	14,023	*(19,055)*		19,430 (MB)	18,940	(Loc)
				(23,000)				
		2,418	4,754	8,689	(UD 1934)	23,201 (MB)	25,564	(Com)
12,344	11,344	11,116	10,744	10,707		16,823 (MB)	20,341	(D)
2,523	2,620	2,418	4,754	4,681		11,183 (MB)	12,206	(Com)
(53,598)	*(50,051)*	*(56,361)*	*(65,632)*	*(78,276)*		305,521 (C.CB)	335,410	(D)
(40,936)	(39,470)	(44,831)	(52,724) (B)	(69,978)				
8,159	17,810	24,385	28,761	42,074		53,159 (MB)	51,421	(D)
4,212	*6,794*	*9,926*	*13,929*	*17,957*		59,166 (MB)	57,497	(Loc)
30,240	*55,652*	78,953	102,795	134,037		252,501 (CB)	333,840	(LB)
993	*1,591*	*2,589*	*4,450*	*6,523*		75,246 (UD)		(Loc)
						As Coulsdon & Purley UD		(Loc)
16,762	*(30,298)*	*(36,666)*	*(39,450)*	*(45,958)*		84,184 (CB)	/ 85,938	(D)
	(27,730)	(35,104)	(38,060)	(44,511)				
6,597	*8,298*	10,162	11,970	18,644		46,146 (MB)	46,510	(D)
4,444	4,978	5,725	6,025	6,579		5,758 (MB)	5,707	(Par)
19,793	*25,154*	*(32,157)*	*(37,253)*	*(42,035)*		29,475 (MB)	28,926	(Loc)
		(29,744)	(39,192)	(38,212)				
4,124	4,051	3,859	3,939	3,780		5,860 (MB)	11,815	(D)
7,531	8,009	8,500	8,891	10,581		24,815 (MD)	25,432	(Loc)
5,946	6,322	6,535	6,412	6,438		8,059 (MB)	8,101	(Com)
43,091	49,793	81,168	94,146 (B)	105,912		132,408 (CB)	219,582	(D)
6,638	6,839	6,645	6,426	6,532		8,495 (MB)	10,179	(Par)
18,148	24,773	29,637	29,847	28,060		52,963 (CB)	51,326	(Loc)

TOWN	Pre-1801	1801	1811	1821	1831	1841	1851
DONCASTER, Yorks (WR)*	1750:2,500	5,678	6,935	8,544	10,801	10,455	12,052
	1775:3,500						
DORCHESTER, Dorset		2,402	2,549	2,743	3,033	3,249	3,513
DOVER, Kent	1750:4,000	7,084	8,804	10,327	11,922	13,872	15,076
	1775:5,000						
DROITWICH, Worcs*		1,845	2,079	2,176	2,486	2,805	3,152
DUDLEY (34), Worcs	1750:5,000	10,107	13,925	18,211	23,043	31,232	37,962
	1775:8,000						
DUKINFIELD (35), Ches		1,737	3,053	5,096	14,681	22,394	26,418
DUNSTABLE, Beds		1,296	1,616	1,831	2,117	2,582	3,589
DURHAM, Durham*	1750:4,500	7,530	7,953	8,822	10,135	14,151	18,334
	1775:6,000						
EALING (36), Msx		5,035	5,361	6,608	7,783	8,407	9,828
Also: *Acton, Msx (Southall)*		(1,425)	(1,674)	(1,929)	(2,453)	(2,665)	(2,582)
Northolt, Msx		(336)	(392)	(455)	(447)	(653)	(614)
Hanwell, Msx		817	803	977	1,213	1,469	1,547
EASTBOURNE, E.Suss		1,668	2,623	2,607	2,726	3,015	3,433
EASTLEIGH (37), Hants		–	–	–	–	–.	–
EAST RETFORD, Notts		1,948	2,030	2,461	2,491	2,680	2,943
ECCLES, Lancs		16,119	19,502	23,331	28,083	33,792	41,497
ELLESMERE PORT (38), Ches		–	–	–	–	–	–
ELY (39), Cambs	1753:3,000	3,886	4,177	4,989	6,121	6,752	8,045
	1775:3,400						
ENFIELD, Msx		5,881	6,636	8,227	8,812	9,367	9,453
Also: *Edmonton, Msx* *		5,093	6,824	7,900	8,192	9,027	9,708
Southgate, Msx (in Edmonton)		–	–	–	–	–	–
EPSOM & EWELL, Surrey		3,628	3,803	4,627	5,082	5,400	6,315
EVESHAM, Worcs		2,837	3,068	3,487	3,991	4,245	4,605
EXETER, Devon	1700:14,301	16,827	18,896	23,479	28,242	31,312	32,818
	1775:16,500						
EYE, E.Suff		1,734	1,893	1,882	2,313	2,493	2,587
FALMOUTH, Corn	1750:3,000	3,684	3,933	4,392	4,761	4,844	4,953
	1779:3,800						
FARNWORTH, Lancs		1,439	1,798	2,044	2,928	4,829	6,389
FAVERSHAM, Kent	1753:2,145	3,488	3,872	4,208	4,429	4,621	5,047
	1775:2,700						
FLEETWOOD (40), Lancs		617	739	875	842	3,847	4,134
FLINT, Flints		1,169	1,433	1,612	2,216	2,860	3,296
FOLKESTONE, Kent		3,704	4,232	4,541	4,296	4,413	(7,549
							(6,726
GATESHEAD, Durham		8,595	8,782	11,767	15,177	(19,505)	(24,805
						(20,123)	(25,568
GILLINGHAM, Kent		4,135	5,135	6,209	6,734	7,640	9,321
GLASTONBURY, Som.		2,035	2,337	2,630	2,984	3,314	3,125
GLOSSOP (41), Derbs		2,759	4,012	1,351	2,012	3,548	5,467
GLOUCESTER, Glos	1743:5,211	7,718	8,339	9,744	11,933	14,152	(16,015
	1773:6,500						(17,572
GODALMING, Surrey		3,405	3,543	4,098	4,529	4,328	4,657
GOOLE, Yorks (WR)		294	348	450	1,671	2,850	2,218
GOSPORT (42), Hants		11,295	12,212	10,963	12,637	13,510	16,908
GRANTHAM, Lincs	1750:2,500	3,303	3,646	4,184	4,590	4,683	5,375
	1775:2,800						
GRAVESEND (43), Kent	1775;2,500	4,539	5,589	6,583	9,445	15,670	16,633
GREENWICH, Kent		14,339	16,947	20,712	24,553	29,595	35,028
GRIMSBY (44), Lincs		1,524	2,747	3,064	4,225	3,700	8,860
GT YARMOUTH, Norf	1750:10,000	14,845	17,977	18,040	21,115	24,086	30,879
	1784:12,608						

1861	1871	1881	1891	1901	.....	1961	1971–77	
16,406	18,758	21,139	25,933	28,932		86,322 (CB)	82,668	(D)
3,760	3,855	3,866	3,486	3,408		12,263 (MB)	13,736	(Par)
16,261	15,580	14,953	13,893	14,540		35,554 (MB)	34,359	(D)
3,144	3,538	3,761	4,021	4,164		7,976 (MB)	12,748	(Par)
44,975	43,791	46,252	45,740	48,744		62,965 (CB)	185,581	(D)
29,953	26,329	29,675	29,239	18,929		17,316 (MB)	17,315	(Loc)
4,470	4,558	4,627	4,513	5,157		25,645 (MB)	31,828	(Loc)
20,308	21,431	23,452	23,173	24,693		20,514 (C.MB)	24,776	(D)
11,963	18,189	25,748	36,267	47,510	1901	183,087 (MB)	300,580	(LB)
(3,151)	(8,306)	(17,126)	(24,206)	(37,703)	1921	65,586 (MB)		(Loc)
(658)	(479)	(496)	(538)	(589)	Loc in Ealing, Harrow, Southall MBs			(Loc)
2,687	3,766	5,178	6,139	10,438	(for Hanwell: 1961):Loc in Ealing MB			(Loc)
5,795	10,361	21,595	24,278	42,701		60,918 (CB)	70,921	(D)
—	515	1,017	3,582	7,779	1936	36,642 (MB)	45,361	(D)
2,982	3,194	9,748	10,603	12,340		17,792 (MB)	18,413	(Loc)
52,679	67,770	98,187	121,817	149,154		43,173 (MB)	38,502	(Loc)
—	—	—	—	10,366	(UD 1955)	44,681 (MB)	61,637	(D)
7,841	8,002	8,029	7,894 (B)	7,673		9,803 (C.UD)	9,020	(Par)
12,424	16,054	(19,104)	(31,811)	(43,042)	1955	109,542 (MB)	266,230	(LB)
—	—	(18,944)	(31,536)	(42,738)	(UD)			
10,930	13,860	23,463	36,351	61,892	1937	92,062 (MB)		(Loc)
						72,359 (MB)		(Loc)
7,085	8,811	10,305	12,168	15,007	(UD 1937)	71,159 (MB)	72,301	(D)
4,680	4,888	5,112	5,836	7,101		12,901 (MB)	13,855	(Par)
33,738	34,646	37,447	37,404	47,185		80,321 (Co.C.CB)	95,729	(D)
2,430	2,396	2,296	2,064	2,004		1,583 (MB)	1,603	(Par)
5,709	5,294	5,973	4,737	11,789		17,621 (MB)	18,041	(Par)
8,720	13,550	20,708	23,758	25,925	(UD 1939)	27,502 (MB)	26,862	(Loc)
6,383	7,973	9,484	10,550	11,488		12,984 (MB)	14,818	(Par)
5,084	5,203	(7,580)	(10,270)	(15,190)		27,686 (MB)	28,599	(Loc)
		(6,733)	(9,274) (B)	(12,082)				
3,428	4,277	5,096	5,247	4,625		13,707 (MB)	14,662	(Com)
(9,678)	(12,951)	(19,297)	(24,232)	30,969		44,154 (MB)	43,801	(Loc)
(8,507)	(12,694)	(18,816)	(23,711)					
(32,749)	(47,808)	65,041	(84,728)	(108,024)		103,261 (CB)	94,469	(D)
(33,587)	(48,592)		(85,692)	(109,888)				
14,608	19,930	20,644	27,872	42,643		72,910 (MB)	86,862	(D)
3,593	3,802	3,828	4,215	4,141		5,602 (MB)	6,558	(Par)
6,130	17,046	19,574	22,416	21,562		17,500 (MB)	24,272	(Loc)
(15,214)	(16,233)	(15,733)	(15,476)	(15,169)		69,773 (Co.C.CB)	90,232	(D)
(16,512)	(18,330)	(36,513)	(39,444)	(47,955)				
(5,778)	(6,862)	(8,640)	(10,500)	(11,356)		15,780 (MB)	18,669	(Par)
(2,321)	(2,455)	(2,505)	(2,797)	(8,748)				
3,479	4,186	10,418	15,416	16,576	(UD 1933)	18,891 (MB)	18,072	(Loc)
22,653	22,637	21,581	25,432	28,873	(UD 1922)	62,457 (MB)	76,116	(D)
4,954	5,028	16,886	16,746	17,593		25,048 (MB)	27,943	(Loc)
18,782	21,265	23,302	23,876	27,196		51,389 (MB)	54,106	(Loc)
40,002	40,412	46,580	57,240	67,174	(1930)	85,546 (Met.B)	217,790	(LB)
11,067	20,238	46,010	51,934 (B)	63,138		96,712 (CB)	95,540	(D)
34,180	41,972	46,767	49,334 (B)	51,316		52,970 (CB)	50,236	(D)

TOWN	Pre-1801	1801	1811	1821	1831	1841	1851
GUILDFORD, Surrey*		2,634	2,974	3,161	3,924	4,074	4,835
HACKNEY (45), Msx*		12,730	16,771	22,494	31,047	37,771	53,589
Also: *Stoke Newington, Msx*		1,462	2,149	2,670	3,480	4,490	4,840
Shoreditch, Msx		34,766	43,930	52,966	68,564	83,432	109,257
HALESOWEN, Worcs		5,867	6,888	8,187	9,765	13,589	18,827
HALIFAX, Yorks (WR)	1750:5,000	8,886	9,159	12,628	15,382	**19,881**	33,582
	1775:6,750						
HAMMERSMITH, Msx		5,600	7,393	8,809	10,222	13,453	17,760
Also: *Fulham, Msx*		4,428	5,903	6,492	7,317	9,319	11,886
HARINGEY —		—	—	—	—	—	—
See: *Hornsey, Msx*		2,716	3,349	4,122	4,856	5,937	7,135
Wood Green, Msx (in Tottenham)		—	—	—	—	—	—
Tottenham, Msx		3,629	4,711	5,812	6,937	8,584	9,120
HARROGATE (46), Yorks (WR)		1,195	1,583	1,934	2,812	3,372	3,434
HARROW, Msx	1750:2,500	2,485	2,813	3,017	3,861	4,627	4,951
	1775:3,000						
Also: *Pinner, Msx*		761	1,078	1,076	1,270	1,331	1,310
and *Stanmore, Msx*		1,146	1,387	1,702	2,020	2,007	1,911
HARTLEPOOL, Durham		993	1,047	1,249	1,330	5,236	9,503
HARWICH, Essex		2,761	3,732	4,010	4,297	3,829	4,451
HASLINGDEN, Lancs		4,040	5,127	6,595	7,776	8,063	9,030
HASTINGS, W.Suss		3,075	3,952	6,185	10,097	11,617	17,088
HAVERING (47), Essex (as H-atte-Bower)		4,698	5,055	6,067	6,812	8,143	8,699
includes Romford, Essex		3,179	3,244	3,777	4,294	5,317	5,868
HAVERFORDWEST, Pembs		2,880	3,093	3,055	3,915	5,941	6,580
HEDON, Yorks (ER)		592	780	902	1,080	998	1,029
HELSTON (48), Corn		2,248	2,297	2,671	3,293	3,584	3,355
HEMEL HEMPSTEAD, Herts		3,680	4,222	5,193	6,037	7,268	8,508
HENLEY-on-**THAMES**, Ox.	1738:2,250	2,948	3,117	3,509	3,618	3,622	3,733
	1775:2,650						
HEREFORD, Herefs	1757:5,592	6,828	7,306	9,090	10,280	10,921	12,108
	1785:5,638						
HERTFORD (49), Herts	1747:2,660	3,360	3,900	4,265	5,247	5,450	(5,703
	1775:2,800						(6,605
HEYWOOD, Lancs		—	—	—	—	—	12,194
HIGHAM FERRERS, Nthants		726	823	877	965	1,030	1,140
HIGH WYCOMBE, Bucks*		4,248	4,756	5,599	6,299	2,002	2,000
HILLINGDON, Msx		1,783	2,252	2,886	3,842	6,027	6,352
Also: *Harlington, Msx*		363	461	472	648	841	872
Uxbridge, Msx		2,111	2,411	2,750	3,043	3,219	3,236
Hayes, Msx		1,026	1,252	1,530	1,575	2,076	2,076
Ruislip, Msx		1,012	1,239	1,343	1,197	1,413	1,392
Harefield, Msx		951	1,079	1,228	1,285	1,516	1,498
Harmondsworth, Msx		879	926	1,076	1,276	1,330	1,307
Ickenham, Msx		213	257	281	297	396	364
Cowley, Msx		214	382	349	315	392	344
West Drayton, Msx		515	555	608	662	802	906
Hornchurch, Msx							
HONITON, Devon		2,377	2,735	3,296	3,509	3,895	3,427
HOUNSLOW, Msx		—	—	—	—	—	—
Also: *New Brentford, Msx*		1,442	1,733	2,036	2,085	2,174	2,063
Chiswick, Msx		3,235	3,892	4,236	4,994	5,811	6,303
Cranford, Msx		212	267	288	377	370	437
Heston, Msx		1,782	2,251	2,810	3,407	4,071	5,202
Isleworth, Msx		4,346	4,661	5,269	5,590	6,614	7,007
Bedfont, Msx		456	577	771	968	982	1,035
Feltham, Msx		620	703	962	924	1,029	1,109
Hanworth, Msx		334	533	552	671	751	790

1861	1871	1881	1891	1901	. . . . .	1961	1971-77	
4,902	5,553	7,442	8,242	9,222		53,976 (MB)	57,213	(D)
76,687	115,110	163,681	198,606	218,998		164,766 (Met.B)	219,240	(LB)
6,608	9,841	22,781	30,936	34,293		52,301 (Met.B)		(Loc)
129,364	127,164	126,591	124,009	117,706		40,465 (Met.B)		(Loc)
23,905	25,509	30,190.	33,580	38,868		44,445 (MB)	53,980	(Loc)
37,014	65,124	81,117	89,832 (B)	104,936		96,120 (CB)	91,272	(Loc)
24,519	42,691	71,939	97,239	111,970		110,333 (Met.B)	184,750	(LB)
15,539	23,350	42,900	91,639	137,249		111,791 (Met.B)		(Loc)
—	—	—	—	—As Harringay, Loc in Hornsey MB			238,200	(LB)
11,082	19,357	37,078	61,097	87,626	1903	97,885 (MB)		(Loc)
—	—	—	—	—	1933	47,897 (MB)		(Loc)
13,240	22,869	46,456	97,174	136,774	1934	113,126 (MB)		(Loc)
4,563	6,775	9,482	13,917	28,423		56,345 (MB)	62,427	(D)
5,525	8,537	10,277	12,988	22,157	(UD 1954)	209,080 (MB)	205,000	(LB)
1,849	2,332	2,519	2,727	3,366	Loc in Harrow MB			(Loc)
2,209	2,173	2,174	2,399	2,896	Loc in Harrow MB			(Loc)
12,245	13,166	(12,361)	(14,585)	(14,074)		17,675 (CB)	97,094	(D)
		(16,998)	(21,271) (B)	(22,723)				
5,070	6,079	7,842	8,202	10,072		13,699 (MB)	14,926	(Par)
10,109	12,000	16,298	18,225 (B)	18,543		14,360 (MB)	14,924	(Loc)
22,910	29,398	42,436	52,340	52,440		66,478 (CB)	72,410	(D)
9,260	11,084	12,311	15,013	20,724	Loc in Romford MB;		246,700	(LB);
6,604	8,239	9,050	10,722	13,915	1937	114,584 (MB)		(Loc)
7,019	6,622	6,398	6,179	6,007		8,892 (MB)	9,104	(Com)
975	992	996	979	1,010		2,345 (MB)	2,530	(Par)
3,843	3,797	3,432	3,198	3,088		7,086 (MB)	9,978	(Par)
9,347	10,100	10,358	10,915	12,490		55,270 (MB/NT)	76,000	(NT)
3,676	3,736	3,692	3,415	3,521		9,114 (MB)	11,431	(Par)
15,585	18,355	19,821	20,267	21,382		40,434 (C.MB)	46,503	(D)
(5,747)	(6,206)	(6,595)	(6,441)	(6,446)		15,737 (MB)	20,362	(Par)
(6,769)	(7,164)	(7,747)	(7,548)	(9,322)				
17,591	19,653	22,979	23,185	25,458		24,090 (MB)	30,400	(Loc)
1,152	1,232	1,468	1,810	2,540		3,753 (MB)	4,390	(Par)
2,161	2,343	(2,390)	(2,599)	3,466		49,981 (MB)	59,530	(Loc)
4,221	4,811	(10,618)	(13,435)					
7,522	8,237	9,295	10,622	11,832	North H. and H.Heath Locs in		230,020	(LB)
					Uxbdge MB			
1,159	1,296	1,538	1,542	1,690		67,915 (UD)		(Loc)
3,236	3,364	3,346	3,154	3,063	1955	63,762 (MB)		(Loc)
2,650	2,654	2,891	2,651	2,594	& Harlington UD (above)			(Loc)
1,365	1,482	1,455	1,836	3,566	1932	72,541 (MB)		(Loc)
1,567	1,579	1,503	1,867	2,008	Loc in Uxbridge MB			(Loc)
1,385	1,584	1,812	1,914	1,971	Loc in Yiewsley & W.Drayton UD			(Loc)
351	386	376	368	329	Loc in Uxbridge MB			(Loc)
371	491	498	525	601	Loc in Uxbridge MB			(Loc)
951	984	1,009	1,118	1,246	As Yiewsley & W.Drayton UD			(Loc)
						23,723 (UD)		
3,301	3,470	3,358	3,216	3,271		4,718 (MB)	5,072	(Par)
—	—	—	As Hounslow Heath, Loc in Heston & Isleworth MB				206,650	(LB)
1,995	2,043	2,138	2,069	2,029)	1932	54,832 (MB)		(Loc)
6,505	8,508	15,663	21,344	28,513)	as Brentford and Chiswick (MB)			(Loc)
530	557	503	507	488	Loc in Heston and Isleworth MB			(Loc)
7,096	8,432	9,754	10,389	11,690)	1932 102,897 (MB)			(Loc)
8,437	11,498	12,973	15,884	19,874)	as Heston and Isleworth MB			(Loc)
1,150	1,288	1,452	1,815	2,131	Loc in Feltham UD			(Loc)
1,837	2,748	2,909	3,661	4,534		51,047 (UD)		(Loc)
763	867	1,040	1,309	2,159	Loc in Feltham UD			(Loc)

TOWN	Pre-1801	1801	1811	1821	1831	1841	1851
HOVE, E.Suss		101	193	312	1,360	2,509	4,104
HUDDERSFIELD, Yorks (WR)*	1775:3,500	7,268	9,671	13,284	19,035	25,068	30,880
HUNTINGDON, Hunts		2,035	2,397	2,806	3,267	3,507	3,882
Also: Godmanchester		1,573	1,779	1,953	2,146	2,152	2,337
HYDE, Ches		1,063	1,806	3,355	7,144	10,170	11,569
HYTHE, Kent		1,365	2,318	2,181	2,287	2,265	2,675
ILKESTON, Derbs		2,422	2,970	3,681	4,446	5,326	6,122
IPSWICH, E.Suff*	1755:12,124	11,277	13,670	17,186	20,454	25,264	32,914
	1775:11,500						
ISLINGTON, Msx*		10,212	15,065	22,417	37,316	55,690	95,329
Also: Finsbury (in Clerkenwell)		—	—	—	—	—	—
JARROW, Durham*		15,624	21,468	24,189	27,995	33,945	42,448
KEIGHLEY, Yorks (WR)		5,745	6,864	9,223	11,176	13,413	18,258
KENDAL, Westm*	1784:7,571	6,892	7,705	8,984	10,015	10,225	10,377
	1793:8,039						
KENSINGTON, Msx*		8,556	10,886	14,428	20,902	26,834	44,053
Also: Chelsea, Msx*		11,604	18,262	26,860	32,371	39,896	56,185
KETTERING, Nthants	1724:2,654	3,011	3,242	3,668	4,099	4,867	5,125
	1750:2,800						
	1775:2,900						
KIDDERMINSTER, Worcs*	1750:5,000	6,110	8,038	10,709	14,981	14,399	(17,03:
	1773:5,749						(18,46:
	1793:6,199						
KING'S LYNN, Norf*	1775:9,000	10,096	10,259	12,253	13,370	16,039	19,35!
KINGSTON-upon-HULL (50), Yorks (ER)*	1750:6,250	22,161	24,299	28,591	32,958	41,629	50,67(
KINGSTON-on-THAMES, Surrey*		4,438	4,999	6,091	7,257	9,760	12,14·
Also: Chessington, Surrey		137	146	150	189	226	22!
Malden and Coombe, Surrey		210	221	250	209	232	28.
Surbiton: as part of Kingston							
parish, Surrey		—	—	—	—	—	—
LAMBETH (51), Surrey		27,985	41,644	57,638	87,856	115,888	139,32:
Also: Clapham, Surrey		3,864	5,083	7,151	9,958	12,106	16,29(
Streatham, Surrey		2,357	2,729	3,616	5,068	5,994	6,90.
LAMPETER, Cards		969	692	827	1,197	1,417	90
LANCASTER, Lancs*	1750:6,500	9,030	9,247	10,144	12,167	13,531	14,37
	1789:8,584						
LAUNCESTON, Corn		1,483	1,758	2,183	2,231	2,460	3,39
LEEDS (52), Yorks (WR)*	1771:16,380	53,162	62,534	83,796	123,393	151,874	172,27
	1775:17,117						
LEICESTER (53) (54), Leics*	1712:6,450	16,953	23,146	30,125	(39,904)	(48,167)	60,58
	1750:8,000				(40,512)	(50,753)	
	1785:12,784						
LEIGH, Lancs*		12,976	15,565	18,372	20,883	22,229	25,99
LEOMINSTER, Herefs		3,966	4,136	4,646	5,249	4,916	5,21
LEWES, E.Suss	1750:2,600	3,309	6,221	7,083	8,592	9,199	9,09
	1775:3,600						
LEWISHAM, Kent*		4,007	6,625	8,185	9,659	12,276	15,06
Also: Deptford, Surrey (55)		18,282	19,833	20,818	21,350	25,617	31,97
LICHFIELD, Staffs	1750:3,400	4,842	5,151	6,181	6,627	6,851	7,10
	1781:3,771						
LINCOLN, Lincs*	1721:4,250	8,676	10,217	11,776	13,903	16,172	(20,39
	1775:5,500						(17,53
LISKEARD, Corn		1,860	1,975	2,423	2,853	3,001	4,38
LIVERPOOL (56), Lancs*	1750:22,000	86,778	110,792	151,173	222,686	309,736	(433,73
	1773:34,407						(375,95
LLANDOVERY (57), Carm		1,242	1,442	1,292	1,766	1,709	1,92
LLANELLI (58), Carm*		2,972	3,891	5,649	7,646	6,846	8,41
LLANIDLOES, Mont		2,282	2,386	3,145	4,189	2,742	3,04
LONDON (59), Msx*		127,528	120,909	125,434	125,573	123,563	127,86

1861	1871	1881	1891	1901	.....	1961	1971–77	
9,624	11,277	20,804	26,097	35,535		72,973 (MB)	73,086	(D)
34,877	70,253	86,502	95,420 (B)	95,047		130,652 (CB)	131,190	(Loc)
3,816	4,243	4,228	4,346	4,261		8,821 (MB)	16,557	(D)
2,438	2,363	2,188	2,095	2,017	As Huntingdon & Godmanchester MB			
13,722	14,223	28,630	30,670	32,766		31,741 (MB)	37,095	(Loc)
2,871	3,289	· 3,522	3,465	4,234		10,045 (MB)	11,959	(Par)
8,374	9,662	14,122	19,744	25,384		34,672 (MB)	34,134	(Loc)
37,950	43,136	50,546	57,360	66,630		117,395 (CB)	123,312	(D)
155,341	213,778	282,865	319,143	335,238		228,345 (Met.B)	200,730	(LB)
—	—	—	—	—	1900	32,887 (Met.B)		(Loc)
52,925	85,616	115,216	152,196	182,363		28,811 (MB)	28,907	(Loc)
15,005	19,775	50,546	57,360	41,564		55,845 (MB)	55,345	(Loc)
12,029	13,442	13,696	14,430	14,183		18,599 (MB)	21,596	(Par)
70,108	120,299	163,151	166,308	173,073		171,272 (Met.B)	186,570	(LB)
63,104	70,738	88,128	96,253	95,086		47,256 (Met.B) as K. and Chel. LB		
5,845	7,184	11,095	19,454	28,653	(UD 1938)	38,659 (MB)	42,668	(D)
(13,979)	(17,791)	(22,299)	(22,818)	(22,513)		41,671 (MB)	47,326	(Loc)
(15,399)	(19,463)	(24,270)	(24,803)	(24,681)				
16,170	16,459	18,539	18,360	20,288		27,536 (MB)	30,107	(Loc)
97,661	121,598	165,690	200,044 (B)	240,259		303,261 (Co.C.CB)	285,970	(D)
17,792	27,073	35,829	44,237	54,119		36,461 (MB)	140,550	(D)
219	280	243	261	388	Loc in Surbiton MB		—	(Loc)
320	416	525	699	641		46,572 (MB)		(Loc)
—	—	—	—	—				
—	—	—	—	—		62,977 (MB)		(Loc)
162,044	208,342	253,699	275,203	298,951		223,763 (Met.B)	304,410	(LB)
20,894	27,347	36,380	43,698	54,325	Loc in Wandsworth MB			(Loc)
8,027	12,148	21,611	42,972	70,933	Loc In Wandsworth Met			(Loc)
989	1,225	1,443	1,569	1,772		1,855 (MB)	2,189	(Com)
14,324	17,034	20,558	26,380	31,224		48,235 (C.MB)	49,584	(D)
2,790	2,935	3,808	4,345	4,053		4,524 (MB)	4,670	(Par)
207,165	259,201	309,119	367,505	428,968		510,676 (C.CB)	496,009	(D)
68,056	95,220	(122,376)	174,624 (B)	211,579		273,470 (C.CB)	284,208	(D)
		(136,593)						
30,052	33,592	46,959	59,984	73,878		46,174 (MB)	46,181	(Loc)
5,658	5,865	6,044	5,675	5,826		6,405 (MB)	7,079	(D)
9,400	10,434	11,199	10,997 (B)	11,249		13,645 (MB)	14,159	(D)
22,808	36,525	53,065	72,272	109,689		221,753 (Met.B)	266,700	(LB)
45,973	60,188	84,653	108,173	116,890		68,267 (Met)		(Loc)
7,008	7,472	8,520	7,986	8,140		14,087 (Co.C.MB)	22,600	(D)
(24,476)	(30,414)	(42,075)	(46,242)	(54,054)		77,077 (Co.C.CB)	74,269	(D)
(20,999)	(26,762)	(37,313)	(41,491)	(48,704)				
4,689	4,700	4,536	3,984	4,010		4,492 (MB)	1,289	(Par)
(551,448)	(668,007)	(788,192)	(771,368)	(838,733)		745,750 (C.CB)	610,113	(D)
(443,938)	(493,346)	(552,508)	(517,980)	(684,958)				
1,855	1,861	2,035	1,728	1,809		1,911 (MB)	2,002	(Com)
11,446	15,281	19,760	23,937	25,617	(UD 1913)	29,979 (MB)	26,383	(D)
3,127	3,426	3,421	2,574	2,770		2,381 (MB)	2,350	(Com)
112,063	74,732	51,405	38,320	26,923		4,767 (Co.C)	4,245	(C)

TOWN	Pre-1801	1801	1811	1821	1831	1841	1851
LOUGHBOROUGH, Leics		*4,564*	*5,400*	*7,365*	*10,800*	*10,025*	*11,210*
LOUTH, Lincs		4,236	4,728	6,012	6,927	8,848	10,467
LOWESTOFT, E.Suff		2,332	3,189	3,675	4,238	4,647	6,580
LUTON, Beds		2,152	3,716	2,986	3,961	5,827	10,648
LYDD, Kent		*1,303*	*1,504*	*1,437*	*1,357*	*1,509*	*1,605*
LYME REGIS, Dorset		*1,451*	*1,925*	*2,269*	*2,621*	*2,756*	*2,852*
LYMINGTON, Hants		*2,378*	*2,641*	*3,164*	*3,361*	*3,813*	*4,182*
LYTHAM ST ANNES, Lancs		*920*	*1,150*	*1,292*	*1,523*	*2,082*	*2,698*
MACCLESFIELD, Ches*	1722:4,500	8,743	12,299	17,746	23,129	24,137	39,048
	1750:4,750						
	1775:6,000						
MAIDENHEAD (60), Berks		949	797	945	—	3,215	3,608
MAIDSTONE, Kent	1750:5,000	8,027	9,443	12,508	15,790	18,086	20,801
	1781:5,650						
	1782:5,775						
MALDON, Essex		2,358	2,679	3,198	3,831	3,967	4,558
MALMESBURY, Wilts		*1,491*	*1,609*	*1,876*	*2,169*	*2,367*	*2,443*
MANCHESTER (61), Lancs*	1758:19,839	*(70,409)*	*(79,459)*	*(108,016)*	*(142,026)*	*(163,856)*	*(186,986*
	1775:30,000	*(76,788)*	*(91,130)*	*(129,035)*	*(187,022)*	*(242,983)*	*(316,213*
MANSFIELD, Notts	1750:2,500	5,988	6,816	7,861	9,426	9,788	10,667
	1775:3,000						
MARGATE (62), Kent		*4,766*	*6,126*	*7,843*	*10,339*	*11,050*	*10,099*
MARLBOROUGH, Wilts		*2,367*	*2,579*	*3,038*	*3,426*	*3,391*	*3,908*
MERTHYR TYDFYL, Glam*		7,705	11,104	17,404	22,083	34,977	46,378
MERTON, Surrey		813	905	1,177	*1,447*	*1,914*	*1,876*
Also: *Mitcham, Surrey*		3,466	4,175	4,453	4,387	4,532	4,644
Wimbledon, Surrey		1,591	1,914	2,195	2,195	2,630	2,693
Morden, Surrey		512	549	638	655	685	628
MIDDLETON, Lancs		*7,991*	*10,408*	*12,793*	*14,379*	*15,488*	*16,790*
MONMOUTH, Mon		3,345	3,503	4,164	4,916	5,446	5,710
MONTGOMERY, Mont		972	932	1,062	1,188	1,208	1,243
MORECAMBE (63), Lancs (*in Poulton*)		—	—	—	—	—	—
MORLEY, Yorks (WR)		2,108	2,457	3,031	3,819	4,087	4,82
MORPETH, Nthbld		2,951	3,244	3,415	3,890	3,610	4,09
MOSSLEY, Lancs		—	—	—	—	—	—
NEATH, Glam*		2,502	2,740	2,823	4,043	4,970	5,84
NELSON, Lancs		—	—	—	—	—	—
NEWARK, Notts	1750:3,500	6,730	7,236	8,084	9,557	10,220	11,33
	1775:4,000						
NEWHAM, Essex		—	—	—	—	—	—
East Ham, Essex		*1,165*	*1,267*	*1,424*	*1,543*	*1,461*	*1,55*
West Ham, Essex *		*6,485*	*8,136*	*9,753*	*11,580*	*12,738*	*18,81*
Barking (63a), *Essex*		*3,906*	*5,543*	*6,374*	*8,036*	*8,718*	*9,88*
Woolwich, Kent *		*9,826*	*17,054*	*17,008*	*17,661*	*27,785*	*32,36*
NEWBURY, Berks	1768:3,732	4,275	4,898	5,347	5,959	6,379	6,57
	1775:3,900						
NEWCASTLE-u-LYME, Staffs	1750:2,800	4,604	6,175	7,031	8,192	9,838	10,29
	1775:3,500						
NEWCASTLE-on-TYNE, Nthbld*	1750:29,000	28,366	27,587	35,181	42,760	49,860	87,78
	1775:33,000						
NEWPORT, Hants*		3,585	3,855	4,059	4,081	3,858	(3,99
							(8,04
NEWPORT (63b), Mon*		1,135	2,346	4,000	7,062	10,815	19,32
NEW ROMNEY, Kent		*755*	*841*	*962*	*983*	*955*	*1,05*
NORTHAMPTON, Nthants*	1746:5,136	7,020	8,427	10,793	15,351	21,242	26,65
	1775:6,000						
NORWICH (64), Norf*	1752:36,169	36,854	37,256	50,288	61,116	62,344	68,19
	1775:38,500						

1861	1871	1881	1891	1901	.....		1961	1971–77	
10,830	*11,456*	**14,681**	*18,123*	*21,382*			38,638 (MB)	45,875	(Loc)
10,560	10,500	10,691	10,040	9,518			11,564 (MB)	11,170	(Par)
10,663	15,246	**19,702**	23,347 (B)	29,850			45,730 (MB)	52,267	(Loc)
15,329	17,317	23,960	30,006	36,404			131,583 (CB)	161,405	(D)
1,667	1,936	2,129	2,051	2,675			2,698 (MB)	4,800	(Par)
2,537	2,603	2,290	2,365	2,095			3,526 (MB)	3,290	(Par)
4,098	*4,298*	*4,366*	*4,511*	*4,165*			28,721 (MB)	35,733	(Loc)
3,194	*3,904*	*5,268*	*7,218*	*13,992*			36,189 (MB)	40,299	(Loc)
36,101	35,450	37,514	36,009	36,624			37,644 (MB)	44,401	(D)
3,895	6,173	8,220	10,607	12,971			35,411 (MB)	45,288	(Loc)
23,058	26,237	26,647	32,197	33,572			59,790 (MB)	70,987	(D)
4,785	5,586	5,468	5,397	5,565			10,509 (MB)	13,891	(D)
(2,400)	*(2,250)*	**(2,220)**	*(2,144)*	2,854			2,610 (MB)	2,680	(Par)
(6,881)	(6,880)	(3,176)	(2,964) (B)						
(185,410)	*(173,988)*	*(148,794)*	*(145,100)*	*(132,316)*			661,791 (C.CB)	543,650	(D)
(357,979)	*(379.374)*	*(393,585)*	*(416,185)*	*(426,944)*					
10,225	11,824	13,653	15,925	21,445			53,218 (MB)	57,644	(D)
10,019	*13,903*	*18,226*	*21,367*	*26,734*			45,739 (MB)	50,347	(Loc)
3,684	*3,660*	*3,343*	*3,012*	*3,046*			4,852 (MB)	6,108	(Par)
49,794	51,949	—	58,080	69,228			59,039 (CB)	55,317	(D&Com)
1,822	*2,139*	2,480	3,360	4,594	(UD)		68,01 (UD)	177,150	(LB)
5,078	6,498	8,960	12,127	14,903		1934	63,690 (MB)		(Loc)
4,644	9,087	15,950	25,761	41,568		1905	37,312 (MB)		(Loc)
654	*787*	694	763	960	(UD)	As Merton & Morden UD			(Loc)
19,635	*21,191*	25,213	28,362	*34,042*			56,668 (MB)	53,512	(Loc)
5,783	5,874	6,111	5,470	5,095			5,504 (MB)	6,570	(D&Com)
1,276	1,285	1,194	1,098	1,034			972 (MB)	990	(D&Com)
—	—	3,931	6,746	11,798	(UD 1902)		40,228 (MB)	41,908	(Loc)
6,840	9,607	17,267	21,068 (B)	23,636			40,338 (MB)	44,345	(Loc)
4,296	4,510	4,968	5,219 (B)	6,158			12,571 (MB)	14,054	(Loc)
—	5,500	13,850	14,162 (B)	13,452			9,776 (MB)	10,086	(Loc)
6,810	9,134	10,409	11,113	13,720			30,935 (MB)	28,619	(D&Com)
—	5,580	10,381	22,700	32,816			32,292 (MB)	31,249	(Loc)
11,515	12,218	14,018	14,457	14,992			24,651 (MB)	26,646	(D)
—	—	—	—	—			—	236,490	(LB)
2,264	*4,334*	*9,713*	*28,744*	*69,758*		1904	105,682 (CB)		(Loc)
38,331	*62,919*	*128,953*	*204,893*	*267,191*		1886	157,367 (CB)		(Loc)
10,996	*12,523*	*16,848*	*25,214*	*62,781*		1931	72,293 (MB)		(Loc)
41,695	*35,557*	*36,665*	*40,848*	*41,625*		1930	146,603 (Met)		(Loc)
6,161	6,602	(7,017)	(7,102)	(6,983)			20,397 (MB)	23,634	(D)
		(10,144)	(11,002)	(11,061)					
12,638	15,538	16,838	17,805	19,147			75,688 (MB)	77,126	(D)
109,108	128,160	145,359	186,300	215,328			269,678 (Co.C.CB)	222,209	(D)
(3,819)	*(3,556)*	*(3,237)*	*(3,058)*	*(2,684)*			19,479 (MB)	22,309	(Loc)
(7,934)	*(7,976)*	(9,375)	(10,216)	(10,911)					
23,249	26,957	38,469	54,707	67,270			108,123 (CB)	112,286	(D)
1,062	*1,129*	*1,026*	1,402	1,376			2,555 (MB)	3,650	(Par)
32,813	41,040	51,881	61,012	87,021			105,421 (CB)	151,000	(D&NT)
74,891	80,390	87,842	100,970	111,733			120,096 (Co.C.CB)	122,083	(D)

TOWN	Pre-1801	1801	1811	1821	1831	1841	1851
NOTTINGHAM (65), Notts*	1739:19,720	28,861	34,253	40,415	50,680	53,091	57,407
	1779:17,711						
NUNEATON, Warwks	1750:2,500	*4,769*	*4,947*	*6,610*	*7,799*	*7,105*	*8,133*
	1775:3,500						
OKEHAMPTON, Devon		1,430	1,440	1,907	2,055	2,194	2,165
OLDHAM (66), Lancs*	1775:5,000	12,024	16,690	21,662	32,381	42,595	52,820
OSSETT (67), Yorks (WR)		3,424	4,083	4,775	5,325	6,078	6,266
OXFORD (68), Ox. & Berks*	1751: 8,292	*10,837*	*12,245*	*15,337*	*19,514*	*22,266*	*24,398*
	1775:10,500						
PEMBROKE, Pembs		1,117	2,415	4,925	6,511	7,412	10,107
PENRYN, Corn		2,324	2,713	2,933	3,521	3,337	3,959
PENZANCE, Corn*		3,382	4,022	5,224	6,563	8,578	9,214
PETERBOROUGH, Nthants*		3,449	3,674	4,598	5,553	6,107	8,672
PLYMOUTH, Devon*	1750:15,000	43,194	56,060	61,212	75,534	80,059	52,221
	1775:25,000						
PONTEFRACT, Yorks (WR)*	1764:2,515	3,097	3,605	4,447	4,832	4,669	5,106
	1775:2,650						
POOLE (69), Dorset	1750:2,500	*4,761*	*4,816*	*6,390*	*6,459*	*6,093*	*(6,718*
	1775:3,500						*(9,255*
PORTSMOUTH (70), Hants	1750:5,500	(25,387)	(34,484)	(39,514)	(42,306)	(43,678)	(61,767
Also: Portsea	1791:6,490	(7,839)	(7,103)	(7,269)	(8,088)	(9,354)	(10,329
PORT TALBOT (71), Lancs		2,084	2,124	2,412	3,475	4,816	7,127
PRESTON (71a), Lancs*		11,887	17,065	24,575	33,112	50,131	68,557
PRESTWICH (72), Lancs*		1,881	2,175	2,724	2,941	3,180	4,096
PUDSEY (73), Yorks (WR)		4,422	4,697	6,229	7,450	*10,002*	*11,603*
PWLLHELI, Caern		1,166	1,383	1,876	2,091	2,367	2,331
RADCLIFFE, Lancs		2,497	2,792	3,089	*3,904*	*5,099*	*6,293*
RAMSGATE, Kent		3,110	4,221	6,031	*7,985*	*10,909*	*11,838*
RAWTENSTALL, Lancs (*in Whalley*)		—	—	—	—	—	—
READING (74), Berks*	1750:7,500	9,770	11,093	13,264	16,042	19,521	22,17
	1775:8,000						
REDBRIDGE –		—				—	
Ilford, Essex (75)		*85*	*119*	*87*	*115*	*189*	*18.*
Wanstead, Essex		*918*	*1,127*	*1,354*	*1,403*	*1,608*	*2,20*
Woodford, Essex		*1,745*	*2,056*	*2,699*	*2,548*	*2,777*	*2,77.*
Dagenham, Essex		*1,057*	*1,488*	*1,864*	*2,118*	*2,294*	*2,49.*
REIGATE, Surrey		*2,246*	*2,440*	*2,961*	*3,397*	*4,584*	*4,92*
RHONDDA, Glam (75a)		542	973	985	1,047	1,363	1,998
RICHMOND, Yorks (NR)*		2,861	3,056	3,546	3,900	3,992	4,10
RICHMOND-upon-THAMES, Sy (76)		4,628	5,219	5,994	7,243	7,760	9,25.
Also: *Twickenham, Msx*		*3,138*	*3,757*	*4,206*	*4,571*	*5,208*	*6,25.*
Teddington, Msx		*699*	*732*	*863*	*895*	*1,199*	*1,14.*
Barnes, Surrey		*860*	*994*	*1,240*	*1,417*	*1,461*	*1,87.*
Mortlake, Surrey		*1,748*	*2,021*	*2,484*	*2,698*	*2,778*	*3,11.*
Petersham, Surrey		*422*	*406*	*516*	*610*	*636*	*65.*
RIPON, Yorks (WR)	1750:2,500	3,211	3,633	4,563	5,080	5,461	6,08
	1775:2,800						
ROCHDALE (77), Lancs*	1750:2,750	*29,092*	*37,229*	*47,109*	*58,441*	*67,889*	80,24
	1775:3,250						
ROCHESTER, Kent		*7,989*	*9,070*	*10,770*	*11,440*	*12,631*	*(14,32.*
							(14,93.
ROMSEY (78), Hants		*4,274*	*4,297*	*5,128*	*5,432*	*5,347*	*5,65*
ROTHERHAM (81), Yorks (WR)*	1750:2,500	*3,070*	*2,950*	*3,548*	*4,083*	*5,505*	*6,31*
	1775:3,500						
ROYAL LEAMINGTON SPA, Warwks*		*315*	*543*	*2,183*	*6,209*	*12,864*	*15,72*
ROYAL TUNBRIDGE WELLS, Kent*		*4,371*	*5,932*	*7,406*	*10,380*	*12,530*	*16,54.*
RUGBY, Warwks		*1,487*	*1,805*	*2,300*	*2,501*	*4,008*	*8,86.*
RYDE (82), Hants		*2,039*	*2,847*	*3,945*	*4,928*	*5,840*	*7,14*

1861	1871	1881	1891	1901	.....	1961	1971–77	
74,693	86,608	186,577	213,877	239,743		311,899 (Co.C.CB)	300,630	(D)
7,666	*7,399*	8,465	11,577	19,209	1907	57,376 (MB)	67,027	(D)
1,929	1,900	1,695	1,879	2,569		3,864 (MB)	3,830	(Par)
72,333	82,629	111,343	131,463	137,246		115,346 (CB)	105,913	(D)
7,950	9,190	10,957	10,984	12,903		14,737 (MB)	17,183	(Loc)
25,080	*27,418*	*30,651*	*31,387*	*32,088*		106,291 (C.CB)	108,805	(D)
15,071	13,741	14,156	14,978	15,853		12,751 (MB)	14,197	(Com)
3,547	3,679	3,466	3,256	3,190		4,451 (MB)	5,135	(Par)
9,414	10,406	12,409	12,432	13,136		19,281 (MB)	19,415	(Par)
11,735	17,434	21,288	25,171	30,872		62,340 (C.MB)	87,568	(D&NT)
62,599	68,080	73,858	84,248	107,636		204,409 (C.CB)	239,452	(D)
5,346	5,372	8,798	9,702	13,427		27,128 (MB)	31,364	(Loc)
(6,815)	*(6,604)*	*(7,179)*	*(7,890)*	*(7,670)*		92,111 (Co.MB)	107,161	(D)
(9,759)	*(10,129)*	*(12,310)*	*(15,438)*	*(19,463)*				
(83,995)	*(102,000)*	*(120,021)*	*(151,253)*	*(180,800)*		215,077 (C.CB)	197,431	(D)
(10,804)	*(11,569)*	*(7,967)*	*(7,998)*	*(7,295)*				
8,924	9,886	10,389	12,360	16,567		51,322 (MB)	50,729	(Com)
81,101	83,515	91,578	99,185	101,295		113,341 (CB)	98,088	(D)
5,288	6,820	8,627	10,485	12,378		34,209 (MB)	32,911	(Loc)
12,912	*13,977*	*12,314*	*13,444* (B)	*14,907*		34,851 (MB)	38,143	(Loc)
2,818	3,040	3,242	3,231	3,675		3,647 (MB)	4,180	(Com)
8,838	*11,446*	16,267	20,021	*(20,595)*	(UD 1935)	26,726 (MB)	29,278	(Loc)
				(25,368)				
11,865	*14,640*	**16,234**	*16,253*	*16,503*		36,914 (MB)	39,561	(Loc)
–	–	22,683	24,733	31,053		23,890 (MB)	21,432	(Loc)
25,866	34,340	*(43,494)*	*(51,694)*	*(59,018)*		119,937 (CB)	132,939	(D)
		(49,117)	*(60,054)* (B)	*(72,217)*				
–	–	–	–	–		–	239,880	(LB)
594	*675*	*993*	*3,969*	*26,241*	1926	178,210 (MB)		(Loc)
2,742	*5,119*	*9,414*	*26,292*	*31,657*	1937	61,259 (MB)		(Loc)
3,457	*4,609*	*7,154*	*10,984*	*13,738*	*with Wanstead*			(Loc)
2,708	*2,879*	*3,411*	*4,324*	*6,091*	1938	108,363 (MB)		(Loc)
9,975	*15,916*	*18,662*	*22,639*	*25,999*		53,751 (MB)	56,223	(Loc)
3,857	*17,777*	*44,046*	*68,721*	*113,735*	(UD 1955)	100,287 (MB)	88,994	(D&Com)
4,290	*4,443*	*4,502*	*4,216*	*3,837*		5,776 (MB)	7,245	(Par)
10,926	*15,113*	*19,066*	*22,684*	*25,557*		41,024 (MB)	174,310	(LB)
8,077	*10,535*	*12,479*	*16,027*	*20,991*	1926	100,822 (MB)		(Loc)
1,183	*4,063*	*6,599*	*10,052*	*14,037*	Loc in Twickenham MB			(Loc)
2,359	*4,197*	*6,001*	*8,445*	*10,047*	1932	32,797 (MB)		(Loc)
3,778	*5,119*	*6,330*	*7,714*	*10,581*	Loc in Barnes MB			(Loc)
637	*683*	*566*	*629*	*589*	Loc in Richmond MB			(Loc)
6,172	6,805	7,390	7,511	8,230		10,486 (C.MB)	10,989	(Par)
(100,900)	*(119,191)*	*(131,149)*	*(132,757)*	*(140,545)*		85,787 (CB)	91,454	(D)
(38,114)	*(44,556)*	*(68,866)*	*(71,401)*	*(83,114)*				
(16,226)	*(16,992)*	*(19,649)*	*(23,407)*	*(27,619)*		50,143 (C.MB)	55,519	(Loc)
(16,862)	*(18,144)*	*(21,307)*	*(26,290)*	*(30,590)*				
5,848	5,681	*(5,579)*	*(5,635)*	*(5,688)*		6,350 (MB)	10,043	(Par)
		(4,104)	*(4,274)*	*(4,365)*				
8,390	**11,248**	*16,257*	*42,050*	54,349		85,478 (CB)	84,801	(D)
17,402	*20,910*	*22,979*	*23,124*	*22,889*		42,561 (MB)	45,064	(Loc)
21,004	*29,756*	35,919	*41,849*	*49,302*		39,869 (MB)	44,612	(D)
7,818	*8,385*	9,891	11,262	16,830	1932	51,698 (MB)	59,396	(D)
9,269	11,234	11,461	10,952	11,043		19,845 (MB)	23,204	(Loc)

TOWN	Pre-1801	1801	1811	1821	1831	1841	1851
RYE, E.Suss		2,187	2,681	3,599	3,715	4,031	(4,592
							(4,071
SAFFRON WALDEN, Essex		3,181	3,403	4,154	4,762	5,111	5,911
ST ALBANS (79), Herts	1750:2,500	3,872	4,362	5,733	6,582	7,745	8,208
	1775:2,700						7,000
ST AUSTELL, Corn		3,788	3,686	6,175	8,758	10,320	10,756
Also: Fowey		1,155	1,319	1,455	1,767	1,643	1,606
ST HELENS, Lancs* (*in Windle*)		—					
ST IVES, Corn		2,714	3,281	3,526	4,776	5,666	6,525
SALE (80), Ches		819	901	1,049	1,104	1,309	1,720
SALFORD, Lancs*		13,611	19,114	25,772	40,786	53,200	63,425
SALISBURY, Wilts	1750:7,000	7,668	8,243	8,763	9,876	10,086	11,657
	1775:6,856						
	1782:7,720						
SALTASH, Corn		1,150	1,478	1,548	1,637	1,541	1,621
SANDWICH, Kent		2,452	2,735	2,912	3,136	2,903	(3,023
							(2,966
SCARBOROUGH, Yorks (NR)*	1750:6,000	6,668	7,067	2,852	8,760	10,048	12,91
	1796:7,350						
SCUNTHORPE (83), Lincs		169	174	210	240	289	305
SHAFTESBURY, Dorset*		2,433	2,635	2,903	3,061	3,170	3,07.
SHEFFIELD (84), Yorks (WR)	1736: 9,695	31,314	35,840	42,157	59,011	68,186	135,31
	1755:12,983						
	1775:27,000						
SHREWSBURY (85), Salop*		14,739	16,606	19,602	21,227	20,921	19,68
SLOUGH (86), Bucks		—	—	—	—	—	—
SOLIHULL, Warwks*		2,473	2,581	2,817	2,878	3,401	3,27
SOUTHAMPTON, Hants*	1757:3,297	7,913	9,617	13,353	19,324	27,744	35,30
	1775:4,500						
SOUTHEND-on-SEA, Essex		—	—	—	—	—	—
SOUTHPORT (87), Lancs (*in N.Meols*)		2,456	2,887	3,177	5,650	8,311	9,31
SOUTH SHIELDS (88), Durham*	0:6,000	11,011	15,165	16,503	18,756	23,072	28,97
	5:8,000						
SOUTHWARK, Surrey*		66,638	72,119	85,905	91,501	98,098	106,93
Also: *Newington, Surrey* *		14,874	28,853	33,047	44,526	54,606	64,81
Bermondsey, Surrey *		17,169	19,530	25,235	29,741	34,947	48,12
Camberwell, Surrey *		7,059	11,309	17,876	28,231	39,868	54,66
Rotherhithe, Surrey		10,296	12,114	3,616	5,068	5,994	6,90
SOUTHWOLD, E.Suff.		1,054	1,369	1,676	1,875	2,186	2,10
SPENBOROUGH (89), Yorks (WR)		8,777	10,556	12,647	14,771	18,317	22,07
STAFFORD, Staffs*	1750:2,500	3,898	4,868	5,736	6,756	9,245	(10,77
	1775:3,000						(11,82
STALYBRIDGE (90), Ches.& Lancs		—	—	—	—	—	14,28
STAMFORD, Lincs & Nthants	1750:2,600	4,022	4,582	5,050	5,837	6,385	8,93
	1785:3,137						
STOCKPORT, Ches*	1759:3,101	14,830	17,545	21,726	25,469	28,431	40,17
	1765:3,713						
	1779:5,000						
STOKE-on-TRENT, Staffs*		16,414	22,495	29,223	37,220	47,951	57,94
STOURBRIDGE (91), Worcs		3,431	4,072	5,090	(6,148)	(7,481)	(8,32
		7,197	8,452	10,070	(12,638)	(15,974)	(18,18
STRATFORD-on-AVON (92), Warwks		2,982	3,803	4,229	5,171	6,022	(6,45
							(3,37
STRETFORD, Lancs*		1,477	1,720	—	2,463	3,524	4,99
SUDBURY, W.Suff	1750:2,700	3,283	3,471	3,950	4,677	5,085	6,04
	1775:3,400						

1861	1871	1881	1891	1901	.....	1961	1971–77	
(4,288)	(4,366)	(4,667)	(4,368)	(4,337)		4,438 (MB)	4,434	(Par)
(3,738)	(3,864)	(4,224)	(3,871)	(3,900)				
5,474	5,718	6,060	6,104	5,914		7,817 (MB)	9,971	(Par)
9,090	10,421	10,659	12,478	16,171		50,293 (C.MB)	52,174	(D)
7,675	8,303							
11,893	11,793	3,582	3,477	3,340	(UD)	25,074 (UD 1968)	32,265	(Loc)
1,429	1,394	1,656	1,957	2,285	(C&E.P 1912)	2,263 (MB)		
37,971	45,240	57,403	71,288	84,410		108,674 (CB)	104,341	(D)
7,027	7,007	6,445	6,094	6,699		9,346 (MB)	9,839	(Par)
3,031	5,573	7,915	9,644	12,088	(UD1935)	51,336 (MB)	55,769	(Loc)
(71,002)	(83,277)	(101,584)	(109,732)	(105,335)		155,090 (C.CB)	130,976	(D)
(102,449)	(124,805)	(176,235)	(198,139) (B)	(220,957)				
12,278	12,903	14,792	15,533	17,117		35,492 (C.MB)	35,302	(D)
1,900	2,293	2,563	2,745	3,357		7,425 (MB)	9,926	(Par)
	(3,060)					4,264 (MB)	4,467	(Par)
2,944	(3,096)	2,846	2,796	3,170				
18,377	24,244	30,504	33,776	38,161		43,061 (MB)	44,440	(D)
368	710	2,126	3,481	6,750	(UD1936)	67,324 (MB)	70,907	(D)
2,960	3,054	2,884	2,658	2,530		3,372 (MB)	3,976	(Par)
185,172	239,947	284,508	324,243	380,793		494,344 (C.CB)	520,327	(D)
22,163	23,300	26,481	26,967	28,395		49,566 (MB)	56,188	(Loc)
—	4,509	5,095	5,462	11,453	(UD1938)	80,781 (MB)	87,075	(D)
3,329	3,741	4,510	5,053	5,832	1954	95,977 (CB)	107,095	(D)
46,960	53,741	60,051	65,325	76,935		204,822 (Co.C.CB)	215,118	(D)
—	—	7,979	12,333	28,857		165,903 (CB)	162,770	(D)
15,947	(25,649)	(42,468)	(55,413)	(64,105)		82,004 (CB)	84,674	(Loc)
	(18,085)	(32,206)	(41,406)	(48,083)				
35,239	45,336	56,875	78,391	97,263		109,521 (CB)	100,659	(Loc)
110,736	101,200	99,270	99,612	94,537		86,249 (Met.B)	260,780	(LB)
82,220	88,722	107,850	115,804	122,172	Loc in Southwark Met.B			(Loc)
58,355	80,429	86,652	84,682	82,124		51,860 (Met.B)		(Loc)
71,488	111,306	186,593	235,344	259,425		17,304 (Met.B)		(Loc)
8,027	12,148	21,611	42,972	70,933	Loc in Bermondsey Met.B			(Loc)
2,032	2,155	2,107	2,311	2,800		2,234 (MB)	1,991	(Par)
25,637	32,121	36,863	38,498	38,785	1955	36,417 (MB)	40,690	(Loc)
(10,996)	(12,212)	(14,399)	(13,946)	(14,060)		47,806 (MB)	55,001	(D)
(12,532)	(14,437)	(19,977)	(20,270)	(20,895)				
(18,130)	(15,323)	(16,384)	26,783 (B)	27,673		21,947 (MB)	22,806	(Loc)
(24,921)	(21,043)	(25,977)						
8,047	7,846	8,773	8,358	8,229		11,743 (MB)	14,662	(Par)
(40,843)	(39,827)	(45,003)	70,263	78,897		142,543 (CB)	139,644	(D)
(54,681)	(53,001)	(59,553)						
71,308	89,262	(104,968)	(122,101)	(140,335)		265,306 (C.CB)	265,258	(D)
		(41,660)	(49,708)	(30,458)				
(8,783)	(9,376)	(9,757)	(9,386)	(10,372)	1914	42,631 (MB)	54,344	(Loc)
(20,345)	(22,198)	(24,757)	(25,056)	(27,278)				
(6,823)	(7,384)	(8,359)	(8,626)	8,593		16,859 (MB)	19,452	(Par&D)
(3,672)	(3,872)	(8,054)	(8,318)					
8,757	11,945	19,018	21,751	30,436		60,364 (MB)	54,297	(Loc)
6,879	6,908	6,584	7,059	7,109		6,642 (MB)	8,166	(Par)

TOWN	Pre-1801	1801	1811	1821	1831	1841	185
SUNDERLAND (93), Durham	1719: 6,000	12,412	12,289	14,725	17,060	17,002	19,05
	1755:16,000						
SUTTON, Surrey		*579*	*638*	*911*	*1,121*	*1,304*	*1,38*
Beddington–Wallington, Surrey		*1,146*	*1,250*	*1,327*	*1,429*	*1,453*	*1,40*
Carlshalton, Surrey		*1,449*	*1,532*	*1,775*	*1,919*	*2,228*	*2,41*
Cheam, Surrey		*616*	*757*	*792*	*997*	*1,109*	*1,13*
SUTTON COLDFIELD, Warwks		*2,847*	*2,959*	*3,466*	*3,684*	*4,300*	*4,57*
SWANSEA, Glam*	1750:3,000	*6,099*	*8,005*	*10,007*	*13,256*	*16,787*	*31,46*
	1775:4,000						
SWINDON, Wilts		*1,198*	*1,341*	*1,580*	*1,742*	*2,459*	*4,87*
SWINTON, Lancs (in Eccles)		—	—	—	—	—	—
TAMWORTH (94), Staffs		(3,748)	(4,060)	(4,917)	(4,967)	(5,337)	(6,06
		(2,786)	*(2,991)*	*(3,574)*	*(3,357)*	*(3,789)*	*(4,05*
TAUNTON, Som	1703:3,880	*5,794*	*6,997*	*8,534*	*11,139*	*12,066*	*13,11*
	1750:4,600						
	1790:5,472						
TEESSIDE		—	—	—	—	—	—
As: *Middlesbrough (Yorks NR)*		239	212	236	383	5,709	7,89
Redcar (Yorks NR)		431	411	673	729	794	1,03
Stockton (Co. Durham)		4,009	4,229	5,006	7,763	9,825	10,17
TENBY (98), Pembs		984	1,176	1,554	2,128	2,912	2,98
TENTERDEN, Kent		*2,370*	*2,786*	*3,259*	*3,177*	*3,620*	*3,78*
TEWKESBURY, Glos	1723:2,866	*4,199*	*4,820*	*4,962*	*5,780*	*5,862*	*5,87*
	1750:3,100						
	1792:3,768						
THETFORD, Norfolk		2,246	2,450	2,922	3,462	3,934	4,05
TIVERTON, Devon	1750:4,500	6,505	6,732	8,651	9,766	10,388	11,14
	1775:5,000						
TODMORDEN, Yorks (WR) (and Lancs)		—	—	—	—	—	—
TORBAY (95), Devon (as Torquay)		—	—	—	—	—	7,90
TORRINGTON (96), Devon		2,044	2,151	2,538	3,093	3,419	3,30
TOTNES, Devon		2,503	2,725	3,128	3,442	3,849	4,41
TOWER HAMLETS, —		—	—	—	—	—	—
As: *Stratford-le-Bow Msx*		*2,101*	*2,259*	*2,349*	*3,371*	*4,626*	*6,98*
Limehouse, Msx		*4,678*	*7,386*	*9,805*	*15,695*	*21,121*	*24,56*
*Bethnal Green, Msx **		*22,310*	*33,619*	*45,676*	*62,018*	*74,088*	*90,19*
Wapping, Msx		*5,889*	*3,313*	*3,078*	*3,564*	*4,108*	*4,47*
*Poplar, Msx **		*4,493*	*7,708*	*12,223*	*16,849*	*20,342*	*28,38*
Bromley-by-Bow, Msx		*1,684*	*3,581*	*4,360*	*4,846*	*6,154*	*11,78*
*Whitechapel, Msx **		*23,666*	*25,578*	*29,407*	*30,733*	*34,053*	*37,84*
*Stepney, Msx **		*20,767*	*27,491*	*36,940*	*51,023*	*63,723*	*80,21*
Tower of London, Msx		*563*	*1,192*	*668*	*713*	*1,417*	*1,77*
Shadwell, Msx		*8,828*	*9,855*	*9,557*	*9,544*	*10,060*	*11,70*
TRURO, Corn		2,358	2,482	2,712	2,952	3,043	10,73
TYNEMOUTH (97), Nmbld*	1750:6,000	3,856	5,834	9,454	10,182	11,890	29,17
	1775:8,000						
WAKEFIELD, Yorks (WR)*	1750:3,500	8,131	8,593	10,764	12,232	14,754	22,06
	1775:5,500						
WALLASEY, Ches		*663*	*943*	*1,169*	*2,737*	*6,261*	*8,33*
WALLINGFORD, Berks		*1,719*	*1,943*	*2,131*	*2,597*	*2,813*	*2,90*
WALLSEND, Nmbld		*1,312*	*1,626*	*5,103*	*5,510*	*4,758*	*5,92*
WALSALL, Staffs*	1750:3,000	10,399	11,189	11,914	15,066	20,852	(26,82
	1775:4,000						(25,68
WALTHAM FOREST, Essex & Msx		—	—	—	—	—	—
As: *Chingford (Essex)*		*612*	*693*	*837*	*963*	*971*	*96*
Leyton (Essex)		*2,519*	*3,162*	*3,374*	*3,323*	*3,274*	*3,90*
Walthamstow (Essex)		*3,006*	*3,777*	*4,304*	*4,258*	*4,873*	*4,95*

1861	1871	1881	1891	1901	.....	1961	1971–77	
17,107	*16,861*	*15,333*	*14,558*	*14,238*		189,686 (CB)	217,079	(D)
		116,526	131,015	146,077				
3,186	*6,558*	*10,344*	*13,977*	*17,223*	& Cheam MB	79,008 (MB)	168,090	(LB)
1,556	*2,834*	*5,492*	*6,430*	*8,996*	1937	32,603 (MB)		(Loc)
2,538	*3,668*	*4,841*	*5,425*	*6,746*		57,484 (UD)		(Loc)
1,156	*1,629*	*2,117*	*2,146*	*3,404*	As Sutton & Cheam MB			(Loc)
4,662	5,936	7,737	8,685	14,264		72,165 (MB)	83,291	
40,802	51,702	41,606	51,720	94,537		167,322 (CB)	173,413	(D)
6,856	*11,720*	19,904	33,001	45,006		91,739 (MB)	91,033	(Loc)
—	*(14,052)*	*(18,107)*	*(21,637)*	*(27,005)*	(UD 1934)	40,470 (MB)	40,167	(Loc)
	(8,791)	*(11,113)*	*(12,905)*	*(15,250)*	As Swinton & Pendlebury MB			
(7,486)	*4,589*	*(4,891)*	*(5,498)*	*(6,062)*		13,646 (MB)	40,285	(D)
(4,362)		*(5,778)*	*(6,614)* **(B)**	*(7,271)*				
(13,720)	*(14,368)*	*(15,620)*	*(17,485)*	*(19,535)*		35,192 (MB)	37,444	(Loc)
(10,192)	*(11,502)*	*(16,614)*	*(18,026)*	*(21,087)*				
—	—	—	—	—		— 1968	396,230	
19,416	39,415	55,367	74,592	90,936		157,395 (CB)	157,313	(D)
1,330	1,943	2,297	2,619	2,956	1922	31,460 (MB)		(Loc)
13,487	28,021	41,719	50,023	51,753		81,274 (MB)	163,258	(D)
2,982	3,788	4,750	4,542	4,400		4,752 (MB)	4,994	(Com)
3,656	3,557	3,511	3,314	3,136		4,948 (MB)	5,930	(Par)
5,876	5,409	5,100	5,269	5,419		5,822 (MB)	8,749	(Par&D)
4,208	4,167	4,032	4,247	4,613		5,399 (MB)	13,727	(Par)
10,447	10,025	10,462	10,892	10,382		12,397 (MB)	15,566	(Par&D)
11,797	11,998	23,862	24,725	25,418		17,428 (MB)	15,163	(Par)
16,419	21,657	24,767	25,534	33,625		54,046 (MB)	109,257	(D)
						As Torbay MB		
3,298	3,529	3,445	3,436	3,241		2,920 (MB)	3,536	(Par)
4,001	4,073	4,089	4,016	4,035		5,502 (MB)	5,772	(Par)
—	—	—	—	—		—	164,650	(LB)
11,590	26,055	37,074	40,365	42,181		Loc in Stepney Met.B		(Loc)
29,108	29,919	32,041	32,202	35,538	Loc in Stepney Met.B			(Loc)
105,101	120,104	126,961	129,132	129,727		47,078 (Met.B)		(Loc)
4,038	3,410	2,225	2,123	2,125	Loc in Stepney Met.B			(Loc)
43,529	48,611	55,077	56,383	58,334	1907	66,604 (Met.B)		(Loc)
24,077	41,710	64,359	70,000	68,371	Loc in Poplar Met.B			(Loc)
37,454	34,874	30,709	32,326	33,640	Loc in Stepney Met.B			(Loc)
98,836	120,383	132,393	133,823	140,532		92,000 (Met.B)		(Loc)
1,409	*1,329*	*1,161*	*933*	*779*	Loc in Stepney Met.B			(Loc)
8,499	*8,230*	*8,170*	*8,123*	*8,633*	Loc in Stepney Met.B			(Loc)
11,337	10,999	10,619	11,131	11,562		13,336 (C.MB)	14,849	(Par)
34,021	38,960	14,118	46,588	51,366		70,091 (CB)	69,338	(Loc)
23,350	28,079	30,854	33,146	41,413		61,268 (C.CB)	59,590	(D)
10,723	*14,944*	*21,192*	33,229	53,579	1910	103,209 (CB)	97,215	(Loc)
2,869	*3,089*	*2,904*	*3,096*	2,916		4,833 (MB)	6,182	(Par)
2,371	4,169	6,351	11,257	20,918		49,822 (MB)	45,797	(Loc)
(39,690)	*(48,524)*	*(58,453)*	71,397 **(B)**	87,464		118,498 (CB)	184,734	(D)
(37,760)	*(46,452)*	*(59,402)*						
—	—	—	—	—		—	233,960	(LB)
1,174	*1,268*	*1,387*	*2,737*	*4,373*	1938	45,777 (MB)		(Loc)
4,794	*10,394*	*22,200*	*43,098*	*75,091*	1926	93,857 (MB)		(Loc)
7,137	*11,092*	*22,531*	*47,754*	*96,720*	1929	198,788 (MB)		(Loc)

TOWN	Pre-1801	1801	1811	1821	1831	1841	185
WANDSWORTH, Surrey*		4,445	5,644	6,702	6,879	7,614	9,611
Also: *Putney, Surrey*		2,428	2,881	3,394	3,811	4,684	5,280
Battersea, Surrey (99)		3,365	4,409	4,764	5,311	6,617	10,560
Tooting Graveney, Surrey		1,189	1,626	1,863	2,063	2,840	2,122
WAREHAM, Dorset		1,627	1,709	1,931	2,325	2,745	3,078
WARLEY (100), Worcs		1,097	1,328	1,950	2,676	5,020	8,379
WARRINGTON, Lancs & Ches*	1750:3,500	10,567	11,738	13,570	16,018	18,981	(20,800
	1781:9,770						(22,873
WARWICK, Warwks*	1730:4,600	5,592	6,497	8,235	9,109	9,775	10,973
	1775:5,200						
WATFORD, Herts		3,530	3,976	4,713	5,293	5,989	6,546
WELLS, Som	1775:2,600	4,505	5,516	5,888	6,649	7,050	7,401
WELSHPOOL (101), Mont		2,872	3,303	3,535	4,536	6,185	6,564
WEST BROMWICH, Staffs*	1775:2,700	5,687	7,485	9,505	15,327	26,121	34,591
WESTMINSTER, Msx*		157,890	166,438	186,584	206,116	226,241	241,450
Also: *Paddington, Msx*		1,881	4,609	6,476	14,540	25,173	46,305
St Marylebone, Msx *		63,982	75,624	96,040	122,206	138,164	157,696
WESTON-s-MARE, Som		138	163	738	1,310	2,103	4,034
WEYMOUTH, Dorset		2,350	2,985	4,252	5,126	5,039	5,273
Melcombe Regis		1,267	1,747	2,370	2,529	2,669	2,95
WHITEHAVEN, Cumb*	1713:4,000	8,742	10,106	12,438	11,393	—	—
	1750:8,000						
	1762:9,063						
WHITLEY BAY (102), Nmbld		251	375	554	632	749	43
WIDNES, Lancs		3,252	4,294	4,820	5,825	6,918	9,37
WIGAN, Lancs*	1750:4,000	10,989	14,060	17,716	20,774	25,517	31,94
	1775:4,500						
WILTON, Wilts		2,144	1,963	2,058	1,997	1,698	1,80
WINCHESTER, Hants	1750:4,000	3,089	3,653	4,318	4,923	6,641	(8,48
	1786:4,900						(13,70
WINDSOR, Berks *Old Windsor*	1750:3,000	669	932	1,050	1,453	1,600	1,78
New Windsor	1775:4,000	3,436	4,340	4,648	5,650	7,887	6,87
WISBECH (103), Cambs	1750:3,000	5,541	6,300	7,877	8,777	10,461	12,70
	1775:3,800						
WOKINGHAM, Berks		2,281	2,365	2,810	3,139	3,342	3,75
WOLVERHAMPTON (104) Staffs*	1750:7,454	12,565	14,836	18,380	24,732	36,382	49,98
	1775:9,665						
WOODSTOCK, Oxon		1,322	1,419	1,455	1,380	1,412	1,26
WORCESTER (104a), Worcs*	1750:10,300	14,842	18,565	23,532	27,641	28,738	29,33
	1775:11,000						
WORKINGTON, Cumb		5,716	5,807	6,439	6,415	—	—
WORKSOP, Notts		3,263	3,702	4,567	5,566	6,197	7,21
WORTHING (105), W,Suss		1,018	2,692	3,725	4,576	4,702	5,37
WREXHAM (106), Denbg	1750:3,000	3,039	3,006	4,795	5,481	5,818	5,98
	1775:3,500						
YEOVIL (107), Som		2,774	3,118	4,655	5,921	7,043	7,74
YORK (108), Yorks*	1735:10,800	16,145	18,217	20,787	26,260	27,818	36,30
	1750:11,400						
	1781:12,800						

For Notes to the above section, please turn to page 332.

1861	1871	1881	1891	1901	.....	1961	1971-77	
13,346	*19,783*	*28,004*	*46,717*	*68,332*	1904	347,422 (Met)	300,530	(LB)
6,481	*9,439*	*13,235*	*17,771*	*24,139*	Loc in Wandsworth Met.			(Loc)
19,600	*54,016*	*107,262*	*150,558*	*168,905*		105,758 (Met)		(Loc)
2,055	*2,327*	*3,942*	*5,784*	*16,473*	Loc in Wandsworth Met.			(Loc)
3,076	*3,067*	*3,024*	*3,074*	*2,736*		3,098 (MB)	4,379	(Loc)
13,379	17,158	25,084	36,170	54,539		68,372 (CB) as Sandwell		
(24,050)	*(29,894)*	*(40,957)*	*(49,126)*	*(56,892)*		75,964 (CB)	133,400	(D&NT)
(26,431)	*(32,083)*	*(42,554)*	*(52,743)*	*(64,242)*				
10,589	11,002	11,800	11,905	11,909		16,051 (MB)	18,296	(D)
7,418	*12,071*	*(15,507)*	*(20,269)*	*(32,599)* (UD)		75,622 (MB)	78,465	(D)
		(12,162)	*(18,826)* **(B)**	*(29,327)*				
7,446	*7,793*	*8,098*	*8,313*	*8,390*		6,715 (C.MB)	8,604	(Par)
7,304	*7,178*	*7,107*	*6,501*	*6,121*		6,330 (MB)	7,030	(Com)
41,795	*47,918*	*56,295*	*59,474*	*65,114*		96,041 (CB)	166,593	(Loc)
254,463	*246,592*	*228,993*	*198,249*	*180,397*		85,735 (C.Met.B)	218,500	(C.LB)
75,784	*96,813*	*107,218*	*118,054*	*127,557*		116,923 (Met.B)		(Loc)
161,680	*159,254*	*154,910*	*142,404*	*132,295*		69,045 (Met.B)		(Loc)
8,038	*10,568*	*12,884*	*15,524*	*18,275*		43,938 (MB)		(Loc)
6,498	*7,533*	*7,920*	*7,626*	*7,473*		41,045 (MB)	42,349	(Loc)
3,515	*3,828*	*3,630*	*3,591*	*4,497*	As Weymouth & Melcombe Regis MB			(Loc)
—	*17,003*	*19,295*	*18,038*	*19,324*		27,566 (MB)	26,724	(Loc)
419	731	1,800	3,008	7,705 (UD 1954)		36,517 (MB)	37,817	(Loc)
12,229	*15,016*	*(19,473)*	*(25,581)*	*(27,747)*		52,186 (MB)	56,949	(Loc)
		(24,935)	*(30,011)*	*(28,580)*				
37,658	39,110	48,194	55,013	60,764		78,690 (CB)	81,147	(D)
1,930	*1,871*	*1,826*	*2,120*	*2,203*		3,402 (MB)	3,815	(Par)
(8,830)	*(8,928)*	*(9,037)*	*(8,526)*	*(7,122)*		28,770 (MB)	31,107	(D)
(14,776)	*(14,705)*	*(17,780)*	*(19,073)*	*(20,929)*				
1,835	2,112	2,521	2,976	3,379		27,165 (MB)	30,114	(Loc)
7,036	7,814	8,079	8,523	10,003				
11,163	*11,527*	*11,373*	*11,282*	*11,796*		17,528 (MB)	17,016	(Par)
4,144	*4,652*	*(5,043)*	*(5,314)*	*(6,002)*		11,392 (MB)	21,069	(D)
		(3,099)	*(3,254)*	*(3,551)*				
60,860	68,291	75,766	82,662	94,187		150,825 (CB)	269,112	(D)
1,201	*1,195*	*1,133*	*1,136*	*1,106*		1,818 (MB)	1,940	(Par)
33,237	*36,243*	*37,435*	*45,748*	*49,790*		65,923 (Co.C.CB)	73,452	(D)
6,467	8.413	14,109	23,490 **(B)**	26,143		29,552 (MB)	28,431	(Loc)
8,361	10,409	11,625	12,734	16,112 (UD 1931)		34,311 (MB)	36,098	(Loc)
5,805	7,413	11,821	16,606 **(B)**	20,015		80,329 (MB)	88,407	(D)
7,562	8,576	10,978	12,552	14,966		33,438 (MB)	39,052	(Com)
(8,486)	*(9,368)*	*(9,507)*	*(10,943)*	*(11,704)*		24,598 (MB)	25,503	(D)
(7,957)	*(8,476)*	*(8,479)*	*(9,648)*	*(9,861)*				
45,385	50,761	*61,789*	*67,004* **(B)**	*77,914*		104,392 (Co.C.CB)	104,782*	(D)

NOTES TO CENSUS RECORDS, CHAPTER ELEVEN

(1) Abingdon: includes part of St Helens; (2) Accrington: Old and New Townships; (3) Aldershot: The Camp was built between 1851 and 1871; (4) Altrincham: Chapelry, part of Bowdon A.P. until 1861; (5) Appleby: St Michael includes townships of Crackenthorpe, Murton, Hilton, Bongate; St Lawrence includes Appleby, Scarthgate, Colby, Burrals, Hoff and Drybeck; (6) Bacup: Part of New-church-in-Rossendale, parish of Whalley; (7) Barking: *Abstract* figure for 'town only'. *VCH* for Civil Parish of Ilford created 1888; (8) Barnet: A strangely indented and inconvenient boundary of Herts and Middlesex; (9) For all Hampshire towns see: *An Index to the 1851 Census for Hampshire* (2 vols.) Ed.: Smith, S. (Hampshire Genealogical Soc. 1980); (10) Bebington: includes Higher and Lower towns, also Storeton, Poulton and Tranmere. From 1881 as Bebington CP and UD; (11) Birkenhead: in Bidston Ancient Parish until 1871; (12) Birmingham: *VCH* figures include Aston, but this does not account for the whole discrepancy; (13) Blackpool: *Layton with Warbreck in 1841* also the town of Blackpool containing 1,304 persons (*VCH*); (14) Bournemouth: the parish of St Peter Bourne-mouth was formed in 1845 from parts of Holdenhurst and Christchurch; (15) Brackley: St James and St Peter parishes; (16) Bradford: see *Poverty and Progress: Social Conditions in Early and Mid-Nineteenth Century Bradford* (Bradford Library Service 1980); (17) Brighton: see *East Sussex Workhouse Census 1851* by Burchall, M. J. (Sussex Family History Group 1978); (18) Brighouse: As Hipperholme-cum-Brighouse in the parish of Halifax; (19) See: *The Streets of Bristol* by Ralph, E. (Hist. Assoc. 1981); (20) Burton-on-Trent: part in Derbyshire. Here only B-o-T Township, not includ-ing Branston, Burton Extra, Horninglow or Strettenton; (21) Bury: in both Blackburn and Salford Hundreds; (22) Caernarfon: In Llanbeblig (Is-Gorfai); (23) Cambridge: includes University popula-tion; (24) Chard: *Chard in 1851* (Chard History Group 1980); (25) Chester: Haygarth, V. R.: 'Obser-vations on the Population and Disease of Chester in the year 1774' *Roy. Soc. Phil. Trans.*, 68 (1900 (26) Chipping Norton: includes Over Norton; (27) Cleethorpes: with Thrunscoe in 1841, increase attributed to 'visitors'; (28) Colwyn Bay: Llandrillo yn Rhos Parish; (28a) Congleton: part of Astbury Ancient Parish until 1841; (29) Coventry: includes part of Holy Trinity. See Bateson, J., *Mid-Victorian Coventry; the City its workers and its Industry, based on Census returns 1851-1861* (Univ. Birmingham Extra-Mural Dept. 1975); (30) Crewe: Ancient Parish of Monks Coppenhall; (31) Crosby: includes Great Crosby Chapelry and Little Crosby Township; (32) Darlington: Township, also Archdeacon, Newton and Blackwell; (33) Darwen: Over and Lower Townships: *VCH* lists under Blackburn; (34) Dudley: also Kingswinford*. For this region see; *Some Copy Census Returns held by the West Midlands Libraries* (Typescript: W. Midlands Branch of the Library Assoc.); (35) Dukinfield: part of Stockport Ancient Parish until 1871; (36) Ealing: see: Rowland, R. N. G. *Street Names of Acton* (London Borough of Ealing Library Service, 2nd edn. 1978); (37) Eastleigh: and Bishopstoke. Eastleigh was created an ecclesiastical parish in 1868 from the civil parish of South Stoneham and included the tithings of Barton Peveril, Eastleigh and Boyatt. The town grew as a railway junction. (38) Ellesmere Port: was created a Municipal Borough in 1933 from Ellesmere Port-and-Whitby Urban District. Ellesmere Port C.P. was created in 1981; (39) Ely: includes Holy Trinity and St Mary; (40) Fleetwood: in Thornton; (41) Glossop: a massive parish which included the townships of Glossop Dale, Hadfield, Padfield, Dinting, Witfield, Chunall, Simmondley, Charlesworth, Chisworth, Ludworth, Hayfield, Mellor, Beard, Thornset, Ollersett and Whittle, Glossop was incorporated in 1866 which accounts for the change in population; (42) Gosport: in Alvestoke Liberty, including Gosport Chapelry; (43) Gravesend: includes Mitton-next-Gravesend; (44) Grimsby: decline in 1841 was the result of the failure of a ropeworks and the previously inaccurate inclusion of Clee parish; (45) Hackney: see *The Hub of Hoxton: Hoxton Street 1851-1871, a Study based on the Censuses.* (London Borough of Hackney Library Services 1980); (46) Harrogate: Bilton and Harrogate in Knaresborough; (47) Havering: includes Hornchurch and Romford; (48) Helston: in Wendron Parish; (49) Hertford: see Munby, L., *Herts Population Statistics 1563-1801* (Hitchin 1964); (50) Kingston-upon-Hull: 1831 figure is 46,426 including Sculcoates; (51) Lambeth: see: *Lambeth, Battersea and Wandsworth: Urban Development in Nineteenth Century London, 1838-1888*, by Roebuck, J. (1979); (52) Leeds: Beckwith, F., 'The Population of Leeds during the Industrial Revolution', *Thoresby Soc.*, Miscellany, 12 (2) (1945); (53) Leicester: see *VCH Leics.*, vol. III, p. 179 note (e); 'Leicester was made a County Borough in 1888; its area was not altered until the Leicester Extension Act 1891'. For the areas added see notes: a, d, e, f, g, h, i and j and m; (54) Leicester: from 1892 add the civil parishes, not included, of Aylestone, Belgrave, Evington, Humberstone, Knighton, Leicester Abbey and Newfound Pool; (55) Deptford: part of Deptford, St Paul was in Surrey; (56) Liverpool: NB also Toxteth Park and West Derby not included here; (57) Llandovery: in Llandingat parish; (58) Llanelli: 'Parish including Borough'; (59) London: adds London Within and Without the Walls. See George, M. D., 'Some Causes of the Increase in Population in the Eighteenth Century as illus-trated by London', *Economic Jnl.*, 32 (1922). The population of London in 1700 and 1750 is given in an Appendix to the 1801 *Census Report*. There were 97 parishes within the walls (381.8 acres) and 12 parishes without (271.1 acres); the Inns of Court are separately entered. — *continued on next page*

(60) Maidenhead: part in Bray, part in Cookham; not separately entered as Maidenhead town until 1841; (61) Manchester: Township only in upper figure; total population below; (62) Margate: see *Visitors to Margate in the 1841 Census Returns* (Local Population Studies 1972). Here, originally, as Thanet; (63) Morecambe: in the township of Poulton-le-Sands and parish of Lancaster. Change of name in 1891, earlier as Heysham; (63a) Barking: a civil parish of Ilford, created out of Barking 1888; (63b) Newport (Mon): St Woollas-with-Newport; (64) Norwich: Local census of 1751; original in County Record Office; (65) Nottingham: Chambers, J. D., 'Population Changes in a Provincial Town: Nottingham 1700–1800' in Pressnel, L. S. (ed.) *Studies in the Industrial Revolution* (1968); (66) Oldham: as Prestwich-cum-Oldham; (67) Ossett: -with-Gawthorpe; (68) Oxford: excluding the University; (69) Poole: includes Hamworthy, Longfleet, Parkstone and St James; (70) Portsmouth: see Stanford, J., and Temple-Patterson, A.: *Condition of the Children of the Poor in Mid-Victorian Portsmouth*, Portsmouth Papers No. 21 (Portsmouth City Council, 1974); (71) Port Talbot: originally Abermouth or Aberavon Port, including the village of Taibach. Named Port Talbot by Act of Parliament in 1835, but does not then appear under this name. The present town's returns are found under two parishes, Taibach and Margam; these are totalled in the Table; (71a) Preston: Spencer, K. M., 'Census Enumeration Schedules', *Loc. Hist.*, vol. 11, No. 3 (1974); (72) Prestwich: as Prestwich-cum-Oldham; here Prestwich township only; (73) Pudsey: a Chapelry in the parish of Calverley; (74) Reading: includes part of St Giles and part of St Mary's; (75) Ilford: part of Barking parish before 1830; (75a) Rhondda comprises the ancient parish of Ystrad y fodwg which covered the valley and included many small townships; (76) Richmond-upon-Thames: *Street-Names of Barnes, Mortlake and East Sheen* (Barnes and Mortlake History Society, 1977); (77) Rochdale: part in Salford Hundred, part (Saddleworth with Quick) is Asbrigg Wapentake (Yorkshire); (78) Romsey: includes both Romsey Extra and Infra; (79) St Albans: after 1881 excludes part of St Michael's; (80) Sale: part of Ashton-upon-Mersey; (81) Rotherham: township only 1801–1881; (82) Ryde: Newchurch parish; (83) Scunthorpe: see *Workers and Community: the People of Scunthorpe in the 1870s, a study based on the 1871 Census*; (84) Sheffield: *Population in Sheffield 1086–1967* (Sheffield City Libraries 1967); (85) Shrewsbury: The original of the 1750 local census is held by the Public Library; (86) Slough: *Slough in 1851: a Town in the Making*; Slough and Eton W.E.A. Local History Class (Berkshire County Council, 1980); (87) Southport: in North Meols; (88) South Shields: under Jarrow, includes Westoe; (89) Spenborough parish of Birstall; combines Cleckheaton, Gomershall and Liversedge; (90) Stalybridge: part of Dukinfield township, part in Stayley township and part in Ashton-under-Lyne. In both Cheshire and Lancashire; (91) Stourbridge: the Township was part of Old Swinford, with Upper Swinford, Wollaston, The Lye and Wollascote; part in Staffordshire, Seisdon Hundred. Township of Stourbridge above. Old Swinford the larger figure, total below; (92) Stratford on Avon: as Old Stratford, including the Borough; (93) Sunderland: Fox, R. C., *The Development of Sunderland in 1851* (Sunderland Polytechnic Dept. of History and Geography. Occasional Paper No. 1, 1980); (94) 'Tamworth Ancient Parish was situated in Offlow Hundred, North and South Divisions, and in Warwickshire (Hemlingford Hundred) Syersote Township was included with part of Tamworth township in 1811' (*VCH*); (95) Torbay: as Torquay; (96) Torrington: Great Torrington; see also Little Torrington; (97) Tynemouth: with North Shields; (98) Tenby St Mary, Within and Without: (99) Battersea: not including Penge Hamlet now in Bromley; (100) Warley: As Smethwick before West Midlands reorganization of 1966. Smethwick was in Staffordshire, Warley in Worcestershire; now part of Sandwell; in 1841–1871 Smethwick, as part of Harborne parish and a member of King's Norton Poor Law Union will be found in Worcestershire; (101) Welshpool: or Pool; (102) Whitley Bay: Castle Ward in Tynemouth parish; (103) Wisbech: Includes St Mary and St Peter; (104) Wolverhampton: see 'Individual Behaviour and Social Change: the Irish in nineteenth century Wolverhampton' by Mack Shaw, in *West Midlands Studies (A Journal of Regional History)*, vol. 14, winter 1981; (104a) Worcester: includes St John in Bedwardine, St Martin and St Peter; (105) Worthing: Broadwater parish; (106) Wrexham: see both Wrexham Regis and Wrexham Abbot; (107) Yeovil: see Leslie Brooke, *Street Names in Yeovil* (Yeovil Arch. and Loc. Hist. Soc. 1979); (108) York: City only.

CHAPTER TWELVE

PHOTOGRAPHS AS EVIDENCE 1840–1983

ANY OF THE DOCUMENTS which we have examined in earlier Chapters is capable of conjuring a mental picture of its time and people. Whenever we are able to add document to document, or take the written record to the street which it describes, then more and more detail will be added to the pictures formed in our imagination. It is as if people of the past could be alive again through our reconstruction of their environment; it is in this sense that scholars of the census refer to their ability to 'repopulate' the houses of a 19th-century town. We turn finally to a more recent kind of evidence which leaves little to our imagination, but instead brings reality to life. Photographs are a unique form of visual record of a living past; each preserves its moment of past time for us to see, not only with an inward eye. For the local historian they have the extra attraction that they are one type of document which he can collect, even as originals, for himself, or even make, as his own photographic record of the places which he studies. In his 'Agenda for Urban Historians' H. J. Dyos has stressed 'the real need for a collection of photographs and plans illustrating the history of our towns . . . with instruction and delight . . .'.[1]

The widespread acknowledgement of the historical importance, as well as the delight, of old photographs within the past ten years is remarkable. As hoards of well-kept glass plate negatives have come to light in town after town, a spate of collections has been published. Densely packed albums of reprints, such as *Victorian Life in Photographs*[2] contain startling images which present moments of time in sharp focus. The high quality of much of the early photographic process and the sheer quantity of production has made a new set of national archives available to the student of local history. Libraries and museums have unearthed their stores of forgotten prints to produce extensive local picture postcard collections for sale. The postcard view itself has now a widespread and respectable following. Many towns have their own Postcard Societies and this fancy has its own guide books.[3]

Black-and-white photographs as we know them today began to appear in 1838 with the development of the daguerreotype, which, in spite of requiring inordinately long exposures and an immobile subject, remained popular from the 1840s to the 1860s. Meanwhile, William Fox Talbot's invention of the paper negative in 1838–41, with the possibility of shorter exposures, permitted further progress. It was the introduction of the wet-plate in the 1850s which produced a ubiquitous generation of professional photographers, each with his wagon-load of equipment and mobile darkroom, who could create 'instant history' from the war-fronts of the Crimea and Gettysburg to the exploration of deserts and rain-forests, from the summits of mountain peaks to the main streets and alleys of almost every substantial English town. In 1860 the

DUDLEY

Pictures 1, 6, and 7 are reproduced by courtesy of Dudley Art Gallery; numbers 4, 5, and 8 are from Dudley Library's collection of local photographs. Descriptions and dates of the titles are as attributed by the Art Gallery and Library. The modern views in 3 and 9 are by Frank Power.

. The 'chairing' of Thomas Hawkes in 1834 by an unknown artist. Sometimes referred to as 'Hawkes at the Hustings'. Major Thomas Hawkes of Himley, a local Tory, defeated the Liberal Member for Dudley, John Campbell, in 1834 and retained the seat against Reform candidated in 1835, '37 and '41. Numerous posters survive for those elections. The shopfronts of (Edward) 'Terry' (a grocer) and (John) 'Bagott Tailor' identify, by reference to the 1841 Census (HO 107/1196:ED 11 pp. 21-2) the nearer building. This was the 'establishment' club and Town Commissioners' meeting-place, the *Dudley Arms Hotel*. Built in 1786, the Hotel was demolished in 1968 to provide site for Marks and Spencer's store. By coincidence number 8 shows a later shop on the other side of the *Dudley Arms*.

2. Tower Street, 1900.

3.   Tower Street, 1983. The modern police and fire stations are on the left and the Baylies' Charity School, founded in 1732 and named on Treasure's map, is on the right. Only the Castle tower appears to be unchanged since 1910, but its grounds now house a zoo.

4. Dudley Old Town Hall before its demolition in
1860. This is possibly the earliest Dudley photograph.
The Middle Row of houses which divided the Market
Place, forming Queens Street, stood behind this
building. These had been cleared in the 1840s, though
still shown on Treasure's map.

5. The Dudley Fountain, Market Place; presented to
the town by the Earl of Dudley, was built on the site
of the Old Town Hall in 1867 where, after some
slight modifications it still stands in the new pedestrian
precinct of the Market Place. Both 5 and 8 are more
fully illustrated and described in David F. Radmore's
Dudley As It Was (1981).

6. A view of Dudley from Easy Hill *c.* 1775 by T. Saunders. The churches of St Edmund and St Thomas can be identified, also several of the town's eighteenth century public buildings.

7. Dudley High Street in 1812 by 'Paul Braddon' the pseudonym of William Henry Cress (1838-1927) and James Leslie Crees (1864-1938) who produced a series of watercolour views of Dudley Streets. As in this case, the scenes are retrospective 'reconstructions'.

8. George Mason's shop *c.*1900. The shop was demolished in 1971; its site is now occupied by a jeweller.

9. Stone Street in 1983. These are the houses built for William Bagott in 1840. (1) The rounded corner of the building (2) the only surviving original window (3) the alley way between numbers 4 and 5 (4) the *Griffin* public house.

BIRMINGHAM

All the Birmingham pictures are from the Central Reference Library, Local History Department. Identification and data for numbers 11-15 are as found in *Birmingham As It Was* by Joseph McKenna (1979).

10. The 'Theatre Royal' in 1834 stood in New Street on the present site of Woolworths. It was demolished in 1956.

11. Holder's Concert Hall, *c.*1851-57 in Coleshill Street next to the *Rodney Inn*. This became Holder's Music Hall in 1857 and the 'Gaiety' in 1886. It closed in 1920.

12. Lench's Trust Almshouses stood in Steelhouse Lane from 1764 to 1880, later the site of Birmingham General Hospital.

13. Moor Street in 1886. The founder of Lench's Trust lived here in the 16th century.

14. New Street, *c.*1886. The site of the present General Post Office is occupied by houses.

15. No. 6 Court, Bagot Street in 1903. It still survives (vestigially) in the vicinity of Aston University.

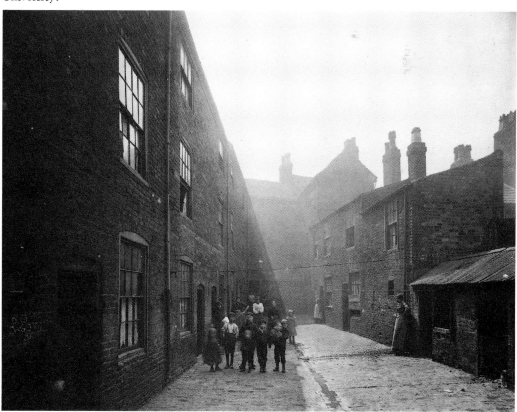

16. Toll Gate on Birchfield Road, Perry Barr, *c.*1870. The inn on the left of the picture was *The Crown and Cushion*, kept by E. Bowen. Birchfield Road is now a motorway.

17. High Street, Harborne, *c.*1905. Note the two types of omnibus and the total absence of motorcars. Harborne was one of the Domesday manors of Greater Birmingham but was not incorporated into the city until 1891.

WORCESTER

All the Worcester pictures are from Worcester City Library and Museum. Identification and data for Nos. 18 to 25 are given in *Worcester As it Was* by Thomas Stafford (1977) with particular thanks to Mr Stafford for provision of several of the originals.

18. Elgar Brothers' Music Shop, *c.*1906 at No. 10 High Street, now occupied by Russell and Dorrell. Sir Edward Elgar occasionally worked here as a youngster.

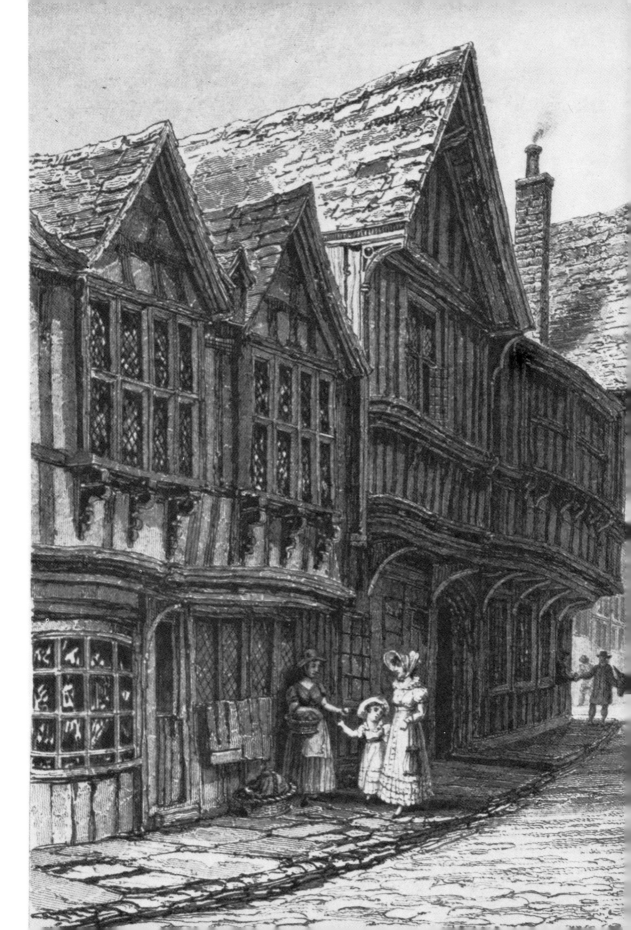

19. Friar Street in 1829 from an engraving by
W. H. Bartlett and W. H. Brooke to illustrate Britton's
Picturesque Antiquities of English Cities.

20. Buildings in Fish Street, now Deansway. The house in the foreground, built *c.*1500, was demolished to make the inner ring-road but the *Farriers Arms* still survives.

21. The Cross, *c.*1910 showing both a double decker horse 'bus and an electric tram.

22. The Volunteer Training Corps in 1915 made up of Reservists and men not (at first) accepted for the Army, but still determined to 'do their bit'; most of these men appear to be over military age. This was their first route march.

23. Foregate Street in 1893. On the right is the site of the present City Library, then occupied by a boarding house. The picture shows horse-tramlines, a hansom cab and gaslights.

24. High Street in 1906 with the Cathedral in the background; the shops on the left are now the Lichgate Precinct.

25. Laying tramlines in Broads Street in 1903-4. This upheaval is graphically described in the contemporary local press.

lighter hand-held camera made 'snapshots' possible, and by the '80s dry plates and inexpensive cameras had turned photography into a popular hobby for thousands of amateurs.

Usually we find that a town's photographic history begins with a few rare examples from *c.* 1850–55, with top-hats at their tallest and crinolines at their widest. A few towns, including Lincoln, Warrington, Rugby and Blackpool, list a few earlier scenes of the 1840s, but these are rare. The world's earliest known crowd scene is a photograph of a massed Chartist meeting in London in 1848; the Duke of Wellington's funeral was photographed in 1852, and there were photographers at the Crystal Palace Exhibition in 1853. Dudley's oldest street photograph is probably that of the old Town Hall on Middle Row, which was demolished in 1860; it offers an interesting comparison with Rowlandson's drawing, made a century earlier (see illustrations on page 172, and Nos. 20 and 21). From the 1870s and 1880s to the turn of the century local photographs became commonplace, both in private collections and in public archives. 'There, at last, was daily life in all its spontaneity and fragility, the light reflected from an ephemeral particle of time fixed and rendered timeless'.[4]

Each town seems to have had its own Victorian photographer and its own collection of plates. Some eminent professionals like Francis Frith ranged far afield, from Wales to the Isle of Wight, throughout the West Country, and northward to Lancashire and Durham. Birmingham Central Library's Local History Department refers to its collection of over 120,000 engravings, prints, photographs and transparencies as 'the largest local history illustrations collection in the Midlands'. The reason for this wealth of illustration is that 'between the years 1842 and 1914 Birmingham had no fewer than 633 photographic studios. The first was opened in 1842 by Joseph Whitlock who for £1,000 purchased the exclusive right to take daguerreotype photographs in Warwickshire. As to the number of amateur photographers it is impossible to say, but the number must surely run into thousands' according to J. McKenna.[5]

There is little if any need to explain the nature of Victorian and Edwardian photographs — they speak for themselves. Their many aspects of social life, invention and fashion are also self-evident. In countless instances we see buildings demolished long ago and people long since dead. Contemporary fashion, from crinoline to bustle, then to leg-of-mutton sleeves and tailored skirt, and cutaway coat to frock-coat then to Norfolk jacket, costumes every street scene. The streets are thronged with public and commercial transport, which changes, in print after print, from coach-and-four or hackney carriage and horse-bus to tramways, first with steam-cars, later electricity then trolley-buses, to the inevitable motor-cars and buses. Photographs of shopfronts (see illustration No. 22) demonstrate a different style of display and availability of goods, a larger number of aproned staff; here we see sides of bacon by the dozen, brushes, baskets, saddlery and vegetable stalls. Street traders and itinerant entertainers are there, from organ-grinders to Punch and Judy shows, 'sandwich-men' and chimney sweeps.

Crowd scenes are a fascinating source of massed information on appearances and attitudes, and many were the occasions for public celebration which brought the Victorians into the market-places. There were photographers to record Coronations, Jubilees, Fêtes, elections, balloon ascents, armistices and recruiting drives, church parades, tattoos, ox-roastings, carnivals and circus processions. The market itself might be a horse-fair or a hiring-fair, a cattle market in a busy town centre or stalls with awnings. Crowds and the rarer busy weekday shopping streets with oblivious passers-by are of particular value as, in most cases, photography was a Sunday occupation finding relatively empty streets and people in their best clothes with an inquisitive awareness of the cameraman. This often results in wooden, open-mouthed poses. More everyday scenes, such as those captured in Birmingham's New Street, *c.* 1880 are especially revealing, unselfconscious documents (see illustration No. 5).

The sense of *difference* is always there — in hundreds of hats, bonnets, parasols, swagger canes, pillbox hats and military tunics, Eton collars, pinafores, knickerbockers and boaters. Different too is the abundance of beards and moustaches, the unfamiliar, unpressed, and heavy cut of even expensive clothes, the curious fixed stares of the poor and their evident disadvantages, the clumsy, dusty roughness of boots of all classes and the raw heaviness of men and women's hardworked hands, horse-dung on the streets and the occasional startling evidence of barefoot poverty; all speak aloud of a different age.

The very street furniture echoes this sense of difference in large shop-signs, giant spectacles and barbers' poles, huge locks and pawnbrokers' brass balls. The clutter of facia boards and irregular shopfronts is less unfamiliar, being different only in style from those we see today. The 19th-century litter of projecting name-boards, lanterns, clocks, awnings and inn-signs is neither more nor less aesthetically pleasing than the garish uniformity of multiple stores and snackbars; there appears to be less refuse on the Victorian pavements, but more for the crossing-sweepers. A distinctive feature of earlier streets is the profusion of large-scale black and white posters; wordy advertising matter of all sorts plasters walls and hoardings but there is rarely a picture. A particularly nostalgic sight are the numerous theatre frontages and posters, the music halls and opera houses, the Grands and Hippodromes which give way to the 'kinemas', the 'bioscopes' and later, the Bingo halls and motor-car showrooms.[6]

Even at the turn of the century we see frequent evidence of the towns' earlier origins, alongside the new railway stations and civic buildings. There are cows tethered outside the *Swan* inn at Stafford in 1860, a thatched cottage in Wolverhampton's Canal Street in 1870, stocks outside Coventry police station in 1854, half-timbered houses at Deritend in Birmingham as late as 1890, and windmills in many town centres. In picture after picture we are aware of cobbled streets which remained amongst the tram-lines in Dudley until the 1930s. Of our three Midland towns, the cathedral city of Worcester is the most recently and suddenly modernised, as the photographs in the City Library show. Most of all one sees a picture of the longer survival of heavily timbered jettied buildings, a contrast with the more recent 'improvements' of the industrial towns, described in Chapter Eight. In Fish Street (illustration No. 11), the picture of a ghost-street, now under the Deansway motor carriageway, is preserved by the camera. So also is the horrendous experience of the city in 1903, when for weeks on end the centre of the town was immobilised by the laying of the electric tramlines by hand and muscle only (illustration No. 16).

There are several national photographic archives, housed in the Public Record Office (13,000 black-and-white prints from *c.* 1920 including 'townscapes'); London's Guildhall (10,560 photographs of London topography since 1857); and the National Library of Wales at Aberystwyth. The Royal Commission on Historical Monuments houses a National Monuments Record for England. This contains 800,000 prints of historic architecture from 1859, including collections of photographs and measured drawings of buildings, and has indexes to photographs and drawings in other regional collections. Local depositors, such as Worcestershire County Record Office, send their contributions to this central record. Similar collections are held by the Department of the Environment and the National Trust, each offering a catalogue or index to their collection and prints for sale.

Locally, most County Record Offices now offer a comprehensive collection of photographs of particular local interest. Sometimes the County Library holds many other local originals. Universities often have photographic collections, as do other educational institutions. Many specialised folk museums include town photographs in their collections and are well worth a search. Quantities of old negatives still remain in private hands, with individual photographers or collectors, or as the stock-in-trade of photographic companies and dealers. The archives of any well-established provincial newspaper (see Chapter Ten) will usually offer a longstanding local collection of photographs. Local authors sometimes offer their personal collections for sale or loan, from which a selection may have been previously published. Learned societies add their own local photographic collections, for reference by bona-fide students; nor should actual photographic societies be forgotten. Of course, not only the municipal boroughs of our base-list are well-endowed; many smaller towns also have collections of historic note. Many local building surveys and urban townscapes continue to be recorded by Civic Trusts. They remind us of another vital feature, indeed a peculiar value of photographic evidence, in that even up-to-date photographic surveys of any town become invaluable records of streets and buildings old and new, rapidly assuming as much significance as earlier, Victorian originals. Many building surveys begun in the 1950s-60s are now historic documents in their own right, an essential complement to earlier photographic and documentary evidence. Several towns, like Blyth and Huddersfield, have collected photographs of buildings about to be demolished and some towns, as at Pinner and Hackney, have published parallel views of their streets 'yesterday and today'.

Even the most unskilled amateur Instamatic cameraman who begins his own 'before-and-after' survey of his town's streets at different stages of their development may soon find that he has the only surviving picture of a noteworthy 'lost' building. In 1976, the author made a hurried collection of about 30 transparencies of schools, factories, chapels, churches, terraced houses and Victorian villas in Wolverhampton, which were then exactly 100 years old. Today, more than half of those buildings are gone, and Bilston Town Hall has since been restored to an elegant and unfamiliar dazzling brightness. Occasionally, initiative for photographic survival lies with an enterprising town hall. In an important article Professor Norman McCord has pointed out the peculiar affinity between the skills of photographic interpretation and the disciplines of archaeology which he describes as 'related development'.[7] He affirmed that 'no category of structure is more threatened with destruction nowadays than those of the recent past'. Indeed, there may well come a time when students have a more complete archaeological record of the Roman villa, than of the Victorian working-class slum court or 'rookery'. 'The student of history who studies Victorian social conditions from books and reports, while ignoring the physical evidence lying about him in a provincial city is', according to Professor McCord, 'studying history in blinkers'. As if to take up his point the *Local Historian* has printed an issue-by-issue series of historical photographs ranging from a Ragged School at Ipswich in 1859, to a railway accident at Wolverhampton in 1899.[8]

Most numerous of all are the collections of town photographs which are stored in libraries and borough archives. The central reference libraries of all the greater cities, house collections of daguerreotypes, glass plates and negatives, lantern slides and prints, numbered in tens and even hundreds of thousands. Most smaller towns also have collections which are usually kept in the borough library's local history department. Additionally the museum and art gallery may also hold another collection. These are usually well indexed and annotated with considerable local knowledge, often providing the source of a lively set of postcards for sale (see illustrations Nos. 7, 8 and 22).

The most essential aid to any student's search for photographic archives is the *Directory of British Photographic Collections*, compiled by Dr. John Wall.[9] This mine of information (based on the findings of the National Photographic Record) lists no less than 1,580 collections, ranging from small assemblies of rare early Victorian prints to the resources of a modern news agency or public institution. The entire index covers international subjects, such as zoology, numismatics and recreation; there are also major entries for genealogy, street scenes, counties, towns etc., industrial archaeology, and schools. The *Directory*'s listing (under 'Geography') of almost all our base-list towns' Local Studies collections has made the compilation of this Chapter's Gazetteer possible but the *Directory* should also be used for more specific reference. As well as the location, title and dates of each collection it includes a complete analysis of subjects, the numbers of photographs available and details of the photographers. The *Directory* will also offer further detail of hundreds of other local collections not listed here, and many other types of subject. Students of towns not included in our municipal base-list, such as Frome, Bradford-on-Avon, Stevenage, Llandaff and all the major Scottish and Irish towns will find material for their study there; the *Directory* is cross-indexed by subject, title of collection, owners, locations and photographers. To the basic facts offered by Wall's *Directory* the Gazetteer adds a bibliography of published books of local photographs, town by town, also the addresses of local Postcard Societies for which I am personally indebted to the Chairman of the Mercia Postcard Club, Maurice L. Palmer.[10]

FURTHER READING

Batley, J., 'Pictures as a Source of Local History', *Loc. Hist.*, vol. 10 (7) (1973).
Bentley, N., *Edwardian Album* (1974).
Creasy, J., *Victorian and Edwardian Social Life from Old Photographs* (1977).
Gernsheim, H. and Gernsheim, A., *A Concise History of Photography* (1965).
Hannavy, J., *The Victorian Professional Photographer* (Shire Publications pamphlet, 1981).
—— *Masters of Victorian Photography* (1978).
Radmore, D. F., 'Suggestions for a Photographic Survey', *Loc. Hist.*, vol. 9 (5) (1971).

GAZETTEER OF TOWN COLLECTIONS OF PHOTOGRAPHS 1840–1983

This handlist shows that at least 230 of the municipal boroughs of our base-list have major photographic collections. A few additional non-corporate boroughs have also been included; these names are given in lower case print, e.g. Bridgnorth. Reference should be made to Dr. Wall's *Directory of British Photographic Collections* to ascertain the size of any collection, also details, not given here, of facilities for loans to lecturers and researchers of slides and negatives for reproduction. The *subjects* are more fully described in the *Directory*. Addresses do not usually repeat the name of the town if the library or museum is in the centre of the town itself, e.g. under HARTLEPOOL: the Central Library indicates an adequate address; in cases of conurbations, suburbs and new 'districts', if any doubt might exist, the situation of the library is given. Wall's *Directory* should be consulted for full postal addresses. A particularly attractive and easily accessible source of Victorian town photographs is recently available in the commercial production of sepia-toned prints from the Francis Frith Collection which includes over 66,000 views of 2,000 towns and villages.

ABBREVIATIONS

Abbreviations used are as follows:

(1) Referring to the whereabouts of photographic collections

AG	= Art Gallery	M	= Museum
Arch	= Archives Dept. of Library	P	= Private collection*
CH	= County Hall	PCC/PS	= Postcard Club or Society
Civ	= Civic Trust	Poly	= Polytechnic
CoL	= County Library	PhS	= Photographic Society
CRO	= County Record Office	S	= Sale of prints
FE	= College of Further Education	TC	= Technical College
FF	= The Francis Frith Collection	TH	= Town Hall
Hist	= Historical Society	Un	= University
L	= Library		

* Names after P, e.g. P(Sankey) are surnames of owners of private collections.

(2) Referring to the circumstances of access to the collection

App = A written application to view is always essential.
St = Collection available for serious students; a written application advisable.
G = Collection open to general public without written application.
Req = Details by request.

(3) Referring to the available aids for examining the collection

Acc = Accessions lists or similar available.
Cat = Collection has catalogue.
Gu = Collection has guide.
I = Collection has Index.
Pc = Postcards on sale.

ABERGAVENNY FF M(G,I): from 1870.

ABERYSTWYTH FF L(G,I): customs, folk-
lore, architecture, from 1880.

ABINGDON FF.

ACCRINGTON FF.

ALDEBURGH FF TH(G): from 1880.

ALDERSHOT L(G): social life, historic events;
(*Prince Consort*'s) L (St,I) army life from
1850.

ALTRINCHAM (FF) L(G,Cat,S): expansion of
industrial town from 1880.

ARUNDEL: Cartland, J., *Arundel: A Picture
of the Past* (1978).

ASHTON-UNDER-LYNE: Leek, A., *Ashton,
Cheshire in Old Photographs* (1981).

AYLESBURY FF.

BANBURY FF M(G,Acc,S): social life, occupations, transport from *c.* 1920.

BANGOR FF.

BARKING L(St,S): architecture and social life
from *c.* 1900.

BARNSLEY P(St,I): street scenes 1822–1972;
Tasker, E. G., *History of Barnsley Streets*
(9 vols., 1974-79).

BARNSTAPLE FF L(St): 1885 onwards.

BARROW-IN-FURNESS P (Sankey Req):
views, launchings, transport 1900–70; P
Wignall (St,I): local history, industrial
archaeology from *c.* 1850.

BARRY FF L(G,Gu): from *c.*1890.

BEAUMARIS FF.

BEBINGTON L(G): Wirral Collection from
late 19th-c.

BECCLES FF.

BEDFORD FF.

BEVERLEY FF L(St): Local Studies collection from *c.* 1860; CRO(G,Cat,S): from
1880.

BEWDLEY FF Davis, S., *Bewdley As It
Was* (1979).

BEXHILL FF: Guilmant, A., *Bexhill-on-Sea:
A Pictorial History* (1982).

BEXLEY FF L(St) local history from *c.* 1880.
Also Foots Cray FF and Sidcup FF.

BIDEFORD FF.

BIRMINGHAM FF L(G,I,Pc): all aspects of
town life, street scenes, from *c.* 1870;
(*Handsworth*) Hist (St,App,I): views from
1875; P(Whybrow) (St,Cat,S): buildings and
streets from 1870; John Whybrow: *How
Does Your Birmingham Grow ?* (1972);
Joseph McKenna: *Birmingham as it Was
1857-1914* (1979); Langhorne, R., *Yardley
Through the Camera 1890-1900* (1972);
McCulla, D. & Gray, J. S.; *Victorian &*

(*Birmingham — continued*)
Edwardian B (1978); Price, S., *Birmingham
Old and New* (1976).

BLACKBURN FF L(G,I,S): local studies from
1850; M(St): social life from *c.* 1850.

BLACKPOOL FF L(G,I): local history from
1840; Eyre, K., *Bygone Blackpool* (1971).

BLYTH L(G,S): includes demolished buildings
and re-development.

BODMIN FF TH(St,Cat): town life, entertain-
ments etc. from *c.* 1860.

BOGNOR FF Library & Archives Service: *A
Picture of Bognor as Shown in Old Photo-
graphs* (W. Sussex County Council 1976);
Cartland, J., *Bygone Bognor* (1979).

BOLTON FF M(G,I,S,Pc): social life from *c.*
1890; Driver, C., *Photographs of Old
Bolton* (1980).

BOOTLE: Merseyside PS.

BOSTON FF.

BOURNEMOUTH FF L(G,I): social history
from 1860.

BRADFORD FF L(G,I,S): Local Studies
collection from late 19th-c. and survey of
city from 1959; TH(G,S): survey of buildings from 1962; M(G,App,I) local history,
people, views from *c.* 1850; Yorks. Arts
Assocn (St,App,I): industrial buildings of N
and E Yorks. 1972; Bradford & District PCC;
Firth, G., *Bradford As It Was* (1978);
Ayers, J. & J., *Bradford Old and New* (1972).

BRECON FF.

BRENT L(G,I): town life, occupations, services
from *c.* 1800; M(G,I): town life and architecture from 1850.

Bridgnorth: W. C. Macefield: *Bridgnorth As It
Was* (1978).

BRIDGWATER FF L(G,S): buildings from
1966; Squibbs, P. J., *Squibbs' History of
Bridgwater* (1982).

BRIDLINGTON FF L(G,I): architecture, seaside holidays etc., from *c.* 1870.

BRIDPORT FF M(St,I): town life from 1900.

BRIGHTON FF M(St,App,Cat): architecture
from 1970; (*Brighton*) L(G): Frith's photo-
graphs, all aspects of town life from *c.* 1870;
(*Hove*) L(G,I): social life from 1900;
P(*Gray*) (St,App,S): buildings, streets,
beach scenes, transport, slums, from 1850;
Gray, J. S., *Victorian and Edwardian
Brighton from Old Photographs* (1974); and
Brighton Between the Wars (1976); Dale, A.
& Gray, J. S., *Brighton Old and New* (1976).

BRISTOL FF L(St,Acc,S): local history and
development of Bristol from *c.* 1855;
M(St,App,S): views 1865-1900, street

(Bristol — continued)
scenes etc.; P(Winstone):
Bristol as it Was 1840-1970 (1957-81); Bristol
PS; Winstone, R., Victorian and Edwardian
Bristol from Old Photographs (1976);
Buchanan, A. & Cossons, N., Industrial
History in Pictures; Bristol (1970).

BROMLEY FF L(G,S): buildings and streets
from c. 1863; Hist (Hayes) (G,I,S): architecture of district. Also BECKEBHAM FF;
CHISLEHURST FF; PENGE FF.

BUCKINGHAM: Lawson, M. & Sparks, I.,
Victorian and Edwardian Buckinghamshire
from Old Photographs (1976).

BURNLEY FF L(St,I,S): architecture and social
life from 1880; AG(G,I,S): social life from
1870; Burton, R. C., Burnley As It Was
(1972); Douglas, A., Burnley Once Upon a
Time (1976).

BURY FF L(G,I,S,Pc): transport and local
government from c. 1852; Barratt, H., Bury
As It Was (1976).

BURY ST EDMUNDS FF: Jarman, G.,
Victorian Bury St Edmunds in Photographs
(Suffolk CRO, 1980).

BUXTON FF L and M(G): N. Derbyshire
collection from 1870.

CAERNARVON FF.

CALNE Civ(App): Old Calne from 1870.

CAMBRIDGE FF L(G,I): architecture, social
life, transport from 1855; CRO(G,I,S):
architecture and biography from c. 1900;
Un(St,I,S): architecture and topography
from c. 1860; university views; M(G,I):
social life from 1860; P(Ramsey & Muspratt
G,Acc,S): street scenes and buildings 1860-
1900; House, M., Cambridgeshire in Early
Postcards (1978); Reeve, F. A., Victorian
and Edwardian Cambridge from Old Photographs (1971).

CAMDEN L(G,I): Camden life from 1867; also
HAMPSTEAD HEATH FF.

CANTERBURY FF Beaney Institute (G,I):
views, topography, architecture from late
19th-c; Canterbury and E. Kent PCC.

CARDIFF FF L(G): Cardiff from c. 1864.

CARLISLE FF M(G): museum collections
from late 19th-c; CRO(G,I,S): topography,
industry, architecture from c. 1856.

CARMARTHEN FF.

CASTLEFORD L(St,I): town life, transport,
architecture from 1850.

CHARD FF.

CHATHAM FF.

CHELMSFORD FF L(G,I,S): from 1870; CRO
(G,Gu,S): all aspects of Essex life from c.1895;

Marriage, J., Chelmsford: A Pictorial History
(1982); Beacham, R., Chelmsford As It Was.

CHELTENHAM FF.

CHESTER FF M(St,Cat): social life, occupations from late 19th-c; L(G,I,S): photographic survey, Chester and Cheshire from
c. 1870. aerial photographs from 1965;
Cath(St,I): cathedral and precincts c. 1910;
CRO(G,Acc): street scenes, fire brigade
1866-1974; Chester PCC; Ward, T. E.,
Chester As It Was (1980).

CHESTERFIELD FF L(G,I,S): local history
from c. 1880.

CHICHESTER FF Price, B., Bygone Chichester
(1974); The Valiant Years (1978); Changing
Chichester (1982).

CHIPPING NORTON: Old photographs of
Blockley, Chipping Camden, Chipping
Norton and Moreton-in-the-Marsh (1982).

CHORLEY TH(St,App): buildings, transport,
roads from 1922.

CLITHEROE FF.

Cirencester FF Viner, D. J., Cirencester As It
Was (1976).

CHRISTCHURCH FF.

CLEETHORPES FF.

COLCHESTER FF L(G,I): customs, architecture, biography from 1870; M(G,I,S):
museum collection from c. 1875; Colchester
and District PCC; Gifford, P., Colchester
As It Was (1972).

COLNE L(G,S): social life from 1870; P
(Spencer) (St,App): Spencer, W., Colne
As It Was (1971); Wightman, P., Bonnie
Colne (1976).

CONGLETON FF.

CONWAY FF.

COVENTRY FF L(G,I,S): local studies collec-
tion from c. 1865; Gilbert, V., Coventry As
It Was (1973); Newbold, E. B., Coventry
Old and New (1974).

CREWE L(G,Acc): The Crewe Story: A Photographic Survey of Crewe 1955-71.

CROYDON FF Croydon Nat. Hist. Soc.:
Survey of Surrey 1902, published as The
Camera as Historian (1916); L(G,Acc,S):
topography and buildings; Croydon Old and
New in Photographs (Croydon Nat. Hist.
Sci. Soc.); Gent, J. B., Edwardian Croydon
Illustrated by Photographs of the Period
1901-19 (Croydon Nat. Hist. Sci. Soc.,
1981); also NORBURY PARK FF;
NORWOOD FF; PURLEY FF.

DARLINGTON FF L(G,I,S): County Durham
and Darlington, especially railways, from
1856; P(St,App): buildings and railways,

(*Darlington – continued*)
Darlington and Stockton from *c.* 1880;
Dean, S. C. & Clough, U. M., *Darlington As
It Was* (1974); Tees Valley PS.

DARTFORD FF L(G,I,S): all aspects from
1860.

DARTMOUTH FF M(G): local and maritime
history from mid-19th-c.

DARWEN FF.

DEAL FF M(St,S): local history and town life
from *c.* 1860.

DERBY FF L(G,I,S): architecture and transport from *c.* 1860; M(St,I,S): aerial views
from *c.* 1920; Rodgers, F., *Derby Old and
New* (1975).

DEVIZES FF.

DEWSBURY L(G,Cat): topography, events and
personalities from 1859; Dewsbury and
District PS.

DONCASTER FF L(G,S): social life and town
life from late 19th-c.

DORCHESTER FF L(G,I,S): Dorset life from
late 19th-c.; M(G,S): Dorset Photographic
Record from *c.* 1850; Irvine, P., *Victorian
and Edwardian Dorset from Old Photographs* (1977).

DOVER FF.

DROITWICH FF.

DUDLEY L(G,I,S,Pc): local history collection and photographic survey from *c.* 1850
Radmore, D. F., *Dudley As It Was* (1977).

DUKINFIELD :Wilkins-Jones, C.,
Dukinfield in Old Photographs (Tameside
Metropolitan Borough 1980).

DUNSTABLE FF.

DURHAM: CRO(G,I,S): social life from late
19th-c.; Un(G,Cat,S): local history of
Durham from *c.* 1860; Edis collection of
historical buildings and people 1880–1950;
(*Bowes*) M(G,I,S): social life, occupations,
architecture from 1862; L(G,Acc): Durham
life from *c.* 1870; (*Beamish*) M(G,Cat,S):
domestic life, architecture of Durham,
Tyne-Wear, Cleveland from 1850; Nelson, I.,
Durham As It Was (1974); McCord, N.,
Durham from the Air (CRO 1971).

EALING: L(G): all aspects from *c.* 1860;
M(G,I,S): Ealing and Hounslow from 1927;
Ealing Library Service: *Ealing As It Was*
(1980): Rowland, R. N. G., and Ealing
Library Service: *Acton As It Was* (1981).

EASTBOURNE FF L(G,I): street scenes from
c. 1880; Elleray, D. R., *Eastbourne – A
Pictorial History* (1978).

ECCLES TH(G,I,S): all aspects of life from
1858.

ELLESMERE PORT L(G,Acc,S): canals,
architecture, transport, from *c.* 1900.

ELY FF Rouse, M. & Holmes, R., *Cathedral
City and Market Town – Pictorial Records
1900-53* (Ely Society 1975).

ENFIELD FF (*Forty Hall*) M(G,I,Pc): local
history and town life; (*Broomfield*) M(G)
and TH(G): historical and modern photographs of Edmonton, Enfield and Southgate
from *c.* 1900.

EPSOM FF and EWELL FF.

EVESHAM FF L(G,I): buildings and events
from *c.* 1905.

EXETER FF.

FALMOUTH FF L(G,I): local history collection, buildings etc. from *c.* 1920.

FARNHAM M(G,I,S): industry and transport
from 1880.

FAVERSHAM FF.

FOLKESTONE FF L(G): Folkestone and
Hythe from *c.* 1880; Sandgate Society (G,I):
Slides of Old Stansgate from *c.* 1890.

FULHAM L(G,I,S): social life from *c.* 1860.

GAINSBOROUGH: *Six Historic Postcards of
Gainsborough* (Lincs. Library Service 1978).

GILLINGHAM L(G): the Medway towns from
1860.

GLASTONBURY FF.

GLOUCESTER FF L(G,I); Gloucestershire life
from 19th-c.; CRO(G,I,S): County survey
from *c.* 1840; Woodman V. & Kent, A.,
Gloucester As It Was (Hendon 1973).

GODALMING L(G,I): social life from *c.* 1950.

GODMANCHESTER FF.

GOSPORT FF.

GRANTHAM FF TC(St): slides of architecture
and streets

GRAVESEND FF L(G,S,Pc): Gravesend from
c. 1875; *Bygone Gravesend and Bygone
N-W Kent, Compiled from a Postcard
Collection* (1979).

GREAT YARMOUTH FF L(G,I): transport
and social life; Hedges, A., *Great Yarmouth
As It Was* (Hendon 1973).

GREENWICH M(App.S): Shipping, ports and
harbours, docks and canals.

GRIMSBY L(G,Cat,S): all aspects of Humber-
side from *c.* 1850; Boswell, D. & Storey,
J. M., *Grimsby As It Was*, vols. I and II
(Hendon 1974 and 1976).

GUILDFORD FF L(G): local history and
topography of Surrey; Surrey PS; Alexander,
M., *Guildford As It Was* (Hendon 1978) and
Vintage Guildford (Hendon 1981).

HACKNEY: Tongue, S., *Six Views of Nineteenth Century Hackney* (Library Services

(*Hackney – continued*)

Tongue, S. & Worpole, K., *A Hackney Camera 1883-1918* (1974); Worpole, K., Renson, I. & Silver, M., *Hackney, A Second Look; Record of a Walk through Hackney in the 1890s and Today* (1974): also STAMFORD HILL FF.

HALIFAX FF L(G,I): Calderdale Buildings from 1965; a photographic survey; (*Bank-field*) M(St,I): town life, horse-drawn vehicles, architecture from 1890; (*Shibden Hall*) M(G,I): social life of W. Yorks. from c. 1870; Porritt, A., *Halifax As It Was* (1973); Porritt, A. & Ogden, J., *Halifax Old and New* (1978).

HAMMERSMITH L(G,I,S): social life from 1860; *Fulham and Hammersmith in Pictures* (Fulham and Hammersmith Hist. Soc. 1973).

HARROGATE FF: Gopel, G., *Harrogate As It Was* (1972).

HARROW FF L(G,I,S): (Hist): photographic and street survey from 1864; Cooper, E., *Pinner Streets Yesterday and Today* (Pinner and Hatch End Loc. Hist. Arch. Soc., vol. 5, 1976); also STANMORE FF.

HASTINGS FF; Elleray, D. R., *Hastings: A Pictorial History* (1979).

HAVERFORDWEST FF.

HAVERING FF; also HORNCHURCH FF; UPMINSTER FF.

HELSTON FF.

HENLEY-ON-THAMES FF.

HEREFORD FF L(G,I,S): social life from c. 1870; M(St,S): social history from 1900.

HERTFORD FF CRO(G,I,S): county views collection, local history and buildings, Hertfordshire PCC.

HEXHAM Civ(St,I,S): photographic library general survey from 1970.

HIGHAM FERRERS: Rushdon Postcard Collectors' Circle.

HIGH WYCOMBE FF: Sparkes, I. G., *High Wycombe As It Was* (1975).

HILLINGDON L(G,I): from late 19th-c.

HONITON FF.

HOUNSLOW (*Hounslow*) L(G,I,S): social history from 1864; (*Chiswick*) L(G,I,S): social history of Brentford and Chiswick from 1870; Hounslow and Dist. Hist. Soc.: *Hounslow As It Was* (1977); Libraries Division, Hounslow: *Old Photographs of Bedfont, Feltham and Hanworth* (1980); Cameron, A., *Isleworth As It Was* (1982).

HOVE FF L(G,I): social history of Brighton and Hove from 1900.

HUNTINGDON FF.

HUDDERSFIELD L(G,I,S): survey of demolished buildings in Huddersfield, Batley, Cleckheaton, Colne Valley, Derby Dale, Dewsbury, Heckmondwike, Kirkburton, Meltham and Mirfield, begun in 1965: Huddersfield PS.

HYDE: Leck, A., *Hyde, Cheshire in Old Photographs* (1981).

HYTHE FF.

ILKESTON L(G,I): local government, transport, buildings from c. 1880; CH(G,I); town and village life in Derbyshire from the 19th-c.

ILKLEY FF L(G): town life from 1860.

IPSWICH FF CRO(G,App,I,S): Suffolk building record from c. 1860; M(G): photographs from 1880; Suffolk PS.

ISLINGTON L(G,Gu): survey of Islington and Finsbury from 1890.

KEIGHLEY L(G,I,S): town life and architecture from c. 1860 P(*Dewhirst*) (St): street scenes, fairs, from c. 1850; Dewhirst, I., *Old Keighley in Photographs* (1972); and *More Old Keighley in Photographs* (1973).

KENDAL FF CRO (G,S): survey of Westmorland from 1971; prints from CoL.

KENSINGTON FF L(G,S): local history, topographical views, buildings, from c. 1860.

KIDDERMINSTER FF L(G,S): architecture, transport from c. 1850; M(G,S): architecture and religion from 1870. Wyre Forest PCC.

KIDWELLY P(*Morris*) (G): occupations and services, Carmarthen.

KING'S LYNN FF M(St,Acc,S): architecture, factories from late 19th-c.; Winton, M., *Vintage King's Lynn* (1976) and *King's Lynn As It Was* (1972).

KINGSTON-UPON-THAMES FF L(G,I,S): local illustrations of history, architecture, topography from c. 1870; CH(G,I,S): Surrey antiquities, buildings; Woodriff, B., *Kingston-on-Thames As It Was* (1980); also MALDEN FF and SURBITON FF.

LAMBETH FF L(G,I,Pc): Surrey Collection; architecture, social life of South London from 1850; also CLAPHAM FF and STREATHAM FF.

LANCASTER FF M(St,I,S): local architecture, transport, from 1923: Docton, K., *Lancaster As It Was* (1973); Makepeace, C., *Lancashire in the 20s and 30s from Old Photographs* (1977).

LAUNCESTON FF.

LEEDS FF L(G,I,S): local history Print Collection from *c.* 1875; Civ(G): street views and architecture from 1870; Thoresby Soc. (St,App,I): buildings and views from 1889; Arch(G): street scenes, aerial photographs, Boer War, from 1890; (*Rothwell*) L(G): local collection from late 19th-c; Leeds PS; Payne, D. & B., *Leeds As It Was* (1974); P(*Connell*) (St): Industrial archaeology from *c.* 1900; Nuttgens, P., and Rutherford, A., *Leeds Old and New* (1976).

LEICESTER TH(St,I): architecture, topography from 1903-24; Broadfield, A., *Leicester As It Was* (1972); Elliott, M., *Leicester: A Pictorial History* (1983); Kidd, W., *Leicester Old and New* (1975).

LEIGH: Bundock, J. F., *Old Leigh, Essex, A Pictorial History* (1978).

LEOMINISTER FF.

LEWES FF L(G,I): architectural survey from 1968; CRO(F,Cat): architecture, genealogy from *c.* 1870; Sussex Arch. Soc.(St.): Reeves Collection: houses, views and portraits from 1855; P(*Davey*) (App.); Brent, C., and Rector, W., *Victorian Lewes* (1980).

LEWISHAM L(G,I,S): local history from 1880; *One Man's Deptford: A Selection from the Photographs of Thankfull Sturdee* (Archives Dept., Lewisham 1980); also SYDENHAM FF.

LINCOLN FF CoL(G,I,S): architecture, social life, Lincolnshire from *c.* 1857; L(G,I,S): photographic survey, architecture, street scenes, begun *c.* 1970; CRO(St,I): local history 1845-1956; Elvin, L., *Lincoln As It Was*, vols. I-IV (1976–80) and *Lincoln in the 1930s and 40s* (1982): Lincoln PS.

LISKEARD FF.

LIVERPOOL FF L(G): social history from 1852; Un(St,Acc,S): architecture from 1948; Lloyd-Jones, T., *101 Views of Edwardian Liverpool and New Brighton* (1978); Lloyd-Jones, T., *Liverpool Old and New* (1975).

LLANELLI FF.

LONDON CH(G,I,S): GLC photograph library on changing face of London from *c.* 1860; CRO(G,I,S): GLC records, architecture, transport, schools from *c.* 1900; Bishopsgate Institute (G,I,S): topography and London street scenes from *c.* 1860; Guildhall Library (G): London life and topography from 1857; Royal Photographic Soc. (App) and British Library (App): National Photographic Record, buildings and street scenes 1875-85; Betjeman, J., *Victorian and*

(*London – continued*)
Edwardian London from Old Photographs (1969); Howgego, J., *London in the Twenties and Thirties* (1978); and *Victorian and Edwardian City of London* (1977).

LOUGHBOROUGH L(G,I): occupations, architecture, factories from *c.* 1850.

LOWESTOFT FF L(G,S): shipping, docks and harbours from 1860.

LUTON FF M(G,I,S): social history, Bedfordshire and Luton from *c.* 1860; TH(St,App): Luton Redevelopment Record from 1958.

LYTHAM ST ANNES FF.

MACCLESFIELD FF: Horne, R., *Macclesfield As It Was* (1978).

MAIDSTONE FF TH(G,Cat,S): aerial surveys, buildings of Kent from *c.* 1850; Kent PS.

MALDON FF M(St,App,I,S); street scenes and buildings from 1912.

MALMESBURY FF CivL(G): photographic survey 1964-65.

MANCHESTER FF L(G,I,S): social life from 1851; AG(G,I,S): topography from 1860; Civ(St,App,S): buildings, Victoria Park area from 1830; Poly(St,App): Recollections of Trafford Park 1896-1939; Makepeace, C., *Manchester As It Was*, vols. I-VI (1973-77); Megson, M., *Victorian Manchester in Photographs – A 1981 Calendar* (Megson 1981); Palliheux, F., *Manchester Old and New* (1975).

MANSFIELD M(St,App,I): local history, streets, buildings from *c.* 1880.

MARGATE FF.

MARLBOROUGH FF Civ(G,S): local history and photographic survey from *c.* 1969.

MERTON AND MITCHAM L(G,I): local history of Merton, Mitcham and Wimbledon from the early 20th-c.

MIDDLESBROUGH FF: Moorson, N., *Middlesbrough As It Was* (1976).

MIDDLETON L(G,I): local history from 1840; Garratt, M., *Middleton Retrospect* (1982).

MONMOUTH FF M(G,I,S): all aspects from 1860; Lower Wye Preservation Soc. (St,App) architecture of Monmouth, Chepstow etc. from late 19th-c.

MORECAMBE AND HEYSHAM FF FE(St, App): local history from 1887.

MORLEY P(*Atkinson*) (St,S): streets and buildings from 1962.

NEATH FF.

NEWARK FF M(G,I,S): social life from *c.* 1875.

NEWCASTLE-UPON-TYNE FF L(G,I,S): social life, views from 1850, Newburn and district from 1890; M(G,I,S): architecture,

(Rochdale – continued)
   Was (1973); Cole, J. & Fish, G., *Bygone
   Heywood* (Rochdale M.B.Council, 1978).
ROMSEY FF.
ROTHERHAM FF: Rotherham PS (G):
   Photographic survey from *c.* 1900; Neville,
   R. G. & Benson, J., *Rotherham As It Was*
   (1976).
ROYAL LEAMINGTON SPA FF.
RUGBY FF L(G,I): survey of town life and
   architecture from 1841; Davies R. J. and
   Rugby Loc. Hist. Gp., *Rugby As It Was*
   (1979).
RYDE FF P(Brinton) (St,App,I,S): town life,
   seaside scenes, architecture from 1860.
RYE FF.
SAFFRON WALDEN FF M(St,Acc): local
   history and historic buildings of Essex.
ST ALBANS FF L(G,Cat): St Albans Visual
   History from *c.* 1900; Toms, E., *St Albans
   As It Was* (1973).
ST AUSTELL FF.
ST HELENS L(G,S): local history from *c.*
   1860; Serrio, G., *St Helens As It Was*
   (1973); *Vintage St Helens and District*
   (1976).
ST IVES FF P(*Studio St Ives*) (G,S): town life
   from *c.* 1880.
SALFORD L(G,I): architecture and social life
   from 1868; M(St,I): architecture and social
   life from 1854; Smith, A., *Salford As It Was*
   (1973).
SALISBURY FF.
SALTASH FF.
SANDWICH FF.
SCARBOROUGH L(G,I,S): local history from
   c. 1855; Berriman, B., *Scarborough As It
   Was* (1972) and *Vintage Scarborough in
   Photographs* (1976).
SCUNTHORPE FF M(G,Cat,S): social life and
   architecture, N. Lincs from *c.* 1860;
   L(G,I,S): local history from 1890.
SHEFFIELD FF L(G,Cat,S): local history and
   topography from *c.*1860; P(*Vickers*) (St,
   App); Vickers, J. E., *Sheffield Old and New*
   (1980).
SHREWSBURY FF L(G,I): Shropshire
   collection from 1888; CoL(G,I,Acc):
   Shropshire Local Collection from *c.* 1860;
   CRO(G,Acc): topography, landscapes,
   churches 1900-10; M(G,App): Shropshire
   topography, buildings, townscape from *c.*
   1950; Shropshire County Library:
   Shropshire in Pictures; The Street Scene
   (1971); Carr, A. M., *Shrewsbury As It Was*
   (1978).

SOLIHULL CRO and P(Jewsbury) (St,App):
   Jewsbury Collection of Solihull celebrities
   and Victorian scenes from 1850; Bell, S.,
   Woodall, J. & Varley, M., *Solihull As It
   Was* (1980).
SOUTHAMPTON FF L(G,I): aerial photo-
   graphs and buildings from mid-19th-c.;
   CRO (G,Cat,S); local history of Southamp-
   ton and Hampshire from *c.* 1880; South-
   ampton and District PS; Hampson, G.,
   Southampton Old and New (1975); Gadd,
   E. W., *Southampton in the 20s, How It
   Looked* (1979).
SOUTHEND-ON-SEA M(St,I,S): architecture
   and social life from *c.* 1890.
SOUTHPORT FF L(G,I): local history from
   c. 1850; Tarbuck, J., *Southport As It Was*
   (1972).
SOUTH SHIELDS FF L(St,I,S): social history
   from *c.* 1880.
SOUTHWARK L(G,Acc): local history from
   c. 1850; Pearson, D. & Boast, M., *Looking
   Back; Photographs of Camberwell and
   Peckham 1860-1918* (Peckham Publicity
   Project 1979); also DULWICH FF.
SOUTHWOLD FF.
STAFFORD CRO(G,Cat): social life of
   Staffordshire from 1860; (*Shugborough*)
   M(St,Cat,S): Department of Social History
   Photographic Collection from *c.* 1880;
   Lewis, R. & Anslow, J., *Stafford As It Was*
   (1980).
STALYBRIDGE: Jones, C. W., *Stalybridge,
   Lancs. in Old Photographs* (1979).
STAMFORD FF: Stamford Survey Group (St,
   App): photographic survey of town and its
   buildings from 1969; (*Sleaford*) CH(G,I,S):
   old town buildings from 1947.
STOCKPORT Aerial views (Metropolitan
   Borough Local History Guide No. 6 1976);
   scenes of Old Stockport (Six Postcards)
   Stockport Public Libraries 1979.
STOKE-ON-TRENT L(G): the Bentley
   Collection from *c.* 1962; (*Hanley*)L and
   P(*Morris*) (St,App): industrial buildings and
   bottle-ovens from 1956; Talbot, R., *Stoke
   Old and New* (1977).
STOURBRIDGE FF.
STRATFORD-ON-AVON FF: Bearman, R.,
   Stratford-on-Avon As It Was (1979).
STROUD: Cotswold (Cirencester and Stroud)
   PCC; Tucker, J., *Stroud As It Was* (1978).
SUDBURY FF.
SUNDERLAND M(G,I,S): transport, occupa-
   tions, architecture, costume from 1950;
   Pickersgill, A., *Sunderland As It Was* (1974).

SUTTON FF L(G,I): local history collection from *c.* 1860; Burgess, F., *Old Cheam, A Photographic Record and Commentary* (Sutton Library and Arts Service 1978); also BEDDINGTON FF; BENHILTON FF; CARSHALTON FF; CHEAM; WALLINGTON FF.

SWANSEA FF Un(St,S): South Wales Indus. Arch. Soc. Collection; Bowden, D. G. & Thomas, N. L., *Swansea Old and New* (1974).

SWINDON M(G,I,S): social life from 1860.

SWINTON L(G,I,S): town life from 1858.

TAUNTON FF CRO(St,Acc): urban views of Taunton, Bath, Bridgwater, Frome, Minehead and Wells from *c.* 1890; Somerset PS.

TENBY FF.

TENTERDEN FF Civ(St,App): Loc. Hist Soc. collection of scenes and buildings from *c.* 1866.

TEWKESBURY FF M(G,I): museum photographic file on town life from late 19th-c.

THETFORD FF.

TIVERTON M(G): Tiverton PhS collection on town life from *c.* 1880; P(*Hulland*) (St,I): social history of S. Devon from *c.* 1860.

TOTNES FF.

TOWER HAMLETS L(G,I): local history of Stepney, Poplar and Bethnal Green from *c.* 1863; Fletcher, G. (Foreword), *Bricks and Mortar; The Buildings of Tower Hamlets in Pictures* (Directory of Community Services, Tower Hamlets 1975); Norse, B., *Tower Hamlets, London in Photographs 1914-39* (Central Library, Tower Hamlets, 1980); also BROMLEY FF.

TRURO FF Arch(G): industrial and street scenes from 19th-c.; M(G): social life, harbours and shipping from 1890; Chesher, V., *Boscawen Street Area, Truro* (Truro Civic Society 1980); and *Ryader Street and the High Cross Area* (Truro Buildings Research Group 1979).

TUNBRIDGE WELLS FF: Mauldon, J., *Tunbridge Wells As It Was* (1977).

TYNEMOUTH: Tynemouth PhS (St,I,S): Tynemouth past and present from 1860.

WAKEFIELD: Speak, H. & Forrester, J., *Old Wakefield in Photographs* (1972).

WALLASEY L(G,I): local history from late 19th-c.

WALLINGFORD FF.

WALSALL L(G,I,S): local history from 1845; Black Country Society: all aspects of Black Country life since 1869; Benon, J. & Raybould, T., *Walsall As It Was* (1978);

(*Walsall – continued*)
Lewis, M. (ed.), *Willenhall and Darlaston Yesterdays in Photographs* (Walsall M.B. Archive Service 1981).

WALTHAM FOREST L(App, I): Leyton and Essex Collection from *c.* 1880: (*Vestry House*) M(G,S): town life, architecture from 1853; (*Chingford*) (G,I,S): South Chingford Library Collection from 1870; Hist(St,I): Parish of Chingford 1939; *Chingford As It Was: A Selection of Photographs* (Chingford Hist. Soc. Bull. 10, 1977); also CHINGFORD FF.

WANDSWORTH FF; also BALHAM FF; TOOTING FF.

WARLEY L(G,I,S): Warley Pictorial Record, now Sandwell Pictorial Record from 1900.

WARRINGTON FF L(G,S) architecture and landscape from 1974; also Warrington Broadside Collection on Cheshire and Lancashire from 1848; M(G): social life, occupations and architecture from *c.* 1890; Williams, P. & Hayes, J., *Warrington As It Was* (1979).

WARWICK FF L(App): Warwick and district, including Leamington Spa, Coventry, Kenilworth, Birmingham and Stratford from 1841.

WATFORD FF Ind. Hist. Soc. (St,S): housing and shops from *c.* 1971; Ball, A. W., *Watford, A Pictorial History 1922-1972* (Watford Borough Council 1972).

WESTMINSTER L(G,I): architecture from *c.* 1850.

WELLS FF.

WESTON-SUPER-MARE FF Somerset PS.

WEYMOUTH FF.

WHITBY P(*Tindales*) (St,I,S): N. Yorks and area from 1947.

WHITEHAVEN L(G,I,S): changing Whitehaven from 1960.

WIDNES FF L(G,I,S): town life, architecture and costume from *c.* 1880.

WIGAN FF.

WINCHESTER FF CRO(G,S): architecture and views from *c.* 1880-90; M(St,I): social life, transport, from 1860.

WINDSOR FF: Underhill, M., *Windsor As It Was* (1972).

WISBECH FF M(G,I,S): town life and architecture from *c.* 1850.

WITNEY: Worley, T., *Witney, Oxon, As It Was* (1981).

WOLVERHAMPTON L(G): buildings, streets, transport from 1870; Roper, J., *Wolverhampton As It Was*, vols. I-III (1974-76).

WOODSTOCK M(St,I): architectural survey
1967-70.
WORCESTER FF L(G,Acc): street scenes,
buildings, from 1890; CoL(G): local studies
library; CRO(G): all aspects of old County's
history from *c*. 1880; Stafford, T., *Worcester
As It Was* (1977).
WORKSOP L(St): local history collection from
1900.
WORTHING FF: Harmer, H. R. & Elleray,
D. R., *A Picture of Worthing — Scenes over
the last 80 years* (County Library Service
1975); L(G,I): Worthing and Sussex Photo-

(*Worthing — continued*)
graphic Survey from *c*. 1870; Elleray, D. R.,
Worthing — A Pictorial History (1977).
WREXHAM FF.
YEOVIL FF: Hayward, L. C. & Brooke, L.,
Bygone Yeovil, Somerset (Yeovil Arch.
Hist. Soc., 1980).
YORK FF L(G): architecture from *c*. 1850;
Arch(G): health, sanitation and slums,
buildings of York from *c*. 1909; York
Georgian Society (G): Georgian architecture
of York — photographs from *c*. 1909;
Willis, R., *York As It Was* (1973).

CONCLUSION

HISTORY is about change. Just as other institutions grow or decline, so towns must change continually in the course of time. We need to remind ourselves that history is also about survival and tradition. Unfortunately we now live in an age when government is persuaded by precedents that it can change *anything* at short notice, with a minimum of apparent justification. It is not enough that taxes reach heights which would amaze the robber barons, or cause Charles I to reflect wryly on the inadequacy of Ship Money. To become completely dependent upon government the subject must be conditioned also to realise that no part of his environment, his livelihood or his domestic life is beyond Their reach. The currency of a thousand years can be inflated into alien cents; foundation charters can be torn up or ignored; laws of free speech, free employment, even *habeas corpus* can be subverted by the State in the name of Equality or Defence. Nothing is too trivial to change — even the traditional date of Boxing Day can be altered to make television's 'Christmas Sunday'. No building is too venerable to be razed for carpark or supermarket site, no ancient town centre is safe from 'ring-roads' which as in Wolverhampton, bulldoze the heart of the place. 'Planners rule — OK?' When the liturgy of the Church, the language of Cranmer, and even the words of the Lord's Prayer can be translated into advertising copy, then it must be assumed that literally nothing is sacred. For governments which could react so hastily to the 'wind of change' as to give away an Empire which had lasted nowhere near Churchill's optimistic thousand years, to re-draw the boundaries of Saxon and Mercian kingdoms presented little difficulty. There is far more to come.

An insidious aspect of modern improvements is that they are never complete; upheaval is inexorably followed by revision. Just as within our lifetimes we may expect the revaluation of a new or 'heavier' pound sterling, litres-to-the-kilometre or yellow telephone boxes, so we must expect continuing reorganization of local government and its districts. It is not surprising to discover that by 1981 there had been at least 24 changes of 1974's 'new' boundaries and more than a dozen changes of names. We must be thankful that the crude attempt at 'Salop' gave way to Shropshire and that the renaming of 'North Wolds' as East Yorkshire is at least reminiscent of one lost Riding. It is too much to wish that some future reorganization might enhance the functions of the ex-municipal boroughs. These are now long gone, the official view of many a district official being that 'they had very little to lose'. The situation of the ex-county boroughs which are at present metropolitan districts is already in the melting pot.

Since the General Election of 1983 the Conservative government is fully committed to the abolition of the six metropolitan counties and the Greater London Council; the massive implications for the metropolitan districts appear to have been left to the imagination. In the absence of any White Paper the districts' future position *sans*-county remains a matter of conjecture. It may be that, surviving this reorganization, they will indeed gain autonomy, with delegated 'agencies' for the *ad hoc* administration of the wider functions of the present counties; for example transport, police, fire services and highways. This could be interpreted as a return to an enhanced 'county-borough' all-purpose status. For the first time in history those 'boroughs' would stand not only separate from an administrative county – though presumably geographical names may survive – but in the total *absence* of any county authority. So the sway of relative influence between county and 'town', which is as old as the Five Danish Boroughs and the Domesday entries 'above the line', will take yet another historic turn, this time to the counties' disadvantage.

On the other hand, one might foresee the abolition of the metropolitan counties as only another interim step towards further reorganization of a different type of 'region' and a new concept of its 'districts'. At least one Wolverhampton Conservative candidate in June 1983 confidently advertized that 'Tories will abolish the Metro-politan Districts including the West Midland County Council'. This possibly Freudian misprint was hastily amended in later printing of the leaflet, but one is left with a suspicion of more to come. So we move inexorably into 1984.

Faced with continuing uncertainty, the most that townsmen can ask in self-defence is that the good names of some of their towns be saved or reinstated. Just as Dagenham, Fulham and Rochester have successfully reclaimed their names as districts, so the real identity of Halifax, Huddersfield, Devizes, Kidderminster, Sudbury, Worksop, Bangor, Widnes and many more towns should be restored. Inevitably, many other erstwhile boroughs would still be overlooked in the final choices. It was sad that both Crediton and Tiverton lost their names *after* 1974 to the anonymity of 'North Devon'. Other towns in their position, such as Bewdley and Kidderminster, should be prepared to come to an agreement to save one of their identities, rather than jealously compromise on such inventions as 'Wyre Forest'. Otherwise we may expect to see even Dudley vanish into the melting-pot – presumably to emerge as 'Swinford' or 'Halesbridge' in 'Beacon' or 'Medium' county. Where, then will the records of the earlier towns ever be found?

GENERAL BIBLIOGRAPHY

Anderson, J. P., *The Book of British Topography* (1881, facsimile edition 1976).
Beresford, M., *New Towns of the Middle Ages* (1976).
Braithwaite, L., *The Historic Towns of Britain* (1981).
Brown, L. M. and Christie, I. R. (editors), *Bibliography of British History, 1789–1851* (1977).
Chalklin, C. W., *The Provincial Towns of Georgian England 1740–1820* (1974).
Clark, P. (editor), *The Early Modern Town, A Reader* (1976).
Clark, P. and Slack, P., *English Towns in Transition, 1500–1700* (1976).
Dyos, H. J., *The Study of Urban History* (1968).
Dyos, H. J. and Woolff, M., *The Victorian City* (2 vols.).
Foster, J. and Sheppard, J., *British Archives: a guide to archive resources in the United Kingdom* (1983).
Gross, C., *A Bibliography of British Municipal History* (1897, repr. 1966).
Gross, C. (ed. E. B. Graves), *A Bibliography of British History to 1485* (revised edn. 1975).
Guiseppe, M. S., *Guide to the Contents of the Public Record Office* (various vols., 1960–1968).
Lawless, P., *Britain's Inner Cities: Problems and Policies* (1981).
Martin, C. T., *The Record Interpreter* (1892, facsimile 1982).
Meller, H. E., *Leisure and the Changing City 1870–1914* (1976).
Richardson, J., *The Local Historian's Encyclopaedia* (1974).
Stephens, W. B., *Sources for English Local History* (1973).
Wacher, J., *Towns of Roman Britain* (1974).

FINAL WORDS

'This is what I will: that every man be under surety, both within the boroughs and without, and let witness be appointed to every borough and to every hundred.'

(Laws of King Edgar: 959-962)

'We intend and grant that all cities, boroughs, towns and ports shall have all their rights and freedoms.'

(King John: Magna Carta: 1215)

'Town air makes a man free.'

(Traditional)

'On that date (1 April 1974) the municipal corporation of every borough outside Greater London shall cease to exist.'

(Local Government Bill, 1972)

'When London government reform was being debated in the early 1960s flesh-creeping horrors were forecast by its many opponents. *By and large* none of these has come to pass. Nearly 90 assorted councils ranging from rural districts to the L.C.C. itself disappeared without trace *and are rapidly slipping from public memory*' (author's italics).

(Mr. Roland Freeman, former Chairman of the G.L.C. Finance Committee, writing in the Local Government Chronicle.)

NOTES TO CHAPTERS ONE TO TWELVE

Chapter One

1. Trevelyan, G. M., *History of England* (1926), p. 637.

Chapter Two

1. Ekwall, E., *The Concise Oxford Dictionary of English Place-Names* (4th edn, 1980).
2. Rivet, A. L. F. and Smith, C., *The Place-Names of Roman Britain* (1979).
3. Stephenson, C., *Borough and Town* (1933).
4. Tait, J., *The Medieval English Borough* (1968 edn).
5. Stenton, F., *Anglo-Saxon England* (1970), p. 527, quoted Biddle, M., 'Towns', in *The Archaeology of Anglo-Saxon England* (ed. D. M. Wilson, 1981), p. 119.
6. Garmonsway, G. N. (ed.), *The Anglo-Saxon Chronicles* (1954).
7. Loyn, H. R., 'Boroughs and Mints, AD 900-1066', in *Anglo-Saxon Coins* (ed. R. H. M. Dolley, 1961), pp. 122-135.
8. *Ibid.*, p. 132.
9. Gelling, M., 'A note on the name "Worcester"', in *Trans. Worcs. Arch. Soc.*, 3rd series, vol. 2 (1968-9), p. 26.
10. *Victoria County History of Worcestershire* (hereafter VCH Worcs.), vol. IV, p. 378.
11. *Ibid.*; see also Barker, P. A., 'The origins of Worcester; an interim survey', in *Trans. Worcs. Arch. Soc.*, 3rd series, vol. 2 (1968-9).
12. Birch 608.
13. VCH Worcs., vol. IV, p. 378.
14. *Ibid.*

Chapter Three
No Notes.

Chapter Four

1. Platt, C., *The English Medieval Town* (1976).
2. Ballard, A., *The English Borough in the Twelfth Century* (1914), p. 30.
3. Platt, *op. cit.*, p. 146.
4. *Ibid.*, p. 147.
5. VCH Worcs., vol. IV, p. 380.
6. Roper, J. S., *Dudley: The Medieval Town* (Dudley Borough Libraries, Transcript No. 3, 1962).
7. West, J., *Village Records* (1982 edn), Chapter III.
8. Beresford, M. and Finberg, H. P. R., *English Medieval Boroughs, A Handlist* (1973), p. 29.
9. Willard, J. F., 'Taxation Boroughs and Parliamentary Boroughs', in *Historical Essays in Honour of James Tait* (ed. J. G. Edwards, 1933).
10. Beresford and Finberg, *op. cit.*, p. 55.
11. Beresford, M., *New Towns of the Middle Ages* (1967).

Chapter Five

1. Gross, C., *The Gild Merchant* (1897); Toulmin Smith, J., 'The English Gilds', *Early English Text Society*, vol. 40 (1870).
2. Phythian-Adams, C., 'Sources for Urban History, 3: Records of the Craft Gilds', *Local Historian*, vol. 9 (6) (1971).
3. Gross, C., *A Bibliography of British Municipal History* (1897), p. 83.
4. Everitt, A., 'The primary towns of England', *Local Historian*, vol. 11 (5) (1975).
5. See any reliable dictionary of surname, for instance, Hassall, W. O., *History Through Surnames* (1967).
6. Sawyer, P. H., The wealth of England in the 11th century', *Trans. Roy. Hist. Soc.*, 5th series, vol. 15 (1965).
7. Hilton, R. H., *A Medieval Society* (1966), p. 206.
8. Unwin, G., *The Gilds and Companies of London* (1966), Appendix B, pp. 372–389.
9. *Ibid.*, facsimile on p. 267; transcription, pp. 370–71.
10. Roper, J. S., *The Dudley Chantry Lands* (1970).
11. Noake, J., 'The Ancient Worcester Cordwainers' Company', *The Gentleman's Magazine*, vol. 3 (1857).
12. Hooper, J. H., 'The Clothier's Company, Worcester', *Trans. Worcs. Diocesan Archit. & Arch. Soc.*, vol. 15 (1880).
13. Miller, E., 'The Fortunes of the English textile industry during the 13th century', *Economic Hist. Rev.*, 2nd series, vol. 18 (1965).
14. Dobson, R. B., 'Urban Decline in Late Medieval England', *Trans. Roy. Hist. Soc.*, 5th series, vol. 27 (1976).

Chapter Six

1. Barley, M. W., *The Plans and Topography of Medieval Towns in England and Wales* (Council for British Archaeology Research Report No. 14, 1976).
2. Lobel, M. D., 'The value of early maps as evidence for the topography of English Towns', *Imago Mundi*, vol. 22 (1958).
3. Arlott, J., *John Speed's England* (1953).
4. Lobel, *op. cit.*, p. 59.
5. Hartley, J. B., *The Historian's Guide to Ordnance Survey maps* (1964).
6. Gibson, J. and Mills, D. (eds), *Land Tax Assessments c. 1690–1956* (Federation of Family History Societies Publications, 1983).
7. Aspinall, P. J., 'Sources for Urban History, 11: The use of 19th century fire insurance plans', *Local Historian*, vol. 11 (6) (1975).
8. *Ibid.*, p. 346; see also Hayward, R. J., 'Sources for Urban Historical Research: Insurance Plans and Land-Use Atlases', *Urban Historical Review*, vol. 1 (1973).

Chapter Seven

1. The data which is given in this Chapter is largely taken from the *First Report of the Commissioners on the Municipal Corporations of England and Wales in 1835* (vol. 2, 1969), published by the Irish University Press as a volume of the British Parliamentary Papers Series.
2. Chandler, G., *Dudley As It Was and Is Today* (1949).
3. Everitt, A., 'Urban Growth 1570-1770', *Local Historian*, vol. 8 (4) (1968); and 'Urban Growth and Inland Trade 1570-1770', *ibid.*, vol. 8 (6) (1968).
4. Roper, J. S., *Dudley: The Town in the 18th Century* (Dudley Public Libraries Transcript No. 12, 1968).

Chapter Eight

1. Mason, F., *Wolverhampton: The Town Commissioners 1777-1848 – Their Story in Their Minutes and the Files of the 'Wolverhampton Chronicle'* (Wolverhampton Libraries typescript, 1976).
2. Lee, W., *Report to the General Board of Health* . . . (1852).
3. Davies, V. L. and Hyde, H., *Dudley and the Black Country 1716-1860* (Museums and Arts Dept., Transcript No. 16, 1970), p. 24.
4. Thorne, T., *Report on a prevalence of typhus in Dudley* . . . (Medical Dept. of the Privy Council Office, 18 August 1871).

Chapter Nine
No Notes.

Chapter Ten
No Notes.

Chapter Eleven

1. Law, C. M., 'Sources for Urban History, 6: A short bibliography of 18th century population history', *Local Historian*, vol. 10 (3) (1972).
2. The author is indebted to the County Archivist of Lancashire for this lucid identification of several otherwise 'missing' towns.
3. Beresford, M. W., 'The unprinted census returns of 1851 and 1861 for England and Wales', *Amateur Historian*, vol. 5 (8) (1963).
4. Smith, R., 'Demography in the 19th century; an introduction to the local history', *Local Historian*, vol. 9 (1) (1970).
5. Chaplin, R., 'Discovering lost "new towns" of the 19th century', *Local Historian*, vol. 10 (4) (1972).
6. Gibson, J. S. W., *Census Returns 1841-1881 on Microfilm: A Directory to Local Holdings* (4th edn), 1982; Federation of Family History Societies Publications.
7. Ballard, Dr. E., 'Report for the Local Government Board on the Sanitary Conditions of the Municipal Borough of Dudley, 2nd December 1874'.
8. Mills, D. R., 'The technique of house repopulation; Experience from a Cambridgeshire village', *Local Historian*, vol. 13 (2), 1978.
9. Mumford, L., *The Culture of Cities* (1938), p. 148.
10. Williams, H., 'Public Health and Local History', *Local Historian*, vol. 14 (4) (1980).
11. 3rd edn, 1981.

Chapter Twelve

1. Dyos, H. J., *The Study of Urban History* (1968), p. 43.
2. Sansom, W. (ed.), *Victorian Life in Photographs* (1974).
3. For example, Duval, W., and Monahan, V., *Collecting Postcards* (1978); *Stanley Gibbons Postcard Catalogue* (2nd edn, 1981).
4. Chapman, T., 'The Victorian Camera, Development and Technique', in Sansom (*op. cit.*), p. 30.
5. McKenna, J., *Birmingham As It Was* (1979).
6. Williams, N., *Cinemas of the Black Country* (1982).
7. McCord, N., 'Photographs as Historical Evidence', *Local Historian*, vol. 13 (1), (1978).
8. See *Local Historian*, vol. 14 (1) (1980), onwards.
9. Wall, J., *Directory of British Photographc Collections* (Royal Photographic Society, 1977).
10. See also *The Picture Postcard Annual* (published yearly).

INDEX

Those towns which are included in the *Gazetteer of English and Welsh Boroughs* at the end of Chapter One are listed in BLOCK CAPITALS but references to them which have already appeared in the Chapters' Gazetteers (q.v.) are not indexed here. Present-day county names are attributed, these may vary historically in text and Gazetteers. Welsh and Romano-British place-names are added.

UNITY AND PROGRESS

TO ALL AN

Knight Commander of the Royal
upon whom has been conferred the
Order, Notley and Ulster King of A
Laws of the University of Birmingham; Chief
Duke of Norfolk Knight of the Most Noble O
ship upon whom has been conferred the herite
deemed that pursuant to the provisions of
day of May 19? duly constituted a body corpo

County Borough of Dudley and the Boroughs of Halesowen and of Stourbridge that Her Majesty the Queen by
status of a Borough on and from the First day of April 1974 and accordingly The Dudley District Council is
lished under lawful authority and he therefore as Chief Executive of the said Borough and on behalf of the Co
same Patent such Supporters and such Device or Badge as We may consider fit and proper to be borne and used
the said Earl Marshal did by Warrant under his hand and Seal bearing date the Twenty-sixth day of Jun
the said Garter, Clarenceux and Notley and Ulster in pursuance of His Majesty's Warrant and by virtue of
and assign unto The Borough Council of Dudley the arms following that is to say—Ver
and Vert each supporting a Beacon fired proper and in base a Salamander reguardant
ry wavy Argent and Azure between two Pears slipped and leaved Or And for the Crest
a representation of Sedgley Beacon Tower proper between two Roses Gules barbed and
depicted And by the Authority aforesaid We do further grant and assign the following Device or
central tower a Golden Fleece proper each flanking tower charged with an Escallop Sable, as
The Borough Council of Dudley the Supporters following that is to say To the dexter a C
sinister an Angel proper winged Argent habited Gules girdled and holding in the exterior
and used for ever hereafter by The Borough Council of Dudley on its Common Seal or otherwise accordi

Dudley's latest Charter of Incorporation, 1974. (By permission of Birmingham Reference Library)